Real Estate Law

Eleventh Edition

Raymond J. Werner

Arnstein & Lehr
Chicago, Illinois

SOUTH-WESTERN
THOMSON LEARNING

Australia · Canada · Mexico · Singapore · Spain · United Kingdom · United States

Real Estate Law, Eleventh Edition, by Raymond J. Werner

Executive Publisher: Dave Shaut
Senior Acquisitions Editor: Scott Person
Production Editor: Amy McGuire
Editorial Assistant: Jennifer Warner-Stephens
Manufacturing Coordinator: Charlene Taylor
Cover Design: Casey Gilbertson
Internal Design: WordCrafters Editorial Services, Inc.
Production House: WordCrafters Editorial Services, Inc.
Compositor: Publishers' Design and Production Services, Inc.
Printer: Courier Westford, Inc.

Printed in the United States of America
3 4 5 04

For more information contact South-Western, 5101 Madison Road, Cincinnati, Ohio, 45227 or find us on the Internet at http://www.swcollege.com

For permission to use material from this text or product, contact us by
• **telephone: 1-800-730-2214**
• **fax: 1-800-730-2215**
• **web: http://www.thomsonrights.com**

Library of Congress Cataloging-in-Publication Data

Werner, Raymond J.
    Real estate law / Raymond J. Werner.—11th ed.
        p.   cm.
    Includes index.
    ISBN 0-324-14362-1
    1. Real property—United States. 2. Vendors and purchasers—United States. 3. Mortgages—United States. I. Title.

KF570 .K7   2002
346.7304′3—dc21

2001020742

To
Lenore, Beth, and Jeff

With a Special Dedication to
the Memory of
Robert Kratovil

Preface

Social, economic, and political changes drive many developments in the law. This fact is evident in changes to the real estate economy, and thus real estate law, caused by the robust economic times in which we are operating. This is in part caused by a vibrant real estate economy that reflects the vibrant general economy of the country.

Another facet of these heady times for real estate is the greater unification of the real estate capital structure with the capital structure of the economy in general. Ownership of much real estate is in the hands of corporations who are typically the users of the property, or real estate investment trusts, both of whom draw their funds from Wall Street. Similarly, real estate financing competes for funds directly with other financings, again on Wall Street. The growth of securitized mortgage lending has been incredible and is the device used to funnel mortgage loans, both residential and commercial, to investors, pension funds, and the like.

Each turn of the economic cycle has had a different effect, building upon the effects of the prior economic cycle. Real estate recessions were marked by temporary credit shortages and an oversupply of completed or partially completed projects. That cycle brought about more discipline in the lending community and perhaps even to the developer set. Projects are more economically feasible and less speculative. Loan-to-value ratios have been reduced, and the loan securities are rated by the same securities rating agencies that rate commercial paper. The doom of the mid and late eighties has been replaced with an economic confidence that permeates the entire economy, including the real estate economy.

Recent developments in the law found in this revision include discussions of the following:

- The refinements to the law of fixtures caused by increased customization of single-family properties and the high-tech environment in which we live;
- New survey standards promulgated by the American Land Title Association and the American Congress of Mapping and Surveying;
- The new environment in which real estate brokers are functioning, including a discussion of dual agency and the potential that a selling broker may become the agent of the buyer;
- Letters of intent in real estate transactions and an expanded emphasis on draftsmanship tips for real estate documents;
- The use of the "as is" clause in real estate sale contracts;
- Environmental issues confronting the real estate industry, including an entirely new chapter on environmental liabilities;
- Today's forms of lending devices, including the impact of securitized mortgage lending;
- The increasingly important impact of bankruptcy law on the real estate and lending community;

- Developments in the law of prepayment of mortgage debts, including limitations on the amount of prepayment penalties or premiums;
- The continued expansion of the liabilities of a broker for fraud and nondisclosure of defects;
- The relationship of several mortgagees secured by the same property;
- Recent United States Supreme Court cases dealing with land use regulation;
- Land use regulation as it affects the social issues of our times, such as AIDS and homelessness;
- Current trends in land development regulation;
- The impact of federal requirements such as the Endangered Species Act and wetlands regulation on land development;
- The interrelationship between clubs, such as country clubs, and homeowners' association membership;
- A thorough discussion of topical commercial lease provisions and issues; and
- Modern trends in the law of discrimination as it relates to real estate, such as discrimination based upon age, family status, and disability.

Contents

CHAPTER 1

Sources of Real Estate Law

1.01 Lack of Uniformity in Laws Governing Real Estate

In each of the United States, two separate systems of law are in force: federal law and state law. With few exceptions, federal laws operate uniformly throughout the country. Each state, however, has its own constitution, laws, and court decisions. Although differences in local conditions cause laws relating to real estate to vary from state to state, and even from area to area within the same state, the basic legal principles governing real estate are much the same throughout the country. This book will describe these basic principles, mentioning, as space permits, the more important state-to-state variations.

1.02 Sources of and Trends in Real Estate Law

The sources of real estate law include the Constitution of the United States; federal laws; regulations adopted by various federal agencies, boards, and commissions; state constitutions; state laws; regulations adopted by various state and municipal agencies; ordinances of the various local governments; and court decisions. While traditionally the latter have been the most important source of real estate laws, developments of recent years give a great deal of prominence to statutes and regulations enacted on a federal, state, and even local level. For example, the Federal Bankruptcy Code has a tremendous impact on real estate law and practice, especially in the mortgage law context.

Decisions by the courts become the law because they form a basis for decision in later cases. In announcing a decision, a court will usually state its reasons and discuss the legal principles governing the particular case. Such a decision, with its accompanying discussion, is called an *opinion*. The opinions from the more significant courts are preserved for reference in later cases. These decisions are then bound into books called *reports*. Today, these decisions are also available online through various data banks, to which courts, lawyers, and others may subscribe. Since these decisions are stored electronically, they can be quickly searched and retrieved.

Since our American real estate law stems in large part from the real estate law of England, it is not uncommon for courts to have based their decisions on similar cases that arose several hundred years earlier in England. This is especially the case in the area of real estate law, where many theories still in use today trace their roots to England. In recent times, federal laws and regulations, together with state laws, have assumed increasing importance in real estate law, especially in the law of real estate finance.

Also of great importance in modern times is the "private law" that lawyers create in the preparation of real estate documents. Those who are new to real estate may fail to understand that the "battle of the forms" is an everyday reality. Landlords' lawyers battle tenants' lawyers over lease language. Mortgage commitments and other loan documents are endlessly redrafted in large deals. In virtually every major real estate transaction the word processors are kept busy with the constant reworking of the transactional documents that set the law of that particular transaction for the parties.

One limitation on the rights of the parties to thus declare the "law" applicable to their situation is found in the tendency of courts to refuse to enforce contract terms regarded as "unconscionable," or grossly unfair. While the concept of unconscionability finds its modern roots in the Uniform Commercial Code (UCC), which applies mainly to personal property, courts choose to regard the UCC as an expression of public policy applicable to all types of transactions, including real estate transactions.

> **EXAMPLE:** Landlord leased a filling station to Tenant. The lease gave Tenant an option to purchase. Tenant exercised the option. Due to awkward phrasing of the option, it appeared that it would take more than fifty years for full payment of the purchase price. The court said that Tenant would have to accept reasonable terms of payment or pay all cash. *Rego v. Decker*, 482 P.2d 834 (Alaska 1971).

We long ago moved into the age of consumerism. Large corporations are compelled to respect the needs of the consumer. The real estate arena is not excluded from this trend. For example, the Federal Truth-in-Lending Act compels the disclosure of interest rates in terms that the ordinary consumer should be able to understand. Similar state laws have also been enacted. The Interstate Land Sales Act requires disclosures that are intended to assist the unwary prospective purchaser of vacant lots in making a purchase decision. Again, similar state laws have also been enacted.

Where there is inequality of bargaining power and where the sophisticated is pitted against the unsophisticated party, the courts will intervene to protect the weaker party. Another manifestation of this tendency is found in the judicial tendency toward rewriting contracts of adhesion. Wherever a relatively weak consumer is confronted with a contract full of fine print, such as a lease, mortgage, or sell-and-build contract, modern courts will pull the teeth of a clause that bears oppressively on the weaker party.

All of this is merely the present manifestation of older concepts. As far back as 1600, English courts decided that it was unconscionable to permit a mortgagor's default to end his rights in the mortgaged land. Toward this end, the courts invented the equitable right of redemption. When mortgagees, in turn, began to insert a waiver of this right in the mortgage contract, the courts struck the clause down as being unconscionable. Manifestations of this tendency can be found today, as courts do not always enforce contracts as written, but infer what they think is reasonable, or fair, under the circumstances.

1.03 The Impact of Economic and Social Change upon the Law

The law has always been shaped by economic and social forces. As the age of consumerism swept the country in the late 1960s and early 1970s, many time-honored rules of law were changed. The law recognized the economic power and social force of consumerism. In the late 1970s and early 1980s, inflation altered so many economic relationships that the law surrounding those relationships also changed. Similarly, the economic downturn of the late 1980s and early 1990s led to decisional and legislative developments as courts and legislatures tried to adjust to the economic realities of the time.

Nowhere was the legal impact of inflation and then recession felt more than in the area of real estate law. The changes that inflation brought to mortgage law alone were dramatic. Inflationary pressures on interest rates brought about the advent of variable rate, rollover, and shared appreciation mortgages. Prior law largely did not allow these transactions, which are now somewhat common. Federal law has preempted state usury laws covering many forms of mortgage transactions. New regulations promulgated for today's forms of financing are much more disclosure oriented so as to allow the consumer to make an informed decision. The next set of developments, especially in the consumer transaction area, will likely be driven by the explosion of electronic processing of real estate transactions. Before this book is published, loan applications will be largely filed and approved electronically at the time the real estate contract is signed, the survey and the title commitment will be ordered, and the appraisal, by way of electronic comparison to comparable properties, will be completed. This will allow the time between contract execution and closing to be greatly compressed. All of this will require some changes in the form of evidence that documents these segments of the transaction.

These changes are not limited to consumer transactions. The ultimate source of real estate financing has shifted away from the thrift institutions, which were fed by depositors, to the public and private securities markets where mortgagors will have to compete for funds on an equal footing with other borrowers. Pension funds, real estate syndications, and other pools of investments are powerful forces in the real estate market.

All of these changes brought about by economic factors are causing a reshaping of the law. This is nothing new. The law has always been responsive to these types of changes and will continue to adjust the relationship of the parties even as the underlying economic assumptions change.

CHAPTER 2
Land and Its Elements

2.01 Land Defined Land, or real estate, includes not only the ground, or soil, but everything that is attached to the earth, whether by course of nature, as are trees and herbage, or by the hand of man, as are houses and other buildings. Ownership rights in land include not only the surface of the earth but everything under and over the surface. Thus, in legal theory, the surface of the earth is just part of an inverted pyramid having its tip, or apex, at the center of the earth, extending outward through the surface of the earth at the boundary lines of the tract, and continuing on upward to the heavens.

2.02 Minerals Since ownership rights in real estate extend to the center of the earth, it is clear that the owner of the land also ordinarily owns the minerals, which are a part of the land, and when the property is sold, the buyer ordinarily acquires such minerals, even though they are not expressly mentioned in the deed. However, a landowner may decide to sell any part or all of the land, such as by selling the minerals only, retaining title to the rest of the land, or by selling the land only and retaining or reserving the minerals. In this way, the former owner of the whole of the real property would keep the minerals for later sale or development, perhaps by selling rights to mine the minerals to a third party who would pay the mineral owner a royalty.

> **EXAMPLE:** Landowner signs a deed conveying to Mineral Buyer all of the coal underlying Landowner's land. Now we have two layers of ownership. Landowner continues to own the surface and may farm or develop it. Mineral Buyer owns the coal. Landowner can sell or mortgage his or her ownership, and Mineral Buyer can do the same. Mineral Buyer automatically has the right to sink shafts from the surface and build roads and tracks over the surface for the purpose of mining and transporting the coal. But Mineral Buyer must not remove the coal in such a manner that the surface of the land will collapse.

Suppose that Farmer sells and grants the coal under his farm to Coal Co. Coal Co. tunnels under the farm as it mines the coal, using the tunnels for transporting coal mined from adjoining areas. The courts agree that Coal Co. may do this, though the explanations vary from state to state. In some states, the interesting theory is advanced that a sale of coal and minerals includes not only the coal and minerals but also the space they occupy, so that when the coal is removed by mining operations, the coal company remains the owner of the space the coal formerly occupied. *Middleton v. Harlan-Wallins Coal Corp.*, 66 S.W.2d 30 (Ky. 1933). W.C. Crais III, Annotation, *Right of Owner of Title to or Interest in Minerals Under One Tract to Use Surface or Underground Passages, in Connection with Mining Other Tract*, 83 A.L.R.2d 665 (1962); Annotation, *Grant, Reservation, or Lease of Miner-*

als and Mining Rights as Including, Without Expressly so Providing, the Right to Remove the Minerals by Surface Mining, 70 A.L.R.3d 383 (1970).

2.03   Oil and Gas   Contrary to popular opinion, oil does not occur in underground pools or reservoirs, but is tightly held in the tiny pores or the openings of porous rocks. Natural gas is held in solution in this oil under great pressure. When a well is drilled into the rock that contains oil and gas, pressure is released and oil and gas gush forth just as a carbonated drink gushes from a warm pop bottle when the cap is removed. The oil will then flow to the low pressure area, namely, the well bore. Some states, impressed with the fact that oil, in its natural state and before drilling occurs, is immovably trapped in the rocks in which it is found, say that the landowner owns the oil beneath his land in much the same way that the landowner owns coal or other minerals. These states are called *ownership states.* Other states, impressed with the fact that oil does move from one underground location to another when wells are drilled, hold that the landowner does not own the oil until it has been pumped, with the landowner thereby taking possession of it. This is called the *law of capture. Atlantic Richfield Co. v. Tomlinson,* 859 P.2d 1088 (Okla. 1993); *Frost v. Ponca City,* 541 P.2d 1321 (Okla. 1975). In all states, when the oil is pumped and brought to the surface, it becomes personal property. Even if the oil or gas is then restored in the ground and migrates to another's property, the stored oil or gas is not then subject to capture by others. *Pacific Gas and Electric Co. v. Zuckerman,* 234 Cal. Rptr. 630 (1987).

All oil states, including the ownership states, follow the rule of *capture,* which holds that a mineral owner who drills from one site will own all of the oil and gas produced, even though some of the oil or gas has migrated from a neighbor's land. The neighbor, of course, can prevent such a result by drilling *offset* wells on his or her land and pumping the oil that would otherwise move to the neighbor's land. All oil-producing states now have laws regulating and controlling the drilling of wells and the production of oil.

The rule of capture is subject to regulation, and some states have moved away from its strict application in some instances, such as where secondary recovery techniques are used. Under these methods, water or gas is injected into the well to cause the recovery of oil or gas that would not be recoverable under primary methods. This injection may affect portions of the pool that lie under other lands, thereby resulting in the drainage of the pool underlying those adjacent lands. Some jurisdictions have taken the view that where these secondary recovery operations result either in drainage of valuable minerals from or damage to the adjacent lands, the adjoining landowner or mineral lessee is entitled to damages. Vitauts M. Gulbis, Annotation, *Rights and Obligations with Respect to Adjoining Landowners Arising Out of Secondary Recovery of Gas, Oil and Other Fluid Minerals,* 19 A.L.R.4th 1182 (1983).

Landowners lack the skill, experience, capital, and entrepreneurial instinct necessary to drill for oil. Therefore, when the presence of oil is suspected, a landowner enters into an oil lease with an oil company. The basic structure of an oil and gas lease was developed by 1895. Its usual elements are as follows: (1) a cash bonus is paid to the lessor for granting the lease, (2) a royalty is paid to the lessor if oil or gas is discovered, (3) the lease is for a fixed term and (4) the term can be extended if the lessee drills a well or pays *delay rentals* to compensate the lessor for the lessee's failure to drill. This delay rental is the price the oil company pays for the privilege of keeping the lease in force without drilling. Delay rentals will continue to fall due as long as the oil company delays drilling. The lease will come to an end if no drilling takes place unless delay rentals are paid. This is known as the *unless lease.*

In contrast to the unless lease is the *drill or pay lease.* A drill or pay provision requires the lessee to produce oil or to pay rent. In an unless lease, the lessee's rights are terminated unless production is begun. A drill or pay lease allows the lessee to pay rent as a means of keeping the lease in effect even though the primary period has expired. 2 Summers, *Oil and Gas,* § § 331–351 (1959); Williams, *Oil and Gas,* §§ 601.5, 605 (1977).

The original *Producers 88* lease set out three rules for the payment of royalties. The lessor would receive (1) one-eighth of the oil delivered to tanks or pipelines, (2) quarterly payments of one-eighth of the value at the well of gas produced from an oil well, and (3) monthly payments of one-eighth of the value at the well of gas produced from a well producing only gas.

Since much litigation has revolved around controversies as to whether the lessee paid the rental required to keep the lease alive, the lease may have a clause protecting the lease from termination if the lessee has made a good faith effort to make the payment. The lease will usually also require the lessee (1) to bury pipelines below plow depth, (2) not to drill nearer than 200 feet from a house or barn, and (3) to pay for crop damages caused by the lessee's operations. These clauses appear to be for the lessor's benefit. Actually, they are inserted by the lessee to negate any contention that he has other obligations or liabilities. The lease also provides that once oil production begins, the lease will continue as long as oil is produced in paying quantities.

It is difficult to generalize about oil and gas lease terms. As is the case with most other legal relationships, there is no such thing as the "usual" form of oil and gas lease. Many years ago, oil companies in Oklahoma used a form that was called the "Producers 88." While this form has been copied extensively, many changes have also been made as various oil lease forms have evolved over the years. Now there is considerable variation, even among the forms bearing the Producers 88 designation.

> **REFERENCES:** Cage, *The Modern Oil and Gas Lease—A Facelift for Old 88;* 31st Annual Institute on Oil & Gas Law 177 (1980); Everett, *Wyoming Decisions Relative to the Law of Oil and Gas and Comments with Respect to Form "88" Leases,* 6 Wyo. L.J. 223 (1952); Williams & Meyers, *Oil and Gas Laws* (2d ed. 1985 & Supp. 1987).

Nomenclature. The word *royalty* originated in England, when it was used to designate the share of the production reserved by the king from those to whom the right to work mines and quarries was granted. In oil and gas law, it is the term used to designate the rent due for the right or privilege to take oil or gas out of a designated tract of land. It is the compensation provided in the lease to the landowner for the lessee's privilege of drilling and producing oil and gas and consists of a share in the oil and gas produced. It does not include either delay rentals or a bonus.

The *working interest* is the lessee's share of oil, as distinguished from the landowner's interest, or royalty interest.

An *overriding royalty* is an interest carved out of the working interest, often by means of an assignment of the working interest that reserves to the assignor a part of the oil and gas produced by the assignee.

2.04 Air Rights   A landowner may sell the space above the surface of the earth in much the same way that the mineral interest may be conveyed to another party. For example, a railroad company may own a tract of land, needing only enough of the space above the surface of the earth as will provide ample clearance for its trains. The space above that height has proved to be valuable for building purposes and may be sold or leased to a developer. *Indiana Toll Road*

Comm'n. v. Jankovich, 193 N.E.2d 237 (Ind. 1963); 1960 Law Forum 303; Mickelson, *Space Law and Air Rights From the Ground Up,* 49 Ill. B.J. 812 (1961).

In the case of the Merchandise Mart in Chicago, which was erected over the tracks of the Chicago and Northwestern Railroad, a plat or map was made and recorded, showing a subdivision in three dimensions:

1. An *air lot,* which consists of the space lying above a plane several feet above the earth's surface;

2. Quadrangular prism or *column lots* (for steel columns to support the building), which extend from the surface of the earth up to the air lot and occupy portions of the surface not occupied by railroad tracks; and

3. Cylindrical or *caisson lots,* which extend from the surface of the earth down to the center of the earth. The bottom of each column lot rests within a caisson lot.

The column lots, which share the level through which the trains move, were made narrower than the caisson lots to eliminate interference with the movement of trains. The railroad sold the air lot, the column lots, and the caisson lots to the Merchandise Mart, but retained ownership of the remainder of the tract. Bell, *Air Rights,* 23 Ill. L. Rev. 250 (1928).

Another conspicuous instance of such utilization of space above the earth's surface is the Park Avenue development in New York, where enormous sums have been invested in buildings that have been developed over railroad tracks.

2.05 Trespass The unauthorized entry upon the land of another is a *trespass.* The landowner may sue the trespasser even though no damage was caused by this trespass. The court may award *nominal damages* of $1.00.

> **EXAMPLE:** I have no right to go upon the land of my neighbor for the purpose of putting up screens, or painting, or repairing my house. *Taliaferro v. Salyer,* 328 P.2d 799, 803 (Cal. 1958).

Because of the three-dimensional nature of the ownership of real estate, trespass may occur above, on, or below the surface of the land.

> **EXAMPLE:** *A* and *B* own adjoining lands. *B* sinks an oil well near the boundary line. This well is angled so that it crosses the boundary beneath the surface and *B* is therefore pumping oil from below *A*'s land. This is called crooked-hole drilling. *A* can sue *B* for damages.

> **EXAMPLE:** Thrusting one's arm across a boundary fence is a trespass. *Hannabalson v. Sessions,* 90 N.W. 93 (Iowa 1902). A building owner cannot maintain shutters that swing across adjoining land. *Homewood Realty Corp. v. Safe Deposit & Trust Co.,* 154 A. 58 (Md. 1931).

The old theory that one's land extends to the sky was adequate when courts were dealing with simple questions. However, common sense revolts at the notion that the mere flight of aircraft over one's land is a trespass. Hence, it has been held that the flight of aircraft at high altitudes, causing no inconvenience to the landowner, is not a violation of the landowner's rights. It is only when the flight is low, as when a plane is taking off or landing and causing damage, that the landowner's rights have been invaded. Such was the case in *United States v. Causby,* 328 U.S. 256 (1946), where flights at level of eighty-three feet forced the landowner to give up the chicken farm.

On another front, a landowner may be liable to those passing from the landowner's land for injuries sustained on adjoining land, if the landowner knew of a dangerous condition on the adjoining land and did not warn or divert those crossing onto the adjoining land. *Alcaraz v. Vece,* 46 Cal. Rptr. 2d 571 (Cal. App. 1995).

2.06 Adjoining Owners

Of the frequently occurring property disputes, none seem more emotional than those between adjoining landowners. Often business concerns give way to heated and irrational battles between parties who once were close friends or business associates. The basic nature of these rights is fairly simple, but the facts of the controversies can become fairly complex. Adjoining owners owe each other the right of lateral support of the land.

> **EXAMPLE:** North and South are adjoining landowners. North wants to build a new structure on his land. To do so, North must excavate for a basement and footings. North must take care that his excavation does not cause South's land to slip into the excavation and damage South's building.

This is generally not a problem in suburban areas, but can raise to great significance in urban areas where lots are narrow, even in commercial zones.

Under the common law, this obligation only extended to the protection of adjoining land in its natural or undeveloped state (i.e., without buildings and improvements). State laws and municipal ordinances have largely changed the common law by requiring the excavating landowner to protect the structures on adjoining lands by giving them lateral support.

Another frequent source of controversy comes from the trees and plants growing on or near the boundary line. If the tree or plant is on the boundary line, it is the property of both owners and neither may injure or destroy it. *Ridge v. Blaha,* 166 Ill. App. 3d 662, 520 N.E.2d 980 (Ill. App. 1988). If the tree or plant is on the land of one of the neighboring owners, it is owned by that landowner. The neighboring landowner may cut or trim intruding branches and roots, but only to the extent that they invade the nonowner's property, *see* Robert Roy, Annotation *Encroachment of Trees, Shrubbery or Other Vegetation Across Boundary Line,* 65 A.L.R.4th 603 (1988), and not to the extent that such action would endanger the tree. *Booska v. Patel,* 30 Cal. Rptr. 2d 241 (Cal. App. 1994).

Where the occupancy of the adjoining property is rather insignificant, the cost of removal is great, and the encroaching owner acted innocently, the court may not require the encroachment removed. *Urban Site Venture II Ltd. Partnership v. Levering Assocs. Ltd. Partnership,* 665 A.2d 1062 (Md. 1995).

> **EXAMPLE:** *A* built a structure on its lot after obtaining a survey to determine that the structure was within the lot lines. After being told that the structure encroached upon a neighbor's land, *A* had the property surveyed again and determined that the structure was within the lot lines. Later, it was determined that the structure did indeed encroach upon the neighbor's land by 1.3 square feet. The value of the encroached area was $200, and the cost of removal was $500,000. The court allowed the encroachment to remain, but ordered *A* to pay damages for the continuing encroachment.

2.07 Real and Personal Property

The distinction between real and personal property is an important one. An article of personal property, such as an automobile, is called a chattel. It is sold by a bill of sale. In fact, sales of chattels need not even be in writing when the sale price is under a figure fixed by law. Ownership of real estate, on the other hand, is transferred by means of a deed.

It is a historical fact that rules of law come into existence when and as society feels a need for them. In early times when men were nomadic, driving their cattle north for the summer and south for the winter, there was no need for a law relating to real estate. People did not aspire to the ownership of land. But there was need for a law of personal property to help men decide how cattle could be sold or who would succeed to ownership at the owner's death. And so the first crude rules of property law evolved, relating to cattle. The word *chattel* derives from cattle, the earliest subject of legal ownership. Later, when men learned to cultivate the soil, real estate law evolved to deal with questions regarding the ownership of land. Differences still persist between the law relating to personal property and the law relating to real estate.

2.08   Trees and Crops   All trees, plants, and other things that grow are divided into two classes:

1. Trees, perennial bushes, grasses, etc., which do not require annual cultivation, are called *fructus naturales* and are considered real estate or real property; and

2. Annual crops produced by labor, such as wheat, corn, and potatoes, are called *fructus industriales* and are considered personal property. *Leigh v. Lynch*, 133 Ill. App. 3d 659, 662, 479 N.E.2d 346, 348 (1985); David M. Holliday, Annotation, *Conveyance of Land as Including Mature but Unharvested Crops,* 51 A.L.R.4th 1263, 1276 (1987).

Since growing crops are personal property, they may be sold orally if the sale price is under the figure fixed by law for oral sales of personal property, *Stem v. Crawford,* 105 A. 780 (Md. 1919), or by bill of sale, as any other chattel.

CHAPTER 3
Fixtures

3.01 In General   A *fixture* is an article that was once personal property, but that has been installed in or attached to land or a building in some more or less permanent manner, so that the article is then regarded in law as part of the real estate.

> **EXAMPLE:** While in a plumber's shop, a kitchen sink is personal property, a chattel. It becomes a fixture and part of the real estate when it is installed in a building.

The distinction of whether an item is classified as a fixture is important for three reasons. First, does a conveyance of real estate automatically pass ownership to these items, even though they are not expressly included in the deed? Ownership will pass to the buyer if the items are fixtures—part of the real estate. Ownership will not pass to the buyer, unless the items are expressly transferred by a bill of sale, if the items are chattels—personal property.

> **EXAMPLE:** Seller contracts to sell his or her house to Buyer. All that is described in the contract is the land. Buyer is entitled to receive the house as well as the land because the house is a fixture and is legally part of the land. Buyer is also entitled to receive the kitchen sink, furnace, toilets, and all other articles installed in the building with a view to remaining there permanently. Buyer is not, however, entitled to Seller's furniture. Articles of furniture are chattels. They do not pass with a sale of land unless specifically mentioned in the contract. Seller can take the furniture with him or her when he or she moves. Seller cannot remove the sink, furnace, or toilets.

Second, if a tenant installs these items in leased premises, do they become so much a part of the real estate that they cannot be removed when the tenant moves out? See section 3.04.

Third, the special rules that lenders must follow to obtain a security interest or mortgage lien upon these items are in part dependent upon the item's classification as realty or personalty. See section 3.05.

3.02 Tests to Determine Whether an Article Is a Fixture   It often becomes important to determine whether a particular article is a fixture. To make this determination, courts apply the following tests:

> 1. The manner in which the article is attached to the real estate. If an article is attached to a building in such a permanent fashion that it could not be removed without substantial injury to the building, it is usually held to be a fixture. This test, which was once the only test of a fixture, has lost its preeminence in modern times. *Finley v. Ford,* 304 Ky. 136, 200 S.W.2d 138 (1947).

> **EXAMPLES:** Water pipes or linoleum cemented to the floor. Cable television wires from the utility pole to the subscriber's home have been held to be a fixture of the house. *T-V Transmission, Inc. v. County Board of Equalization,* 338 N.W.2d 752 (Neb. 1983).

2. The character of the article and its adaptation to the real estate. The fact that an article was specially constructed or fitted with a view to its location and use in a particular building, or the fact that the article was installed in the building in order to facilitate the purpose for which the building was constructed, tends to show that the article was intended to become a permanent part of the building. If this is the case, the article will likely be considered a fixture.

EXAMPLES: Pews in a church; a theater sign constructed for a particular theater; screens and storm windows specially fitted to the house; electronic computing equipment installed to run the security system of an office building. Z. Fineberg, Annotation, *Electronic Computing Equipment as Fixtures*, 6 A.L.R.3d 497 (1966). *But see Allstate Ins. Co. v. County of Los Angeles*, 161 Cal. App. 3d 877, 207 Cal. Rptr. 888 (1984) (holding that normal computers are personalty).

3. The intention of the parties. Today's courts place great weight on the intention of the parties in determining whether an article is a fixture. *American Tel. & Tel. Co. v. Muller,* 299 F. Supp. 157 (D.S.C. 1968). The courts will ask was the article attached with the intention of making it a permanent part of the building? Tests 1 and 2 are helpful in determining the intention of the parties, but once that intention is determined, it must govern.

EXAMPLES: Gas stoves are often installed in apartment buildings by the building owner for the use of tenants. The stoves are intended to remain there permanently, since they increase the rental value of the apartments and form the integrated and operating building. Therefore, they are considered fixtures, even though they can be removed from the building with comparative ease. *Leisle v. Welfare B. and L. Ass'n.,* 232 Wis. 440, 287 N.W. 739 (1939). The same is true of electric refrigerators installed in apartment buildings. *Guardian Life Ins. Co. v. Swanson,* 286 Ill. App. 278, 3 N.E.2d 324 (1936). Air conditioners are necessities, not luxuries, in a modern apartment and are treated as fixtures when installed by the owner in a more or less permanent fashion. *State Auto Mutual Ins. Co. v. Trautwein* , 414 S.W.2d 587 (Ky. 1967); Michael J. Yaworsky, *Air-conditioning Appliance, Equipment or Apparatus as Fixture*, 69 A.L.R.4th 359, 395 (1989). *But see LaFleur v. Foret*, 213 So. 2d 141 (La. App. 1968) (rejecting the argument that air conditioners should be placed in the same category as furnaces and heating units, which the law considers immovables, by analogy to the functions they fulfill).

Again, it is important to remember that conservative courts are accustomed to stress Rule 1 above and would not consider a gas stove, electric range, or refrigerator installed in an apartment building a fixture. *Elliott v. Tallmadge,* 207 Or. 428, 297 P.2d 310 (1956); R.P. Davis, Annotation, *Electric Range as Fixture,* 57 A.L.R.2d 1103 (1958). There is substantial agreement on the point that a gas stove or refrigerator installed in a private home, unless the installation is custom, is not a fixture, since the owner usually intends to take it with him when the property is sold. *State v. Feves,* 228 Or. 273, 277–78, 365 P.2d 97, 99 (Or. 1961). Intention is of controlling importance if there is doubt about the outcome as a result of the application of the other tests.

The law of fixtures is an example of how the law develops, expands, and changes as customs, technology, and our society have changed. The luxuries of one generation become the necessities of the next. Since intention is the factor that dominates the determination of whether an article is a fixture, the same type of article may be a fixture in one factual setting and a chattel in another. For example, a free-standing gas stove may well be a chattel in a private home and would not be transferred automatically to the buyer with a sale of the land. In an apartment building, exactly the same kind of stove would, in many cases, be considered a fixture, passing automatically with a sale of the land. Articles of furniture (tables, chairs, and so forth), whether in a home, hotel, or furnished apartment, are universally considered chattels. *State v. Feves,* 228 Or. 273, 365 P.2d 97, 101 (Or. 1961). The decisions on carpeting are in hopeless confusion. J.H. Crebb, Annotation, *Carpets, Linoleum or the Like as Fixtures*, 55 A.L.R.2d 1044 (1957). Obviously, the better rule is that wall-to-wall carpeting installed by the owner is a fixture, especially where installed on a concrete slab or rough plywood floor.

The secret intention of the party installing the articles will not govern. The test for determining whether an article is a fixture measures the objective manifestations of the intent of the parties. This test requires an analysis of the nature of the article, the relation of the parties, the adaptation of the article to the property, the mode of annexation, and all other surrounding circumstances.

> **EXAMPLE:** The question is whether an air conditioner in an apartment is a fixture. As stated, the question is absurd. Who put it there? The tenant or the landlord? Tenants usually intend to take their property with them. Permanent annexation is not in the tenant's mind. The opposite is true if the landlord installed the air conditioner. Is it an easily removable window unit? Or is it one of 100 identical air conditioners built into apertures in the masonry wall of the building? If the latter, it is almost certainly a fixture.

It will help you understand these fixture tests if you understand a little about the history of fixture law. Hundreds of years ago in agricultural England, where we find the beginnings of this law, buildings tended to be rather simple, and the annexation test worked well enough. In America, some problems developed even in early times. A Virginia rail fence rests on the ground, but is not attached to it. The courts thought that, for obvious practical reasons, it ought to go with a sale of land, and they so decided. Later, when factories began to appear, it became evident that the annexation test was obsolete. A purchaser of a factory who is also buying the seller's business wants and rightfully expects to buy a going concern. Yet, under the old annexation test, the seller would be allowed to remove the machinery, because this could be done without injury to the building. Partly in response to circumstances such as this, the courts invented the intention test, which enabled the buyer to claim the machinery. *Hopewell Mills v. Taunton Savings Bank,* 150 Mass. 519, 23 N.E. 327 (1890). Still later, when landlords began to put stoves and refrigerators in apartments, the courts faced the same problem, and some of them decided in favor of the intention test, but some did not. Those that did not were bothered by the flimsy connection between the appliance and the building by simply plugging a refrigerator into a wall socket.

Builders equip homes with a variety of appliances that are attractive to the buyers. A prime example is the "package kitchen." It is best for the buyer to ask the builder for a bill of sale as well as a deed, the bill of sale being used to transfer ownership of the appliances. Probably most courts will treat package kitchen items as fixtures.

> **EXAMPLE:** Standard-size dishwasher installed in a well under a Formica counter top next to sink and attached to electric wiring of house by flexible metal conduit through junction box; standard-model garbage disposal attached to underside of sink; standard-model range hood located over a drop-in counter-top range were permanent fixtures, although removable without damage to the building. *Builders Appliance Supply Co. v. A.R. John Const. Co.,* 455 P.2d 615 (Or. 1969); *State Dept. v. Town & Country, Inc.,* 256 Md. 584, 261 A.2d 168 (1970).

Another fairly recent development is the use of garage door openers. These are generally permanently installed and are viewed as being fixtures. *Ablin v. Morton Southwest Co.,* 802 S.W.2d 788. 791 (Tex. Civ. App., 1990).

As you can see, in determining the intention of the party installing the fixture, the courts consider the nature of the party's interest in the property. It is unlikely that a tenant would wish to make permanent additions to the landlord's property. Hence, the rules concerning tenant's fixtures have evolved. Under these rules, most of the tenant's installations are treated as removable chattels. But, when the installations are made by the landlord, they are more likely to be thought of as true fixtures, which go to a buyer landlord even though not mentioned in the deed.

3.03 Constructive Annexation

Certain objects, though in no way attached to the building, are regarded as so strongly connected with the building that they are fixtures under the doctrine of *constructive annexation.*

> **EXAMPLE:** Ownership of the keys to a building passes when the deed is delivered to the buyer. *United States v. 967.905 Acres of Land,* 305 F. Supp. 83, 88–89 (D. Minn. 1969) *rev'd on other grounds,* 447 F.2d 764 (8th Cir. 1971).

> **EXAMPLE:** In the sale of a factory, spare or duplicate parts go with the land as fixtures because of their logical connection with the machinery.

> **EXAMPLE:** Car unit for an electric garage door opener.

The doctrine of constructive annexation has special application in the area of the financing of large industrial complexes. Heavy machinery and computer equipment that is installed for permanent use in an industrial facility, thereby becoming a constituent part of the factory or office building, will usually be deemed constructively annexed to the real estate under the *integrated industrial plant* rule. Parties to large commercial financings must deal with the potential application of this doctrine by carefully setting out their rights in their transactional documents. See section 3.05 *infra.*

3.04 Articles Removable by Tenants

Special rules are applicable in the landlord and tenant situation. Articles that a tenant is allowed to remove are classified into the following three categories:

1. Trade fixtures. In order to encourage a tenant to equip itself with the tools and implements of its trade, articles installed by a tenant for a trade or business purpose are classified as trade fixtures and may be removed by the tenant at the expiration of his lease. Intention is a significant factor in this area of the law, for it is obvious that the tenant intends to take such articles with it when it moves.

   EXAMPLES: Airplane hangars; bowling alleys; greenhouses; booths, bars, and other restaurant equipment; gasoline pumps and tanks in a filling station; barber chairs; soda fountains; oil derricks.

2. Agricultural fixtures. Articles installed by a tenant farmer for the purpose of enabling it to farm the land are called agricultural fixtures and may be removed by the tenant when it quits the land.

   EXAMPLES: Hen houses; tool sheds; maple-sugar houses.

3. Domestic fixtures. Articles installed in a dwelling by a tenant in order to render it more comfortable and attractive are removable by the tenant.

   EXAMPLES: Bookshelves; venetian blinds.

The three classes of articles that a tenant is allowed to remove are often referred to collectively as *tenant's fixtures.* Fixtures, as described in preceding sections, are real estate. Tenant's fixtures are personal property. Observe, also, that the trade fixtures rule applies only to articles installed by tenants, not to articles installed by the landowner. *Young Electric Sign Co. v. Erwin Electric Co.,* 477 P.2d 864 (Nev. 1970).

> **EXAMPLE:** Gas pumps installed by a tenant in a rented service station are clearly trade fixtures. Pumps installed by a landowner would be true fixtures and would automatically go with a sale of the land. Machinery in a factory is a fixture if installed by the landowner. *Foote v. Gooch,* 96 N.C. 265, 1 S.E. 525 (1887).

Annexations made to the property by a tenant are presumed to be for the tenant's benefit and not to enrich the owner of the land. Annexations made by an owner are presumed to be made with the intent to improve the property. *Commonwealth Edison Co. v. Property Tax Appeal Board*, 219 Ill. App. 3rd 550, 557, 579 N.E.2d 1082, 1086 (1991).

It is important to remember that lease forms, invariably drafted for the landlord's benefit, often contain clauses forbidding removal of the tenant's installations. E.T. Tsai, Annotation, *What Constitutes Improvements, Alterations or Additions Within Provisions of Lease Permitting or Prohibiting Tenant's Removal Thereof at Termination of Lease*, 30 A.L.R.3d 998 (1970).

> **EXAMPLE:** A lease of a filling station provided that at the termination of the lease all improvements on the premises would be the property of the landlord. The tenant was not permitted to remove gas pumps and tanks it had installed. *Id.* at 1034.

It is important also to remember that if the tenant moves out leaving its trade fixtures behind, they become the property of the landlord. L.S. Tellier, Annotation, *Time Within Which Tenant's Right to Remove Trade Fixtures Must Be Exercised*, 6 A.L.R.2d 322 (1948). In the process, they change from chattels to real estate, and ownership passes from tenant to landlord.

3.05 Secured Financing and Fixtures

When only the landowner and the real estate mortgagee are involved, the rule is that fixtures bought, paid for, and installed by the landowner *after* the execution of a mortgage on the land become subject to the lien of the mortgage and cannot thereafter be removed by the landowner. In this situation, in other words, the mortgage lien attaches to *all* fixtures, even trade fixtures, thereafter installed by the mortgagor, as opposed to a tenant, on the mortgaged premises. Such fixtures may not be removed without the mortgagee's consent. *Bowen v. Wood,* 35 Ind. 268 (1871). However, trade fixtures installed by a tenant, whether installed before or after the mortgage, are removable by the tenant, even though the owner of the property encumbered it with a mortgage that covered fixtures. *Standard Oil Co. v. La Crosse SuperAuto Service,* 217 Wis. 237, 258 N.W. 791 (1935).

The Uniform Commercial Code (UCC) has been adopted in nearly all fifty states. Under the UCC, a security interest in a chattel, including a chattel that has been or will be installed as a fixture, is created by means of a security agreement, which replaces the old chattel mortgage and conditional sale contract. This document, however, is not recorded. Instead, a brief notice of the existence of the security agreement is filed. This notice is a financing statement. Where an article has become or is to become a fixture, the financing statement must be filed in the recorder's office where mortgages on real estate are filed. When thus filed, it gives notice to all of the lender's security interest in the article. Subsequent purchasers of the real estate and subsequent mortgagees of the land are bound by this filing, and if a default occurs under the security agreement, the articles can be repossessed and removed by the security holder without liability for any incidental damage to the building occasioned by the removal. If the financing statement is not filed as required by law, a subsequent purchaser or mortgagee of the land is protected against removal of the articles and need not pay the unpaid balance due on the articles.

An important distinction must be made here. The UCC will not generally apply to the conflict between the ownership interest of a fixture lessor and a subsequent purchaser or mortgagee. In a number of jurisdictions, the fixture lessor's interest will be superior to the purchaser or lender's, even if those parties have no knowledge of the fixture lessor's interest. As a practical matter, however, fixture lessors often make a fixture filing to protect themselves in the event that the fixture lease is held to be a security interest. Garfinkel, *How Objects Become Fixtures,* 1 Prac. Real Est. Law. 19, 25 (1985).

Where the article is purchased and installed on the land after the recording of a mortgage on real estate, the holder of the chattel security lien may remove the article from the real estate in case of default, regardless of the incidental damage to the building. However, the security interest holder must reimburse the real estate mortgagee for the cost of repairing the physical injury to the building caused by the removal.

An interesting situation develops when a home buyer installs special options or extras in a home under construction.

EXAMPLE: Buyer entered into a contract to purchase a home from Builder. As construction progressed, Buyer installed some special equipment, including kitchen cabinets and lighting fixtures. Problems developed, and Builder's lender foreclosed, claiming the extras installed by Buyer. The court held that as between Builder and Buyer the extras were personal property and not fixtures and that the lender's security interest could not include that which Builder did not have. Thus, Buyer could remove the extras. *Saver's Bank v. Anderson,* 480 A.2d 82 (N.H. 1984).

3.06 Agreement of the Parties	All of the rules are statements of law that the courts have framed. The parties may, however, avoid the result that would follow from the impact of these rules by their agreement. Stated differently, the agreement of the parties may, by their agreement, make personal property out of what the law would consider real property and vice versa. *Lilenquist v. Pitchford's, Inc.,* 525 P.2d 93 (Or. 1974).

EXAMPLE: Landowner and Tenant agree that, notwithstanding the fact that the law would cause items installed in the leased premises to be tenant fixtures and removable by the tenant at the end of the lease term, the items shall become part of the realty and thus not removable at the end of the term. This agreement will be enforced by the courts.

Electronic systems, which are common in many real estate developments, create opportunities for the use of this concept.

EXAMPLE: A cable television company installed the necessary wiring and facilities to provide a master antenna system for a condominium complex. The agreement between the developer and the television company provided that the wiring and facilities would remain the property of the television company. The wiring and facilities could be removed without material damage to the real property. The court, after considering other evidence, held that the television system was the personal property of the television company. *Country Manors Ass'n, Inc. v. Master Antenna Systems, Inc.,* 458 So. 2d 835 (Fla. App. 1984).

This agreement would not, however, be binding upon third parties unless they took with notice of its terms. 35 Am. Jur. 2d *Fixtures* § 18.

As can be seen from the preceding examples, the rules for determining whether an item is a fixture can sometimes produce opposite results. At a minimum, the matter might be left to a court for determination. Parties entering into any type of real estate transaction should do so with a full agreement upon exactly what they consider to be fixtures and what they consider their rights and interests in those items to be. Whether it is a real estate contract, lease, or financing transaction, the documentation should set out the intention of the parties with respect to the items of related personal property and come to an agreement as to their respective rights in that property.

3.07 Severance

If the landowner actually removes an article from the land or from the building to which it has been attached, with the intention that the removal shall be *permanent,* such article becomes personal property again and does not pass by a deed of the real estate. Thus, if a landowner tears down a fence and piles the material on the land, such material does not pass by a deed of the land. The fixture has again become personal property by *severance.* If the removal is for a *temporary purpose,* as the removal of a piece of machinery for repairs, the article remains a fixture, notwithstanding its removal from the soil, and passes by a deed of the real estate.

3.08 Building Erected on Wrong Lot

A perpetual source of legal controversy concerns the rights of a party who through innocent mistake erects an improvement on the land of another party, usually land adjoining that actually owned by the improving party. Some states allow compensation to the builder in such cases. *Voss v. Forgue,* 84 So. 2d 563 (Fla. 1956); *Olin v. Reinecke, 336* Ill. 530, 168 N.E. 676 (1929); *Hard v. Burroughs,* 251 Mich. 578, 232 N.W. 200 (1930). *See generally* C.R. McCorkle, Annotation, *Compensation for Improvements Made or Placed on the Premises of Another by Mistake*, 57 A.L.R.2d 263 (1958). Other states deny any compensation on the grounds that an improving party has the obligation or duty to see to it that the improvement is built on the right land.

The basis for the court decisions awarding compensation to the party making the innocent mistake is the law of *restitution,* which is designed to accomplish precisely that. The newer cases go strongly in this direction.

> **EXAMPLE:** Landowner hired Builder to erect a house on Landowner's lot. Builder hired Surveyor to place survey stakes to define the boundary of the lot. Surveyor, by mistake, placed the stakes on the adjoining lot. Landowner was entitled to a lien on this lot (which was owned by a third party) for the value the building contributed to the lot. *Duncan v. Akers,* 262 N.E.2d 402 (Ind. App. 1970).

Similarly, to prevent the unjust enrichment of the landowner upon whose land the improvement was mistakenly erected, the developer may remove the improvement, but must restore the lot to the condition that existed prior to the work. *Peck v. M.C. Developers, Inc.,* 618 A.2d 940 (1992).

The courts take the view that the innocent improver is entitled to compensation unless he has actual knowledge of the mistake before construction begins. *Johnson v. Stull,* 303 S.W.2d 110 (Mo. 1957). If the true owner, without protest, watches a stranger building on its land, the true owner is sure to be subjected to a lien for the value of the building. It is grossly unfair not to warn the stranger of the mistake. *Benedict v. Little,* 264 So. 2d 491 (Ala. 1972).

CHAPTER 4

Easements

4.01 Easement Defined

An easement is a right acquired by a landowner to use the land of another for a special purpose.

> **EXAMPLE:** Servient and Dominant own adjoining tracts of land. By a written instrument, signed, sealed, and recorded in the proper public office, Servient grants to Dominant the right to cross Servient's tract at a particular place for the purpose of providing access to Dominant's tract from a highway abutting Servient's land. The right created for Dominant is called an easement. Servient remains the owner of the land over which Dominant may travel. Dominant has only the right to travel over the land to and from the highway.

4.02 Easement Appurtenant Runs with the Land

The easement described in the preceding section is an *easement appurtenant.* An easement appurtenant is created for the benefit of a tract of land. Consequently, for such an easement to exist, there must always be two tracts of land owned by different persons; one tract, called the *dominant tenement,* has the benefit of the easement, and the other tract, called the *servient tenement,* is crossed by the easement. In the example given in the preceding section, Dominant's tract is the one enjoying the benefit of the easement. It is therefore the dominant tenement. Servient's tract is the servient tenement since it is the tract that is subject to the easement.

Although the dominant tenement need not adjoin the servient tenement, *Egidi v. Town of Libertyville*, 251 Ill. App. 3d 224, 233–34, 621 N.E.2d 615, 622–23 (1993); *Allendorf v. Dally,* 6 Ill. 2d 577, 129 N.E.2d 673 (1955), it usually does.

An easement appurtenant is regarded as being so closely connected to the dominant tenement that, upon a sale and deed of the parcel benefitted by the easement, the easement will pass to the grantee in the deed, even though the deed does not mention it. Such an easement is said to *run with the land*. In the previous example, if Dominant should sell the land to Purchaser, Purchaser would automatically acquire the right to cross Servient's land. Whoever owns the dominant tenement owns the easement. A separate sale of the easement is not permitted.

Usually an easement is created by one landowner in favor of another landowner. However, an easement can run in favor of the holder of any interest in land.

> **EXAMPLE:** Landlord leases a store to Tenant and in the lease grants Tenant an easement of ingress and egress over Landlord's adjoining land. The easement is valid. Easements in favor of tenants are common.

4.03 Easement and License Distinguished

It is often difficult to distinguish an easement from a license. Ordinarily, an unauthorized entry on the land of another is called a trespass and makes the trespasser liable to pay damages to the landowner. The owner may, however, grant permission to enter for a particular purpose. This permission is called a license. A common example is a theater ticket that authorizes the ticket buyer to enter the theater to view the performance.

An easement is usually created by a written document; a license is often created verbally. An easement is usually a permanent right; a license is temporary. A license is a purely personal right and cannot be sold; the ownership of an easement changes with the ownership of the land to which it relates. An easement cannot be revoked; a license is revocable.

> **EXAMPLE:** *A* and *B* owned adjoining lots. They entered into a verbal agreement to establish a party driveway on the common boundary line between their lots. *B* thereafter built concrete walks and steps to the driveway. After this driveway had been in use for two years, *A* notified *B* that *A* intended to construct a driveway entirely upon *A*'s lot and expected *B* likewise to provide for itself. When *A* sought to erect a fence along the common boundary, *B* filed a suit to prevent him from doing so. The court held that *A* was within his rights, since the agreement was merely a verbal license, not an easement, and a license is revocable. *Baird v. Westberg,* 341 Ill. 616, 173 N.E. 820 (1930). With the present aversion to the unconscionable, it is doubtful the court would so hold today. *Monroe Bowling Lanes v. Woodfield Livestock Sales,* 244 N.E.2d 762 (Ohio App. 1969).

Also, courts may treat a license as an agreement for an easement where large sums of money are spent in reliance on it.

> **EXAMPLE:** Landowner owned Blackacre. Buyer wished to purchase the north half of Blackacre to erect a motel and restaurant. The parties entered into a contract of sale. Buyer explained that he would need to install drains over six inches of Landowner's land. Landowner orally agreed that he could do so. The deal was closed. Landowner later demanded that Buyer remove the drains. The court held that this was an oral agreement for an easement that became irrevocable by *part performance* when Buyer erected his buildings. *Anastaplo v. Radford,* 14 Ill. 2d 526, 152 N.E.2d 879 (1959); *Moe v. Cagle,* 385 P.2d 56 (Wash. 1963).

In considering the ruling in the *Anastaplo* case, we should understand that the phrase "part performance" has different meanings. For example, if Seller orally agrees to sell vacant land to Buyer, and Buyer takes possession and builds a home, Buyer can compel Seller to give him or her a deed. Here, part performance is proof that an oral contract of sale was made. 73 Am. Jur. 2d *Statute of Frauds* § 427. But in the *Anastaplo* case, the acts of Buyer placed him in a position where refusal to give him the right to maintain the drain would cause Buyer unjust impoverishment. 73 Am. Jur. 2d *Statute of Frauds* § 408.

As can be seen, some of the strict rules that the courts used yielded some harsh results. The courts responded over time, relaxing requirements to achieve more equitable results.

> **EXAMPLE:** Landowner owned a two-story store and office building. Landowner gave ABC Advertising Co. the right to use Landowner's roof for five years for a large advertising display. The court held that this created an easement in gross. This achieved the fair result of preventing a revocation of the instrument. *Baseball Pub. Co. v. Bruton,* 302 Mass. 54, 18 N.E.2d 362 (1938).

Parenthetically, mortgage lenders are constantly working to clear up problems created by oral agreements between neighbors. Should a neighbor apply for a mortgage, a party driveway existing under oral agreement would instantly be detected and reported by the lender's appraiser. The loan process would be stopped, and the neighbors would be required to sign and record a written agreement that sets forth their rights.

4.04   Easement in Gross

An *easement in gross* resembles an easement appurtenant, but there is no dominant tenement.

> **EXAMPLES:** Right granted to a telephone and utility company to maintain poles and wires over grantor's land; right granted to a city to construct, maintain, and operate a canal through grantor's land; easements for railroads, street railways, pipelines, and power lines.

A commercial easement in gross (i.e., one created for profit) is alienable. It can be mortgaged or sold. Kloek, *Assignability and Divisibility of Easements in Gross,* 22 Chi.-Kent L. Rev. 239 (1944); 3 Powell, *The Law of Real Property* § 419 (1981).

4.04(a)   Easement in Gross—Cable TV

The question of the apportionability of an easement in gross has assumed new and special significance since the advent of cable television and other means of electronic communication. In the usual case, a utility company, by dedication, grant, or condemnation, has acquired from the landowner a broad easement in gross to install electric and telephone lines. A cable television company then approaches the utility and obtains a license or easement to attach its cables to the existing utility poles. Theoretically, this adds a burden to the landowner's land and raises a further question as to whether an easement in gross can be conveyed to a third person or its use divided in favor of a third person. Until a few years ago, there were no decisions in this area and courts were reasoning by analogy to basic concepts of real estate law. As the years have passed and new forms of communication have developed, more cases have been decided and laws passed to deal with the relationship of the landowner and the utility or communication company as the new realities of the communication world are addressed.

We must take the law step by step. As stated previously, a commercial easement in gross is alienable. *Champaign Nat'l. Bank v. Ill. Power Co.,* 125 Ill. App. 3d 424, 465 N.E.2d 1016 (1984). It is equally clear that the grantee of an easement in gross cannot transfer to another rights greater than such grantee was given in the initial easement grant. Thus, it would seem obvious that a company that has acquired an easement for one purpose only, such as the power to cross land for the installation and operation of an electric line, could not transfer to another corporation the power to cross land with a cable TV line. This, indeed, was the precise holding in *Consolidated Cable Utilities, Inc. v. City of Aurora,* 109 Ill. App. 3d 1035, 439 N.E.2d 1272 (1982).

It must be remembered that many existing easements in gross were created long before cable TV and other communication media were invented. The language used in the creation of those easements must now be construed in light of facts that were not specifically in the minds of the parties to the original easement documents.

In *Hoffman v. Capitol Cablevision System, Inc.,* 52 A.D.2d 313, 383 N.Y.S.2d 674 (1976), the easement grant was for electricity and "messages." The court held that this included the right to hang TV cables on the poles and to assign to another the right to do so. TV programs are "messages." The court also gave us a valuable rule of construction. It held that furnishing cable TV is an important public purpose, and grants should be construed to permit cable TV installation wherever possible. Expanding upon the language of the easement grant, the court in *Henley v. Continental Cablevision of St. Louis County, Inc.,* 692 S.W.2d 825 (Mo. App. 1985), held that an easement for electric, telephone, and telegraphic service permitted the installation of cable TV. *See also Jolliff v. Harden Cable Tel. Co.,* 76 Ohio St. 2d 103, 269 N.E.2d 588 (1971).

Many easement grants create "utility" easements. The courts will be left with the task of determining what uses are included within this term. In *Illinois–Indiana Cable Tel.*

Ass'n. v. Ill. Commerce Comm., 55 Ill. 2d 205, 403 N.E.2d 287 (1973), the court held that a cable TV company was not a public utility. *See Consolidated Cable Utilities v. City of Aurora,* 108 Ill. App. 3d 1035, 439 N.E.2d 1272 (1982); *White v. Detroit Edison Co.,* 281 N.W.2d 283 (Mich. 1979).

A further problem must be dealt with. An appurtenant easement is normally regarded as nonexclusive. *Stevens v. Bird-Jex Co.,* 18 P.2d 292 (Utah 1933). Thus, if a landowner grants an easement for ingress and egress over a strip of its land to a third party, the landowner can continue to use that strip for any purpose that does not interfere with the easement holder's rights. The landowner can even cantilever a building over the easement. *Sakansky v. Wein,* 86 N.H. 337, 169 A. 1 (1933). In construing an easement in gross, on the other hand, the courts are inclined to construe the easement as exclusive. *Hoffman v. Capitol Cablevision System, Inc.,* 52 A.D.2d 313, 383 N.Y.S.2d 674 (1976). Thus, if the landowner granted to an electric company an easement to cross the land with a power line, this is usually considered to be an exclusive easement that gives the utility the sole privilege of providing power over that specific right of way. The landowner cannot give another company the right to install an electric line in that strip.

While you will not find this rule in the decisions, an examination of the decisions reveals that *utility* easements in gross are commonly thought of as being exclusive, because utility companies are natural monopolies. It would have been pointless to run two competing electrical services over the same strip of land. But as to easements appurtenant, the rule is different. If a landowner grants a driveway easement over its land, there is no reason why the driveway cannot be shared unless, of course, the grant is of an exclusive easement.

When an easement in gross is *exclusive,* only the easement owner is entitled to use it. Restatement, Property (Servitudes) § 493, Comment C. Therefore, there is a strong inference that the easement is *apportionable. Id.* This means that the easement owner may choose to share its easement with others, so long as the shared use is one permitted by the terms used in the creation of the easement. Restatement of Property (Servitudes) §185.493. The "intention of the parties" determines the true meaning of the terms used. *Id.* Comment B. If the easement in gross is *nonexclusive,* it is usually deemed to be unapportionable by the easement owner. *Id.* Comment D. In such case, the *landowner* may grant others the right to use the easement strip. *Winslow v. City of Vallejo,* 148 Cal. 723, 84 P. 191 (1906).

The U.S. Supreme Court has held that a cable television company seeking to enter upon property to service tenants must pay just compensation for this privilege. *Loretto v. Teleprompter,* 458 U.S. 419, 102 S. Ct. 3164 (1982). Accordingly, the Illinois statutes have a provision for determining just compensation in such instances for acquiring the statutory easement. 55 ILCS 5/5-1096, 65 ILCS 5/11-42-11.1. *See also City of Lansing v. Edward Rose Realty, Inc.,* 502 N.W.2d 638 (Mich. 1993). *See also* 47 U.S.C. § 541(a).

Much of this has been resolved by the enactment of the Cable Communications Policy Act of 1984, which provides cable TV access over public rights of way and through easements dedicated for compatible uses. 47 U.S.C. § 541(a)(2). This does not, however, compel access over a condominium's common areas. *Media General Cable of Fairfax v. Sequoyah Condominium Council of Co-Owners,* 991 F.2d 1169 (4th Cir. 1993). *See generally* Morton I. Hamburg, *All About Cable* (1981); I. Stein, *Cable TV* (1985).

4.05 Creation of Easement

An easement may be created by express grant, express reservation, agreement, mortgages, implied grant, implied reservation, necessity, prescription, condemnation, sale of land by reference to a plat, and by estoppel.

4.05(a)   Express Grant   A landowner may create an easement over its land by express grant, which, because it conveys an interest in land, should contain all the formal requisites of a deed. The grant should be in writing and should sufficiently describe the easement, the land subject to the easement, the character of the easement (easement for ingress and egress, and so forth), and should be signed, sealed, witnessed, acknowledged, delivered to the grantee, and recorded in accordance with local rules governing deeds. No particular words are necessary, and omission of the seal is not a fatal defect.

Although an instrument creating an easement is technically known as a *grant,* the document is not always so labeled. Very often an instrument in the form of a deed will operate as a grant of an easement by reason of the insertion of language limiting the use of the land to a particular purpose.

> **EXAMPLE:** Landowner signed a warranty deed conveying to Buyer, an adjoining landowner, a strip of land "to be used for road purposes." The quoted phrase appeared immediately following the property description in the deed. It was held that this deed did not make Buyer the owner of the strip, but only gave him an easement for road purposes. *Magnolia Petroleum Co. v. West,* 374 Ill. 516, 30 N.E.2d 24 (1940).

A grant of an easement may also be incorporated in a deed that conveys land.

> **EXAMPLE:** Landowner owns Lots 1 and 2 and sells Lot 1 to Buyer. After the property description in this deed, the following is inserted: "For the consideration aforesaid, the grantor grants to the grantee, its heirs and assigns, as an easement appurtenant to the premises hereby conveyed, a perpetual easement for ingress and egress over and across the south ten feet of Lot 2 in the subdivision aforesaid." The deed accomplishes two objects: (1) It transfers ownership of Lot 1 to Buyer and (2) gives Buyer an easement over the south ten feet of Lot 2.

The following drafting tips should be kept in mind as the easement agreement is formed.

1. The dominant and servient estate (i.e., the property that is benefitted and the property that is burdened by the easement) should be specifically described. The easement area should be precisely located within the servient estate so that the easement does not affect the entire burdened parcel. For example, since it would rarely be the intent of the parties that a roadway easement would encumber an entire parcel, as opposed to a strip within the parcel, the specific area of the roadway should be delineated.

2. The consideration for the granting of the easement, if only the agreement of the parties, should be stated. For example, the parties may use the typical drafting language, "for good and valuable consideration, the receipt and sufficiency of which are acknowledged, the parties agree as follows . . . ."

3. Words of grant, such as "the grantor hereby grants to the grantee" should be used, just as in a deed. The additional formality of conveying to the grantee "his heirs and assigns" should be followed so the easement is not deemed to be personal to the grantee and enduring only for the life of the grantee. *Elwell v. Miner,* 174 N.E.2d 43, 46 (Mass. 1961).

4. The easement grant should state whether the easement is appurtenant to a parcel of property or in gross.

5. The easement should state whether it is perpetual or whether it has a shorter duration, such as the life of the grantee or a term of years. *Texas Co. v. O'Meara,* 377 Ill. 144, 36 N.E.2d 256, 258 (1941).

6. The purpose of the easement must be stated. An easement does not exist for itself, but rather exists as an easement for access, parking, utilities, or some other purpose.

7. The use of the easement premises is not limited to the present uses of the property, or present means of technology. *See* F.T. Chen, Annotation, *Extent and Reasonableness of Use*

of Private Way in Exercise of Easement Granted in General Terms, 3 A.L.R.3d 1256, 1287 (1965). As a result, the parties must think of the future and the limits that the parties want and are willing to impose on the use of the easement at a later time. What if the easement serves a building on one of the tracts and that building is destroyed? Can the easement way be used to serve the replacement building? On a related point, the easement cannot be used to serve the additional land acquired by the holder of the easement, even if that land adjoins the dominant parcel, unless the parties so agree. The servient parcel need not be immediately adjacent to the dominant parcel. *Allendorf v. Daily*, 6 Ill. 2d 577, 129 N.E.2d 673, 679 (1955).

8. The grantee of the easement must limit the use of the easement to the purposes for which the easement was granted. For example, an easement for ingress and egress would not allow the holder to install poles and wires above the easement, or conduits under the easement. F.T. Chen, Annotation, *Extent and Reasonableness of Use of Private Way in Exercise of Easement Granted in General Terms*, 3 A.L.R.3d 1256, 1287 (1965).

9. The document should state whether the easement is exclusive to the holder or whether others, including the grantor and its successors and assigns, can share in the use of the easement. This is especially important in the case of a roadway easement.

10. While, generally, the landowner can use the area above the easement if such use does not interfere with the easement holder's use of the easement, the respective rights of the parties should be thought out and drafted into the easement agreement. *Sakansky v. Wein*, 86 N.H. 337, 169 A. 1, 2–3 (1933). There are some easements that by their nature preclude construction over the easement area. *Tide-Water Pipe Co. v. Blair Holding Co.*, 42 N.J. 591, 202 A.2d 405 (1964) (preventing construction of lake over pipeline); *Sumrall v. United Gas Pipe Line Co.*, 97 So. 2d 914 (Miss. 1957). Similarly, the landowner can use the area under the easement way in a manner that does not unreasonably interfere with the easement holder's use of the easement. *Eldorado, M., & S.W. R.R. v. Sims*, 228 Ill. 9, 81 N.E. 782, 785 (1907).

11. If the dominant parcel is later subdivided into two or more parcels, the easement runs in favor of all of those parcels. *See* R.W. Gascoyne, Annotation, *Right of Owners of Parcels into Which Dominant Tenement Is or Will Be Divided to Use Right of Way*, 10 A.L.R.3d 960 (1966). Care should be taken in the drafting process so that the easement is not allowed to be overburdened.

12. The easement grant should set out the nature and extent, if any, of the easement holder's obligations to improve, maintain and repair the easement, or the share in the cost of that improvement, maintenance, and repair.

13. The easement grant should set out the warranties of title given by the grantor, just as would be set out in a deed. The grantee should get title insurance to cover the easement grant. Just as a deed may be a nullity if the grantor does not hold title to the property to be encumbered with the easement, the easement may have no value. A frequent problem is created in the informal deal where a party gives an access easement to a neighboring landowner, without getting a joinder from the lender who holds a mortgage lien on the property. If the lender forecloses, the easement would be extinguished. Similarly, when a landowner conveys a parcel of land to a living trust, and then individually, as opposed to as a trustee of the living trust, grants the easement, the easement would be wild instrument not being given by the party in title to the land, the trustee of the living trust.

14. The servient owner has no right to relocate the easement unless the easement grant confers this right.

15. It is wise to include a clause that terminates liabilities accruing after property is transferred by either the grantor or the grantee. Similarly, liability for matters arising prior to such transfer, such as an unauthorized blocking of a nonexclusive roadway easement, should be preserved.

4.05(b) Express Reservation   A landowner, in selling and conveying part of its land, may reserve in the deed an easement in favor of the tract retained by the landowner. As in the case of grants of easements, reservations of easements, not labeled as such, occur frequently.

EXAMPLE: Landowner owns Lots 1 and 2 and sells Lot 2 to Buyer. After the property description in the deed, the following is inserted: "The grantor reserves to itself, its heirs and assigns, as an easement appurtenant to Lot 1 in the subdivision aforesaid, a perpetual easement for ingress and egress over and across the south ten feet of the premises hereby conveyed."

EXAMPLE: Landowner sold and conveyed certain land to Buyer by a deed containing the following clause: "Saving and excepting therefrom a strip of land forty feet wide along the bank of the east fork of Austin Creek all the way across said land, for a road to be built at some future time." The court held that, although the deed purported to except from its operation the forty-foot strip in question, ownership of the forty-foot strip passed to the grantee in the deed, but the grantor had an easement thereover for road purposes. *Coon v. Sonoma Magnesite Co.,* 182 Cal. 597, 189 P. 271 (1920).

4.05(c)   Creation of Easement by Agreement   The law requires no technical formula of words to create an easement. The only essential is that the parties make clear their intention to establish the easement. *Scanlan v. Hopkins,* 270 A.2d 352 (Vt. 1970).

Thus, easements may be created by contract or agreement, such contract or agreement being, in effect, the grant of the easement. A familiar illustration is the party wall agreement.

4.05(c)(1)   Party Walls   Suppose you own Lot 1 and I own adjoining Lot 2. You plan to erect a building on your lot, and I propose to erect an identical building on mine. If we can get together, we can effect an economy by means of a party wall. We will erect our buildings in such a way that on the common boundary line where our lots meet only one wall will be built, straddling the line, half on each side of it. Each of us will use that wall as a wall of our building. It will support my floors and roof and yours also. The economies of such an arrangement are obvious. The cost of the wall is shared. Land is conserved. Windows are eliminated, as is the expense of maintenance of one outside wall.

Legally, I own the half of the wall that rests on my lot, and you own the half that rests on your lot. I have an easement of support in your half of the wall, and you have an easement of support in my half. Owners planning such an arrangement enter into a party wall agreement. Naturally, a written agreement should be used, for an easement is an interest in land, and the law requires that interests in land be created in writing.

Suppose I plan to build at a time when you are not yet ready to go ahead. Here, the party wall agreement gives me the right to put half of the wall on your lot and further provides that when you decide to build, you will pay me half the cost of the wall.

The duty to repair a party wall falls equally on both owners. If either owner repairs the wall, the repairing owner is entitled to collect from the other owner half the expenses thus incurred.

Unless the party wall agreement provides otherwise, either owner may increase the height of the wall without the consent of the other. However, the entire expense must be borne by the party who heightens the wall, unless the other owner decides to use the added wall.

Additional Points on Party Walls. (1) Each owner has the right to extend the beams of its building into the party wall, but not beyond the center line of the wall. (2) The wall may be used for flues and fireplaces. (3) If an owner chooses not to erect a building on its side of the party wall, it may use that side of the wall for advertising signs. *CJS Party Walls* § 15(a)–(f). (4) As a rule, if one of the owners wishes to demolish its building, it may, but it must leave the wall intact for the support of the adjoining building. *Beasley v. Pelmore,*

259 Ill. App. 3d 513, 516, 631 N.E.2d 749, 751 (1994); *Cino Theatre Co. v. B/G Sandwich Shops,* 24 F.2d 31 (6th Cir. 1928).

4.05(d)   Mortgages   When a landowner owns Lots 1 and 2 and mortgages Lot 1, it may, at the mortgagee's insistence, include in the mortgage a grant of easement over part of Lot 2. Such a clause may run somewhat as follows:

> And as further security for payment of the debt above described, the mortgagor mortgages and grants to the mortgagee, its heirs and assigns, as an easement appurtenant of Lot 1 aforesaid, a perpetual easement for ingress and egress over and across the south ten feet of Lot 2 in the subdivision aforesaid.

Likewise, the landowner may wish to reserve, for the benefit of Lot 2, an easement over part of Lot 1. In such a case, an appropriate clause of reservation may be included in the mortgage.

The foregoing illustrations show how a mortgage can create an easement. When such a mortgage is foreclosed, ownership of the dominant and servient tenements passes into separate hands, and the real existence of the easement begins. Suppose, however, that the landowner owns a lot that enjoys the benefit of a previously created easement and mortgages the lot. In the mortgage, nothing is said concerning the easement. The mortgage is foreclosed. The purchaser at the foreclosure sale enjoys the benefit of the easement, for an appurtenant easement runs with the land even though it is not mentioned in the mortgage or in the foreclosure proceedings. Robert Kratovil, *Easement Draftsmanship and Conveyancing*, 38 Cal. L. Rev. 426 (1950).

An easement that benefits mortgaged property that is acquired by a mortgagor subsequent to the giving of a mortgage automatically comes under the lien of the mortgage and passes to the purchaser at any mortgage foreclosure sale. *First Nat'l. Trust & Sav. Bank v. Smith,* 284 Mich. 579, 280 N.W. 57, J.E. Macy, Annotation, *Loss of Private Easement by Nonuser or Adverse Possession*, 25 A.L.R.2d 1265 (1952).

The effect of a mortgage on an easement and vice versa depends on which is *prior in time*. Prior in time is prior in right.

> **EXAMPLE:** Owner mortgages Lot 1 to Lender in 1991. The mortgage is recorded. In 1992, Owner gives his neighbor an easement of access over Lot 1. In 1993, Lender forecloses his mortgage. The mortgage being prior in time to the easement was prior in right. The foreclosure destroys the easement. *Kling v. Ghilarducci,* 3 Ill. 2d 455, 121 N.E.2d 752 (1954).

> **EXAMPLE:** Owner gives Neighbor an easement of access over Owner's Lot 1 in 1991. It is recorded. In 1992, Owner mortgages the lot to Lender. Later, the mortgage is foreclosed. The easement being prior in time is prior in right and is not affected by foreclosure of the mortgage.

Laypersons are at times disturbed by the notion that foreclosure of a mortgage can destroy an easement that was bought and paid for. It must be remembered that the law assumes that a prudent person will have the title searched before paying for the property or other rights acquired. The title search would reveal the mortgage. One who buys an easement in the face of a prior recorded mortgage does so with eyes wide open and deserves no sympathy. The purchaser should have received the mortgagee's subordination to the easement.

4.05(e)   Implied Grant or Reservation   Often, when the owner of two tracts of land sells or mortgages one of them, there is no mention at all of easements, and yet as a result of the transaction, an easement is created. In such cases, the situation of the land is such that the courts feel the parties intended to create an easement even though they did not actually say so. Such easements are called *implied ease-ments*. They are created by *implied grant* and *implied reservation*. When a landowner uses one part of its land for the benefit of another part, and this use is such that if the parts were owned by different persons the right to make such a use would constitute an easement, then upon a sale of either of such parts an implied easement is created. *Cheney v. Mueller*, 485 P.2d 1218 (Or. 1971).

> **EXAMPLE:** Owner owned two adjoining lots. On each lot there was a two-story building. The buildings were separated by a partition wall. The stairway to the second floor was located entirely on one lot, and there were doors through the partition wall by which occupants of the second floor on the other lot reached their apartments. Owner sold and conveyed the lot on which the stairway was located to Buyer. There was an implied reservation of an easement for the use of the stairway, and Owner could continue to use such stairway even though the deed made no mention whatever of any easement. If Owner had instead sold Buyer the lot that had no stairway and had retained the lot on which the stairway was located, there would have been an implied grant of an easement to Buyer to use the stairway. *Powers v. Heffer-man*, 233 Ill. 597, 84 N.E. 661 (1908).

4.05(e)(1) Requirements for Creation of Implied Easement

The following are the requirements for the creation of an implied easement:

1. The prior use of one part of the land for the benefit of the other part must have been apparent. That is, the use must have been such that it would have been disclosed on a reasonable inspection of the premises. The theory is that the parties intended to continue the obvious arrangements existing when the sale took place. *Burns Mfg. Co. v. Boehm*, 356 A.2d 763 (Pa. 1975).

> **EXAMPLE:** Suppose *A* owns Lots 1 and 2, and sewage from the house on Lot 1 drains through an underground pipe running across Lot 2. There is a catch basin on Lot 2. If *B* buys Lot 2, the presence of the catch basin with a visible cover on the surface of the ground will give *B* notice and thereby create an implied easement for drainage over Lot 2. Annotation, *Implied Easement in Respect of Drains, Pipes or Sewers upon Severance of Tract*, 58 A.L.R. 824 (1929).

Note that we start with a situation where one person owns two or more adjoining tracts of land and one tract is used for the benefit of the other. This use would be considered an easement if the lands were owned separately. For this reason, the arrangement is often said to create "quasi-easements" or "almost easements," things that resemble easements. Remember that, at this point, *true* easements do not exist, because an easement connotes rights of one person in the land of another person.

2. The prior use must have been continuous.

> **EXAMPLE:** Where *A* owned two adjoining lots and constructed a driveway on the common boundary line between the lots and thereafter sold one of the lots to *B*, an implied easement was created for use of the driveway as a common or party driveway. *Walters v. Gadde*, 390 Ill. 518, 62 N.E.2d 439 (1945); *Gorman v. Overmyer*, 199 Okla. 451, 190 P.2d 477 (1947). Another example would be a party wall, and still another would be a well on the boundary line serving two adjoining properties. *Frantz v. Collins*, 21 Ill.2d 446, 173 N.E.2d 437 (1961).

3. The easement must be "necessary." That is, the easement must be highly convenient and beneficial to the property. The test of whether an easement is necessary is this: Can a substitute for this easement be obtained without unreasonable expense and trouble? If it cannot, the easement is necessary.

4. The ownership of the two tracts of land must be in one person when the use commences and become separated thereafter, so that one person owns the benefitted tract and someone else

owns the burdened tract. Charles C. Marvel, Annotation, *What Constitutes Unity of Title or Ownership Sufficient for Creation of an Easement by Implication or Necessity*, 94 A.L.R.3d 502, 505 (1979). This is obvious, for as long as the same person owns both tracts there can be no easement. By definition, an easement is a right in another's property. The manner in which the separation of ownership takes place is immaterial. Usually, it takes place when the original owner sells either the benefitted or the burdened tract to another person, but any other manner of separating the ownership will do. For example, if the owner of two such tracts places a mortgage on one of them, and such mortgage is later foreclosed, the ownership of the two tracts passes into different hands and an implied easement is created. *Liberty Nat'l Bank of Chicago v. Lux*, 378 Ill. 329, 38 N.E.2d 6 (1941). Or, if the owner of two such tracts dies, leaving a will by which he gives one tract to *A* and the other to *B*, an implied easement will be created. *Hoepker v. Hoepker*, 309 Ill. 407, 141 N.E. 159 (1923). Or, if a tract of land is divided by a partition suit, an implied easement may be created. *Deisenroth v. Dodge*, 7 Ill. 2d 340, 131 N.E.2d 17 (1955).

Implied easements are an unusual feature of easement law. The circumstances outlined above that persuade the courts to hold that an easement exists suggest to the court's mind that an easement should exist whether or not the parties ever gave the matter any thought. Had they been asked, no doubt they would have replied, "Of course, we expected the situation to continue after the sale as it was before the sale." When all the requirements coexist, this is the answer that enables the courts to say that an easement *does* exist. Why does litigation result? Many implied easement cases represent a "shakedown" effort whereby one landowner attempts to extort an unreasonable sum as compensation for the requested formal easement grant to be given to confirm the situation. Also, neighbor fights generate ill will, and litigation results.

4.05(e)(2) An Easement Can Be Implied from the Circumstances

EXAMPLE: Owner owns a lot having lake frontage and a lot landward of the beach lot. Owner sells the landward lot to Buyer with an easement for use of the beach. An easement will be implied to cross the beach lot to reach the beach. *Ames v. Prodon,* 60 Cal. Rptr. 183 (1967).

4.05(e)(3) Implied Easements—Common Scheme or Plan

It has been pointed out that where two adjoining owners erect buildings with a party wall straddling the boundary line, an easement is created even though no written document exists. This idea can be carried a step further. Where two adjoining landowners engage in a scheme of common development that cannot exist without easements, easements exist.

EXAMPLE: Owner 1 owns Lot 1 and Owner 2 owns the adjoining Lot 2. By verbal agreement, they erect buildings with an arcade of shops straddling the boundary line between the lots. Easements for the arcade now exist even though there is no written document. *Blakeney v. State,* 163 S.E.2d 69 (N.C. 1968).

EXAMPLE: Owner owns a large lot on which it erects row houses or town houses at right angles to the street. Owner sells the town houses. Implied easements come into being for ingress, egress, sewer, water, electricity, etc. *Gilbert v. Chicago Title & Trust Co.,* 7 Ill. 2d 492, 131 N.E.2d 1 (1956).

4.05(f) Easement of Necessity

When the owner of land sells a part thereof that has no outlet to a highway except over the remaining land or over the land of strangers, a right of way by necessity is created by implied grant over the remaining land of the seller.

Easements of necessity are often confused with implied easements. Easements by necessity rest on the philosophy that land is a valuable community asset and none of it should be rendered landlocked and useless. To allow a tract of land to be without access is an intolerable waste of a valuable resource. The implied easement, on the other hand, rests on the assumption that the obvious and beneficial use was intended to continue after ownership of the parcels was severed. For this reason, the courts require only that the use be highly beneficial, for this also tends to establish that it was intended to continue.

In the case of an easement by necessity, a totally *new factual situation* is created. A tract of land, previously part of a larger parcel that had access to the outside world, is suddenly converted into an island with no means of access. The courts create a *new* means of access so that the island can remain useful. Easements by necessity are rare; implied easements are common.

It has been held that an easement by necessity will be created even though the landowner has legal access to the property, if that legal access is impractical. *MacCaskill v. Ebbert,* 739 P.2d 414 (Idaho 1987). A similar result will follow if the alternative route is very expensive. *Bean v. Nelson,* 817 S.W.2d 415 (Ark. 1991). *See also,* Michael A. DiSabatino, Annotation, *Way of Necessity over Another's Land, Where a Means of Access Does Exist, but Is Claimed to Be Inadequate, Inconvenient, Difficult or Costly,* 10 A.L.R.4th 447 (1981).

4.05(g) Prescription   *Prescription* is the acquisition of a right by lapse of time. An easement may be acquired by prescription, just as ownership of land may be created by adverse possession. Usually, the period of time required for the acquisition of an easement by prescription is the same period as that required for the acquisition of ownership of land by adverse possession. This period, called the *prescription period,* varies from state to state. Periods of ten, fifteen, and twenty years are common.

> **EXAMPLE:** Owner owned a private alley and an adjoining apartment building. Neighbor owned a neighboring apartment building. Without any permission from Owner, Neighbor's tenants constantly used Owner's private alley in order to enter their apartments from the rear. Whenever Owner's tenants parked their cars in the alley, Neighbor would call the police and have them put out. This continued for more than twenty years. Then, Owner attempted to stop this use of the alley by Neighbor's tenants. It was held that Owner could not do so, since Neighbor had acquired an easement by prescription. *Rush v. Collins,* 366 Ill. 307, 8 N.E.2d 659 (1937).

> **EXAMPLE:** Owner owned a house and lot. Owner constructed a garage in the rear of the lot. Because the space adjoining Owner's house was inadequate for a driveway, Owner constructed one that ran partly across Neighbor's adjoining land. This was done without seeking Neighbor's permission. Owner used this driveway for over twenty years. Owner acquired a prescriptive easement to continue to use it. *Nocera v. De Feo,* 340 Mass. 783, 164 N.E.2d 136 (1959).

The following are the requirements for the creation of an easement by prescription:

1. The use must be *adverse.* If it is under permission or consent of the owner, the use is not adverse. There must be such an invasion of the landowner's rights as would entitle the landowner to maintain a suit against the intruder. If the use is, on its face, permitted as a matter of neighborly accommodation, the use is not adverse or hostile.

    > **EXAMPLE:** Owner had a driveway running to a garage in the rear of his house. Neighbor often used this driveway to get his car into his backyard. Neighbor never sought Owner's permission, although they were good friends. This use will not ripen into a prescriptive easement. It is, on its face, a matter of neighborly accommodation. *Stevenson v. Williams,* 188 Pa. Super. 49, 145 A.2d 734 (1958).

2. The use must be *under claim of right,* in that there must be no recognition of the right of the landowner to stop the use.

3. The use must be *visible, open,* and *notorious,* so that the landowner is bound to learn of it if the landowner keeps itself well informed about its property.

    EXAMPLE: The secret placing of a drainpipe in a wooded gully would not be considered notorious.

4. The use *must not be merely as a member of the public.* The use by the claimant of the easement must be sufficiently exclusive to give notice of an individual claim of right.

5. The use must be *continuous* and *uninterrupted* for the required period of time. That is, the easement must be exercised whenever there is any necessity for its use, and the use must be of such frequency as to apprise the landowner of the right being claimed.

    EXAMPLE: Occasional entries upon a neighbor's land, for example, to put up screens or storm windows, to paint a wall, to trim a hedge, or to clean gutters, are not such continuous uses as will ever ripen into a prescriptive easement. *Romans v. Nadler,* 217 Minn. 174, 14 N.W.2d 482 (1944).

    The use may, however, be seasonal, such as the use of a roadway for access to a summer cabin during the summer months, as long as the use is continuous, uninterrupted, and commensurate with appropriate seasonal uses. *Miller v. Rau,* 597 N.Y.S.2d 532 (1993). It is not necessary that the adverse use be that of one person only.

    EXAMPLE: In Illinois, the prescriptive period is twenty years. Suppose that *A* and *B* are neighbors. *A* builds a driveway over *B*'s land without *B*'s permission. *A* uses the drive for five years. *A* sells his land to *C*, who also uses the driveway for five years. *C* sells to *D*, who uses the driveway for ten years. Now, *D* has a prescriptive easement. The prescriptive uses that *A*, *C*, and *D* made can be tacked, that is, added together to make up the required twenty years. Jeffrey F. Ghent, Annotation, *Tacking as Applied to Prescriptive Easements*, 72 A.L.R.3d 648 (1976). Also, since the easement was used for the benefit of a tract of land, it is an easement appurtenant and will thereafter run with the land so benefitted.

    Nearly all prescriptive easements are appurtenant easements.

Where an easement is acquired by prescription or any other means, the easement owner automatically acquires as rights incidental to the easement all rights needed for the useful enjoyment of the easement.

    EXAMPLE: *A* and *B* owned adjoining Lots 7 and 8. *A* erected a three-story building on Lot 7 and attached a fire escape to the building on Lot 7. The fire escape extended over the space above Lot 8. As is customary, the lowest member of the fire escape extended in a horizontal direction, hinged in such a fashion that it could be lowered to the ground level of Lot 8 in case of fire. After twenty years, *B* threatened to build under this horizontal member. The court held that *A*'s prescriptive easement included, as a right incidental to the right to maintain the fire escape, a right to lower the horizontal member into an unimproved area beneath. *Poulos v. F.H. Hill Co.,* 401 Ill. 204, 81 N.E.2d 854 (1948).

4.05(g)(1) Party Driveways

Suppose you and I own adjoining lots, each with a house on it, and, pursuant to a verbal agreement, we build a party driveway, straddling the boundary line between our lots and serving our garages in the rear of our lots. Each of us uses this driveway continuously for the required period of time. Most courts hold that a party driveway easement has been created by prescription. 98 A.L.R. 1096. This is quite a legal oddity, for obviously such common use is permissive, not adverse. Yet, to prevent injustice, courts allow prescriptive easements to be created by such use. *Petersen v. Corrubia,* 21 Ill. 2d 525, 173 N.E.2d 499 (1975).

4.05(g)(2)   State Laws   State laws have been enacted, as in Illinois, that prevent the creation of an easement by prescription if the landowner posts signs forbidding use of his land. This relieves the landowner of making periodic inspections of his vacant land to see if strangers are using it.

4.05(g)(3)   Public Highways   When the public has used a privately owned strip of land for the purpose of passage for the required period of time, courts often hold that an easement for a public highway has been created by prescription.

4.05(h)   Creation of Easement by Condemnation   Although in some states laws provide that complete ownership of the land may be acquired by condemnation, the general rule is that where land is taken by condemnation for a street, highway, railroad right of way, or telephone or electric power line, the taker acquires only an easement. All such easements are easements in gross.

> **EXAMPLE:** City wishes to open a street across Owner's land, but Owner is unwilling to sell. City files a condemnation suit against Owner, and a judgment is entered fixing the full market value of the strip to be taken for the opening of the street. City pays this amount into court. Although City pays the full market value of the strip, it acquires only an easement thereover, and Owner remains the owner subject to the easement. Thus, Owner may construct subvaults beneath the street without any liability to City for payment of rent.

4.05(i)   Sale by Reference to Plat   Where a developer subdivides land into lots, blocks, streets, and alleys, and thereafter sells lots in the subdivision, each purchaser of a lot automatically acquires an easement of passage over the streets and alleys shown on the plat or map of the subdivision, even though the deed to the lot makes no mention of such right. Such a private easement becomes important where the subdivider attempts to close up a street or alley before the public has acquired the right to insist that such street or alley remain open. The lot owners are in a position to keep the street open by virtue of their easement rights, even though the street never became a public street. V. Woerner, Annotation, *Conveyancing of Lot with Reference to Map or Plat as Giving Purchaser Rights in Indicated Streets, Alleys, or Areas not Abutting His Lot*, 7 A.L.R.2d 607 (1949).

The plat also gives the city rights in the dedicated streets and public rights. In some instances, the city acquires full ownership of the dedicated streets. In other cases, it acquires only an easement. C. S. Tellier, Annotation, *Validity and Construction of Regulation as to Subdivision Maps or Plats*, 11 A.L.R.2d 524 (1950).

4.05(j)   Easement by Estoppel   There are other instances of the creation of an easement by *estoppel*.

> **EXAMPLE:** Owner owns sewer and water pipe in a street running past its property and other vacant land owned by Owner. Owner makes a deed of a vacant lot to Buyer, but nothing is said about the sewer and water pipes. Buyer builds a house and Owner, without objection, watches Buyer tie into the sewer and water pipes. An easement to use the sewer and water services has been created by estoppel. *Monroe Bowling Lanes v. Woodfield Livestock Sales,* 244 N.E.2d 762 (Ohio App. 1969).

> **EXAMPLE:** Corporation leased a co-op apartment in its apartment building to Tenant. Corporation had a plat in its office, showing a recreation area with swimming pool adjoining the building, and its agent always referred to this recreation area when making his sales pitch on apartments. An easement by estoppel has been created. Tenant can use the recreation area. *Hirlinger v. Stelzer,* 222 So. 2d 237 (Fla. App. 1969).

4.05(k) Declaration of Easements

Easements are used so extensively in the planned unit development, town house, condominium, and other new development context, that they are now typically contained in a document that also includes building restrictions, Homeowners' Association liens, and the like. This document is thus called a Declaration of Restrictions, Easements, Liens, and Covenants. As distinguished from the old practice of including all of the restrictions, building lines, and easements in the deed to purchasers in the development, the declaration is executed and recorded, and then merely referred to in the deeds that are given to buyers.

4.06 Unlocated Easements and Relocation

If *R* owns a large tract of land and grants to *E* an easement over that tract, manifestly it is not *R*'s entire tract that comprises the servient tenement, for it is not intended that *E* shall wander aimlessly over the premises. It is, rather, the intention of the parties that some small part of the tract shall become the easement or servient tract. The parties have simply failed to specify the precise location of the easement. In such cases, the owner of the servient tenement has, in the first instance, the right to designate the location of the easement, provided the owner exercises this right in a reasonable manner, having regard to the suitability and convenience of the right of way to the rights and interests of the owner of the dominant tenement. If the owner of the servient tenement fails or refuses to locate the way, the owner of the dominant tenement may select the location, having due regard to the interests, rights, and conveniences of the other party. William B. Johnson, Annotation, *Location of Easement of Way Created by Grant Which Does Not Specify Location*, 24 A.L.R.4th 1053 (1983). Court action may be necessary if the parties cannot agree. Disputes and litigation can be avoided through the simple device of employing a surveyor to locate and monument the easement tract on the ground, whereupon a legal description can be prepared and included in the easement grant.

Once an easement has been located, either by the act of the parties in agreeing upon its location or in the initial easement grant, the location cannot be changed without the consent of the easement owner.

> **EXAMPLE:** Owner owns two lots. Lot 1 abuts on a highway. Owner sells Lot 2 to Buyer, simultaneously granting an easement of ingress and egress to the highway. The easement runs through the middle of Lot 1, rendering it unusable. Owner has no right to change the location of the easement. *Davis v. Bruk,* 411 A.2d 660 (Me. 1980); *Sedillo Title Guar., Inc. v. Wagner,* 457 P.2d 361 (N.M. 1969).

The easement can be relocated if both parties acquiesce, even without a written document.

> **EXAMPLE:** In the last example, suppose Owner and Buyer verbally agree on relocation. Owner blacktops a new driveway along the edge of Lot 1, and the old drive is torn up. The easement has been relocated by acquiescence. F.M. English, Annotation, *Relocation of Easements (Other than Those Originally Arising by Necessity); Rights as Between Private Parties*, 80 A.L.R.2d 743 (1961). *See* William B. Johnson, Annotation, *Location of Easement of Way Created by Grant Which Does Not Specify Location*, 24 A.L.R.4th 1053 (1983) (regarding the location of an easement by necessity).

4.06(a) Pipeline Easements

Most unlocated easements are pipeline easements. Pipelines extend over many miles of ground. The pipeline companies send out right-of-way crews to acquire the easements. Once a member of such a crew has determined the ownership of a farm, he or she uses a simple form that the farmer and spouse sign. It gives the pipeline company an easement over the entire farm. This is perfectly valid. *Collins v. Slocum,* 284 So. 2d 98 (La. App. 1973).

A land developer who buys a farm for development cannot live with an unlocated ease-ment. The developer should contact the pipeline company and obtain a release of the ease-ment over all of the farm except the land through which the pipeline runs. If there is a mortgage on the pipeline, that is also released, except as to the actual line of the pipe.

Once a pipeline has been installed in a pipeline easement, some courts hold that addi-tional pipes or a larger pipe cannot be installed. *Winslow v. City of Vallejo,* 148 Cal. 723, 84 P. 191 (1906). The far better rule is precisely to the contrary. *Standard Oil Co. v. Buchi,* 72 N.J. Eq. 492, 66 A. 427 (1907); *Weaver v. Natural Gas Pipeline Co. of America,* 27 Ill. 2d 48, 188 N.E.2d 18 (1963). This problem should be covered in the grant.

4.07   Complex Easements

Today, complex easements are employed in a number of situations. Wherever two or more parcels of land, whether those parcels are side by side or stacked on top of one another, are used in common, an easement agreement should be entered into between and among the owners so that their mutually dependent rights are defined and memorialized.

A shopping center is a common example. Many department stores own the "pad" on which the store is built. Since the store is dependent upon the adjoining parcels for access and utility easements, among other things, a reciprocal easement agreement is entered into by the neighboring owners. This agreement allows the employees and customers of one owner to cross the land of the other for pedestrian and vehicular access and parking. The REA, as it is called, also allows the utility easements to pass through and service the ad-joining parcels. These agreements may get more complicated and include common area maintenance cost payment arrangements, operating covenants, and other agreements that govern the operation of the shopping center.

It is also commonplace to find a multistory building divided into multiple ownerships and uses. The lower floors may be devoted to office building use and be owned by *A*. The upper floors may be devoted to residential apartments and be owned by *B*. *B* may even choose to divide the apartment area into condominiums so that each apartment is separately owned. Such, indeed, is the situation in the case of the many multiuse buildings found in al-most all major cities.

The structural members of the bottom of the building support the upper floors. Eleva-tor shafts serving the upper floors travel through the lower building. Heating, ventilating, and air-conditioning ducts, as well as water and utilities, travel through both sections of the building. A very lengthy Easement and Operating Agreement is prepared. There are prob-lems, to be sure, but they are all capable of solution.

4.08   Structure Easement–Easement Through Structure

Where an easement is created in a structure without creating any interest in the land, ordi-narily, destruction of the structure destroys the easement.

> **EXAMPLE:** Owner owned Lot 1 on which he erected a two-story apartment building. When the city passed an ordinance requiring second-story apartments to have two exits, Owner ac-quired from Neighbor the right to make an opening into Neighbor's building, which was flush against Owner's building, and to use Neighbor's stairway as the second exit. Neighbor's building was destroyed by fire. The easement is extinguished. Annotation, *Destruction of Building as Terminating Easement Therein,* 154 A.L.R. 82 (1945).

4.08(a)   Easement in Favor of Structure

If an easement is created *in favor of* a structure only, destruction of the structure similarly terminates the easement.

> **EXAMPLE:** *X* and *Y* were neighbors. Intending to build a stable for riding horses, *X* pur-chased from *Y* driveway rights over *Y*'s land to and from the stable to be erected on the rear

of *X*'s land. Ultimately, the stable was destroyed by fire. The easement was terminated. 2 Thompson, *Real Property* § 764, 766 (perm. ed.).

4.09 Right to Profits of the Soil

An easement does not confer on the easement owner any right to the profits of the soil, such as oil, hay, coal, or minerals.

EXAMPLE: County acquired a highway over Owner's land by condemnation. County has no right to drill oil wells on the land covered by the road. The County has only an easement for road purposes.

The landowner whose land is subject to the easement has the right to oil, minerals, and other profits of the soil.

4.10 Use of Easement Premises—Dominant and Servient Tenements

An easement appurtenant can be used only for the benefit of the dominant tenement. It may not be used for the benefit of any other tract of land. The dominant tenement is the land intended to be benefitted *at the time the easement was created*. Land acquired by the owner of the dominant tenement after the creation of the easement has no right to use the easement. It is nondominant land.

EXAMPLE: Owner owned Lot 2. An easement appurtenant to Lot 2 allowed the owner of Lot 2 to use a spur or switch track over Lot 1 to the west of Lot 2. Owner thereafter bought Lot 3, which adjoined Lot 2 to the east, and erected a powerhouse on Lot 3. The switch track could not be used to service the powerhouse since the switch track easement was appurtenant only to Lot 2. *Goodwillie Co. v. Commonwealth Edison Co.,* 241 Ill. 42, 89 N.E. 272 (1909); *Ogle v. Trotter,* 495 S.W.2d 558 (Tenn. App. 1973); *College Inns of America, Inc. v. Cully,* 460 P.2d 360 (Or. 1969).

Particularly in the case of industrial easements, it is well to keep in mind at the time easement is created that the dominant owner may later wish to acquire other neighboring land for plant expansion. The easement grant should provide that such subsequently acquired property shall enjoy the benefit of the easement.

If the dominant tenement is divided, the easement runs in favor of each part into which it is divided. R.W. Gascoyne, Annotation, *Right of Owners of Parcels Which Dominant Tenement Is or Will Be Divided to Use Right of Way,* 10 A.L.R.3d 960 (1966); Annotation, *Conveyance of Right of Way in Connection with Conveyance of Another Tract as Passing Fee or Easement,* 89 A.L.R.3d 767 (1979).

EXAMPLE: Owner, owning the bed of a lake and the land surrounding the lake, sells Buyer a lot that does not have lake frontage. The deed includes an easement of access to the lake and a right to use the lake for recreation. Buyer sells half his lot to his brother, both parts abutting on the easement of access. Both Buyer and his brother can use the easements. There is some limit, not very clearly defined, on how far you can go with this. R.W. Gascoyne, Annotation, *Right of Owners of Parcels Which Dominant Tenement Is or Will Be Divided to Use Right of Way,* 10 A.L.R.3d 960, 968 (1966). Suppose Buyer were to divide his lot into fifty lots. The courts might not permit use of the easements. This is an excessive *increase of burden. Crocker v. College of Advanced Science,* 268 A.2d 844 (N.H. 1970).

Where an easement of ingress and egress is created by grant, it may be used by the easement owner for all reasonable ingress and egress purposes, and use is not restricted to such purposes as were reasonable at the date of the grant.

EXAMPLE: Use of the easement by automobiles will be permitted even though an easement was created when horse-drawn vehicles were in use. F.T. Chen, Annotation, *Extent and Rea-*

sonableness of Use of Private Way in Exercise of Easement Granted in General Terms, 3 A.L.R.3d 1256, 1287 (1965). Use of utility easement may be expanded to add fiber optic cables. *Edgcomb v. Lower Valley Power and Light, Inc.*, 922 P.2d 850 (Wyo. 1996).

With changing conditions, more intensive use may be made of the easement than was contemplated at the time the easement was created.

> **EXAMPLE:** At the time an easement of ingress and egress was created, the dominant tenement was occupied by a private dwelling. Later, this dwelling was replaced by a hotel. It was held that the hotel could continue to use the easement. *White v. Grand Hotel*, 1 Ch. 113 (1913).

> **EXAMPLE:** In another case, the holder of an access easement extended its use to a shopping center that covered both the dominant tenement and an adjoining parcel. This extension of the use resulted in a total loss of the access easement. While the normal remedy for overuse of an easement is an injunction to enjoin the overuse, the exceptional use to which this easement was put so combined the proper and improper use that the only practical remedy was the forfeiture of all of the easement rights. *DND Neffson Co. v. Galleria Partners*, 745 P.2d 206 (Ariz. App. 1987). Where an injunction will protect the servient tenement holder, the easement will not be terminated by its overuse. *McCann v. Dunteman Co.*, 609 N.E.2d 1076 (Ill. App. 1993).

Where an easement is acquired by *prescription,* use of an easement after the prescriptive period has expired must remain pretty much the same as the use that took place during the prescriptive period. Certain current upgrades to the easement way are permissible.

> **EXAMPLE:** A prescriptive driveway easement may be upgraded from dirt to gravel and a bridge may be constructed where a stream was forded because such improvements were foreseeable consequences of the development of the dominant parcel. The installation of utility lines beneath the easement way was not permitted because they were not foreseeable. *Kuras v. Kope,* 533 A.2d 1202 (Conn. 1987).

If the width of an easement is fixed at the time of its creation, it will not grow wider even though conditions change.

> **EXAMPLE:** In 1918, Owner granted Neighbor a ten-foot easement for ingress and egress. The fact that today's big trucks cannot use so narrow a way does not increase the size of the easement. *Feldstein v. Segall,* 198 Md. 285, 81 A.2d 610 (1951).

On the other hand, the servient owner has no right to diminish the easement holder's right of use by placing pillars or other structures in the passageway. The easement holder has the right to use the full passageway. *Rudolph Wurlitzer Co. v. State Bank,* 290 Ill. 72, 124 N.E. 844 (1919). Nonetheless, the servient owner may take reasonable actions to make the use of the easement safe, such as by installing speed bumps. *Wilson v. Palmer,* 622 N.Y.S.2d 882 (1995). *See* Annotation, *Legal Aspects of Speed Bumps,* 60 A.L.R.4th 1249, 1254–56 (1988).

The holder of an access easement can park to load and unload, but cannot park overnight. This does not mean, however, that the owner of an easement for ingress and egress has the exclusive right to use the surface of the land for that purpose. The landowner remains the owner of the easement premises, subject only to the prescribed rights of the easement owner, and has the right to make any use of the easement tract that does not interfere with the easement. Daniel E. Field, Annotation, *Right to Maintain Gate or Fence Across Right of Way,* 52 A.L.R.3d 9 (1974).

> **EXAMPLE:** In the case of an easement of ingress and egress, the landowner may travel over the easement tract as long as such travel does not interfere with the easement holder's right of travel. The landowner, indeed, may even erect structures or run power lines above the easement, so long as the underlying owner leaves space at the surface adequate for travel by the easement owner. *Sakansky v. Wein,* 86 N.H. 337, 169 A. 1 (1933*); Cleveland Railway Co. v. Public Service Co.,* 380 Ill. 130, 43 N.E.2d 993 (1942). Or, a landowner may tunnel and mine minerals beneath an easement for ingress or egress or build over a water pipe easement.

Since an easement is a right to use another's land for a special purpose only, the easement owner must use the easement premises only for that purpose for which the easement exists. Robert Kratovil, *Easement Law and Service of Non-Dominant Tenements: Time for a Change,* 24 Santa Clara L. Rev. 649 (1984).

> **EXAMPLE:** Owner grants Neighbor an easement for ingress and egress over a part of Owner's land. Neighbor has no right to lay gas pipes in the easement premises. F.T. Chen, Annotation, *Extent and Reasonableness of Use of Private Way in Exercise of Easement Granted in General Terms,* 3 A.L.R.3d 1256, 1278 (1965).

4.11 Maintenance and Repair of Easement Facilities

The fact that Owner gives Neighbor an easement over Owner's property imposes no duty on Owner to pave the easement tract, keep it in repair, or do anything at all for Neighbor's benefit. Annotation, *Rights and Duties of Owners* Inter Se *with Respect to Upkeep and Repair of Water Easements,* 169 A.L.R. 1147, 1152 (1947).

> **EXAMPLE:** Owner gave Neighbor an easement to take water from a well on Owner's land. It was held that Owner was not obliged to operate the pump to furnish Neighbor's water even though that was the physical situation at the time the easement was created. *Gowing v. Lehmann,* 98 N.H. 414, 101 A.2d 463 (1953).

Therefore, if the parties agree that the owner of the burdened land is to have some affirmative duties, they must be spelled out in the easement grant.

Of course, the easement owner has the right to take all steps necessary to make this easement usable. For example, in an easement of ingress and egress, the easement owner would have the right to repair or improve an existing road, to lay down a new road, to build bridges across streams, to trim encroaching trees and shrubs, to blast rocks, and to otherwise remove impediments, and so forth. Annotation, *Rights and Duties of Owners* Inter Se *with Respect to Upkeep and Repair of Water Easements,* 169 A.L.R. 1147, 1152 (1947); E.H. Schopler, Annotation, *Right of Servient Owner to Maintain, Improve, or Repair Easement of Way at Expense of Dominant Owner,* 20 A.L.R.3d 1026.

Also, where a private road is used by *both* the landowner and the easement owner, they must divide the cost of repairs in proportion to their use of the road, even though the easement agreement is silent on this score. *Stevens v. Bird-Jex Co.,* 81 Utah 355, 18 P.2d 292 (1933).

If the easement tract is used only by the easement owner and falls into disrepair as a result of neglect, the easement holder has no right to deviate from the prescribed way and travel over other land belonging to the landowner. *Dudgeon v. Bronson,* 159 Ind. 562, 64 N.E. 910 (1902). On the other hand, if the landowner obstructs the easement, the easement owner has the right to travel around the obstruction over other land belonging to the landowner.

<table>
<tr><td>**4.12 Termination of Easement**</td><td>Easements may be terminated in the following ways:</td></tr>
</table>

1. When an easement has been created for a particular purpose, it ceases when the purpose ceases.

   EXAMPLE: A party wall agreement ceases when both buildings are destroyed by fire, unless the party wall agreement provides otherwise. An easement for railroad purposes ends when the railroad tears up its tracks and discontinues service.

2. When the owner of an easement becomes the owner of the land that is subject to the easement, the easement is extinguished by merger.

3. The owner of an easement may release the easement right to the owner of the land that is subject to the easement.

4. The owner of an easement may terminate it by abandonment. For this to occur, there must be an intention to abandon the easement and acts manifesting such intention.

4.12(a) Tax Sale

In some states, a tax sale of the servient tenement extinguishes the easement. In others, it does not. Holly P. Rockwell, Annotation, *Easement, Servitude, or Covenant as Affected by Sale for Taxes*, 7 A.L.R.5th 187 (1992); Annotation, *Easement, Servitude or Restrictive Covenant as Affected by Enforcement of Assessment of Improvement Liens*, 26 A.L.R. 873. In many states, as in Illinois, the matter is governed by statutes that preserve the easement. 35 ILCS 200/22–70. *See also Arizona R.C.I.A. Lands, Inc., v. Ainsworth*, 515 P.2d 335 (Ariz. App. 1973); *Fields v. District of Columbia*, 443 F.2d 740 (D.C. Cir. 1971), citing Restatement of Property § 509(2); 5 *Powell on Real Property* 225; Robert Kratovil, *Tax Sales: Extinguishment of Easements, Building Restrictions and Covenants*, 19 Hous. L. Rev. 55 (1982).

4.13 Special Types of Easements

4.13(a) Streets

Easements vary, of course, as to their scope.

EXAMPLE: Owner grants Neighbor an easement for ingress and egress. This easement cannot be used for installation of water pipes or electric conduits.

However, courts give an easement given to a municipality for street purposes a very broad interpretation. The adjoining owners own the land constituting the street. But, the city's easement permits the use of the street for transportation of all kinds, including transportation of electricity (electric poles) or of messages (telegraph poles). Robert Kratovil, *Easement Draftsmanship and Conveyancing*, 38 Cal. L. Rev. 426 (1950). The city usually grants to utility companies the right to install these poles. This right is called a *franchise*. So far as cable television is concerned, the TV company would have to obtain a franchise from the city. But, if it intends to fasten its cable to existing telegraph poles, it must also obtain an agreement from the telegraph company.

In most, but not all, states, if a deed of land refers to an adjoining street or other way, it automatically creates an easement of access over the street or way if the grantor owns the land comprising the street or way.

EXAMPLE: Owner owns Lot 1 in Block 1 in Chicago Heights and a strip of land east and adjoining known in the neighborhood as Holden Court. Holden Court is not a public street. Owner makes a deed to Buyer of part of Lot 1 described as "bounded on the east by Holden Court." This deed gives Buyer an easement right in Holden Court. This is sometimes called an *easement by estoppel*.

Obviously, this is a poor substitute for a properly planned easement grant.

4.13(b) Scenic Easements

As the population grows, so does concern for the preservation of open spaces, especially for scenic treasures that remain in private ownership. These same sites are also heavily sought after by developers. Under recent legislation and court decisions, a state may condemn or purchase a scenic easement that, in effect, forbids the landowner to build upon his land. The Federal Highway Beautification Act offers incentives to the state to create such easements. *Markham Advertising Co. v. State,* 439 P.2d 248 (Wash. 1968).

> **EXAMPLE:** Owner owns a stretch of rolling farmland through which a lovely river winds. The land abuts a highway that commands an excellent view of the scene. The state condemns Owner's right to build upon the farm and pays Owner compensation for the deprivation of this right. He may continue to occupy and farm the land, but it will never be developed. This right acquired by the state is called a scenic easement. *Kamrowski v. State,* 31 Wis. 2d 256, 142 N.W.2d 793 (1966). The state has acquired the farmer's "development rights."

4.13(c) Solar Easements

England has a doctrine called ancient lights.

> **EXAMPLE:** Owner owns Lot 1 on which a house has stood for many years. Neighbor owns a vacant lot next door. In England, Neighbor would not be permitted to erect a high building on its lot that would cut off Owner's light.

In America, the situation is treated quite differently. In America, Neighbor can build any building that is permitted by local law, even if it cuts off Owner's sunlight.

> **EXAMPLE:** The Fountainebleau Hotel in Miami Beach added fourteen stories to its structure. This cast a shadow on the swimming pool of the nearby Eden Roc Hotel. The court held that the Eden Roc was without any legal remedy. *Fountainebleau Hotel Corp. v. Forty-Five Twenty-Five, Inc.,* 114 So. 2d 357 (Fla. App. 1959). *See also Blumberg v. Weiss,* 17 A.2d 823 (N.J. 1941); 1 Am. Jur. 2d *Adjoining Landowners* § 753.

Of course, if an action is prompted by pure spite, the law will provide a remedy.

> **EXAMPLE:** Owner owns a house, and Neighbor owns an adjoining vacant lot. They quarrel. Neighbor attempts to erect a wall for the sole purpose of blocking light and air from Owner's windows. The courts will stop this.

It goes without saying that the neighboring landowners are able to agree to the creation of such solar easements. *See* Kraemer, *Solar Law* (1978).

> **EXAMPLE:** Owner owns a lot on which Owner proposes to build a solar home. Owner and Neighbor enter into an easement agreement under which Owner made a payment to Neighbor and Neighbor granted Owner an easement that limits the height of any building Neighbor may build so that Owner's solar energy will not be obstructed. The easement agreement is recorded. It is binding on Neighbor and all subsequent owners of his lot.

The energy crisis of the 1970s and resultant attention that solar energy attracted caused a legislative reaction toward the regulation of the creation of solar easements. While laws may vary from state to state, they frequently require that the description of the easement include the vertical and horizontal angles at which the solar easement extends over the servient tenement. *See, e.g.,* Cal. Civ. Code § 801.5; McKinney's N.Y. Real Prop. L. § 335.b.

Also, height restriction ordinances are valid in proper cases.

EXAMPLE: Village zones an area for single-family dwellings and imposes reasonable height, sideline, and frontline restrictions, such that any lot owner can safely build a house utilizing solar energy. The ordinance is valid.

Solar zoning ordinances were also enacted. These ordinances create a zoning envelope. This is a cube of space in which a building may be erected on a lot in such a manner that the land adjoining cannot be improved by a building that obstructs sunlight to the southern exposure of the building roof, where solar panels will be erected. Reiner Lock, *Encouraging Decentralized Generation of Electricity: Implementation of the New Statutory Scheme*, 2 Solar Law Rep. 263 (1980).

In New Mexico, a solar user has the statutory right to prohibit the blockage of his or her solar access. Minan and Lawrence, *Legal Aspects of Solar Energy*, 30 (1981). Thus, the first landowner to use solar collectors is given the right to prevent the erection of improvements by others that cast shade upon them. California and Colorado both declare void any contract or covenant that prohibits the installation of a solar energy system. Minan and Lawrence, at 39. Model ordinances have been drafted that protect the use of solar access. Minan and Lawrence, at 51. A form of a solar access easement has been drafted. Kraemer, *Solar Law* (1976) 45.

It has been held that the owner of a solar-heated building can sue to prevent construction of a building on neighboring land that would place his or her solar collectors in the shade. *Prah v. Maretti,* 108 Wis. 2d 223, 321 N.W.2d 182 (1982). The facts of the case suggest that the neighbor may have acted maliciously or unreasonably, in which case the rule would be like the one that bars erection of a spite fence. At all events, the court held that the part creating the shade would be a nuisance. In Georgia, a statute creates an implied easement for solar access where the owner of a home and adjoining vacant lot sells the house, saying nothing about the access to sunlight. *Goddard v. Irb,* 255 Ga. 47, 335 S.E.2d 286 (1985).

4.13(d)
Conservation
Easements

A number of state laws provide for the grant and donation by a landowner to some public body of a conservation easement. 756 ILSC 120/1. These conservation easements maintain the undeveloped state of the land to protect wildlife and natural resources. After granting the easement, the landowners can continue to farm. At times the statute, as in Illinois, contains a laundry list of uses that can be prohibited (e.g., dumping, removal of trees, erection of signs, etc). Or, it may limit use of the land solely for nature trails or farming. Such a donation may reduce the local tax assessment, reducing the real estate taxes.

It is evident that the conservation easement closely resembles the scenic easement. The scenic easement seems to have more frequently been acquired by purchase or condemnation. The conservation easement has often been donated, with the tax advantages in mind. David J. Dietrich, *Conservation Easements*, Prob. & Prop. 43 (Nov./Dec. 1998). At times the two concepts are lumped together and termed acquisition of development rights, or this may be called an *open space easement.*

As is also evident, the preservation of open space has become an important goal of our time. Other methods are available, for example, coastal zoning, zoning land for agricultural purposes, and large-lot zoning. Use of the planned unit development is another method. The control of wetland development is still another.

The preparation of a conservation easement requires skill and care. Tolan M. Richter, *Conservation Rights in Illinois—Meshing Illinois Property Law with Federal Tax Deduction*

Requirements, 71 Ill. B.J. 430 (1983). Both state law and federal law must be complied with. The title must be searched because foreclosure of a prior mortgage will extinguish the easement. Other state law aspects, marketable title acts, for example, also must be considered.

A special type of conservation easement is a facade easement. It is a gift by the landowner to a public body or nonprofit corporation of the right to prevent any change in the outward appearance of a historic building.

CHAPTER 5

Descriptions of Land; Legal Descriptions

5.01 Legal Descriptions

Every deed, mortgage, or lease contains a description of the land involved. The purpose of such a description, obviously, is to fix the boundaries of the land intended to be sold, mortgaged, or leased. The document describes a specific piece of land and cannot apply to any other. A street address is adequate to guide guests to a home or for mail delivery, but greater precision is needed to fix the exact point where a parcel of land ends and where the adjoining parcel begins. Hence, we have the legal description. In reading a legal description, keep in mind that before the description was written, someone, probably a land surveyor, went out and located the boundaries of the ground and then put into words the directions for locating the lines and directions that were traced on the land. These written directions are called a legal description of the land.

5.02 Surveys

In connection with any purchase or mortgage of land, it is a common and prudent practice to have the land surveyed. The survey serves a variety of purposes. It identifies on the ground the boundaries of the tract of land. This tells us, for example, whether the land has access to a street. Surveys also determine whether a building encroaches on neighboring land or if neighboring buildings encroach on the land being surveyed. Surveys also show if the buildings or other improvements encroach on adjoining streets or alleys. Basement stores and parking spaces often intrude into adjoining streets. This requires examination of the city permit given for this purpose. A building may violate setback lines established by city ordinances or private building restrictions. If the building is not plumb, it may extend into neighboring air space. There may be subsurface problems with electric cables, drainage pipes, etc., unlawfully crossing the property. Neighboring doors or gates may open over the land. A telephone line may cross the land, necessitating relocation before building can begin.

Lawyers, title companies, the Federal National Mortgage Association (FNMA), the Federal Housing Authority (FHA), the Federal Home Loan Mortgage Corporation (FHLMC), and others have requirements concerning surveys they will accept. The survey should be prepared by a surveyor acceptable to the parties to the transaction and accompanied by the survey reports that may be required by these institutions. Some parties to transactions require special certifications from surveyors.

5.02(a) ALTA/ACSM Land Title Surveys

There are several survey standards, many promulgated by state land survey associations. The most exacting and universally accepted are those adopted by the American Land Title Association (ALTA) and the American Congress on Surveying and Mapping (ACSM). The most recent revisions of these standards were made in 1992.

The standards set forth minimum details and criteria for exactness for land title surveys. These standards include both the criteria that one would expect in a professionally drawn survey and certain other matters. For example, the survey boundary is to be drawn to a convenient scale and that scale should be set out. A north arrow must be shown and, where practical, the survey is to be oriented so that north is at the top of the drawing. The point of beginning should be shown as well as the remote point of beginning, if that point is different. Boundaries are to be read in a clockwise direction, if possible, and where record bearings, angles, and distances differ from the measurements made by the surveyor, both shall be clearly indicated. The survey should also indicate the measured and record distances from the corners of the parcels to the nearest right-of-way lines of the streets, and monuments found or placed should be shown.

The ALTA/ASCM survey standards also have a menu of additional survey requirements, some of which should almost always be used and some of which may be used in appropriate circumstances. This menu allows the client to request that the surveyor place monuments at all major corners of the property, set out a legend of symbols and abbreviations, give a flood zone designation, calculate the land area, show the contours of the land, show setback, height, and bulk restrictions of record or disclosed by applicable zoning or building codes, calculate the square footage of all buildings, show the parking areas and, if those areas are striped, the striping and number of parking spaces, and locate utilities serving the property.

5.03 Metes-and-Bounds Descriptions

Metes are measures of length, such as inches, feet, yards, and rods. *Bounds* are boundaries, both natural and artificial, such as streams or streets. In a *metes-and-bounds description,* the surveyor takes the reader by the hand, as it were, leading the reader around the land. In doing this, the surveyor starts at a well-marked point of beginning and follows the boundaries of the land until the courses and distances return to the starting point. Landmarks called *monuments* often mark the several corners of the tract. A monument may be a natural monument, such as tree or river, or an artificial monument, such as a fence, stake, wall, road, or railroad.

> **EXAMPLE:** A tract of land in Chicago, Cook County, Illinois, is described as follows: Beginning at a point in the east line of Mason Street one hundred feet north of the north line of Washington Street; running thence east on a line parallel to the north line of Washington Street 125 feet to the west line of an alley; thence north along the west line of said alley, twenty-five feet; thence west on a line parallel to the north line of Washington Street, 125 feet to the east line of Mason Street; thence south along the east line of Mason Street, twenty-five feet to the place of beginning.

The earliest descriptions in history were metes-and-bounds descriptions. All property in the thirteen original colonies of the United States was originally described by metes and bounds, the descriptions usually running from the mouth of a stream, or from a tree or stump.

5.04 The Government Survey

By the time of the treaty with England at the end of the Revolutionary War, the United States became the owner of the vast Northwest Territory, consisting of the present states of Illinois, Indiana, Ohio, Michigan, and Wisconsin. The end of the war found the United States heavily burdened with debts incurred during the war. It was decided that the new land should be sold and the proceeds used to retire the national debt. However, in selling the land to settlers, metes-and-bounds descriptions could not be used, for the new land was an untrodden wilderness. Hence, some new system of describing land was needed. The system so devised was the rectangular system of land surveys, known as the Government Survey. Under this system, whenever a district, such as part of a state, was ready for private ownership, the government arranged for a survey of the land to be made. To begin a survey of this character, it is necessary to have some substantial landmark from which a start may be made. A place that readily can be referred to, such as the mouth of a river, is usually selected. From such a point, a line is run due north to the margin of the district to be surveyed. This first north and south line is called a *prime meridian,* or *principal meridian.* Some principal meridians have been numbered, such as the First Principal Meridian, which runs north from the mouth of the Great Miami River on the boundary between Ohio and Indiana and that governs the surveys of public lands in Ohio. Others have been named, as the Tallahassee Meridian, the Mount Diablo Meridian, the Humboldt Meridian, and the San Bernardino Meridian.

An east and west line is run intersecting the principal meridians at some prominent point. This line is called the *base line.* Both north and south of the base line, additional east and west lines are run at intervals of twenty-four miles.

Since it is the object of the survey to create a huge checkerboard of identical squares covering the entire tract to be surveyed, it is plain that many north and south lines are needed. Owing to the curvature of the earth's surface, however, all true north and south lines converge as they approach the North Pole. This is obvious, since no matter how far apart two north and south lines are at the equator, they must meet at the North Pole. Hence, if continuous north and south lines were to be used in the survey, it is clear that because of the convergence of the north and south lines the tracts thus formed would grow narrower and narrower as the surveyors worked north. Although this imperfection cannot be altogether eliminated, it can be minimized in the following manner: Along the base line, both east and west of the principal meridian, and at intervals of twenty-four miles, lines running due north are run. These are called *guide meridians.* But they are run only as far north as the next *correction line,* that is, a distance of twenty-four miles. Then, new intervals of twenty-four miles are measured off along this correction line, and a new series of guide meridians based on these new intervals is run for another twenty-four miles. This process is repeated until the boundaries of the tract are reached. Similar guide meridians are run based on the correction lines lying south of the base line.

Thus, the district surveyed is divided into tracts approximately twenty-four miles square. These tracts are further divided into parts six miles on each side. These smaller parts are called *townships.*

Each row, or tier, of townships running north and south is called a *range.* The first row east of the principal meridian is referred to as *Range 1 East* of that meridian. Thus, the first row of townships east of the Third Principal Meridian is referred to as *Range 1 East of the Third Principal Meridian.* The row of townships next adjoining to the east is called Range 2 East of the Third Principal Meridian, and so on. Each row or tier of townships running east and west is identified by the number of townships intervening between it and the base line. Thus, a township in the first row north of the base line is called *Township 1 North.* The township next adjoining to the north is called *Township 2 North,* and so on. To identify a township completely, both the range number and the township number must be given, such as *Township 40 North, Range 13, East of the Third Principal Meridian.* The township thus identified is in the fortieth row north of the base line and in the thirteenth row east of the Third Principal Meridian. Such a description is often abbreviated and becomes *T. 40 N., R. 13 E. of the 3d P.M.*

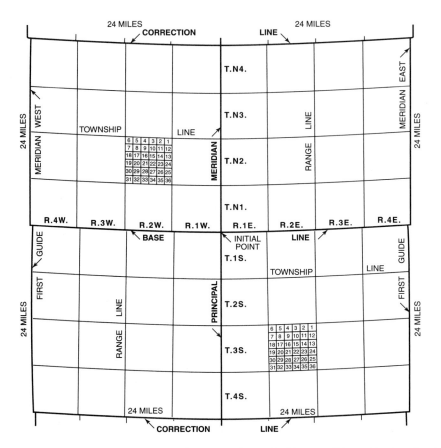

FIGURE 5-1 Correction Lines and Guide Meridians with Division of Townships into Sections

Each township is divided into thirty-six tracts, each approximately one square mile. These tracts are called *sections*. The sections in a township are numbered from one to thirty-six, always commencing with the section in the northeast corner of the township. Sections are often divided into quarters, and these quarters are also often divided into quarters.

The government system of rectangular surveys has been employed in surveying the lands of the states of Alabama, Florida, Mississippi, and all of the states north of the Ohio River and west of the Mississippi River, except Texas.

Local surveys, which in some respects resemble the Government Survey, will occasionally be encountered in the other states.

5.05   Plats   Large tracts of land are often subdivided into building lots. Thereafter, each building lot is conveyed by its lot number.

> **EXAMPLE:** Developer, believing that the tract is ripe for subdivision, buys the Northeast Quarter of the Northeast Quarter of Section 7, Township 40 North, Range 13 East of the Third Principal Meridian, in Cook County, Illinois. Developer hires a surveyor, who divides the tract into blocks, separated by streets. Each block is divided into lots. The lots and blocks are numbered, and the streets and the subdivision are named. For this particular subdivision, Developer selects the name "Highwood." The surveyor prepares a map, called a plat, showing the lots and blocks, their dimensions and numbers, the width and names of the streets, the loca-

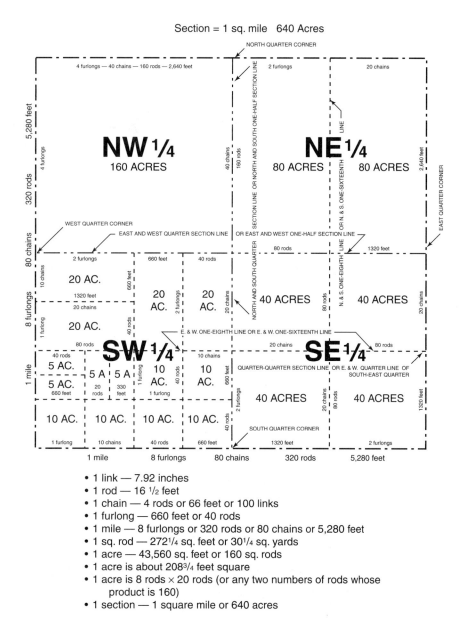

FIGURE 5-2 Section of Land Divided into Quarters and Showing Acreage and Distances

- 1 link — 7.92 inches
- 1 rod — 16 1/2 feet
- 1 chain — 4 rods or 66 feet or 100 links
- 1 furlong — 660 feet or 40 rods
- 1 mile — 8 furlongs or 320 rods or 80 chains or 5,280 feet
- 1 sq. rod — 272 1/4 sq. feet or 30 1/4 sq. yards
- 1 acre — 43,560 sq. feet or 160 sq. rods
- 1 acre is about 208 3/4 feet square
- 1 acre is 8 rods × 20 rods (or any two numbers of rods whose
  product is 160)
- 1 section — 1 square mile or 640 acres

tion of the quarter-section lines, and other similar information. After receiving the approval of local officials, the plat is filed or recorded in the office where deeds and mortgages are recorded. A description of a lot in this subdivision will read somewhat as follows: Lot 2 in Block 5 in Highwood, a subdivision of the Northeast Quarter of the Northeast Quarter of Section 7, Township 40 North, Range 13 East of the Third Principal Meridian in Cook County, Illinois.

5.06   Description by Popular Name

Descriptions by the popular name of the tract have been held sufficient, as where a deed conveys "The Old Merchant Farm." *Hayes v. O'Brien*, 37 N.E. 73 (Ill. 1894).

5.07 General Description

A deed sometimes contains no definite description, but merely purports to convey all land owned by the grantor in a certain district, as "all the land owned by the grantor in Cook County, Illinois." Such descriptions, sometimes called *Mother Hubbard clauses,* are sufficient to pass title from the grantor to the grantee, but they may not be sufficient to impart constructive notice to third parties who do not have actual notice of the deed. *Luthi v. Evans,* 576 P.2d 1064 (Kan. 1978). To overcome this potential problem, the grantee may record an affidavit that specifically describes the property intended to be conveyed. There is a theory espoused by some courts that this type of conveyance cannot be used to convey known parcels of land. *Jones v. Colle,* 727 S.W.2d 262 (Tex. 1987).

5.08 Street Address

A description by street address alone should never be used in a deed or mortgage. Since the proper legal description is not always available when a contract for the sale of land is being drafted, descriptions by street address will be found in contracts. Some contracts provide that the legal description will be substituted or added when it becomes available.

A danger sometimes present in street address descriptions is revealed by the following illustration.

> **EXAMPLE:** Landlord leased to Tenant "certain premises known as 10 East Chicago Avenue, Chicago, Illinois." The building in question bore this address. It was a restaurant. Landlord owned a vacant lot adjoining, which patrons of the restaurant sometimes used as a parking area, although it was not a regular parking lot. It was held that a lease by street number includes only the lot on which the building is situated. *Killian v. Welfare Engineering Co.,* 66 N.E.2d 305 (Ill. App. 1946).

It is not unusual to see, and it is good drafting form, to place the street address after the legal description. The statutory requirements for deeds and other recorded documents often require that this be done. Similarly, some states require that the real estate tax index number be added to the legal description, not as a substitute for the legal description, but as an aid to the recorder and others who index the recorded documents.

5.09 Area

Land may be described by its area, as the "North one acre of the Southeast Quarter of Section 1, Township 44 North, Range 2 East of the Third Principal Meridian, Lake County, Illinois."

5.10 Adjoining Owners

Lands are also described by reference to adjoining lands.

> **EXAMPLE:** A deed described the land as follows: "Bounded on the east by a fifty-acre tract of land owned by G.B. Turner purchased by him from N.W. Rodden; bounded on the north by the right of way of the Texas and Pacific R.R.; and on the west by a fifty-acre tract owned by the said G.B. Turner and known as the J.F. Neal tract of land; bounded on the south by the Katie Moore Boham tract of land." *Cox v. Campbell,* 143 S.W.2d 361 (Tex. 1940).

5.11 Foreign Grant

Portions of this country were once owned by France, Holland, Mexico, and Spain. In fact, the titles to some of the most valuable lands on Manhattan Island are based upon Dutch grants. Hence, descriptions employing foreign units of land measure, such as the *vara* and the *arpent,* are often encountered.

5.12 Indefinite Description

A deed, mortgage, or other document must describe the land conveyed in a way that it can be located and identified.

> **EXAMPLE:** A deed was made of the "southeast half" of a certain section. This deed was held void for uncertainty in the description. *Pry v. Pry,* 109 Ill. 466 (1884).

It is often difficult to determine whether a description is good or bad.

> **EXAMPLE:** A deed was made to "one acre of land in the northwest corner of Block 20" in a certain subdivision. This deed was held good, because a surveyor could go to the northwest corner of the block and measure out a sufficient distance west and south to include one acre of land. *Richey v. Sinclair,* 47 N.E. 364 (Ill. 1897).

A deed of "my house and lot" is not indefinite. Oral evidence can be introduced in court to show what tract of land was intended. *Brenneman v. Dillon,* 129 N.E. 564 (Ill. 1920).

When a deed description is too indefinite to identify the land, but the grantee, by consent of the grantor, takes possession of premises that are within the general terms of the description and erects permanent improvements on them, the defect in the description is thereby cured.

> **EXAMPLE:** Owner made a deed to a railroad of "a strip of land one hundred feet in width over the Northeast Quarter of Section 12, Township 14 North, Range 2 East of the Third Principal Meridian." The railroad, with Owner's consent, actually occupied a strip of land one hundred feet in width and erected railroad tracks on this land. The description, though originally too indefinite, became sufficient by occupation.

The rule that possession cures an indefinite description is also applicable to leases and to contracts of sale.

5.13 Description Containing Omissions

A deed, mortgage, or other document is valid, even though part of the description is omitted, if enough remains to identify the land conveyed.

> **EXAMPLE:** A deed to land described as being in Santa Cruz County, California, failed to name the meridian from which the township and range were numbered. This did not invalidate the deed, since all descriptions of land in that county are numbered from the Mt. Diablo Meridian. *Harrington v. Goldsmith,* 68 P. 594 (Cal. 1902).

5.14 Correction of Deed Description by Court Order

When an error occurs in the land description in a deed and the seller refuses to give a new deed to correct the error, a court order can usually be obtained correcting the erroneous description. This is known as *reformation* of an instrument. And, if in the meantime, the grantee has been in possession of the land, probably no great harm will result from the error. If, however, the grantee has not gone into possession, as where the land is vacant, third persons, such as judgment creditors of the grantor, may acquire rights in the land superior to those of the grantee. *See* 4 *American Law of Property* § 17.23.

5.15 Streets or Highways as Boundaries

As previously pointed out, a city often does not own the land comprising its roads, streets, or alleys, but only has an easement thereover for street purposes. When a deed or mortgage is made of land abutting on such a road, street, or alley, the land sold or mortgaged generally runs to the center of such road, street, or alley. W.W. Allen, Annotation, *Description with Reference to Highways as Carrying Title to Center or Side of Highway*, 49 A.L.R.2d 982 (1965). *See also,* J. Schiffres, Annotation, *Relative Rights and Liabilities of Abutting Owners and Public Authorities in Parkway in Center of Street*, 81 A.L.R.2d 1436 (1962) (dealing with the relative rights and liabilities of abutting owners and public authorities in parkways in the center of streets).

> **EXAMPLE:** Seller gives Buyer a deed selling and conveying that part of a certain section of land "lying south of Dundee Road." By this deed, Buyer acquires all land in that particular section lying south of the center of Dundee Road.

The reason for this rule is obvious. The Seller, having parted with ownership of his land, would have no use for the adjoining strip of road. Hence, it is presumed that he intended half of the adjoining road to pass to the Buyer with the land sold.

When a street is used as a boundary, keep in mind that legally the street usually includes much more than the paved roadway over which cars travel. It often includes the sidewalk, the planted area known as the *parkway,* and may even include a narrow strip of land on the house side of the sidewalk. Check the recorded subdivision plat to locate the true street line.

5.16 Waters as Boundaries If Seller owns land through which a stream flows and this ownership includes the stream bed, a deed, mortgage, or lease of land "lying south of Plum Creek" will, under a rule analogous to the highway rule, include the south half of the creek. George A. Locke, Annotation, *Deeds: Description of Land Conveyed by Reference to River or Stream as Carrying to Thread or Center or Only to Bank Thereof—Modern Status,* 78 A.L.R.3d 604 (1977).

5.17 Parts of Lots Care should be exercised in drafting descriptions of parts of lots.

> **EXAMPLE:** A subdivision plat indicates that Lot 2 in Block 3 is eighty feet wide. Owner gives Buyer a deed to the "east forty feet of Lot 2." When Owner sells the remainder of the lot, his description thereof should be "Lot 2, except the east forty feet thereof," and not "the west forty feet of Lot 2." The reason is obvious. Suppose Lot 2 is actually slightly more that eighty feet in width, as it well may be, for land measurements are not perfectly accurate. Deeds of the east forty feet and the west forty feet of the lot would leave a small strip of land in the middle of the lot still owned by Owner.

When the lot is not a perfect square or rectangle, use of descriptions such as the "east half" or "north half" of the lot should be avoided, since the word "half" usually is considered to mean half by area, and the boundary line will be located with an equal number of square feet on either side thereof. This may result in an unequal division of the frontage of the lot.

A deed of a part of a lot that abuts on a diagonal street should use descriptions like the "northwesterly thirty feet" rather than the "north thirty feet," since, if the diagonal street runs in a true northwesterly or northeasterly direction, it is difficult to determine which side of the lot is the "north" side. Cases will be found where two of the boundary lines may lay equal claim to being the "north" line of the lot.

5.18 Buildings Since buildings are usually fixtures and, as such, are part of the land, a deed of the land will automatically give the buyer the buildings thereon. They need not be mentioned in the deed.

5.19 Tax Bills Tax bills contain abbreviated, vague, and unsatisfactory descriptions of the land. They should never be used in drafting a deed, contract, or lease. Some states, however, require that the assessor's parcel number or taxpayer's identifying number be reflected on the face of the deed in addition to the legal description.

CHAPTER 6
Land Titles and Interests in Land

6.01 Estates in Land

Just as land may be divided into layers by a sale of "air rights" or minerals, so the ownership of land may be divided into various types of interests. Lawyers speak of interests in land as "estates." The highest type of interest, of course, is complete, or fee simple absolute, ownership.

> **EXAMPLE:** *A* owns a tract of land. No one else has any interest whatever in the land. *A* is said to be the owner in fee simple. This is a technical phrase connoting ownership of the land. When one hears it said that "*A* has title" to a particular tract of land, it is understood that *A* is the fee owner, owns the land in fee or in fee simple, or has an estate in fee simple absolute. All these are different ways of expressing the idea that *A* owns the land, that this ownership is of unlimited duration, and that so long as *A* obeys the law, *A* may do as *A* chooses with the land, and, on *A*'s death, it will go to *A*'s heirs, or, if *A* leaves a will, to the persons named in the will.

Suppose, however, that *A,* being the fee simple owner of the land, executes a ten-year lease thereof to *B*. Now *A* has parted with some rights in the land. *A* has given up the right to occupy the land for ten years and, in return, has received *B*'s promise to pay rent for those ten years. *B* has acquired the right to occupy the land in accordance with the provisions of the lease, but has not, of course, become the fee simple owner of the land. *B* has merely acquired a *leasehold estate* or *term for years* in the land. A leasehold estate, even where the lease is for many years, is, for most purposes, legally considered to be personal property of the lessee. *Chicago v. University of Chicago,* 134 N.E. 723 (Ill. 1922) (lease for 1000 years).

For some purposes, a lease is said to be a *chattel real.* That is, it has some of the attributes of real property and some of the attributes of personal property. Thus, a lease is entitled to be recorded in the real estate records, like a deed or mortgage of land. *Lincoln Nat'l Bank & Trust Co. v. Nathan,* 19 N.E.2d 243 (Ind. 1939). The same would be true of a mortgage of the leasehold estate. A leasehold estate can be partitioned in the same manner as real estate. *Pierce v. Pierce,* 123 N.E.2d 511 (Ill. 1954); *McGuire v. Cohen*, 195 N.E.2d 280, 284 (Ill. App. 1964).

The word *estate* is used to express the degree, quantity, nature, duration, or extent of an interest in land. Complete ownership is an estate in fee simple, but there are many other estates, such as life estates and leasehold estates. Each differs from the others with respect to the rights and duties of the owner of the estate in question.

6.02 Divisions of Land Ownership

As can be seen from this and other chapters, ownership of land can be divided according to time (as in the case of a landlord giving a ten-year lease), or vertically (as in the case where a railroad deeds air space to a developer), or according to the substance in the land (as in the case of a farmer giving a deed to a coal company of the coal beneath the farmland), or among co-owners (as where a husband and wife buy property as joint tenants).

6.03   Life Estates   The owner of the life estate can use and enjoy the land only during his lifetime.

> **EXAMPLE:** Landowner dies leaving a will giving land to Widow for her life, and, at her death, to their children, *C* and *D*. Widow thus acquires a life estate in the land and becomes a life tenant. She is entitled to the reasonable and necessary use of the land for her lifetime, but she must not do anything that will in any way injure the permanent value of the property. She may collect and use the rents of the land, but must keep the property in repair and must pay the real estate taxes and the interest on any mortgage encumbering the property. She must not drill any new oil wells or open new mines, but may take oil or minerals from existing wells and mines. On her death, all of her rights in the land will cease.

Life estates may be created by will or deed. Often, to save the expense of probating his will after his death, a father, while still living, will give a deed of his land to his son or daughter, and in the deed will reserve to himself a life estate.

Certain special kinds of life estates are created by law, rather than by will or deed, such as dower, curtesy, and homestead.

6.04   Trusts   A *trust* is an equitable obligation, binding a *trustee* to deal with the *trust property* or *trust estate* for the benefit of the *beneficiaries,* any of whom may enforce the trustee's obligations. There are various kinds of trusts.

> **EXAMPLE:** Landowner dies leaving a will that gives all of his property to Trustee, in trust, with power to sell the property and make investments, the income of the trust to be payable to Widow during her lifetime, and on her death the trust property to be distributed among Landowner's children then living. Since this trust was created by Landowner's last will and testament, it is known as a *testamentary trust.*

> **EXAMPLE:** Landowner signs a deed conveying his land to Trustee, in trust, with power to sell the property and make investments, the income of the trust to be payable to Landowner during his lifetime, and after Landowner's death to Widow during her lifetime, and on her death the property to be distributed among Landowner's children then living. Since this trust becomes effective during Landowner's lifetime, it is known as a *living trust.* This form of trust is becoming increasingly popular as an estate planning device to avoid the time and expense of probate and to efficiently plan the administration of the estate while at the same time minimizing estate tax consequences.

> **EXAMPLE:** Buyer plans to acquire a tract of land while at the same time concealing the fact that he owns the property. He also wishes to prevent his wife and his judgment creditors from acquiring any interest in the land. On purchasing the land, Buyer directs Seller to convey the land to Trustee. The deed gives Trustee full power to sell and mortgage the land, but does not mention Buyer's name. The deed is filed for record. The deed to Trustee and also a separate unrecorded agreement are signed by Buyer, as the beneficiary of the trust, and the Trustee. This agreement recites that all title to the land is vested in Trustee and that the beneficiary's interest is only personal property. The Trustee agrees to deal with the land only when directed to do so by Buyer. Buyer has accomplished his purpose. He has acquired the property through a vehicle that keeps his ownership interest out of the public records, and, since the trust specifically provides that Buyer's interest is only personal property, no dower rights attach, and judgments against Buyer are not liens against the land. Yet, Buyer has complete control over the land. *Chicago Title & Trust Co. v. Mercantile Trust and Sav. Bank,* 20 N.E.2d 992 (Ill. 1939). This is called a "land trust."

The land trust is recognized and valid in Florida, Illinois, Indiana, North Dakota, and Virginia. Henry W. Kenoe, *Kenoe on Land Trusts* (1989); Garrett, *Land Trusts*, 1955 Law Forum 655; Comment, 14 Kans. L. Rev. 97 (1965); Note, 18 U. Miami L. Rev. 699 (1964); Note, 45, N.D. L. Rev. 77 (1968).

6.05 Cemetery Lots

When a cemetery corporation sells a lot, or burial site, the purchaser does not become the absolute owner of the lot. The deed gives the grantee merely an easement right of burial. *Steele v. Rosehill Cemetery Co.,* 19 N.E.2d 189 (Ill. 1939); *Smith v. Rost*, 906 S.W.2d 906, 907 (Mo. App. 1995); Note, 109 U. Pa. L. Rev. 378 (1961). The grantee also has the right to enter the cemetery to care for the graves, subject to the reasonable regulations adopted by the cemetery company as to visiting hours, monuments, grave decorations, and so on. Like any other easement, the easement of the burial may be lost by abandonment. *Trustees of First Presbyterian Church v. Alling,* 54 N.J.S. 141, 148 A.2d 510 (N.J. 1959); *Walker v. Georgia Power Co.*, 339 S.E.2d 728, 730–31 (Ga. App. 1986) (Heir, by virtue of acquiescence without objection to the removal and reinterment of the remains of her ancestors had abandoned easement in the original property.).

6.06 Modes of Acquiring Ownership of Land

While title to or ownership of land is most often acquired by deed, by will, or by descent, there are other modes of acquiring title to land, among them, condemnation and adverse possession.

6.06(a) Condemnation

When land is needed for a public use, it can be acquired by a governmental body through the exercise of the power of eminent domain. The power of eminent domain is held by the United States, the state in which the land lies, cities, villages, school boards, and other public bodies, quasi-public corporations, such as railroads and public utility corporations, and in some states, private individuals have the right of eminent domain in limited instances as, for example, when they are landlocked. The power is subject to two conditions: The use to which the property is to be devoted must be a public one, and just compensation must be paid.

Exercise of the power of eminent domain involves a lawsuit called a condemnation proceeding that is begun by the city or other public body desiring to acquire title. The just compensation to which the landowner is entitled is the fair market value of the land at the time of the taking of the land. This value is often determined by a jury if the parties cannot agree upon the value of the land.

By condemnation, the condemnor acquires either an easement or fee simple title, although federal legislation permits the United States to acquire by condemnation the right to occupy the land for a term of years only, if that is what is what is needed to fulfil the public purpose. If an easement will serve the purpose for which the land is to be acquired, the condemnor will often only acquire an easement.

> **EXAMPLE:** As a rule, an easement only is acquired by a railroad condemning for a right of way, a city condemning for a street, a telephone company condemning for a telephone line, or a drainage district condemning for a drainage ditch. In such cases, even though the landowner receives the full market value of the land condemned, the landowner retains the ownership of the land so condemned. The point is of importance, since if an easement for street or right of way purposes acquired by condemnation is later abandoned, the original landowner still retains his ownership free and clear of the easement. *Bell v. Mattoon Waterworks & Res. Co.,* 92 N.E. 352 (Ill. 1910).

In many cases, however, it is necessary that fee simple title be acquired, as when land is condemned for a courthouse site.

**6.06(b) Adverse
Possession**

Often, the public records will show a complete and perfect succession of deeds from the first conveyance from the government down to the current record landowner. This is known as the *record title* or *paper title*. Yet, the true ownership of the land may be outstanding in someone who holds possession of the land without a single document to show its ownership. This nonrecord ownership may have been acquired by the nonrecord claimant taking possession of the land and staying in possession for a number of years fixed by the law. At the end of that period, which varies from state to state, the party in possession comes into ownership of the land, even though the land was not conveyed to him or her, he or she entered the land without any right whatever to do so, and he or she has not placed any instrument in the public records to show his or her ownership.

The law providing for the acquiring of title to land by adverse possession exists for two reasons: (1) it furthers the public policy that encourages the use of land and (2) ownership of real estate often depends on transactions that occurred so long ago that the witnesses who were familiar with the transaction are dead or have forgotten the facts.

Not every possession of land will ripen into ownership. For this to occur, the possession must be legally adverse; that is, the possession must be *actual, hostile, notorious, exclusive, continuous,* and *under claim of right.*

For possession to be adverse, it must be actual. As the judges put it, the occupant must unfurl his or her flag on the land and keep it flying so that the true owner may see that an enemy has invaded the land and planted the standard of conquest. In other words, the occupant must do something that will make the owner notice that a stranger has occupied his land. This does not mean, however, that the occupant must live or reside on the land.

> **EXAMPLE:** *A* fences and farms some vacant land adjoining his farm in Illinois. This continues for twenty years. He now owns this adjoining land by reason of his adverse possession.

This rule is of importance in boundary disputes, since if a landowner erects a fence on what he or she claims to be the boundary of the land and claims all the land to the fence, this possession will eventually ripen into ownership, even though the fence is actually over on the neighbor's land. The same is true when a building encroaches over and upon adjoining land.

Usually possession is not hostile when the person in possession occupies a relation of trust and confidence toward the holder of the paper title.

> **EXAMPLE:** A father's possession is not hostile to the child, the possession of a husband is not hostile to the wife, and the possession of an agent is not hostile to his employer.

The requirement that possession be *notorious* merely means that the possession of the occupant must be such that the real owner would be likely to notice it.

Adverse possession, in order to ripen into title, must be *continuous.* However, seasonal possession is often sufficient, for the possession need only be such as is usual with respect to land of similar character. For example, it is sufficient if farmland is farmed in the farming season, timberland logged in the logging season, and so on.

> **EXAMPLE:** *A* occupied *B*'s hunting shack each year during the hunting season. Ultimately, *A* acquired good title by adverse possession. *Kraus v. Mueller,* 12 Wis. 2d 430, 107 N.W.2d 467 (1961).

For a person to acquire title by adverse possession, he or she must claim that to be the owner of the land, but it is enough if his or her acts and conduct indicate that he or she claims to be the owner of the land.

> **EXAMPLE:** *A* and *B* owned adjoining lots, *A* owning Lot 9 and *B* owning Lot 8. *A* built a frame cottage on Lot 9, but the cottage extended two feet over on Lot 8. *A* thought the house was entirely on Lot 9 and never made any oral claim to this two-foot strip. *A* paid taxes on Lot 9 and *B* paid the taxes on Lot 8. After twenty years, a survey was made that disclosed the encroachment. Although *A* had made no oral claim to the two-foot strip, *A*'s acts in erecting and maintaining a building on this strip, showed that *A* claimed title to the strip. *A* therefore had acquired title by adverse possession. *Cassidy v. Lenahan,* 128 N.E. 544 (Ill. 1920).

As is evident, adverse possession resembles prescription in the law of easements. However, adverse occupancy often, at the *surface* of the ground, ripens into ownership by adverse possession. Adverse *use* ripens into a prescriptive easement. The utility of this distinction is reasonably obvious.

> **EXAMPLE:** *A* and *B* own adjoining Lots 7 and 8. Both lots have a home on them. *A*'s home is so constructed that the eaves extend over *B*'s lot. When *A*'s home is demolished, it would be absurd to hold that *A*'s prescriptive easement runs in favor of any new home. How in the world would the air space formerly occupied by the eaves be located? A simple solution is to hold that when a prescriptive easement is created, it runs in favor of the house. When the house is gone, the easement is gone.

6.07   Land Ownership by Aliens

The federal government and many states regulate and, in some instances, prevent the acquisition of real property interests in the United States by foreigners. In many cases, these laws and regulations, both state and federal, look through the form of the ownership entity and into the tiers of ownership that lay behind the entity actually acquiring the real estate.

> **EXAMPLE:** A Swiss citizen forms a Delaware corporation to acquire and hold real estate in the United States. The mere fact that the landowner will be a corporation of a state of the United States will not relieve that corporation from compliance with many federal laws relating to the foreign ownership of United States real estate or exempt the corporation from the strictures of many state laws regulating or preventing foreign land ownership.

Beyond regulation, foreigners must be aware of and carefully plan their land acquisitions around a complexity of tax legislation that often changes. While such tax legislation is beyond the scope of this text, its existence must be noted and any investor must consult a qualified tax attorney or accountant for guidance in this area. Silbergleit, *U.S. Tax Considerations in Structuring and Restructuring Foreign (and Particularly Canadian) Investment in U.S. Real Property—Impact of the Tax Reform Act of 1986 and the New FIRPTA Regulations* in Canadian Investment in U.S. Real Estate, A.B.A. Real Prop., Prob. & Tr. L. Sec. Annual Meeting Program Materials (Aug. 9, 1987); Planning for Foreign Investment in U.S. Real Estate after the Tax Reform Act of 1986, A.B.A. Real Prop., Prob. & Tr. L. Sec. Annual Meeting Program Materials (Aug. 10, 1987).

While many states do not prohibit or regulate the ownership of real estate by foreigners, others have a variety of restrictions ranging from outright prohibition to reporting requirements. Brodkey, *Foreign Investment in U.S. Real Estate: The Role of State Restrictions in Structuring the Transaction, Parts I, II, and III,* Lawyer's Supplement to the Guarantor, Jan./Feb., 1987, Mar./April, 1987, & May/June, 1987; James C. McLoughlin, Annotation, *State Regulation of Land Ownership by Alien Corporations*, 21 A.L.R.4th 1329 (1983).

The federal government has a number of laws and regulations relating to alien land ownership. A few of these prohibit foreign land ownership. For example, the Alien Land Act of 1887 prohibits the ownership of land in territories of the United States by other than U.S. citizens and resident aliens, 48 U.S.C.A. §§ 1501, *et seq.,* and another statute prohibits the purchase of mineral interests in lands owned by the United States. 30 U.S.C.A. § 22.

Most federal statutes and regulations on the subject do not prevent foreign ownership of U.S. real estate, but rather impose various, and sometimes oppressive, reporting requirements on the owners of such property. For example, the Agricultural Foreign Investment Disclosure Act of 1978 requires that any foreign person who acquires or transfers an interest in U.S. agricultural, ranching, or timber land file a report with the Secretary of Agriculture. 7 U.S.C.A. §§ 3501 *et seq.*; 7 C.F.R. §§ 481.1 *et seq.* There are other federal statutes that apply to the general business activities of foreigners and therefore apply to real estate transactions and ownership as well. These include the requirement of the International Investment Survey Act of 1976, which requires that reports be filed by every business entity in which foreigners have a direct or indirect interest of 10 percent or more, 22 U.S.C.A §§ 3101 *et seq.*; 15 C.F.R. Part 806, the requirement that a report be filed with the Securities and Exchange Commission in the event that a foreigner acquires more than a 5 percent interest in a publicly-traded corporation, 15 U.S.C.A. §§ 78m(d), 78n(d), and the requirement that every domestic and foreign corporation that is controlled by a foreign person file an annual information return with the Internal Revenue Service, 26 U.S.C.A. § 6038A. Richards, *Reporting and Disclosure Requirements for the Foreign Investor in U.S. Real Estate,* 25 Real Prop. Prob. & Tr. J. 217 (1990).

CHAPTER 7
Deeds and Conveyances

7.01 Defined A deed is a written instrument by which an owner of real property transfers or conveys that ownership to another.

7.02 Types of Deeds The forms of deed that are commonly used in the United States are *quitclaim deeds, warranty deeds,* and *deeds of bargain and sale.*

7.02(a) Quitclaim Deed A quitclaim deed purports to convey only the grantor's *present interest in real estate,* if the grantor has any interest, rather than the real estate itself. Since such a deed purports to convey only whatever interest the grantor has at the time, its use does not mean or imply that the grantor has good title, or any title at all. This form of deed does not impose any future obligations on the grantor. If the grantor has an interest, it is conveyed by the quitclaim deed. If the grantor has no interest, none will be conveyed. If the grantor acquires an interest after executing the deed, the interest will be retained as the grantor's property.

Quitclaim deeds are used when the grantor knows that the title held has a flaw, such as where another may have an interest in the real estate, or where the interest of the grantor is doubtful, but a deed is needed to clear that interest. Parties that have acquired title through foreclosure or other involuntary means will often convey by way of a quitclaim deed or other form of deed with limited warranties, since they will want no liability for breach of the covenants that are contained in a warranty deed for title defects that are not of their making.

7.02(b) Warranty Deed A warranty deed (sometimes called a *general warranty deed*) contains certain assurances or warranties by the grantor that the deed conveys a good and unencumbered title. Such warranties are called *covenants of title*. While these covenants differ somewhat in their scope, depending on the local practice, the covenants usually warrant the following:

1. That the grantor has good title to the land conveyed. This is called the *covenant of seizin.*
2. That there are no encumbrances on the land except as stated in the deed. This is called the *covenant against encumbrances.*
3. That the grantee, or his or her grantees, will not be evicted or disturbed by a person having a better title or lien. This is called the *covenant of quiet enjoyment.*

If the grantee suffers a loss because the title is not good as covenanted, the grantor may be liable for the damages suffered by the grantee as a result.

If any encumbrances exist that are not excepted from the coverage of the warranties contained in the deed, the covenant against encumbrances is violated. An encumbrance, within the meaning of this covenant, includes any lien, such as a mortgage, tax lien, or judgment lien; an easement; a restriction on the use of the land; or an outstanding dower right. The grantor's liability on this covenant is not affected by the fact that the grantee knew of the encumbrance. E.L.D., Annotation, *Easements as Breach of Covenant Against Encumbrances*, 64 A.L.R. 1479 (1929). If the grantor wishes to escape liability on this covenant, a "subject to" clause must be inserted to qualify the language of the deed. In this way the deed covenants will not be breached by the existence of a particularly described mortgage, restriction, or other encumbrance. Sometimes the "subject to" clause is drafted without a great degree of specificity, such as when the conveyance is subject to "restrictions of record." Grantees should be reluctant to accept such general limitations on the covenants of warranty without knowing the exact nature of the matters of record. What if the property is being purchased for the construction of a gas station, and the matters of record restrict the property to single-family residential uses only?

It is still customary in many localities to set out in full in the warranty deed the various covenants of title. However, in many states, statutes have been enacted under which the usual covenants of title are implied from the use of certain specified words. When these particular words are used, the deed must be read as though the usual covenants of title were set out in full therein. In Alaska, Illinois, Kansas, Michigan, Minnesota, and Wisconsin, the words *convey* and *warrant* make a deed a general warranty deed. The same result is achieved in Pennsylvania, Vermont, Virginia, and West Virginia by use of the words *warrant generally,* and, in Arkansas, Florida, Idaho, Missouri, and Nevada, by the words *grant, bargain,* and *sell.*

The fact that the seller is willing to give a general warranty deed is little or no assurance to the grantee that the grantor has good, clear title to the land. Suppose that the grantor gave a warranty deed conveying the Empire State Building, which was not owned by the grantor. Clearly, this warranty deed would pass no title to that valuable property for the simple reason that the grantor did not own it. 26 C.J.S. *Deeds* § 117. The grantor would, of course, have the right to sue the grantee for breach of the covenants of warranty.

7.02(b)(1) Special Warranty Deed

A *special warranty deed* is one in which the grantor covenants only against the lawful claims of all persons claiming by, through, or under the grantor. This type of deed is called a *grant deed* in some states. The grantor is liable in such case if the grantee is disturbed by some claim arising through an act of the grantor, but not the grantor's predecessors in title. For example, if, prior to the execution of the deed, the grantor had placed a mortgage on the land that the deed failed to set out in its "subject to" clause, and thereafter the grantee is compelled to pay off the mortgage, the grantor is liable for damages thus sustained by the grantee. But, if the grantor's predecessor and not the grantor gave the mortgage, the grantor is not liable. In some states (e.g., Mississippi, Pennsylvania, Vermont, Virginia, and West Virginia), use of the words *warrant specially* is sufficient to create a covenant of special warranty. In California, Idaho, and North Dakota, use of the word *grant* achieves the same purpose.

7.02(c) Deed of Bargain and Sale

There are deeds that convey the real property and not merely the grantor's interest; therefore, they are not quitclaim deeds. They do not include warranties of title; therefore, they are not warranty deeds. Such a deed is a *deed of bargain and sale,* or a *deed without covenants.*

7.03 Requirements of a Valid Deed

The essential elements of a deed are a competent grantor, a grantee, recital of consideration, words of conveyance, an adequate description of the land, the signatures of grantor and spouse, and delivery of the completed instrument to the grantee. In addition, a deed may (though it need not) contain warranties of title, recitals showing mortgages and other encumbrances, a date, witnesses, an acknowledgment, and documentary stamps. Delivery is followed by the filing or recording of the deed in the proper public office.

7.03(a)   Grantor

Every deed must have a grantor. The grantor conveys the property. The fact that the name used by the grantor differs from the true name of the grantor does not invalidate the deed.

The name of the grantor must appear in the body of the deed.

> **EXAMPLE:** *A, B,* and *C* own certain land. A deed is made, and the names of *A* and *B* appear in the body thereof, but all three owners sign the deed. *C*'s interest does not pass under the deed.

However, a deed beginning "in consideration of ten dollars, I do hereby convey" is sufficient if signed by the landowner, even though the grantor's name does not appear in the body of the deed. *Bowles v. Lowery,* 62 So. 107 (Ala. 1913). The same is true where the deed begins with the phrase "The undersigned." *Frederick v. Wilcox,* 24 So. 582 (Ala. 1898).

A mistake in the spelling of the grantor's name or a variance between the spelling of the name in the body of the deed and the spelling in the signature will not invalidate the deed where the identity of the person intended to be designated is obvious.

> **EXAMPLE:** A deed is good even though it names "Emmonds" as grantor, but is signed "Emmens." And a deed is good even though it names "Abraham B. Kain" as grantor but is signed "A. Boudoin Kain." *Lyon v. Kain,* 36 Ill. 362 (1865).

7.03(a)(1)   Grantor—Competency

The grantor and spouse must be of legal age and of sound mind. In many states, a deed by a person who has been declared insane by a court is void. Even if the grantor has not been declared insane, the deed may later be set aside if, as a matter of fact, the grantor lacked the mental capacity to understand in a reasonable manner the nature of the transaction in which he or she was engaged and its consequences and effects on his or her rights and interest.

> **EXAMPLE:** Widower has three children, Alice, Beth, and Charles. When Widower becomes too feeble to take care of himself, Alice, a married but childless daughter, moves into Widower's home with her husband. As time passes, Widower becomes senile and requires constant care. Alice, feeling she should be rewarded for her care of her father, prepares a deed of the home running to herself as grantee and has Widower sign it. After Widower's death, Beth and Charles learn of the deed. They file a suit to set it aside. If they can show that Widower was too senile to understand that he was parting with ownership of his home when he signed the deed, the court will set it aside. Cases of this sort occur by the thousands.

7.03(a)(1)(i)   Fraud, Coercion, and Mistake

A deed obtained by fraud, misrepresentation, or coercion may be set aside by proper court proceedings. This is particularly true when through old age, mental weakness, ignorance, illness, or some other cause, the grantor was incapable of coping with the grantee, and, due to such incapacity of the grantor, the grantee has obtained the property for substantially less than its value.

A mutual mistake occurs where both parties are under some misapprehension.

> **EXAMPLE:** Seller owns Tracts 1 and 2. Believing he is buying Tract 1, Buyer receives and pays for a deed conveying Tract 2, because Seller believes Buyer wishes to buy Tract 2. The deed will be set aside, and the money refunded to Buyer.

**7.03(a)(1)(ii)
Grantor—Infancy**

In most states, an individual achieves majority (comes of age) at the age of eighteen. A person who is not of age is an *infant* and, after achieving majority, may sue to set aside any deed executed while an infant. If it is necessary that the real estate of an infant or an insane person be sold for his or her support or for some other proper purpose, court proceedings may be instituted for that purpose.

**7.03(a)(2)   Grantor—
Corporations**

A favorable vote of the directors of a corporation is usually necessary to authorize the sale of corporate real estate. Laws will often be encountered requiring a vote of the holders of two-thirds of the corporate stock to authorize any sale of substantially *all* the corporate assets. Alternatively, a vote of the majority of the members of a church corporation or a non-profit corporation may be necessary for a sale of the property.

Where the property is owned by a close corporation (a corporation with few shareholders), it should have a meeting of all of its shareholders and all of its directors to adopt the resolution authorizing the sale. The secretary's certificate to the resolution should state that it was unanimously adopted at a meeting of *all* shareholders and *all* directors.

**7.03(a)(3)   Grantor—
Partnerships**

The power of a general partner to convey partnership property is addressed in the Uniform Partnership Act (UPA), the Uniform Limited Partnership Act (ULPA), and the Revised Uniform Limited Partnership Act (RULPA), which comprise the dominant organic partnership laws in the United States. In general, the general partner of a limited partnership has all of the rights and powers of a partner in a general partnership. ULPA § 9(1). The UPA gives every partner the status of agent for the partnership for the purpose of carrying on its business, and the partner may bind the partnership by the execution in the partnership name of any instrument that apparently carries on the business of the partnership in the usual way. UPA § 9(l). The partnership is not bound by a partner's unauthorized acts if the person with whom the partner is dealing knows that the partner has no authority to so act. UPA § 9(1). An act of the partner that is not apparently for the carrying on of the business in the usual way does not bind the partnership unless the act is authorized by the other partners.

Under the old Limited Partnership Act, the general partner of a limited partnership did not have the power to execute any act that would make it impossible to carry on the ordinary business of the partnership unless all of the limited partners had given their written consent or ratification of the "specific act." ULPA § 9(1)(b). Real estate lawyers expressed the fear that this provision required unanimous consent of all limited partners to a specific transaction. If that were the law, real estate syndications would be unable to efficiently deal with their assets. Unanimous consent would be very difficult, if not impossible, to obtain. Agreeing that such a ridiculous result could not have been intended, the drafters of many limited partnership documents included a provision whereby the limited partners gave their consent in advance to a voting arrangement that did not require unanimous consent for the conveyance of partnership property.

The RULPA, as approved by the National Conference of Commissioners on Uniform State Laws in 1976, contains a section that specifically authorizes the partnership agreement to grant to all or a specified group of limited partners the right to vote on a per capita or other basis upon any matter. R.U.L.P.A. § 302. It gives the general partner broad powers.

REFERENCE: Robert Kratovil & Raymond J. Werner, *Fixing up the Old Jalopy—The Modern Limited Partnership Under the ULPA,* 50 St. John's L. Rev. 51 (1975); *See also Publicly Traded Limited Partnerships: An Emerging Financial Alternative to the Public Corporation,* 39 Bus. Law. 709 (John W. Slater, Jr. ed. 1984).

7.03(a)(4) Grantor's Spouse   Whether the grantor's spouse must join in the deed depends on the local law. Generally speaking, however, it is necessary for the grantor's spouse to join in the deed for one or more of the following reasons:

1. In most states, land occupied by a husband and wife as their home is known as the homestead. Any deed or mortgage of the homestead must be signed by both husband and wife, the theory being that the home should not be disposed of unless a new home satisfactory to both parties has been furnished.

2. In most states, a wife has certain rights in her husband's land, and her rights in any particular parcel of land are not defeated or affected by any deed made by her husband unless she has joined in making the deed.

3. Depending on the local law, a husband may have *curtesy, dower,* or other rights in the land owned by his wife, and his signature on his wife's deed is required in order to relinquish these rights.

4. Some of the western states have the community property system, and, in most of these states, it is required that deeds of community property be signed by both husband and wife.

5. In some states (e.g., Illinois), laws have been passed that seem to give some property interest in the land that is awarded to the other spouse in a divorce. This appears to make it prudent to have both spouses join in any deed of the real estate that is owned by either spouse.

It is obvious from the foregoing that the marital status of the grantor should be clearly stated in the deed, as *bachelor, widow, spinster,* or *divorced and not remarried.*

Often a spouse will join into a deed merely to convey any marital or spousal rights that the spouse may hold. This is the case where the spouse does not have an estate in the land. Such joinder should be done cautiously. If the deed contains warranties, the joining spouse will be liable under those warranties unless the joinder is limited. *Nordberg v. Green*, 638 So. 2d 91 (Fla. App. 1994).

7.03(b) Grantee   Every deed must have a grantee. If it does not, it is void.

EXAMPLE: *A* makes out a deed to *B*, who, unknown to *A*, is dead at the time. The deed is void. A dead grantee is no grantee at all. H.A.W., Annotation, *Death or Extinction of Corporate Existence of Grantee, or One of the Grantees Prior to Execution of Deed*, 148 A.L.R. 252 (1944).

The grantee need not be named in the deed if the grantee is sufficiently described.

EXAMPLE: A deed to "John Smith and wife" transfers ownership to John Smith and his wife. *Ballard v. Farley,* 226 S.W. 544 (Tenn. 1920).

A deed running directly to an unincorporated association is void for want of a grantee.

EXAMPLE: A number of persons attended a particular church that was known as the "First Avenue Baptist Church." The church, however, was not incorporated. One of the members of the congregation made a deed of gift of his real estate to "First Avenue Baptist Church." The deed was void. *Heiligenstein v. Schlotterbeck,* 133 N.E. 188 (Ill. 1921).

The fact that the name inserted in the deed is not the grantee's true name does not invalidate the deed. In other words, for the purpose of any particular real estate transaction the grantee may assume any name. *See Roeckl v. FDIC*, 885 P.2d 1067 (Alaska 1994).

EXAMPLE: If the grantee should direct the seller to insert the name "Robert Cook" as grantee in the deed, intending to hold ownership of the land by that assumed name, the deed is perfectly valid. *Chapman v. Tyson,* 81 P. 1066 (Wash. 1905).

This situation frequently occurs with respect to persons who pass as husband and wife although they are not legally married.

EXAMPLE: A deed designated as grantees Fabrio Casini and Lucy Casini, his wife. Actually, Lucy was not the wife of Fabrio, although they passed as husband and wife. The deed was a valid deed, and the grantees became co-owners of the property. *Casini v. Lupone,* 72 A.2d 907 (N.J. 1950); *Michael v. Lucas,* 137 A. 287 (Md. 1927).

A misspelling of the grantee's name will not invalidate the deed where the identity of the person intended to be designated is obvious. This is also true of deeds to corporations.

EXAMPLE: The grantor attended a church whose proper corporate name is First Avenue Methodist Church, and, intending to convey land to this church, he made out a deed to The Methodist Church of First Avenue. The deed is valid. *Church of Christ v. Christian Church,* 61 N.E. 1119 (Ill. 1901). This defect is technically termed a misnomer. Misnomer does not invalidate a deed.

In a few states, a husband cannot convey directly to his wife, or vice versa, since according to the ancient view, the husband and wife together are but one person, and it takes two persons to make a deed. However, both husband and wife may join in a deed to a third person, who may thereupon convey to the wife.

In community property states, a deed to a married person should indicate whether the grantee holds the land as community property, with the husband and wife sharing the property equally, or as "separate property," wholly free of all interest or claim of the other spouse. Since this is a choice made by the grantee, the grantee should sign the deed indicating acceptance of the conveyance in that form.

If, in such a state, a husband and wife wish to hold the property in joint tenancy, it is best that the deed be drafted with a place for the grantees' written express acceptance of this form of ownership.

In any event, where the grantee executes the deed to show acceptance of the form of ownership, assumption of obligations, or for any other reason, the grantee's signature should be acknowledged.

A deed to a minor or an insane person is valid.

In many states it is required that the deed show the address of the grantee, and a deed will not be accepted for recording unless this appears in the deed. However, failure to show the address does not invalidate the deed.

In the case of a deed involving a corporation, partnership, or trust, there are a number of matters to check.

1. Does the corporation exist?

   EXAMPLE: A deed to ABC Corp. is dated December 8, 1980. The corporate charter issued by the state is dated December 15, 1980. The deed runs to a grantee that did not exist on December 8. There is a problem.

   EXAMPLE: ABC Corp. was created by a charter dated November 1, 1975. On July 1, 1978, it was dissolved by the state for failure to pay its corporation tax. A deed to this corporation is dated December 8, 1980. A dissolution is like the death of an individual. A problem exists. *But see Lighthouse Church v. Texas Bank*, 889 S.W.2d 595 (Tex. App. 1994).

2. Is any foreign corporation in the deal duly licensed in the state?

   EXAMPLE: ABC Corp. is formed in Delaware in 1975. It buys an office building in Illinois in 1980. But it has no license to do business in Illinois. A tenant in the building fails to pay his rent. ABC Corp. cannot file an eviction suit. Most states will not allow unlicensed foreign corporations to sue in their courts.

3. If a partnership is involved, how should the deed read?

   EXAMPLE: *A, B,* and *C* are partners doing business as Unity Associates. In most states, the deed to the partnership may go either way, to *A, B,* and *C* or to Unity Associates.

4. Does the partnership exist? A limited partnership does not exist until its certificate has been filed as required by law.

5. If a foreign limited partnership is involved, has it been licensed to do business in the state?

6. How should a deed to a trust run?

   EXAMPLE: A business trust has ten beneficiaries. The trust document names *A* as trustee, and the trust is known as Prudence Trust. The deed should run to *A* as trustee of Prudence Trust. *See* Herbert B. Chernside, Annotation, *Modern Status of the Massachusetts Business Trust*, 88 A.L.R.3d 704 (1978).

7.03(b)(1) Deeds in Blank

The problem of whether a deed is void for want of a grantee often arises in connection with deeds where the name of the grantee is left blank at the time the deed is signed by the grantor. Of course, if the blank space for the grantee's name is never filled in, the deed cannot be a good deed, for a deed must convey the land to someone. Where the name of the grantee is inserted by an agent of the grantor after the grantor has signed the deed, the deed is usually valid.

EXAMPLE: Landowner signs a deed complete in all respects, except that the name of the grantee is left blank. The deed is delivered to Agent, with directions to sell the property for not less than a certain sum. Agent interests Buyer in the purchase of the property. Buyer is willing to pay the stipulated price. Agent fills in Buyer's name as grantee and delivers the deed to Buyer. Buyer pays the purchase price, not knowing that his name was filled in after the deed was signed. Such a deed is generally held valid, even though Agent's authority was merely verbal. *West v. Witschner,* 428 S.W.2d 538 (Mo. 1968); W.R. Habeeb, Annotation, *Validity and Effect of Deed Executed in Blank as to Name of Grantee,* 175 A.L.R. 1294 (1948). But, a deed delivered with the land description left blank is held void in many states. *West v. Witschner,* 428 S.W.2d 538 (Mo. 1968).

7.03(c) Consideration

Consideration is the value given for a conveyance of land. For many years, payment of a "consideration" or price was thought to be necessary in order to create the "use" in the purchaser. Today, consideration is usually recited in the deed, but actual presence of consideration is not necessary.

The deed usually recites that it was given for "$10.00 and other good and valuable consideration." In some states, the actual consideration must be stated.

Deeds are usually drafted with a general statement of nominal consideration to keep the private business dealings of the parties from becoming part of the public record. These efforts are not entirely successful. People who want to know the selling price of land can usually compute that price from the transfer stamps placed on the deed.

EXAMPLE: If the transfer tax is $1.00 per $1,000 dollars of the selling price, a deed with $10.00 of transfer tax affixed was given for $10,000, notwithstanding the fact that the consideration clause read "$10.00 and other valuable consideration."

If the deed recites a consideration, the fact that the deed represents a gift of the land and that no money actually changed hands will not invalidate the deed. An individual may give away land if he or she wishes. However, a person must be just before being generous. If the grantor is indebted at the time of the making of the gift, creditors may thereafter have the deed set aside as in fraud of their rights. The payment of a nominal consideration, such as $10, will not suffice to sustain the deed in such a case. A fair consideration is needed to sustain a deed against existing creditors of the grantor.

7.03(c)(1)
Consideration—
Support Deeds

Parents often convey their real estate to a son or daughter on the understanding that such son or daughter will support the parents for the rest of their lives. Similarly, an elderly person without close relatives may convey real estate to a stranger or to a retirement or nursing home in return for a promise of support. While, ordinarily, a deed cannot be set aside for *failure of consideration,* that is, for the reason that the grantee failed to receive what he or she bargained for, support deeds form an exception to the rule. *Bruno v. Bruno,* 172 A.2d 863 (Pa. 1961). Where the grantee fails to keep the promise to support the grantor, the deed can usually be set aside.

> **EXAMPLE:** A father and mother conveyed real estate to their son. The mother had owned the property, and it had been the parents' home. The deed recited a consideration of $2,500. The actual consideration, however, was the son's agreement to support the parents and give them a home for the rest of their lives. Several years later, the son stopped supporting the parents and became so abusive that they moved out and went to live with another son. The deed was set aside. *Worrell v. West,* 296 P.2d 1092 (Kan. 1956). The grantee is not living up to his promise unless he furnishes kindness and attention, as well as physical necessaries. *Zarembski v. Zarembski,* 48 N.E.2d 394 (Ill. 1943).

7.03(d)   Words
of Conveyance

Every deed must contain words of conveyance. These differ from state to state. In warranty deeds, *convey and warrant* or *grant, bargain,* and *sell* are often used. In quitclaim deeds, the words usually are *convey and quitclaim* or *remise, release,* and *forever quitclaim.*

7.03(e)   Description
of Land

A deed must describe the land conveyed.

7.03(f)   Waiver of
Dower and Homestead

In some states, a deed must contain a clause releasing and relinquishing all homestead, dower, and curtesy rights in the premises.

7.03(g)   Date

A date is not essential to the validity of a deed, though it is the universal custom to date all deeds.

7.03(h)   Execution;
Signature

The signature of the grantor is essential to the validity of the deed. A *forgery* (a deed to which some unauthorized third person has affixed the grantor's signature) is a nullity and conveys no title whatever. The fact that the grantor's signature is misspelled will not invalidate the deed. If the grantor is unable to write, he or she may sign by mark, in which case the signature line appears as follows:

His
"John X Smith (Seal)"
Mark

Everything but the "X" may be typed. The "X" must be affixed by the grantor.

Occasionally, a deed is signed not by the grantor him- or herself, but by an *attorney-in-fact.* An attorney-in-fact is simply an agent authorized by the landowner to sell and convey his or her real estate. In order for such a deed to be valid, the following requirements exist:

1. The landowner must first sign and deliver to his or her attorney-in-fact a written instrument, called a *power of attorney,* authorizing such attorney to sell and convey the land in question. Such an instrument must be as formal as the deed itself. In states that require a deed to be sealed, the power of attorney must be sealed. In states that require a deed to be witnessed, the power of attorney must be witnessed. All the other requirements relating to deeds should be observed, including acknowledgment and recording.

2. The deed must name the landowner, not the attorney-in-fact, as the grantor.

3. The name signed to the deed should be that of the landowner. Under the usual method, the attorney signs the grantor's name and then places his or her name beneath that of the grantor as follows:

"John Smith (Seal)"
"By Henry Brown, his Attorney-in-Fact"

4. The grantor must be alive on the date of the delivery of the deed, since death of the grantor automatically terminates the power of attorney. Insanity of the grantor may have the same result. Some states have enacted "durable power of attorney" laws. These statutes provide that the power continues notwithstanding the incompetency of the grantor.

5. Since the landowner ordinarily has the power to terminate the agency at any time and thus take away the attorney's power to execute deeds on his behalf, it should be established that the agency actually had not been terminated or revoked at the date of the delivery of the deed.

The technical mode of executing the deed of a corporation is for the proper officer to sign the corporate name, adding his or her own signature and official title beneath the name of the corporation. Usually, the corporate bylaws provide that deeds shall be signed by a president or vice president and attested to and sealed by a secretary or assistant secretary.

The mere fact that the grantor's name on the deed is signed by someone other than the grantor does not invalidate the deed. The execution of the deed may be ratified or otherwise authorized by the true grantor. If this is the case, the deed is as effective as though the actual grantor signed the deed.

7.03(i)   Seal   In some states, principally eastern states, a seal is essential to the validity of a deed. In most states, however, a seal is unnecessary, though the custom of using a seal persists. But even in those states where a deed by an individual need not bear a seal, a deed executed by a corporation should have the official corporate seal affixed.

7.03(j)   Witnesses   In many states, a deed must be witnessed, two witnesses being the number commonly required. Most states require witnessing where the deed is signed by mark.

7.03(k)   Taxes   Many states, counties, and municipalities have enacted laws that impose a tax upon the transfer of property. Under some of these laws, the recorder must refuse to accept a deed for recording unless proper tax stamps are affixed. These taxes vary from state to state and municipality to municipality. Local law and practice must be reviewed.

7.03(l)   Delivery of Deeds   Delivery is essential to the validity of a deed. The word *delivery* is somewhat misleading, since it would lead one to believe that it is necessary that the deed be actually handed by the grantor to the grantee. This is not the case. Delivery is simply the final act by which the grantor, who has previously signed the deed, signifies his or her intention that the deed shall take effect. Whether a deed has been delivered depends primarily on the *intention* of the grantor. The test is as follows: Did the grantor *do* or *say* anything to show the intention to pass ownership of the land to the grantee? A deed may be delivered by acts without words or by words without acts, though ordinarily there are both words and acts in the making of a delivery.

> **EXAMPLE:** At the closing of a deal, Buyer hands Seller a check. Seller signs the deed and, without saying a word, hands it to Buyer. There is a delivery.

> **EXAMPLE:** At the closing of a deal, all the papers, including Seller's signed deed, are on the closing table. Having received the check, Seller tells Buyer (the grantee) to take the deed. There is a delivery.

> **EXAMPLE:** Seller signs a deed conveying real estate to Buyer and hands it to Buyer, not with the intention of passing title, but with the understanding that Buyer will check the legal description to see if it is sufficient. There is no delivery.

> **EXAMPLE:** Seller signs a deed conveying real estate to Buyer but leaves it at his office while still thinking over the deal. Buyer steals the deed from Seller's office and shows it to Third Person, who purchases from Buyer, relying on Buyer's possession of the deed. Third Person acquires no title. There was no delivery of the deed.

7.03(I)(1) Delivery—Several Grantors

Suppose *A* and *B* own certain real estate, and both of them sign a deed running to *C* as grantee. *A* hands the deed to *B* for the sole purpose of having the deed checked by their lawyer. Without *A*'s permission, *B* hands the deed to *C* and collects the sale price from *C*. This is not a good deed so far as *A* is concerned. *A* still owns his half interest. One joint grantor, who is not authorized by the co-tenant, cannot make a valid delivery of the deed that will be binding on the latter. K.A. Dreschsler, Annotation, *Delivery of Deed or Mortgage by One or More but Not All of the Grantors or Mortgagors*, 162 A.L.R. 892 (1946).

When land is owned by several persons, all of them named as grantors in one deed, and one of the grantors signs the deed and hands it to the grantee with the statement that his or her consent to the sale of the land is conditioned on the other grantors also signing the deed, such deed is inoperative unless all grantors sign. *Logue v. Von Almen,* 40 N.E.2d 73 (Ill. 1941); *Cities Service Oil Co. v. Viering*, 89 N.E.2d 392, 397 (Ill. 1949); Herbert T. Tiffany, Note, *Conditional Delivery of Deeds*, 14 Colum. L. Rev. 389 (1914).

7.03(I)(2) Delivery—Lifetime of the Grantor

Delivery of a deed must be made in the lifetime of the grantor.

> **EXAMPLE:** On Seller's death, an envelope with Seller's name on it is found in Seller's safe-deposit box. The envelope is opened and found to contain a deed from Seller to Buyer. The deed is void for want of delivery.

A deed is the proper instrument for transferring ownership of land from one living person to another, and, in general, this means that the deed, to be effective, must operate while both parties are alive.

However, a grantor may effectively deliver a deed to the grantee with a clause therein stating that the deed is to take effect only at the grantor's death. The deed gives the grantee the present right to enjoy the property at the grantor's death. V. Woerner, Annotation, *Effect on Validity and Character of Instrument in Form of Deed of Provisions Therein Indicating an Intention to Postpone or Limit the Rights of Grantee Until After the Death of the Grantor*, 31 A.L.R.2d 532 (1953). *See also* V. Woerner, Annotation, *Sufficiency of Delivery of Deed Where Grantor Retains or Recovers Physical Possession*, 87 A.L.R.2d 787 (1960).

7.03(l)(3)   Delivery—Third Persons

Where the grantor gives the deed not to the grantee but to some third person, a wholly new set of rules comes into play. A number of different situations present themselves.

> **EXAMPLE:** Seller executes a deed running to Buyer as grantee and gives the deed to Buyer's lawyer, with the intention of giving Buyer ownership of the real estate here and now. This is delivery to an *agent of the grantee* and is good delivery.

> **EXAMPLE:** Seller executes a deed running to Buyer as grantee and gives the deed to his own lawyer to check its form. There is no intention to transfer ownership and no delivery. Here, the deed has been handed to the *agent of the grantor.*

> **EXAMPLE:** Seller enters into a contract to sell land to Buyer and pursuant thereto executes a deed to Buyer. However, Seller gives the deed to XYZ Bank with directions to deliver the deed to Buyer when certain moneys are paid by Buyer to the bank. This is an escrow. If the conditions for the delivery of the deed by the escrowee are not met, delivery by the escrowee in error will not vest title in the grantee. *LaSalle Nat'l Bank v. Kissane,* 546 N.E.2d 790 (Ill. App. 1987).

> **EXAMPLE:** Seller executes a deed running to Son, as grantee, gives the deed to Custodian and directs Custodian to deliver the deed to Son after Seller's death. This brings up the subject of *death escrows.* This is a good delivery as long as it is clear that Seller intended to part with all control over the real estate once Seller gave the deed to Custodian. Oddly enough, the courts allow Seller, in such cases, to use the real estate during Seller's lifetime. They do not regard this as inconsistent with the passing of ownership to Son. It is as though Seller had conveyed outright to Son, but had reserved a life estate in the property. *Bury v. Young,* 33 P. 338 (Cal. 1893).

7.03(l)(4)   Delivery—Family Transactions

If a father executes a deed to a minor child, the deed is beneficial to the child, and if the father indicates by his words and conduct that he intends the deed to operate at once, actual delivery is unnecessary. The courts are most reluctant to upset a deed that is made as a gift by a parent to a child.

7.03(m)   Acceptance

For a deed to transfer ownership of real estate, it is necessary that the grantor intends to transfer ownership to the grantee and that the grantee intends to accept ownership of the real estate. *Blankenship v. Myers,* 544 P.2d 314 (Idaho 1975). That is to say, delivery by the grantor must be accompanied by acceptance of the deed by the grantee. C.R. McCorkle, Annotation, *What Constitutes Acceptance of Deed by Grantee,* 74 A.L.R.2d 992 (1960). Only rarely will disputes arise regarding acceptance, and the courts are not disposed to be technical about it. Indeed, the courts have gone so far as to hold that if the grantor makes and records a deed without the knowledge of the grantee, ownership will nevertheless pass if the grantee, on being informed of the deed, assents to it, even though this takes place after the death of the grantor. *Mann v. Jummel,* 56 N.E. 161 (Ill. 1899). Also, if the grantee dies before learning of the deed, acceptance will be presumed and the deed held good. *Lessee of Mitchell v. Ryan,* 3 Ohio St. 377 (1854). A parent may accept for an infant. *Whitworth v. Whitworth,* 210 S.E.2d 9 (Ga. 1974).

7.04   Recording

Virtually all deeds are filed for record in some public office.

7.05   Official Conveyances

Deeds by executors, administrators, guardians of minors, conservators or guardians of insane persons, sheriffs, masters in chancery, receivers, trustees in bankruptcy, and other similar conveyances usually depend for their validity on prior court proceedings. In addition, numerous technical requirements exist that frequently expose such deeds to attack.

7.06 After-Acquired Title

If the grantor in a warranty deed does not have title or does not have complete title at the time of executing the deed, but thereafter acquires title, such title will automatically pass to his or her grantee without any additional conveyance. The opposite is true when the grantor conveys by quitclaim deed. If the grantor did not have title to the property at the time of the giving of a quitclaim deed, the grantee would not automatically be vested with title that the grantor subsequently obtained. *Tuttle v. Burrows*, 852 P.2d 1314 (Colo. App. 1992).

7.07 Title Conveyed

If the grantor owns the real estate in fee simple, and the deed contains no qualifying language, the deed gives the grantee good fee simple title to the property. However, deeds often contain qualifying language, which results in the grantee's acquiring something less than the fee simple title.

> **EXAMPLE:** Seller makes a deed conveying land to Buyer "and the heirs of his body." In some states, Buyer acquires only a life estate by such deed, and his children acquire the remainder. In other states, such a deed will give Buyer the full fee simple title to the land.

> **EXAMPLE:** Seller conveys land to Buyer by a deed that contains the following clause: "To have and to hold for and during the grantee's life." Buyer acquires only a life estate by this deed.

The law on this subject is so complex and contains so many refinements of reasoning that no one but an experienced attorney should attempt to interpret a deed containing any qualifying language whatever. In particular, words such as *heirs, heirs of the body, issue,* and *death without issue* are danger signals. Indiscriminate use of such language is an invitation to a lawsuit.

7.07(a) Title Conveyed by Deed— Fee or Easement

If language is added to the deed indicating the purpose for which the land is to be used, this may result in giving the grantee something less than full ownership of the land. Lawyers talk about the nature of the *estate* conveyed by the deed.

> **EXAMPLE:** By warranty deed, Seller deeded to Buyer "a right of way one rod wide" over certain land. This deed gave Buyer only an easement of travel. A deed that conveys a right, especially a right of way, rather than land, gives the grantee only an easement. As can be seen, the word "easement" is not necessary for an easement to be created. A.E. Korpela, Annotation, *Deed to Railroad Company as Conveying Fee or Easement*, 6 A.L.R.3d 973 (1966).

Also, if the deed conveys the land, with the words of purpose following the property description, the courts are not in agreement on the legal effect of the conveyance.

> **EXAMPLE:** Seller made a deed to Buyer of a strip of land "to be used for road purposes." The court held that Buyer acquired only an easement for road purposes. *Magnolia Petroleum Co. v. West,* 30 N.E.2d 24 (Ill. 1940). The reason for this is that courts apply rules of interpretation. One of these is that courts cannot ignore any language in a written instrument. If any meaning is to be given the phrase "to be used for road purposes," it is that the land must be used *only* for road purposes. This makes the deed a grant of right to use the land for a specific purpose. That is what an easement is. The estate conveyed is not an *estate in fee simple.* Here, the court interprets the language in a way that would surprise a layperson. But, in other states, exactly the same kind of deed will be held to give Buyer full ownership of the strip. *Biggs v. Wolfe*, 178 A.2d 482 (Del. 1962).

> **EXAMPLE:** Where a deed runs to a charitable corporation, frequently some reference is made in the deed to the use of the land for the charitable purposes of the corporation. Normally, this nevertheless leaves the corporation with a salable ownership in the land. Bogert, *Trusts* § 54 (6th ed. rev. 1987); 4 Scott, *The Law of Trusts* § 348.1 (4th ed. 1987).

EXAMPLE: Seller deeds his vacant land to Hospital "for hospital purposes." Hospital finds the land not well adapted to hospital purposes. It sells the land to Third Person. This is a valid transaction. Third Person gets good title to the land.

Where a deed runs to a city, village, park district, or other public body, and contains language descriptive of the use to which the land is to be put, questions may arise as to the nature of the ownership thus acquired, particularly when such use is abandoned, though in most cases, the courts struggle to find that the public body acquired a good, salable title to the land. 28 Am. Jur. 2d *Estates* § 149; 10 McQuillin, *Municipal Corporations* § 28.19 (3d ed. 1990).

EXAMPLE: Seller sold and deeded his land to City "to be used for the use and benefit of the citizens of City." City found the land unusable for city purposes and sold it to Third Person. This can be done. Third Person acquires good ownership of the land. *City v. Jones,* 122 N.W.2d 503 (Neb. 1963).

The fact that the deed was made because of the threat of condemnation by the public body does not alter this rule. *Mattion v. Trustees,* 279 N.E.2d 66 (Ill. 1971); *Contra, Kendrick v. City of St. Paul,* 6 N.W.2d 449 (Minn. 1942).

There is an exception to this rule in some states:

EXAMPLE: Seller deeded real estate to the City of Milwaukee "for highway purposes." By this deed, the city acquired only an easement to use the land for highway purposes and could not sell the land. This exception is confined to deeds for street, alley, and highway purposes, and even then, in some states, the city gets good, salable ownership of the land.

Where a deed runs to some public body "for park purposes" there is no agreement whatever as to what such a deed conveys. V. Woerner, Annotation, *Nature of Estate Conveyed by Deed for Park or Playground Purposes*, 15 A.L.R.2d 975 (1951).

7.08 Exceptions and Reservations

In conveying land, the grantor often wishes to retain some part of the land described or to reserve some right therein. This is accomplished by inserting in the deed the proper clauses of exception and reservation. An exception withholds from the operation of the deed title to a part of the land described in the deed. Thus, a deed of Lot 1 *excepting the north twenty feet thereof* does not pass ownership of the north twenty feet of the lot. That portion was *excepted* from the conveyance. A *reservation* is the creation by the deed of a new right in favor of the grantor, usually an easement or life estate. Thus, in a deed of Lot 1 *reserving to the grantor an easement for ingress and egress over and across the north twenty feet of Lot 1,* ownership of the north twenty feet passes to the grantee, but an easement is reserved in favor of the grantor. Sometimes, the terms *excepting* and *reserving* are used inaccurately, and the courts will hold that a true reservation was created by the use of the word *excepting* or that a true exception was created by the use of the word *reserving.*

EXAMPLE: Seller conveys certain land to Buyer "except the north ten feet for a right of way." Ownership of the entire tract, including the north ten feet, passes to Buyer, but the quoted clause reserves an easement for Seller over the north ten feet. 139 A.L.R. 1348.

It is possible for the grantor in a deed to reserve a life estate in the property conveyed. Often, to save the expense of probating a will after his death, a father, while still living, will give a deed of his land to his son or daughter and, in the deed, will reserve to himself a life estate. The grantee becomes the owner of the land, and the grantor retains the use thereof for his lifetime. The use of this form of deed must be accompanied with a warning. Once such a deed is executed and delivered, the grantor cannot recall it. The psychological effect of this change in circumstances often brings about friction between the parent and child. Hence, such transactions should be avoided, if possible.

7.09 Suggestions

1. *Form of deed.* If there is a contract for the sale of real estate, find out if the contract specifies the form of deed to be given. If the contract specifies that the seller is to give a warranty deed, then, of course, a warranty deed form must be used. If the contract does not specify the form of the deed, in most states, a quitclaim deed will suffice. The seller will prefer to use this form, since it subjects the seller to no personal liability for defects in title. If there is no written contract for the sale of the land, the seller will again prefer to give a quitclaim deed.

2. *Grantor.* Check the deed by which the grantor acquired ownership and see that the grantor's name is spelled the same way in the deed by which the grantor conveys the property. Any difference in spelling may lead to an objection when the title is examined. If a woman acquires title by her maiden name and subsequently marries, the deed should show both names: *Mary Jones, formerly Mary Smith.* Any examiner of the title will thus find a connected chain of title to the land. The grantor's marital status should be given: *bachelor, spinster, widow, widower,* or *divorced and not remarried.* If the grantor is married, the spouse should also be named as grantor, and their marital status given: *John Smith and Mary Smith, his wife.* A married woman or widow should never be described as "Mrs. John Jones." Her legal name is "Mary Jones." Don't describe yourself as "R. John Smith." Legally, your middle name or middle initial is no part of your name. Hence, you should at least describe yourself as "Robert John Smith," for it is poor practice to use initials only in legal documents. If the state law requires, give the street address of the grantor and grantee. Special forms of deeds are used where the grantor is a corporation, trustee, executor, and so on. Of course, all the landowners must convey if the buyer is to get good title, but different landowners may use different deeds. As a rule, it is best for a husband and wife to join in the same deed.

3. *Grantee.* Have the proposed grantee write out his or her name on a slip of paper—first name, middle initial, if any, and last name—and copy the name in this identical form in the proper place in the deed form. The grantee's marital status may, but need not, be given. State the grantee's place of residence. If two or more persons are acquiring title, the names of all must be shown in the deed. If they are taking title as joint tenants, use a joint tenancy form deed. Legal stationers usually print a special form for joint tenancy transactions. Following the names of the grantees in this form is a phrase reading somewhat like this: *As joint tenants with the right of survivorship and not as tenants in common nor as tenants by the entireties.* When husband and wife are taking title, their marital relation should be shown, as *John Smith and Mary Smith, his wife.* If a corporation is taking title, its charter should be checked and the name copied exactly and without the slightest deviation. For example, if the charter states the corporate name as *The Elite Hat Shop, Inc.,* do not omit the *The* and do not spell out the *Inc.*

   A deed to a trustee should clearly identify the trust. Never draft a deed running simply to *John Smith, as trustee.* Have the deed run to *John Smith, as trustee under Trust Agreement dated June 15, 1946, and known as the Pinecrest Liquidation Trust,* or other proper designation. You should have before you the trust instrument creating the trust and describe it accurately in the deed. If the deed to the trustee also creates the trust, it is serving a double purpose: (1) It is operating as a deed of the land and must contain all the necessary elements of a deed and (2) it is creating a trust and must contain all the requisite elements for the creation of a trust. Such a document should be drafted only by one thoroughly conversant with the law of trusts. The deed should conform to the contract of sale with respect to the grantees. For example, if Seller contracts to sell to Buyer 1 and Buyer 2, Seller should not, even though Buyer 1 requests it, make a deed running to Buyer 1 only. That would violate Buyer 2's rights and make Seller liable for damages if Buyer 2 suffers a loss. If you are creating a corporation that is to acquire real estate, be sure that the corporation's charter has been issued and that all other formalities for corporate existence are complied with before the deed to the corporation is made out. In other words, be sure you have an existing, legal grantee to whom to convey.

4. *Consideration.* Let the deed recite a monetary consideration, as *in consideration of the sum of $10 and other good and valuable consideration.* In a few states, it is customary or necessary to recite the true sale price of the land. In deeds by corporations, trustees, executors, and so forth, the deed should recite the true sale price.

5. *Words of grant.* Every printed form of deed contains words of grant. It is not necessary to tamper with these, since the warranty deed form will have words appropriate for a warranty deed and the quitclaim deed form will also have appropriate words.

6. *Description.* Do not attempt to draft a description unless you are sure you know what you are doing. If a title policy, abstract, or Torrens certificate has been previously issued on the land that is being sold, and the land sold is identical with the tract mentioned in the title policy, abstract, or Torrens certificate (i.e., there have been no subsequent conveyances of portions of the tract, etc.), then the description may be copied from the title policy, abstract caption, or Torrens certificate, since such documents usually contain accurate descriptions. After the description has been copied into the deed form, have someone read it aloud to you while you follow the description in the title policy, abstract, or Torrens certificate, since even a microscopic error in typing may throw the whole description off.

7. *Subject to clause.* If the grantor in a warranty deed wishes to avoid personal liability, he or she should include in the subject to clause all defects in title, such as mortgages, unpaid taxes, existing leases, restrictions, and so forth. However, the contract of sale usually specifies as to what objections the title will be subject when conveyed to the buyer; the seller, in preparing the deed, has no right to add items to this list. For example, if the seller agrees, by the contract, to convey the land to the buyer subject only to a certain mortgage, the seller cannot include in the deed the words "subject to mortgage recorded as Document No. 10356789 and also to restrictions of record." The buyer has the right to object to the inclusion of the portion relating to the restrictions, since restrictions were not mentioned in the contract. In a quitclaim deed, a subject to clause is unnecessary and inappropriate.

8. *Mortgages.* If the land is being sold subject to a mortgage that the grantee is to assume and agree to pay, let the deed state "Subject to a mortgage made by *X* in favor of *Y* dated _____, 19__ and recorded _____, 19__, in Book 100, Page 101, as Document No. 999, which the grantee herein assumes and agrees to pay."

Where the buyer is paying part cash and giving back to the seller either a mortgage or trust deed for part of the purchase money, it is better that the deed contain a recital somewhat as follows: "As part of the consideration for this transaction, the grantee herein has this day executed to _____, as trustee, a trust deed, of even date herewith, securing a promissory note in the sum of $_____, which represents part of the purchase price for said premises." This is particularly desirable where a trust deed is involved, since if Seller sells and conveys land to Buyer and Buyer simultaneously executes a trust deed to Trustee, the public records do not clearly show that the trust deed was given as part of the purchase price unless the deed contains the suggested recital. Of course, the trust deed or mortgage should also contain a recital that "this trust deed is given to secure payment of part of the purchase price of said premises."

9. *Statement of purpose of deed.* Inexperienced conveyancers tend to put various legal- sounding phrases in deeds without having any clear idea of the purpose such phrases were intended to serve. This is a very dangerous practice. Do not insert a single syllable in a deed unless you are certain what the legal effect of that insertion will be. Remember that if you add in your deed phrases like "to be used for road purposes," the result may be to create a grant of an easement out of what started to be a deed of the real estate. It is neither necessary nor desirable to state in the deed the purpose for which the land is to be used.

10. *Restrictions and conditions.* Restrictions and conditions must be drafted with care. Because of the drastic consequences attendant upon the enforcement of a reverter clause, the grantee should view with suspicion any attempt to insert a reverter clause in the deed. If there is a written contract for the sale of the land, the grantor has no right to insert in the deed any restrictions

or conditions not provided for in the contract. If the contract provides for a building restriction, but says nothing about a condition or reverter clause, the grantor has no right to provide in the deed for a reverter of title in the event of a breach of condition. Be sure you understand the words you use in drafting restrictions, as, for example, residence purposes, dwellings purposes, or business purposes. Certain words have a well-known technical meaning, and if such words are used in a deed, courts will give them their usual meaning, regardless of what special, individual meaning they may have in the mind of the grantor. The grantor will not even be allowed to testify that such a word had a special meaning. On the other hand, inexperienced draftspersons often use words that have no meaning at all, such as the provision that "only houses of standard construction shall be erected on said premises." It would be difficult to get two people to agree on the definition of "standard construction." Such a phrase is so devoid of meaning that courts cannot enforce it.

11. *Easements.* A deed may contain a grant to the grantee of an easement over other lands of the seller. If there is a written contract of sale, and it makes no mention of such an easement, the seller is under no obligation to include it in the deed. A deed may reserve to the grantor an easement over the land conveyed. If there is a written contract of sale, and it makes no mention of such an easement, the grantor has no right to insert such a clause in the deed.

12. *Waiver of dower and homestead.* Almost without exception, deed forms prepared by your local stationers include the necessary waivers of dower and homestead rights. For this and other reasons, it is dangerous to use a deed form printed in your state in conveying land lying in some other state. Obtain a form printed in the state where the land lies.

13. *Date.* It is the custom to date all deeds.

14. *Signature.* Before permitting the grantor to sign, have him or her write his or her name on a piece of paper. Check the spelling with the spelling of the name in the body of the deed. Be sure that the two correspond, since even trivial variations are frequently objected to by title examiners. Type the name of the grantor beneath the signature line and direct him or her to sign exactly as the name is typed.

15. *Seal.* If a seal is needed on deeds of land in your state, deed forms printed in your state will show a seal on the signature line. If there are more signatures on the deed than there are printed signature lines, be sure the word *Seal* appears after each signature. The corporate seal is always necessary on deeds made by corporations.

16. *Tax stamps.* The necessary tax stamps should be attached where the state law requires.

17. *Witnesses.* Always have two or more witnesses sign the deed if any grantor has signed by mark. If all grantors are able to write, their signatures need not be witnessed unless the state law requires witnesses. Some states require that all deeds be witnessed.

18. *Acknowledgment.*

19. *Recording.* File your deed in the proper public office immediately after it has been acknowledged. Delay may prove disastrous.

20. *Statutory requirements.* Make sure to comply with all applicable state laws relating to various recitations that are required to appear on the face of the deed (i.e., compliance with local subdivision ordinances and plat acts, mailing address of the grantee, and name and address of the person preparing the deed). Readiness avoids recording problems and delay. Many states have enacted requirements that the deed and other recorded documents be of certain size, have certain margins, be of a certain size type font, and be of a certain color ink. These laws are designed to make automated document storage and retrieval systems work better. If the documents do not comply, they will not be accepted for recording, or will only be recorded if a higher fee is paid. The failure to comply with these requirements will, at a minimum, be an embarrassment.

21. *Take care in preparing the deed.* Erasures and alterations raise danger signals that proper draftsmanship and transcription should avoid. 1 *Merrill on Notice* § 81 at 106 (1952).

CHAPTER 8

Acknowledgments; Notaries

8.01 In General An acknowledgment is a formal declaration made before some public officer, usually a notary public, by a person who has signed a deed, mortgage, or other instrument, that the instrument is his or her voluntary act and deed. *In re McCauley's Adoption,* 131 N.W.2d 174 (Neb. 1964); *D.T. McCall & Sons v. Seagraves,* 796 S.W.2d 457, 463 (Tenn. Ct. App. 1990). This act of acknowledgment, memorialized by the public official, furnishes formal proof of the authenticity of the execution of the instrument.

8.02 Certificate The officer before whom this declaration is made attaches a certificate to the instrument or fills in the printed form of certificate that appears on virtually all deeds, mortgages, and other documents meant to be recorded. This is known as the *certificate of acknowledgment.* It usually recites that the grantor appeared before the officer and acknowledged the execution of the instrument as the free and voluntary act and deed of the signing party. However, the form of the certificate of acknowledgment varies considerably from state to state and from situation to situation. An acknowledgment taken from an individual differs from an acknowledgment taken from a corporate officer. It is important that the proper form be followed. *In re Viking Co., Inc.,* 389 F. Supp. 1230 (1974).

An acknowledgment must not be confused with an affidavit. An affidavit is a written statement made under oath. At the conclusion of the affidavit, the officer, usually a notary, recites that it was subscribed and sworn to. An affidavit is not acceptable as a substitute for an acknowledgment. The two serve different purposes. *Hatcher v. Hall,* 292 S.W.2d 619 (Mo. 1956). The acknowledgment merely makes the prima facie showing that the instrument was duly executed. The affidavit or verification goes to the truth of the matters set forth therein. *D.J. Fair Lumber Co. v. Karlin,* 430 P.2d 222 (Kan. 1967); *Trane Co. v. Bakkalapulo,* 672 P.2d 586, 588 (Kan. 1983).

8.03 Waiver of Dower and Homestead Rights In some states, the certificate of acknowledgment must specifically state that dower and homestead rights were understandingly relinquished.

8.04 Necessity In a few states, Arizona and Ohio, for example, an unacknowledged deed is not valid. In a number of states, certain types of instruments, such as deeds of married women or deeds or mortgages of homestead land, must be acknowledged. Other deeds, however, are legally valid, though not acknowledged. This statement is without significance, since, as a practical matter, every deed or mortgage should be acknowledged. In the great majority of the states, an unacknowledged instrument is not entitled to be recorded. H.D. Warren, Annotation, *Record of Instrument Without Sufficient Acknowledgment as Notice*, 59 A.L.R.2d 1299, 1302 (1958). If the deed is not given the effect of a recorded document, the title of the holder of the deed is precarious indeed. Lack of an acknowledgment on a deed may render title unmarketable. Other technical reasons make an acknowledgment a practical necessity.

8.05 Who May Take an Acknowledgment

A deed or mortgage may be acknowledged before a notary public or some other officer designated by the local law. Such a person, it is said, *takes* the acknowledgment of the grantor. Generally, a notary who is an attorney is competent to take the acknowledgment of his or her client. D.E. Evins, Annotation, *Disqualification of Attorney, Otherwise Qualified to Take Oath or Acknowledgment from Client*, 21 A.L.R.3d 483, 523 (1968). However, a notary with a financial interest in the transaction is disqualified. For example, a grantee in a deed would be clearly disqualified from taking the grantor's acknowledgment. Other disqualified parties include the grantor in a deed, mortgagor and mortgagee in a mortgage, and the trustee in a trust deed. In some states, a stockholder of a corporation that is a party to the instrument is disqualified from taking the acknowledgment of the corporation. In other states, the rule is the reverse.

8.06 Venue

The venue of the certificate of acknowledgment is the caption, which is usually shown as follows:

STATE OF ILLINOIS
COUNTY OF COOK } (SS)

The venue shows the place where the acknowledgment took place, that is, the place where the grantor appeared before the notary and made his or her formal declaration that the deed was his or her voluntary act.

8.07 Effect of Invalidity

It is important to keep in mind the fact that invalidity of the acknowledgment does not make the deed void. However, in most states, a valid acknowledgment is essential for proper recording; that is, if the acknowledgment is void, the deed, though recorded, is treated as an unrecorded deed. If that is the result, subsequent owners of the property are not on constructive notice of the rights of the grantee of the defectively acknowledged instrument.

8.08 Foreign

It is not uncommon for a document to be executed and thus acknowledged in a state other than the state in which the land lies.

The acknowledgment will be valid if it conforms either to the law of the state of execution or to the law of the state where the land lies. An acknowledgment taken outside of the state where the land lies is known as a *foreign acknowledgment*. In some states, it is required, either by custom or by law, that every acknowledgment taken outside of the state have attached a certificate by a court clerk to the effect that the officer taking the acknowledgment was authorized by law to do so. This is known as a *certificate of authenticity,* or a *certificate of magistracy*. If the certificate goes on to recite that the acknowledgment is in due form, it is known as a *certificate of authenticity and conformity,* or *certificate of magistracy and conformity*.

8.09 Date The date of the certificate of acknowledgment is unimportant. Hence, omission of the date of the certificate or insertion of an incorrect date will not invalidate the acknowledgment. Care should be taken to make sure that the date of the acknowledgment correlates with the date of the execution of instrument. While the date of the acknowledgment should be the date of the execution, it is not uncommon for instruments to be dated "as of" a date different from the actual date of execution. In such case, the "as of" date and the acknowledgment date will not be the same.

8.10 Signature of Officer Taking Acknowledgment The certificate of acknowledgment must be signed by the officer taking the acknowledgment. Otherwise, it is not valid. The certificate should also show the official character of the person taking the acknowledgment such as, notary public, or justice of the peace.

8.11 Seal An acknowledgment taken by a notary public is usually invalid unless the notary's official seal is placed on the certificate. The requirements as to seals of officers other than notaries vary from state to state. If there is a trend in this area, it is toward the use of rubber stamps instead of the traditional metal seal. Rubber stamps are more readable when recorded documents are placed into the microfilm or other imaged records of the county recorders and secretaries of state.

8.12 Date of Expiration of Commission Failure of the notary public to show the date his or her commission expires does not invalidate the certificate.

8.13 Liability of Notary—False Acknowledgment Both the notary public and the surety on his or her official bond will be liable for damages caused by the notary's willful misconduct, as where the notary falsely certifies to a forged mortgage and the mortgage is sold to an innocent purchaser. John D. Perovich, Annotation, *Liability of Notary Public or His Bond for Wilful or Deliberate Misconduct in Performance of Duties*, 44 A.L.R.3d 1243 (1972). The notary and the notary's surety will also be liable when the notary's negligence causes damage, as when the notary acknowledges the signatures on a forged mortgage without knowing the parties who appear before the notary and without procuring any evidence or information as to their identity. *Id. See also* D.E. Ytreberg, Annotation, *Measure of Damages for False or Incomplete Certificate by Notary Public*, 13 A.L.R.3d 1039 (1967).

8.14 Foreign-Speaking Persons and Handicapped Persons A problem has arisen relating to the relationship and business practices between notaries public and people who have immigrated to the United States from countries where the civil law prevails. In those countries, the notary public is a public official of considerable importance and legal training. In this country, notaries are not to give legal advice unless, of course, they are lawyers. To emphasize the importance of this point, the recent revision of Illinois' notary public law expressly prohibits notaries who are not attorneys from preparing any legal instrument or filling in the blanks of an instrument other than a notary certificate. 5 ILCS 312/1–101 *et seq.*

To further address this problem, which is especially important in the Latin communities, Illinois notaries who are not attorneys and who advertise notarial services must include in the ad a notice that the notary is not an attorney and may not give legal advice or accept fees for legal advice. 5 ILCS 312/3–103.

The notary must read the instrument to a blind person before taking an acknowledgment. If the party executing the document does not speak or understand English, the notary shall not take the acknowledgment unless the nature and effect of the document are translated into a language that the person understands. 5 ILCS 312/6–104

CHAPTER 9

Recording and Constructive Notice

9.01 Necessity of Recording

Every state has a recording law. These laws provide, in substance, that, until recorded, a deed, mortgage, or other instrument conveying an interest in real property is ineffective and void as to subsequent purchasers or mortgagees of the same land. The policy behind these laws is that the ownership of real estate should be disclosed by the public records. Purchasers of land should be able to rely on those records and be protected against secret, unrecorded deeds and mortgages.

Under these laws an unrecorded deed or mortgage is good and valid *as between the parties to the instrument*. A subsequent grantee or mortgagee, however, may acquire its interest in the property free of the interest created by the earlier grant, if the grant to the subsequent grantee or mortgagee is recorded before that grantee or mortgagee has actual or constructive notice or knowledge of the prior rights. The public policy behind this concept is that persons who deal with real estate in ignorance of the unrecorded interests should be protected against those unrecorded rights.

> **EXAMPLE:** Seller, the owner of a parcel of vacant land, sells the land to Buyer 1 and gives Buyer 1 a deed. Buyer 1 fails to record the deed. Later, Seller dies, and Seller's heirs, not knowing that Seller had previously sold the land, deed the land to Buyer 2, who records his deed. Buyer 2 purchases in ignorance of the earlier deed to Buyer 1. Buyer 2 gets good title to the real estate. Buyer 2 is an innocent purchaser or bona fide purchaser.

> **EXAMPLE:** Seller owns a parcel of land. Seller mortgages it to Lender in 1985. The mortgage, through error, is not recorded. Seller sells the land to Buyer in 1986, concealing the existence of the mortgage. Buyer acquires the land free and clear of the mortgage. The innocent purchaser is protected against the unrecorded mortgage.

9.02 Constructive Notice from the Records

The recording laws have a double operation or effect. First, they protect a purchaser or mortgagee who acts in ignorance of an earlier unrecorded deed or mortgage. Second, they also provide that if a deed or mortgage is recorded, all persons who thereafter deal with the property will be deemed to have full knowledge of the recorded document. The courts will not permit a party to act in ignorance of a recorded document. Every purchaser or mortgagee of the land is said to be *charged with notice* of prior recorded documents. The courts say that the public records impart *constructive notice* of all prior recorded deeds and mortgages.

> **EXAMPLE:** Seller conveys land to Buyer 1, who records the deed. Thereafter, Seller persuades Buyer 2 to buy the same land, telling Buyer 2 that Seller still owns the land. Buyer 2 fails to examine the public records relating to this tract of land. Buyer 2 acquires nothing. Buyer 2 has constructive notice of the deed to Buyer 1.

REFERENCE: Taylor Mattis, *Recording Acts: Anachronistic Reliance,* 25 Real Prop., Prob. & Tr. L.J. 17 (1990); Ray E. Sweat, *Race, Race-Notice and Notice Statutes: The American Recording System,* Prob. & Prop. (May/June 1989) at 27.

9.03 Office Where Deeds Are Recorded

The name of the officer charged with the duty of keeping the public records of deeds and mortgages varies from state to state. This officer may be known as the recorder of deeds, county recorder, clerk and recorder, register of deeds, or registrar of deeds. For convenience, the public officer is hereinafter referred to as the *recorder,* and the public office where deeds are filed or recorded is referred to as the *recorder's office.*

9.04 What Constitutes Recording

A person wishing to record a deed or mortgage simply deposits it with the recorder. Such a deed or mortgage is said to be recorded. All the world must take notice of its existence. The recorder copies the document in his or her record books, indexes it, and returns the original to the person who left it for recording. The recorder does not determine the validity of the document.

9.05 Persons Protected by Recording Laws

The recording laws are designed primarily to protect a subsequent bona fide purchaser of the land. A bona fide purchaser is one who has paid the purchase price in good faith and without knowledge of the prior unrecorded deed or mortgage. A mortgagee who loans money in reliance on the public records is a bona fide encumbrancer and is entitled to the protection of the recording laws similar to the protections given to a bona fide purchaser.

EXAMPLE: Owner mortgages his land to Lender 1, without recording the mortgage. Thereafter, Owner mortgages the same land to Lender 2, and Lender 2 records his mortgage. Lender 2 does not know of the earlier mortgage to Lender 1. Lender 2 has a first mortgage on the land.

A number of states add the requirement that, to be entitled to these protections, the subsequent purchaser or mortgagee must file the deed or mortgage for record before the recording of the earlier deed or mortgage. Under this rule, for example, it will not suffice that the purchaser has acquired a tract of land in good faith and in ignorance of an earlier unrecorded mortgage. The purchaser must also record the deed before the prior mortgage is recorded. But, if the purchaser records the deed in apt time, the purchaser is protected, even if the mortgagee later discovers the oversight and proceeds to record the mortgage.

In some states, the grantee under a quitclaim deed is, by definition, not a bona fide purchaser. *Polhemus v. Cobb*, 653 So. 2d 964 (Ala. 1995); *Pankins v. Jackson*, 891 S.W.2d 845 (Mo. App. 1995). The theory is that the fact that the grantor does not make full assurances that the grantor is the owner of the property being conveyed is enough to put the purchaser on notice. This theory is not entitled to much weight in today's society. There are many instances in which the grantor simply does not have adequate knowledge to prudently give the warranties that go with a deed with covenants. For example, the buyer of property from a foreclosing lender may have no basis to give covenants of warranty upon a sale of the property. Title insurance is available to protect the purchaser from most of the risks that the warranties would cover. It should be noted, however, that the coverage under a title insurance policy may be more restrictive than the warranties of title contained in a warranty deed.

In some states, a judgment creditor is also protected against prior unrecorded deeds and mortgages.

EXAMPLE: Owner makes a mortgage to Lender on November 15. The mortgage is recorded on November 20. On November 17, Creditor obtains a judgment against Owner.

> The judgment enjoys priority of lien over the mortgage, since it was rendered prior to the recording of the mortgage.

A substantial number of states, however, do not extend this protection to judgment creditors.

A person who has acquired land by gift is not protected by the recording laws, because the donee or recipient had not paid any consideration for the property.

> **EXAMPLE:** Owner mortgages land to Lender. Lender fails to record the mortgage. Owner thereafter gives Daughter a deed to the land as a gift, and Daughter records her deed. Lender can nevertheless enforce the mortgage against Daughter. But if, prior to the recording of the mortgage, Daughter should sell the land to Buyer, Buyer, being a purchaser, would get good title free and clear of the prior unrecorded mortgage.

Similarly, a person who acquires title by will or as an heir of the landowner is not protected.

> **EXAMPLE:** Owner makes a mortgage to Lender, but Lender fails to record this mortgage. Thereafter, Owner dies leaving a will whereby the land is given to Son. Lender may enforce the mortgage against Son.

9.06   Effect of Actual Knowledge

Of course, one who actually knows of a prior unrecorded deed or mortgage is not protected against it. After the knowledge or notice is acquired, the party cannot be a bona fide purchaser.

> **EXAMPLE:** Owner owns certain land and mortgages it to Lender in 1985. Through error, the mortgage is not recorded. Owner enters into a contract to sell the land to Buyer in 1990. The contract of sale describes the mortgage. Buyer must pay off the mortgage or take the land burdened with the mortgage. Buyer is not protected. Buyer is not an innocent purchaser.

Similarly, where a subsequent purchaser takes with *actual knowledge* of an instrument that was recorded, but because of some defect, this instrument does not impart *constructive notice,* no bona fide purchaser protection attaches. A.M. Swarthout, Annotation, *Record of Instrument Which Comprises or Includes an Interest or Right that Is Not a Proper Subject of Record,* 3 A.L.R.2d 571, 589 (1949).

> **EXAMPLE:** Purchaser obtained a title report that showed a defectively recorded deed to Stranger. This deed, though taken by the recorder, did not legally give constructive notice because it bore no acknowledgment. Purchaser will not be a bona fide purchaser and will take subject to Stranger's right. *See* H.D. Warren, Annotation, *Record of Instrument Without Sufficient Acknowledgment as Notice*, 59 A.L.R.2d 1299, 1318 (1958).

9.07(a)   Prerequisites to Valid Recording—Instruments Entitled to Be Recorded

Deeds, mortgages, release deeds, satisfactions of mortgages, assignments of mortgages, and other instruments affecting the title to land should be recorded. Only the original instrument is entitled to be recorded. The recording of an unsigned copy of an instrument is without legal effect. *Herzer v. Dembosz,* 167 N.E.2d 210 (Ill. 1960).

9.07(b)   Prerequisites to Valid Recording—Defective Instruments

In a great majority of the states, an instrument must be properly acknowledged by the grantor or mortgagor in order to be entitled to recording. In a number of states, proper witnessing is accepted as a substitute for an acknowledgment. But if the instrument is neither witnessed nor acknowledged, or the witnessing or acknowledgment is fatally defective, the instrument is not considered as a recorded instrument, even though the recorder accepts it and copies it on the public records. H.D. Warren, Annotation, *Record of Instrument Without Sufficient Acknowledgment as Notice*, 59 A.L.R.2d 1299, 1318 (1958).

9.07(b)(1)
Prerequisites to Valid
Recording—Defective
Instruments—Legal
Descriptions

Since a purchaser or mortgagee is under no obligation to examine the records affecting land other than that which the purchaser is buying or upon which the mortgagee is loaning money, the record of an instrument that was intended to convey or affect the property, but which has such an erroneous description that it does not appear to affect the land in question, does not bind any subsequent purchaser, mortgagee, or judgment creditor.

> **EXAMPLE:** Owner owns the West Half of the Northwest Quarter of Section 14, Township 38 North, Range 13 East, of the Third Principal Meridian. Owner executes a mortgage to Lender that is intended as a mortgage on this same land but which inadvertently describes the land as falling in Section 24 instead of Section 14. The mortgage is recorded. A person searching the records as to Owner's title has no way of knowing that this mortgage was intended for the particular land in question. Therefore, this mortgage does not impart constructive notice, and subsequent purchasers, mortgagees, and judgment creditors will be protected against this mortgage. *See Landis v. Miles Homes, Inc.,* 273 N.E.2d 153 (Ill. App. 1971).

9.08 Possession
as Notice

The law requires every prospective purchaser or mortgagee to examine into the possession of the real estate and to ascertain what rights are claimed by the parties in possession. Whether or not the prospective purchaser or lender actually makes this inspection, such purchaser or mortgagee is deemed to know the facts that the investigation would have disclosed. In other words, possession imparts constructive notice in much the same way as the recording of a deed.

> **EXAMPLE:** Owner sells and conveys a home to Buyer 1. Buyer 1 fails to record the deed, but moves into the house. Owner offers to sell the land to Buyer 2. Buyer 2 examines the records in the recorder's office and finds title in Owner, but fails to examine into the possession of the premises. Buyer 2 takes a deed from Owner. This deed passes no title. Buyer 1's possession gave Buyer 2 constructive notice of this deed.

> **EXAMPLE:** Tenant leased the laundry rooms in a building being converted to condominiums under an arrangement that later proved to be economically unattractive to the purchasers of the condominium units. Before the condominium units were sold, Tenant affixed signs and stickers to the walls of the laundry room and to the laundry machines. These signs and stickers identified Tenant as the lessee of the laundry room. The condominium purchasers brought suit to declare the laundry room lease to Tenant as being of no force against them. The court ruled otherwise, stating that the placement of the signs identifying an occupant different from the record owner was sufficient to place a prospective purchaser of the condominium units on inquiry notice. *See Dana Point Condominium Ass'n, Inc. v. Keystone Serv. Co.,* 491 N.E.2d 63 (Ill. App. 1986). *See also Clean Corp. v. Foston,* 634 A.2d 1200 (Conn. App. 1993).

It should, however, be noted that the prospective purchaser's duty of inquiry does not necessarily exist in all situations. For example, there may be no such obligation where the tenant occupied only a part of the property or where the tenant's possession was not sufficiently visible so as to put a prospective buyer on inquiry notice. *Cohen v. Thomas & Son Transfer Line, Inc.,* 586 P.2d 39 (Colo. 1978).

It is obvious that the failure to record or a defective recording of a deed is usually less dangerous than the failure to record or the defective recording of a mortgage. This is understandable, since the purchaser usually goes into possession of the land after receiving the deed. This possession gives all the world notice of the purchaser's rights. On the other hand, a mortgagee rarely goes into possession before a default has occurred and is therefore entirely dependent on the public records to give other persons notice of the mortgagee's rights.

In a few states (e.g., South Carolina and Virginia), possession does not impart constructive notice.

9.09   Chain of Title   Except in a few states, a title searcher tracing title by means of the public records employs an official index of names, called the "Grantor-Grantee Index." Suppose, for example, that the United States sold a particular tract of land to John Jones on March 15, 1840. The title searcher will turn to the Grantor Index, which is arranged alphabetically, and, beginning with the date March 15, 1840, he will look under the letter "J" for any deeds or mortgages made since March 15, 1840, by John Jones. Naturally, the searcher would not expect to find any deeds or mortgages of that land made by Jones prior to March 15, 1840, because Jones did not become the owner until that date. Therefore, the law does not require the purchaser to look for any such deeds or mortgages prior to that date. *Glen Ellyn Sav. & Loan Ass'n v. State Bank of Geneva,* 382 N.E.2d 1267, 1273 (Ill. App. 1978).

Suppose that John Jones conveyed the land to Joseph Smith by deed dated September 10, 1860, and recorded November 1, 1860. The search now turns to any deeds or mortgages made by Smith on or after September 10, 1860, the date when Smith acquired title. This process is repeated until the title has been searched down to the present and is called "running the chain of title."

To be considered properly recorded, a deed or mortgage must be in the *chain of title;* that is, it must be dated in the proper chronological order.

> **EXAMPLE:** At a time when negotiations for the purchase were virtually concluded, Joseph Smith made a mortgage on the land dated September 5, 1980, and recorded September 6, 1980. Both of these dates were prior to the date of the deed by which Smith later acquired ownership, namely, September 10, 1980. A title searcher would not find this mortgage, since the searcher would not look under the name "Smith" for any deed or mortgage prior to September 10, 1980. Such a mortgage is not in the line or chain of title. *The legal result is the same as though the mortgage had not been recorded at all.* A person buying the land not knowing of the existence of this mortgage would get good title free and clear of the mortgage.

In other words, the records show the ownership of land passing from one person to another. The name of each successive owner as that name appears on the public records must be searched only during the period of ownership, as such period is revealed by the public records, to see what recorded deeds and mortgages the owner has executed.

Because of the *chain-of-title theory,* it is important that names be spelled correctly in deeds and mortgages.

> **EXAMPLE:** A deed runs to John O. Malley. A mortgage is thereafter made by John O'Malley. The mortgage is not in the chain of title and is treated as an unrecorded mortgage. The deed is indexed under M, the mortgage under O.

The chain-of-title theory is a two-edged sword. One, constructive notice is given of those instruments that are in the chain of title. Two, instruments outside of the chain of title do not impart constructive notice. *Pease v. Frank,* 105 N.E. 299, 301 (Ill. 1914).

9.10   Tract Indexes   In a few states (e.g., Iowa, Louisiana, Nebraska, North Dakota, Oklahoma, South Dakota, Utah, Wisconsin, and Wyoming), the name index (Grantor-Grantee Index) has been supplemented by a Tract Index. This index allocates a separate page to each piece of property in the county, and, if you are interested in a particular piece of property, you simply locate the page in the index where you will find listed all recorded deeds and other documents relating to this piece of property.

9.11   Record as Notice of Contents of Deed or Mortgage

An instrument duly recorded is notice to subsequent purchasers and mortgagees not only of the instrument itself, but also of all of its contents.

> **EXAMPLE:** A warranty deed contained a covenant that the premises were free and clear of all encumbrances "except a certain mortgage for $900." The referenced mortgage had not been recorded. This was notice to the grantee and to all other persons of the existence of the mortgage.

9.12   Foreign Language

A deed or mortgage written in a foreign language, though valid as between the parties, does not impart constructive notice and must be treated as an unrecorded document. *Moroz v. Ransom,* 285 N.Y.S. 846 (N.Y. App. 1936).

9.13   Liens that Need Not be Recorded

There are certain liens, such as real estate tax liens, inheritance tax liens, and franchise tax liens, that are binding on subsequent takers of the property, though not recorded.

9.14   Short Leases

In a number of states, leases that exceed one year in duration (in other states, three years) must be recorded. Possession under a longer lease does not impart constructive notice. In consequence, a purchaser or mortgagee of an apartment building, for example, may assume that occupants are there under short leases where no leases have been recorded. This is a practical approach to the problem of large buildings where checking possession is a burdensome task. In point of fact, purchasers and mortgagees never do check all the tenants in a large building. Instead, they accept a written statement by the building manager describing the leases and the terms of the leases.

CHAPTER 10
Real Estate Brokers

10.01 Defined A real estate broker is an agent employed by the buyer or seller in negotiating the sale, purchase, lease, or exchange of real estate. The broker's compensation is usually paid in the form of a commission, or a percentage of the selling price or rentals to be paid in the case of a lease.

10.02 Brokers' Functions in Today's Market The old idea that the broker's task is simply one of finding another party to the transaction has totally disappeared. Today's brokers are highly skilled professionals with a great breadth of knowledge in real estate law, finance, real estate economics, and market conditions. Among the matters they must be familiar with are as follows:

1. Zoning, including the ability to determine whether a basement apartment in a home is illegal; whether occupancy by unmarried persons who are not related may be unlawful; whether an area that has numerous apartments scattered among single-family homes may be unable to keep out additional apartments; or what kind of development local laws will allow at the subject site.

2. Building codes, especially those that require replacement of plumbing and old electrical wiring where extensive rehabbing is contemplated.

3. Private building restriction problems—for example, those that prohibit building near lot lines and would thus bar an addition to an existing structure.

4. Methods of financing where financing by an institution is unavailable: for example, purchase money mortgage; installment contract; wraparound mortgage; second mortgage; assumable mortgage; and all the mechanical difficulties, advantages, and disadvantages of each financing method, including income tax advantages; the ability to retain old low-interest mortgages; the availability of high returns on wraparound mortgages; the uses of balloon notes and acceleration clauses; the use of prepayment privileges; and other matters that can be very important in structuring a sale or lease transaction.

5. Benefits and drawbacks of the manner in which title is to be taken, including in a corporation, limited liability company, partnership and the like; in the case of commercial property, and in trust, joint tenancy, or tenancy by the entireties; and in the case of property acquired by an individual. While these issues involve careful consideration in light of the acquiring entity's organizational structure, tax situation, and estate plan—matters that are beyond the responsibility of most real estate brokers—the broker needs an understanding of these concepts so as to better understand and implement the client's desires. Proper structuring of the deal from this perspective at the time the contract is being prepared will go a long way in preventing problems later.

6. The pitfalls involved where unmarried persons plan to buy property together, whether as a residence or for an investment.

7. The impact of the failure of the property to comply with local zoning, building, and other laws and ordinances, and the compliance of the purchaser's expected use with such laws and

ordinances. Whether the property is to be used for commercial, industrial, or residential purposes, the purchaser should not be surprised after the acquisition by the local zoning inspector preventing the intended use, or frustrating the buyer by preventing the buyer from
earning the income it expects from the property.

8. The pitfalls and benefits in buying a landmark.

9. Where informal party driveways exist, buyers must be advised to obtain counsel for the
preparation of formal agreements.

10. In a condominium or other common-interest community, the broker must know about restrictions on pets, renting, leases, etc. The broker must also be able to explain about assessments and special assessments and the role of the Homeowners' Association. It is especially
important that the broker make the buyer aware of the possibility of special assessments and
the need to inquire whether any such assessments are in the offing.

This list is suggestive only and is not intended to indicate that the broker should usurp
the role of the other advisors to the broker's clients, such as the client's lawyer and accountant. The broker can and should play an invaluable role as a "business" counselor to the
principal. The greatest benefit that the broker provides to the parties is the intimate knowledge of the market and skill in making the deal. Whether the transaction be residential or
commercial, no matter how sophisticated the parties may be in their own business, it is unlikely that they have the local real estate acumen and market knowledge that the broker has.
Most buyers and sellers simply do not participate in property sales and leasing transactions
on a daily basis, as does the broker. Brokers know how to make the deal and bring the parties together, if a deal is to be made.

10.03 Salesmen Virtually every real estate brokerage office maintains a staff of salespeople who do the actual legwork of showing properties, structuring deals, negotiating their terms, and putting
together the term sheets, letters of intent, or sales contracts. Salespeople are required to
have a state license, which is obtained after certain educational and examination requirements are met. The requirements for a salesperson's license are less comprehensive than the
requirements for a real estate broker's license.

Today, the broker makes a determined effort to establish the relation with the salesperson as that of *independent contractor.* There is a distinction between an *employee,* who
must take orders from an employer, and an independent contractor, who is hired to do a job,
but is not subject to the day-to-day control of the manager. The objective is to avoid the employer-employee relationship, so that the broker need not pay employee benefits, and so
forth. Problems may arise. A salesperson may often go to the "boss" on complex deals. If
the broker controls the manner in which the salesperson works, the broker may become an
employer. Many real estate offices prefer the employer-employee relationship. It gives the
broker more control. Many salespeople object to this approach. They want to be on their
own.

Whatever the legal relationship is, courts are bound to hold the broker liable for fraudulent representations made by salespeople. The broker may also be responsible for failing
to properly supervise the salespeople working from the brokerage office. *Nevada v. Soeller,*
656 P.2d 224 (Nev. 1982).

10.04 License In many states, an unlicensed person is not authorized to act as a real estate broker or salesperson. Real estate brokerage is a profession requiring knowledge, experience, and honesty.
In order to obtain a license, a candidate must have the qualifications that are specified by
local law. For a real estate broker to recover commissions, the broker must have a license

when hired to perform the services for which a commission is claimed. *Schoene v. Hickam,* 397 S.W.2d 596 (Mo. 1965).

Where a "business broker" who does not have a real estate license is retained to sell a business that includes real estate, the court decisions seem to be to the effect that the fact that the broker is not a licensed real estate broker will not deprive the broker of its right to the commission. *Winthrop & Co., Inc. v. Milgrom,* 668 A.2d 557 (Pa. Super. 1995); *Bottomley v. Coffin,* 399 A.2d 485 (R.I. 1979); *Business Brokerage Ctr. v. Dixon,* 874 S.W.2d 1 (Tenn. 1994). Of course, the business brokerage concept cannot be a sham. The broker must indeed be retained to sell the business and not the real estate.

Today, state regulators belong to the National Association of Real Estate License Officials. The brokers' examination is standardized to some extent, and educational and ethical standards climb steadily. Many states require brokers to take continuing education courses. Other states are certain to follow. State regulators have shown a strong tendency to hold brokers to high standards of conduct. State laws list many causes for revoking a broker's license. Racial discrimination, whether in the form of steering, blockbusting, or other conduct, is one of them.

> **EXAMPLE:** A broker advertised to buy real estate. The ad did not disclose that the prospective purchaser was a broker. The broker's license was lost. *Land v. Georgia Comm.,* 142 Ga. App. 860, 237 S.E.2d 243 (1977).

> **EXAMPLE:** A broker's license may be lost if the broker acts dishonestly in transactions for the broker's own account. For example, in a deal where the broker was the seller, the broker made a fraudulent misrepresentation. The broker was selling his own property and not acting for another party. The broker lost his license. Jay M. Zitler, Annotation, *Revocation or Suspension of Real Estate Broker's License for Conduct Not Connected with Business as Broker,* 22 A.L.R.4th 136 (1983).

The system of licensing real estate brokers has generally paralleled the growth of professionalism in the real estate business. The standards of competence and professionalism have and will continue to escalate as the financial service industry goes through a period of rapid and systemic change.

10.05 Broker Regulation

In addition to dealing with the several matters discussed elsewhere in this chapter, state licensing laws prohibit brokers and their associates and salespeople from the following:

- Failing to account for or remit any funds or documents of others;
- Commingling the money or property of others with their own, and failing to deposit funds belonging to others into a special account that is maintained separate and apart from their normal business account;
- Displaying a "for rent" or "for sale" sign on any property, or advertising that property for sale or rent without the written consent of the owner;
- Inducing any party to an existing contract of sale to break that contract so that a new contract can be negotiated with a third party;
- Negotiating with a property owner for the sale or lease of the owner's property, if the broker knows that the owner has an exclusive listing agreement with another broker; and
- Continuing to solicit a listing from a property owner who has given notice that the owner has no interest in selling the property. *Curtis v. Thompson,* 840 F.2d 1291 (7th Cir. 1988).

Both state and federal law also preclude a broker from discriminating on the basis of race, color, religion, sex, national origin, or handicap in the manner in which property is offered for sale or lease.

10.06   Code of Ethics   Many controversies involving brokers, especially those involving conflicts between two brokers, are settled by reference to the code of ethics established by the National Association of Realtors or by the local real estate board. Penalties vary with the nature of the offense—the most severe being expulsion from the board and loss or suspension of the broker's or salesperson's license. Mere suspension from the board prohibits the broker's access to the multiple listing service maintained by the board and is an effective punishment indeed.

10.07   Employment–
Necessity of Contract
of Employment

A real estate broker acts as an *agent*. The person who hires the broker is known as the *principal*. Usually the broker is hired by the landowner for the purpose of procuring a buyer. In return for finding a buyer willing to buy on the landowner's terms, the broker is to receive a commission from the landowner. Occasionally, the broker is hired by a person wishing to buy real estate. In either case, in order to recover a commission, the broker must demonstrate a contractual relationship with the person from whom a commission is claimed. While it is not the ideal situation, a broker's agency agreement may be *implied* from the conduct of the parties.

> **EXAMPLE:** Landowner gave Broker a description of the property and requested that Broker sell it at a designated price. This is a contract of employment, and Broker is entitled to a commission if Broker finds a buyer. The fact that compensation was not discussed is immaterial. Landowner must have understood that Broker would expect to be paid if a buyer was produced. *Long v. Herr,* 10 Colo. 380, 15 P. 802 (1887).

> **EXAMPLE:** Broker, without any prior request from Landowner, submitted an offer of $3,000 for the purchase of the land. Landowner declined, stating that the price for the land was $4,000. Broker thereupon procured a buyer who was willing to buy for $4,000. Landowner refused to sell. Landowner is not liable for a commission. The mere statement by a landowner that the landowner will take a certain sum for the land is not sufficient to authorize the person to whom the statement is made to act as agent for its sale. Landowner is entitled to assume that Broker is acting for the buyer and will look to the buyer for his compensation. *O'Donnell v. Carr,* 189 N.C. 77, 126 S.E. 112 (1925).

A broker's commission is usually paid by the seller in the case of a sale transaction and by the landlord in the case of a leasing transaction. This is due to the obvious fact that it is financially easier to collect money from the seller, who is being paid the purchase price of the property, or the landlord who will be collecting the rent. It is not necessarily the case that, as between the buyer and the seller, the seller will be obligated to pay the brokerage commissions. The parties can agree that the buyer is to pay the broker. If this is the case, the broker should have a clear and separate agreement with the buyer.

Legally, the fact remains that the broker cannot collect from the seller unless the broker can show that the broker was hired by the seller. A formal listing agreement is the best evidence of the agreement of the parties. Indeed, in commercial transactions, these agreements can be quite complex and the subject of vigorous negotiations. If there is no formal listing contract, at the very least, the seller or landlord must say or do things that make the broker believe it has been hired by the seller or landlord. *Reeve v. Shoemaker,* 200 Iowa 938, 205 N.W. 742 (1925). Or, the broker must so conduct itself that it is clear to the seller or landlord that the broker expects to be paid a commission. *Korzendorfer Realty, Inc. v. Hawkes,* 178 S.E.2d 524 (Va. 1971).

> **EXAMPLE:** Suppose in the example last given, the broker had asked, "When will my commission be paid?" Suppose the owner had replied, "At closing." This is enough to show a contract of employment.

Ordinarily, a broker hired by the seller has no claim against the buyer.

> **EXAMPLE:** Seller hired Broker, who found Purchaser. Seller and Purchaser entered into a contract of sale. However, difficulties arose and Purchaser refused to perform. Broker cannot collect anything from Purchaser. Broker's contract of employment is with Seller only. P.G. Guthrie, Annotation, *Liability of Defaulting Purchaser for Owner's Broker or Auctioneer*, 30 A.L.R.3d 1395, 1399 (1970).

10.07(a)
Employment—
Persons Who May
Employ a Broker

A person other than the property owner may list the property for sale or lease and become liable for a commission. 12 Am. Jur. 2d *Brokers* § 163 (1997).

> **EXAMPLE:** Wife owned certain real estate. Husband listed the property for sale with Broker, who knew that Wife owned the property. Broker found a buyer for the property, but Wife refused to sell. Husband was liable to Broker for a full commission. Broker was entitled to assume that, at the proper time, Husband would procure Wife's consent to the sale. *Aler v. Plowman,* 190 Md. 631, 59 A.2d 196 (1948); *Pose v. Knobelock,* 194 S.W.2d 943 (Mo. App. 1946).

> **EXAMPLE:** The land was held in community property, but the husband alone signed the listing. He is liable for the full commission. *C. Forsman Real Estate Co. v. Hatch,* 547 P.2d 1116 (Idaho 1976).

> **EXAMPLE:** Property was owned by Husband and Wife, in joint tenancy. Husband alone, without Wife's permission, listed the property for sale with Broker, who found a buyer for the property, but Wife refused to sign the contract of sale and the deal fell through. Husband was held liable to Broker for a full commission. Charles C. Marvel, L.L.B., Annotation, *Recovery of Damages for Breach of Contract to Convey Homestead Where Only One Spouse Signed Contract*, 5 A.L.R.4th 1310 (1981).

10.07(b)
Employment—
Necessity for Written
Contract

Because of the endless litigation that has arisen concerning the existence of an employment contract, in many states, the contract of employment must be in writing in order for the broker to be entitled to a commission. The agreement must state the amount of commission to be paid. B. Olin, Annotation, *Statutory Necessity and Sufficiency of Written Statement as to Amount of Compensation in Broker's Contract to Procure Purchase, Sale, or Exchange of Real Estate*, 9 A.L.R.2d 747 (1950).

10.07(c)
Employment—Form
of Contract

Often, the hiring of a broker is an informal, oral affair. However, written contracts, called *listing contracts,* are also used. The essential elements of such an agreement are as follows: (1) names of seller and broker; (2) description of property, usually by street address, W.R. Habeeb, Annotation, *Sufficiency, Under Statute of Frauds, of Description or Designation of Property in Real Estate Brokerage Contract*, 30 A.L.R.3d 935 (1970); (3) terms of sale, including sale price, whether sale is for cash or on terms, and so forth; (4) duration of broker's employment; (5) amount of commission to be paid or the basis upon which the commission is to be calculated; and (6) special agreements, such as the provision for an exclusive agency. Each of the countless local real estate boards is likely to have its own listing form.

10.07(d)
Employment—
Unconscionability

The law requires that the broker use a listing form that is fair to the employer. John A. Moffet, Jr., Note, *Let the Seller Beware—Unconscionability and the Real Estate Broker's Employment Contract,* 5 Memphis St. U.L. Rev. 59 (1974).

10.07(e)   Contract
Provisions

Quite commonly, a *contract of sale* will contain a provision that a commission will be paid by the seller to the broker at closing. Even if there is no proof of a *contract of employment,* this provision in the contract of sale or lease suffices to make the seller or landlord liable to the broker. *Moran v. Audette,* 217 A.2d 653 (D.C. 1966); *Woodworth v. Vranizan,* 539 P.2d 1055 (Or. 1975). The broker is what the lawyers call a "third-party beneficiary." Of course, the broker's rights rest on the terms of the contract.

> **EXAMPLE:** The contract of sale provided that the seller would pay the broker a commission at closing. This contract, however, was contingent on the buyer's ability to obtain financing. The buyer was unable to obtain financing. The broker collects no commission. *Shumaker v. Lear,* 235 Pa. Super. 509, 345 A.2d 249 (1975).

10.08 Open Listing

There are several different types of listing contracts. The *open listing* contains no provision forbidding the landowner from selling the land or hiring other brokers. Ordinarily, an owner may hire two or more brokers, unless the owner has specifically agreed not to do so. *Kelly v. Beaudoin,* 298 A.2d 831 (Vt. 1972). Virtually all informal verbal listing arrangements are open listings. The disadvantage of this type of contract is that it is likely to produce quarrels over the commission where several brokers produce buyers.

> **EXAMPLE:** Landowner employed Broker to obtain a purchaser. Broker obtained a purchaser on the specified terms, but Landowner refused to pay a commission on the ground that Landowner had already concluded an agreement to sell to a purchaser obtained by another broker. Broker cannot recover a commission from Landowner.

The primary object to be attained in the employment of agents to sell or lease real estate is the production of a single purchaser or tenant for such real estate. That object is attained where one of several agents produces a purchaser who is ready, able, and willing to buy or lease the real estate on the owner's terms. Where several agents are employed, the sale of the property, either by the owner in person or by any of the brokers, operates at once to terminate the authority of all the brokers, although they had no actual notice of the sale. Courts "read" this provision into every open listing agreement unless the agreement is to the contrary.

In every open listing there is an unspoken, implied precondition that, to receive compensation, the broker must find a willing buyer or tenant before such a buyer or tenant is procured by the owner or some other broker.

When different brokers have the property for sale or lease, and no one of them has the exclusive right to make the sale or lease, the broker who first finds a buyer or tenant ready, able, and willing to buy is the procuring cause of the sale or lease and is the one entitled to the commission. Nonetheless, sellers are well advised to make the payment of commission conditioned upon the closing of the sale to the buyer. In the case of a leasing transaction, the owner will typically condition the payment of the commission upon some event that indicates that the owner will get the economic benefit of the transaction, such as the tenant's taking occupancy of the premises and the commencement of rent payments.

Open listings are used quite often in sales of commercial property or apartments.

10.09 Exclusive Agency

Unless there is an agreement to the contrary, the landowner may hire two or more brokers to sell the same property and will be liable only to the broker who first finds a buyer. Fear that time and money spent in locating a buyer may be wasted if another broker is working on the deal has led brokers to favor a listing contract that assures the broker that as long as the employment continues, no other broker will be hired. Such a listing is called an *exclusive agency.* If the owner hires a second broker who finds a buyer for the property, the owner will have to pay both brokers. *Dean Vincent, Inc., v. Chef Joe's, Inc.,* 541 P.2d 469 (Or. 1975). However, in some states, the second broker must not accept employment if he or she knows a prior exclusive arrangement exists. Dale R. Agthe, Annotation, *Validity and Application of Regulation Prohibiting Licensed Real Estate Broker from Negotiating Sale or Lease with Owner Known to Have Exclusive Listing Agreement with Another Broker*, 17 A.L.R.4th 763 (1982).

The giving of an exclusive agency does not bar the landowner from selling the property, even while the listing agreement is outstanding, without the assistance of other brokers. If the property owner sells the property without the assistance of the broker, the exclusive agency automatically comes to an end without any liability on the landowner's part for a commission, regardless of the employment period specified in the listing contract. *Martin Realty Co. v. Fletcher,* 103 N.J.L. 294, 136 A. 498 (1927); *Des Rivieres v. Sullivan,* 247 Mass. 443, 142 N.E. 111 (1924); C.C. Marvel, Annotation, *"Exclusive Right to Sell" and Other Terms in Real Estate Broker's Contract as Excluding Owner's Right of Sale,* 88 A.L.R.2d 936 (1963). This is a provision the court "reads into" the listing. 88 A.L.R.2d 936 *supra.* In every exclusive agency there is an unspoken, implied precondition that the broker must find a willing buyer before such a buyer is procured by the owner.

The mere fact that the listing contract refers to the broker as an exclusive agent is enough to create an exclusive agency. *Harris & White v. Stone,* 137 Ark. 23, 207 SW 443 (1918).

10.10 Exclusive Right to Sell

The *exclusive right to sell* goes one step further than the exclusive agency. It not only makes the broker the sole agent of the landowner for the sale of the property, it also provides that the named broker will receive a commission in the event the property is sold by the named broker, by the owner, *or by anyone else.* The key difference between the exclusive agency and the exclusive right to sell is found in the result that, even if the owner sells the property during the listing period, the broker must be paid a commission. *Bourgoin v. Fortier,* 310 A.2d 618 (Me. 1973); *Flynn v. La Salle Nat'l. Bank,* 9 Ill.2d 129, 137 N.E.2d 71 (1956).

A broker who desires an exclusive right to sell should draft the listing contract with great care.

> **EXAMPLE:** A form simply gave the broker "the exclusive right to sell" the property. The court felt that this did not sufficiently warn the seller that he could not sell the home through his own efforts. 88 A.L.R.2d 948, *supra.*

In time, brokers developed forms that state explicitly that the broker will get a commission if, during the listing period, the property is sold by the named broker, any other broker, or the owner. This has become the common form used almost everywhere. It is the "exclusive right to sell."

Of course, every form can be changed by the parties.

> **EXAMPLE:** *A* has been negotiating with *B* for the purchase by *B* of *A*'s home. At times, agreement was almost reached. *A* decided to wait no longer and listed the property with *X,* a broker. *A* insisted on typing into the listing a clause stating that no commission will be paid if the property is sold to *B.* This protects *A* because of the time and effort already devoted to trying to sell the property to *B.*

10.11 Multiple Listing

Multiple listing is simply a means by which brokers in a given area pool their efforts to sell properties listed with any other member of the pool. The original, or *listing broker,* obtains from the property owner an exclusive right to sell. The listing broker then furnishes a copy of the listing to all members of the pool. Today, this is done through local and even national computer networks so the information on new listings is quickly given to the members of the multiple listing pool or board and even to Realtors in other states so they can serve their relocating customers. If any member other than the original broker sells the property, the commission is divided between the original or listing broker and the *selling broker* who effects the sale. In some systems, the central registration office also shares in the commission.

Only the original broker may sue the property owner for a commission. The property owner has no contract of employment with the other members of the pool. *Goodwin v. Glick,* 139 Cal. App. 2d 936, 294 P.2d 192 (1956). The members of the pool working on the sale owe the landowner the usual duties of a broker, such as loyalty. *Frisell v. Newman,* 71 Wash. 2d 520, 429 P.2d 864 (Wash. 1967).

In some listing agreements, a paragraph is included stating that the listing will be furnished to members of the multiple listing service (MLS). Arguably, the selling broker is hired, through the MLS, by the listing broker. This makes the selling broker a "subagent." *Frisell v. Newman,* 71 Wash. 2d 520, 429 P.2d 864 (1967). This may become important if the selling broker makes a misrepresentation and the buyer sues the seller. *See also* 1 H. Miller & M. Starr, *Current Law of California Real Estate,* 4.8 at 18–19 (1975); Case Note, *Real Estate Broker's Duties to Prospective Purchasers,* 1976 B.Y.U.L. Rev. 513 (1976); Paul A. Longton, Comment, *A Reexamination of the Real Estate Broker-Buyer-Seller Relationship,* 18 Wayne L. Rev. 1343, 1353 (1972); L.S. Tellier, Annotation, *Real Estate Broker's Power to Bind Principal by Representations as to Character, Condition, Location, Quantity, or Title of Property,* 58 A.L.R.2d 10, 41 (1958).

10.11(a)   Antitrust   Since multiple listing systems may either set a commission rate or specify a recommended rate, their practices have come under fire as violations of the antitrust laws. Court decrees have been entered prohibiting the fixing of commission rates. The U.S. Supreme Court has held that federal antitrust laws are applicable to brokers' groups that bring about a fixed rate of commission in a given area. *McLain v. Real Estate Board,* 444 U.S. 232, 100 S. Ct. 502 (1980). The states also have laws that forbid price fixing or restraint of trade. Examples of such legal requirements are found in cases that have held that a real estate board that has operated a multiple listing system, limiting the persons who could be admitted to membership, has violated the antitrust laws, *Grillo v. Board of Realtors,* 219 A.2d 635 (N.J. Super. 1966), and that the exclusion of licensed brokers from an MLS is illegal. *Marin County Board of Realtors v. Palsson,* 16 Cal. 3d 920, 549 P.2d 833, 130 Cal. Rptr. 1 (1976). As a result, the combined pressure of federal and state laws has caused brokers' groups to liberalize their membership rules and pricing structures. Vitauts M. Gulbis, Annotation, *Application of State Antitrust Laws to Activities or Practices of Real-Estate Agents or Associations* 22 A.L.R.4th 103 (1983).

10.12   Performance Required of Broker   Suppose that *A* contracts with *B* to perform some act for *A,* such as building a house. *A* will pay *B* a stated sum for such performance of the contract. *B* has earned the contract price when *B* has performed the contract. The same is true of a broker; the commission has been earned when the obligations imposed upon the broker under the listing agreement have been fulfilled. Generally, a broker has earned the commission when a ready and able buyer is produced who is willing to buy on either the terms specified in the listing contract or on other terms acceptable to the *seller. Bonanza Real Estate, Inc. v. Crouch,* 517 P.2d 1371 (Wash. App. 1974).

> **EXAMPLE:** Landowner hires Broker to find a buyer. Broker finds Prospect who signs a contract at less than the price asked by the Landowner. Landowner and Prospect negotiate until they agree on a price. Broker has earned the commission even though the property will be sold for less than specified in the original listing agreement.

At times, the broker may submit a contract signed by the buyer for the full contract price requested by the seller. Such a contract is a mere *offer to buy*. Until the seller signs and executes the contract, the seller is not bound to the potential buyer to sell the property. The broker, on the other hand, has performed and therefore has earned a commission even if the seller does not execute the contract.

Likewise, if the seller and buyer reconsider after a contract of sale has been executed, thereby canceling or terminating the deal, the seller remains liable to the broker for the commission. W.R. Habeeb, Annotation, *Real Estate Broker's Right to Commission as Affected by Failure or Refusal of Customer (Prospect) to Comply with Valid Contract*, 74 A.L.R.2d 437, 459 (1960). Also, if the buyer has signed a contract that the seller has also signed and thereafter refuses to complete the deal, the broker has nevertheless earned the commission. 74 A.L.R.2d 437, 443, *supra*.

The word *able* in the phrase "ready, willing and able to buy" refers to financial ability. The buyer must be able to command the necessary funds to close the deal within the time required. *Pellaton v. Brunski*, 69 Cal. App. 301, 231 P. 583 (1924). The buyer must have the money necessary to meet any cash payment required, be able to obtain a loan for the balance of the purchase price, and be financially able to meet any further payments. *Reynor v. Mackrill*, 196 Iowa 1298, 164 N.W. 335 (1917). Otherwise stated, the buyer must have the present ability to pay. *Boutelle v. Chrislaw*, 35 Wis. 2d 665, 150 N.W.2d 486 (1967). Thus, a newly organized corporation having limited funds might be considered not *able* to buy. However, it is not necessary to show that the buyer is standing outside the office door with all cash in hand. It is sufficient if the buyer is *able* to command the necessary funds. *Perper v. Edell*, 160 Fla. 447, 35 So. 2d 387 (1948). Thus, a buyer is *able* to buy if it has arranged to borrow the funds necessary to pay for the property. *Schaaf v. Iba*, 73 Ohio L. Abs. 46, 136 N.E.2d 727 (1955).

To *produce* a willing buyer requires that the broker must reveal the buyer's identity to the seller. C.C. Basham, Annotation, *Duty of Real Estate Broker to Disclose Identity of Purchaser or Lessee*, 2 A.L.R.3d 1119, 1128 (1965). A *willing* buyer is one who is willing to enter into the contract that is acceptable to the seller. If the contract is *conditional,* the buyer becomes a willing buyer only when the condition is satisfied.

This point is of great importance because most contracts contain some conditions, whether they relate to the buyer's ability to obtain financing, the ability to sell an existing property, the ability to obtain subdivision, zoning, or other approvals, or other matters. It is normal and expected that the broker will tender a contract signed by the buyer that differs from the contract called for by the listing contract. Once this takes place, the broker's rights rest on the terms of the tendered contract, if that contract was accepted by the seller. If the condition inserted by the buyer is his or her ability to obtain financing, the broker's right to a commission depends on the buyer's ability to obtain financing.

> **EXAMPLE:** Owner hires Broker to sell property for $100,000. Broker finds Purchaser, who is willing to pay the price, but needs a loan of $80,000. Owner and Purchaser sign a contract contingent on Purchaser's ability to get the loan of $80,000. Owner was not obliged to accept this condition. Legally, Purchaser was not a buyer ready, able, and willing to buy under the terms of the listing agreement. Hence, Broker has not yet earned the commission. If Purchaser fails to get the loan, Broker earns no commission. *Woodland Realty, Inc. v. Winzenried,* 82 Wis. 2d 218, 262 N.W.2d 106 (1978); *Cooper v. Liberty Nat'l Bank,* 75 N.E.2d 769 (Ill. 1947); *Slonim Ltd. v. Bankers Mortgage & Realty Co.,* 42 A.2d 396 (N.J. 1945).

Since every contract by implication requires a good faith effort on each party to perform, the buyer must make a good faith effort to obtain financing. If the buyer fails to do so, this condition drops out of the contract, and the buyer is unconditionally liable to the seller. Hence, the broker has earned his commission.

Buyer, to protect himself, should apply to at least two lenders. If each gives Buyer a letter refusing to grant a loan, that is evidence that buyer has made a good faith effort to obtain a loan and failed.

There are numerous other examples that illuminate the matter of the performance required of the broker.

> **EXAMPLE:** No commission is payable if the buyer is willing to sign only an installment contract. J.E. Keefe, Annotation, *What Deviation in Prospective Vendee's Proposal from Vendor's Terms Precludes Broker from Recovering Commission for Producing Ready, Willing, and Able Vendee*, 18 A.L.R.2d 376, 382 (1951). But, if the *seller* also is willing to sign the installment contract with the buyer, the broker earns the commission when the first installment is paid, unless the listing agreement provides otherwise. 18 A.L.R.2d 376, 382, *supra*.

> **EXAMPLE:** Where the contract of sale is contingent on the buyer's ability to procure an existing lender's consent to an assumption of a mortgage, the broker earns no commission until the required consent has been obtained. *Kopf v. Milam,* 60 Cal. 2d 600, 387 P.2d 390 (1963).

> **EXAMPLE:** Listing calls for sale on "cash or contract." Broker's buyer signs an installment contract, but terms are unacceptable to seller. No commission is due to the broker. *White v. Turner,* 164 Kan. 659, 192 P.2d 200 (1948).

> **EXAMPLE:** When the broker tenders a buyer who insists on a condition that the buyer's obligation to perform is contingent on some official action, the broker has not earned the commission unless and until that action has taken place. Illustrations include the requirement of city approval of buyer's plat, *Larkins v. Richardson,* 502 P.2d 1156 (Or. 1972), obtaining a license to operate the facility in the case of a contract of sale of a hospital or convalescent home, *Urbanski v. Halperin,* 30 Conn. Super. 575, 307 A.2d 180 (1973), or obtaining a state liquor license, in the case of a contract to purchase a restaurant or tavern, *Blaine v. Stinger,* 79 Ariz. 376, 290 P.2d 732 (1955).

The broker is entitled to no compensation or reimbursement whatever for unsuccessful efforts to sell unless the listing contract expressly so provides.

Often, after a seller has listed property with a broker, and after the broker has found a buyer who is ready, able, and willing to buy at the listed price, the seller changes his or her mind and looks for some way to turn down the buyer without being liable to the broker for a commission. Such a seller often seeks to take refuge behind the rule that if the terms offered by the prospective buyer differ from the terms specified in the listing agreement, the broker is not entitled to a commission. 18 A.L.R.2d 376, *supra*. If the listing agreement is silent on other terms of the transaction, the law will read various implications into the agreement. If the terms of the proposed contract of sale do not harmonize with the terms of sale set forth or *implied* in the listing contract, the seller may reject the prospective buyer without incurring any liability for a commission.

> **EXAMPLE:** If the listing agreement is silent, the seller is required to convey only the land, building, and articles that are technically fixtures. If the contract of sale tendered by the broker requires the seller to convey furniture and other personal property, the seller may reject the contract without any liability for commission. *Sharkey v. Snow,* 13 Ill. App. 3d 448, 300 N.E.2d 279 (Ill. 1973).

Customary contract provisions, like those requiring a seller to have good title, cannot be used by the seller as an excuse to reject the buyer. *Adelman v. Caputi,* 181 S.E.2d 608 (Va. 1971).

When the broker procures a purchaser ready, willing, and able to purchase on the authorized terms and, through the fault of the owner, the sale is not consummated, the broker is entitled to a commission. A commission must be paid to the broker when

1. The deal falls through because the owner decides not to sell and refuses to execute the deed or contract. The rule is the same where the land has increased in value, and the owner rejects the broker's buyer for this reason. If the seller refuses to execute the sales contract, giving as the only reason the fact that it has decided not to sell, the seller cannot thereafter shift positions and claim that the buyer's offer was not in compliance with the listing. *Russell v. Ramm,* 200 Cal. 348, 254 P. 532 (1927).

2. The deal falls through because the owner's spouse refuses to execute the contract or deed. J. Evans, Annotation, *Real Estate Broker's Right to Compensation as Affected by Failure or Refusal of Principal's Spouse to Join in Contract of Sale,* 10 A.L.R.3d 665 (1966). This assumes that state law requires the spouse's joinder in the contract.

3. The deal falls through because of defects in the owner's title. *Triplett v. Feasel,* 105 Kan. 179, 182 P. 551 (1919); Diane M. Allen, Annotation, *Real Estate Broker's Right to Recover Commission from Seller Where Sale Fails Because of Seller's Failure to Deliver Good Title—Modern Cases,* 28 A.L.R.4th 1007 (1984).

4. The deal falls through because of the owner's fraud. *Hathaway v. Smith,* 187 Ill. App. 128 (1914).

5. The deal falls through because the owner is unable to deliver possession within a reasonable time.

6. The deal falls through because the seller insists on terms and provisions not mentioned in the listing contract, such as the right to remain in possession after the deal has closed. *Brown v. Ogle,* 75 Ind. App. 90, 130 N.E. 147 (1927).

7. After the contract of sale has been signed, the seller and buyer get together and cancel the contract. *Steward v. Brock,* 60 N.M. 216, 290 P.2d 682 (1955).

8. Both parties sign a contract of sale, but the buyer later defaults. 74 A.L.R.2d 454, *supra.*

   EXAMPLE: Seller and Buyer sign an installment contract and Buyer later defaults. *Engelking v. Boyce,* 278 Or. 237, 563 P.2d 703 (1977). To offset the effect of this rule, Seller may wish to limit his liability to the amount of the residue of the earnest money after payment of Seller's expenses.

10.12(a)   Statutes   A broker must comply with laws governing brokers. If the broker fails to furnish the seller a copy of the listing agreement, as local law may require, the broker cannot recover a commission. *Carnell v. Watson,* 578 P.2d 308 (Mont. 1978).

**10.12(b)
Performance After
Expiration of Listing
Period—Withdrawal
from Sale**

Most listing contracts fix an expiration date. Indeed, some state laws require that such a date be set in the listing agreement. Several rules exist as follows:

1. If the period expires, and the seller thereafter refuses to consider prospects brought in by the broker, the seller is within its rights. Performance must take place within the time specified in the agreement.

2. Some listings specify that the broker has earned the commission if, within the listing period, the broker "introduces" a buyer to the seller and, within _____ days after expiration of the listing, a contract of sale is signed with that buyer. This clause is valid. The broker has performed within the listing period by introducing a prospect to the seller before the listing has expired. L.S. Tellier, Annotation, *Broker's Right to Commission on Sales Consummated After Termination of Employment,* 27 A.L.R.2d 1348, 1408 (1953). The property must, however, be sold to the buyer introduced by the broker within the period set forth in the listing agreement. If the sale occurs after the expiration of that period, the broker does not have a right to a commission, unless the listing agreement specifically provides to the contrary. *Edmonds v. Coldwell Banker Residential Real Estate Services, Inc.,* 377 S.E.2d 443 (Va. 1989).

Sometimes, the listing agreement speaks of a buyer "submitted by the broker" or a buyer with whom the seller has "negotiated" within the listing period. "Negotiation" is more than merely introducing a potential buyer to the property. The broker must participate in deliberation, discussion, and conference on the terms of the proposed contract. *P.J. Berry Co., Inc. v. Denver American Family Lodge West, Inc.,* 663 P.2d 264 (Colo. App. 1983). Again, the broker is entitled to a commission if such negotiations take place. J.R. Kemper, L.L.B., Annotation, *Construction of Provision in Real Estate Broker's Listing Contract that Broker Shall Receive Commission on Sale After Expiration of Listing Period to One with Whom Broker Has Negotiated During Listing Period,* 51 A.L.R.3d 1149 (1973).

The listing agreement may award the broker a commission if the seller withdraws the property from sale before the listing expires. *Blank v. Borden,* 115 Cal. Rptr. 31, 524 P.2d 127 (1974). In these cases, the seller has agreed to a special kind of performance or event under which the broker need not be the procuring cause of sale. Obviously, such provisions are introduced because sellers often engage in sharp practices in order to deprive the broker of a commission.

3. To preserve the broker's rights under a clause such as that described previously, the listing contract may include a provision permitting the broker to "register" with the seller the names of all prospects to whom the broker has shown the property. Many brokers, even in the absence of such a clause, send the seller a letter when they have shown the property to a prospect and request the seller to "protect" the broker if the property is sold to this prospect. The seller is concerned that it not be exposed to frivolous claims by brokers that buyers contacting the seller after the expiration of the listing period were introduced to the property by the broker during the listing period. Sellers may be cautioned to amend the listing agreement to include a provision that the broker's protection only extends to those potential purchasers who were introduced to the property by the broker and whose names are provided to the seller in writing before the end of the listing period. These clauses will be strictly construed by the court. If the broker does not give the owner the prospect's name within the prescribed time, the broker may have no right to a commission. *Century 21 Parker Real Estate, Inc. v. Amos,* 894 P.2d 1131 (Okla. App. 1994).

4. A special problem arises in this context when the listing period expires and the original broker is replaced by a second broker. If the first listing agreement protected the broker for sales made after the expiration period to buyers who were introduced to the property by the first broker, as would normally be the case, what happens when the seller lists the property with the second broker who sells the house to a party introduced to the property by the first broker during the first broker's listing period? Many form residential listing agreements expressly negate the first broker's right to a commission in this case. Obviously, the agreement must be analyzed and a provision added to address the agreement of the parties in this regard. Listing agreements for commercial property are usually specially negotiated and modified. These provisions should get a great deal of attention.

10.12(c) Performance on Price or Terms Differing from Listing Agreement

In the ordinary situation in which the principal promises a broker a commission for finding a purchaser and the asking terms are stated to the broker, the usual interpretation is that the asking terms are intended merely to guide the broker in starting negotiations, and the broker will have a right to the commission if the broker produces a customer ready and willing to purchase at such price or on such modified terms as the principal may accept. *Bonanza Real Estate, Inc. v. Crouch,* 517 P.2d 1371 (Wash. App. 1974).

10.12(d) *Ellsworth Dobbs*

There is some thinking that because the broker is so much better informed than the seller as to the potential buyer's financial ability to consummate the purchase of the property, the seller should not be liable for a commission if the deal falls through because the buyer cannot command the necessary financial resources. This is so especially in the residential or consumer setting as opposed to the commercial setting.

The case of *Ellsworth Dobbs* comes to the rescue of the parties who have neglected to insert in the contract of sale a clause making it contingent on the buyer procuring financing. As stated, if the purchaser insists on such a clause in the purchase contract, the broker has not procured a willing and able buyer unless and until financing is procured. If such a clause is not inserted, technically, the seller has accepted the broker's buyer as a willing and able buyer. *Ellsworth Dobbs* bars the broker from recovering a commission if the deal falls through for lack of financing. *Ellsworth Dobbs, Inc. v. Johnson,* 50 N.J. 528, 236 A.2d 843 (1967).

As between seller and buyer, the mortgage contingency clause is essential. If the contract lacks this clause and the deal falls through because financing cannot be obtained, the buyer will be in default and forfeit the earnest money.

Predictably, this is generally the law because it squares with the normal expectation of the parties. *See generally Tristram's Landing, Inc. v. Wait,* 367 Mass. 622, 327 N.E.2d 727 (Mass. 1975); *Shumaker v. Lear,* 345 A.2d 249 (Pa. 1975); John A. Moffet, Jr., Note, *Let the Seller Beware—Unconscionability and the Real Estate Broker's Employment Contract,* 5 Memphis St. U.L. Rev. 59, 71 (1974). *But see Gordon v. Bauer,* 177 Ill. App. 3d 1073, 532 N.E.2d 855 (Ill. App. 1988).

10.12(e) "No Deal, No Commission" Provision

While ordinarily the broker has earned the commission as soon as a buyer who is ready, able, and willing to buy is produced by the broker, the parties may validly contract by means of the so-called *no deal, no commission clause.* This clause is inserted in the listing agreement and provides that the payment of the commission is contingent upon the closing of the deal and full payment of the purchase price to the seller. Thus, if the seller cannot clear the title, or if the buyer refuses to go through with the deal, the seller need not pay a commission. 74 A.L.R.2d 437, *supra.* However, if the seller's refusal to complete the sale is arbitrary and without reasonable cause or in bad faith, the broker is entitled to the commission. *Huntley v. Smith,* 153 Minn. 297, 190 N.W. 341 (1922); *Goldstein v. Rosenberg,* 331 Ill. App. 374, 73 N.E.2d 171 (1947).

In effect, the *Ellsworth Dobbs* case makes every broker's listing agreement contingent on the buyer's ability to obtain financing and satisfy all of the other conditions of the contract. Also, it is a rule of some real estate boards that no commission be collected unless the deal closes. Indeed, some real estate board listing agreements so provide.

10.13 Procuring Cause of Sale

A broker that has been hired by the landowner has earned the commission when its efforts were the primary and procuring cause of the sale. When the owner or several brokers have been active and a sale is concluded, the broker, to justify a claim to a commission, must show that it was the efficient cause of the sale. The mere introduction of the buyer to the property may not be enough to earn the commission. *Mollyann, Inc. v. Demetriades,* 614 N.Y.S.2d 437 (App. Div. 1994). The following are typical situations in which the problem arises:

1. The broker introduces a prospect to the owner. Thereupon, the owner and the prospect, without the broker's intervention, negotiate and conclude a sale. The broker is the procuring cause of the sale and is entitled to a commission. *Ranney v. Rock,* 135 Conn. 479, 66 A.2d 111 (1949). A sham transaction will be disregarded and the courts will award the broker its due commission when the parties try to disguise what they are really doing. *Farm Credit Bank v. Miller,* 872 S.W.2d 376 (Ark. 1994).

2. When several brokers are involved, the rule appears to be substantially that if the first broker's efforts result in a disagreement, or if negotiations are abandoned, and thereafter a second broker steps in and brings the parties together, the second broker is the procuring cause of the sale. M.C. Dransfield, Annotation, *Broker's Right to Commission Where Owner Sells Property to Broker's Customer at Less than Stipulated Price,* 46 A.L.R.2d 848, 865 (1956). But, if the first broker brings about a substantial agreement, and the second broker merely works out details of the transaction, the first broker is the procuring cause of the sale. In other words, the broker whose efforts predominate in bringing about the sale gets the commission.

There are cases where the broker is entitled to damages or compensation even though it has not been the procuring cause of the sale. For example, in the case of an exclusive agency, the broker will be entitled to compensation from a seller who hires another broker who in turn succeeds in selling the property, because the employer breached the listing agreement with the first broker, which obligated the owner to refrain from hiring other brokers. This exposes the seller to payment of two commissions. J.F. Ghent, Annotation, *Liability of Purchaser of Real Estate for Interference with Contract Between Vendor and Real Estate Broker*, 29 A.L.R.3d 1229 (1970). In the case of an exclusive right to sell, the broker may be entitled to compensation, even if the property is sold by the seller. Here, the seller has breached the contract not to try to sell the building through its own efforts. *Bell v. Dimmerling,* 149 Ohio St. 165, 78 N.E.2d 49 (1948). Or, the listing contract may provide that the broker will be entitled to compensation if the property is sold to a person with whom the broker has negotiated, or whose name has been furnished the seller by the broker. Here, a broker who engages in negotiations with a prospect collects a commission, even though a deal is ultimately clinched by the landowner him- or herself or another broker. *Delbon v. Brazil,* 134 Cal. App. 2d 461, 285 P.2d 710 (1955).

10.13(a)   Effect of Seller's Ignorance That Buyer Was Procured by Broker

When a seller hires a broker to sell the property and thereafter sells the property to a buyer procured by the broker, in most states, the broker is entitled to a commission, despite the fact that the seller is ignorant of the fact that the buyer was procured through the broker. *Ranney v. Rock,* 135 Conn. 479, 66 A.2d 111 (1949); T.C. Williams, Annotation, *Real Estate Broker's Right to Commissions as Affected by Owner's Ignorance of Fact that Purchaser Had Been Contacted by Broker*, 142 A.L.R. 275 (1943). *But see Bear Kaufman Realty, Inc. v. Spec Development*, 645 N.E.2d 244 (Ill. App. 1994) (which was decided on the basis of the "innocent seller" defense). This theory absolves the seller from the payment of a commission when the seller, after due inquiry, reasonably believes that there is no broker involved in the transaction and sells the property at a lower price as a consequence. Having hired a broker, the seller should know that the appearance of a buyer may have been caused by the broker. The seller should check with the broker whenever a prospective buyer comes in. Inquiring of the buyer is rather pointless, for obviously many buyers, hoping to get a reduced price, will conceal the fact that a broker interested them in the property.

Suppose, however, that *A,* a landowner, hires *B,* a broker, and *B* interests *C* in the purchase of the property. *C* procures a dummy or strawman, *D,* to make an offer for the property. *A* inquires of *B* if *B* had interested *D* in the purchase of the property. Not knowing that *D* is only a nominee for *C, B* says no, and *A* cuts his price by the amount of the commission he would have paid to *B. B* gets no commission. *A* has done all he could to protect his broker. *Zetlin v. Scher,* 217 A.2d 266 (Md. 1966).

If the seller reduces the price to a prospect in ignorance of the fact that the prospect was procured by the seller's broker, some states, as stated previously, allow the broker to collect the commission. The seller is at fault because it failed to check with the broker. Other states refuse the broker a commission. 46 A.L.R.2d 872, 877 *supra*. These latter states feel that the broker should notify the seller of each prospect it procures. The answer is obvious from the broker's perspective. As soon as the broker finds a prospect, the broker should notify the seller in writing of the name and address of the prospect.

The broker can collect damages from a buyer who attempts to cheat it out of a commission.

EXAMPLE: Owner hired Broker, and Broker interested Buyer in the purchase of the property. Buyer then contacted Owner directly and got Owner to cut the price. Buyer did this by representing to Owner that no broker was involved. Owner, feeling there would be no liability for the payment of a commission, cut the price. Broker can sue Buyer for damages. 29 A.L.R.3d 1229, 1251, *supra.* Buyer was guilty of a wrongful interference with Broker's business relationship.

10.14   Duration and Termination of Employment

Many controversies arise as to the duration and termination of the broker's employment. The listing agreement should specify when it expires. In many states, statutes or regulations require the listing agreement to state the date on which the term ends.

10.14(a)   When No Term Limit Is Specified

If the listing contract specifies no duration, the broker's authority automatically lapses after expiration of a reasonable time. 27 A.L.R.2d 1346, 1390, *supra.* Of course, the determination of what is a reasonable time is left to chance. Obviously, it is better that the listing agreement is specific in this regard so that the owner and broker both know where they stand. Without certainty, the owner does not know whether it can relist the property in the event it is not sold after a period of time.

10.14(b)   Where the Listing Contract Fixes the Period of Employment

Listing contracts usually provide that they are to continue for a specified time. In such case, the broker is not entitled to a commission unless, within the time limit, a customer is procured who is ready, able, and willing to buy.

In the following cases, the broker will recover a commission even if it fails to find a purchaser within the listing period.

1. When the expiration of the listing time is attributable to the bad faith of the owner, as when the owner deliberately postpones agreement with the broker's buyer, hoping thereby to defeat the broker's claim for compensation. 27 A.L.R.2d 1346, 1357, *supra.*

2. If negotiations are begun within the time specified in the listing contract, continue without interruption, and are completed after the time has expired, the broker is entitled to the commission, particularly where the delay is due to the fault of the owner, as where it is occasioned by a defect in title. The seller is considered to have waived or extended the time limit.

3. When the listing contract contains some clause protecting the broker. For example, some listing forms, in large type, purport to run for a fixed period of time, such as thirty days, but following this will be a provision continuing the listing until a termination notice has been served on the broker.

4. Courts are unfriendly to these provisions for automatic extension of the listing period. Even if the listing contract is an exclusive agency or exclusive right to sell, it will be considered *an open listing during the extended period* if it is at all ambiguous. *Central Realty Co. v. Clutter,* 406 N.E.2d 515 (Ohio 1980). When a listing stated it was to be "sole and exclusive for three months and thereafter until sixty days written notice had been given," it was exclusive only for the initial three-month period. Thereafter, it was only an open listing. *Boggess Realty Co. v. Miller,* 227 Ky. 813, 14 S.W.2d 140 (1929); *Wilson v. Franklin,* 282 Pa. 189, 127 A. 609 (1925).

10.14(c)   Revocation Based upon the Nature of the Listing Agreement

Up to relatively recent times, the broker's listing agreement was what lawyers term a *unilateral contract.* Such a contract is one that contains a promise by *one* of the parties to the agreement, but no promise by the other.

EXAMPLE: "I, the owner of 1234 Main Street, Anytown, U.S.A., promise to pay Broker a commission of 6 percent if you sell said house for not less than $100,000 within the next sixty days." Signed by both parties and dated. Note that the broker makes no promise to do anything.

If the listing agreement is unilateral in form, the owner may terminate it before the termination date, but only if the owner does so before the broker has expended any money or effort. Put another way, such an agreement is revocable by the owner only up to the time the other party, the broker, begins performance. *McMenamin v. Bishop,* 493 P.2d 1016 (Wash. App. 1972); *Stone v. Reinhard,* 183 S.E.2d 601 (1971); *Hutchinson v. Dobson-Bainbridge Realty Co.,* 31 Tenn. App. 490, 217 S.W.2d 6 (1946); *Patton v. Wilson,* 220 S.W.2d 184 (Tex. Civ. App. 1949); 1 Arthur Linton Corbin, *Corbin on Contracts* 154 (1993); William E. Wallace, *Promissory Liability Under Real Estate Brokerage Contracts,* 37 Iowa L. Rev. 350, 370 (1952); 12 Am. Jur. 2d *Brokers* § 32 (1964); G.M.H., Annotation, *Character and Extent of Right of Broker Who Has Exclusive Contract, Where Sale Is Effected Without His Agency,* 64 A.L.R. 404 (1929).

In these cases, any revocation after the broker has begun performance is wrongful and makes the owner liable to the broker for damages.

Most real estate boards have adopted the *bilateral listing contract* wherein the seller employs the broker to sell the property and the broker promises to take certain actions, such as advertising and showing the property. Such a listing is irrevocable from the moment it is signed. The broker has a legal obligation to perform as promised. A sale is not the required performance; what is required is the effort to bring about a sale. Any revocation by the owner before the listing period has expired will be wrongful, so long as the broker is keeping its part of the bargain.

10.14(d) Revocation After Broker Has Performed

Of course, the landowner has no right to revoke the broker's employment after the broker has brought in a buyer ready, able, and willing to buy.

10.14(e) Revocation in Bad Faith

In all types of listings, the owner will be liable to the broker for damages if it acts in bad faith in revoking the broker's employment. 27 A.L.R.2d 1348, 1395, *supra.* Even when no time of employment is specified, when the broker is concluding negotiations with a prospective purchaser, the owner cannot revoke the agency in bad faith for the purpose of avoiding the payment of commission. In other words, when the broker has found a prospect and is concluding negotiations with that prospect, so that the commission is virtually earned and the broker is approaching success, the owner cannot discharge the broker and thereupon step in and consummate the transaction. Such a result would defeat the broker's right to compensation. Restatement (Second) of Agency § 46 (1958).

> **EXAMPLE:** Landowner hired Broker to sell a tract of land. While Broker was negotiating with a prospect, Landowner sold the land to its spouse and discharged Broker. Thereupon, Landowner and spouse sold to Broker's prospect. They were liable for Broker's commission. *Alexander v. Smith,* 180 Ala. 541, 61 So. 68 (1912).

> **EXAMPLE:** Immediately after the listing expires, the seller sells the property to a prospect found by the broker. This is bad faith. *Feeley v. Mullikin,* 44 Wash. 2d 680, 269 P.2d 828 (Wash. 1954).

10.14(f) Revocation by Sale

A wrongful revocation of the broker's exclusive right to sell takes place if the owner contracts to sell the land to a purchaser not procured by the broker or even if it gives the purchaser only an option to purchase. The option removes the property from the market. *Hunt Real Estate Corp. v. Smallidge,* 321 N.Y.S.2d 825 (1971); *Coleman v. Mora,* 263 Cal. App. 2d 137, 69 Cal. Rptr. 166 (1968).

10.14(g)   Notice of Revocation of Employment

When a landowner decides to withdraw property from sale, it must give the broker notice of the revocation of employment before the broker has performed. If the broker brings in a buyer ready, able, and willing to buy, no judge will allow the owner to say, "I fired you mentally five days ago." 12 C.J.S. *Brokers* § 127; 12 Am. Jur. 2d *Brokers* § 61 (1964).

10.14(h)   Revocation by Sale by a Person Other than the Broker

A different situation is presented when the revocation of employment takes place by virtue of the fact that the land has been sold by someone else. As previously explained, in an *open listing* the employment of all brokers hired by the owner automatically ends when a ready, able, and willing buyer is found, either by the owner or by one of the brokers. In an *exclusive agency,* the broker's employment automatically ends if the owner, through its own efforts, finds a willing buyer. No duty to notify the broker rests on the owner in most states, because all brokers understand that in these situations their employment is subject to such automatic termination. *Des Rivieres v. Sullivan,* 247 Mass. 443, 142 N.E.111 (1924); 12 Am. Jur. 2d *Brokers* § 61 (1964). These termination provisions are "read into" the listing contract by the courts.

Suppose that in an open listing a broker finds a willing buyer. However, it fails to notify the owner of this fact, and thereafter the owner signs a contract with some other buyer, procured, let us say, through another broker, the owner being still ignorant of the first broker's successful efforts. The first broker loses its commission. It is its duty to notify the owner promptly on finding a buyer. *Wilson v. Franklin,* 282 Pa. 189, 127 A. 609 (1925). The broker is well advised to notify the owner as soon as a willing buyer is found.

10.14(i)   Damages for Wrongful Revocation of Employment

Suppose that under one of the rules discussed in this section the owner's revocation of the broker's employment is legally wrongful. How much should the courts award the broker? Some courts give the broker only the expenses incurred for advertising and so forth and a sum that will compensate it for the reasonable value of its services. These are restitutionary damages. *Ferguson v. Bovee,* 239 Iowa 775, 32 N.W.2d 924 (1948); *Nicholson v. Alderson,* 347 Ill. App. 496, 107 N.E.2d 39 (1952); 12 Am. Jur. 2d *Brokers* § 64 (1964). Most courts, however, on one theory or another, award the broker a full commission. 37 Iowa L. Rev. 350, 367, *supra*; Bruce I. McDaniel, Annotation, *Validity, Construction, and Effect of Provision in Exclusive Listing Agreement for Payment of Commission on Termination by Owner,* 69 A.L.R.3d 1270 (1976).

The broker will have a better chance of collecting a full commission if the listing contract has a clause covering the possibility of the seller withdrawing the property from sale. Such a provision would allow the broker to receive a full commission "if, within the time above specified, the premises are sold by the broker, owner, or anyone else, or if, within said period, the owner withdraws the property from sale or terminates the broker's employment." *Baumgartner v. Meek,* 126 Cal. App. 2d 505, 272 P.2d 552 (1954).

10.15   Amount of Compensation

In a case where the broker has found a buyer, it is entitled to the commission agreed upon, and if no commission has been fixed by the parties, it is entitled to the usual and customary commission for such services. The broker is usually not entitled to extra compensation for incidental services.

The compensation typically is computed on the basis of the gross sales price.

EXAMPLE: Owner owns property that is encumbered by a $120,000 mortgage. Owner lists the property with a broker at $150,000, and the broker finds a buyer. Although Owner will obtain a net of only $30,000 ($150,000 less the $120,000 required to pay the mortgage), Owner must pay a commission based on a price of $150,000.

10.16 Time of Payment of Commission

Typically, the broker is entitled to the payment of the commission when a ready, willing, and able buyer is procured. Obviously, the seller does not want to pay a commission until the closing proceeds are available as a source of funds for the payment. As we have discussed, the seller wants the listing agreement to provide that the commission is not payable unless the deal closes. Brokers may insist that the seller be liable for the commission if the deal does not close because of the seller's fault.

Another issue arises in the context of the transaction that fails to close because of the buyer's default. In such case, the seller is frequently entitled to forfeit the earnest-money deposit as liquidated damages. If that fund is forfeited to the seller, should the broker be entitled to its commission? Should the broker be entitled to a proportionate share of its commission? The seller will contend that the broker was employed to obtain a buyer who will close, and that the seller is entitled to retain all of the forfeited earnest money as compensation for keeping the property off the market for a time. The seller will also feel that if litigation ensues as a result of the buyer's objection to the forfeiture of the earnest money, the costs of that litigation should be deducted from the earnest money before it is paid to the broker. These issues must be negotiated before the listing agreement is signed.

Another issue as to the timing of the payment of the commission arises in the context of a sale where the purchase price is to be paid part in cash at the time of the closing and part over time. Is the seller to pay all of the commission to the broker at the time of the closing? What if the amount of the cash paid to the seller at the closing is less than the commission payable to the broker? Again, these issues must be negotiated before the listing agreement is signed.

10.17 Lien for Commission

A broker hired by the seller has no lien on the seller's land for the payment of its commission unless the listing contract or statute so provides. W.W.A., Annotation, *Real Estate Broker's Rights and Remedies in Respect of Property or Proceeds for Payment or Security of His Commission*, 125 A.L.R. 921 (1940). In other words, even though the broker has earned its commission, its only remedy, if the seller fails to pay, is to sue the seller and obtain a judgment against it. The broker cannot do anything to block the sale of the land by the seller to the broker's customer or anyone else. Recent legislation in Illinois gives brokers in commercial transactions a lien for their commissions.

10.18 Earnest Money

The seller's broker ordinarily has no authority to accept an earnest-money deposit. M.O. Regensteiner, Annotation, *Payment to Broker or Agent Authorized to Sell Real Property as Payment to Principal*, 30 A.L.R.2d 805, 810 (1953). Quite commonly, however, the broker is permitted to hold the earnest money with no written agreement regarding disposition of such money. If the sale is completed, the money must be returned to the seller. *Mader v. James*, 546 P.2d 190 (Wyo. 1976). If the sale is not completed and the buyer is not at fault, the broker must return the money to the buyer. *Mader v. James*, 546 P.2d 190 (Wyo. 1976); 12 Am. Jur. 2d *Brokers* § 103 (1964); E. LeFevre, Annotation, *Broker's Liability to Prospective Purchaser for Refund of Deposit or Earnest Money Where Contract Fails Because of Defects in Vendor's Title*, 38 A.L.R.2d 1382 (1954). But, if the seller is not at fault, the broker may not collect its commission if the broker returns the earnest money to the buyer. *Lake Co. v. Molan*, 269 Minn. 490, 131 N.W.2d 734 (Minn. 1965). A seller's broker who returns the earnest money to a defaulting purchaser also loses its commission. V. Woerner, Annotation, *Broker's Return of Deposit to Purchaser as Waiver of Right to Demand Commission from Seller*, 69 A.L.R.2d 1244 (1960). Most cases hold that where the seller's title proves defective, or the deal falls through for some other fault of the seller, the broker must return the earnest money to the buyer. 38 A.L.R.2d 1382, *supra.*

The better rule is that when a deal falls through, the broker should return the earnest money to the seller, the employer of the broker, leaving it to the buyer to collect from the seller. *Scholz v. Clements,* 7 Ill. App. 2d 510, 130 N.E.2d 1 (1955); 12 Am. Jur. 2d *Brokers* § 103 (1964). The broker should not be asked to assume the role of judge and thus determine, as between seller and buyer, who is entitled to the return of the deposit. Of course, either the listing contract or the contract of sale can give the broker specific directions in this regard, and the broker should follow them. Unless the broker is clearly instructed in the earnest-money agreement or sales contract, the broker should go to court to get instructions if there is any dispute as to the disposition of the earnest money.

10.18(a) Risk of Loss Caused by Broker's Embezzlement

Where the earnest money is in the hands of the seller's broker, the rule is a simple one. If the broker is not authorized *by the seller* to accept a deposit, the money is the buyer's money entrusted to the broker, and the buyer must bear the loss resulting from the embezzlement. 30 A.L.R.2d 805, 808, *supra.* If the listing contract authorizes the broker to accept a deposit, risk of loss is on the seller.

Even when a seller accepts a *down payment* taken by the broker from the buyer, this does not constitute authority by the seller to the broker to accept the balance of the purchase price. The seller is entitled to assume that the broker was acting as the *buyer's agent* in transmitting the down payment. Suppose that the listing contract authorizes the broker to sign a contract of sale on behalf of the seller. Here, the broker necessarily has implied authority to accept the down payment, for a down payment is made when the contract is signed. 30 A.L.R.2d 805, 816, *supra.* The broker holds the money as agent of the seller, and if the broker embezzles the money, the loss falls on the seller. If the listing contract authorizes the broker to *sell and convey* the property, or if the seller entrusts the deed to the broker for delivery to the buyer, then the broker has implied authority to receive all of the purchase price. This must be so, for the seller's agent, not the seller, will be present at the closing of the deal, and the buyer must pay someone.

A number of states have adopted statutes under which brokers are required to contribute to a fund that is used to compensate victims of a broker's defalcations.

10.19 Splitting Commission— Multiple-Broker Deals

Agreements to divide commissions are common and are usually enforced.

> **EXAMPLE:** Broker *A* (who has no office) uses the office of Broker *B*. *A* stated to *B*, "If I ever get a deal in your office, I'm going to split my commission with you." *B* was entitled to half the commission. John D. Perovich, Annotation, *Construction of Agreement Between Real Estate Agents to Share Commissions*, 71 A.L.R.3d 586, 601 (1976).

In general, the participating broker will collect its share of the commission if and when the commission is collected.

> **EXAMPLE:** Broker *A* was hired to sell some parcels of land. Broker *A* contacted Broker *B* offering to split the commission in any parcel *B* sold. *B* is entitled to his share as and when *A* collects the commission on sales engineered by *B*. 71 A.L.R.3d 586, 606, *supra.*

A broker may become liable to another broker for wrongful deprival of a commission.

> **EXAMPLE:** Owner listed land for sale with Broker 1. Broker 2 contacted Owner and was told to obtain Owner's terms from Broker 1, which Broker 2 did. Broker 2 found Buyer 1, ready

able, and willing to buy, and Owner accepted him. Broker 1 and Broker 2 agreed that they would share the commission equally. Then, Broker 1 persuaded Owner to sell the land to Buyer 2 in a deal with Broker 1, obtaining all of the commission. Broker 1 is liable to Broker 2 for the commission of which Broker 2 was deprived by Broker 1's wrongful conduct. It is wrongful to interfere with a contract right. Jeffrey F. Ghent, Annotation, *Liability of Real Estate Broker for Interference with Contract Between Vendor and Another Real Estate Broker*, 34 A.L.R.3d 720, 730 (1970).

If the broker hired by the seller asks a second broker to help sell the property, and the second broker finds a buyer and collects a commission, the commission must be divided between brokers. *Wheeler v. Waller,* 197 N.W.2d 585 (Iowa 1972). The brokers have engaged in a joint venture, and each party in a joint venture owes a duty of good faith to the other.

If Seller hires Broker and Broker finds Buyer, but Buyer offers less than Seller is willing to accept, Broker may legally share its commission with Buyer. This is often done. J.R. Kemper, Annotation, *Failure of Real Estate Broker to Disclose to Principal Fee-Splitting Agreement with Adverse Party, or Adverse Party's Broker as Breach of Fiduciary Duty Barring Claim for Commission,* 63 A.L.R.3d 1211, 1219 (1975).

10.19(a) Splitting Commission with Buyer

The seller's broker may split the commission with the buyer where this concession is necessary to obtain the buyer's signature on the contract. This is simply a sacrifice on the broker's part. It does not harm the seller. *Lageschulte v. Steinbrecher,* 35 Ill. App. 3d 909, 344 N.E.2d 750 (1976); 63 A.L.R.3d 1211, *supra*. The broker must disclose to its principal, the owner, that part of the commission was being paid to the buyer. Failure to do so is a breach of the broker's fiduciary duty to the seller and could result in the forfeiture of the entire commission. *Goldberg Realty Group v. Weinstein,* 669 A.2d 187 (Me. 1996).

Splitting commission in the multiple listing system is legal.

Programs through which a broker offers potential homebuyers merchandise discounts if they deal with the broker have also been upheld. *Coldwell Banker Residential Real Estate Services of Illinois v. Clayton,* 475 N.E.2d 536 (Ill. 1985). In a technical sense, these arrangements are a splitting of the broker's commission with the buyer.

The broker must not split the commission with "finders" or other persons lacking a broker's license. Doing so will defeat a broker's claim for a commission. *Thorpe v. Carte,* 250 A.2d 618 (Md. 1969).

10.20 Duties of the Broker—Loyalty and Double Agency

In general, the duties of a broker are the same as those of any other agent. They arise because the broker is an agent. They need not be spelled out in the listing contract. An agent must be loyal to his or her principal. If the broker is also acting for the other party to the transaction, the principal may, when this fact is discovered, declare the contract void. This is true even though the transaction is a good one for the principal and the other party acts in good faith and was unaware of the double agency. *Gordon v. Beck,* 196 Cal. 768, 239 P. 309 (1925). It is in the interest of the seller to obtain the highest possible price. This interest is diametrically opposed to the buyer's interest, which is to pay the least. Clearly, no one agent can serve both of these conflicting interests. *Duffy v. Setchell,* 38 Ill. App. 3d 146, 347 N.E.2d 218 (1976). Such a broker also loses its commission.

EXAMPLE: Owner hired Broker 1 to sell a parcel of land, and Buyer hired Broker 2 to find land of this character for purchase. Broker 1 and Broker 2 conferred and agreed to split their commissions down the middle. Neither broker can collect any commission. 63 A.L.R.3d 1211, 1219, *supra*. The impact of this rule is typically negated in the listing agreement, which allows the seller's broker to sell the property through the multiple listing service and split the commission in the manner provided in the multiple listing contract among the brokers.

By engaging in undisclosed dual-agency arrangements, the broker exposes itself to more than civil liability to its clients.

An interesting twist to this issue arises where the broker is a representative of a buyer. The representation of one potential buyer may preclude the broker from representing other potential buyers, especially where one buyer has given the broker confidential information. *Conant v. Karris,* 520 N.E.2d 757 (Ill. App. 1987); *Stefani v. Baird & Warner, Inc.,* 510 N.E.2d 65 (Ill. App. 1987).

Suppose a broker is hired by the buyer to find property in a certain area, with the buyer to pay a commission. Suppose that thereafter a property owner lists land of this description for sale with this broker. The broker reveals this fact *to the buyer only,* and a deal is closed between the seller and buyer, without, however, any knowledge on the seller's part that the broker was originally hired by the buyer. The broker collects the commission from the seller and now sues the buyer. To the broker's surprise, the buyer claims that the broker cannot collect any commission whatever in a double-agency situation. This is correct. The fact that the buyer knew of the double agency makes no difference. A fraud was perpetrated on the *seller,* and the law will not help a party to the fraud, the broker, to collect from the other party to the fraud, the buyer. *McConnell v. Cowan,* 44 Cal. 2d 805, 285 P.2d 261 (1955); C.V. Venters, Annotation, *Acceptance by Principal of Services of Broker with Knowledge that He Acted Also for the Other Party as Affecting Broker's Right to Compensation,* 80 A.L.R. 1077, 1087 (1932). The fact that the broker felt it was acting in the best interests of both parties is immaterial.

Of course, if a full disclosure of the dual-agency situation is made by the broker to the client and the client makes a knowing waiver of the dual representation, the broker may represent both parties. *Cole v. Brundage,* 344 N.E.2d 583 (Ill. 1976). The broker should be cautioned, however, that the courts will carefully inquire into its conduct to ensure that the broker has not favored one party over the other. This is a very difficult position for the broker.

The rule against double agency is often applied with great strictness.

EXAMPLE: Buyer requested that Broker find him a home. Broker contacted Homeowner, and a contract of sale was signed. Both Buyer and Broker expected that Broker would receive the commission from Homeowner. Buyer did not expect to pay a commission to Broker. This was also Broker's understanding. Nevertheless, Broker was working for both parties and should have revealed this to Homeowner. *Duffy v. Setchell,* 347 N.E.2d 218 (Ill. App. 1976).

A dual-agency type of problem develops because many buyers feel that the broker who works with them represents them. This is especially the case in the residential as opposed to the commercial setting. In commercial transactions, buyers and tenants are often represented by their own broker, but that is typically not so in residential transactions.

The factual pattern is very familiar. The prospective residential purchaser begins working with a broker who is attempting to find a home for the buyer by looking to listings of the office in which the broker or salesperson is employed and then to properties on the multiple listing service. Under the traditional legal analysis, the seller has employed the listing broker as an agent for the sale of the home. The others in the listing agent's office and those who use the multiple listing service to find properties for their sales prospects are subagents of the listing broker. All of the brokers and salespeople in this chain are linked by the law of agency to the seller. They all owe the duties of an agent to the seller, and none of them are the agents of the buyer owing to the buyer the duties of an agent.

These duties are significant and meaningful in a transaction such as the purchase of a home. The broker may have a duty to disclose defects in the property, even if an investigation into the existence of such defects must be undertaken. *Enright v. Jonassen*, 931 P.2d 1212 (Idaho 1997). The duty of loyalty and confidentiality are especially important. For example, it is very important that someone who is negotiating on behalf of the buyer keep in confidence the fact that the buyer must act quickly because the buyer's existing house has been sold, or that the buyers must move out of the apartment they rent in a very short time. Similarly, the seller is entitled to trust the confidences that it may give to its agent, the broker, about the necessitous financial condition that the seller may be in. These circumstances are at polar opposites from one another, and the broker or salesperson in the traditional setting must keep the information obtained from the seller confidential and not inform the seller what was learned from the buyer.

To react to this situation, many states have enacted statutes that permit dual agencies, under certain circumstances, and disclosure laws that require the broker give a written notice informing the buyer that the broker represents the seller. Further, some states have legislated the agency relationship created by multiple listing services out of existence. 225 ILCS 455/38.55. In addition, the true buyer-broker relationship has been statutorily approved in many jurisdictions, breaking the chain of agency relationships leading from the seller to each real estate professional involved in the transaction. In some states, these rules have been changed to such an extent that even different salespeople working in the same office can be the representative of the buyer and the seller, respectively. Of course, disclosure of the relationship must be made and the consequences explained to the parties. 225 IlCS 455/38.45.

Under these new rules, a brokerage office can legally, within a structure that has removed the uncertainties of the situation for the benefit of the brokers and the parties, have a salesperson represent the seller and another salesperson represent the buyer. The buyer's salesperson becomes just that, an agent of the buyer, with loyalty and duties to the buyer and not the seller. This is perfectly sensible in that it meets with the expectations of the parties in today's real estate community. There is an incidental benefit to the seller in all of this. The seller will not be liable for misrepresentations made by the buyer's broker unless, of course, the seller was in some way responsible for them. *See* Pancak, Miceli, & Sirmans, *Real Estate Agency Reform: Meeting the Needs of Buyers, Sellers and Brokers*, 25 Real Est. L.J. 345 (1997).

A middleman, who merely brings the parties together, leaving them to negotiate, may serve both parties. Here, the double-agency rule does not apply. H.N.G., Annotation, *Validity of Contract by Agent for Compensation from Third Person for Negotiating Loan or Sale with Principal*, 14 A.L.R. 464, 472 (1921); L.S. Tellier, Annotation, *Real Estate Broker's Power to Bind Principal by Representations as to the Character, Condition, Location, Quantity, or Title of Property*, 58 A.L.R.2d 10, 42, 58 (1958). But, if the broker assists either party, or in some degree influences the parties, the broker is not a middleman. It is obvious that very few agencies fall in the middleman category.

10.20(a) Duties of the Broker—Conflict-of-interest Problems

An agent must not have any individual interest in the transaction without the knowledge and consent of the principal.

EXAMPLE: Owner placed property with Broker. Negotiations resulted in a sale by Owner to Buyer for $3,200; the Broker received a commission of $160. After the deed was given, Owner discovered that Buyer was one of Broker's employees. Owner was entitled to have the conveyance set aside. *Johnson v. Bernard,* 323 Ill. 527, 154 N.E. 444 (1926). Owner was also entitled to a return of the commission.

This rule even precludes a sale by the broker to its spouse unless the seller is informed of the relation. If, however, the broker fully discloses the facts to the landowner, the broker may buy for itself, for a relative, or for itself and others.

10.20(b)   Duties of the Broker—Disclosure and Nondisclosure

An agent must make full disclosure to the principal of all matters that may come to the broker's knowledge pertaining to the subject of the agency. C.E. Basham, Annotation, *Duty of Real Estate Broker to Disclose Identity of Purchaser or Lessee,* 2 A.L.R.3d 1119, 1123 (1965).

EXAMPLE: Owner placed property with Broker. Broker wrote Owner stating that Broker together with several other parties would buy the land at $400 per acre. The contract was signed, and Broker received a commission. Later, Owner discovered that, prior to making this offer, Broker had received a $500 per acre offer for this property. Owner was entitled to have the contract canceled. *Rieger v. Brandt,* 329 Ill. 21, 160 N.E. 130 (1928); A.E. Korpela & J. Kraut, Annotation, *Liability of Real Estate Broker or Agent to Principal for Concealing or Failing to Disclose Offer,* 7 A.L.R.3d 693 (1966).

EXAMPLE: The broker is liable if it transmits an offer to the principal, but conceals a more favorable offer. 7 A.L.R.3d 693, 696, *supra.*

EXAMPLE: While the property is listed with Broker, it increases in value. Owner is ignorant of this fact, but Broker knows of it. Broker fails to disclose this circumstance to Owner. Broker has violated the duty of full disclosure. *Eastburn v. Joseph Espalla, Jr. & Co.,* 112 So. 232 (Ala. 1927); Eunice A. Eichelberger, Annotation, *Real Estate Broker's or Agent's Misrepresentation to, or Failure to Inform, Vendor Regarding Value of Vendor's Real Property,* 33 A.L.R.4th 944 (1984).

EXAMPLE: Buyer, procured by Broker, has a poor financial status. Broker knows this, but fails to reveal it to Seller. A contract is signed, but the deal fails to go through because Buyer cannot raise the necessary funds. Broker has violated the duty of full disclosure. *McGarry v. McCrone,* 97 Ohio App. 543, 118 N.E.2d 195 (1954); *Nugent v. Scharff,* 476 S.W.2d 414 (Tex. App. 1971); *Mason v. Bulleri,* 543 P.2d 478 (Ariz. App. 1975); Theresa Ludwig Kruk, Annotation, *Real Estate Broker's Rights and Liabilities as Affected by Failure to Disclose Financial Information Concerning Purchaser,* 34 A.L.R.4th 191 (1984).

EXAMPLE: Buyer, procured by Broker, is a distant relative of Broker. Broker must reveal this fact to Seller. F.G. Madara, Annotation, *Duty of Real Estate Broker to Disclose that Purchaser is a Relative,* 26 A.L.R.2d 1307 (1952). Broker must also disclose the true identify of the purchaser. 2 A.L.R.3d 1119, *supra.*

In other words, the broker's duty is not discharged simply by handing a contract to the seller for signing. The broker must give the seller all facts that might influence the seller in accepting or rejecting the offer, or else the broker is liable for damages. The broker must give its opinion as to the price that can be obtained, the likelihood of a higher price being offered in the future, the possibility of making a favorable trade or other use of the property, etc. *Moehling v. W.E. O'Neil Construction Co.,* 20 Ill. 2d 255, 170 N.E.2d 100 (1960).

The converse of the broker's duty of disclosure is the duty not to reveal secret information to prospective buyers. Thus, the seller's broker violates these duties if it reveals to a prospective buyer that the seller will take less than the listed price for the property, for obviously no buyer will pay the listed price if it knows that the seller will take less. *Haymes v. Rogers,* 70 Ariz. 257, 219 P.2d 339 (1950), *modified on reh.* 70 Ariz. 408, 222 P.2d 789 (1950).

Some state laws have been passed to protect brokers from liability for the failure to disclose (as opposed to misrepresentating) information relating to psychologically impacted property, such as the fact that the property was the scene of a murder or that a past occupant was an AIDS victim. Ronald Brown & Thomas H. Thurlow, *Buyers Beware: Statutes Shield Real Estate Brokers and Sellers Who Do Not Disclose that Properties Are Psychologically Tainted,* 49 Okla. L. Rev. 625 (1996). Further, disclosure of the seller's HIV infection may violate the Fair Housing Act. 42 U.S.C. § 3604(f).

10.20(c) Duties of the Broker— Misrepresentations, Nondisclosure

A broker hired by the seller will be held liable to the buyer in damages if the broker, acting on its own, makes a willful misrepresentation that induces the buyer to enter into the contract of sale. L.S. Tellier, Annotation, *Real Estate Broker's Power to Bind Principal by Representations as to Character, Condition, Location, Quantity, or Title of Property,* 58 A.L.R.2d 10, 27 (1958); D.P. Grawunder, Annotation, *Liability of Vendor's Real Estate Broker or Agent to Purchaser for Misrepresentations as to, or Nondisclosure of, Physical Defects of Property Sold,* 8 A.L.R.3d 550, 553 (1966).

> **EXAMPLE:** The broker falsely represented that the house was stucco-covered brick. It was not. *Perkins v. Gross,* 26 Ariz. 219, 224 P. 620 (1924). He was liable to the buyer.

> **EXAMPLE:** A house is in an area that had flood problems over a period of time. After each flood, Owner had the storm drains cleared. Broker advised Owner not to note the prior flooding on the disclosure statement because the problem had been corrected. The disclosure statement said there were no drainage problems or standing water. Buyer purchased the house and a flood occurred. The Broker was liable to Buyer for failure to disclose the past flooding problems. *Swendsen v. Stock,* 979 P.2d 475 (Wash. App. 1999).

If the buyer chooses to rescind (cancel the deal and obtain return of the down payment) because of a misrepresentation made by the broker, the broker loses all right to a commission from the seller. L.S. Tellier, Annotation, *Real Estate Broker's Right to Commission Where Purchaser Refuses to Go Through with Executory Contract Because of Reckless Misrepresentations Made to Him by Broker Respecting Property,* 9 A.L.R.2d 504 (1950).

Most state licensing laws provide that the broker's license may be suspended or revoked if the broker makes substantial misrepresentations or false promises.

10.20(d) Duties of the Broker—Skill and Care

Like other agents, a broker must exercise skill and care in the service of its employer. J.C. Vance, Annotation, *Liability of Real Estate Broker to Principal for Negligence in Carrying Out Agency,* 94 A.L.R.2d 468 (1964).

> **EXAMPLE:** A broker, hired to sell land, found a buyer and drew a contract of sale, which the parties signed. Thereafter, the buyer refused to go through with the deal. The court held that the contract was so poorly drawn that the buyer was not legally bound. The broker thereby forfeited its commission. *Dingman v. Boyle,* 285 Ill. 144, 120 N.E. 487 (1918). Moreover, the broker is liable to the seller for any damages the seller has suffered. *Mattieligh v. Poe,* 57 Wash. 2d 203, 356 P.2d 328 (1960).

> **EXAMPLE:** A broker hired to buy or trade has a duty to determine the value of the real estate acquired for the principal. If the broker fails in this respect and the property turns out to

be a poor buy, the broker is liable and forfeits its commission. *Smith v. Carroll Realty Co.,* 8 Utah 2d 356, 335 P.2d 67 (1959).

EXAMPLE: A broker employed to find a property for a buyer must exercise skill and care if it undertakes to close the deal for the buyer without an attorney. Thus, if the broker fails to procure a clear title for the buyer, the broker is liable to buyer for damages. *Lester v. Marshall,* 143 Colo. 189, 352 P.2d 786 (1960).

EXAMPLE: A broker can be held liable for loss caused by its ignorance of the applicability and effect of zoning laws. *Burien Motors, Inc. v. Balch,* 513 P.2d 582 (Wash. 1973).

EXAMPLE: A broker was held liable for not adequately explaining the nonrecourse provision in the sales contract or recommending that the seller retain a lawyer. *Crutchley v. First Trust & Sav. Bank,* 450 N.W.2d 877 (Iowa 1990).

EXAMPLE: A seller's broker may be liable to a purchaser for negligently selecting a home inspector or other professional who does a poor job and does not discover defects in the property being sold. *Thomson v. McGinnis,* 465 S.E.2d 922 (W. Va. 1995); *Fowler v. Westair Enterprises, Inc.,* 906 P.2d 1053 (Wyo. 1995).

10.20(e)   Duties of the Broker—Liabilities and Penalties for Breach of Duty

Where the broker breaches its duties toward the employer, one or more of several penalties may result.

1. In almost every case, the broker will lose its commission. If the broker has already been paid, the commission must be refunded. 2 A.L.R.3d 1119, 1126, *supra.*

2. If the broker has made a profit, as where the broker had bought the property from the principal through a nominee and resold it at a profit, the broker must pay such profit over to the principal.

3. If the principal has suffered any damages as a consequence of the broker's breach of duty, the broker will be liable for such damages.

4. Where the broker's misconduct is deliberate, as where it secretly buys the property from the principal, the court may see fit to punish the broker by compelling it to pay exemplary damages, that is, damages greater than the damage the employer has actually suffered. *Ward v. Taggart,* 51 Cal. 2d 736, 336 P.2d 534 (1959).

5. For a serious offense, such as secretly buying the principal's property, failing to disclose material facts to the principal, embezzling the principal's funds, etc., the broker may have its license suspended or revoked altogether. L.S. Tellier, Annotation, *Grounds for Revocation or Suspension of License of Real Estate Broker or Salesman,* 56 A.L.R.2d 573 (1957). Fraud in his or her own land transactions may also result in the loss of the broker's license. *Holland Realty Inv. Co. v. State,* 436 P.2d 422 (Nev. 1968).

As is true with respect to lawyers, doctors, architects, and others, the courts are holding brokers to increasingly higher standards of professional ethics and competence. This is a desirable trend and is likely to continue.

It should be noted, however, that the broker's liability is not without limits. The broker may not be liable to third parties who are not intended beneficiaries of the broker's services.

EXAMPLE: A structural engineer examined a balcony overlooking the Pacific Ocean in Malibu. The brokers were informed of the defects that the engineer found, but either misrepresented the condition of the balcony or did not disclose the engineer's findings. The balcony collapsed during a housewarming party and several people were injured. The injured persons did not include the buyer or the seller. The court held that these third parties were not intended beneficiaries of the brokers' services, and therefore the brokers were not liable to them. *FSR Brokerage, Inc. v. Blanco,* 41 Cal. Rptr. 2d 404 (Cal. App. 1995).

10.20(f) Duties to Purchaser

As described earlier, a broker is normally hired by the seller. One would think that the broker therefore has no duties to the purchaser. This is not necessarily the case. The more recent decisions take the position that the broker is a special type of agent. The broker is licensed by the state after passing a comprehensive examination. The broker enjoys a monopoly in that unlicensed persons are barred from the profession. In effect, the state holds the broker out as being a responsible and capable person. The broker, therefore, has duties to the purchaser as well as to the seller. *Ward v. Taggart,* 51 Cal. 2d 736, 336 P.2d 534 (1959); *Sawyer Realty Group, Inc. v. Jarvis,* 89 Ill. 2d 379, 432 N.E.2d 849 (1982); *Dugan v. Jones,* 615 P.2d 1239 (Utah 1980); 12 C.J.S. *Brokers* § 104 (1980). *See also* Chapter 13.

In a notable case, *Easton v. Strassburger,* 199 Cal. Rptr. 383 (Cal. App. 1984), the court held a broker responsible to the purchaser for damages resulting from shifting soil conditions. The home was built on filled land, and massive soil movement occurred because of poor soil compaction. Although the broker did not know that the home was built on fill, indicators were present that should have put the broker on notice of the problem. This duty may not apply in commercial transactions or where the buyer is sophisticated. *Smith v. Rickard,* 254 Cal. Rptr. 633 (Cal. App. 1988).

Of course, where the broker makes a misrepresentation or false statement, liability will follow.

> **EXAMPLE:** Seller's broker misrepresented the zoning of the subject property to Buyer. Broker held liable. *Barnes v. Lopez,* 544 P.2d 694 (Ariz. 1976).

> **EXAMPLE:** If the listing broker furnishes false information to its listing service and a member of the service transmits this false information to a buyer, the listing broker is liable to the buyer, just as if the listing broker made the misrepresentation directly to the buyer. *Granberg v. Turnham,* 333 P.2d 423 (Cal. 1958); *First Church v. Cline J. Dunton Realty, Inc.,* 19 Wash. App. 275, 574 P.2d 1211 (1978). This result is altered by statute in some states, if the broker providing the false information to the buyer does not know that the information is false. 225 ILCS 455/38.25.

> **EXAMPLE:** If the broker arranges "creative financing," such as balloon-note financing, it may be liable if the buyer suffers damage. Zumpano & Marsh, *Creative Financing Arrangements: Risks and Liabilities,* 12 Real Est. L.J. 151 (1983).

Brokers are finding comfort in the fact that many states have enacted laws requiring the seller to give a prescribed form of written disclosures to the purchaser. *See, e.g.*, 765 ILCS 77/20; Mich. Comp. Laws Ann. § 565.951. By giving these disclosures, the seller and the seller's broker are protected against the buyer later claiming that the seller and the seller's broker did not disclose defects that are inherent in the property. Of course, the seller and the broker must be forthcoming in the manner in which the disclosure form is completed. Indeed, the seller must be forthcoming and deal in good faith. Playing cute with the facts will not be a defense. *Engelhart v. Kramer*, 570 N.W.2d 550 (S.D. 1997). If a known defect is not disclosed, the disclosure statement documents the nondisclosure.

The broker may also have a duty to ensure the safety of prospective purchasers who tour the property offered for sale at an open house. This duty requires the broker to advise prospects of defects that are reasonably discoverable through an ordinary inspection undertaken for the purpose of selling the property. *Hopkins v. Fox & Lazo Realtors*, 625 A.2d 1110 (N.J. 1993).

Just as a broker must not have an individual interest that conflicts with the interest of the seller, the broker must not have an individual interest that conflicts with the interest of the purchaser.

> **EXAMPLE:** Seller's broker, after receiving an inquiry from a buyer, rechecked the property and secretly had a partner buy the property. Broker is liable to buyer. *George v. Bolen,* 580 P.2d 1357 (Kan. App. 1980).

It is curious to find the courts are holding the seller's agent liable to the buyer, who is, in fact, the seller's adversary. This is explained in *Walter v. Moore,* 700 P.2d 1219 (Wyo. 1985). In that case, the court pointed out that the salesperson spent weeks or months in a close relationship with the buyer, driving side-by-side in the salesperson's car, going through homes together, and probably getting on a first-name basis. This confidential relationship placed on the salesperson the burden of dealing fairly with the purchaser.

10.21   Unauthorized Practice of Law

The law appears to differ from state to state with respect to the propriety of a broker's filling in a form contract of sale where this is merely incidental to the earning of the commission for procuring a sale. 53 A.L.R.2d 788, 796, *supra.* However, if the broker makes a separate charge for filling in a form, it may be guilty of the unauthorized practice of law. 53 A.L.R.2d 788, 804, *supra.* Likewise, if a broker prepares a will or deed to put land in joint tenancy, it is guilty of the unauthorized practice of law. 53 A.L.R.2d 788, 807, *supra.*

In a significant departure from prior decisions, it was held that a real estate broker could draft, close, and record a real estate sales transaction and charge a $250.00 drafting fee. The court felt that this was not the unauthorized practice of law because the transaction was "simple." *Cardinal v. Merrill Lynch Realty/Burnet, Inc.,* 433 N.W.2d 864 (Minn. 1988). Similarly, in New Jersey, brokers are not engaged in the unauthorized practice of law when they handle real estate transactions. *In re Opinion No. 26 of the Committee on the Unauthorized Practice of Law,* 654 A.2d 1344 (N.J. 1995).

10.22   Authority of Broker to Sign Contract

Ordinarily, a broker does not have authority to sign a contract on behalf of his or her employer. H.D. Warren, Annotation, *Power of Real Estate Broker to Execute Contract of Sale on Behalf of Principal,* 43 A.L.R.2d 1014 (1955).

10.23   Franchising

In the franchising context, the real estate broker retains his or her independent status. The franchiser furnishes advertising, training, procedure manuals, forms, and so forth. Each franchiser is furnished a list of the franchisees in other areas. This enables each franchiser to have a national referral service—for example, in employee-transfer situations. If the franchising agreement gives the franchiser the right to allocate territory, that portion of the agreement is likely to draw fire from the federal government. The laws against monopolies forbid territory allocation. Dowling & Hines, *Here Comes the Real Estate Franchise,* 7 Real Estate Rev. 48 (Summer 1977).

10.24   Integrated Financial Organizations

Large national corporations have embarked upon the business plan of furnishing the consumer with total financial services. The theory goes that the consumer can have "one-stop" service from these organizations. By shopping in one place, the consumer can obtain banking, stock brokerage, insurance, and real estate brokerage services. From the business point of view, one customer base feeds the other. From the consumer's point of view, there is comfort in dealing with a business concern that the consumer has come to know and trust. In some instances, the customer can obtain a discount on a bundle of goods and services provided by the same entity. This packaging of services has been upheld. *Coldwell Banker Residential Real Estate Services of Illinois, Inc. v. Clayton,* 475 N.E.2d 536 (Ill. 1985).

Another development is found in the business plan to concentrate many of the services that relate to a purchase of residential real estate at the title company's or broker's office. The title examination, survey, flood-plain certification, appraisal, and other related services are being integrated into the same service provider. It is likely that these services will come to all be focused at the point of sale, the broker's office, as the deal is signed. The broker will then initiate all of the orders for related services that will enable the parties to close the transaction on time and with the utmost efficiency.

10.25 Mortgage Finder   Brokers may now put a homebuyer into contact with a mortgage lender and receive a fee from the homebuyer. This is not a violation of the federal Real Estate Settlement Procedures Act.

CHAPTER 11

Contracts for the Sale of Real Estate

11.01 In General Any discussion of a real estate purchase and sale contract must necessarily presume that the reader is knowledgeable in many aspects of real estate law and practice. The contract itself brings together many concepts of real estate law and practice, and the parties can only bind themselves to one another after they thoroughly understand those concepts or have had them explained by a knowledgeable attorney. For example, by contracting to buy the property subject to covenants, conditions, and restrictions of record, the buyer must accept the conveyance even if one of those restrictions would prevent the use of the property for a purpose intended by the buyer.

For this reason, the contract must be considered only in light of the knowledge of the various aspects of real estate law that it brings into play. A knowledge of title evidence and the nature of title defects, a working knowledge of the closing process, a basic understanding of land development issues, and an understanding of mortgage financing principles and the like are essential before one can meaningfully enter into a contract for the purchase of a parcel of real estate.

11.02 Why a Contract of Sale of Land Is Needed Where a landowner and a buyer agree to buy and sell a parcel of land, one may ask why it is necessary that a contract be signed. The landowner could right then and there give a deed to the buyer and the buyer could immediately pay the purchase price to the seller. This is not possible because there are too many other details to attend to before the transaction can close. The seller may not want to give up the property, whether it be a home or business property, until a replacement property can be purchased and an orderly move arranged. Most contracts give the parties several weeks or months between the signing of the contract, the closing, and the exchange of possession. This could be worked out with the buyer effectively renting the property to the seller for a similar period of time. The buyer may need the proceeds from the sale of an existing house before closing on the purchase of the new home. To meet this situation, a bridge loan could be arranged to provide the needed funds, but that will only increase the cost of the transaction for the buyer.

There are many details to be attended to between the signing of the contract and the closing. The buyer will have to arrange for the financing of the purchase, and the seller will have to arrange for the payoff of existing mortgages. While today's automated credit processing systems are moving us toward quick loan approvals, we have not yet achieved instant loan documentation and funding. Inspections and appraisals must be conducted and title evidence produced and examined. While many title companies can produce title commitments within a day or two, we have not yet achieved instant, on-line title evidence to facilitate the instant transaction.

Perhaps the single most important factor standing in the way of the instant closing is that the parties desire to have some time between the contract and the closing to take care of their business and personal needs. For example, many contracts, both for commercial and residential property, require that certain contingencies be met before the obligations of the parties become fixed. Many contracts are contingent upon the buyer obtaining financing that meets the buyer's needs. Many other contracts are contingent upon the successful completion of a check of the property to ensure that it is structurally sound, free from environmental defects, rezoned, or otherwise suitable for the buyer's purposes.

Even without contingencies, the parties must arrange their personal and business affairs to accommodate the acquisition or sale of the property. For commercial property, management companies must be terminated, work forces relocated, service contracts terminated or assigned, and dozens of other details attended to before the transaction can close. In residential transactions, the children must be transferred from one school to another, service contracts must be terminated, and various services transferred from the old to the new home. Sometimes more importantly, it takes time for people to sever emotional ties to their old home while they acclimate to the idea of living somewhere else.

While the electronic integration of the service providers that assist and participate in real estate transactions will eliminate many of the delays and uncertainties in the process that commences with the execution of the contract and ends at the closing, there is probably no need for the instant closing, and we will continue to see an interval of time between the contract and closing.

11.03 Types of Contracts

The cash sale contract contemplates that the deal will be promptly closed. There is also a type of contract called the *installment contract, contract for deed,* or *land contract.* An installment contract provides for a down payment, with the balance of the purchase price payable in installments. The buyer receives the deed when all of the installments have been paid or when the unpaid balance of the purchase price has been paid down to an agreed figure, whereupon the buyer is to receive a deed and pay the balance of the purchase price, either in cash or through the giving of a purchase money mortgage for the balance of the purchase price.

11.04 Necessity for a Written Contract

It is necessary that the fundamentals of an agreement of the parties for the purchase and sale be in writing. Oral contracts to sell real estate cannot be enforced. The law that so provides is known as the *Statute of Frauds.* To satisfy the Statute of Frauds, the contract must contain the names of the seller and buyer, a sufficient description of the land, the contract price, the terms of sale if other than cash, and the signature of "the party to be charged," that is, the signature of the party against whom suit is brought to enforce the contract. A few states require both parties to sign the contract. There appears to be a trend in this direction. As a rule, oral testimony cannot be introduced in court for the purpose of supplying omissions in the written document.

The Statute of Frauds may leave the parties in an uncertain situation. Suppose that *A* enters into an oral contract with *B* to buy *B*'s land, and *A* gives *B* a down payment. Thereafter, *A* changes its mind. Although *B* cannot sue *A* for the balance of the contract price, neither can *A* get its down payment back as long as *B* is willing to go through with the deal. *See* R.J. Fox, Annotation, *Vendor's Willingness and Ability to Perform Contract Which Does Not Satisfy Statute of Frauds as Precluding Purchaser's Recovery Back of Payments Made Thereon,* 169 A.L.R. 187 (1947).

Where the only memorandum of the agreement contains only the bare bones of the understanding of the parties, the courts will read into the contract some of the missing terms.

EXAMPLE: If the contract is silent on these matters, the courts will assume a cash sale was intended with the closing to take place in a reasonable time; that the sale price and deed will change hands simultaneously; that the deed will be a quitclaim deed; that the buyer will be entitled to marketable title free from all encumbrances; that any defects in marketability must be raised before the deal is closed; that the buyer will determine marketability at its own expense, and so on.

No particular form of contract is required. A binding contract may be in the form of one or more letters, escrow instructions, receipt, a check, a promissory note, and so on.

EXAMPLE: A contract was as follows:

Chicago, January 8, 1904
Received of Anton Ullsperger $100 on said purchase of property No. 1031 Milwaukee Avenue, Chicago, Illinois at a price of $14,000.

C. Meyer

Meyer refused to perform. The court compelled Meyer to give Ullsperger a deed. *Ullsperger v. Meyer,* 217 Ill. 262, 75 N.E. 482 (1905).

It should be noted that Ullsperger, who had *not* signed the contract, was allowed to enforce the contract against Meyer, who *had* signed it. This is an example of the "party to be charged" concept discussed previously. Meyer could not have enforced the contract against Ullsperger. This is in accord with the general rule that, in a land contract, a seller may legally compel performance if it can produce a contract signed by the buyer, and the buyer can demand performance if it can produce a contract signed by the seller. Signature by both parties is not necessary. Such a contract, although it meets the minimum requirements of the law, is altogether unsatisfactory, as will become apparent from the subsequent discussion. Obviously, it is best to have both seller and buyer sign the contract, and this is the usual practice.

Many documents that are legally sufficient as contracts for the sale of land are quite short, as the previous example demonstrates. Moreover, such documents are often given misleading names, such as deposit receipt or offer to purchase. People sign such documents without realizing that they have obligated themselves to buy or sell property. Sometimes, such brief documents state that the parties will later sign a "regular" real estate contract. The court decisions are conflicting as to the effect of the inclusion of this phrase. As long as the main terms of the sale are stated in the shorter, initial document, most courts hold that the failure to sign a formal, detailed contract is not controlling, especially where the parties proceed with the details of the transaction as though a binding contract existed. *Sewel v. Dolby,* 171 Kan. 640, 237 P.2d 366 (1951). Other states feel that the parties do not intend to be bound until a formal, detailed contract is executed, as called for in the short form, and therefore hold that the short document is not binding. *Brunette v. Vulcan Materials Co.,* 119 Ill. App. 2d 390, 256 N.E.2d 44 (1970); *Lippman v. Featherston,* 247 Mich. 153, 225 N.W. 489 (1929); 17A Am. Jur. 2d *Contracts* § 6 (1991). The better thinking of modern decisions is that these short-form contracts are binding to at least require that the parties undertake in good faith to negotiate and execute the formal, detailed contract.

11.05 Letters of Intent

The letter of intent is frequently used in connection with the sale of commercial properties. The letter of intent is used to set out the principal business terms of the deal before the parties embark on the more detailed, and sometimes long, process of negotiating and documenting the full contractual relationship. Often, the parties will agree in the letter of intent that the property will be kept off the market for a period of time while the parties work in good faith toward the execution of the formal agreement. This is a binding covenant of the letter of intent, even if the letter of intent itself is not a binding agreement for the purchase and sale of the property.

A frequent area of dispute lies in whether the letter of intent is a binding contract for the sale of the property. It is best that this not be left to chance. If the parties intend that the letter is a binding agreement for the sale of the property, they should so state. If not, it should be expressly stated that the parties are not bound to any agreement for the purchase of the property unless and until a formal agreement to that effect is executed. Even in this circumstance, the parties may be bound to bargain in good faith in an effort to reach a formal agreement. Georgette C. Poindexter, *Letters of Intent in Commercial Real Estate*, 28 R.E.L.J. 195 (2000); Charles L. Knapp, *Enforcing the Contract to Bargain,* 44 N.Y.U. L.Rev. 673 (1969).

11.06 Drafting the Purchase and Sale Agreement

There are many ways that contracts for the purchase of real estate are drafted. In residential transactions, the contract is usually on a preprinted form adopted by the various real estate brokers' groups or boards or is drafted by the developer in the case of the sale of a new home. The broker or salesperson then merely fills in the blanks with the business points of the deal and has the parties sign the contract. These forms may have preprinted riders to address the typical situations that confront the home buyer and seller. For example, a rider may allow the buyer to have the home inspected and to opt out of the deal if the inspector's report reveals defects in the property. Another may make the parties' obligations contingent upon the approval of the contract by the attorneys for the buyer and seller. Occasionally, these forms are in a computer word-processing system, the broker fills in the blanks on a master screen, and the contract is printed out on a computer printer.

Commercial deals are more complex and generally do not lend themselves to preprinted forms. The parties usually bring the deal to their lawyers, outline the business terms, and then negotiate the final form of the agreement, which one or the other of the attorneys drafts.

Whatever method is used for the drafting of these agreements, all real estate contracts have, or should have, provisions that address the following points.

1. The basic agreement of the buyer and seller to purchase and sell the property.
2. The identification of exactly what is to be purchased and sold. The real property should be described by the use of its legal description. The personal property should be described as specifically as possible or at least by good generic descriptions. If any intangible property is to be transferred, such as certificates of occupancy, service contracts, insurance policies, or causes of action against third parties, that property should be described as specifically as possible.
3. The amount of the purchase price and an agreement on the way in which the purchase price is to be paid, all in cash at the closing, or part in cash at the closing and part over time as a purchase money mortgage or pursuant to an installment contract.
4. The amount of earnest money must be established, and the parties must determine whether any additional earnest money will be paid as conditions are satisfied or as the contract moves closer to the closing. The parties must agree where the earnest money is to be deposited, and if it is to earn interest, for whom that interest will accrue. The parties must agree upon how the

balance of the purchase price will be paid. Will it be paid all in cash at the closing or will the seller accept the buyer's promissory note for all or some of the balance? If the buyer's obligation to pay the balance is to be deferred and paid in full or in part over time, will the buyer's deferred obligation to pay be secured by the property or by something else?

5.   How the seller's title is to be evidenced and whether the property is to be surveyed. Once the evidence of title and survey are obtained, there must be a mechanism to eliminate title and survey matters that are unacceptable to the buyer and an agreement upon what will result if those matters cannot be eliminated.

6.   Representations and warranties of the parties. For example, the seller may represent and warrant that it has not received any notice from any governmental body that the property violates any zoning, building, health, or safety code.

7.   Conditions to the obligations of the parties to close the transaction. For example, the buyer's obligation to close may be conditioned upon the receipt by the buyer of a mortgage commitment and the fulfillment of the conditions of that commitment.

8.   Matters occurring between the time of the execution of the contract and the closing. For example, the seller may wish to continue to operate the property as though the contract did not exist and enter into leases and operational contracts, while the buyer may not want the property saddled with new matters without its approval. The parties must also agree upon the responsibility for any change in the condition of the property between the contract execution and the closing, including the risk of loss as a result of casualty, such as fire or flood, or condemnation of part or all of the property.

9.   The time and place of the closing.

10.   Deliveries to be made by the parties at the closing.

11.   Adjustments to the purchase price, prorations, and the allocation of the costs and fees relating to the closing.

12.   The rights and obligations of the parties in the event of a default.

13.   Any additional matters, such as indemnifications of the parties for liabilities relating to the property for pre- and postclosing matters.

11.07   Questions that Should be Asked by Parties Intending to Enter into a Contract

Before listing the property with a broker for sale, the seller should determine that it really wants to sell. If the property is listed with a broker, and the broker finds a buyer ready, able, and willing to buy at the listing price and on the listing terms, the seller must pay a commission, even if the seller later decides that it really does not want to sell.

Similarly, a married property owner must determine whether its spouse wants to sell. Again, if a broker with a listing agreement finds a buyer, and the spouse that did not sign the listing agreement refuses to sell, the broker will be entitled to a commission. In most states, the buyer will refuse to go through with the deal because, unless the reluctant spouse signs the contract, that spouse is not legally obligated to execute the deed, and this will leave spousal rights outstanding.

The seller should also determine that it is really in a position to sell. Suppose the broker finds a willing buyer, but if it is found that the seller's title is defective, the seller cannot pay off the existing mortgage, or the replacement property will not be ready for occupancy for a long time, the deal may fall through, and the seller will be obligated to pay a commission.

Before signing a contract of sale, the buyer should ask itself the following questions and attend to the following matters:

1.   Are there any zoning or environmental laws or ordinances that forbid or hamper the use the buyer wishes to make of the land? Suppose a buyer signs a contract to buy a vacant lot with the intent to erect a filling station on the land and then discovers that the lot is zoned for residences only. The buyer must go through with the deal or breach the contract and suffer the

consequences. Even if the intended use complies with the ordinance, will the plans be approved by the local municipality? For example, will there be adequate off-street parking to comply with the ordinance? For these reasons, contracts for the purchase of land on which a development is to be built will often be conditioned upon the zoning and planning approval of the intended project.

2. Under local ordinances, how far from the front, side, and rear lines must buildings be erected? Does this leave room for the type of building that the purchaser has in mind?

3. If the buyer plans to use a septic tank for sewage disposal, is the lot big enough to qualify under local ordinances?

4. If there is an airport in the vicinity, are there any regulations prohibiting the erection of electric poles or other structures that might prove a hazard to aircraft?

5. Does the building on the property violate existing zoning or building ordinances? If it does, the buyer may be compelled to bring the structure into conformity with the law or even to tear it down.

6. Is the building a nonconforming use? If it is, the buyer cannot enlarge or alter it, or even rebuild it if it is substantially damaged by fire. If the building is legally abandoned, the municipality can forbid its reuse for the nonconforming purpose.

7. Especially if the building is new, has a certificate of occupancy been issued?

8. Does the seller have a permit for any structure that requires a special municipal permit, such as a swimming pool, a water tank on a roof, or a sign that extends over a sidewalk? If the property has a facility that serves alcoholic beverages, can the buyer obtain the necessary liquor license?

9. If the contract of sale states that title will be subject to building restrictions, easements, mineral rights, and so on, how will these affect the buyer's building plans?

10. Are there sewers, water lines, or other utilities in adjoining streets? If so, will the buyer have the legal right to connect to these lines, and what is the connection charge?

11. Are there any utility lines, such as underground lines, drainage ditches, drain tiles, and so on, that will interfere with the building plans?

12. Are existing streets, walks, sewer, and other utilities fully paid for? If not, will they be paid for by the seller or buyer, or by future special assessments?

13. Will the development interfere with the drainage from neighboring land?

14. Keeping in mind that the law often says, "let the buyer beware," are there any defects in the building (e.g., termites, a defective heating plant, a basement that floods, or an inadequate well or septic tank)?

15. Is the soil adequate for the planned building? Should soil tests be performed?

16. Is the building on the land to be purchased or adjoining land so close to the boundary line that, if an owner of one property excavates, there is danger that the building will fall into the excavation?

17. Keeping in mind that the buyer will become personally liable for personal injuries as soon as the deal is closed, are the elevators, boilers, gas, water, and sewer in the building in safe condition? Will the insurance that covers casualty damage to the property, rent loss, and liability be in place before the property is acquired?

18. Are any public projects scheduled for the area that may result in the taking of this property for public use? It is discouraging for a businessperson to build up neighborhood goodwill over a period of time and then find the property taken for a public improvement.

19. Are any zoning or building code changes likely to take place that will interfere with the building plans?

20. Are there any judgments against the buyer? Once the buyer signs a contract to purchase the property, the seller will be obligated to convey the property to the purchaser. The purchaser's creditors may obtain a lien on that property and even take it away from the purchaser through an execution, or judgment, sale.

21. Where the contract calls for the buyer to accept the property subject to "existing leases," what do the leases provide? If the leases contain clauses that are very burdensome to the landlord, the buyer may wish to reconsider purchasing the property or changing the economic terms to account for these unexpected burdens. Estoppel certificates must be obtained from the tenants to ensure that the leases are properly identified, and to verify the basic terms of the lease and determine whether there are any defaults by the landlord or tenant. Certainly, the buyer, who is depending on the rent flow from tenants, does not want to acquire the property only to learn that the tenants claim that the existing landlord is in default under the lease obligations, and the tenants are threatening to terminate their leases or claim material damages against the landlord as a result of those defaults.

22. If the contract requires the buyer to accept the property subject to the existing mortgage, the contract should require the seller to furnish, at closing, a statement signed by the mortgagee showing the balance due on the mortgage and the absence of any defaults. The buyer should check the mortgage to make sure it does not give the mortgagee the right to declare the mortgage debt due in case the mortgagor sells the property without the mortgagee's permission.

23. Has the building been designated as a landmark or historical site? Is it in a flood plain?

24. The buyer should inquire about proposed new construction in the area that might make the neighborhood undesirable for the use intended by the buyer.

25. The buyer should confirm operating costs and taxes and determine whether special property assessments are planned, which could impose an unexpected financial burden on the buyer.

26. Local regulations may require that various certificates be obtained or inspections done to determine whether the property complies with energy laws, building codes, and other ordinances and regulations.

27. Parking should be checked. Does the existing parking satisfy local regulations? Will the planned development satisfy local parking requirements? Is street parking permitted? Is the parking of certain types of vehicles, such as trucks and recreational vehicles, prohibited?

28. The area should be checked for mud slides, floods, or earthquakes. Flood insurance is usually available under a federal program. If earthquake insurance is available, an additional premium probably is required.

29. Questions should be asked about the need for new schools or other public works. Any such governmental improvements may result in tax increases, or the local municipality may require that the buyer contribute to the cost of those projects as a prerequisite to obtaining the approval of the plans for the development.

30. There are many sites where toxic chemicals have been stored or dumped. An environmental audit must be undertaken to determine whether the land has underground storage tanks, hazardous wastes, asbestos, or radon. As an owner, the buyer could become liable for the cost of cleaning the property, even if that cost exceeds the property value.

31. If the buyer plans to rehab an older building, an architect should be consulted before the contract is executed, or during an applicable contingency period. The local municipality may have a "grandfather clause" that insulates older buildings from enforcement of the current building code. When a major rehab occurs, the ordinance may require that the entire building be brought "up to code." This means new wiring, new plumbing, and so forth. The expense may be great.

32. A buyer of an office building must check it carefully. For example, buildings may have inadequate electrical, heating, ventilating, and air conditioning systems that will not accommodate the needs of a modern-day occupant.

33. If the building is new, there may be warranties relating to the roof, heating plant, etc. The contract should require that these warranties be assigned to the buyer.

34. If the buyer intends to occupy parts of the building that are currently leased, the lease cancellation clause must be analyzed for its validity and applicability, and the contract should specify when and how the lease is to be canceled and who is to pay the costs related to any such cancellation. Under some lease cancellation clauses the seller and buyer must both join in the notice of cancellation and attach the contract of sale to the notice.

Before signing the contract, the seller should ask the following questions:

1. Is title to the property is clear? If not, the buyer may be liable for damages if the title cannot be cleared. At a minimum, extra transaction costs will be incurred.

2. What problems may arise with the existing mortgage on the property? If the existing mortgage is to be released, the seller should check to see whether the mortgage has a prepayment clause. The seller should agree with the existing lender on the mechanics for the payment and release of the mortgage at the closing. Will the lender agree to accept payment at the closing and promise to deliver a release to the title company that will insure title in the buyer free of the mortgage, or will the lender deposit the mortgage papers and release or satisfaction in escrow to be delivered when the agreed payoff amount is received? Typically, the seller will use the purchaser's funds to pay off the existing loan at the closing and will not use its own funds to pay off the mortgage debt before then.

3. Does the contract itself contain representations and warranties as to the obligations of the parties to pay brokerage commissions and identify any brokers with whom the parties have dealt?

4. Does the seller know whether it can comply with all ordinances applicable to the property? A number of laws and ordinances have been enacted that require the seller to have the property inspected immediately prior to sale. The inspector is sent by the local building department. If the inspector finds that there are no violations of the building code, the transaction will be allowed to proceed. If the inspector finds violations of the building code or other ordinances, these must be corrected before the deal is closed.

11.08   The Seller

Just as a deed must have a grantor, a contract must have a seller.

EXAMPLE: A hotel known as the Glen House, together with its furniture, was sold at auction to Joseph Grafton for $90,000. He refused to go through with the deal. The only document signed by Grafton was the following:

I, the subscriber, do hereby acknowledge myself to be the purchaser of the estate known as the Glen House, with furniture belonging to it, in Green's Grant, New Hampshire, and sold at auction, Tuesday, May 16, 1871, at 11 o'clock a.m., and for the sum of $90,000, the said property being more particularly described in the advertisement hereunto affixed; and I hereby bind myself, my heirs, and assigns to comply with the terms and conditions of the sale, as declared by the auctioneer at the time and place of sale.

Joseph Grafton

The court held that this was not an enforceable contract of sale, since the seller was not named. *Grafton v. Cummings,* 99 U.S. 100 (1878).

The following are the principal contractual requirements relating to the seller.

1. If title to the property is held by co-owners, all should be named as seller.
2. The seller should be an adult of sound mind.
3. If the seller is a corporation, the sale must be authorized by its directors and, sometimes, by its stockholders.
4. Where the seller is a trustee or executor, it must be determined that the trustee or executor, or other party acting as a representative, has the power to sell the property. Neither an executor nor trustee has the power to sell property unless the will or trust instrument expressly gives that power.

A contract by a shareholder of a corporation to cause the corporation to sell and convey corporate land is valid. *Borg-Warner Corp. v. Anchor Coupling Co.,* 16 Ill. 2d 234, 156 N.E.2d 513 (1958).

**11.08(a)
Subpurchase**

It is not uncommon for a seller in one contract to be the buyer under another contract relating to the same land. This is not necessarily objectionable.

> **EXAMPLE:** Seller contracts to sell to Buyer 1, and Buyer 1 contracts to sell to Buyer 2. They can hold a double closing, preferably in escrow, and Seller and Buyer 1 will get their money, and Buyer 2 will get ownership of the land. *Waggoner v. Saether*, 207 Ill. 32, 107 N.E. 859 (1915).

**11.08(b)   The Seller's
Spouse**

In some states, the spouse of a landowner has certain spousal rights in the land, and these rights cannot be extinguished without the spouse's signature. When the seller's spouse, in such a state, has not signed the contract of sale and refuses to sign a deed to the property, courts differ as to the courses open to the buyer. In general, the buyer may decline to go through with the deal and may obtain return of the down payment on the grounds that the seller is unable to deliver clear title.

In those community property states that require the spouse's consent to a disposition of the community property, the spouse's consent is needed for a valid contract to convey community real estate.

Where land is occupied by a family as their home, regardless of whether the land is owned by the husband or the wife, both must join in any deed of the land. Laws relating to homestead require the signature of both spouses on the deed. Both must join in the contract to sell.

Some states permit either spouse to convey its own property without the signature of the other spouse. In such states, the spouse's signature is not necessary, either on the contract of sale or on the deed, unless, of course, the land to be sold is a homestead.

In states that have abolished dower, but have substituted some statutory interest that the wife retains if she fails to sign the husband's deed, the courts show the same conflict of opinion as prevails in the states that still have dower. Some allow a deduction from the purchase price to compensate the buyer when the seller's spouse refuses to sign the deed and some do not. *Free v. Little,* 31 Utah 449, 88 P. 407 (1907).

The failure of the spouse to join in the contract is considered a harmless mistake if he or she is willing to join in the deed. *Davis v. Dean Vincent, Inc.,* 465 P.2d 702 (Or. 1970).

11.09   The Buyer

Just as a deed must have a grantee, so a contract must have a buyer. The buyer should be named in the contract. If there are two or more buyers and they wish to acquire title as tenants by the entireties, in the case of married people, or as joint tenants, the contract should so state. Special language is needed in many states to accomplish either result. For example, in some states, the deed will describe the grantees "as joint tenants with the right of survivorship and not as tenants by the entireties." In community property states, the contract may call for a deed to " _____ a married man, as his sole and separate property." Or if, in a community property state, the husband and wife wish to own as tenants in common (as may well be the case if each has children by a prior marriage), the contract and deed both will need a clause stating that the buyers have agreed that each will hold a half interest as tenant in common with the other. In such event, the deed must be signed by the grantees to reflect this agreement, and the contract should indicate that the buyers will sign the deed.

If the buyer is a general or limited partnership, a written partnership agreement should have been executed. If a limited partnership is involved, a certificate of partnership should have been recorded.

If the buyer is a corporation, the bylaws and charter should be examined for special requirements, if any, for acquiring the property. A foreign corporation needs a certificate of good standing from the state of its incorporation and should be qualified to do business in the state where the property is located.

11.10 Purchase Price—Payment Provisions

The contract of sale must state the purchase price. A common fault in contracts is the failure to state precisely how the purchase price will be paid. The parties should consider stating what part of the price is allocated to realty and what part is allocated to personal property. Real estate taxes, for example, are based on the value of the real estate. Personal property will have a shorter depreciable life for income tax purposes.

11.11 FIRPTA Withholding

The Foreign Investment in Real Property Tax Act requires that buyers of property withhold a tax equal to 10 percent of the sales price if the seller is a person from another country. 11 U.S.C. § 1445. While the act requires that the transferee withhold only in the case of a disposition of U.S. Real Property Interest by a Foreign Person, the only safe way for the transferee to protect itself is to withhold or fall within the exemptions of the act.

If the seller falls within an exemption from the act's withholding requirements, the seller will want to have the contract drafted in such a manner so as to allow the seller to document the exemption as an alternative to withholding. If an exemption does not apply, the contract should allow the buyer to withhold the appropriate amount from the closing proceeds and, in turn, bind the buyer to make the appropriate payments to the Internal Revenue Service. The seller will probably want this payment to be made through the closing escrow or by the closing agent.

11.12 Property Sold

Disputes over a deficiency in the quantity of land sold are common, especially in the case of farmland. The usual rule is that a deficiency in quantity is immaterial if the sale is *in gross*. A sale in gross is a sale of a specific tract of land by name or description. *See* C.T. Drechsler, Annotation, *Relief by Way of Rescission or Adjustment of Purchase Price for Mutual Mistake as to Quantity of Land, Where the Sale is In Gross,* 1 A.L.R.2d 9, 18 (1948).

> **EXAMPLE:** Seller contracts to sell to Buyer "the Evergreen Ranch in Coles County, Colorado, containing 640 acres, more or less, at a price of $500,000." A survey shows the ranch contains only 620 acres. No deduction will be allowed from the sale price. The sale was of the ranch, not of 640 acres. The fact that the price was a gross price, not a *per acre* price, helps establish this. *See* C.T. Drechsler, Annotation, *Relief by Way of Rescission or Adjustment of Purchase Price for Mutual Mistake as to Quantity of Land, Where the Sale is In Gross,* 1 A.L.R.2d 9, 18 (1948). This rule will be applied unless the deficiency is very great. *Maxwell v. Redd,* 496 P.2d 1320 (Kan. 1972).

Where the sale is on a price-per-acre basis, the buyer is sometimes given relief if there is a deficiency in quantity. *See* Annotation, *Measure and Elements of Damages Recoverable from Vendor Where There Has Been a Mistake as to Amount of Land Conveyed,* 94 A.L.R.3d 1091 (1979).

> **EXAMPLE:** Seller contracted to sell to Buyer "the North seven acres of the Hawkins Tract at a price of $5,000 per acre." The deal was closed and $35,000 paid to Seller. Thereafter, it was discovered the tract conveyed was short three-fourths of an acre. Buyer can sue Seller for the deficiency. *See* E.H. Schopler, Annotation, *Relief by Way of Adjustment of Purchase Price, for Mutual Mistake as to Quantity of Land Where Contract of Sale Fixes Compensation at a Specified Rate per Acre or Other Area Unit,* 153 A.L.R. 37 (1944).

When property is sold by the acre, the parties may want to set the price on a usable acre basis. If this is done, the parties must agree upon the definition of *usable* so that the calculation of the purchase price can be easily accomplished and disputes avoided. For example, if the property to be sold includes a private roadway, or an area that is burdened by an easement in favor of a third party, that area may be disregarded from the computation of the purchase price, if the parties so agree. The surveyor then determines the size of the usable area and the unusable area. The purchase price is then calculated on the basis of the size of the usable area. The important task is to define the parties' intent at the contract stage.

The property sold includes all fixtures that comprise part of the real estate. In the case of commercial buildings, there may be items of personal property that are used in connection with the property that are to pass to the buyer. If so, they should be described in the contract. Without such provision, the buyer is not entitled to any of the items that are not fixtures. It is also a good idea for the contract to specify any items that are excluded from the sale, if that is the parties' intent. Where those items are fixtures, if they are not excluded by the contract, the buyer is entitled to receive them at the closing.

11.12(a) Description of the Land Sold

The contract must contain a reasonably certain description of the land sold. While the description need not be as formal as that contained in a deed, it must be sufficiently definite to identify the land sold with reasonable certainty. *See* W.W. Allen, Annotation, *Sufficiency of Description or Designation of Land in Contract or Memorandum of Sale Under Statute of Frauds,* 23 A.L.R.2d 6 (1952).

There are two views as to the sufficiency of a contract that contains some description of the property but that requires resort to oral testimony to identify the particular property intended to be sold. In states that take a strict view, such contracts are not enforceable.

> **EXAMPLE:** A contract described the land as "real estate situated in the County of Cook and State of Illinois, to wit: One five-room flat and two six-room flats at 3517 Palmer Street." The city in which the land was located was not mentioned. It was held that this description was too indefinite. *Heroux v. Romanowski,* 336 Ill. 297, 168 N.E. 305 (1929). Since verbal evidence would be needed to establish the city and state in which the land is located, the contract is not sufficient. This rule is followed in most states.

On the other hand, liberal courts enforce such contracts.

> **EXAMPLE:** A contract identified land as "305 S. Negley Avenue." Oral testimony was admitted to prove that the seller owned property of this address in Pittsburgh, Pennsylvania, and the contract was enforced. *Sawert v. Lunt,* 62 A.2d 34 (Pa. 1948).

If the city and state are given, a description by street address is sufficient. *See* W.W. Allen, Annotation, *Sufficiency of Description or Designation of Land in Contract or Memorandum of Sale Under Statute of Frauds,* 23 A.L.R.2d 6, 39 (1952). But it is preferable, of course, to use a correct legal description of the land sold.

Where a contract contains a defective street address description but also states that the legal description may be inserted later, the court decisions are conflicting. One line of cases state that the buyer can insert the proper legal description. *Schmalzer v. Jamnik,* 407 Ill. 236, 95 N.E.2d 347 (1950). Other courts hold the contract void. *Murphy v. Morse,* 96 Ga. App. 623, 100 S.E.2d 623 (1957).

Where the seller owns a house and an adjoining vacant lot, great care must be exercised in preparing the description. Likewise, care should be taken where the building has several addresses. *Goebel v. Benefit Trust Life Ins. Co.,* 88 Ill. App. 2d 19, 232 N.E.2d 211 (1967).

At times, a contract for the sale of land refers to a building that the seller is to construct on the land, but the description of the building is totally inadequate. The contract cannot be enforced. *Landgraver v. DeShazer,* 398 P.2d 193 (Or. 1965).

11.13 Completeness   To be enforceable, all the terms of the contract must be settled and none must be left to be determined by future negotiation. *See* W.E. Shipley, Annotation, *Validity and Enforceability of Contract Which Expressly Leaves Open for Future Agreement or Negotiation the Terms of Payment for Property*, 68 A.L.R.2d 1221 (1959),

> **EXAMPLE:** A contract called for a sale price of $75,000, $5,000 cash at "time of possession and balance of payment to be arranged at a later date." This contract is not enforceable, even if the buyer wishes to pay cash. *Murphy v. Koll Grocery Co.,* 311 Ky. 771, 225 S.W.2d 466 (1949). Note that if the contract had simply stated a price of $75,000 and had said nothing regarding terms, the contract would have been enforceable. The court would have read into the contract that a cash deal was intended and that the deal was to be closed in a reasonable time. But since the parties intended something other than a cash deal, and left the exact terms unsettled, the contract was incomplete and unenforceable. Similar holdings followed where a contract stated that the balance of the price was payable "by future agreement on or before January 1, 19_____," *Bentzen v. H.N. Ranch Inc.,* 320 P.2d 440 (Wyo. 1958); where the contract stated that a price of $85,000 was payable "as per terms agreed on," *Roberts v. Adams,* 164 Cal. App. 2d 312, 330 P.2d 900 (1958); where the contract stated "balance in monthly payments," *Cefalu v. Breznik,* 15 Ill. 2d 168, 154 N.E.2d 237 (1958); where the contract said that the balance of $50,000 was payable "as lots are released at purchaser's convenience," *Edward H. Snow Dev. Co. v. Oxsheer,* 62 N.M. 113, 305 P.2d 727 (1957); where the contract called for a purchase money mortgage but failed to specify the due date, *Sweeting v. Campbell,* 8 Ill. 2d 54, 132 N.E.2d 523 (1956); and, where a contract provided that the seller would give the buyer a deed that would reserve a vendor's lien for the balance of the purchase price, and that "the rate of interest will be agreed upon later," *Hume v. Bogle,* 204 S.W. 673 (Tex. Civ. App. 1918).

In other words, where what is written by the parties indicates on its face that parties intended additional terms to be negotiated at some future time, the contract is incomplete. The courts explain that while they can enforce a contract that the parties have made, the courts cannot make or complete a contract that the parties have failed to complete by leaving some provisions for future bargaining. This rule is commonly applied when it appears that some sort of credit sale was contemplated but the terms were not agreed upon. Today's more liberal courts will supply minor or, in some cases, important terms that the parties have omitted. 1 Arthur Linton Corbin, *Corbin on Contracts* §§ 2.8, 4.1–4.5 (rev. ed. 1993 & Supp. 1997); 11 Samuel Williston & Walter H.E. Haeger, *Contracts* § 1424 (3d ed. 1968 & Supp. 1996).

11.13(a) Certainty   In addition to being complete, the contract must be definite and certain. If the court cannot tell what the parties agreed upon, it cannot force them to carry out their agreement.

> **EXAMPLE:** Seller agreed to sell certain land to Buyer for $5,000, "one-half cash, balance one to four years, with interest at 7 percent." This contract is too vague and indefinite to be enforced. No one can be certain what the quoted language means. *Crawford v. Williford,* 145 Ga. 550, 89 S.E. 488 (1916).

11.14 Type of Title, Deed, and Evidence of Title   There are three separate ideas that are sometimes confused.

> **EXAMPLE:** A contract of sale is silent as to the *type of title* the buyer is to receive. In such case, the buyer is entitled to a marketable title, free of all encumbrances. This will be explained later.

> **EXAMPLE:** The contract is silent as to the *type of deed* the buyer is to receive. In some states, the buyer must be content with a quitclaim deed.

> **EXAMPLE:** The contract is silent as to the *type of evidence of title* (abstract, title policy) the buyer is to receive. In such case, the buyer must procure its own evidence of title at its own expense.

11.14(a) Type of Deed

A contract will be enforceable even though it does not specify the type of deed to be given. Nevertheless, since there is a vast difference between a quitclaim deed and a warranty deed, the contract should state the type of deed to be given.

If the contract is silent regarding the type of deed to be given, in some states, the seller need only give a quitclaim deed or a deed of bargain and sale without covenants. *Morris v. Goldthorp,* 390 Ill. 186, 60 N.E.2d 857 (1945); *Boekelheide v. Snyder,* 71 S.D. 470, 26 N.W.2d 74 (1947); *Vitra Seal Co. v. Jaycox,* 62 A.2d 431 (N.J. 1948); Ty*mon v. Linoki,* 16 N.Y.2d 293, 213 N.E.2d 661 (1965); J.R. Kemper, Annotation, *Variance Between Offer and Acceptance in Regard to Title as Affecting Consumation of Contract for Sale of Real Property,* 16 A.L.R.3d 1424, 1430 (1967). This does not excuse the seller from giving a marketable title. It simply means that once the title has been shown to be marketable, the seller may deliver a quitclaim deed and be rid of any possibility of future worry regarding presently unknown title defects. Other states imply that a warranty deed was intended.

It is best for the buyer to insist on a warranty deed. In a few states, the mere fact that the buyer is content to take a quitclaim deed is enough to prevent the buyer from being a bona fide purchaser. Lacking bona fide purchaser status, the buyer will take the land subject to unrecorded deeds, mortgages, liens, and so forth.

> **EXAMPLE:** Pursuant to a contract, Seller gave Buyer a quitclaim deed. Buyer then discovered that Seller had placed an unrecorded mortgage on the property. In some states, a grantee in a quitclaim deed is not a bona fide purchaser and the unrecorded mortgage would be good against Buyer.

The deed should comply with the contract in all respects.

> **EXAMPLE:** Seller contracts to convey to Husband and Wife in joint tenancy. Seller made the deed to Husband only. Wife is entitled to have the deed reformed to run to Husband and Wife as joint tenants. *Wahl v. Fairbanks,* 405 Ill. 290, 90 N.E.2d 735 (1950).

> **EXAMPLE:** Seller contracts to sell to Buyer. The contract calls for a warranty deed. Nothing is said about encroachments. A survey shows the building encroaches three inches into the street. Seller wants to make the warranty deed subject to the encroachment. Seller cannot do so. The deed must follow the contract.

> **EXAMPLE:** Seller contracts to sell to Buyer and to give Buyer a warranty deed. Actually, Seller owns the property in the name of Nominee and offers Buyer a warranty deed signed by Nominee. Buyer does not have to accept the conveyance from Nominee, but may insist upon the conveyance from Seller. A.G.S., Annotation, *Marketable Title,* 57 A.L.R. 1253, 1507 (1928). Some may ask what difference does it make who the grantor may be. The grantor makes certain warranties of title in all but a quitclaim deed. The nominee is typically a shell entity without any assets to enable it to respond to any demands made by the buyer for breach of these warranties. The buyer is entitled to rely upon the creditworthiness of the seller and not the empty-shell nominee.

One must not attach too much importance to the giving of a warranty deed. After all, a crook could execute and deliver a warranty deed purporting to convey title to valuable real estate, and the buyer would receive absolutely nothing. The crook cannot convey what it does not own. A warranty deed is like the frosting on a cake. It's nice to have if the grantor really owns the land. But, if the buyer really wants to know that the seller owns what he or she purports to convey, the buyer must insist on receiving evidence of title, written proof that the seller really owns the land he or she is attempting to convey. Typically, this proof and assurance is in the form of title insurance.

11.14(b)
Marketable Title

Unless the contract provides otherwise, the seller must convey marketable title. Such title is also described as a *merchantable title*. This means that the seller must have good title, free from liens, encumbrances, or defects other than those specified in the contract. As a general rule, every buyer of land has a right to demand a title that shall put it in all reasonable security against loss or annoyance by litigation. The buyer's title should be free from doubt and enable the buyer to hold the property in peace, free from the hazard of litigation. If the buyer wishes to sell the land, the buyer should be reasonably sure that no flaw will come up to disturb its market value. *Firebaugh v. Wittenberg,* 309 Ill. 536, 141 N.E. 379 (1923).

The contract should contain a *subject to* clause specifying the permitted objections. These are the matters that are known to encumber the title. Many of these matters may have encumbered the title when the buyer acquired the property. Others may have been created by the buyer, such as an easement for the benefit of a local utility. These matters are usually of a character such that they cannot be removed. Easements and building restrictions are a good example. In many cases, the buyer finds these matters unobjectionable. As long as they are listed in the subject to clause, they do not render the title unmarketable under the contract.

The marketable title problem has two aspects. First, the earlier history of the title may contain defective deeds and other such matters. Second, the title must not be subject to easements, liens, or other "encumbrances," except those specified in the contract.

In every state, and even in different localities within a state, lawyers have struggled to evolve lists of permitted objections appropriate to the locality. Such lists often find their way into printed contract forms prepared by bar associations, real estate boards, and title companies. Several dangers must be considered when using these forms. Since new laws are enacted constantly, there is always danger that a form may be outdated. A form appropriate to one locality must not be used elsewhere. A form suitable for a residential transaction may be totally inapplicable to a purchase of vacant land or an office building.

Law students are puzzled at times by an apparent conflict between two situations. They know that *recording imparts constructive notice.* All persons are deemed to know what the public records reveal. Why, then, is it customary to set forth in the contract of sale the permitted encumbrances that the buyer must accept, even in generic form, such as building restrictions of record? The problem lies in the resolution of three competing factors. At this point, the parties want to come to agreement, the buyer will accept title to the property subject only to certain matters, and the seller wants to know the buyer has agreed to accept title to the property encumbered by certain generalized exceptions. In point of fact, the parties cannot be certain what encumbrances exist until the title search has been completed. This search is made *after* a bargain has been struck and a contract signed.

As can readily be seen, the rules of law that operate on a point that the parties have failed to cover in their contract are often hopelessly impractical, and the parties cannot leave the outcome to chance and litigation. It is for this reason that lawyers and form writers constantly "draft around" these rules. And, of course, even the forms are often imperfect and require modification. This is usually the task of the lawyer. Real estate brokers or salespeople are, in many states, forbidden to change forms to fit the situation. This is considered the unauthorized practice of law.

One of the important functions of contracts, then, is to spell out the rights and duties of the parties so as to reach a result different from that offered by the rules of law. This is perfectly legal and is done constantly.

> **EXAMPLE:** The contract of sale should list the encumbrances the seller is powerless to remove and which the buyer agrees to accept. Building restrictions contained in the plat of subdivision are an example if they are not violated by present uses of the property.

> **EXAMPLE:** The contract of sale may provide that within _____ days the seller will deliver to the buyer a title commitment.

The question of marketability of title must be disposed of before the deal is closed. In other words, if the buyer wishes to avail itself of the right to insist upon a marketable title, the buyer must point out such defects as they are discovered and before the purchase price is paid and the deed delivered. Once the deal is closed, the buyer cannot demand the money back if the title proves defective. A.G.S., Annotation, *Marketable Title*, 57 A.L.R. 1253, 1261 (1928); Charles S. Parnell, Annotation, *Deed as Superseding or Merging Provisions of Antecedent Contract Imposing Obligations upon the Vendor,* 38 A.L.R.2d 1310 (1954); 92 C.J.S. *Vendor & Purchaser* §§ 184, 552 (1955). However, if the buyer has received a warranty deed from the seller and that deed does not list an objectional encumbrance in its subject to clause, the buyer may sue the seller for damages.

11.14(b)(1) Marketable Title— Mortgages and Other Liens

Unless the contract provides otherwise, the buyer has the right to demand a title free and clear of all mortgages, tax liens, judgment liens, mechanics' liens, and all other liens. It is not sufficient for the seller to offer to deduct the amount of such liens from the purchase price. The buyer may reject the title unless it is actually cleared of such liens. Suppose, however, that there is a mortgage or other lien on the property, and the seller can arrange to have the mortgage paid in full out of the purchase money due to the seller and cause the mortgagee to deliver a release of the mortgage to the escrowee or title company that is closing the deal. Must the buyer go through with the deal in this manner if the contract does not require it to do so? In most states, the answer is in the affirmative. The title is not considered unmarketable if the seller can arrange to have the owner of the mortgage, judgment, or other lien present at the closing of the deal ready to turn over proper releases to the buyer on receiving payment of the amount due from the buyer. *Kaiser v. Wright,* 629 P.2d 581 (Colo. 1981); Jack W. Shaw, Jr., Annotation, *Vendor and Purchaser: Marketability of Title as Affected by Lien Dischargeable Only Out of Funds to Be Received from Purchaser at Closing,* 53 A.L.R.3d 678 (1973).

Nonetheless, the contract should specifically allow the seller to apply the purchase money to the payment of the liens and encumbrances. In reality, the lienholder is rarely at the closing. Rather, in what is more commonly the case, the title company that closes the deal takes a payoff statement from the lienholder and withholds an amount from the seller's proceeds so that this lien can be paid in full. The title company then insures the buyer and the buyer's lender without exception for the prior lien, even though the lien itself has not yet actually been released of record.

11.14(b)(2) Marketable Title— Easements

In general, easements render the title unmarketable unless, of course, the contract requires the buyer to take title to the property subject to easements. Recent decisions have held, however, that title is not rendered unmarketable by the existence of visible easements that benefit the property.

> **EXAMPLE:** The contract is silent regarding easements. A utility company has an easement over the rear five feet of the land for an electric power line, and such a power line is, in fact, located on the rear five feet of the land. The power line services the property in question. In many states, the title would be considered marketable. A.G.S., Annotation, *Marketable Title*, 57 A.L.R. 1253, 1426 (1928)

The seller should check its title insurance policy or other evidence of title to see if it shows the title to be subject to an easement. If the title evidence reveals the presence of such an easement, the contract should specifically include the easement in the subject to provision. For example, the contract should state that the title will be subject "to easement recorded with the Recorder of _____ County, _____ on _____ ___, 19__, as Document No. 1234567." The buyer, on the other hand, should not sign a contract with such a provision until the easement has been reviewed and its terms deemed to be acceptable to the buyer, or sign a contract stating that the seller will deliver title subject "to easements of record." The buyer would be obligated to take the title subject to the identified easement in the first instance and any recorded easement in the second instance, even if the easement was for a one-hundred-foot highway running right through the middle of the land.

11.14(b)(3)
Marketable Title—
Building Restrictions

Often the use to which a tract of land may be devoted is controlled by building restrictions contained in recorded deeds, declarations of covenants, conditions and restrictions, or subdivision plats. Unless the contract provides otherwise, the buyer is not required to accept a title encumbered with restrictions as to the character of the buildings that may be erected, the use to which the property may be put, and so on, even though such restrictions may in fact enhance the value of the property.

> **EXAMPLE:** Seller contracts to sell to Buyer a vacant lot in an upscale residential development. The contract does not mention restrictions. The recorded plat of the subdivision contains a restriction providing that only single-family dwellings may be built on the lots. Buyer may reject the title encumbered by this restriction. A.G.S., Annotation, *Marketable Title*, 57 A.L.R. 1253, 1414 (1928)

Suppose the contract requires the buyer to accept title to the property subject to "building lines and building restrictions," and the building on the property violates existing restrictions. The buyer may decline to go through with the deal, for a *violation of a restriction* is a defect or encumbrance separate and distinct from the restriction itself.

> **EXAMPLE:** A contract required the buyer to accept the title subject to building and use restrictions. There was a building restriction prohibiting the erection of buildings within five feet of any side lot line. The buildings actually extended into the prohibited area. It was held that the buyer could refuse to go through with the deal. *Hebb v. Severson,* 32 Wash. 2d 159, 201 P.2d 156 (1948); *Lohmeyer v. Bower,* 170 Kan. 442, 227 P.2d 102 (1951).

The buyer should never sign a contract that states that title will be subject to "restrictions of record." This provision obligates the buyer to take title to the property subject to any restriction, no matter how absurd, even a restriction that the only building permitted on the land is a chicken coop. If the seller's title insurance policy is available, the buyer should review that policy, as a source of information about the seller's title. If time permits, the buyer should obtain current title evidence before entering into the contract. If that title evidence shows a restriction, it also should be reviewed. If the buyer has no objection to it, let the contract read that title will be subject to the specifically identified restriction. Where the contract must be signed at a time when information on existing building restrictions is not available, and the land is improved with a building that is the principal subject matter of the sale, you might employ the following clause: "Subject to covenants and restrictions of record, provided same are not violated by the existing improvements and the use thereof." When you are buying *vacant* land you *must* insist on reading the restrictions in full before signing the contract.

An approach that favors the buyer, while at the same time allowing the contract to be executed, is to include a contract provision that requires the seller to deliver to the buyer a current title commitment that is accompanied by copies of all recorded and other documents referenced in the commitment. The contract will then expressly allow the buyer to reject the title and cancel the contract if any of the encumbrances are unacceptable to the buyer.

**11.14(b)(4)
Marketable Title—
Zoning and Building
Code Violations**

Building restrictions imposed by deeds or plats must be distinguished from zoning and building ordinances. Such ordinances, though they may greatly restrict the use that may be made of the land, do not render the title unmarketable. Generally, the attitude of the courts is that zoning and building ordinances are part of the law of the land, and all persons are supposed to take notice of them. Peter G. Guthrie, Annotation, *Zoning or Other Public Restrictions on the Use of Property as Affecting Rights and Remedies of Parties to Contract for the Sale Thereof,* 39 A.L.R.3d 362, 370 (1971). Ignorance of the law excuses no one.

Suppose, however, that the property contains existing violations of zoning or building ordinances. Here, the rule is different. Courts tend to hold that substantial existing violations of zoning ordinances render a title unmarketable. 3 *American Law of Property* § 11.49 (1952); *Lohmeyer v. Bower,* 170 Kan. 442, 227 P.2d 102 (1951); *Moyer v. De Vincentis Constr. Co.,* 107 Pa. Super. 588, 164 A. 111 (1933); *Hartman v. Rizzuto,* 123 Cal. App. 2d 186, 266 P.2d 539 (1954); Peter G. Guthrie, Annotation, *Zoning or Other Public Restrictions on the Use of Property as Affecting Rights and Remedies of Parties to Contract for the Sale Thereof,* 39 A.L.R.3d 362, 375 (1971).

> **EXAMPLE:** A building containing three apartments was erected in an area where the ordinance prohibited construction of a building containing more than two apartments. The court held that the buyer could terminate the contract and obtain return of his down payment. *Oatis v. Delcuze,* 226 La. 751, 77 So. 2d 28 (1954).

In many cities, violations of building ordinances (like those forbidding basement apartments, requiring certain minimum sanitary arrangements, separate exits for each apartment, or fireproof material, etc.) now entail drastic punishment. Cities have come to recognize that the fight against slums and blight is a fight for survival. Building ordinance violations, like zoning ordinance violations, are being recognized as flaws in the marketability of title, for they impose on a purchaser the same hazards of litigation that the rule of marketability of title was designed to avoid. *Brunke v. Pharo,* 3 Wis. 2d 628, 89 N.W.2d 221 (1958), *noted in* Wis. L. Rev. 641 (1958); *Bronen v. Marmer,* 206 N.Y.S.2d 909 (1960). *But see Stone v. Sexsmith,* 28 Wash. 2d 947, 184 P.2d 567 (1947); *Ableman v. Slader,* 80 Ill. App. 2d 94, 224 N.E.2d 569 (1967).

The prudent buyer of commercial or multifamily property will insist that the contract of sale provide that the seller will deliver the property "free from all violations of zoning and building ordinances," and undertake a due diligence check with local municipal officials for such violations before being obligated to close the deal.

> **EXAMPLE:** The transaction involved a house with an illegal basement apartment. The seller could not bring the building into compliance by tearing out the illegal apartment, because the

contract contemplated the seller getting a permit from the city to legalize the condition as it was when the contract was signed. As it stands, the title is unmarketable. *Hammer v. Michael,* 243 N.Y. 445, 154 N.E. 305 (1926). *See* Peter G. Guthrie, Annotation, *Zoning or Other Public Restrictions on the Use of Property as Affecting Rights and Remedies of Parties to Contract for the Sale Thereof,* 39 A.L.R.3d 362 (1971).

Advertising for sale a building that contains ordinance violations with the implication that the property does not violate the zoning law may constitute a fraud upon the buyer. A comparable problem arises when a warranty deed is given that makes no mention of zoning or building code violations. Some courts say that the grantor is not liable. *Domer v. Sleeper,* 533 P.2d 9 (Alaska 1975); *Marathon Builders, Inc. v. Polinger,* 263 Md. 410, 283 A.2d 617 (1971). Other courts hold the grantor liable. *Wilcox v. Pioneer Homes, Inc.* 41 N.C.A. 140, 254 S.E.2d 214 (1979).

11.14(b)(5)
Marketable Title—
Leases and Tenancies

Unless the contract so provides, the buyer need not accept a title subject to existing leases or existing tenancies without leases. *Haiss v. Schmukler,* 201 N.Y.S. 332 (1923). If any such leases or tenancies exist, the contract should provide that the title is subject to the rights of tenants under leases, written or oral. The buyer, however, should not execute a contract binding itself to accept title subject to existing leases and tenancies, unless the buyer has satisfied itself that the leases and occupancy rights are acceptable. Alternatively, the buyer may be given a stated period of time after the execution of the contract to examine the leases and terminate the contract if, within the time period, the buyer finds the leases to be unacceptable and so notifies the seller.

There are many reasons for the purchaser to take these precautionary steps. The leases may be below market and therefore not provide the expected economic return to the buyer. Alternatively, a lease may have the effect of preventing a use that the buyer wishes to make of the property. For example, if the buyer wants to redevelop the property, the term of existing tenant leases may frustrate the buyer's plans, unless the buyer enters into a favorable settlement with the tenants to encourage them to terminate their leases. In the worst of cases, a tenant may have an option to purchase the property, perhaps at a stated price that is less than the price the buyer is willing to pay.

Since the existing leases may be disadvantageous to the property owner, the contract should include a schedule of the leases and all amendments thereto represented as being accurate and complete by the seller. The buyer's attorney will then read the leases to advise the buyer of their terms.

11.14(b)(6)
Marketable Title—
Encroachments

Encroachments are generally of three kinds: (1) The building on the land sold may encroach onto neighboring land; (2) the building on the land sold may encroach onto adjoining streets or alleys; (3) buildings on adjoining land may encroach upon the land sold. L.S. Tellier, Annotation, *Encroachment of Structure on or over Adjoining Property or Way as Rendering Title Unmarketable,* 47 A.L.R.2d 331 (1956). The survey should depict these encroachments.

When the seller's buildings extend onto neighboring land, the factor that renders a title unmarketable is the danger that the neighbor may initiate litigation to obtain a court order directing removal of the offending portion of the structure, a task that may involve great expense. The buyer also will be put to the expense of defending the litigation. This concept is in harmony with the principle that a title is not marketable if there is an appreciable risk of litigation. *Very slight* encroachments will not render the title unmarketable, as where a wall of the building on the premises sold extends three-quarters of an inch onto neighboring land. *Traxler v. McLeran,* 116 Cal. App. 226, 2 P.2d 553 (1931). The reason such property remains marketable is that if the encroachment of a building onto adjoining land is slight, the cost of removal is great, and the benefit to the adjoining landowner from removal of the building is slight, courts will not compel removal of the encroachment. *Nitterauer v. Pulley,* 401 Ill. 494, 82 N.E.2d 643 (1948). The application of the same theory may yield a different result when the building that encroaches on neighboring land is old or dilapidated, or a temporary structure of small value, or a structure that is removable at only slight effort or expense. In these instances, the title is deemed marketable.

It is hard to draw the line between objectionable and unobjectionable encroachments when permanent structures are involved. The encroachment of a house one and one-half inches on neighboring land has been held to render title unmarketable. *Stokes v. Johnson,* 57 N.Y. 673 (1874). When buildings on neighboring land encroach on the premises being sold, courts are more liberal. At the worst, the buyer will be deprived of some portion of the land that the seller has agreed to sell. If the area occupied by the encroaching building is insignificant when compared with the total area of the land being sold, the title is marketable. *Merges v. Ringler,* 54 N.Y.S. 280 (1898).

When buildings on the land sold extend over adjoining streets or alleys, as in the case of buildings extending over and upon neighboring privately owned land, there is danger that a suit will be instituted to compel removal of the encroachment. The title is unmarketable. Still, if the encroachment is trivial, so that action by the city authorities is highly improbable and it is unlikely that a court would order the encroachment removed, the title is marketable.

> **EXAMPLE:** A building encroached two inches onto an adjoining street. The title was held to be marketable. *Mertens v. Berendsen,* 213 Cal. 111, 1 P.2d 440 (1931).

Suppose the contract provides that the seller agrees to deliver a title "subject to questions of survey" or "subject to such a state of facts as an accurate survey would show." Such clauses are inserted to relieve the seller of all responsibility with respect to encroachments. If the existence of encroachments is revealed, the buyer must nevertheless go through with the deal. *McCarter v. Crawford,* 245 N.Y. 43, 156 N.E. 90 (1927). If, on the other hand, the contract requires the seller to deliver title "free from all encumbrances and encroachments," the existence of trivial encroachments, such as would ordinarily not render title unmarketable, will nevertheless justify the buyer's rejection of the title.

11.14(b)(7)
Marketable Title—
Chattels

Many sales of land specifically include chattels that are valuable in themselves, or essential to the operation of the property as a whole, as, for example, when a hotel is being sold. The buyer is entitled to marketable title to the chattels. *Peters v. Spielvogel,* 163 So. 2d 59 (Fla. App. 1964). To determine whether the chattels are encumbered by liens, Uniform Commercial Code financing statement searches are ordered and typically updated just prior to the closing. These searches do not , however, show who owns the chattels. The buyer will typically rely upon the seller's representations as to ownership. Where the chattels are especially valuable, due diligence into the ownership of the chattels may be conducted.

11.14(b)(8)
Marketable Title—
Miscellaneous
Defects

There are many other defects or encumbrances that may render a title unmarketable. For example, a deed signed by some prior landowner may be defective in that the property is not properly described in that old deed, or a signature may be lacking, or the grantor's spouse may have failed to sign the deed. Court proceedings on which the title depends, such as mortgage foreclosures, sales by guardians, and the like, may have been defectively conducted. Estates of deceased prior landowners may have been improperly probated. An example is found in the recent case of *Create 21 Chuo, Inc. v. Southwest Slopes, Inc.,* 918 P.2d 1168 (Haw. App. 1996), in which the court found that archaeological sites and possible customary rights of native tenants impair the marketability of property purchased for development purposes.

An undisclosed, abandoned underground storage tank will not of itself render title unmarketable. *See generally Holly Hill Holdings v. Lowman,* 619 A.2d 853 (Conn. App. 1993), *aff'd.,* 226 Conn. 748, 628 A.2d 1298 (1993). Similarly, the title to land that is environmentally contaminated is not unmarketable merely because of the environmental contamination. *HM Holdings, Inc. v. Rankin,* 70 F.3d 933 (7th Cir. 1995).

Marketability of title plays an important part in those situations where the buyer, after having executed a purchase contract, regrets the bargain and wishes to get out of the deal. The buyer's attorney will then subject the title to a minute scrutiny, hoping to find some defect that renders the title unmarketable, so that the client may declare the contract at an end and obtain the return of the down payment.

**11.14(b)(9)
Marketable Title—
Title Insurance**

The fact that a title company is willing to insure the seller's title does not make it marketable.

> **EXAMPLE:** Seller entered into a contract to sell real estate to Buyer. The contract required Seller to furnish a clear policy of title insurance. The title search revealed a recorded easement. The title company was willing to issue a clear policy. Buyer was permitted to back out of the deal. Buyer is entitled to a marketable title and title insurance under these circumstances. *New York Investors, Inc. v. Manhattan Beach Bathing Parks Corp.,* 243 N.Y.S. 548 (1930), *aff'd,* 176 N.E. 6 (1931).

From the seller's perspective, the contract should provide that the title policy is conclusive evidence that the title is good as therein stated, but it shall not be evidence of any matters not insured by said policy. This relieves the seller of the obligation to deliver a marketable title, and eliminates the possibility that the buyer may attempt to flyspeck the title to get out of the deal.

**11.14(b)(10)
Marketable
Title—Laws**

As time goes by, it has grown increasingly difficult to prove that any real estate title is marketable. Year by year, the chain of deeds, mortgages, wills, and other recorded matters relating to the title, beginning with the original grant from the government, grows longer and more complex. In consequence, abstracts of title and title searches grow longer, more difficult, and more complex. The sheer number of transactions affecting the title to a parcel of property gives rise to many more opportunities for technical errors that impair the marketability of title. A solution for these difficulties had to be found.

In many states, laws have been passed to promote the marketability of title. In general, such laws select a particular period of time. In Illinois, for example, the period is forty years. 735 ILCS § 5/13-118 0. If an examination of the public records shows that for the last forty years title to a particular tract of land has passed from one person to another in a connected fashion, that this connected chain of title culminates in a deed to *X,* and that *X* is in peaceable possession of the land in question, *X* will be deemed to have good and marketable title to that tract of land, free and clear from any adverse claims to the title that antedate the forty-year period.

This does not mean that all claims that are beyond the statutory period are automatically wiped out. Each of these marketability laws provides a period of time during which a person claiming an interest that is more than the statutory period may record an affidavit or other claim stating the nature of its interest in a particular piece of land. In this fashion, any claim to the title of land must appear on the records within the statutory period, or it is automatically outlawed. Consequently, a person searching the title to the land need only search the title during the statutory period, and if a connected chain is found, the title search may disregard recorded matters that antedate the period.

This does not mean that all matters that were first recorded prior to the statutory period may be disregarded. Each of these marketability laws lists certain interests that are not affected or outlawed by the marketable title legislation.

> **EXAMPLE:** A common provision of marketability of title laws is to the effect that a person claiming an easement need not record its claim of easement if the existence of the easement is revealed by a physical examination of the land itself. Thus, if a neighbor claims party wall rights or an easement for a driveway extending over the premises, it is fairly clear that a mere glance at the property will reveal the existence of such easement claims. Therefore, they need not be rerecorded.

Another common exception relates to claims of the U.S. Government. No state has the power to pass laws that extinguish the rights of the U.S. Government. Whatever the claim may be, if it does not fall within the list of claims not affected by the legislation, it is outlawed unless a document in proper form showing the existence of such claim is recorded within the statutory period. See Jay M. Zitter, Annotation, *Construction and Effect of "Marketable Record Title" Statutes,* 31 A.L.R.4th 11 (1984); Walter L. Barnett, *Marketable Title Acts—Panacea or Pandemonium?,* 53 Cornell L. Rev. 45 (1967); Note, *Constitutionality of Marketable Title Legislation,* 47 Iowa L. Rev. 413 (1962); Robert E. Adams, Note, *Real Property—Promoting the Marketability of Land Titles,* 46 Ky. L.J. 605 (1958); Ralph W. Aigler, *A Supplement to Constitutionality of Marketable Title Acts,* 56 Mich. L. Rev. 225 (1957); Ray J. Aiken, *Proposed Title Legislation: A Suggested Solution to the Problem of Marketable Title,* 50 Marq. L. Rev. 15 (1966); Lewis M. Simes, *The Improvement of Conveyancing: Recent Developments,* 34 The Journal (Okla. B. Ass'n) 2357 (1963); Ann Litherland, *Marketablity Acts: A Step Forward for Title Examination Procedure in Illinois,* 1957 U. Ill. L.F. 491; Basye, *Clearing Land Titles* §§ 171–189 (2d ed. 1970).

11.14(c)   Time of Existence of Good Title

Ordinarily, the seller need not have good title on the date of the contract. It is sufficient if the seller has good title at the time the deed is to be delivered, or even later, for example, at the time the court, in a specific performance suit, orders the contract to be enforced. *Gibson v. Brown,* 214 Ill. 330, 73 N.E. 578 (1905).

If the contract provides that time is of the essence and also provides that the seller will furnish the buyer an abstract of title or other evidence of title within a specified period of time, the seller must meet this deadline, or the buyer will have the right to declare the contract at an end.

11.14(d)   Evidence of Title

It is important to distinguish between the seller's duty to deliver good title and the seller's duty to furnish evidence that title is good. As stated previously, unless the contract provides otherwise, the seller must furnish the buyer a *marketable title*. But, if the contract does not require the seller to do so, the seller is under no obligation to furnish the buyer *any evidence that the title is good.* The buyer gets its own title evidence unless the contract specifies otherwise. Indeed, this is the custom in some areas.

11.14(d)(1) Time for Furnishing Evidence of Title and Curing Defects in Title

If the contract requires the seller to furnish evidence of title, but does not fix a time limit for the furnishing and examination of the abstract or other evidence of title, it is assumed that a reasonable time was intended. In such case, the seller has a reasonable time to furnish the buyer the abstract or other evidence of title, the buyer has a reasonable time to examine the abstract and point out defects in title, and the seller has a reasonable time to eliminate or cure the defects.

To eliminate uncertainties and speculation by either party on the rise or fall of the value of the property before choosing to perform its part of the contract, the contract should

1. Fix the time allowed the seller to furnish the buyer evidence of title. When the contract requires the seller to furnish evidence of title by a certain date and provides that time is of the essence, and the title evidence is not furnished by the agreed date, the buyer may rescind (i.e., declare the contract terminated) and may recover its deposit. *Johnson v. Riedier,* 395 Ill. 412, 70 N.E.2d 570 (1941). Most contracts fix a specific time for furnishing the evidence of title and provide that time is of the essence.

2. Fix the time allowed to the buyer to examine the title evidence and point out any defects in title. Failure to do so constitutes an acceptance of the title in the condition presented.

3. Fix the time allowed the seller to cure defects in title.

4. Fix a time within which the buyer must choose to accept or reject a defective title that the seller cannot cure within the time allowed.

11.15 Earnest Money

Earnest money is a deposit or down payment made by the buyer as a guaranty that the contract will be performed on its part. If the buyer does perform, the earnest money applies as a part payment of the purchase price. If the buyer defaults, the earnest money may be retained by the seller. Usually, the contract specifically permits the seller to retain the earnest money where the buyer defaults. But even in the absence of such a provision, a buyer who is in default cannot recover its earnest money from the seller. *Zirinsky v. Sheehan,* 413 F.2d 481 (1969). *See also* James O. Pearson, Jr., Annotation, *Modern Status of Defaulting Vendee's Right to Recover Contractual Payments Withheld by Vendor as Forfeited,* 4 A.L.R.4th 993 (1981). Courts have allowed the seller to retain rather substantial down payments—for example, $300,000 on a sale price of $3,000,000, and $35,000 on a sale price of $140,000. Arthur L. Corbin, *The Right of a Defaulting Vendee to the Restitution of Installment Unpaid,* 40 Yale L.J. 1013 (1931). But retention of an earnest money deposit of $30,000 on a sale for $95,000 is unconscionable. *Hook v. Bomar,* 320 F.2d 536 (5th Cir. 1963).

For its protection, the seller should require a deposit large enough to cover the broker's commission, the costs incurred in negotiating the contract and preparing for the closing of the aborted deal, and compensation to the seller for the loss of its bargain should the buyer default. For the buyer's protection, the contract should provide that the earnest money will be held in escrow by a third person pending the closing of the deal. This helps to ensure that the buyer will experience a minimum of difficulty in obtaining the return of the deposit should it prove impossible for the seller to deliver clear title, or should the seller otherwise be unable or unwilling to perform. If the seller insists that its broker hold the earnest money, let the contract provide that if the broker fails to return the money to the buyer when the buyer is entitled to it, the seller will pay the amount of the earnest money to the buyer. This will force the seller to think twice about entrusting a large amount of money to an individual. Banks, title companies, and trust companies charge a very small fee for holding earnest money deposits.

If the buyer deposits a check as earnest money, the buyer should be sure there are adequate funds in the bank account to cover the check. If the seller attempts to have the check certified, and the bank refuses because funds are lacking, the seller then has the right to refuse to carry out the deal. *Gallinaro v. Fitzpatrick,* 267 N.E.2d 649 (Mass. 1971).

There is a common misconception shared by the seller and the broker with respect to earnest money. They tend to view the earnest money as belonging to the seller. This is not the case.

> **EXAMPLE:** Buyer pays Seller earnest money, but Seller's title proves defective. Obviously, Seller must refund Buyer's earnest money. This suffices to show that the money is held by Seller for the benefit of both parties at least until Seller shows that the seller is able to perform. 40 Yale L.J. 1030, *supra.* Until then, Seller's right to the earnest money is inchoate, that is, it has not yet ripened. E. LeFevre, Annotation, *Broker's Liability to Prospective Purchaser for Refund of Deposit or Earnest Money Where Contract Fails Because of Defects in Vendor's Title*, 38 A.L.R.2d 1382, 1384 (1954).

11.16   Mortgages and Financing in Real Estate Sales

Several possibilities are present in the financing of real estate sales:

1. The property may be unencumbered, and the buyer may be ready to pay cash. No mortgage figures in the sale of the land.
2. The property may be unencumbered, but the seller may be willing to accept the purchase price partly in cash and take a purchase money mortgage for the remainder of the purchase price. For example, a lender may own a building that it has acquired by foreclosure of a mortgage. To induce a buyer to purchase the building, the lender may be willing to accept part of the purchase price by way of a purchase money mortgage.
3. The property may be unencumbered, but the buyer will need to mortgage the property in order to raise the full purchase price.
4. The property may be subject to an existing mortgage, and the buyer may be willing to acquire the property subject to that mortgage.
5. The property may be subject to an existing mortgage, but that mortgage may be too small, or its payments may not fit the buyer's cash flow needs. In such case, it will be necessary for the buyer to put a new mortgage on the property for the required amount, payable on such terms as will meet the buyer's needs. The sale will involve paying off the seller's existing mortgage and simultaneously placing the buyer's new mortgage on the property.
6. The sale may be by an installment contract with a clause reserving the right to the seller to mortgage the land, with the buyer's agreement to take title subject to the mortgage.
7. The sale may be by an installment contract with a provision that the buyer will receive the deed when a specified amount is paid. The buyer will then give a mortgage to the seller for the balance of the purchase price.
8. The sale may be by an installment contract with no mortgage provisions. Some states have special laws that apply in such circumstances. For example, in Maryland, a law provides that when the purchaser in an installment contract has paid 40 percent of the purchase price, it is entitled to demand a deed upon executing a purchase money mortgage to the seller for the balance. Md. Code Ann., Real Property § 10-105.

Unless the contract provides otherwise, the buyer need not accept a title subject to a mortgage. If there is a mortgage on the land and the buyer is to accept the land with the mortgage remaining unpaid, the contract should specify that the land being sold is subject to such mortgage, the amount of the unpaid balance of the loan, and whether the buyer will *assume and agree* to pay the mortgage, since if the buyer does agree, the buyer will become personally liable to the mortgagee for the mortgage debt. If the buyer does not assume and agree to pay the mortgage, the buyer may lose the land by foreclosure should it default in the payment of the mortgage, but no personal judgment can be rendered against the buyer for the unpaid debt.

The contract should also specify whether the seller requires that it be released from liability by the lender. If the seller is not, or cannot be, so released from liability with respect to the loan, the seller may want the buyer to indemnify the seller from loss that the seller may suffer as a result of the buyer's defaults under the loan documents. If the contract calls for the buyer to take the land subject to a mortgage, but misdescribes the mortgage, the buyer can back out of the deal. *Crooke v. Nelson,* 195 Iowa 681, 191 N.W. 122 (1922).

11.17 Contingent Contracts

Often, a clause will be inserted in a contract making it subject to some contingency, so that if the specified event does not occur, the buyer will be released from its obligation to close the transaction and be entitled to the refund of the earnest money. Usually, such clauses are inserted at the buyer's request. A common example is a clause making the contract contingent on the buyer's ability to procure a mortgage loan of a specified sum. Other examples include a clause making the contract contingent on the buyer's ability to procure a liquor license, or a clause making the contract contingent on the rezoning of the premises within a specified time. Peter G. Guthrie, Annotation, *Zoning or Other Public Restrictions on the Use of Property as Affecting Rights and Remedies of Parties to Contract for the Sale Thereof,* 39 A.L.R.3d 362, 385 (1971). For example, if a buyer plans to redevelop industrial property for residential use and the property is zoned for industrial use, the buyer will insist that the contract contain a provision rendering it void unless appropriate rezoning is obtained within a certain number of days. Today, contracts are often contingent upon the purchaser receiving certain economic benefits that make a proposed project economically feasible.

At times, contingency clauses tend to be rather vague. Nevertheless, some courts will enforce them.

> **EXAMPLE:** Where the contract called for a soil compaction report satisfactory to the buyer, the court held that this meant a report satisfactory to a reasonable person. *Collins v. Vickter Manor,* 47 Cal. 2d 875, 306 P.2d 783 (1957).

Some, but not all, modern decisions sanction a good bit of indefiniteness in contingency clauses.

> **EXAMPLE:** A contract stated it was contingent on the buyer's procuring a mortgage loan of a stated sum "with interest at current prevailing rate." The clause was held to be sufficiently definite. *Barto v. Hicks,* 124 Ga. App. 472, 184 S.E.2d 188 (1971).

> **EXAMPLE:** A contract of sale for $28,000 stated it was contingent on the buyer obtaining a mortgage of $_____. The court held that a mortgage for a "reasonable amount" was intended, and when the buyer tried to get a mortgage of $21,000 and failed, the contract was at an end. *Grayson v. LaBranche,* 225 A.2d 922 (1967).

11.17(a) Contingent Contracts—Financing

Where a contract has a financing contingency, the buyer must make a reasonable effort to procure that financing. *Fry v. George Elkins Co.,* 327 P.2d 905 (Cal. App. 1958). What a reasonable effort may be is not always clear. A buyer who fails to make a reasonable effort is guilty of *bad faith.* As a result, the contingency clause becomes void and the buyer will lose the earnest money if the buyer does not close. The buyer must act in good faith. Ray J. Aiken, *"Subject to Financing" Clauses in Interim Contracts for the Sale of Realty,* 43

Marq. L. Rev. 265 (1960); Patricia Jursik, *Subject to Financing Clause—Escalator Provision in Mortgage Commitment Fails to Satisfy Specificity Requirement in Offer to Purchase,* 62 Marq. L. Rev. 123 (1978); Donald M. Zupanec, Annotation, *Sufficiency of Real-Estate Buyer's Efforts to Secure Financing upon Which Sale Is Contingent,* 78 A.L.R.3d 880 (1977).

It is best that the contract give details of the mortgage to be obtained, such as the interest rate, time of payment, and so forth. Often the contract gives the buyer a period of time to procure financing, and, if the buyer fails, the seller is then given an additional period to procure financing for the buyer. A seller may procure a mortgage loan of the desired amount for the buyer and the buyer reject it in horror because the interest rate or the loan costs and points are too high. Obviously, all such details should be covered in the clause. If, however, the details are omitted, the courts are likely to insist that the terms of the offered mortgage be "reasonable," otherwise the buyer is not required to accept it. *Lach v. Cahill,* 138 Conn. 418, 85 A.2d 481 (1951); *Chambers v. Jordan,* 262 A.2d 505 (Md. 1970). Minds differ as to what is reasonable, and controversy and litigation easily develop in such a situation. Some older decisions indicate that stating the terms of the desired mortgage in detail is not necessary. *Smith v. Vernon,* 6 Ill. App. 3d 434, 286 N.E.2d 99. Reasonable terms, they say, will be implied. These decisions should be ignored. There are many mortgage plans available today, and they vary greatly. What is an acceptable loan to one party may be totally unacceptable to another. *Neiss v. Franze,* 422 N.Y.S.2d 345 (1979). *See also* Harvey L. Temkin, *Too Much Good Faith in Real Estate Purchase Agreements? Give Me an Option,* 34 U. Kan. L. Rev. 43 (1985).

If the contract is contingent on the buyer obtaining a mortgage, and if the buyer acting in good faith cannot procure the mortgage, the buyer is entitled to a return of its earnest money deposit. *Lewicki v. Chrachol,* 56 Ill. App. 2d 54, 205 N.E.2d 491 (1965). To show that the buyer is acting in good faith, the buyer should make a written application to a mortgage company for the type of loan described in the contract. If the lender rejects the buyer, the buyer should insist upon receiving a written, signed rejection that can be used in court if litigation develops. The buyer should be careful to follow the terms of the financing condition. If, for example, the condition requires the buyer to apply to an institutional lender, applying to a mortgage broker may not be adequate. *Vafa v. Cramer,* 622 N.Y.S.2d 567 (App. Div. 1995). While the result of this case may be criticized, it demonstrates the need to closely follow the terms of the contract.

One application may not be enough to show good faith in some cases. As a precaution, the buyer should make application to a second lender and procure a second letter of rejection. Donald M. Zupanec, Annotation, *Sufficiency of Real-Estate Buyer's Efforts to Secure Financing upon Which Sale Is Contingent,* 78 A.L.R.3d 880 (1977).

The buyer must also confront the reality that almost all loan commitments are conditional, at least upon the buyer's execution of the final loan documents, the lender obtaining a lien on property that is not encumbered by title defects, and the borrower's financial condition not changing. The buyer must take care that these conditions are in fact satisfied or the lender will not make the loan and the buyer's earnest money may be forfeited. The typical financing contingency does not continue to protect the buyer against the failure of the loan commitment conditions to be satisfied. *Cowern v. Norris*, 634 A.2d 992 (N.H. 1993).

Nearly all contingency clauses require the buyer to notify the *seller* in writing within a specified time of its inability to obtain financing. This must be done, or else the seller will be entitled to keep the earnest money if the purchaser does not close the deal. Merely phoning the broker is inadequate. Written notice to the seller is required. It is important the contract provisions relating to the giving of notice and the time in which the notice is effective be followed.

Often, a "kick out" will be inserted by a seller in a contingent contract.

> **EXAMPLE:** Broker finds Purchaser, who has $15,000 cash to apply on a sale price of $100,000. Purchaser, of course, insists on a clause making the contract contingent on his ability to get a loan of $85,000. Seller is unwilling to take the property off the market while Purchaser seeks financing. Seller therefore is willing to sign the contract only if the contract is subject to sale to a third party prior to Purchaser obtaining the loan commitment or waiving the contingency clause. Purchaser wants the property and agrees to such a clause. Purchaser must take care that large loan application fees will not be lost if Seller gets another buyer.

11.17(b) Contingent Contracts—Subject to Sale of Buyer's House

Often, the buyer will need the proceeds from the sale of its current house before it can close on the purchase of a new home. Even if the buyer does not need these funds, the buyer will not ordinarily want to pay two mortgages. If the buyer purchases the new house first and market conditions permit, the buyer may insert a clause that makes the buyer's obligation to purchase contingent upon the sale of the buyer's old house. Frequently, sellers demand that clauses of this type have the "kick out" provision discussed previously to allow the seller to keep the property on the market and to allow the buyer to save the deal by waiving the contingency if the seller finds another buyer.

> **EXAMPLE:** Buyer and Seller enter into a real estate contract for the purchase of Seller's house. This contract is contingent upon Buyer selling its existing home. Seller will go along with this as long as a firmer deal does not come along. If it does, Seller may notify Buyer that it has an offer from another buyer. Buyer then has a stated period of time (usually one or two days) to decide whether to waive the contingency. If the contingency is waived, Buyer must go through with the deal or lose the earnest money, whether Buyer sells its existing home or not. If Buyer elects not to waive the contingency, the Seller is allowed to accept the offer of the new buyer and the contract between Buyer and Seller becomes void. Buyer gets the earnest money back at that point.

11.17(c) Contingent Contracts—Approvals

Many contracts for the purchase of homes are signed on Sunday, when advice of legal counsel is not available. It seems advisable for the parties to insert some clause making the terms of the contract, other than price, subject to the approval or amendment by the lawyers for the parties. Also, the buyer is unable to determine the physical condition of the property and needs the help of an expert. *Indoe v. Dwyer,* 424 A.2d 456 (N.J. 1980); Annotation, *Construction and Effect of Clause in Real Estate Contract Making Contract Contingent upon Approval by Attorney for Either Party*, 15 A.L.R.4th 760 (1982).

If the parties agree to make the contract contingent on approval by the buyer's inspector, and the contract requires the inspector to list specific defects discovered during the inspection, the question remains whether the seller should be given the right to cure the defects and, if so, how much time it should be allowed for the cure to be accomplished. This matter presents thorny problems. In some states, the attorney approval provision allows the attorney for a party to simply cancel the contract without stating any reason, providing that the attorney and the party represented by the attorney act in good faith. This rule is said to protect the unsophisticated party. *Groshek v. Frainey*, 654 N.E.2d 467 (Ill. App. 1995). The attorney's statement of conditions upon which the contract will be approved is in law a counteroffer that the other party may or may not accept.

> **REFERENCES:** John E. Blyth, *What You Should Know About "Subject to the Approval of My Attorney" Clauses,* 12 Prac. Real Estate Law., May, 1996, at 81.

11.17(d) Contingent Contracts— Environmental Matters

To protect against the environmental liabilities that a property owner may incur, many contracts for the sale of commercial property now contain a provision that allows the buyer to cancel the contract in the event that an environmental audit of the property reveals the presence of underground storage tanks or unacceptable levels of environmental contamination. A modified version of such a clause is often found in the contract for the sale of residential property. This clause allows a buyer to cancel the contract if unacceptable levels of radon or lead-based paint are found in the property. See Chapter 28.

11.17(e) Contingent Contracts— Lead-Based Paint

As a result of a law that became fully effective at the end of 1996, sellers of housing built before 1978 must disclose to a purchaser the presence, location, and condition of any known lead-based paint hazards in the property being sold. 42 U.S.C. § 4852d. In addition, the seller must deliver to the purchaser any records or reports pertaining to lead-based paint that are in the seller's possession or reasonably available to the seller and a pamphlet prepared by the U.S. Environmental Protection Agency and the U.S. Consumer Product Safety Commission. The purchaser has ten days to conduct a lead-based paint risk assessment or inspection of the property and decide whether to proceed with the transaction. If that inspection reveals the presence of lead-based paint, the seller can opt out of the deal. The ten-day period can be shortened or waived by the purchaser. The act goes so far as to make real estate agents responsible to see to it that the seller complies with the requirements of the law and separately responsible to disclose any information they may have about lead-based paint in the property. Transactions involving the sale of foreclosed properties are exempt from the lead-based paint law.

11.17(f) Contingent Contracts— Requirements of State Laws and Local Ordinances

In reaction to matters of local concern, many states, counties, and local governments have enacted laws and ordinances that interpose contingencies or that require certain filings or governmental approvals be obtained before real estate may be transferred. These laws and ordinances run the gamut from those that require the local fire department to inspect the building to determine whether there are adequate smoke detectors and sprinklers and the building department to inspect the building for violations, to the disclosure of environmental information about the property.

No listing here can be adequate because the state and local legislatures are constantly adopting new measures to react to local concerns. The parties to the real estate purchase and sale contract should contact the units of local government having jurisdiction over the property at the time they enter into the contract to determine whether any such ordinances apply and, if so, their ramifications. If any of these ordinances do apply, the parties must provide in their contract for the required inspections and approvals. In addition, the parties must agree upon what happens if the approval is not issued by the inspecting body or if the parties cannot comply with the law or ordinance. Does the contract terminate, or is the seller obligated to bring the property into compliance with the law, thereby reducing its net proceeds from the sale of the property?

11.18 Possession and Rents

The general rule of law is that the right to possession of real estate follows the legal title. Since the purchaser does not acquire the legal title to the property until it receives the deed, as a rule, it is not entitled to possession until that time. E. LeFevre, Annotation, *Effect of Failure of Contract for Sale or Exchange of Real Estate to Specify Time for Giving of Possession,* 56 A.L.R.2d 1272 (1957). The contract, however, may expressly authorize the buyer to take possession before it receives the deed. Such a provision would normally be included in an installment contract, because a purchaser under such a contract usually expects to take possession long before it is entitled to receive the deed. Also, the contract may, by implication, confer the right of possession on the buyer, as where it contains a provision requiring the buyer to keep the buildings in repair or to give up possession in case of default.

The party who is entitled to possession is entitled to the rents of the land. Ordinarily, therefore, rents falling due before the seller gives the buyer a deed belong to the seller, and rents due after the delivery of the deed are payable to the buyer.

11.19 Taxes   Unless the contract provides otherwise, the seller must give the buyer good title free and clear of taxes that were a lien at the time the contract was made. In fact, if the seller remains in possession after the contract is made, and taxes become a lien while the seller is in possession, the seller must pay these taxes. However, if the buyer goes into possession and taxes thereafter become a lien, the buyer must pay these taxes. To eliminate questions, the contract usually specifies the taxes to which the land will be subject when the deed is made.

11.20 Insurance and Risk of Loss   It sometimes happens that before the deal is closed the building is destroyed or damaged by fire or other casualty. In some states, the loss falls on the buyer. In other words, the buyer must go through with the deal and pay the full contract price, even though the building has been destroyed. John E. Macy, Annotation, *Vendor and Purchaser: Risk of Loss by Casualty Pending Contract for Conveyance,* 27 A.L.R.2d 444, 466 (1953); V. Woerner, Annotation, *Rights and Liabilities of Parties to Executory Contract for Sale of Land Taken by Eminent Domain,* 27 A.L.R.3d 572 (1969); John E. Cribbit, *Insurance and the Executory Contract for the Sale of Real Estate,* 51 Ill. B.J. 124 (1962); Lawrence X. Pusateri, *Risk of Loss After Contract to Sell Real Property—Adoption of Uniform Vendor and Purchaser Risk Act in Illinois,* 52 Ill. B.J. 464 (1964). This risk is not limited to fire. It includes damage from flood, windstorm, earthquake, vandalism, explosion, hurricane, erosion, subsidence, collapse of retaining wall, and crop loss in agricultural properties. Most states give the buyer the benefit of the seller's insurance.

In an increasing number of states, statutes or court decisions put the risk of loss on the seller, so that if a substantial loss by fire or other casualty occurs before the buyer has been given a deed to the property, the buyer may cancel the deal and obtain return of its down payment. *Dixon v. Salvation Army*, 191 Cal. Rptr. 111 (1993). An important factor in some of these states is the fact of possession. The party in possession is in a better position to prevent fires and other casualties. *Skelly Oil Co. v. Ashmore,* 365 S.W.2d 582 (Mo. 1963). Hence, in these states, if the buyer is put in possession before the deal is closed, the risk of loss will fall on the buyer.

In all states, the risk of loss falls on the seller where (1) the contract specifically provides that risk of loss pending closing of the deal rests on the seller; (2) the seller does not have a good marketable title at the time of the loss because it would be unfair to put the risk of loss on a buyer when the seller is in no position to perform its obligations under the contract, *Eppstein v. Kuhn,* 225 Ill. 115, 80 N.E. 80 (1906); (3) the seller is at fault in causing the delay in closing the deal and, during this delayed period, a loss occurs; and (4) the loss is due to the carelessness of the seller, as when he or she leaves the house during a cold spell without draining the heating system and the radiators are cracked by ice formation.

Today, we see many contracts that contain complex formulas for apportioning the risk of loss between the buyer and seller. Often, these provisions shift the risk between the parties based upon whether the damage is *material.* Materiality is determined by reference to a percentage of the purchase price or an absolute amount. Obviously, what is material under some circumstances or with respect to some properties may not be material with respect to others.

If the damage is not material, the seller is often given a period of time to complete the repairs and apply the insurance proceeds to the cost of completion. The closing is delayed while the work is being done. If the buyer does not want to delay the closing until the work is done, the buyer may elect to close and take an assignment of the insurance proceeds. A problem arises when the insurance proceeds are inadequate to pay for the costs of repair and replacement. This will always be the case where the seller has a deductible in the coverage. A similar problem is presented where the coverage is simply inadequate or does not embrace the covered risk. For example, if the seller does not have earthquake coverage and the loss is the result of an earthquake, the buyer does not want to be in a position where it must take the assignment of whatever insurance coverage there may be and repair the damaged property. All of this must be extensively negotiated between the parties prior to the execution of the contract.

A typical solution would involve the following components:

1. The seller should provide notice of the casualty to the purchaser.

2. If the damage is not material, the purchaser will not be afforded the election of opting out of the transaction, but the seller will be obligated to rebuild or restore the premises or give the purchaser a credit against the purchase price for the cost of such restoration or rebuilding.

3. The valuation of the loss is important. What is the definition of *material damage,* and who makes the determination of the extent of the damage? The parties may well want to allow this matter to be submitted to arbitration.

4. The plans and specifications for the restoration of the damage must be considered. This is especially important in the restoration of older properties. Must the seller bear the cost of restoring the property to its former state? For example, will the walls have to be made of plaster and special tin ceilings fabricated and installed to repair those that were damaged, or will today's wallboard and fiber ceilings be acceptable? If building codes have changed since the building was constructed, will the seller be required to bear the extra cost of restoring the property in light of current building codes, or should the purchaser contribute the extra cost?

5. The seller will be obligated to make and prosecute a claim with the insurance company and to commence the rebuilding and restoration of the damaged property. If restoration will not be completed within the time originally set for the closing of the transaction, the closing date may have to be extended for a reasonable period of time, or the purchaser may agree to accept the property in its then "as is" condition and take an assignment of the claims against the insurance company together with any proceeds payable under the insurance policies.

6. The parties should address the issue of the inadequacy of the insurance proceeds and the obligation of the seller to fund any amounts required to restore or rebuild the property that are not paid by the insurer.

11.21 Prorating or Apportionment

Provision is frequently made for prorating, adjustment, or apportionment of rents, taxes, insurance premiums, water taxes, interest accrued on mortgages that will remain after the closing, personal property taxes on personal property transferred to the buyer, gas and electric bills, janitor's salary, management fees on current rent collections, and charges on service contracts, such as exterminator or scavenger service. It is also customary to provide that fuel on hand shall be purchased by the buyer at current prices as of the proration date. Although it is usual to prorate certain items not mentioned in the contract, it must be remembered that, in the event of controversy, the party contending that an item should be prorated will be legally unable to compel proration in the absence of provision in the contract therefor. *Lathers v. Keogh,* 109 N.Y. 583, 17 N.E. 131 (1888); *Antietam-Sharpsburg Museum Inc. v. William H. Marsh, Inc.,* 249 A.2d 721 (Md. 1969); *Wilson v. Campbell,* 425 S.W.2d 518 (Ark. 1968).

It is often the case that the contract will provide that prorations are to be final. As deals become more complex and the matters being prorated become larger in size, there is a tendency away from such requirements. For example, in complex transactions involving multiple sites, it is not possible to finalize all of the items to be prorated at the time of the closing. The parties will agree to give a tentative closing statement at the closing and further adjust accounts between them within a stated period thereafter.

Similarly, with respect to real estate taxes, the parties usually believe that the taxes will increase. As a result, prorations are often based on an agreed-upon percentage that is more than 100 percent of the most recent tax bill. For example, the parties may agree to prorate taxes on the basis of 110 percent of the most recent tax bill. This method reflects the parties' best guess of the amount of the increase. If the actual increase is more or less, each of the parties takes the risk that it may pay more than its fair share.

Another method of handling the proration of any item that is not certain at the closing is to call for the reproration of the item when the actual costs are known. For example, the parties may agree to reprorate real estate taxes when the actual tax bills are issued.

11.22 Insulation   The Federal Trade Commission (FTC) has ruled that sellers of new homes must disclose the type, thickness, and R-value of the insulation installed in each area of the home. The seller must also disclose the areas of the home where insulation will not be installed. The FTC staff compliance guidelines state that this regulation applies to the sale of new homes and to the sale of existing homes if the seller is in the business of selling such properties and insulation was added in the renovation or rehabbing of the property. In this latter instance, however, the disclosure would only relate to the insulation installed as part of the renovation program and not to the insulation that was in the home when it was purchased by the rehabber.

These disclosures must be made in the contract itself, or in some other document that is incorporated by reference into the contract, and reviewed by the purchaser before execution of the contract. 16 C.F.R. § 460; NAHB, *Disclosure and Advertising of Home Insulation: A Guide to the Federal Trade Commission's Trade Regulation.*

11.23 Transfer Taxes   States, counties, and, with increasing frequency, local municipalities have enacted transfer tax legislation. These laws and ordinances impose a tax on the transfer of real property, typically based upon the value of the real estate or the purchase price paid for the property. In some instances, a credit against these taxes may be given for the balance due on a mortgage, which will remain as an encumbrance after the transfer of title. These tax statutes will usually have some exceptions, and certain types of transactions will be exempt from the transfer tax. From a contractual perspective, the parties must agree upon who will pay these taxes and how they will be paid. For example, the parties may agree that the tax imposed by state law and county ordinance will be paid by the seller and the tax imposed by local municipal ordinance will be paid by the buyer. The parties may further agree that the tax will actually be paid by the escrowee out of the funds of the respective parties.

11.24 Date   The contract need not be, but usually is, dated.

11.25 "As Is" Provisions   Many sellers of commercial properties are very concerned that they not be exposed to contingent and unexpected liabilities after they have sold their property. To accomplish this, they attempt to sell the property "as is" and without warranties or representations of any kind except as stated in the contract. These provisions often fit into the purchase and sale of commercial properties where the buyer does extensive due diligence work inspecting the property and its operating results by reviewing the leases and other contracts relating to the property, reviewing the records of the zoning and building departments of the local municipality, conducting environmental audits and engineering inspections of the property, and otherwise satisfying itself that the property is acceptable for purchase. Often this work is done by the buyer after the property is under contract so that the buyer will not incur the cost of the work only to see some other party purchase the property. In such cases, the contract typically has a provision that allows the buyer to terminate the contract if its due diligence reveals matters that the buyer finds unacceptable.

Where such is the case, an "as is" clause is proper and will be upheld by the courts, especially where the parties were represented by counsel and other advisors and agreed upon the allocation of risk between them. *Lenawee County Bd. of Health v. Messerly*, 331 N.W.2d 203 (Mich. 1982). *See generally* Frank J. Wozniak, Annotation, *Construction and Effect of Provision in Contract for Sale of Realty by Which Purchaser Agrees to Take Property "as-is" or in Its Existing Condition*, 8 A.L.R.5th 312 (1992). *See also Prudential Ins. Co. of America v. Jefferson Associates*, 896 S.W.2d 156 (Tex. 1995).

Sellers should not feel overly comfortable just because the contract contains such a clause. Where the seller or the seller's representative makes misrepresentations upon which the buyer relies, the seller may still be liable. *Lance v. Bowe*, 648 N.E.2d 60 (Ohio App. 1994); *Wagner v. Cutler*, 757 P.2d 779 (Mont. 1988). Liability will also befall a seller who knows of a latent defect, but does not disclose the nature or existence of such defect to the buyer. *Haney v. Castle Meadows, Inc.*, 839 F. Supp. 753 (D. Colo. 1993); *Levy v. Creative Constr. Services of Broward, Inc.*, 566 So. 2d 347 (Fla. App. 1990).

Also, the "as is" clause may not protect the seller from liability to the buyer when the buyer is exposed to liability for hazardous waste clean-up costs. *Amoco Oil Co. v. Borden, Inc.*, 889 F.2d 664 (5th Cir. 1989); *Amland Properties Corp. v. Aluminum Corp. of America*, 711 F. Supp. 784 (D. N.J. 1989); *Wiegmann & Rose Int'l Corp. v. NL Industries*, 735 F. Supp. 957 (N.D. Cal. 1990); *New West Urban Renewal Co. v. Westinghouse Electric Corp.* 909 F. Supp. 219 (D. N.J. 1995); *Prospect Industries Corp. v. Singer Co.*, 569 A.2d 908 (N.J. 1989).

Contracts will often contain both an "as is" clause and an "integration" clause. The latter clause contains the agreement of the parties that the contract contains the entire agreement and understanding of the parties with respect to the transaction at hand. Notwithstanding that language, the buyer may sue the seller in tort, and not upon the contract, for misrepresentations relating to the transaction. *Keller v. A.O. Smith Harvestore Products,* 819 P.2d 69 (Colo. 1991).

11.26 Antitrust Compliance

It may come as a surprise to some that the antitrust laws may be applicable to the transfer of a parcel of real estate. Nonetheless, such may be the case. The Hart Scott Rodino Anti-Trust Improvements Act of 1976 was enacted to give the FTC and the Department of Justice the opportunity to review transactions before they are finalized to determine whether they violate the antitrust laws. 15 U.S.C. § 18a. The FTC recently amended its premerger notification rules to exempt certain categories of real property acquisitions from the Act's reporting requirements. This amendment was adopted because the exempt transactions are unlikely to run afoul of the antitrust laws, since the properties that are the subject of the exemptions are abundant and widely dispersed.

A previous exemption is related to certain acquisitions of new facilities, undeveloped real property, office buildings, and residential property sold in the ordinary course of the seller's business. That ordinary course of business exemption continues. While it may overlap with some of the new exemptions, the new exemptions are not limited to the ordinary course of business requirements. The new categories of exempt transactions are as follows: the acquisition of new facilities that have not yet produced income and were either constructed by the seller or held by the seller solely for sale; used facilities that are acquired from the lessor by a lessee who had sole and continuous use of the facility since it was built; unproductive property that has not generated more than $5,000,000 in revenue in the three years preceding the contemplated acquisition; office and residential property; hotels and motels that do not include a gambling casino; recreational land, not including ski facilities, multipurpose arenas and stadiums, or racetracks and amusement parks; agricultural property, not including processing facilities; and rental retail space and warehouses. 16 C.F.R. § 802.2. If the transaction would violate the laws, the FTC is to disapprove of the transaction.

The Act applies where the parties to a transaction are engaged in interstate commerce or where their business affects interstate commerce. This test is easily met in large real property transactions. One of the parties must have net sales or assets of at least $100,000,000 and the other party must have net sales or assets of at least $10,000,000. Again, this second test is easily met in today's large real property transactions, especially because the test is applied not only to the entity involved in the transaction, but also to the aggregation of all of the other entities in the corporate family of the party to the transaction.

The prime test for many real estate transactions measures the size of the transaction itself. It is met when, as a result of the transaction, the acquiring entity will hold either (1) more than $15,000,000 of the voting securities and assets of the acquired entity or (2) 15 percent or more of the voting securities of and assets of the acquired entity.

An exemption applies to the transfer of realty in the ordinary course of business. Definitional problems arise out of the use of these terms. First, certain real estate is really a business unto itself. Accordingly, the FTC considers the transfer of a shopping center and a resort hotel to be the transfer of a business and not the transfer of realty for the purposes of the exemption. The FTC has exempted the transfer of unimproved land, office buildings, and residential properties from the premerger filing requirements. Again, qualifications to these exemptions must be considered. If an office building or residential property also contains retail space, the value of that space must be less than $15,000,000 and the revenue from the retail space for the last two years must not have exceeded 10 percent of the total revenue from the building. Also, the unimproved land may not have structures, agricultural land, timber, or mineral reserves that have a combined value of $15,000,000.

If the Act applies, a preclosing notification must be made and the parties must await the elapse of a thirty-day waiting period before closing the transaction. The contract should accommodate this situation and allow the parties to make the necessary filings, cooperating in good faith as necessary, while awaiting the notice from the FTC. If the FTC objects to the transaction, the contract should give the parties the right to either opt out of the transaction or to cooperate in working toward the closing.

11.27   Execution   As heretofore pointed out, the contract must be signed by the party against whom enforcement of the contract is sought. Of course, in practice, the contract is almost invariably signed by both seller and buyer.

Suppose property is owned jointly by *A* and *B*. *C* negotiates with *A* for the purchase of the property and agrees with *A* that the land will be sold for the sum of $10,000. A contract is prepared, designating *A* and *B* as sellers and *C* as buyer. *A* and *C* sign the contract. *B* refuses to sign. Is the contract binding on *A*? No, for the contract shows on its face that a sale was intended only if both landowners agreed. *Madia v. Collins,* 408 Ill. 359, 97 N.E.2d 313 (1951); W.W. Allen, Annotation, *Contract to Sell Land Not Signed by All of Co-Owners as Operative to Cover Interests of the Signers,* 54 A.L.R 767, 778 (1945); 92 C.J.S. *Vendor & Purchaser* § 548 (1955). *See also Williams v. Singleton,* 723 P.2d 421 (Utah 1986) as to the failure of one of the co-purchasers to execute the contract.

11.28 Contracts Signed by Agents

A person may authorize an agent to enter into contracts on his or her behalf for the purchase or sale of real estate. In many states, this authorization must be in writing, and in all states, it is customary to employ a written authorization. *But see Nelson v. Boone,* 890 P.2d 313 (Haw. 1995), which allowed specific enforcement of a contract signed by the seller's attorney, even without a written authorization from the seller to the attorney. Such an agent is an *attorney in fact,* and the document granting this authority is a *power of attorney.* It is dangerous for the parties to rely on the authority of a representative of the buyer or seller to bind that party, even if the representative is the party's lawyer, and even if the act purports to be an agreement to something minor, such as an extension or amendment of the contract. *Schafer v. Barrier Island Station, Inc.,* 946 F.2d 1075 (4th Cir. 1991); *Diversified Development & Investment, Inc. v. Heil,* 889 P.2d 1212 (N.M. 1995).

11.29 Seal

A seal is not necessary to the validity of a contract.

11.30 Delivery

Suppose you list your land for sale with a broker and he finds a buyer interested in its purchase but who does not wish to pay the price you are asking. The buyer prepares and signs a contract of sale stipulating a lower price. This is an *offer.* He hands the contract to the broker, who hands it to you. You sign the contract and return it to the buyer. This is an *acceptance.* The contract is now in force. Suppose, however, that you simply sign the contract and hold on to it, hoping that a higher offer will appear, and refuse to answer the buyer's telephone calls. This last situation poses the following questions. (1) Must the buyer be *notified* that his offer has been accepted? In other words, can he legally withdraw the offer at any time before he is notified that the offer has been accepted? (2) Is delivery necessary to the validity of a contract? The buyer, you will notice, is in an awkward spot. He cannot risk signing a contract to buy some other property, for if he does, he may find himself obligated to buy two parcels. Some courts protect the buyer and would allow him to revoke his offer in this last situation, stating either that the acceptance is ineffective until the buyer is notified thereof or that delivery is necessary for a written contract to be binding. *Hollingshead v. Morris,* 172 Mich. 126, 137 N.W. 527 (1912); Case Note, *Statute of Frauds; New Requirements for Enforceable Purchase Agreements,* 8 Wm. Mitch. L. Rev. 991 (1982).

The contract should be prepared in duplicate original, with the buyer signing both duplicate originals. Each duplicate original contains a provision that the buyer's liability, if any, is terminated and his or her down payment is to be returned, unless a duplicate original signed by the seller is delivered to the buyer within three days after the date of the contract. The buyer hands both duplicate originals to the seller, but retains a copy, so that the buyer can prove its nonliability if it fails to receive a signed duplicate within the specified time.

**11.31
Acknowledgments**

An acknowledgment is not necessary, although it is desirable since it simplifies proof of the contract in any suit brought thereon. If the contract is to be recorded, acknowledgment is necessary in nearly all states.

11.32   Witnesses

If the contract is not acknowledged, it should, as a practical matter, be witnessed, although this is not necessary as a matter of law. The fact that the signatures are witnessed simplifies use of the contract in any litigation that may develop.

11.33   Recording

Some contracts will go so far as to include a clause providing that the contract is void if the buyer records it. A buyer who is hopelessly in default will sometimes record the contract, hoping thereby to cloud the seller's title and to obtain a return of part of the purchase price paid. In view of the public policy behind recording laws, such provisions are of doubtful validity. Garret Power, *Land Contracts as Security Devices*, 12 Wayne L. Rev. 391, 402 (1966).

**11.34   Effect of
Contract—Interest
of Purchaser**

The signing of a contract for the sale of land does not give the buyer legal title to the land. Ownership can be transferred to the buyer only by a deed. However, the buyer does acquire an interest in the land. This interest is known as equitable title.

The equitable title of the buyer results from the doctrine of equitable conversion. *Shay v. Penrose,* 25 Ill. 2d 447, 185 N.E.2d 218 (1962); 91 C.J.S. *Vendor & Purchaser* § 106. In most states, the buyer's equitable title arises the moment the contract is entered into.

> **EXAMPLE:** Seller enters into an installment contract with Buyer. Buyer dies without a will, leaving Heir as the only heir. Administrator is appointed administrator of Buyer's estate. The equitable interest of Buyer passes to Heir as real estate. 33 C.J.S. *Executors and Administrators* § 112. Suppose Seller dies and ABC Co. is appointed his administrator. ABC Co. will be entitled to collect the contract payments. 33 C.J.S. *Executors and Administrators* § 112. Since Buyer was the equitable owner of the land, the courts will, for most purposes, treat Seller's interest under the contract as personal property, going to his administrator.

As a result of this rule, a contract purchaser can mortgage its contract interest by means of a real estate mortgage.

11.35   Effect of Deed

When the deal is closed and the seller's deed delivered to the buyer, the deal is regarded as consummated. The contract of sale has served its purpose. It is *merged* into the deed. Charles S. Parnell, Annotation, *Deed as Superseding or Merging Provisions of Antecedent Contract Imposing Obligations upon the Vendor*, 38 A.L.R.2d 1310 (1954). The contract no longer exists. For this reason, if matters remain to be attended to after the closing of the deal, it is best that they be set forth in an agreement that expressly states that the obligations of the parties as set forth in that agreement shall survive the closing. This is particularly important as to title matters, for the buyer waives the right to cancel the contract because of defects in title if it accepts the deed and pays the consideration while the title is defective or encumbered. A.G. Shepard, Annotation, *Deed as Superseding or Merging Provisions of Antecedent Contract Imposing Obligations upon the Vendor*, 84 A.L.R. 1008, 1031 (1933).

There are some exceptions to the merger rule. In particular, when the contract expressly calls for performance to be rendered after the deal is closed, the delivery of the deed does not extinguish that aspect of the contract.

> **EXAMPLE:** The contract required the seller to lay water mains and sewers after closing of the deal. The deal was closed, and the deed delivered to buyer. Thereafter, the seller failed to lay the water mains and sewers. The buyer filed a damage suit against the seller, and the

seller was held liable. *McMillan v. American Suburban Corp.,* 136 Tenn. 53, 188 S.W. 615 (1916). The same would be true where the contract requires the seller to build a house on the land sold. A.G. Shepard, Annotation, *Deed as Superseding or Merging Provisions of Antecedent Contract Imposing Obligations upon the Vendor,* 84 A.L.R. 1008, 1023 (1933). If the contract warrants that the building is in sound condition, this warranty survives the closing of the deal, for that obviously was what the parties intended. *Levin v. Cook,* 186 Md. 535, 47 A.2d 505 (1946). Contract provisions as to the date on which possession will be turned over to the buyer are not merged in the deed. In all of these cases, the buyer's only remedy, if the seller fails to perform, is to sue the seller for damages. The buyer cannot sue to rescind the contract and regain the purchase price. *De Bisschop v. Crump,* 24 F.2d 807 (5th Cir. 1928).

When the deal is closed and the deed accepted by the buyer-grantee, all questions of *marketability of title* are at an end. A.G. Shepard, Annotation, *Deed as Superseding or Merging Provisions of Antecedent Contract Imposing Obligations upon the Vendor*, 84 A.L.R. 1008, 1025, 1027, 1032 (1933); A.G.S., Annotation, *Marketable Title*, 57 A.L.R. 1253, 1261 (1928) (a grantee who receives a warranty deed can sue the grantor for damages for breach of the warranties of title set in the deed, if a title defect shows up). The buyer's right to sue the seller for the seller's misrepresentations is not affected by the closing of the deal. Normally, the buyer does not discover these misrepresentations until after taking possession.

11.36   Assignment of the Contract

The buyer may assign his or her interest in the contract. By virtue of the contract, the buyer has the right to demand a deed to the property on performing its part of the contract. The buyer may sell and transfer his or her right to a third party, which is accomplished by means of a brief instrument called an *assignment*. Such a third party is called the *assignee*. The assignee has the right to make the payments required by the contract and to demand a deed from the seller. In other words, the assignee steps into the shoes of the buyer and may compel the seller to perform its obligations under the contract.

The assignee does not, however, become personally liable to the seller for payment of the purchase price, unless the assignment provides that the assignee *assumes and agrees* to pay the purchase price. *Lisenby v. Newton,* 120 Cal. 571, 52 P. 813 (1898).

Of course, the buyer cannot escape personal liability for payment of the purchase price by assigning the contract. The buyer remains liable to the seller notwithstanding the assignment. If the rule were otherwise, a buyer could always rid itself of a burdensome contract by assigning it to a pauper.

The contract may forbid assignment, as many contracts often do.

11.37   Deed by Seller to Stranger

When the seller, after entering into the contract, sells and conveys the land to some third party, the question arises as to whether the buyer under the contract can compel such third party to give the buyer a deed to the land on payment of the contract price. The buyer can compel the conveyance from the third party in the following cases:

1. When the contract was recorded prior to the making of the deed to the third party;
2. When, though the contract was not recorded, the buyer took possession of the land prior to the making of the deed to the third party; and
3. When, even though the contract was not recorded and the buyer did not take possession of the land, the third party actually knew of the earlier contract at the time it received his or her deed.

If the case does not fall within these three rules, the buyer cannot compel the third party to give a deed. In other words, the buyer has lost all of its rights in the land. However, the buyer may then sue the seller to recover any amounts paid on the purchase price.

If the contract requires the seller to give a warranty deed, the buyer need not accept a warranty deed signed only by the seller's grantee. The seller must also join in the deed. *Crabtree v. Levings,* 53 Ill. 526 (1870).

11.38   Time for Performance

The contract should specify the date on which the deal is to be closed. If the contract does not specifically fix the time when performance is due, it will be implied that the contract is to be performed within a reasonable time, and the purchase price must be paid at that time. Most contracts fix a specific time for the performance of all acts thereunder. If the contract provides that *time is of the essence,* each act required by the contract must be done promptly at the time specified. In a cash sale where time is of the essence, if either party fails to perform promptly, the contract will be unable to obtain specific performance.

> **EXAMPLE:** The contract called for an earnest-money down payment, balance to be paid within five days after Seller's title was shown to be good. The contract provided that time was of the essence. Seller delivered evidence of good title on August 5. Buyer did nothing. On August 19, Seller served notice on Buyer to close the deal within five days. Again, Buyer did nothing. On September 10, Buyer tendered the balance of purchase price. Seller refused to accept. Buyer then filed suit for specific performance and the court refused to grant it. Buyer was in default and time was of the essence. *Johnson v. Riedler,* 395 Ill. 412, 70 N.E.2d 570 (1946).

11.39(a)   Remedies of the Seller

If the buyer fails or refuses to perform, the seller, in lieu of declaring a forfeiture, may pursue one of the following courses:

1. The seller may rescind the contract. *Rescission* is not the same as *forfeiture.* By rescinding, the seller declares the contract at an end and surrenders all rights thereunder. Both seller and buyer must be restored, as far as possible, to the situation existing before the contract was made. In an installment contract, the seller, on rescinding, must give back to the buyer the payments made, less a fair rent for the time the buyer has been in possession. *Hillman v. Busselle,* 66 Ariz. 139, 185 P.2d 311 (1947). The right to rescind does not depend upon any provision in the contract. However, most installment contracts give the seller the right to declare the contract forfeited if the buyer defaults. By declaring a forfeiture, the seller terminates the contract, but retains all payments previously made by the buyer, since this right is expressly conferred by the contract. The seller may thereupon file a suit to clear his or her title of the cloud created by the forfeited contract.

   Some states allow the seller to rescind, apply the earnest money in reduction of the damages, and sue the buyer for any other damages sustained. This is a sensible rule. *Anderson v. Long Grove Country Club Estates, Inc.,* 111 Ill. App. 2d 127, 249 N.E.2d 343 (1969).

2. In some states, the seller may tender a deed to the buyer and then sue the buyer for the purchase price.

3. The seller may sue the buyer for damages.

4. The seller may sue the buyer for specific performance of the contract. *Vincent v. Vits,* 566 N.E.2d 818 (Ill. App. 1991).

5. The seller may simply retain the earnest money.

11.39(a)(1) Remedies of the Seller—Forfeiture

The typical remedy of a seller for the default of the buyer is to forfeit the earnest money posted by the buyer. This is why the earnest money should be adequate so as to keep the buyer in the deal rather than allowing the buyer to walk away from the transaction with little loss. Both parties will have typically incurred costs as a result of the pendency of the contract. Legal fees will have been incurred as the parties have negotiated and executed the contract. A survey may have been ordered, as well as a title commitment. More than the direct costs, the seller will have lost sales momentum by taking the property off the market under the belief that the buyer was going to go through with the deal. These damages are difficult to calculate and the courts will typically allow the parties to contract for the forfeiture of the earnest money in the event of the buyer's breach.

It is important that the forfeiture clause provides that the parties have agreed that the seller will be damaged by the buyer's default, that such damages are difficult to compute, and that the parties agree that the earnest money will be forfeited in the event of a breach by the buyer and that such forfeiture is not as a penalty but to pay the seller for the damages that it will incur.

The contract should set out whether the forfeiture of the earnest money is the sole remedy of the seller, or whether the seller can also obtain specific performance. The fact that the contract contains a liquidated damages provision does not preclude the right to obtain specific performance. *Coney v. Commercial Nat'l Realty Co.*, 410 N.E.2d 1181 (Ill. App. 1980). If the contract allows the seller to elect to forfeit the liquidated damages or to sue for actual damages, the forfeiture provision may be unenforceable because the parties did not in fact agree in advance upon the amount of damages that might arise in the event of the buyer's breach. *Grossinger Motorcorp., Inc. v. American Nat'l Bank and Trust Co.*, 240 Ill. App. 3d 737, 607 N.E.2d 1337 (1993).

11.39(b)   Remedies of the Buyer

In case of the seller's refusal or failure to perform, the buyer may pursue one of the following courses:

1. The buyer may *rescind,* that is, declare the contract terminated and recover the earnest money deposit. Rescission is the buyer's normal remedy when the land has decreased in value. One difficulty here is that the seller usually is reluctant to return the buyer's deposit. The buyer, of course, has the right to file a suit against the seller and obtain a judgment, which can be enforced in the usual ways—by levy on property, by garnishment, and so forth. However, while the suit is pending, the seller may very well decide to sell the property to someone else and then spend the earnest money.

2. The buyer has a lien on the land as security for repayment of purchase money paid in and may enforce such lien if the seller is unable or unwilling to convey good title. W.R. Habeeb, Annotation, *Right of Vendee Under Executory Land Contract for Amount Paid on Purchase Price*, 33 A.L.R.2d 1384 (1954). A buyer who wishes to obtain return of the down payment from a defaulting seller would be well advised to file a suit to enforce the purchaser's lien, for this ties up the seller's property and prevents the sale of the land to others. This is not true if the buyer merely sues the seller for a money judgment.

3. The buyer may sue the seller to compel *specific performance* of the contract, that is, to compel the seller to give a deed on receiving payment of the purchase price. The buyer will resort to this remedy when it wants the land for some particular purpose—for example, to keep out a competitor—or when the buyer anticipates that the land will appreciate in value. In general, specific performance is a more effective remedy than a suit for money damages, since damages are always hard to prove and judgments for money are hard to collect.

4. The seller, of course, cannot compel the buyer to accept a bad title. But sometimes the buyer wants to go through with the contract and the seller refuses. The seller's title may be clouded with some unpaid tax, unpaid mortgage, or easement. To make things more difficult for the buyer, the seller refuses to make any effort to eliminate these defects. Here, the buyer may wish to file a suit for specific performance and ask the court to make a deduction from the purchase price because of the defects in title.

   EXAMPLE: The contract price is $10,000. An examination of title reveals the existence of $1,000 in unpaid taxes. The court will order specific performance on the buyer's deposit of $9,000 in court for the seller if the seller refuses to pay the taxes. This remedy of the buyer is called *specific performance with an abatement from the purchase price.*

5. Where the seller will not or cannot go through with the deal, the buyer may sue the seller for *damages.* In such an action, the buyer ultimately will receive a judgment for money damages. In the meantime, however, while the suit is pending, the seller is at liberty to sell the land to others, and any buyer who gets a deed before the buyer obtains a judgment takes the land free of the buyer's claims.

6. The parties may agree that in the event of a default by either of them, the other's only remedy is to be returned to the status quo. *Leet v. Totah,* 620 A.2d 1372 (Md. App. 1993).

11.39(c)   Remedies— Restitutionary Damages— Promissory Estoppel

On occasion, *even where a contract has not been signed,* there will be a liability for damages.

> **EXAMPLE:** Hoffman and his wife owned a small store. Red Owl, a national franchiser, advised Hoffman to sell his store, promising to find a party, to buy some land, build a bigger building, and lease it to the Hoffmans with an option to purchase. The Hoffmans would receive a Red Owl franchise. All this was arranged orally. The Hoffmans sold their store in reliance on Red Owl's promises. Red Owl refused to go through with the deal. Red Owl was held liable for all the damages the Hoffmans suffered. Red Owl made a promise knowing the Hoffmans would rely on it. Under the doctrine of promissory estoppel, the promisor is liable for the damages its promisee incurs. Although the promises were made to Hoffman only, Red Owl could foresee that his wife would also rely on Red Owl's promise. Hence, they are liable to her as well. *Hoffman v. Red Owl Stores, Inc.,* 26 Wis. 2d 683, 133 N.W. 267 (1965). Lawyers often speak of this as *detrimental reliance.*

11.39(d)   Remedies— Election of Remedies

Some remedies are so inherently inconsistent that, if a party chooses one, he or she cannot resort to remedies he or she would otherwise have.

> **EXAMPLE:** In some states, an installment seller has a *statutory right* to cancel the contract by giving the buyer notice of his or her default and forfeiture. Thereafter, he or she cannot sue the buyer for damages, unless the contract so provides. *Zirinsky v. Sheehan,* 413 F.2d 481 (8th Cir. 1969).

Indeed, in some states, if the seller is going to pursue a remedy, other than the forfeiture of the earnest money, the seller must release the earnest money to the buyer. *Palmer v. Hayes,* 892 P.2d 1059 (Utah App. 1995).

11.39(e)   Remedies— Exclusiveness of the Remedies Spelled Out in Contract—Choice of Inconsistent Remedies

In the case of a cash sale, even though the contract is silent on the point, the seller may, in the event of default by the buyer, retain the buyer's earnest money deposit. This is a form of forfeiture that is universally permitted. Often, the contract specifically provides that, in the case of the buyer's default, the seller may declare the contract ended and keep the earnest money. This is not necessarily an *exclusive remedy.* G.H.P., Annotation, *A Provision in Land Contract for Pecuniary Forfeiture or Penalty by a Party in Default as Affecting the Right of the Other Party to Specific Performance,* 32 A.L.R. 584 (1924); W.W.A., Annotation, *Provision in Land Contract for Pecuniary Forfeiture or Penalty by Party in Default as Affecting the Right of the Other Party to Specific Performance,* 98 A.L.R. 887 (1935). In other words, the seller, *in lieu of retaining the earnest money, may have the right to sue the buyer for specific performance or for damages.*

The contract often provides that, in the event the seller's title proves defective, the buyer must either take the title "as is" or be content with a return of the earnest money deposit. This is then the buyer's exclusive remedy if the seller is *in good faith unable* to clear title. *Wolofsky v. Waldron,* 526 S.2d 945 (Fla. App. 1988); *Old Colony Trust Co. v. Chauncey,* 214 Mass. 271, 101 N.E. 423 (1913); *Nostdal v. Morehart,* 132 Minn. 351, 157 N.W. 584 (1916). If the buyer wishes to accept title "as is," it must notify the seller of that decision within the time allowed by the contract. *Miller v. Shea,* 300 Ill. 180, 133 N.E. 183 (1921). However, if the seller's title examination reveals defects that the seller could easily clear, but the seller refuses to do so because of a reluctance to go through with the transaction, or if the seller knew the title was defective when it signed the contract of sale, then the clause is not deemed to provide an exclusive remedy, and the buyer may file for specific performance with an abatement from the purchase price or for damages. *Mokar Properties Corp. v. Hall,* 179 N.Y.S.2d 814 (1958). This clause protects the seller only where it is truly unable to deliver a clear title and was unaware of the defects in its title. *Blau v. Friedman,* 140 A.2d 193 (N.J. 1958).

The crucial point for the parties to keep in mind is that the contract must set out their intent. Is forfeiture of the earnest money to be the sole remedy of the seller, or is the seller also to be able to sue for specific performance and damages? If the seller is able to sue for damages, should the parties agree that damages will be in addition to the forfeited earnest money or in lieu of the forfeiture of the earnest money? Furthermore, should the damages be limited either as to amount or character of loss (e.g., the amount of attorney, surveyor, and title fees incurred by the seller in the aborted transaction), or should damages be unlimited?

From the buyer's side, the parties should agree whether the buyer is limited to the return of the earnest money, or whether the buyer is also entitled to sue for damages and specific performance. Again, if the buyer may sue for damages, are there to be any limits on the amount or character of those damages?

11.39(f) Attorneys' Fees

A companion to the default provision is a clause that entitles the successful party in any litigation, arbitration, or dispute resolution process to recover its attorneys' fees and court costs. Without such a clause, the court will not award attorneys' fees, and the defaulting party is placed at a major advantage.

11.40 Abandonment

Through abandonment, either buyer or seller may lose its rights under the contract. If either party clearly shows by its acts that it does not intend to go through with the contract, the other party may assume that it has abandoned the contract. L.S. Tellier, Annotation, *What Constitutes Abandonment of Land Contract by Vendee,* 68 A.L.R.2d 581 (1959).

> **EXAMPLE:** The buyer, under an installment contract, took possession of the premises. Later, the buyer fell far behind in its payments and eventually accepted a lease from the seller. When oil was discovered, the buyer attempted to enforce the contract. The court held that the buyer's rights had been lost by abandonment. *Dundas v. Foster,* 281 Mich. 117, 274 N.W. 731 (1937).

11.41 Hardship

On occasion, a court will refuse to enforce a contract where enforcement would cause undue hardship.

11.42 Fairness and Inadequacy of Consideration

If the price is far below the real value of the land, and the parties are not on equal terms, as when the buyer is an experienced businessperson and the seller is ignorant, mentally feeble, or inexperienced, the court will refuse to compel the seller to give a deed.

> **EXAMPLE:** Shortly after the Chicago fire, the owner of certain lots in Chicago, a weak-minded man who was ignorant of the value of the land and of business generally and who was unable to understand English well, was persuaded by a shrewd man to sell the lots for $21,000. The lots were worth much more, and their value was rapidly rising. Owners of adjoining lots had just made arrangements to build on these adjoining lots. These facts were known to the buyer but not to the seller. The court refused to compel the seller to give a deed. *Fish v. Leser,* 69 Ill. 394 (1873).

11.43   Mistake   The very word *contract* implies that there must be a meeting of the minds. Occasionally, both parties to the contract are mistaken as to some matter. This is called a *mutual mistake*. When there is a mutual mistake, either party may cancel or rescind the contract.

> **EXAMPLE:** The owner of certain land verbally offered to sell the land for $6,000. The buyer misunderstood the price to be $3,000 and agreed. Under such misunderstanding the deed was executed and delivered. There was no meeting of the minds here, and the owner was entitled to a reconveyance. *Neel v. Lang,* 236 Mass. 61, 127 N.E. 512 (1920).

**11.44
Misrepresentation
and Fraud**

So many statements are made by each party in the course of a sale of land that almost always some untrue statement, called a *misrepresentation,* is made. If the misrepresentation is of some unimportant or trivial matter, generally speaking, it will not affect the contract. Such a misrepresentation is said to be immaterial. Suppose, however, that a misrepresentation is made as to some important matter. It is clear, first of all, that such a misrepresentation does not make the contract null and void. After the misrepresentation has been discovered, the party who was deceived may nevertheless wish to enforce the contract. It may do so. If the contract has not yet been performed—that is, the seller has not yet given a deed—and the buyer who was guilty of the fraud files a suit to enforce the contract, the other party may use the fraud as a defense to such a suit. It will bring to the court's attention the fact that the party who is bringing the suit made a misrepresentation as to an important matter, and the court will refuse to enforce the contract.

If the contract has been performed—that is, the seller has given the deed and the buyer has paid the purchase price—and one party then discovers that an important misrepresentation has been made, it may file a suit to get the land back (rescission), if that party was the seller, or get the money, if that party was the buyer.

Remember that the buyer is seldom in a position to discover the seller's misrepresentation until it has taken possession of the property. The buyer may rescind (get his or her money back), even if the misrepresentation was not intentional.

The topic of fraud and misrepresentation on the part of the seller, the selling broker, and the listing broker has given birth to a vast amount of litigation in recent times; therefore, Chapter 10 is devoted to this topic.

11.45   Hardship   At times, if circumstances change after the contract is signed, and as a result it would be a substantial hardship to compel performance of the contract, the courts have refused to enforce it. W.E. Shipley, Annotation, *Change of Conditions After Execution of Contract or Option for Sale of Real Property as Affecting Rights to Specific Performance,* 11 A.L.R.2d 390 (1950).

> **EXAMPLE:** After the contract was signed, the city rezoned the land for residential purposes. The buyer, as was known to the seller, planned to erect a factory. The court refused to enforce the contract. *Clay v. Landreth,* 187 Va. 169, 45 S.E.2d 875 (1948). To some considerable extent, the concept of hardship is being replaced by the concept of unconscionability.

**11.46   Liability for
Injuries**

The matter of implied warranties of the building is one that deals with (1) new buildings erected by a merchant-builder and (2) damages suffered by the buyer because of defects in the building that the buyer must expend funds to repair. A different question is presented when the buyer (or a member of its family) or a member of the public suffers injuries because of a defect in the building or land sold.

The seller may be liable because it knew of a hidden defect that created a danger to occupants.

EXAMPLE: There is an unused well on the property that Seller has covered with sod. Wife of Buyer steps on the sod and the rotten boards break, plunging her into the well. Seller is liable for failure to warn Buyer. *Cooper v. Cordova Sand and Gravel Co.,* 485 S.W.2d 261 (Tenn. App. 1971).

EXAMPLE: The building in question has a cornice that has been weakened by water freezing in the spaces between lengths of the cornice. There is an obvious danger to members of the public on adjoining sidewalks. Seller sells the property to Buyer. The cornice falls, injuring a pedestrian. Seller is liable because it sold a nuisance. Buyer is liable because it knowingly maintained a nuisance. 58 Am. Jur. 2d *Nuisances* §§ 50–51

Possible liabilities such as these give cautious sellers reason to keep their liability insurance in force after the closing, even though, except as a result of the application of theories such as the above, a seller is not ordinarily liable for defects or injuries occurring after the sale. *Kimberlin v. Lear,* 500 P.2d 1022 (Nev. 1972); Emile F. Short, L.L.B, L.L.M., Annotation, *Liability of Vendor or Grantor of Real Estate for Personal Injury to Purchaser or Third Person Due to Defective Condition of Premises,* 48 A.L.R.3d 1027 (1973).

11.47 Additional Suggestions on Contract Draftsmanship

Preliminary Observations. The goal to be achieved in drafting a contract of sale is twofold. Of course, the parties want a contract that the courts will enforce. However, this is not always the case. Many contracts are so poorly drafted that courts cannot and will not enforce them. In addition, after the seller and buyer have explored all aspects of the deal and reached an agreement as to all their rights and duties, they should specify all of the terms that they have agreed on and state them so clearly that there can be no controversy as to their meaning.

Parties. In general, the suggestions made regarding parties to deeds are applicable to parties to contracts.

Purchase Price. State the purchase price and terms of payment. If the price is determined by reference to the area of the property, the contract should state the method of computing the purchase price.

Earnest Money. For the seller's protection, the deposit should be adequate. The seller should insist on a certified or cashier's check. The buyer should insist that money be held in escrow by a bank or trust company, or by the broker as is typical in a residential deal.

Purpose for Which Buyer Is Purchasing the Property. Careful thought must be given to the purpose for which the buyer is purchasing the property. For example, it may be that the buyer intends to use the property for a purpose prohibited by the zoning ordinance. If so, the contract must contain a clause for the buyer's protection requiring an amendment to the zoning ordinance to be procured within a limited time, and if the zoning is not changed within that time, the buyer should be allowed to cancel the contract and obtain a return of the earnest money. The seller should agree to join in the rezoning petition. If the contract is prepared and signed at a time when information concerning the provisions of recorded building restrictions or applicable zoning and building ordinances is unavailable, but the seller feels that neither restrictions nor ordinances will prevent use for the buyer's intended purpose, a clause may be added giving the buyer the right to terminate the contract within a specified time if it shall appear from recorded covenants, conditions or restrictions, or from zoning or building ordinances, official maps or plans, or applicable statues that the premises cannot legally be used for the intended purposes.

Description of the Property To Be Sold. The parties should adequately describe the land that is being sold.

Streets and Alleys. The seller will usually have some right, title, or interest in and to the streets or alleys adjoining the premises sold, including private streets and vacated streets, and it is desirable that the contract of sale call for the seller to convey, without warranty, all such right, title, and interest.

Items To Be Conveyed to the Buyer or Retained by the Seller. A contract for the sale of land obligates the seller to deliver title to the land and all fixtures, including the building, for it, of course, is a fixture, and fixtures are part of the land. Chattels, however, such as furniture, are not included, unless the contract expressly so provides.

Assignments. If any part of the property is rented, the buyer will typically want an assignment of the leases. The contract should also require seller to assign to buyer any other items that buyer wishes to receive (e.g., service contracts [contracts with exterminators, scavengers, and so on], roof guaranties, or tenant's deposits).

Fixtures. What does the seller expect to retain after the deal is closed? Once the contract is signed, the seller is obligated to deliver to the buyer all fixtures. They are legally part of the land. If the seller expects to retain attached machinery or other items that might be considered fixtures, provision to this effect should be included in the contract.

Encumbrances to Which the Title is To Be Subject and to Which the Buyer Agrees. The seller should see that it has listed in the contract all of the encumbrances or other defects in title that it does not propose to clear before the deal is closed. Most contract forms contain a printed list of common encumbrances, such as leases or building restrictions, but it is intended that the seller will add to this list as necessary. Suppose, for example, that the seller's title is subject to an easement. Is it mentioned in the contract? If not, and the buyer changes its mind and decides to back out of the deal, it may be able to do so, because the title, as finally examined before the deal is closed, must reveal no encumbrances other than those listed either in general or in specific language in the contract.

The buyer should carefully analyze every encumbrance listed by the seller. For example, if in the contract it is agreed that the buyer will take subject to "existing leases," it must accept the property subject to any lease, no matter how ridiculously low the rent may be. If the contract says that the buyer will accept title subject to "building restrictions of record," "easements of record," and "mineral rights," as many printed forms provide, will any of these restrictions, easements, or mineral rights interfere with the buyer's intended use and occupancy of the property? Moreover, will some easement documents to which the land is subject obligate the buyer in some way as owner of this land? For example, an easement for road purposes may obligate the buyer to keep a neighbor's road in repair. Similar personal liability provisions may be contained in restriction documents.

Mortgage Provisions. These should be detailed and complete. For example, if the contract calls for a purchase money mortgage, the amount, interest rate, maturity date, and form of mortgage should be clearly set forth. Similar details should be included in a clause giving the buyer the right to cancel if it cannot procure the mortgage of a specified amount, and specify the time allowed to procure the mortgage. If land is being sold subject to a mortgage, the contract should specify the amount, whether the buyer is to assume personal liability, and that no defaults shall exist. If the seller has a mortgage on the land that must be released, the contract should provide that the seller will have the right to pay it off at the closing, using the buyer's funds for this purpose.

Evidence of Title. Since title insurance has become the almost universal form of title evidence, the contract should identify the title company, state who is to furnish and pay for the title insurance and when it is to be obtained, and allow the buyer to point out defects in title not permitted by the contract for the seller's clearance of objections and for the buyer to decide whether to accept the title "as is" if objections cannot be cured.

Clearing Title by Escrow Deposits. For the protection of the seller, the contract should contain a provision allowing the seller to leave money in escrow with some bank or title company if the title is not clear on the day of the closing. Otherwise, a deal may fall through simply because a seller is not in a position to remove some trivial defect, such as a small mechanic's lien, within the time allowed. While it is common practice for the parties to establish an escrow with the attorney for one of the parties, such an escrow may not be valid. *See Galvanek v. Skibitcky,* 55 Conn. App. 254, 738 A.2d 1150 (1999) (which held that an escrow cannot be validly created with an attorney for one of the parties).

Chattel Lien Search. The contract should specify if the seller is to furnish a search for financing statements or other liens on personal property being sold and, if so, the time allowed to obtain the searches.

Building Ordinance Violations. If the seller is to furnish a formal, official report as to building code violations, the contract should so state and set out the time within which the report is to be delivered. The buyer should try to have the contract provide that the seller "warrants that the building on the premises is now and at the date of closing will be free and clear of all violations of laws and ordinances, and for breach of this warranty, buyer may rescind this contract, before or after closing, or, at his election, may sue for damages."

Survey. The contract should specify whether the seller is to deliver a survey and the time within which this is to be done. The time allowed for the buyer to raise objections based on the survey should tie into the time allowed the buyer for raising objections to the title. If the seller objects to paying for a survey, the buyer may decide to get one at his or her own expense.

Building and Other Restrictions. If the seller wishes to place building restrictions on the land sold, it must make provision for this in the contract.

Risk of Loss. Suppose the building is destroyed or damaged by fire or other casualty before the deal is closed. The right of the buyer to cancel the deal and its right to insurance money if it does not back out should be covered.

Miscellaneous Documents To Be Furnished to the Buyer. If a new building requires a certificate of occupancy or an approval by the underwriters of electrical installations, or if it is customary to obtain similar certificates with respect to plumbing and the like, the contract should provide that the seller will deliver these at the closing. In case of a new building, guaranties by the subcontractors are customary. There is usually a roof guaranty and a guaranty of the plumbing and heating equipment and electrical installations. The contract should provide that the seller will transfer and deliver these to the purchaser at the closing.

The buyer should obtain the "as built" architect's plans and specifications for the building. Also, the buyer should obtain appropriate evidence that the building is free from infestation.

Possession. The contract should state the date on which possession is to be given.

Tenant's Security Deposits. Assignment of the tenant's security deposits to the buyer must be covered specifically. Typically, the seller wants an indemnity from the buyer that the security deposits will be properly applied, and the buyer wants to know that all security deposits are being transferred.

Advance Payments of Rent. The contract should allow the buyer a credit against the purchase price where a tenant has already paid the seller the rent for the last several months of the term.

Prorated Items. These should be covered in great detail to avoid arguments at closing over who pays for janitor's vacation pay, water bills, and so forth.

Documents. All miscellaneous documents that the buyer will need should be provided for in the contract. The seller is under no legal obligation to furnish any document that the contract does not call for.

Signatures, Acknowledgment, and Witnessing. All the parties must sign, taking care to sign as their names appear on the contract. Witnessing and acknowledgment should be considered if the contract is to be recorded. Without witnessing and acknowledgment, the contract is not recordable in many states.

Unions. If the sale is of a substantial property, it is quite possible that the seller employs union members and that a collective bargaining agreement is in place. In such case, a labor lawyer should be consulted, since the buyer must change, recognize, or renegotiate the existing collective bargaining agreement, or terminate it.

Utilities, Etc. If vacant land is being sold, the contract should warrant that utilities, water, sewer, and so on are available at the property lines and are connectable.

Access. As to vacant land, the seller may warrant that the land has access to abutting streets.

Easements. With the help of a surveyor, the buyer should determine if the property is serviced by an easement over adjoining land. If it is, the contract must require the seller to convey the easement and to furnish title insurance or other evidence of title (such as an abstract) to show that the seller owns an unencumbered easement. The land is useless to the buyer if it has no legal access.

If the sale involves granting the buyer an easement over the seller's adjoining land, this must be carefully planned. A title search of that land is needed, and the easement must be in a form a title company will insure.

Contiguity of Parcels. If the land consists of several parcels, the buyer should insist that the title company ensure that the parcels do indeed adjoin each other. Alternatively, the surveyor should draft a new perimeter description that embraces the entire tract. The survey will then reveal if there are strips between the parcels.

Merger. If there are matters (landscaping, paving driveways) that the seller should attend to after closing, add a sentence that these covenants do not merge in the deed.

Inspection before Closing. The buyer is always given the right to inspect the day before closing a home deal to determine if the seller has removed valuable fixtures (chandeliers, etc.).

Zoning and Building Code Violations. In some areas of the country, the building must be inspected by the city before closing, since local law does not permit recording the deed unless it has the building inspector's approval. In larger deals (hotels, office buildings), the seller will have professionals make a careful inspection before signing the contract, always remembering that, in some states, violations of these codes are not considered as affecting the marketability of title. In residential transactions, the private inspector who inspects for the buyer may be able to detect violations and cover this in its report. It is unwise to omit any mention of this in the contract. This becomes a battleground, because the seller argues that every building has some violations and that the buyer will simply use this as an argument to lower the price. At a minimum, the contract should require the building to be free of officially posted ordinance violations.

Warranties of the Condition of the Building. Many home sales require the building to pass a private inspection. This clause appears frequently in contracts because if the buyer simply holds off signing until the inspection is made, another buyer may "steal the deal." If the seller refuses to permit this clause, the buyer may ask the seller to represent and warrant that the heating, electrical, plumbing, etc., are in working order. Some sellers will agree to this. If the buyer wants the seller to warrant that the appliances are in "good working order," the seller may not agree. What is "good" working order? The seller will argue for a clause that *all* buyer's rights in this regard terminate at closing.

Brokers. Some sellers want protection by the buyer against claims of a broker other than the broker paid by the seller.

Service Contracts. In larger deals, the seller may have a variety of service contracts, such as elevator inspection, termite inspection, waste removal, burglar alarm service, and so on. The buyer will want copies of these service contracts and the ability to assume or reject them.

Unrented Space. If it is anticipated that large rental space may become vacant before closing, the parties should agree on who rents the space, who approves, who pays the rental broker, etc.

Water Stock. In some localities, mutual water companies are formed to service the community. Each property owner holds a stock certificate signifying the number of shares in its name. Provision should be made for transfer of this stock.

Subdivisions. If the contract involves vacant subdivided land, the seller will have complied with the local laws that regulate subdivisions.

Lease Schedule. The lease schedule should be complete. Many office leases have rent concessions. The lease schedule should warrant that there are no concessions, no options to renew, etc. The impact of rent control ordinances should be considered. Determine what lease brokerage commissions are payable on existing leases and who pays them.

CHAPTER 12

Installment Contracts for the Sale of Real Estate

12.01 In General
In general, the cash real estate sale contract contemplates that the deal will be closed as soon as the circumstances reasonably permit and the conditions to the closing are satisfied or waived. There is another type of contract called the *installment contract, contract for deed,* or *land contract.* An installment contract provides for a down payment, with the balance of the purchase price paid over time, typically in monthly installments. The buyer receives the deed when all of the installments have been paid or when the unpaid balance of the purchase price has been reduced to an agreed amount, whereupon the buyer is to receive a deed and give the seller a purchase money mortgage for the balance of the purchase price.

Before entering into an installment contract, the seller should remember that it is going into the credit business. For this reason, the seller should do the same evaluation of the buyer as a lender does in the loan underwriting process. Is the buyer creditworthy? A credit check must be made. Does the buyer have the income to make the periodic payments as they come due? The buyer's annual income must be verified by inquiry of the employer or a review of the buyer's income tax returns. A good real estate broker can be of great help to the seller in attending to these details and in evaluating the information.

12.02 Broker's Commission
Where the broker's listing contract permits an installment contract (as distinguished from a cash sale) or the seller decides to accept an installment purchaser, the broker's commission is earned once the contract is signed. For this reason, the seller may want the listing contract to provide for the commission to be payable in installments. The seller does not want to pay a full commission if the buyer defaults in the early months of the sale, or if the cash flow of the sale proceeds does not give the seller adequate funds to pay the commission.

12.03 Spouse's Signature
Both the seller and spouse should join in the execution of the installment contract of sale to waive and release marital and homestead rights.

12.04 Purchasers as Joint Tenants
Where a husband and wife are buying, it is probably wise to have them purchase as joint tenants or as tenants by the entireties. Over the relatively long life of the contract, one of the buyers may die. In such case, the purchaser's interest will devolve to the survivor.

12.05 Title Search and Closing
The installment sale contract is usually used because the buyer does not have enough cash to qualify for a regular mortgage or because mortgage financing is not readily available. Still, the buyer usually must make a substantial down payment. Hence, the buyer will want proof of the seller's title before the payment of any of the down payment. A common method of handling this situation is for the contract to provide that the buyer is to make an earnest money payment to be held in escrow by the seller's broker or some other third party.

A title commitment or report is then obtained, just as in a cash sale. If the title is acceptable or, more exactly, in conformity with the contract, an initial closing is held at which prorations are made as in a cash sale, and the balance of the down payment is paid. The buyer then takes possession of the property.

In some areas, this is handled more formally. A preliminary contract is signed calling for the execution of a formal installment contract. When the title is shown to be in conformity with the preliminary contract and the prorations are agreed upon, the parties sign the installment contract, the balance of the earnest money is paid, and the buyer takes possession. In larger deals, this document may require the seller to prepare and sign a deed running to the buyer. This deed is delivered "in escrow" to a bank or title company, which holds the deed under a formal escrow agreement that may call for the installment payments to be made to the escrowee.

The final payment is a "balloon," that is, a large payment. When it is due, a second title commitment is obtained. If that commitment conforms to the contract requirements, the last payment is made and the escrowee delivers the deed to the buyer. Thus, even if the seller has died during the life of the contract, the deed is available and is quite valid.

In many areas, the buyer's lawyer will insist that the buyer receive a "contract purchaser's" title policy when the down payment is made. This policy is issued in duplicate, one to each party, and shows the buyer's interest under the recorded contract. It ensures the validity of the contract and insures the buyer against future matters involving the seller, such as bankruptcy. Under this method, the buyer is virtually certain that if payments are made regularly, a clear final title policy will be issued.

Where the contract is substantial, the original contract or a memorandum thereof is acknowledged before a notary and recorded in the recorder's office. Title companies usually insist on this.

In small transactions, usually involving old homes sold with a nominal down payment, the unsophisticated buyer signs the contract with no title search to be made until payment has been completed. Such transactions expose the purchaser to an incredible risk of loss of title. Nevertheless, they occur. There are instances where a purchaser has occupied and paid on a home for many years and in the end has been unable to obtain clear title.

12.06 Recording

Some printed forms forbid the recording of the contract. There is some doubt as to the validity of such a clause. The state of Illinois forbids this clause in residential contracts. 765 I.L.C.S. 70/2.

12.07 Assignment by Buyer

To control the occupancy of the property, the seller may wish to include a clause forbidding assignment of the contract by the buyer without the seller's consent. Such a clause is valid. *Immel v. Travelers Ins. Co.,* 373 Ill. 256, 26 N.E.2d 114 (1940); *Dobitz v. Oakland,* 561 P.2d 441 (Mont. 1977).

Where an assignment is made, thought should be given to the liability of the assignee. By the weight of authority, a mere assignment does not create a personal liability of the assignee to the seller. *Quest v. Robertson,* 71 Ill. App. 3d 678, 388 N.E.2d 1335 (1979). In a few states, the assignee does become liable. *Rose v. Vulcan Materials Co.,* 194 S.E.2d 521 (N.C. 1973) (citing authorities pro and con). Of course, if the seller's consent is needed, it may insist that the assignee sign an instrument assuming personal liability in consideration of receiving the seller's consent.

Clauses forbidding assignment of the contract by the buyer do not prevent the buyer from signing an installment contract to sell his or her interest. Such a contract is called a *subpurchase. Covington v. Clark,* 346 P.2d 229 (Cal. 1959); *Lake Shore Club v. Lake Front Realty Corp.,* 398 N.E.2d 893 (Ill. App. 1979). Comment, *Specific Performance by Partial Vendee,* 4 Stan. L. Rev. 443; *Recent Case,* 100 U. Pa. L. Rev. 1073 (1952); *Decision,* 27 N.Y.U. L. Rev. 174 (1952); Edward H. Clyde, *Subvendee of Portion of Realty May Obtain Specific Performance,* 3 Utah L. Rev. 257 (1952) (all dealing with subpurchase contracts).

In point of fact, the restriction on assignment can take one of three forms. The contract may contain a covenant not to assign. Presumably, for a breach of this covenant, the remedy would be a suit for damages. The contract may state that an assignment without the required consent is void. Alternatively, an assignment without the required consent may make the *contract* void at the option of the injured party. John Edward Murray, Jr., *Murray on Contracts* § 306 (1974). It is therefore important to frame the clause carefully, making the choice with care. Again, in states where forfeitures are frowned upon, and this is a long list of states, one wonders if the last alternative will be valid.

Actually, a fourth option exists, namely, inclusion of a due-on-sale clause that is triggered either by an assignment or subpurchase contract.

12.08 Prepayment Privilege

The buyer will insist that the contract give it the right to prepay the installment balance of the purchase price. If the contract does not expressly give this privilege, the contract balance cannot be prepaid. *Burns v. Epstein,* 413 Ill. 476, 109 N.E.2d 774 (1952). Sellers are concerned about the income tax impact of prepayment and may require deferred payments. To ensure this result, sellers may even exact a stiff prepayment penalty. Courts will uphold the penalty if it is reasonably related to the seller's risk of incurring increased income tax liability. *Williams v. Fassler,* 167 Cal. Rptr. 545 (1980).

12.09 Impounds

Many installment contracts in home sales require the buyer to make monthly payments that include one-twelfth of the yearly real estate tax and fire insurance premium. This, of course, is a common provision in home mortgages. In such case, failure of the buyer to include these *impound payments* in its monthly remittance would be a default under the contract and might eventually lead to a forfeiture.

12.10 Acceleration Clause

From the seller's point of view, it is desirable that an installment contract authorize the seller to declare the entire purchase price due in case of default. Otherwise, a chronically delinquent buyer can drive a seller to distraction by curing the defaults each time the seller serves notice of the seller's intent to declare a forfeiture.

> **EXAMPLE:** Owner contracts to sell real estate to Buyer at a purchase price of $20,000 payable in monthly installments. Buyer is constantly late in making payments. The contract contains an acceleration clause. Owner sends Buyer notice to cure all his defaults within thirty days, otherwise Owner will declare the entire purchase price due. This is permitted under the acceleration clause. After acceleration has taken place, Owner is in a position to forfeit unless Buyer can pay the entire purchase price. This is helpful in getting rid of the chronic delinquent. But, as in the case of mortgage law today, the seller must not exercise its rights unfairly.

The acceleration clause is commonly regarded as valid. *Benincasa v. Mihailovich,* 188 N.W.2d 136 (Mich. App. 1971). However, it is probably necessary for the seller to give the purchaser notice and an opportunity to cure the defaults within a reasonable time. *Brannock v. Fletcher,* 155 S.E.2d 532 (N.C. 1967). If the seller accelerates unfairly, courts will set the acceleration aside.

> **EXAMPLE:** The seller cannot declare an acceleration where there is an honest dispute as to the amount due. *Moore v. Bunch,* 185 N.W.2d 565 (Mich. App. 1971).

12.11 Insurance

It seems wise for the contract to spell out all the appropriate insurance requirements and to require the buyer to furnish evidence periodically that the insurance is in force. Both the seller and the buyer should have liability coverage. To be sure, the brunt of liability will fall on the buyer/occupant, but the seller may be named a defendant in personal injury suits, and an insured seller will be entitled to have the insurer defend the lawsuit without charge. The hazard insurance should have a "manuscript" rider covering both the seller and the buyer. The seller should require an endorsement that provides that acts of the buyer (e.g., arson) that would invalidate the buyer's coverage, will not invalidate the seller's coverage.

12.12 Judgments Against Seller— Equitable Conversion

In many states, the buyer is regarded as the equitable owner of the property. In these states the interest of the seller is commonly a bare, naked legal title. Judgment liens against the seller do not attach to such a title. *Bank of Sante Fe v. Garcia,* 102 N.M. 588, 698 P.2d 458 (1985), *cert. denied,* 698 P.2d 886 (1985); A.G.S., Annotation, *Right of Vendee Under Unrecorded Executory Land Contract as Against Subsequent Deed or Mortgage Executed by, or Judgment Rendered Against Vendor,* 87 A.L.R. 1505, 1512 (1933). State law must be checked. Some contract forms contain a provision that the purchaser acquires no title, legal or equitable, until the sale price is paid in full. The validity of these clauses has been sustained. *Cox v. Supreme Sav. & Loan Ass'n,* 126 Ill. App. 2d 74, 262 N.E.2d 74 (1970) (holding valid a clause that buyer acquires no interest in land until the contract price is paid in full). This clause is objectionable to the purchaser. It negates the equitable conversion that would result from the signing of the contract and deprives the purchaser of the protection against judgments against the seller.

At times, during the life of the contract, the buyer will learn that a judgment or other lien has, in fact, been filed against the seller. This raises a problem of great difficulty. The seller may, in good faith, be appealing or otherwise contesting the lien. But the buyer is put to the hazard of continuing its payments on a title that may be clouded when it is conveyed to the buyer. Some relief is obtained by a clause providing that, in such cases, the buyer may elect to make its payments to a bank in escrow for both parties until satisfactory assurances have been given that these liens will not affect the buyer's title.

There is no device that is really satisfactory to both parties. A long-term escrow may help if accompanied by a title policy protecting the buyer against future liens. Alternatively, the title may be placed in a trust at the time the contract is signed with directions to the trustee to give a deed to the buyer when the last payment is made.

Again, a title company may be persuaded to give the buyer a clear policy on the theory that, in states where equitable conversion exists, the seller holds a naked legal title in trust for the buyer and such a title is not subject to judgment liens. *Reuss v. Nixon,* 272 Ill. App. 219 (1933); *Bunch v. Eifler,* 191 Ill. App. 344 (1915); 87 A.L.R. 1505, 1515, *supra.*

12.13 Mortgages

Both the seller and the buyer have interests that may be mortgaged. *Tanglewood Land Co. v. Byrd,* 42 N.C. App. 251, 256 S.E.2d 270 (1979), *aff'd,* 299 N.C. 260, 261 S.E.2d 655 (1980). As to the seller's interest, the contract should provide that the buyer's interest is subordinate to any mortgage that does not exceed the balance due on the contract. The contract should also provide that in case of any default in the mortgage, the buyer may make the payments on the mortgage and such payments shall reduce the contract balance.

As to the buyer, a clause is needed under which the seller joins in the mortgage or subordinates its interest thereto. Some rehab contractors accept a mortgage on the buyer's interest only. This is legally valid, but unsound. If the buyer's interest is terminated for default, this wipes out the mortgage.

REFERENCES: *Nelson v. Bailey*, 54 Wash. 2d 161, 338 P.2d 757 (1959); *Simonson v. Wenzel*, 27 N.D. 638; 147 N.W. 804 (1914); *Eade v. Brownlee*, 29 Ill. 2d 214, 193 N.E.2d 786 (1963) (all holding that contract purchaser has interest that may be mortgaged). *Norlin v. Montgomery*, 367 P.2d 621 (Wash. 1961) (seller's interest is not subject to mortgages executed by buyer). *Eade v. Brownlee*, 29 Ill. 2d 214,193 N.E.2d 786 (1963); *Miles Homes, Inc. v. Grant*, 134 N.W.2d 569 (Iowa 1965) (both holding buyer's mortgagee not entitled to notice of forfeiture). *Contra Kendrick v. Davis*, 452 P.2d 222 (Wash. 1969). As to notice to lien creditors of buyer generally, see *Hayes v. Carey*, 287 Ill. 774, 122 N.E. 524 (1919); *MGIC Mtg. Corp. v. Bowen*, 572 P.2d 547 (N.M. 1977). *Knauss v. Miles Homes, Inc.*, 173 N.W.2d 896 (N.D. 1970) (holding that purchaser's mortgagee is a necessary party to seller's suit to quiet title). 87 A.L.R. 1505, 1515, *supra;* Thomas A. Henzler, *Mortgages—Mortgage of a Vendee's Interest in an Installment Land Contract—Mortagee's Rights on Default*, 43 Mo. L. Rev. 371 (1978); *Recent Development*, 45 Wash. L. Rev. 645 (1970) (all dealing with situation where, after installment contract is recorded, the seller mortgages its interest. The issue is whether buyer can claim priority over mortgage for payments made after it learns of the mortgage. *In re* Heide, 915 F.2d 531 (9th Cir. 1990) (holding that the Uniform Commercial Code applies when the seller uses his or her interest as security). *But see In re Shuster*, 784 F.2d 883 (8th Cir. 1986); *In re Hoeppner*, 49 B.R. 124 (Bky. E.D. Wis. 1985).

12.14 Bankruptcy of Seller

The new Bankruptcy Code protects a buyer in possession against the bankruptcy of the seller. The former Bankruptcy Act did not.

12.15 Building Code Regulations

Laws will be encountered that require an installment seller, prior to signing the contract, to furnish information as to reported building code violations. A question remains as to the liability of the seller for building code violations that develop later. The buyer, of course, is liable, since it has possession and control of the building. *Cox v. Supreme Sav. & Loan Ass'n,* 126 Ill. App. 2d 293, 262 N.E.2d 74 (1970). However, the code language may be broad enough to impose liability on the seller as well. *Cocanig v. City of Chicago,* 21 Ill. 2d 464, 173 N.E.2d 482 (1961); *City of Chicago v. Porter,* 26 Ill. App. 2d 323, 168 N.E.2d 468 (1960). Of course, the seller will be liable to the city for building code violations existing when the contract was signed. *Cox v. Supreme Sav. & Loan Ass'n,* 126 Ill. App. 2d 293, 262 N.E.2d 74 (1970).

In some states, the fines for building code violations are substantial. Obviously, the seller should require the buyer to keep the building free from building code violations and make violation of this agreement grounds for forfeiture. The seller should retain the right to make reasonable inspections of the building and exercise this right. If substantial code violations appear, the seller should declare the contract forfeited.

12.16 The Forfeiture Process

Every installment contract contains a forfeiture clause. If the buyer fails to make its payments, this clause gives the buyer the right to terminate the contract and to retain the payments the buyer has made. This is what lawyers call an *agreed remedy.* It exists only if the forfeiture clause is found in the contract. *Realty Securities Corp. v. Johnson,* 93 Fla. 46, 111 So. 532 (1927). In this respect, *forfeiture* differs from *rescission.* Rescission is a right the courts give the seller even where the contract is silent. The seller may terminate the contract if the buyer fails to make its payments, but should "restore the status quo." This means the seller should return to the buyer the payments made by the buyer less a fair rent for the time the buyer has been in possession. *Hillman v. Busselle,* 66 Ariz. 139, 185 P.2d 311 (1947). Obviously, the seller wishes to keep those payments. Hence the importance of the forfeiture clause. By declaring the contract forfeited, the seller terminates the contract and retains all payments previously made by the buyer. 77 Am. Jur. 2d *Vendor and Purchase* § 500.

Just as we so often find that tenants do not pay their monthly rent exactly on the day it is due, we often find that purchasers under installment contracts do not pay their payments exactly on the day they are due, or they may from time to time make payments of less than the amount due. The overwhelming majority of installment sellers go along with the buyer, hoping that it will be able to straighten out its finances. Ultimately, the seller may decide that it can no longer be indulgent. Then, the seller faces a problem that its own indulgence has created.

> **EXAMPLE:** An installment contract provided that time was of the essence, but the seller often accepted payments after the dates fixed for payment. This constituted a waiver of the provision that time was of the essence. The reason is that the seller, by accepting payments after the dates fixed, had led the buyer to believe that it would not insist on the provision that payments must be made strictly on the specified dates. It would therefore be highly unjust to permit the seller suddenly to declare a forfeiture of the contract for the buyer's failure to pay one of the installments promptly. *Fox v. Grange,* 261 Ill. 116, 103 N.E. 576 (1913); James O. Pearson, Jr., Annotation, *Modern Status of Defaulting Vendee's Right to Recover Contractual Payments Withheld by Vendor as Forfeited,* 4 A.L.R.4th 993 (1981).

The seller may revive the provision that time is of the essence. To do this, the seller simply serves a warning notice on the buyer that, in the future, the seller will insist on strict performance of the contract according to its terms, and thereafter the buyer must make payments promptly or the seller may declare a forfeiture. This warning notice must be followed by a declaration of forfeiture if the buyer fails to cure defaults within the allotted time. Such a warning notice must not be a mere dun. It must state unequivocally that the contract will be forfeited if the defaults are not cured within the specified time. *Monson v. Bragdon,* 159 Ill. 61, 42 N.E. 383 (1895). Many contracts contain a provision that acceptance of late payments shall not constitute a waiver of the provision that time is of the essence. Some courts refuse to give this provision effect. *Morrey v. Bartlett,* 288 Ill. App. 620, 6 N.E. 290 (1937); *Scott v. Cal. Farming Co.,* 4 Cal. App. 2d 232, 40 P.2d 850 (1935). In many states, a warning notice must always be given before an installment contract is forfeited. *County of Lincoln v. Fischer,* 216 Or. 421, 339 P.2d 1084 (1959); W.W. Allen, Annotation, *Right of Vendee in Default to Recover Back Money Paid on the Contract and Withheld by the Vendor as Forfeited,* 31 A.L.R.2d 14 (1953).

It is obvious that forfeiture involves a number of steps. The first step is the giving of notice to the purchaser. Where there are two or more purchasers, each is entitled to separate notice. In short, the seller should never send a notice addressed to "Mr. and Mrs. John Smith."

Sending a notice to the wrong address is a fatal defect if the seller knows or with reasonable diligence can obtain the correct address. *Kingsley v. Roeder,* 2 Ill. 2d 131, 117 N.E.2d 82 (1954).

If the purchaser has assigned its interest to a third party or placed a mortgage on its interest, obviously the better practice is to serve all notices on all such parties. Whether failure to so notify these parties will invalidate the forfeiture is a difficult question to answer. *Eade v. Brownlee,* 29 Ill. 2d 214, 93 N.E.2d. 786 (1963) (purchaser's mortgagee not served). *Holiver v. Dept. of Public Works,* 127 N.E.2d 790 (Mass. 1955); *Miles Homes, Inc., v. Grant,* 134 N.W.2d 569 (Iowa 1965) (purchaser's mortgagee not entitled to notice). *Kendrick v. Davis,* 452 P.2d 222 (Wash. 1969) (purchaser's mortgagee is entitled to notice).

12.16(a) Trifling Defaults At times, the buyer will argue that forfeiture ought not be permitted where the default is trifling in amount.

> **EXAMPLE:** A buyer in a $30,000 contract deliberately defaulted in a payment of $10.48. The court sustained the forfeiture. Where a default is deliberate, the buyer is, in effect, demanding a reduction in the sale price. He cannot force this decision on the seller. *Miller v. American Wonderlands, Inc.,* 275 N.W.2d 399 (Iowa 1979).

But, where there are minor defaults not due to stubborn defiance, the courts often set aside or refuse forfeiture. *Fisel v. Yoder,* 320 N.E.2d 783 (Ind.).

12.16(b) Forfeiture Procedure— Acceleration Improper

For some unexplained reason, many installment contracts lack an acceleration clause. In such case, a seller seeking to declare a forfeiture may demand payment of only those installments that are delinquent. However, on occasion a seller will, quite improperly in such cases, declare an acceleration in his or her notice of his or her intention to declare a forfeiture. By the better view, this is a fatal defect. The forfeiture must be set aside. *Rader v. Taylor,* 333 P.2d 480 (Mont. 1958). A buyer facing a demand for the entire balance due when it is having a hard time making the regular monthly payments will despair. It is unfair to give the buyer the impression that it can save the interest only by paying the entire balance due.

12.16(c) Forfeiture Procedure— Declaration of Forfeiture

Of course, following the seller's notice to the buyer to cure defaults or suffer a forfeiture, the seller must declare the forfeiture. A forfeiture cannot be made in the seller's mind. It must be communicated to the buyer. *Lovins v. Kelley,* 19 Ill. 2d 25, 166 N.E.2d 69 (1960). If, and only if, the contract requires it, the declaration of forfeiture must be recorded. *Tobin v. Alexander,* 380 N.E.2d 45 (Ill. 1978).

12.16(d) Forfeiture Procedure—Recovery of Money Paid by Buyer

Even where a forfeiture has been declared, the buyer's rights may be revived. This occurs where the seller waives the forfeiture by conduct indicating that it considers the contract still in force, as by negotiating with the buyer concerning the title of the property, possible repurchase by the seller, extension of time of payment, and the like. W.W. Allen, Annotation, *Waiver of, or Estoppel to Assert, or Election Not to Assert, Forfeiture of Executory Land Contract Because of Default in Payment,* 107 A.L.R. 345 (1937). All owners of the land must join in the notice of forfeiture. 91 C.J.S. *Vendor and Purchaser* § 139 (1937).

Where a recorded contract has been properly forfeited, the seller can obtain a court decree declaring the buyer's rights terminated.

Where the buyer is in military service, the contract cannot be forfeited without a court order. The court may either postpone the forfeiture or order the repayment of prior installments before permitting forfeiture of the contract.

In California, Georgia, Montana, South Dakota, Wisconsin, and Utah, a purchaser whose contract has been forfeited is allowed to get back the amount it has paid, less a reasonable compensation to the seller for the use of his or her land. Illinois, Iowa, and Minnesota allow the purchaser to cure defaults within a specified grace period and thus preserve the contract. Arizona also provides a grace period that increases in proportion to the amount paid on the contract. *Real Property Installment Contracts—Vendee's Right to Equity of Redemption Denied,* 13 Rutgers L. Rev. 620, 624 (1959); Terence C. Porter, Comment, *Installment Contracts for the Sale of Land in Missouri,* 24 Mo. L. Rev. 240, 244 (1959). In Florida, Illinois, Indiana, and Maryland, the contract must be foreclosed like a mortgage. *Mid-State Inv. Corp. v. O'Steen,* 133 So. 2d 455 (Fla. App. 1961), *cert. denied,* 136 So. 2d 349 (Fla. 1961); *Skendzel v. Marshall,* 301 N.E.2d 641 (Ind. 1973); 735 ILCS 5/15-1106(a). However, in most states, the forfeiture provisions in the contract will be enforced. *Coe v. Bennett,* 46 Idaho 62, 266 P. 413 (1928); 4 A.L.R.4th 993, *supra.*

Perhaps the most important clause in an installment contract, from the seller's point of view, is the forfeiture clause.

In various circumstances, courts will allow the buyer to recover a portion of the purchase price he or she has paid. 4 A.L.R.4th 993, *supra.*

12.16(e) Relief Against Forfeiture— Forfeiture and Damages

Courts will, on occasion, set aside a forfeiture of an installment contract. Allen E. Korpela, Annotation, *Specific Performance of Land Contract Notwithstanding Failure of Vendee to Make Required Payments on Time*, 55 A.L.R.3d 10 (1974); *Restatement (Second) of Contracts,* § 214(d), 276. The more money the buyer has paid, the more likely the court is to do this. Where the buyer has made substantial improvements, it is quite likely to obtain this sort of relief. *Krentz v. Johnson,* 36 Ill. App. 3d 142, 343 N.E.2d 165 (1976). The more lenient the seller has been in accepting short payments or delayed payments, the greater the likelihood that the forfeiture will be set aside. *Krentz v. Johnson, supra.* Where the buyer's breach consists of failing to make repairs, the seller's notice must give the buyer a reasonable time to make repairs. Otherwise, the forfeiture cannot stand. Where the forfeiture notice was sent to the wrong address, the forfeiture cannot stand. *Kingsley v. Roeder,* 2 Ill. 2d 131, 117 N.E.2d 82 (1954). Whenever it would be unreasonable to let the seller keep the buyer's payments and, at the same time, oust the buyer from the land, the forfeiture will be set aside. *McWilliams v. Urban Am. Land Dev. Co.,* 194 N.W.2d 920 (Mich. App. 1972). In such cases, the court may order foreclosure by sale, which gives the buyer a right to redeem. *Ruhl v. Johnson,* 159 Neb. 810, 49 N.W.2d 687 (1951). Where the buyer's payments amount to little more than the rental value of the land, the case for relief is poor. But where the seller is in default, any forfeiture declared will be set aside.

Some states that normally allow the remedy of forfeiture, nevertheless insist on foreclosure where the buyer has paid in substantial amounts.

> **EXAMPLE:** Court refused forfeiture and ordered foreclosure where buyer had paid 30 percent of sale price. *Morris v. Weigle,* 383 N.E.2d 341 (Ind. 1978).

Some courts put this on the ground that a forfeiture in such cases is *unconscionable. Williams v. Havens,* 444 P.2d 132 (Idaho 1968). Other courts state that forfeiture in such cases "shocks the conscience of the court." *Kay v. Wood,* 549 P.2d 709 (Utah 1976); *Jenkins v. Wise,* 574 P.2d 1337 (Haw. 1978). Of course, some courts are more liberal with purchasers than others. It is not possible to state a definite rule as to what size of an investment will protect a buyer against forfeiture. *Clements v. Castle Mtg. Service Co.,* 382 A.2d 1367 (Del. 1977).

12.17 Foreclosure

A seller may file a foreclosure suit if the buyer defaults. The foreclosure may be a *strict foreclosure. Walker v. Nunnenkamp,* 373 P.2d 559 (Idaho 1962); A.G.S., Annotation, *Vendor's Remedy by Foreclosure of Contract for Sale of Real Property,* 77 A.L.R. 270, 282 (1932). In such a foreclosure, the purchaser will be given a period of time to pay up, and if it fails to do so, the buyer's rights will be extinguished. Alternatively, the court may order a foreclosure sale of the land. 77 A.L.R. 270, 276, *supra.* If foreclosure is by sale, some states allow some sort of redemption period. L.S. Teller, Annotation, *Redemption Rights of Vendee Defaulting Under Executory Land Sale Contract After Foreclosure Sale or Foreclosure Decree Enforcing Vendor's Lien or Rights*, 51 A.L.R.2d 672 (1957). Other states allow no redemption period.

As in the case of forfeitures, the court may hold in foreclosure cases that the seller has waived the contract provision that time is of the essence.

EXAMPLE: Seller entered into an installment contract with Buyer. The contract contained an acceleration clause. From time to time, Buyer was delinquent in its payments and Seller wrote dunning letters. Finally, Seller, in exasperation, declared all the contract price due and filed a suit to foreclose. Buyer tendered all back payments into court. The court dismissed the foreclosure. *Stinemeyer v. Wesco Farms, Inc.,* 487 P.2d 65 (Or. 1971).

This last example is relatively new law, but is likely to become the law in many states. The courts, in their desire to ameliorate hardships, are quite likely to set aside accelerations.

12.18 Statutory Remedies of Seller   In some states, Minnesota, for example, the seller uses a statutory remedy to terminate a defaulting buyer. 77 Am. Jur. 2d *Vendor & Purchaser* § 585 (1975).

CHAPTER 13

Fraud and Misrepresentation
in Real Estate Transactions

13.01 In General   Suits for fraud or misrepresentation have been in our courts for many years. Of course, virtually all of these suits are filed by disappointed purchasers who discovered that the seller had made a false statement, or a misrepresentation, concerning some important, material aspect of the property that was the subject of the transaction. In the usual situation, the falsity of the statement is discovered after the deal has closed and the buyer has taken possession of the property. It is then that the buyer discovers the misrepresentation. At that point, the buyer has a choice. It could file a suit for money damages in a law court. If successful, the buyer would keep the property and be compensated for the damages caused by the seller. Alternatively, the buyer could file a suit in a chancery court, or equity court, and seek to have the transaction set aside or rescinded. If the buyer succeeds in the rescission suit, it would get its money back and return the property to the seller.

    If the buyer chooses to sue the seller for damages, the earliest rule required the buyer to prove that the seller knew the statements were false and intended to deceive the buyer. In effect, the law courts would only punish a deliberate lie. The chancery court, however, did not insist on proof of a deliberate lie. If the misrepresentation was as to some material fact, the chancery court would set the transaction aside, even though the seller was ignorant of the defect. The chancery or equity court does not require proof of an intention to deceive. The seller may be innocent, yet chancery will set the deal aside. *Norton v. Poplos,* 443 A.2d 1 (Del. 1981). Of course, chancery would also rescind if the seller had deliberately lied. Dobbs, *Remedies,* Ch. 4.

13.02 Fraud by Conduct   While most fraud consists of spoken or written words, fraud may also be found in the conduct of the seller.

> **EXAMPLE:** Seller owns a home. The basement floods whenever it rains heavily and there are marks along the entire basement wall showing the level which flood water reaches. Seller decides to sell the home, and paints the basement, obliterating the flood line or mark. Buyer inspects the basement. Not seeing any evidence of the flooding, Buyer buys the home. The first heavy rain reveals the problem. Buyer can sue Seller for damages or to set the deal aside. *Russow v. Bobola,* 2 Ill. App.3d 837, 277 N.E.2d 769 (1972).

> **EXAMPLE:** Seller used deodorant to conceal the fact that carpets were soaked with dog urine. Seller is liable for damages. *Campbell v. Booth,* 526 S.W.2d 167 (Tex. Civ. App. 1975).

> **EXAMPLE:** The seller showed the property to the buyer as a multiple-family dwelling and commented on the rents generated by the building. This was a tacit representation that the premises were legally usable as an apartment building, which was false, for such use violated the city ordinances. It was held that the buyer could declare the contract void and rescind the deal upon discovering the fraud. *Gamble v. Beahm,* 198 Or. 537, 257 P.2d 882 (1953).

This same result would follow if there is any statement in the contract itself or the advertisements or promotional material for the sale of the property that can be construed as representing that the existing use of the building is legal, as when the contract describes the building as a "store and dwelling" when such use is actually illegal.

13.03 Nondisclosure

Failure of the seller to disclose some basic fact or flaw known to the seller that would not be evident on any ordinary inspection of the premises furnishes grounds for a suit for damages or rescission.

> **EXAMPLE:** Seller (a builder) builds a home on filled ground. Building on landfill usually results in serious settling and cracks in the house. Seller says nothing to Buyer. The house looks fine. Buyer buys it and, later, cracks begin to develop. Buyer can sue for damages or rescission. Vitauts M. Gulbris, Annotation, *Statutes of Limitation: Actions by Purchasers or Contractees Against Vendors or Contractors Involving Defects in Houses or Other Buildings Caused By Soil Instability*, 12 A.L.R.4th 866 (1982).

> **EXAMPLE:** Seller owns a home that it knows to be termite infested. Seller sells the home to Buyer, saying nothing. Again, most courts today say that Buyer can sue for damages or rescission. E.T. Tsai, Annotation, *Duty of Vendor of Real Estate to Give Purchaser Information as to Termite Infestation*, 22 A.L.R.3d 972 (1968).

> **EXAMPLE:** Seller failed to disclose to Buyer that a woman and her four children had been murdered in the home. This is fraud. No one wants to be a landlord to ghosts. *Reed v. King,* 193 Cal. Rptr. 130 (1983).

This is an example of the ever-changing nature of the law. The seller says or does nothing to deceive the buyer. In former times, the buyer would have no remedy. The law said, "Let the buyer beware." This attitude has virtually disappeared. *Passive concealment* is as reprehensible as a deliberate lie. *Holcomb v. Zinke,* 365 N.W.2d 507 (N.D. 1985). *See also* Janet Fairchild, Annotation, *Fraud Predicated on Vendor's Misrepresentation or Concealment of Danger or Possibility of Flooding or Other Unfavorable Water Conditions*, 90 A.L.R.3d 569 (1979) (flooding), and 90 *id.* 592 (roof leaks). *Johnson v. Davis,* 480 So. 2d 625 (Fla. 1986).

Recent cases have focused on the duty of the seller to disclose the fact that the property being sold may be "psychologically tainted." The taint arises from the fact that a suicide, murder, or rape may have occurred in the property, or that an AIDS patient may have lived in the property.

> **EXAMPLE:** Buyer asked Seller why bars were on some of the windows in the house. Seller responded that there was a break-in several years ago. Seller withheld information about crime in the neighborhood and that Seller's daughter was raped in the house only a year prior to the sale. The court held that the Seller did not make adequate disclosure of the facts. *Van Camp v. Bradford*, 623 N.E.2d 731 (Ohio Com. PL. 1993).

> **EXAMPLE:** A seller failed to disclose reports that a house was haunted. Stories of poltergeists in the house were in the local and national press. The purchaser could not have been expected to discover the situation. For the court to rule otherwise would place an impossible burden upon the buyer. *Stambovsky v. Ackley*, 572 N.Y.S.2d 672 (1991).

Several states have enacted laws that relieve the seller from liability for not revealing such matters.

13.04 Buyer's Failure to Investigate

Where the buyer has information readily available to it, but does not attempt to learn the true facts, the buyer may not be able to pursue the seller for the seller's misrepresentation or nondisclosure. *Halbrooks v. Jackson,* 495 So. 2d 591 (Ala. 1996); *Brakebill v. Hicks,* 388 S.E.2d 695 (Ga. 1990). *But see Chapman v. Rideout,* 568 A.2d 829 (Me. 1990); *Soursby v. Hawkins,* 737 P.2d 145 (Or. App. 1987).

**13.05
Nondisclosure—
Environmental
Matters**

As is often the case, developments in different areas of the law converge. One set of such converging developments is the law requiring the disclosure of facts or defects in the property that are not evident upon an ordinary inspection of the property with the law relating to environmental matters. It may be prudent for a property seller to disclose the known existence of environmental defects in the property being sold. In commercial transactions where the buyer has retained environmental consultants, it may be argued that the buyer had adequate opportunity to discover the environmental defects and thus has no right against the seller for nondisclosure.

It is also crucial that the seller analyze carefully the general representations given in a real estate sales contract so that representations against material defects and the like do not include environmental matters.

**13.06 Broker's
Liability**

The seller's broker is the seller's agent and the seller is liable for the agent's fraud, misrepresentation, or fraudulent concealment of facts.

> **EXAMPLE:** Seller's broker knew that several earth movements and slides had damaged the building. This was not disclosed to Buyer. The broker was held liable to Buyer. *Easton v. Strassburger,* 199 Cal. Rptr. 383 (Cal. App. 1984).

Thus, the seller's broker is under a duty to disclose to the buyer any material defects known to the broker but unknown to the buyer and not observable on ordinary inspection. The court went on to say that the broker is liable for negligence, that is, for failure to inspect and discover defects and reveal them to the purchaser. This last liability of the broker is a relatively new development in the law. Negligence is very different from fraud.

As noted in the chapter dealing with real estate brokers, the multiple listing system (MLS), and the liability it creates, is a somewhat changing area of the law. Some decisions follow:

> **EXAMPLE:** Seller listed his home with Weagley, a broker-member of the MLS. Weagley prepared the listing sheet, which stated, "All In Top Shape." The listing sheet was furnished to Graham, a member of the MLS. He showed it to Buyer. The house turned out to have severe defects. Buyer sued Graham and was awarded damages. *Gouveia v. Citicorp Person-to-Person Fin. Center, Inc.,* 686 P.2d 262 (N.M. 1984).

> **EXAMPLE:** The listing broker put an incorrect area statement in the listing sheet, and this false information was transmitted by the MLS to the selling broker. The selling broker gave this false information to the buyer. The buyer sued *both* brokers and *both* were held liable. *First Church, etc. v. Cline J. Duntom Realty,* 574 P.2d 1211 (Wash. 1978). The court held that a listing broker, the agent of the seller, has authority to hire another broker to help sell the property. This is done through the MLS and the selling broker becomes the subagent of the seller. This so-called "subagency" makes the selling broker liable to the buyer.

In addition to the common law, or the law made by court decisions, statutory law may have application to fraud and nondisclosure situations.

> **EXAMPLE:** Seller wished to sell his home, but needed the proceeds of sale to buy another home. Seller explained this to his broker. Seller asked the broker what price he could expect to receive from the home sale. The broker stated a sale price of $162,000. The seller bought

a new home, but could not sell the old home even at the reduced price of $137,000. The broker was totally innocent, and believed the old home could be sold for much more. Nevertheless, under the Consumer Fraud Act (which many states have enacted) the broker is liable for damages. *Duhl v. Nash Reality, Inc.,* 102 Ill. App. 3d 474, 429 N.E.2d 1267 (1982).

EXAMPLE: Seller's broker represented to Buyer that the existing mortgage (which Buyer intended to assume) bore an interest rate of 9%. It later turned out the interest rate was 12%. The broker was held liable to Buyer under the Consumer Fraud Act. *Beard v. Gress,* 90 Ill. App. 3d 622, 413 N.E.2d 448 (1980).

As is evident, new and terrifying liabilities are being thrust upon the broker. It is a Catch-22 situation. If the broker reveals the facts and defects, the deal may die. If the broker does not, the broker will be liable for damages suffered by the buyer.

These state consumer fraud acts can be traced back to federal legislation. Deceptive acts and practices are declared unlawful by Section 5(a) of the Federal Trade Commission Act. 15 U.S.C. § 45. The state laws are modeled after this federal law. They usually provide for public or private enforcement.

The Illinois Consumer Fraud Act was amended in 1982 to protect a broker or its salesperson from liability for the communication of any false, misleading, or deceptive information provided by the seller of real estate located in Illinois unless the salesperson or broker *knows* of the false, misleading, or deceptive character of such information.

Some courts are beginning to hold the broker liable for *innocent misrepresentation.*

EXAMPLE: Broker innocently stated to buyer that hotel was on five acres of land. Buyer later found land was only half that size. Broker was held liable. *Gauerke v. Rozga,* 332 N.W.2d 804 (Wis. 1983).

EXAMPLE: Broker innocently represented that a well supplied an adequate amount of water. The supply was found to be inadequate. Broker was held liable. *Bevins v. Ballard,* 655 P.2d 757 (Alaska 1982).

EXAMPLE: Seller's broker represents to Buyer that the land is zoned commercial when in fact part of it is zoned residential. Broker is liable to Buyer. *Barnes v. Lopaz,* 25 Ariz. App. 477, 544 P.2d 694 (1976).

A broker must have general knowledge of the building code and zoning ordinances applicable to the property being sold. *Amato v. Rathbun Realty, Inc.,* 647 P.2d 433 (N.M. 1982). The philosophy here seems to be that since a broker holds itself out as an expert, and its business consists of supplying information to others, the broker must accept this added liability. In other words, the broker must carefully analyze the property offered for sale.

In a recent decision, a purchaser of a home sued the seller and the seller's broker for fraud. *Munjal v. Baird & Warner, Inc.,* 485 N.E.2d 855 (Ill. App. 1985). The defect complained of was extensive flooding of the basement, of which the seller was aware. The seller failed to disclose this fact to the buyer. The broker was unaware of the flooding, but when the buyer drew the broker's attention to a leak, the broker urged the seller to consult an attorney. The court held the seller liable, stating that its failure to disclose the problem constituted fraud. This, of course, is the modern rule.

As to the broker, the court held that no liability had been shown. The broker was unaware of the problem, and the court was unwilling to impose on the broker a duty to make an exhaustive inspection to ascertain the presence of the defect. This is a sensible decision. It is the practice of Realtors to examine a home before accepting a listing. This is done to determine the probable market value, to fix a suggested listing price, and to point out matters that might make the home more attractive and salable, such as repairing leaking faucets, washing or painting walls, etc. The broker, after all, will represent the seller. It is his or her duty to help the seller.

However, the buyer should not expect the broker to make the kind of inspection that a professional inspector will make for a buyer. Professional inspectors will inspect the home for the buyer and assume the negligence liability this entails. Many of them give written warranties.

13.07   Mandatory Disclosure

As discussed in Chapter 10, many states have enacted laws requiring written disclosures to be made to the purchaser by the seller prior to the execution of the contract. While there was initial reluctance about the effect of these disclosure laws, now that they are prevalent and every seller must comply, the initial concern over these laws has eased. While the seller must be truthful in completing the disclosure statement, the statement protects both the seller and the buyer. The buyer is protected by knowing more about the property, and thus can make an informed purchase decision with knowledge of the typical factors that may be material defects, such as flooding, termites or other pests, filled ground, environmental contamination, inoperable building systems, and the like. The seller is protected because a written disclosure has been made and preserved in the file for use in defense of claims by the purchaser that it was duped and misinformed about the condition of the property.

13.08   Conclusion

Clearly, the courts are imposing stricter standards of liability on sellers of real estate and their brokers. Predictably, the development of this trend will be spotty. Some states will move faster and farther than others. Brokers, in particular, will be faced with some serious problems. Craig A. Peterson, *Tort Claims by Real Estate Purchasers Against Sellers and Brokers: Current Illinois Common Law and Statutory Strategies,* 1983 So. Ill. U.L.J. 161; M. David LeBrun, Annotation, *Recovery of Punitive Damages in Action By Purchaser of Real Property Charging Fraud or Misrepresentation,* 19 A.L.R.4th 801 (1983).

CHAPTER 14

Closing Real Estate Transactions: Loan Closings; Escrows

14.01 Closing or Settlement Defined

After the contract of sale has been signed, a number of details must be addressed. For example, the title must be examined to determine if the seller really owns the property and what mortgages, liens, restrictions, and the like encumber the seller's title. A survey must be obtained. The property must be inspected to ascertain whether there are any encroachments, unrecorded easements, and unrecorded rights of parties in possession. When all of this is completed and the seller is able to perform in the manner required by the contract, the seller gives the buyer a deed, and the seller is paid the balance of the purchase price. All of this is the process of *closing the deal*. In some states, this actual closing of the transaction is referred to as *settlement*. Often, much the same process is taking place with respect to the buyer's mortgage, and there will be a simultaneous *loan closing*.

Although the two closings, sale and loan, involve simultaneous processing and may culminate in a single meeting when both transactions are finalized, each process will be discussed separately. This is in recognition of the two distinct sets of relationships, which, although they involve the same subject matter, give rise to different rights and obligations.

As can be seen, the time necessary to take a real estate deal from contract through closing generally takes several weeks. While the length of time varies from deal to deal, there are several different phases of work to be done in the closing process. First, the postcontract deliveries must be made. For example, in commercial property transactions, the buyer will often receive many documents relating to the construction of the buildings, the income and expenses derived from the property, and the permits, warranties, and other matters that relate to the operation of the property. The parties must also attend to the fulfillment of the contingencies or conditions that must be satisfied or waived before one or the other of the parties is obligated to close the deal. Title evidence for the real property and lien searches covering the personal property involved in the transaction are ordered along with a survey of the property. The seller will work on clearing liens and other encumbrances from the title or survey to satisfy the contractual agreement relating to the quality of title to be conveyed. The closing documents must be prepared and exchanged for approvals of counsel, and the parties must agree on closing statement items. The buyer will obtain insurance and order the opening of accounts with local utility companies and other service providers so that the property will be operating without interruption through and after the closing. Finally, the closing takes place and the title and possession of the property are transferred from the seller to the buyer.

14.02 The Lawyer's Role

The need for counsel in a real estate transaction is demonstrated by the following examples:

EXAMPLE: Buyer signed a contract of sale to buy a vacant corner lot upon which the buyer intended to erect a service station. Buyer had no lawyer. After the deal closed, Buyer discovered that the lot was zoned for single-family dwellings and that service stations were a prohibited use of the property. A lawyer would have inquired into the zoning of the property before the contract was signed or would have called for the production of adequate evidence that the intended use could be had of the property.

EXAMPLE: Without counsel, Buyer entered into a contract for the purchase of a vacant lot upon which Buyer intended to construct a veterinary hospital. The preprinted form contract called for Buyer to accept title subject to "building restrictions of record." When the title search was produced, it showed that the title was subject to a building restriction that permitted only residential uses. Buyer was faced with either going through with a transaction that would result in Buyer's acquisition of land that was not suitable for the intended purpose or being in breach of the contract and possibly forfeiting the earnest money. This predicament could have been avoided if Buyer had retained counsel before signing the contract.

Obviously, examples such as these take place all the time. They need not occur. An attorney is needed from the precontract stage through the closing. Many people fail to recognize this need until it is too late. This is particularly true in residential transactions, perhaps the largest single transaction many people ever have in their lifetimes. Rather than rely upon the advice of counsel, many consumers eagerly execute the purchase contract and rely on sheer luck to pull them through. Many "average" homes have selling prices of several hundreds of thousands of dollars, but buyers and sellers of these properties only rarely have representation when the blueprint for the transaction, the real estate sales contract, is executed. What is more incredible is the number of people who carry the transaction through to closing without counsel, only to find to their chagrin that they were penny-wise and dollar foolish.

14.02(a) Conflict of Interest

It has long been a rule of legal ethics that a lawyer is forbidden from representing conflicting interests in a transaction without full disclosure and consent by all of the parties. This disclosure must not only be of the multiple representation, but also of the effect of this representation upon the exercise of the lawyer's professional judgment on behalf of each party. The real estate sales transaction is a somewhat frequent scene for this practice, as in the case of a developer's attorney who is automatically denominated as buyer's counsel as a form of repayment for services rendered to the developer. *See In re Kamp,* 194 A.2d 236 (N.J. 1963). This activity may lead to professional sanctions being taken against the lawyer. *The Florida Bar v. Tietelman,* 261 So. 2d 140 (Fla. 1972). It may also have repercussions for the clients.

EXAMPLE: A purchaser was entitled to rescind a real estate sales contract when it was represented by the seller's counsel, who failed to disclose to the purchaser the existence of a lien on the property. The court found this to be a material fraud on the part of the seller. *Holley v. Jackson,* 158 A.2d 803 (Del. 1959).

Some lawyers are also real estate brokers and insurance brokers. They should maintain separate offices for each business. The real estate brokerage, the insurance business, and the law practice must be operated completely separately. H. Lee Roussel & Mose K. Rosenberg, *Lawyer-Controlled Title Insurance Companies: Legal Ethics and the Need for Insurance Department Regulations*, 48 Fordham L. Rev. 25, 38 (1980). *See also* Ill. St. Bar Ass'n Ethics Opinion No. 84-14; Raymond J. Werner, *Real Estate Closings,* 5 (2d ed. 1988).

14.03   Matters to Be Considered Before Closing

The first step in preparing for the closing is to read the contract and identify the obligations of the parties. For example, the contract will typically require that the seller deliver evidence of title to the buyer within a set time period. The seller must know of this requirement and order the title commitment from the title company sufficiently in advance so that the delivery requirement is met.

The parties should calendar the critical dates set out in the contract so that they have an eye on the time requirements set by the contract and are acting to meet those requirements without waiving any rights that the contract terms may give them.

> **EXAMPLE:** If the contract contains a mortgage contingency clause, the buyer will usually have to make good-faith efforts to obtain the mortgage financing and, if a loan commitment is not received, notify the seller of the inability to fulfill the commitment within the period of time allowed by the contract. If this notice is not given on time, the buyer will typically waive its right to avoid the contract.

It is best to prepare a closing checklist that lists the critical dates and the pre- and post-closing tasks to be performed. This is an efficient device to be used by the client and counsel to assign these tasks between them as a device for controlling legal fees.

14.03(a)   Evidence of Title

If the contract requires the seller to furnish an abstract or other evidence of title, the seller should do so within the time allowed by the contract, for if the seller fails to do so, a reluctant buyer may seize the opportunity to cancel the deal. The buyer, in turn, should within the time allowed by the contract, draw attention to any defects in title not permitted by the contract. Otherwise the buyer will be regarded as waiving such defects. The seller should then, within the permitted time, cure any defects pointed out by the buyer. When the contract specifies that the seller shall furnish an abstract of title showing clear title, the buyer has a right to insist that quitclaim deeds and other documents needed to clear the buyer's title objections be recorded and included in an update to the abstract of title. *Kincaid v. Dobrinsky*, 225 Ill. App. 85 (1922). When the contract calls for a title insurance policy showing clear title in the seller, the buyer has the right to insist that all unauthorized objections be cleared from the title policy by the seller.

The buyer should consider whether special coverage endorsements (i.e., zoning coverage or an encroachment endorsement), should be ordered from the title insurance company. Even if the contract does not require the seller to provide these special endorsements, or the transaction may not be contingent upon the title company's willingness to issue such coverage, the buyer may be well advised to order the special endorsements that are appropriate for the transaction. Werner, *Real Estate Closings,* Ch. 2 (2d ed. 1988).

14.03(b)   Closing Documents

Closing document preparation takes a great deal of time and care. In larger deals, it is usual for the closing documents to be identified in, or even made exhibits to, the real estate sale contract. In other transactions, the exact nature and form of the closing documents must be worked out as the closing approaches. Typical closing documents are as follows:

1. Deed.
2. Sellers' affidavit stating that there are no adverse matters affecting title that are not shown on the title commitment or preliminary title. The title insurance company may also require an ALTA Loan and Extended Coverage Owner's Policy Statement. A misrepresentation in the affidavit will support an action for damages. *Somerset County v. Durling,* 415 A.2d 371 (N.J. 1980).
3. Bill of sale for personal property.
4. Evidence of compliance with fire, health, building, and zoning laws and ordinances.

5. Bulk sales affidavit.

6. Updated chattel lien search.

7. Closing statement that contains the itemization of the purchase price, adjustments to the purchase price, prorations of rents, taxes and other revenue and expense items relating to the property, and the allocation of the costs of the transaction between the buyer and the seller, all ultimately calculating the amount that the buyer must pay at the closing and the closing proceeds that the seller will take from the closing.

8. Condominium association's waiver of the right of first refusal.

9. Corporate resolutions.

10. Declaration of homestead.

11. Environmental audit. The typical approach is to obtain a "Phase 1" audit, which is based upon a review of the property, its prior uses, surrounding properties and their uses, and a check of the records of the EPA and the local building department and the chain of title. The Phase 1 audit is intended to determine whether there is a reason to go further to determine that hazardous materials are present. In residential properties, the analysis is typically somewhat less extensive, focusing on the presence of radon, asbestos, and lead-based paint., If the Phase 1 audit reveals the possible presence of hazardous materials, the next step is to conduct a more rigorous examination of the property, which will entail testing and sampling for the actual presence of these materials.

12. Foreign Investment in Real Property Tax Act (FIRPTA) documentation needed to establish an exemption or to meet withholding requirements of the act.

13. Indemnity agreements called for by the contract or otherwise agreed upon by the parties to take care of contingencies and further performance that the parties agree can be performed after the closing.

14. Inspections of the property by a qualified property inspector, architect, or engineer. With more frequency, buyers are requiring that the property be inspected as a contingency for the closing of the deal. These inspections go beyond the environmental audit and address the physical condition of the buildings and improvements on the property. Often these inspections are conducted promptly after the contract is signed. If the property does not pass inspection, the buyer may terminate the contract or perhaps negotiate for a reduction in the purchase price.

15. Insurance policies, if they are to be assigned, together with evidence of premium payments and the insurer's consent to the assignment. Assignment of insurance policies was typically the norm in real estate transactions. Today, most buyers, whether consumers or businesses, have their own insurance packages and agents with whom they deal. As a result, the seller typically cancels its insurance shortly after the closing, and the buyer typically obtains its own insurance shortly before the closing.

16. Internal Revenue Service reporting forms, including IRS form 1099-B, to report the gross proceeds of the sale. See Section 14.03(e), *infra*.

17. Originals of all leases and contracts that will continue in effect after the closing, together with any needed consents to the assignment from other parties to the contracts.

18. Mortgages to be assumed at the closing. A buyer who is taking subject to existing financing should obtain a copy of the outstanding mortgage and note. The existing mortgagee should also give an estoppel statement showing the amount due on the existing mortgage so that it cannot later assert that a larger amount is due. If the buyer is taking title subject to an existing mortgage, the contract should be contingent upon, and the closing documents should include, the lender's written consent to the sale, if the mortgage has a due-on-sale clause. As a condition to giving its consent, the lender will typically want the buyer to assume the mortgage and other loan documents.

19. Opinions of counsel regarding the validity of corporate documents, usury, zoning, etc.

20. Memorandum of closing, stating that all contract requirements have been fulfilled, is sometimes signed by the buyer and seller to preclude bickering over what should have been done prior to the closing.

21. Payoff statements on encumbrances to be paid off and released at the closing and that can be relied on by the parties. *Mid-State Homes, Inc. v. Startley,* 366 So. 2d 734 (Ala. App. 1979). A

special problem is presented when the existing mortgage is a revolving credit or credit line mortgage. The outstanding balance on these loans fluctuates as the borrower, often unilaterally, obtains an additional advance. This can be done by going to the lender to obtain additional funds to be secured by the mortgage, or, in some consumer loan settings, by simply writing a check or using a charge card. Lenders are unwilling to give binding payoff statements in this setting unless the borrower is deprived of the ability to increase the loan balance. Obviously, these payoffs must be carefully worked out on a case-by-case basis. Most importantly, the underlying loan must first be identified as a revolving credit or credit line mortgage to enable the problem to even be addressed. If the existing lender is consenting to the sale subject to the existing mortgage, on the condition that the interest rate be increased, loan term altered, or the like, the documents recasting the loan must be drawn and executed. Here, too, the lender should give a statement of the current status of the loan, stating the date through which payments have been made; the loan balance, including both principal, interest, and late charges; and the balance in the real estate tax and insurance escrow accounts.

22. Permits for curb cuts, awnings, etc.

23. Pest control report.

24. Plans and specifications. On big buildings, the buyer wants to get the plans that depict the building "as built." No building is ever built 100 percent according to the original plans. For example, pipes and conduits are often relocated when construction reveals that the planned locations are impractical.

25. Power of attorney.

26. Real estate tax bill upon which the tax proration will be based.

27. Real estate transfer tax declaration or return.

28. Receipt for broker's commission.

29. Soil test report.

30. Survey.

31. Tenant roster, rent roll, outstanding leases, assignment of leases, letter to tenants. Where a building is managed by a responsible management firm, buyers and lenders customarily accept a manager's letter as to apartment leases. On commercial properties, space leases are usually checked unless they are short-term office leases. The manager's letter always covers renewal options, purchase options, advance payments of rent, and security deposits.

32. Owner's title insurance policy.

33. Warranties from the builder, roofer, appliance manufacturers, etc.

14.03(c) Prior Approvals

Since closings are apt to be fairly hectic, it is a good idea for the parties to submit to each other, in advance of closing, all the documents that will then be exchanged, such as the deed, mortgage note, survey, leases, and assignments. The documents are then checked in the quietude of one's office and pencil initials are placed in a corner of the document. Further scrutiny of the form at the time of closing is then omitted, although a check of signatures and acknowledgments will still be needed at that time. If documents affecting the title are at all unusual, it is best to have them approved by the title officer before they are put into final form and executed.

14.03(d) Income Tax Withholding—FIRPTA

Foreign investors in U.S. real estate are required to make certain disclosures or filings. The Deficit Reduction Act of 1984 requires that the buyer deduct and withhold 10 percent of the purchase price on the sale of a U.S. real property interest. If the buyer fails to deduct and withhold this amount and the transaction is not otherwise exempt, the buyer will be exposed to liability to the IRS. 26 U.S.C. § 1445; 26 C.F.R. § 1.1445-1T, *et seq.,* 49 Fed. Reg. 50,667, *et seq.* (Dec. 31, 1984).

The parties should have their real estate sales contract drawn to accommodate the handling of this withholding requirement. When the deal works its way to the closing stage, the buyer must ensure that the transaction either falls within an exemption to the act or that a withholding is made. Either of these approaches will typically involve the preparation and execution of additional closing documentation. If a withholding is to be made, the transferee is to report and pay the amount withheld to the IRS within ten days after the transfer date. IRS forms 8288 and 8288A are used for this purpose.

FIRPTA allows exemptions to its withholding requirement. If exempt, all but the most sophisticated real estate transactions will fall within one of three categories. Perhaps the most common exemption applies in situations where the property is acquired by the buyer for use as a residence and the purchase price is $300,000 or less. For this exemption to apply, the buyer must plan to live in the property for at least 50 percent of the days that the property is in use during the first two twelve-month periods after the sale. The danger in relying upon this exemption lies in the fact that the buyer's change of plans could make the buyer liable for the tax if the seller does not pay it.

If the buyer relies upon this residential exemption, no special documentation is required, but the possible need to prove to the IRS that withholding was not required on the transaction is one more reason for the buyer to retain the transactional documents, such as the contract, closing statement, deed, and title policy.

Another exemption applies if the seller is not a foreign person. While the buyer may use any, or no, means to determine whether the seller is a foreign person, the Foreign Investment in Real Property Tax Act establishes a means by which the buyer can be protected from tax liability if it is later determined that the seller is a foreign person. This is accomplished by the buyer simply obtaining a Certificate of Nonforeign Status, wherein the seller, under penalty of perjury, states that it is not a foreign person and gives its name, address, and taxpayer identifying number. The buyer may rely upon this certificate, and make no withholding, even if the certificate is false, unless the buyer knows that the certificate is false or receives notice of its falsity. The buyer must retain this certificate for five years after the year of transfer and make it available to the IRS upon request.

Another exemption applies when the parties rely upon a Withholding Certificate, which is issued by the IRS and which states either that no withholding or a reduced withholding is appropriate.

Whatever device is used, the contract must set out a blueprint for handling this withholding requirement, and the transactional documents either must evidence the applicability of an exemption or a withholding must be made. If not, the buyer is exposed to tax liability for the foreign seller's failure to pay the tax relating to a gain realized upon the disposition of the property.

14.03(e) Income Tax Reporting

The Internal Revenue Code requires brokers to file an informational return showing the gross sales proceeds of transactions in which they were involved, I.R.C. § 6045(a), and to furnish customers with a statement reflecting the information shown on the return, I.R.C. § 6045(e). This return is to be made on form 1099-B promulgated by the IRS.

This reporting requirement has direct impact upon attorneys, title companies, mortgage lenders, and real estate brokers. This is because the term *real estate broker* is defined in the Code in such a way so as to place the responsibility for this reporting upon a hierarchy of participants in the closing in the following order:

1. The person (including any attorney or title company) responsible for closing the transaction.
2. The mortgage lender.
3. The seller's broker.

4. The buyer's broker.

5. Any such other person designated in the regulations.

These reporting requirements cause increasing use of the settlement services of escrowees to thereby shift the responsibility and the cost of providing these returns and statements to that closing agent. Real estate purchase and sale contracts should be drafted with that possibility in mind. They should at least contain the standard provision that either party may require that the transaction be closed in escrow with both parties bearing one half of the escrow fee. The escrow closing will cause the title company to be responsible for compliance with the IRS requirements.

Further, revisions should be made to standard real estate contract forms to require that the identification of the seller include the seller's social security number or taxpayer identification number to facilitate the filing of these returns.

In the event that the taxpayer fails to properly furnish its taxpayer identifying number, and in certain other instances, the "broker" may have to deduct and withhold 20 percent of the amount that would otherwise be paid to the taxpayer. The Tax Reform Act imposes this backup withholding requirement on real estate brokers. I.R.C. § 3047(B)(3)(C).

In the event that the real estate broker fails to file the return, a penalty of $50 for each failure shall be imposed. I.R.C. § 6652 (a)(1)(B). In the event that the failure to file amounts to an intentional disregard of the filing requirement, the penalty shall be 5 percent of the gross proceeds required to be reported. I.R.C. § 6652(a)(3).

14.03(f)   The Survey   The survey delivered by the seller must be carefully checked. A survey made ten years ago, for example, obviously will not cover buildings and other improvements erected since then. Does the survey locate the property with reference to known monuments, such as government section corners? Does it show the location of all buildings located on the land? Does it show the location of all buildings located on adjacent land? Are all buildings, walks, and so on well within the lines of the lot on which they belong? Do any structures extend over the setback lines established by city ordinances or building restrictions? Does the survey show whether upper portions of the buildings, such as bay windows or eaves, extend over the lot lines? Are there possible subsurface encroachments, such as footings on the building, extending into adjoining land?

The certificate of the survey should also be checked for an express declaration that it is intended to be relied upon and, if erroneous, can be sued upon by the buyer, his or her mortgagee, and their title companies. *Rozny v. Marnul,* 250 N.E.2d 659 (Ill. 1969); Note, 64 N.W.U. L. Rev. 903 (1961). *See* Robert Kratovil, *Modern Real Estate and Documentation,* Ch.7 (1975).

The standards by which surveys are to be prepared are established by local surveyors' associations and, on a national level, by the American Land Title Association and the American Congress on Surveying and Mapping. The most recent national standards were adopted in 1999. If the survey is prepared in accordance with those standards, it will be called an ALTA/ASCM land title survey. The standards establish technical requirements for the survey and what is to be shown on the survey. In addition, the standards include "Table A," which is a checklist of additional requirements that may be ordered with the survey. Those optional items include the following:

1. The placement of monuments at all major corners of the property;

2. A vicinity map;

3. The designation of the flood zone applicable to the property;

4. The area of the property;

5. The property contours and the datum of the elevations;

6. The identity and drawing of record setback, height, and bulk restrictions affecting the property;

7. The exterior dimensions of buildings at ground level, the area of the exterior footprint of the buildings or gross floor area of all buildings at ground level, and the height of all buildings;

8. The depiction of substantial visible improvements;

9. A drawing of the property's parking areas, and if the parking areas are striped, the striping, type, and number of parking spaces;

10. The location of access to a public highway;

11. The location of utilities serving the property;

12. Governmental agency survey-related requirements; and

13. Other significant observations.

14.03(g)   Chattel Lien Search

If valuable chattels are included in the sale, a search of the Uniform Commercial Code records should be made for financing statements affecting such chattels. This search requires care. Code filings relating to fixtures, crops, and consumer goods (stoves, refrigerators, and other appliances found in the ordinary home) are found in some local office, often the recorder's office, but in some states, in a department separate from the department where deeds are filed. Filings covering furniture and other chattels in a hotel or furnished apartment or raw materials in an industrial plant are likely to be found in some central office, usually that of the secretary of state.

14.03(h)   Ordinance Violations Search

If, in the particular community, it is possible to procure a title company or other search of city records as to building ordinance violations, this should be done. If such a search cannot be obtained, an architect or engineer should check the building carefully for violations and also examine the building's files in the office of the local building and zoning department.

14.03(i)   Inspection of the Property

Before closing the deal, the buyer should make a careful physical inspection of the property. Possession imparts constructive notice, and the buyer will take the property subject to the rights of the grantee under an unrecorded contract, or others whose interest is disclosed by their possession. If the premises are occupied by tenants, their occupancy is notice of their rights. Therefore, tenants' leases should be checked for options to renew or purchase. The buyer should not accept the seller's assurance that the tenants are on month-to-month tenancies. The buyer should check with the tenants to determine such things as the term of their tenancy; what furniture, appliances, equipment, and so on they claim; what security deposit they have made; whether they have paid any advance rent; the status of their rental obligation; and whether they claim that the landlord, and now the seller, is in default under the leases.

The buyer checks for the existence of unrecorded easements, for the buyer takes the property subject to unrecorded easements if the existence of the easement would be revealed by an inspection of the premises. The buyer should also check to see whether this particular transaction will result in the creation of any implied easements. It should be determined whether rear or side exits run over adjoining property, or whether shutters or doors open over adjoining premises thus making an easement necessary with the neighboring owner. If heat or other utilities are furnished by an adjoining building, a written agreement will be necessary. If vaults, marquees, and so forth extend into public streets or alleys, permits will be necessary.

If the buyer defers inspection until after the abstract or other evidence of title has been furnished, the buyer can check to see if the building violates any recorded building restrictions. Even if the contract requires the buyer to take subject to "building restrictions," the buyer is not required to take subject to violations of restrictions. Violations constitute a separate and distinct defect in title. The buyer should check for violations of zoning or building ordinances and for recent repairs or construction that might ripen into a mechanic's lien.

It is also customary to have an inspection shortly prior to the closing so that mechanical systems (heating, air conditioning, and so forth) can be checked to determine whether they are in operating condition and how they function. Sometimes, the buyer may want an inspection by a qualified home inspection company, in the case of residential property, or by an architect or engineer, in the case of commercial property. An appropriate contingency clause is often inserted in the contract, stating that the sale will close only if the inspection shows that all systems are in working order. This is also a good time for the seller to set out the drawings, blueprints, plans and specifications, warranties, instruction manuals, and so forth for the buyer and its staff. If the seller is reluctant to actually surrender these items until the sale closes, at least the buyer will know where to find these materials when possession is transferred.

Certainly, where the buyer is purchasing a newly constructed or rehabbed property, the buyer will want a certificate of occupancy issued by the local building department.

14.03(j) Impact of Local Ordinances

Until recently, real estate transactions were largely controlled by state law. Local ordinances, such as the zoning and building code, merely regulated how a building was used and whether a building was safe. In recent years, the extent of real estate regulation by municipalities has increased dramatically.

Initially drafted as revenue measures, local ordinances imposed taxes on real estate transactions. For example, the taxes imposed on a transfer of a parcel of Cook County real estate include a $1.00 per thousand dollar tax to the State of Illinois and a $0.50 per thousand dollar tax to Cook County. Local cities and villages impose an additional transfer tax ranging from $1.00 per thousand to $10.00 per thousand. These municipal taxes bring an extra $1,000 to $10,000 of cost to a $1,000,000 real estate transaction. Obviously, the buyer and seller must allocate the liability for the payment of these taxes in the real estate sales contract and, if possible, structure the transaction in a manner to properly minimize or avoid the tax.

Many cities have tacked other requirements onto the transfer tax process. Inspections are routinely required to determine whether the property is in compliance with the building and zoning code. Some villages require that the sewer and water charges be paid in full before the property is transferred. The transfer tax mechanics give the local authorities a convenient mechanism to enforce these local requirements. If they are not met, the village clerk will not sell the transfer tax stamps. Without the tax stamps, the county recorder will not accept the deed for recording and the transaction will not close.

Local transfer tax and inspection-type requirements vary considerably from town to town and often change without a great deal of publicity. Before any transaction is negotiated, the local municipality should be contacted to determine its current requirements. In addition to the penalties prescribed for violation of the ordinance, typically, transfer tax stamps will not be sold unless the buyer or seller presents evidence that the property is registered or exempt from the registration requirements of the ordinance. Without the transfer tax stamps, the deed cannot be recorded.

14.03(k)   Maintenance of Property from Date of Contract to Date of Closing

It is the seller's responsibility to maintain the property in a reasonable manner between the date of contract and the date of closing. If the seller permits the property to deteriorate, the buyer may sue the seller for damages, even after the deal is closed. Goldberg, *Sales of Real Property* 442; 92 C.J.S. *Vendor & Purchaser* § 286a.

14.04   Closing Practices

Closing practices vary from locality to locality and even within the same county. Depending upon local custom, closings are conducted by lending institutions, title insurance companies, escrow companies, real estate brokers, and attorneys for the buyer or seller. The "New York" style of closing has spread to many parts of the country, especially in large transactions. A title company representative is present at this closing to "mark up" a copy of the most recent title commitment, waiving matters that are cleared at the closing, and accepting the deed and other documents for recording. The buyer leaves the closing with a title policy or a marked-up commitment assuring the buyer's title, even if the deed is not yet recorded and the seller leaves the closing with the proceeds of the sale.

14.05   Bulk Sales Affidavits and Notices

A sale of real estate may incidentally involve the sale of the entire stock of goods, wares, or merchandise of the seller. It is necessary that such a sale comply with the local Bulk Sales Act, which usually involves giving notice of the pending sale to the creditors of the business so that they can protect their rights. U.C.C. § 6-101, *et seq.* Some states have enacted laws that require a preclosing filing with the state authorities. The state then searches its records to determine whether the seller is in arrears in its payment of taxes, unemployment compensation payments, and the like. Some cities have enacted similar ordinances. If the buyer proceeds to close without getting a clearance from the governmental office, the buyer may be liable for the seller's unpaid taxes and the like.

14.06   Closing Date

The contract of sale should fix a closing date, the time the deed is to be delivered, and the balance of the purchase price to be paid. If no closing date is fixed in the contract, it is presumed that the deal is to be closed within a reasonable time, and either buyer or seller may select a reasonable date and notify the other that it will be prepared to close at such time. Often, one of the parties is not prepared to close on the date specified in the contract and requests an adjournment of the closing. In such case, the other party, in granting the request for adjournment, specifies that the prorations or apportionment will be computed as of the original date or the adjourned date, whichever is more favorable to the party granting the concession. For example, if the adjournment is made at the request of the seller and the income of the building is greater than the carrying charges, the buyer will insist that the apportionment or prorations be computed as of the original date. The buyer will receive the rents from the date originally fixed for closing, and the seller will be entitled to interest on the unpaid balance of the purchase price and the purchase money mortgage from the original closing date. Of course, if the contract fixes a closing date and provides that time is of the essence, the party who is ready to close on the date fixed need not grant a request for an adjournment.

Some contracts fix a date that is to govern the prorations, regardless of the date of the delivery of the deed and actual closing. Other contracts provide that prorating or apportionment shall be computed as of the date of the delivery of the deed.

The buyer should not rely on any extension of time granted by the seller's lawyer or broker. Normally, neither of them has the power to grant extensions.

14.07 Matters to Be Attended to at Closing

14.07(a) Title

The buyer should make a final check to see that the title is clear and subject only to the encumbrances permitted by the contract. If the deal is not closed in escrow, the title commitment or preliminary title report should be dated down to cover the period between the date of the earlier commitment or report and the closing of the deal. Judgments or other liens may attach during the interval and will, of course, encumber the title acquired by the buyer. The buyer should at least insist that the seller's attorney give a written statement that the buyer's check will not be delivered to the seller until after the deed to the buyer has been recorded and the title is searched to cover that date. Of course, these dangers can be avoided. If, by agreement, the seller is to clear certain objections after closing, the buyer should retain part of the purchase price, usually double the amount of the lien involved, to ensure performance on the part of the seller.

14.07(b) Form and Contents of Documents Involved

The documents should all be checked to see if they are in proper form and comply with the contract. For example, if the deed to be given is a warranty deed, the "subject to" clause of the deed should be checked to make certain that it does not include any encumbrances that were not included in the "subject to" clause of the contract. The deed should also be checked to see if the recorder of deeds will accept it for recording. For example, in many states, laws forbid metes-and-bounds subdivisions, that is, the division of a tract of land into plots for sale without the formality of recording a subdivision plat. The recorder will often reject such a deed, and the buyer is left with a deed that it has paid for but cannot record to protect itself against claims by third parties.

If, as is so often the case, the major portion of the purchase price is being furnished by the buyer's mortgage lender, the attorneys will make a final check of the mortgage and note to see that the principal amount, interest rate, and monthly payments are in accordance with the loan commitment. If this has not previously been attended to, a similar check should be made of the other loan documents, such as the assignment of rents and waiver of defenses.

14.07(c) Water and Other Utility Bills

The buyer should call for the production of paid water and other utility bills. If these bills have not been paid, service to the building may be cut off. The water and other utility and service providers should be ready to change the accounts from the seller to the buyer on the closing date.

14.07(d) Payment of Purchase Price and Delivery of Documents

The balance due according to the closing statement should be paid and the documents to which each party is entitled delivered.

14.08 Closing Statement— Prorations

The contract of sale usually provides that various items shall be adjusted or prorated. Items not mentioned in the contract are nevertheless often prorated according to local custom. *O'Donnell v. Lutter,* 156 P.2d 958 (Cal. App. 1945); *Valley Garage, Inc. v. Nyseth,* 481 P.2d 17 (Wash. App. 1971). The prorating or adjustment results in credits and debits against each party. These are usually shown on a closing statement, which is also called a settlement statement. Forms of closing statements vary, but the HUD RESPA closing statement has become the norm in all but large commercial deals. Although the HUD closing statement may be used by the title and escrow companies in closing commercial transactions, parties to commercial transactions typically provide an additional closing statement on their own form.

A commonly used form lists in one column all credits due the seller and in a separate column all credits due the buyer. The completed statement is approved by the buyer and the seller. An extended discussion of the closing statement and its elements can be found in Raymond J. Werner, *Real Estate Closings,* Ch. 4 (2d ed. 1988).

While these calculations traditionally have been made by the use of proration tables, prorations today are often made by using pocket calculators or computers specially programmed to produce closing documents, including the closing statement and prorations.

14.08(a)   Closing Statement— Prorations—Merger

The concept of merger arises in various ways in the closing of a real estate transaction. The basic idea is that notwithstanding what is stated in the contract, the parties' actions in closing the transaction restate the obligations of the parties if they are at variance with the contract terms. For example, in a recent case, a court held that merger occurred and the seller was not entitled to reprorate real estate taxes, even though there was a clear mistake in the amount of the real estate taxes upon which the proration was based. *Batler, Capitel, & Schwartz v. Tapanes,* 517 N.E.2d 12 16 (Ill. App. 1987).

Obviously, if the parties want to avoid this result, they should agree otherwise in the contract or place a short provision into the closing statement itself to provide that errors may be corrected. It is typical to find a so-called "oops agreement" in a lender's closing package to expressly require the parties to correct any errors in the closing documents. This only relates to the agreement between the borrower and the lender and not to the agreement between the buyer and the seller.

14.08(b)   Closing Statement—Credits Due Seller

The usual credits due the seller are as follows:

1. Full purchase price.
2. Taxes and insurance reserves in existing lender's impound account, if buyer is taking subject to an existing mortgage.
3. Unearned insurance premiums, if an insurance policy is to be assigned to buyer.
4. Fuel on hand and building supplies, and other inventory to be sold to the buyer.
5. Any charges paid by the seller in advance, such as water tax, prepayments on exterminator or other service contracts, real estate taxes paid in advance.

14.08(c)   Closing Statement—Credits Due Buyer

The usual credits due the buyer are as follows:

1. Earnest money.
2. The principal, accrued interest, and other amounts due on any existing mortgages, if the purchaser is to take subject to or assume such mortgages. These amounts should be determined by reference to an estoppel statement obtained from the underlying lender.
3. Amount of the purchase money mortgage that the seller has agreed to take back in part payment of the purchase price.
4. Unearned rents that have already been collected. Since rents are usually collected on the first day of the month, the buyer, under most contracts, will be entitled to its proportionate share of the current month's rent collections together with any other rent prepayments. This includes unearned rent on all leases, including such unusual leases as advertising space, satellite dish and antennae space, and the like. The contract should set out the manner in which delinquent rents are to be handled. In some circumstances, delinquent rents may be treated as being paid, especially if security deposits have been applied against unpaid rents for the month of the closing.
5. Security deposits made by tenants, to the extent that they have not been applied by the seller to amounts due from tenants, or to cure other defaults of the tenants. The leases and local law should be reviewed to determine whether interest accrues on the security deposits. If it does, the buyer is entitled to a credit in the amount of the accrued interest that has not been paid to the tenants.

6. Real estate taxes. Since the seller has had the rents of the property for prior years and for part of the current year, it is only fair that the seller pay all real estate taxes for those prior years and its proportionate share of the current year. Often, tax prorations are based on *the most recent ascertainable tax bill.* Tax bills are based upon many factors, such as the assessed value, equalization factors, and the tax rate. A change in any of the factors will not yield an *ascertainable tax bill* until the other factors are set. Until those other factors are determined, a change in any one of the factors will not justify a change in the basis of the proration from the most recent tax bill. *Lenzi v. Morkin,* 469 N.E.2d 178 (Ill. 1984). If the seller has not already paid those taxes and the contract so provides, the taxes should be apportioned with the buyer getting the appropriate credit. In some localities, however, it is not customary to apportion current taxes. In periods of rising taxes, a clause in the contract may call for proration of taxes at a base in excess of the latest tax bill, for example, "107 percent of the latest available tax bill." As an alternative, the contract may call for reproration of taxes, if the actual bill, when received, substantially exceeds the latest available tax bill, say by 10 percent or more. Without such a provision, neither party can seek adjustment, even if the variation is costly. *3700 S. Kedzie Bldg. Corp. v. Chicago Steel Foundry Co.,* 156 N.E.2d 618 (Ill. App. 1959). Buyers should be advised of the timing of changes of any of the factors that make up the real estate tax bill, and address protective measures in the contract. For example, if the property is scheduled for a periodic reassessment, the resulting impact on taxes that may have been prorated may be dramatic. This may call for a reproration provision and result in a postclosing adjustment between the parties. Real estate taxes should not be confused with special assessments. While the former may be proratable, the latter are not, unless the contract so provides. *Alder v. R.W. Lotto, Inc.,* 517 P.2d 227 (Wash. App. 1973). Note also that proration of real estate taxes between the buyer and the seller will not transfer the personal liability for the payment of those taxes from the owner on the date of assessment or levy to the buyer. The seller may retain this liability under local real estate tax law.

7. Items based on meter readings, such as water, electricity, and gas charges, if not paid in advance.

8. Wages and other charges accrued and unpaid, such as janitor's salary, scavenger service, and so on.

14.08(d) Closing Statement— Other Items

Some charges are allocated to either the buyer or seller, depending upon the terms of the contract and local custom. Those charges include the following:

1. Condominium and PUD assessments must be prorated with appropriate credits given to buyer and seller, depending upon whether the assessments are paid in advance or in arrears.

2. In the Midwest, the contract often requires the title charges to be borne by the seller. These are, therefore, a debit against the seller. In New York, the buyer bears this cost.

3. The cost of the survey. This is a matter of negotiation. Most often, the contract allocates this cost to the seller.

4. The chattel lien search fee and termite and other inspection costs are usually paid by the seller.

5. Real estate transfer taxes imposed by states, counties, and cities are subject to varying practices.

6. The buyer pays the recording fee for the deed, and the contract usually requires the buyer to pay for the recording of any purchase money mortgage and the cost of title evidence covering that mortgage. Release fees and recording charges to obtain and record a release of the seller's mortgage and other title encumbrances that are not permitted under the contract are to be paid by the seller.

7. Escrow fees are often divided between the buyer and the seller.

8. The broker's commission is usually paid out of the proceeds of sale and charged against the seller. It is not altogether unusual to have a contract provide that the buyer is to pay the brokerage commission. Obviously, the closing statement should follow the contract.

14.09 Matters to Attend to After Closing

After closing, the buyer, the escrowee, or title company should immediately record the title clearance documents delivered at the closing, the deed and the other recordable documents delivered at the closing. The title evidence should be brought down to cover the recordation of the closing documents. Title insurance policies should be obtained to cover the owner's interest and any purchase money mortgage given by the buyer to the seller. Tenants should be notified to pay rent to the buyer. If the contract documents did not obligate the seller to notify the janitor, building manager, scavenger service, exterminator, and so forth of the termination of their employment, the buyer should give those termination notices. The buyer should also (1) have the water, gas, and electric accounts changed to its name; (2) have the name of the assessee changed on the local real estate tax collector's books; (3) arrange for janitor, scavenger, building manager, and other services; (4) once again check to see that appropriate insurance is issued to protect the buyer's interest and that the mortgagee loss clause is included in the insurance package; (5) obtain worker's compensation and employer's liability insurance, if necessary; and (6) make sure that tenants are notified of the transaction and that future rental payments are made to the buyer.

14.09(a)   The Closing Letter

After the deal has been closed, the buyer's lawyer usually writes a closing letter to the buyer. This letter encloses and describes the documents that the buyer is receiving and describes the documents that are still to come. For example, it often takes some time for the recorder of deeds to complete the recording process and send the recorded deed to the buyer's attorney, who will send it on to the buyer.

The letter should suggest to the buyer what it is to do in the future. For example, the letter should suggest the date on which tax bills should be received, that the buyer retain the contract and closing statement for income tax records, and that the deed and title policy be placed in a safe-deposit box.

14.10   Mortgage Closing

Just as a sale is closed by delivery of the deed to the buyer and the purchase price to the seller, a mortgage transaction is closed by delivery of the mortgage and note to the lender and the disbursement of the mortgage funds to the mortgagor or pursuant to the mortgagor's direction.

14.10(a)   Borrower's Concerns

In shopping for a lender, the borrower should have numerous areas of concern. This is especially so in light of the wide range of mortgage programs available today. Beyond the obvious questions of interest rate, timing and maximum amount of increases in the interest rate on adjustable rate loans, loan charges or points, loan-to-value ratio, and loan term, the borrower should determine the following:

1. Is the borrower required to carry life or disability insurance? Must it be obtained from a particular company? The borrower may prefer no insurance or may wish to obtain it at a better premium rate elsewhere.

2. Is there a late payment charge? How much? How late may the payment be before the charge is imposed? The borrower should be aware that late payments may harm a credit rating. In addition to late charges, loan documents usually provide for default interest if payments are not made within a number of days after they are due.

3. If the borrower wishes to pay off the loan in advance of maturity (e.g., if the buyer sells the property or refinances), will a prepayment penalty be imposed? If so, how large is that prepayment penalty or premium.

4. If the buyer is dealing with the lender who holds the existing mortgage, the buyer might be able to take title subject to that loan in a transaction called an *assumption*. This form of transaction usually saves the borrower some settlement costs and benefits the buyer if the interest rate on the prior loan is lower than current market rates. Since the assumption transaction will typically involve a higher down payment than the transaction wherein the buyer obtains institutional financing, the buyer may want to ask the seller to take back a second mortgage to finance all or

part of the difference between the sales price and the balance on the existing mortgage, or otherwise arrange for a loan to fill this gap. If it is to be the case that the seller is to remain obligated on the loan rather than a novation being worked, where the buyer is substituted for the seller as the obligor under the loan documents, the seller will typically want an indemnity agreement. Through this document, the buyer agrees to indemnify and hold the seller harmless from any loss, cost or expense that the seller may incur or pay as a result of the buyer's breach of the underlying loan documents.

5. The borrower may want this same flexibility when it becomes the seller and should inquire whether the loan will be assumable by a purchaser at the time. If so, will the lender have the right to charge an assumption fee or raise the rate of interest, and will the lender release the borrower from personal liability?

6. Will the borrower be required to pay monies into a special reserve (escrow or impound) account to cover taxes, insurance, or replacements and repairs or other recurring expenses? If so, how large a deposit will be required at the closing of the loan? In lieu of making these periodic payments, may the borrower post an account, letter of credit or other security for its promise to pay real estate taxes and insurance premiums, replace obsolete furnishings, fixtures and equipment, and otherwise fulfill its obligations under the loan documents?

7. In looking for the best mortgage to fit the borrower's particular financial needs, the residential borrower may wish to compare the terms and requirements of a private conventional loan with the terms of a loan insured through the Federal Housing Administration (FHA) or Farmers Home Administration, or guaranteed by the Veterans Administration (VA). The FHA, VA, and Farmers Home Administration loans involve federal ceilings on permissible charges for some settlement services, which may be of interest to the borrower.

14.10(b) RESPA The Real Estate Settlement Procedures Act (RESPA), 12 U.S.C. § 2601, has an impact upon lenders, brokers, and real estate attorneys. The Act's primary impact upon the closing process is directed toward lenders of "federally related mortgage loans." These are loans that are both secured by a first lien on residential (one- to four-family) real property and meet any one of the following four criteria: (1) the loan is made by a lender that has its deposits insured by or that is regulated by the federal government; or (2) the loan is insured, guaranteed, supplemented, or assisted under a federal housing or urban development program; or (3) the loan is intended to be sold to FNMA, GNMA, or FHLMC; or (4) the loan is made by any creditor who makes or invests in residential loans aggregating more than $1,000,000 per year. 12 U.S.C. § 2602. The coverage of the act is very broad, with most residential lenders being subject to its strictures.

The Act requires that most residential loans be closed through the use of the HUD settlement statement, 24 C.F.R. § 3500.8(d), which must be available to the borrower before the closing, 12 U.S.C. § 2603(b); that within three days of the application, the lender make a good-faith estimate of likely settlement service charges, 12 U.S.C. § 2604(c)–(d), 24 C.F.R. §§ 3500.6–3500.7(a); and that a HUD booklet on settlement costs be given to the borrower with the estimate. 12 U.S.C. § 2604. The buyer should ask for an explanation of all settlement charges.

The Act also limits impound or escrow accounts for the payment of real estate taxes and insurance. 12 U.S.C. § 2609.

14.10(c) Title Defects The typical lender wants a first lien position subject only to a permissible set of encumbrances on the title, such as easements and restrictions on the use of the property. Other lenders make their loans on the security of junior liens and charge a higher rate for the greater risk involved in the transaction. Among the precautions that should be taken in this regard are the following:

1. The mortgage should be checked for errors in filling in the blanks, signatures, witnesses, acknowledgments, and the like. Before the mortgage proceeds are disbursed, the mortgage should be recorded, or delivered to the title company for recording with the assurance from the title company that the required priority will be insured, no matter what is discovered after the mortgage is recorded and the title is searched to cover that recording. If the lender is forwarding funds to a title company's agent or approved attorney, the lender should insist upon receiving the title company's *insured closing letter or statement of settlement service responsibility,* which insures the mortgagee against embezzlement of loan funds or the agent's failure to follow the mortgagee's directions. If the mortgage is being assigned, the assignee should obtain a mortgage assignment endorsement insuring the validity of the assignment and substituting the name of the assignee as the insured.

2. All objections to the mortgagor's title disclosed by the examination of title should be analyzed. All defects in title should be cleared. If the title search reveals building restrictions or conditions, ascertain whether existing buildings violate such restrictions. Of course, copies of the instruments creating restrictions, easements, and so forth should be obtained and analyzed.

3. The mortgagee should inquire into the rights of parties in possession for the purpose of discovering unrecorded leases with options to purchase, unrecorded deeds and contracts, unrecorded easements, and so on. It must keep in mind the fact that the mortgagee, in nearly all states, takes its mortgage subject to the interests of all parties in possession of the premises.

4. The mortgagee should (1) inspect the building carefully for signs of recent work and, if any appears, demand to see paid bills and mechanic's lien waivers for any such work; and (2) get an affidavit from the mortgagor that all work or materials furnished to premises have been paid in full that, if false, will subject the mortgagor to criminal prosecution.

5. A survey should be obtained and examined to determine whether any encroachments or other survey defects exist.

6. The mortgagee should obtain the usual mortgagor's affidavit to the effect that there are no judgments, bankruptcies, and so on against the mortgagor.

7. The lender must comply with the Federal Truth-in-Lending Act (15 U.S.C.A. §§ 1601–1665).

14.10(d)   The Loan Closing Statement

Seldom does the borrower receive the full amount of the mortgage loan. Various deductions are made for title searches, surveys, recording fees, and other costs of the loan transaction. Therefore, on disbursement of the loan, the mortgagee will prepare a loan settlement statement similar to that prepared for the buyer and seller. This form should be used for three reasons: (1) it furnishes the borrower with a complete record of all disbursements and withholdings made by the mortgagee from the proceeds of the loan; (2) it provides the mortgagee a signed authorization by the borrower for all such disbursements and thus tends to eliminate the possibility of any legal action that might be taken if the mortgagor claims improper charges were made against its loan; and (3) in those cases where there is no binding loan commitment, it fixes the date on which the mortgage becomes a lien on the land, since where there is no binding commitment, the mortgage does not become a lien on the land in some states until the date on which the loan is paid out to the mortgagor. In general, the settlement statement shows the full amount of the loan and all deductions from it and their amount. It also shows the net amount available to the mortgagor and contains an acknowledgment by the mortgagor that it has received that amount. The statement should be dated and signed by both mortgagor and mortgagee when the loan is closed.

Many miscellaneous items are debited against the borrower upon the closing of the mortgage loan. It is important that each debit be provided for in the loan contract documents, that is, the application, commitment, and acceptance. Among the items often debited against the borrower are as follows:

1. Lenders usually require that borrowers pay at settlement the interest accruing on the mortgage loan from the date of settlement to the beginning of the period covered by the first mortgage payment.

   EXAMPLE: Suppose settlement takes place on April 16 and the buyer's first regular monthly payment is due on June 1. At settlement, the lender will collect interest for the period from April 16 to May 1. The June 1 mortgage payment will pick up the interest that accrued during May.

2. The fees for the appraisal, credit report, and lender's title protection.

3. On some mortgage loans, the mortgagee insists on *private mortgage insurance* to insure the mortgagee against loss in the event of default and foreclosure. The premium for this insurance is debited against the borrower.

4. Most home buyers take out a new *homeowners' insurance policy* to cover fire loss, liability, etc. The first year's premium is usually a debit against the borrower, unless the borrower obtains the insurance from its own insurance agent.

5. Most residential lenders insist that the monthly payment include one-twelfth of the estimated real estate taxes and hazard insurance premiums for the current year. These are called impounds. In these cases, there is an initial payment that is debited against the borrower.

6. There may be miscellaneous fees that are debits against the borrower.

   EXAMPLE: Lender's attorney's fee, mortgage tax, fees for recording mortgage, and accompanying documents.

7. Lenders may charge both points and miscellaneous loan origination fees, which may be debits against the borrower on the loan closing statement.

14.10(e) Zoning and Building Code Violations

A check should be made for violations of local zoning and building ordinances that the mortgagee might be compelled to remedy at its own expense were it to acquire title by foreclosure.

14.10(f) Insurance

Existing fire insurance policies should be checked to determine that the amounts and coverages are adequate and that the policies are properly written with the mortgage clause attached.

14.10(g) Documents of the Loan File

The mortgagee's loan file should include the following papers:

1. Application for the loan, signed by the borrower, and a copy of the mortgagee's letter of commitment and the borrower's acceptance.

2. Plat of survey.

3. If the loan is made to finance the purchase of property, the mortgagee should have a copy of the contract of sale in its files. This will prove helpful in making an appraisal of the property and establishing that the loan-to-value requirements were fulfilled.

4. Appraisal.

5. Mortgagee, mortgage note, UCC financing statements evidencing the lien on personal property in building, assignment of rents and leases, and other loan documents executed by the borrower and delivered at the closing.

6. Assignment of mortgage and waiver of defenses, if loan was purchased from original lender.

7. Credit reports on the borrowers.

8. Insurance policies, with mortgagee loss clauses attached.

9. Mortgage title policy.

10. Mortgagor's affidavit as to judgments, divorces, recent improvements, and other pertinent facts.

11. Copy of escrow agreement, if the loan was closed in escrow.

12. Loan closing statement, including receipt for loan proceeds signed by borrowers.

13. If loan was a refinancing loan, a copy of the canceled mortgage and note that were replaced by the new loan.

14. If the loan is part of a federal program—that is, VA guaranteed, FHA insured, or sold in the secondary market to the Federal Home Loan Mortgage Corporation or some other similar purchaser—the special documents that make up such a loan package and are required by those entities must be a part of the loan file.

15. The requirements of any loan servicing contract relating to document retention must also be followed. Many of these servicing contracts require that the loan file be retained for a stated period after the loan is repaid.

16. Subordination of reverter if one was obtained. If any other prior mortgage or other lien was subordinated to the current mortgage, the subordination agreement, of course, should also be in the loan files.

17. Certificate of good standing and certified copy of corporate resolutions, if the mortgage was made by a corporation. If the property mortgaged is all, or substantially all, of the assets of the corporation, resolutions by both directors and stockholders may be necessary. If the borrower is a partnership, the loan file should contain a certified copy of the partnership agreement or the certificate of limited partnership, if the borrower is a limited partnership. If the borrower is a limited liability company, the loan file should contain a certificate of good standing, a certified copy of the articles of organization, and the operating agreement, if one exists, evidence that the LLC has not been dissolved, and a certificate of the incumbent members if the LLC is managed by its members, or a certificate of the incumbent managers, if the LLC is managed by a manager.

18. Will, trust indenture, or other trust instrument, or a copy of these, if mortgagor is a trustee.

19. Full copy of building restrictions affecting the mortgaged premises, particularly if the loan is a construction loan.

20. Leases to key tenants and assignments thereof to mortgagee.

21. The statements, waivers, and so forth necessary to document compliance with federal and state disclosure laws, the Real Estate Settlement Procedures Act (12 U.S.C.A. § 2601, *et seq.*), and similar local laws.

14.11   Nature of Escrow

An escrow is created when documents, funds, or other items are deposited with a third person with directions to deliver the deposits only upon the performance of the conditions set forth in the escrow instructions. The third person, to whom the deed is delivered, is called the *escrow holder, escrow agent, escrow trustee,* or *escrowee.* The document that sets out the conditions to be fulfilled prior to delivery and the other instructions to the escrowee is called the *escrow agreement* or *escrow instructions.*

14.11 (a)   Operation and Purpose of Escrows

A contract for the sale of land usually requires the seller to furnish title evidence showing the condition of the seller's title. Suppose that on May 10, the seller agrees to sell a parcel of land to the buyer for $50,000. The contract is not recorded, and the seller remains in possession of the property. The seller orders the title commitment, which is received on May 20, and shows the condition of title sometime between May 10 and May 20, say, May 15. The title evidence shows that, as of May 15, the seller held clear title and the buyer paid its money and received a deed. It then develops that on May 16, the IRS filed a tax lien against the seller. Other liens and encumbrances, such as judgments, suits attacking title, or mortgages, may also arise during this interval or gap between the effective date of the title evidence and the recording of the deed to the buyer. The seller may even die, leaving minor heirs, who obviously would be incapable of signing any deed.

To avoid these and other similar risks, sales are often closed in escrow. In an escrow transaction, the deed, mortgage, and other closing documents are delivered to the escrowee, a disinterested third party, often a title insurance company, with written instructions to record the deed, mortgage, and other documents; order an examination of title covering the date of the recording; and, if the title shows clear *in the buyer,* insure that title, pay over the purchase price to the seller, and otherwise deliver the documents and other deposits as instructed. The escrow agreement also provides that, if the seller's title is defective and the defects are not cured within a specified period of time, the buyer shall be entitled to the return of the purchase money upon reconveying the title to the seller. In those cases where the seller has not recently had its title examined, the procedure is often divided into two steps. Before the deed is recorded, the escrowee is instructed to cause the seller's title to be examined down to a current date. This step may even be taken before the escrow agreement is signed. Then, if title shows clear in the seller, the instructions provide that the deed be recorded and the examination of title brought down to cover the recording of the deed.

When the transaction follows the procedure outlined previously, it is common for the grantee to deposit with the escrowee a quitclaim deed, called a *reconveyance deed,* conveying the land back to the grantor. Then, if the title proves defective, the escrowee is instructed to record the quitclaim deed so that record title will once more be in the grantor.

A concern is raised as to the quality of the title being reconveyed to the seller. Will it be subject to those matters that are binding against the buyer, such as judgments and tax liens? The buyer's interest was recorded, the buyer acquired only a conditional title. This title, by the very words of the escrow, will be defeated if the deal cannot close. Hence, when the buyer's title vanishes, the judgment or tax lien against the buyer's interest automatically is terminated.

The question is also asked, If the title shows clear in the buyer except for liens against the seller, such as the seller's old mortgage, on what theory can the escrowee use the buyer's funds to pay those liens? The answer is that as soon as the title shows clear in the buyer, subject only to the old mortgage, the seller's proceeds in the escrow belong to the seller. The typical escrow agreement contains an instruction to the escrowee to use enough of those proceeds to pay the old mortgage.

In counties where it is possible to examine titles very quickly, the procedure may follow these lines: The seller will have its title examined to a current date. If title shows clear, the seller will deposit its deed with a title company as escrowee. The escrowee orders a second examination of title to cover the period intervening between the date of the prior examination and the close of recording hours on the day the deed is deposited. This examination can be made quickly, for it covers a period of only a few days. If title is clear, the seller's deed is recorded the next morning, the moment the recorder's office opens.

Under either system, the buyer's money is not paid to the seller until the buyer is assured of receiving clear title.

Escrow practices and the frequency of their use differ quite a bit from state to state. In many communities, escrows are virtually unknown. This is particularly true of small communities where seller and buyer know and trust each other. The danger here that the seller will make a deed or mortgage to some third person is not so great as in large communities, where relationships are apt to be more impersonal.

Another benefit of the escrow is that if objections to the title that can be removed by use of the purchase money appear, such as judgments against the seller or unpaid taxes, the buyer may with absolute safety, after the title is recorded in its name, allow the escrow holder to use part of the purchase money for the purpose of removing such objections.

Escrows are also used in land assemblies. In this context, the seller who has given an option is required to put a deed in escrow to be given to the buyer upon the buyer's timely performance of the conditions of the option agreement. Through this device, the seller who learns that its deal is part of a large assembly is powerless to hold up the larger transaction, having already given the deed to a neutral third party.

Even where a sale transaction is not closed in escrow, some of the closing proceeds are often put into an escrow to take care of some element of the seller's performance that remains incomplete (i.e., new construction that is not finished or damage to the property that occurred between the contract date and the closing date that is the seller's responsibility to repair).

14.11(b) Requirements of an Escrow

Good escrow practice requires the following:

1. There must be a valid and enforceable contract for the sale of the land. *Johnson v. Wallden,* 173 N.E. 790 (Ill. 1930). The escrow agreement may in itself contain all the essential requirements of a contract of sale. *Wood Bldg. Corp. v. Griffitts,* 330 P.2d 847 (Cal. App. 1958). The existence of a valid contract of sale, either in the escrow instructions or in a separate instrument, is, however, indispensable for a binding escrow. If this were not true, it would be possible to have what is in effect a contract for the sale of land without the written agreement that the law requires for land sales.

   EXAMPLE: Two landowners executed deeds to each other pursuant to an oral exchange agreement and delivered such deeds to an attorney with verbal directions to deliver each deed to the grantee named therein when each landowner had presented a receipt showing payment of back interest on existing mortgages. Before these receipts were delivered, one of the landowners demanded return of its deed. The court held that it was entitled to the return of the deed. The contract of exchange was only oral and therefore unenforceable. *Jozefowicz v. Leickem,* 182 N.W. 729 (Wis. 1921).

2. The escrow agreement should contain a *condition,* something that must be done before the deliveries are to be made and the buyer's money paid to the seller. The usual condition is that all deposits be made and the title be in a defined condition, subject only to those objections listed in the contract of sale and escrow instructions.

3. The deed must be a good and valid deed.

4. The escrow holder must be a third person. Neither the buyer nor seller may act as escrow holder.

14.11(c) Contents of Escrow Agreement

The following are usual terms of an escrow agreement:

1. The names and signatures of the buyer and seller with the written acceptance of the escrow by the escrowee.

2. A list of the deposits into escrow to be made by the seller. These deposits will typically include the deed, bill of sale, leases, assignments of leases, notices to tenants to pay the rent to the buyer, paid tax bills, service contracts, warranty contracts, and the like.

3. A list of deposits to be made by the buyer. These deposits will typically include the purchase price and purchase money mortgage, if one is to be given, or the proceeds of the mortgage obtained by the buyer. These mortgage proceeds often come from a separate money lender's escrow established with the same escrowee, with the funds "poured over" into the buyer-seller escrow when the conditions for the closing of the money lender's escrow are met. Often this occurs simultaneously with the closing of the buyer-seller escrow.

4. An instruction on when the deed is to be recorded, that is, immediately, upon the proper title evidence being produced, or when the buyer's funds clear.

5. The type of title evidence to be obtained.

6. A list of permitted title exceptions that the buyer agrees to accept as a condition of title to the conveyed property.

7. The time allowed for the seller to clear the title of unpermitted title exceptions.

8. How and when the purchase price is to be disbursed, with directions as to which items are to be prorated or apportioned. Often, the buyer and seller will agree upon or jointly deposit a closing statement to be used by the escrowee.

9. Directions for the delivery of the escrow deposits upon the close of escrow.

10. Directions for the return of deposits to the respective parties if the conditions for closing the escrow are not met within the allotted time period.

11. Directions for the payment of escrow, title and recording charges, broker's commissions, and attorney's fees.

12. A notice procedure for the parties to use in the event of a default and a mechanism for resolving the default.

While an escrow often takes the form of instructions by the buyer and seller to the escrowee, the legal fact remains that the escrow instruction is an agreement or contract among its parties.

**14.11(d)
Irrevocability
of Escrow**

When a valid escrow agreement has been executed and the instruments provided for are delivered to the escrow holder, neither party can revoke the escrow and obtain the return of its deposit. At times, one party to a transaction changes its mind and makes a demand on the escrowee for return of the deposit. The escrowee is justified in refusing to comply with an unwarranted demand. If the situation is legally doubtful, the escrowee may insist on a court adjudication of the rights of the parties. *Franks v. North Shore Farms, Inc.,* 253 N.E.2d 45 (Ill. App. 1969); *Cocke v. Transamerica Title Ins. Co.,* 494 P.2d 756 (Ariz. App. 1972).

**14.11(e) Conflict
Between Contract
of Sale and
Escrow Agreement**

Since the escrow is a means of carrying out the terms of the contract of sale, there should be no conflict between the two agreements. In the event of conflict, however, disposition of the deed and money deposited in escrow must be governed by the escrow instructions. *Widess v. Doane,* 112 Cal. App. 343, 296 P. 899 (1931). Similarly, the escrow agreement may extend the closing date set by the contract. *Eastern Motor Inns, Inc. v. Ricci,* 565 A.2d 1265 (R.I. 1989).

**14.11(f) When
Title Passes**

Prior to the performance of the conditions specified in the escrow, title to the land remains in the seller, even though the deed to the buyer may be recorded. This is a technical, but important concept. Since ownership of the land remains in the seller until the conditions specified in the escrow instructions have been met and performed, even though a deed from seller to buyer has been recorded, the seller remains in possession, collects the rents, and pays taxes, until the escrow conditions have been satisfied. Even an innocent purchaser or mortgagee from the grantee is not protected in such cases. *Osby v. Reynolds,* 103 N.E. 556 (Ill. 1913); *Clevenger v. Moore,* 259 P. 219 (Okla. 1927).

> **EXAMPLE:** An escrow agreement required the buyer to deposit the purchase price in escrow. Before this was done, the buyer persuaded the escrow holder to deliver the deed, which the buyer thereupon recorded. Buyer then placed a mortgage on the property. When the seller discovered this mortgage, he filed suit, and the court canceled the mortgage as a cloud on his title, even though the mortgagee had acted in entirely good faith. *Blakeney v. Home Owners' Loan Corp.,* 135 P.2d 339 (Okla. 1943).

If, however, the grantor allows its deed to be recorded, an innocent purchaser from the grantee in that deed will usually be protected, if the grantor has also allowed the grantee to take possession of the land, for in such case *both the records and the possession show the grantee as the apparent owner,* and an innocent purchaser from such grantee should be protected, for there is nothing to apprise it of the grantor's rights. *Mays v. Shields,* 45 S.E. 68 (Ga. 1903).

Immediately upon the performance of the conditions specified in the escrow agreement, ownership of the land passes to the buyer and ownership of the purchase price passes to the seller. Thereupon, the escrow holder becomes the agent of the buyer as to the deed and of the seller as to the money. *Shreeves v. Pearson,* 230 P. 448 (Cal. 1924). At that moment, the escrow holder holds the deed for the grantee. It is as though the grantee itself held the deed. Thus, delivery of the deed has been completed and actual manual delivery of the deed by the escrow holder to the grantee adds nothing to the grantee's title. *Shirley v. Ayres,* 14 Ohio 307 (1846). However, it is the practice to provide for a delivery of the deed by the escrow holder to the grantee. This is the so-called *second delivery.*

14.11(g)   Relation Back   Where the grantor delivers a deed in escrow, then dies, and thereafter the condition of the escrow is performed, the deed is considered as passing title as of the date of the delivery of the deed to the escrow holder. It is said that the title *relates back* to such time.

> **EXAMPLE:** Seller entered into a written contract to sell a parcel of property to Buyer. Seller signed the deed and delivered it to the escrowee. Buyer deposited the purchase price with the escrowee. The escrowee recorded the deed as permitted by the escrow instructions, which also provided that the purchase price was to be delivered to Seller when the title evidence showed the title to be clear of unpermitted objections. Before the title examination was completed, Seller died, leaving minor children as heirs. Thereafter, the title evidence was produced showing acceptable title in Seller. The deed was good since the transfer of title related back to the time when Seller was alive.

So too, if the grantee dies after the deed has been delivered in escrow, and the condition of the escrow is thereafter performed, the deed will be treated as relating back to the delivery in escrow and may be delivered for the benefit of the grantee's heirs. *Prewitt v. Ashford,* 7 So. 831 (Ala. 1890).

The same theory follows when the seller marries or becomes insane after the delivery of the deed into escrow.

The rule that title relates back to the time of the original delivery of the deed to the escrowee is confined to the examples given previously. In other situations, *transfer of ownership of the land takes place as of the time when the terms and conditions of the escrow are performed.* For example, if the escrowee absconds with the buyer's purchase money before the conditions of the escrow have been fulfilled, the loss must fall on the buyer, because *at the time of the defalcation, the purchase money still belonged to the buyer. Hildebrand v. Beck,* 236 P. 301 (Cal. 1925); G.V.I., Annotation, *Who Bears Loss of Funds While in Hands of Escrow Agent,* 39 A.L.R. 1080 (1925). On the other hand, if the terms of the escrow have been performed and thereafter the escrowee absconds with the money, the loss falls on the seller, because *after the conditions of the escrow have been fulfilled, the money on deposit belonged to the seller. Lechner v. Halling,* 216 P.2d 179 (Wash. 1950); *Lawyers Title Ins. Co. v. Edmar Constr. Co.,* 294 A.2d 865 (D.C. 1972).

Thus, if a lender is a party to an escrow and the escrowee embezzles the mortgage money before the title has been cleared as required by the escrow instructions, the mortgage funds still belong to the mortgagee who must suffer the loss of its funds and cannot collect from the mortgagor even though it holds the mortgagor's promissory note. *Ward Cooke, Inc. v. Davenport,* 413 P.2d 387 (Or. 1966).

14.11(h) Mortgages

Since, as against third parties, a mortgage, in some states, does not become a lien until a debt that the mortgage secures exists, mere recording of a mortgage does not create a lien. Liens attaching to the land *prior to the time that the mortgage money is disbursed to the mortgagor* may obtain priority of lien over the mortgage. But, if the mortgagee deposits its mortgage money in escrow, with directions to pay the money over to the mortgagor if an examination of title shows the mortgage as a first lien on the date of its recording, then immediately upon the recording of the mortgage, its position as a first lien is established. Payment into escrow is treated as payment by the mortgagee to or for the benefit of the mortgagor.

Again, there are cases where a buyer is borrowing money to complete its purchase. The mortgagee does not want its money paid out until title shows clear in the buyer, who is the mortgagor. The seller will not want to give a deed until and unless it is assured of receiving the purchase price. This difficult situation is easily taken care of through an escrow. The deed, mortgage, and mortgage money are deposited with an escrowee under written instructions to record the deed and mortgage and pay the mortgage money to the seller if the title examination shows the mortgage as a first lien. The interests of all parties are protected.

> **EXAMPLE:** The contention has been advanced by the creditors of the mortgagor that they can garnishee such funds. The courts have rejected this contention. Robert Kratovil & Raymond J. Werner, *Modern Mortgage Law and Practice,* § 5.34 (2d ed. 1981). The same result occurs where creditors attempt to garnishee construction money held by the mortgagee. The funds cannot be garnisheed.

14.11(i) Long-Term Escrows

The long-term escrow is used in the sale and financing of real estate as an alternative or supplement to the installment contract. This device operates somewhat as follows: The seller enters into a contract for the sale of real estate with a buyer who is unable or unwilling to pay the entire purchase price at the time of closing. The seller desires to retain a security interest in the property to secure the deferred payment of the purchase price and to swiftly terminate the buyer's interest upon the buyer's default. To accomplish these objectives, the property is conveyed to a bank or title company, as trustee. The trust agreement incorporates the installment contract. The trustee is authorized to collect the payments due under the contract, remitting them to the seller. When the final payment is made, the trustee conveys the property to the buyer. If the buyer defaults, the property is conveyed to the seller. In some states, this conveyance to the seller occurs after a statutory forfeiture procedure is conducted. In other areas, the seller conducts the forfeiture of the buyer's interest after the return conveyance from the trustee. George G. Bogert, *Trusts and Escrows in Credit Conveyancing,* 21 Ill. L. Rev. 655 (1927). The disadvantages of this arrangement are as follows:

1. Until completion of the payments, the public records show title in the seller. This gives the seller the opportunity to defraud the buyer by making a deed or mortgage to some third person who is unaware of the contract's existence. *Waldock v. Frisco Lumber Co.,* 176 P. 218 (Okla. 1918). This would not be true if the contract were recorded or if the buyer went into possession of the land.

2. The depositary may deliver the deed to the buyer notwithstanding the fact that the buyer has not completed its payments and recording of this deed will cloud the seller's title.

3. Default on the buyer's part after it has made substantial payments may result in a lawsuit against the depositary. *Phoenix Title & Trust Co. v. Horwath,* 19 P.2d 82 (Ariz. 1933). To avoid

becoming involved in forfeiture proceedings, the escrowee often insists that after a lapse of time without payments by the buyer, the escrowee may return the seller's deed to the seller. The seller then proceeds to declare the forfeiture.

4. In some states, a buyer in an escrow deal takes subject to judgments rendered against the seller while the deal is in escrow but before the purchase price is fully paid and the deed recorded. *May v. Emerson, 96* P. 454 (Or. 1908); R.T. Kimbrough, Annotation, *Relation Back of Title or Interest Embraced in Escrow Instrument upon Final Delivery or Performance of Condition,* 117 A.L.R. 69, 85–88 (1938). The danger from this is increased when the escrow extends over a long period of time. In addition to the danger of judgments, there is the danger that while the escrow is running, federal income tax liens may be filed against the seller or the seller may go into bankruptcy. Robert Kratovil & Raymond J. Werner, *Modern Mortgage Law and Practice* § 9.11 (2d ed. 1981).

To avoid becoming involved in forfeiture proceedings, the escrowee often insists that after a lapse of several days without any payments by the buyer, the escrowee may return the seller's deed to him or her. The seller then proceeds to declare the forfeiture.

14.11(j)   Closer's Liability   Whether the closing is conducted by an escrowee, lending institution, or lawyer, the closer may incur liability for improper or mistaken performance of its closing duties.

> **EXAMPLE:** Where an escrowee breaches the escrow instructions, the escrowee will be liable for damages proximately caused by the breach.

> **EXAMPLE:** Where a lender fails to obtain the proper insurance coverage for a buyer who has instructed the lender to obtain the insurance, the lender will be liable if a loss occurs. *Parnell v. First Fed. Sav. & Loan Ass'n,* 336 So. 2d 764 (Miss. 1976); *Taylor v. Colonial Sav. Ass'n,* 533 S.W.2d 61 (Tex. 1976).

> **EXAMPLE:** A lender that closed a real estate transaction was held liable to the buyer for failing to disclose the results of a termite inspection. *Miles v. Perpetual Sav. & Loan Ass'n,* 388 N.E.2d 1364 (Ohio 1979).

Courts have gone beyond the situation of mere breach of contract to hold that the closer has a fiduciary duty to the buyer and seller to transmit information in its possession and make reasonable inquiry when it knows of matters that might create a problem. *Cano v. Lovato,* 734 P.2d 762 (N.M. App. 1986). Also, the closer must take great care in what is said at the closing, since the parties may justifiably rely on the closer's expertise.

> **EXAMPLE:** A settlement attorney retained by the lender assured the buyer that the property being purchased was located within described boundary lines. In fact, a well and other facilities encroached upon neighboring property. The court held the settlement attorney liable to the buyer. *Flaherty v. Weinberg,* 492 A.2d 618 (Md. 1985).

While the parties to the escrow or closing may be comforted by knowing that the closer is liable for failure to follow the closing instructions or misappropriation of the deposited funds, the real comfort is found in the financial standing of the closer or a party standing behind the closer's obligations. When the parties deal with a branch office of a title insurance company, they have comfort that the closing entity has the wherewithal to stand behind its mistakes. To achieve this same comfort when dealing with a title insurance agent, the parties may request a statement of settlement services responsibility or insured closing letter. Through this document, the title insurance company that underwrites the agent promises to be responsible for the agent's failure to follow instructions and misappropriation of funds. There are conditions of these letters that must be followed if the title insurer is to be liable. Notably, to be protected, the party must be the recipient of the title insurance issued by the agent. This is not the case for a seller who does not take back a purchase money loan that is insured by the title insurer, or a lender who is receiving the payoff of an existing loan. The closing protection letter must be tailored to address these situations. Similarly, the parties may be protected when they deal with a closer that has been approved by the title insurer. *Sears Mortgage Corp. v. Rose*, 634 A.2d 74 (N.J. 1993).

14.11(k) Today's Escrow Practices— Residential Transactions

Several years ago, most home sales were closed in the lender's office. In part, the lender's wish to close residential transactions stemmed from the lender's desire to pressure the seller to deposit the proceeds of sale in a savings account. These deposits are a vanishing species. The seller is in the stock market, money markets, and so forth. More important, financial service providers today seek to cut their overhead and keep staff costs low. An effective way to accomplish that end is to not employ many employees in the loan origination operation. In this way, the loan transaction will be closed through an escrow with a title company, with the closing charges paid by the borrower. Lenders have a form agreement with a title or escrow company stating, in essence, that the lender is sending loan documents and funds to the title company, and when the title company is prepared to issue its mortgage policy, clear of objections, to the lender, it may disburse the lender's funds. The title company personnel examine the title, call in the sellers and buyers, get all necessary documents executed, do the prorations, record the deed and mortgage, and pay the seller. In some areas, the parties have their lawyers present to make sure the closing is being handled correctly and to check into problems that arise, but the mechanics are handled by title company personnel.

The buyer's lawyer has a copy of the title search. When the title company tells the lawyer all objections have been cleared, the lawyer can advise the buyer that the money can safely be applied. This does not minimize the lawyer's role. He or she reads the easements, the building restrictions, the survey, and leases, if any. But the lawyer is relieved of the burden of paying state and city document taxes, prorating rents on a four-flat, and so on.

14.11(l) Large Transactions

Where a sale escrow is set up on a large transaction between seller, buyer, and a title company, the lender that is financing the purchase of the property may seek to protect itself by giving a written instruction to the title company that it will wire funds to the title company's escrow bank account when the conditions to funding the loan have been met. These conditions are derived from the lender's loan commitment. They include such matters as (1) the willingness of the title company to insure the mortgage as a first lien, subject only to permitted exceptions; (2) confirmation of the validity of the leases that provide cash flow for payment of the mortgage; (3) confirmation of the validity and priority of the lender's chattel lien documentation; and (4) the existence of adequate hazard insurance, etc.

CHAPTER 15
Title Insurance and Other Evidence of Title

15.01 Historical Background

It is obvious that a purchaser of land cannot merely rely upon the fact that it receives a warranty deed as conclusive evidence that it is receiving good title. For example, anyone could give a deed to the World Trade Center in New York. That deed would convey nothing to the grantee. It is a worthless piece of paper. It would merely give the grantee the right to sue the grantor, a right that may be quite empty.

The buyer must receive evidence that the seller has title to the property and what, if any, defects, liens, and encumbrances are against that title. The form of this evidence of title is agreed upon in the contract of sale. In the past, the nature of title evidence varied from area to area and it was necessary for the buyer and seller to conform their needs to the customs of the area where the land lies. Today, however, title insurance is the almost universally accepted form of title evidence.

In all events, the history of the development of title evidence is interesting and useful. In the early days of this country, the nation was predominantly agricultural. Transfers of ownership were infrequent. Indeed, farmers tended to hold the land in the family, passing it from generation to generation. Hence, the land record books in the county courthouse were not numerous, and it was easy for a lawyer to go to them to examine the title to a particular tract of land.

Also, going back to the old days, when villages were relatively small, business was done largely on a first-name basis. The lawyer for the buyer in a real estate transaction would go to the courthouse to examine the land records, and have a friendly conversation with the recorder of deeds who was thoroughly familiar with everything that had happened in the courthouse in recent memory. The recorder could probably tell the lawyer what transactions there were relating to the land in question. The lawyer would make a formal check of the land records and would then go to the tax office and again have an informal talk with the tax collector followed by a quick search of the tax records. The lawyer would then prepare an opinion of title, which would reflect the result of these searches. The whole process was quite informal.

As time went on, other factors caused this friendly format to become more formalized. One of these factors was the opening of the Erie Canal in 1825. When that occurred, it became possible for ships to move from the Atlantic seaboard through the Great Lakes to Chicago. It was also no longer necessary for people traveling westward to use the old Indian trail roads, which were at times impassable. This in turn created a flow of commerce that sharply increased land values. A good deal of land speculation resulted. Land transactions became numerous and the land record books in the courthouse multiplied. The number of recordings increased again when railroads entered the picture. The speculation became feverish. It was no longer easy for a lawyer to check the growing number of land records. It was no coincidence that abstract offices began to open at this time.

As recorders would leave their elected office, they would often open an abstract office near the courthouse. A courthouse clerk would be hired to make trips to the recorder's office to note all documents filed in the public record on a particular day. The clerk would also check the tax records to determine what tax sales or payments were made. These transactions would then be entered in the separate books kept in the abstract company's office. The records kept at the abstract company were in a far more convenient form than existed in the courthouse. For example, suppose that we are involved in a sale of Lot 1 in Block 1 in Sheffield's Addition to Chicago. The abstractor would open a page in its book for that particular parcel of property, and every transaction involving that parcel would be entered in chronological order on that page. This was done in anticipation of future title examination orders that might be placed with the abstractor for that parcel.

When the lot was being sold, the contract of sale would call for the seller to furnish the buyer an abstract of title. At that time, the abstractor would look at its books and make a list of all the transactions appearing on that particular page. This list is sometimes referred to as a *chain*. The chain would be taken to the courthouse and brief copies of each instrument appearing in the chain would be made. The abstractor would then prepare a brief history of the title beginning with the first grant from the United States. Each transaction would appear in chronological order, but in a highly abbreviated form.

Today, many title companies prepare their abstracts by photocopying or imaging each document in the chain of title. The abstract would be handed to the buyer's attorney for examination and the preparation of an *opinion of title*. This was a very important step forward in the process of examining and evidencing title. The lawyer was liberated. He could examine the title to the property in the comfort and convenience of his office by merely using the abstract. Today, the work is largely done by title companies in their electronic plants. Even where the lawyer continues to participate in the process as an examining attorney or title agent, the lawyer's work is electronically automated and extensively computerized.

For many years, the abstract system worked very well. Indeed, it is still used in the agricultural parts of the Midwest. However, from time to time, defects in the abstract system came to light.

> **EXAMPLE:** Owner is selling an apartment building that is encumbered with a $200,000 mortgage. Owner could, of course, clear the mortgage by paying it off. But, for a much lower cost, Owner could merely forge the lender's execution of a mortgage release and record the document. While this apparently rids the record title of the mortgage, the release is really a nullity. Buyer would actually be acquiring the property subject to the $200,000 mortgage.

Many other such defects that are hidden in the recording system also exist. Abstracts do not protect against these hidden risks.

Beginning around 1880, the abstractors took on an additional chore. They would prepare their abstract as usual. Subsequently, an in-house attorney would examine the abstract and render a title opinion. Then the abstractor would issue an insurance policy, insuring the purchaser of the property that it was acquiring good title to the property. In this fashion, the insurer took the risk of forgeries, misrepresentation of marital status, and so on.

In the early days of title insurance, the abstractor was unwilling to inspect the property. Nonetheless, there are certain defects in title that do not appear on the public records but appear only from an examination of the property itself. For example, if the property is occupied by a purchaser under an unrecorded contract, the contract will be valid and binding on any later purchasers, because possession by the first purchaser imparts constructive notice of the possessor's rights. If there is an unrecorded easement crossing the property, it will be valid and binding against a purchaser. If there are any encroachments, such as the encroachment of a building onto the adjoining property, the encroachment will not appear from the public records, but may be revealed only by a survey. Because of this, the title insurance policies set up certain exclusions for those facts that could be found only upon an examination of the property, such as the unrecorded rights of parties in possession. The title insurer refused to insure against title defects that could not be seen from a review of the public records, because the title insurer did not visit the premises to look for such defects.

However, as time went on, purchasers of title policies came to demand more protection. As a result, the title insurance companies, which had replaced the abstractor-insurer, began to inspect the property to determine if exceptions relating to parties in possession, encroachments, unrecorded easements, and mechanic's liens could be removed. As the title insurance companies began this practice, they also discovered the need for other special coverages. For example, if a building violates a building restriction, a special endorsement could be given insuring the purchaser against loss arising by reason of this violation.

Finally, title insurers formed the American Land Title Association (ALTA), a national trade association, and a degree of uniformity in title policies and endorsements made its appearance.

15.02 Abstractor's Liability

The abstractor is in no sense a guarantor of title, but rather undertakes to exercise due care in the preparation of the abstract. The abstractor renders no opinion as to the title. If the abstract includes all recorded instruments affecting the title and, as a consequence, discloses a fatally defective title, the abstractor has fully discharged its responsibilities. But, if an intending purchaser orders an abstract and the abstractor negligently omits a mortgage, judgment, or other lien that the purchaser is thereafter compelled to pay, the purchaser can obtain reimbursement from the abstractor. W.W. Allen, Annotation, *Abstractor's Duty and Liability to Employer Respecting Matters to Be Included in Abstract*, 28 A.L.R.2d 891 (1953). The abstractor's liability may also extend to third persons not parties to the contract for abstracting services. William B. Johnson, Annotation, *Negligence in Preparing Abstract of Title as Ground of Liability to One Other than Person Ordering Abstract*, 50 A.L.R.4th 314 (1986).

> **EXAMPLE:** Purchasers relied upon an abstract prepared for sellers by an abstract company. The court held that the purchasers could recover even though the abstract was prepared before the contract of purchase. *Williams* v. *Polgar,* 204 N.W.2d 57 (Mich. 1972), *aff'd* 391 Mich. 6, 215 N.W.2d 149 (1974).

To be safe, it is best for anyone who relies upon the abstract to have it certified by the abstractors to that person.

15.03 Certificate of Title

In some localities, the making of an abstract was omitted. The attorney would merely examine the public records and issue a certificate, which is an opinion of title based on the public records that were examined. Like an abstractor, such an attorney is liable only for damages occasioned by his or her negligence. Joseph T. Bockrath, J. D., Annotation, *Liability of Attorney for Negligence in Connection with Investigation or Certification of Title to Real Estate*, 59 A.L.R.3d 1176 (1974). The same is true when a certificate of title is issued by a title company. *Lattin* v. *Gillette,* 30 P. 545 (Cal. 1892); *Bridgeport Airport, Inc.* v. *Title Guaranty & Trust Co.,* 150 A. 509 (Conn. 1930).

15.04 Risks Involved in Relying on Record Title

There are certain defects in title that even a perfect abstract or certificate of title will not disclose because these hidden defects or hidden risks cannot be discovered by an examination of the public records. These hidden risks include the following:

1. *Forgery.* A deed in the chain of title may seem entirely regular but may nevertheless be a forgery. Such a deed is totally void and a purchaser or mortgagee of such title is not protected. Likewise, a forged release of mortgage does not discharge the mortgage lien.

2. *Insanity and minority.* A deed or release of mortgage executed by a minor or insane person may be subject to cancellation by subsequent court proceedings.

3. *Marital status incorrectly given.* A deed or mortgage may recite that the grantor or mortgagor is single, whereas in fact the party may be married. This may later result in a dower or other claim by the grantor's spouse.

   EXAMPLE: *H* owns an apartment building and is married to *W*, but is separated from her. *H* has an opportunity to sell the building and does so. *H* signs *W*'s name to the deed. The spouse's right in the property remains outstanding, and if *W* survives *H*, she will be able to force a sale of the building and her rights will be paid her out of the sale price.

4. *Defective deeds.* A recorded deed may not have been properly delivered. For example, it may have been found by the grantee among the grantor's effects after the grantor's death and then placed on record. Such deeds, of course, pass no title.

   EXAMPLE: *A* owns an apartment building. He is a bachelor. He shares a safe-deposit box with his nephew, *X*. *A* dies. *X* opens the box and finds a deed from *A* to *X* to the apartment building, with a note pinned to it stating that *A* wants *X* to have the building. *X* records the deed. The deed is void. The mere fact that the deed was recorded after *A*'s death discloses that there is something wrong with the deed.

There are other risks not of a legal character that are encountered when a deal is closed in reliance on a certificate of title or abstract and opinion. One of these risks is the risk of unwarranted litigation attacking the title. A landowner's title may be good as a matter of law, but if some other person entertains the notion that it has some title to, or interest in, the land, litigation may follow. Such litigation, even though successfully defended, may prove costly. Again, a competent attorney examining an abstract for a purchaser may reach an entirely correct opinion that the title is good. But when the purchaser, in turn, is selling or mortgaging the land, the attorney for the subsequent buyer or mortgagee may arrive at a different conclusion. This may necessitate the institution of litigation to clear the title. It is this fear of objections to the title by a subsequent examiner that prompts attorneys to scrutinize abstracts closely and raise every technical objection possible. This practice is known as *fly-specking.*

15.05 Title Insurance

It is the function of title insurance to shift or transfer to a responsible insurer risks such as those mentioned in the preceding section. Title insurance is a contract to make good a loss arising through defects in title to real estate or liens or encumbrances on real estate. As a rule, a title company will not insure a bad title any more than a fire insurance company would issue a policy on a burning building. However, title companies disregard many of the technical objections that would be raised by an attorney examining an abstract. If an examination of the title discloses that good title is vested in a particular person, the company will issue its policy, to indemnify the insured against any loss sustained by reason of defects in title not enumerated in the policy and to defend any lawsuit attacking the title where such lawsuit is based on a defect in title covered by the policy.

15.05(a)   The Title Insurance Policy

Title companies issue both *owner's policies and loan policies.* The owner's policy is usually issued to the landowner, typically at the time of purchase. Mortgage or loan policies, of course, are issued to lenders. Unlike other types of insurance policies, which insure for limited periods of time and are kept in force by the periodic payment of renewal premiums, an owner's title insurance policy is bought and paid for only once, and then continues in force without any further payment until a sale of the property is made. At that time, the title is examined to cover the period of time since the issuance of the policy, and a new policy is issued to the purchaser. A charge is then made for the issuance of the new policy.

It may help to understand title insurance if it is compared with casualty insurance.

> **EXAMPLE:** *X* buys a home and the deed to *X* is received on April 1, 1996. *X* receives a title insurance policy insuring his title as of April 1, 1996. On the same day, *X* takes out a one-year fire insurance policy. The title insurance policy insures *X* against any defects in title not shown in the policy where such defects occurred *on or prior to April 1, 1996.* No annual premium need be paid. Casualty insurance insures against any fire and other damage *occurring after April 1, 1996.* Annual premiums must be paid to keep the casualty policy in force.

The mortgage policy terminates when the mortgage debt is paid. However, if the mortgage is foreclosed, then the protection of the mortgage policy continues in force, protecting against any defects of title that existed on, or prior to, the date of the policy. In both policies, the company undertakes to defend at its own expense a lawsuit attacking the title where the lawsuit is based on a defect in title covered by the policy. This is one of the attractive features of title insurance to property owners, since "nuisance" litigation affecting real estate is quite common and expensive to defend, even though not well founded. A policy of title insurance usually shows the name of the party insured and the character of its title, which is usually fee simple title, although title policies are also issued on other interests, such as leaseholds or easements. It also contains a description of the land and, if the policy is a mortgage policy, a description of the mortgage. The policy lists those matters that affect that particular tract of land, such as any mortgage, easement, lien, or restriction thereon. Like other insurance policies, it contains printed conditions and stipulations.

Common printed exceptions found in owner's policies relate to the rights of parties in possession and questions of survey. Often, real property is in the possession of those whose rights are not disclosed by the records. Common instances are tenancies under oral or unrecorded leases and rights of those in possession under unrecorded contracts to purchase. When no survey has been furnished to the company, it has no means of knowing what encroachments exist, if any. The policy will therefore be subject to encroachments and other matters that a survey would reveal, as well as the rights of persons in possession claiming under some unrecorded document.

Title policies exclude certain risks from coverage. Those risks include matters that arise by reason of zoning, subdivision, building code and environmental laws, the exercise of the governmental right of police power, eminent domain, defects and other matters created by the insured, and claims relating to certain creditor's rights matters. While this listing is an oversimplification of the intricacies of the exclusions themselves, their application is quite complex and beyond the scope of this chapter.

While the policies promulgated by the ALTA are the most frequently issued, some states mandate the form of policy and regulate the forms of coverage that may be issued by the title companies doing business in that state. For example, Texas prescribes that a form of title policy be issued that affords a lesser amount of insurance than that available in other states. Further, Florida and several other states restrict the type of endorsements that may be offered by the title companies in those states.

15.05(b)   Title Insurance— Residential Policy

A new residential form of owner's title insurance is in use in many areas. This policy, is-sued only to consumers for residential transactions, is a dramatic innovation for two rea-sons. First, it is written in plain language both for marketing reasons and as a response to laws in some states that require insurance policies to be written in clear and understandable language. Second, the residential policy offers expanded coverage to the home buyer. This additional coverage includes the following:

1. Protection against unrecorded matters, such as survey problems, unrecorded easements, and unrecorded mechanic's liens.
2. To protect against the effects of inflation, the policy amount automatically increases by 10 per-cent per year for the first five years of coverage.
3. Insurance for actual loss incurred as a result of the forced removal of the existing structure be-cause it extends onto adjoining land or onto any easement or because it violates a restriction shown in the policy or because it violates the zoning law.
4. Insurance against actual loss incurred if the insured cannot use the land for a single-family res-idence because such a use violates a restriction shown in the policy or an existing zoning law.
5. In the event that the insured cannot use any of the land because of a claim against the title, the insurer will repay the insured for rent paid until the cause of the claim is removed.

15.05(c)   Title Insurance—Short-Form Residential Loan Policy

The Short-Form Residential Loan Policy was promulgated by ALTA to address the con-cerns of residential loan originators that the loan package, including the lender's title pol-icy, be available for delivery into the secondary mortgage market as soon as possible. In many instances, the issuance of the long-form loan policy was delayed for various factors. When finally received, the policy had to be checked and placed into the proper file. All of this increased the delay and cost of delivering the loan into the secondary market. To elim-inate these delays and costs, the title industry developed the short-form loan policy.

This policy, while providing the same coverage as the ALTA loan policy, is unique in that it is a one-page, preprinted form with little deal-specific information other than the identification of the policy date, mortgage amount, loan number, name of insured, name of borrower, and property address. Unlike standard loan policies, it does not contain the legal description of the mortgaged premises. Rather, the short-form policy refers to the legal de-scription set forth in the mortgage. If standard-form endorsements are to be issued, the cov-erage is provided merely by checking a box, thereby incorporating the endorsements into the policy coverage.

This form does not identify each of the defects, liens, and encumbrances affecting the title to the subject property. Rather it incorporates the coverage of the ALTA loan policy and takes generic exception to certain matters. For example, the policy takes exception for covenants, conditions, and restrictions, if any, appearing in the public records, but goes on to insure that those restrictions have not been violated and that any future violation will not result in a forfeiture or reversion of title, and that there are no provisions under which the lien of the insured mortgage can be extinguished, subordinated, or impaired. Similarly, the policy takes exception for easements and servitudes appearing in the public records, but goes on to insure that none of the improvements encroach upon the easements and that use of the easements for the purposes for which they were granted will not interfere with or damage the improvements, including lawns, shrubbery, and trees.

Through this style of coverage, the policy takes generic exceptions to the types of matters that might affect the title while at the same time giving the lender the protection it requires.

15.05(d) Title Insurance— Endorsements

Where the evidence of title reveals defects not permitted by the sale contract (or permitted by the contract only where title insurance thereover is available), the parties may choose to avail themselves of title insurance coverage afforded against the potential loss or damage that could be incurred by the existence of such defects. Also, the insured may desire greater coverage than that given by the standard form of policy. Title companies offer endorsements to cover special assessments, contiguity, encroachments, restrictions, foundations, zoning, and many other matters. Some special endorsements are available only to lenders to cover usury, truth in lending, negative amortization, and revolving credit loans. In some states where the forms of coverage are not limited or regulated, the title companies have a lot of flexibility to craft endorsements to cover special circumstances that are unique to the transaction at hand.

15.06(e) Title Insurance— Leasehold Policies

Suppose a tenant is about to take a lease on a store, theater, restaurant, or other commercial location in which it plans to make a substantial investment for remodeling and then make a substantial investment in developing a market in the area. Just as a buyer of land needs to know that the seller has a good, clear title, this tenant needs to know that the landlord has a good, clear title to the leased premises and that the tenant will not be dispossessed in the middle of the lease by foreclosure of mortgages or other liens on the landlord's title. Further, the tenant needs assurance that it will be allowed to conduct its business in the premises and not be prohibited because of building restrictions or zoning laws. Many leases require the landlord to furnish the tenant a leasehold title policy issued by a title company insuring the validity of the tenant's lease, free from mortgages or other encumbrances. Also, when the leasehold is the security for a mortgage, the lender will require a leasehold loan policy.

ALTA has also promulgated standard forms of leasehold owners and loan policies. Prior to that time, various title companies insured leaseholds by "doctoring up" regular owner's and loan policies. The leasehold policies define the insured leasehold estate to include the right of possession for the term of the lease subject to the conditions of the lease. The policies also describe a method of evaluating the leasehold estate and list the items of incidental damage to be paid if the insured is forced to surrender occupancy of the premises due to matters insured against.

15.05(f) Title Insurance— Easement Policies

Suppose a tract of industrial property accesses a railroad by means of an easement for a spur track over adjoining land. The validity of the easement is important to the value of the property and its use for industrial purposes. A sophisticated purchaser of the industrial tract will insist that the owner's title policy to be furnished at the closing insures the validity of the easement.

15.05(g) Title Commitments

Suppose that *A* had purchased some land in 1940 and had received a title policy at that time. *A* is now selling this same land to *B*. Naturally, *B* would not want to rely on such outdated title evidence. Therefore, the contract of sale will call upon *A* to have the title company bring its title search down to the present date. The title company will then issue a current title *commitment* obligating the company to issue its policy to *B*, subject only to the matters shown in the commitment. If any defects appear on the commitment that the seller must clear up (e.g., unpaid back taxes), the seller pays off the item, receives paid tax bills or other documents, and exhibits them to the title company, which thereupon waives the exception. When the title is clear, and the land conveyed to the buyer, a title policy will be issued naming the buyer as the insured.

15.05(h)   Title Insurance— Transactional Context

In a transactional context, considerable negotiation is directed toward agreeing upon the title insurer and the matters to be covered by the title insurance policy. In large transactions, the issues of reinsurance and coinsurance are heavily negotiated. Sellers are typically concerned over price, service, and the willingness of the title insurer to give the coverages requested by the buyer and any lenders who may be involved in the transaction. Buyers are typically concerned with the financial standing of the title insurer, service, underwriting capability, and the willingness of the company to effectively facilitate the deal. The competition among title companies is intense, sometimes with deals switching from one title company to the other in midstream. In any event, the parties are well served if they establish a good working relationship with the title companies so that a degree of comfort and trust is established.

15.06   The Torrens System

In a few counties in the United States, the Torrens system is also in place to give title protections to purchasers and lenders. Under the recording acts, when a deed is made conveying land, the grantee in the deed is recorded. The recorder makes a copy of the deed, places this copy in the record books, which are available to the public, and returns the original deed to the grantee. The recorder does not pass upon the validity of the deed. If the grantee wishes to satisfy itself that it has received a good title, the grantee may obtain title insurance, an abstract, and opinion of title, or a title certificate.

The Torrens system operates quite differently. The records of the Torrens office actually reflect the status of the title. While the Torrens office keeps the various deeds, mortgages, easement grants and the like, as those documents are registered, they are inscribed by reference on the official certificate of the title kept in the Torrens office. These certificates are bound into books as public records. At the same time that the registrar prepares the original certificate, a duplicate certificate of title is delivered to the owner.

When a tract of land has been registered under the Torrens system, no subsequent transaction binds the land until that transaction has been registered in the Torrens office, as opposed to recorded in the recorder's office. When the land is sold, the deed itself does not pass ownership of the land. The deed must be taken to the Torrens office, and if the registrar is satisfied that the deed is valid, the old certificate of title is canceled and a new one issued to the buyer. It is this *registration* that puts ownership in the grantee. The deed is not returned to the grantee but remains in the Torrens office. Similarly, a mortgage is not effective against the property until the registrar has checked it as to form and signature and entered it on the certificate of title. However, the registrar does not check on or guarantee the essential validity of the mortgage, for example, to see whether the mortgage money has been paid out or whether the interest rate is usurious.

No judgment or other lien is valid against property that has been registered under the Torrens system until a copy of that judgment or lien has been filed in the Torrens office and the lien noted on the certificate of title.

Use of the Torrens system is largely confined to a few metropolitan areas, such as Boston, Duluth, Minneapolis-St. Paul, and New York City. Even in those areas, it is falling into disuse. Chicago had perhaps the largest Torrens system, and that system is now in the final stages of being terminated; all of the registered properties are being deregistered and put into the recording system. The system, while idealistic, does not allow the flexibility of title insurance. As a result, even where the property in question is in the Torrens system, the parties to sophisticated transactions will often obtain title insurance, in addition to Torrens protection.

The Torrens certificate purports to be conclusive proof that the title is as therein stated. As in the case of other evidences of title, there are exceptions and objections that the Torrens certificate does not cover. These vary somewhat from state to state. Unlike a policy of title insurance, the Torrens certificate does not require the registrar to assume the defense of litigation attacking the title of the registered owner. The property owner must defend the litigation at its own expense and, if successful, be reimbursed by the Torrens office for the expenses of the litigation.

CHAPTER 16

Insurance Relating to Real Estate

16.01 In General

In the past, insurance was purchased in pieces. A fire policy with extended coverage was bought from one carrier, a liability policy from another, and so on. Today, coverage on both commercial and residential properties is offered as a package. Indeed, entities that own many parcels of real estate have a single package of coverages for their entire portfolio of property. Nonetheless, a historical perspective is in order.

16.02 Development of Standard Fire Policy

The need for fire insurance first became apparent after the Great Fire of London in 1666. However, the policies that came into use in England following that catastrophe contained numerous and varied fine-print exceptions that led to much litigation and disappointment on the part of the policyholders. These conditions also prevailed in America, and, in 1873, agitation for a standard policy led to the adoption of a standard policy form in Massachusetts. In 1886, New York adopted a standard policy form, which was revised by a law effective in 1918. This policy still strongly favored the insurer, and, in 1943, New York adopted a form more favorable to the insured. This old form was widely adopted everywhere and used for many years. It is still used on some commercial properties. This policy covers loss by fire only. Loss from the following other hazards are covered by a rider known as the extended coverage endorsement:

1. Explosion damage. If an explosion not caused by fire occurs on the premises and no fire results, none of the damage is covered. If a fire starts *first* and the fire causes an explosion, all loss is covered whether due to fire or explosion, for the fire is the cause of the loss. B. Fineberg, Annotation, *Construction and Application of Provision in Fire Policy Specifically Excepting Loss by Explosion Unless Fire Ensues*, 82 A.L.R.2d 1128 (1962). If an explosion occurs first and fire results, the policy covers the damage caused by the fire but not the damage caused by the explosion.

2. Water damage not resulting from a fire, such as damage from water seepage in a basement or from a leaking sprinkler system.

3. Windstorm damage. As in the case of explosions, if a fire results from windstorm damage, the fire loss is covered by the policy.

4. Loss from hail, riot, civil commotion, aircraft, and many other hazards.

Breakage, water damage, and damage from chemicals caused through efforts to extinguish the fire are considered to be caused by fire and are therefore covered by the policy.

16.03 Extended Coverage Endorsement

As can be seen, the fire policy provides very rudimentary coverage. Except in unusual circumstances, it is not adequate to protect a property owner from many of the causes of loss or damage to property. As a result, the extended coverage rider or endorsement was developed. Its content varies according to locality and insurer, but it often covers loss from windstorm, hail, explosion, riot, civil commotion, aircraft, vehicles, and smoke from friendly fires, except those in fireplaces. The windstorm damage coverage of the extended coverage endorsement does not cover rain, snow, or other water damage as such, except where caused by or resulting from windstorm or another peril specified in the extended coverage endorsement.

> **EXAMPLE:** In a heavy rain, the sewer backs up and floods the basement. The damage is not covered by the extended coverage endorsement.

> **EXAMPLE:** A tornado tears off a roof and the debris breaks water pipes. The water rushes out of the pipes, causing damage. All the damage is covered by the insurance, for the basic cause of the entire loss is the windstorm.

> **EXAMPLE:** A hailstorm breaks windows, and the rain and wind sweep in, causing damage. All the damage is covered, because the original cause is a hailstorm, which is a peril specified in the extended coverage endorsement.

Damage caused by explosion of a steam boiler on the premises is not covered, nor is damage caused by vehicles driven *by the landowner,* but if, for example, a delivery truck entering a drive runs into the building, this damage is covered.

16.04   Hazards Covered— Homeowners' Policies

For many years after the adoption of the New York 1943 form, the traditional fire insurance policy was offered as a basic form of coverage, which together with a rider or endorsement covered loss by windstorm and other perils. For residential properties, this policy has been replaced by the package of coverage offered in the homeowner's policy. The current forms of homeowners' policies do away with fine print, long sentences, and lawyers' language, opting for a booklet type of presentation with readable type, simple sentences, and the absence of hypertechnical language.

There are two basic types of homeowners' policies. One is the old-fashioned "named peril" policy. This form names the risks or perils insured against. There are presently two forms of this policy, the HO-1 and the HO-2. The HO-1 covers losses caused by fire or lightning, windstorm or hail, explosion, riot or civil commotion, vehicles, smoke, vandalism and malicious mischief, theft, and glass breakage. The HO-2 form expands the coverage of the HO-1 form, also insuring against losses caused by falling objects, weight of ice, snow, or sleet, collapse of a building or any part of a building, Annotation, *What Constitutes "Collapse" of a Building Within Coverage of Property Insurance Policy*, 71 A.L.R.3d 1072 (1976), accidental discharge or overflow of water or steam, sudden and accidental tearing apart or bulging of a heating, air conditioning, or hot water system, freezing of plumbing, heating, air conditioning system, or household appliances, and the sudden and accidental damage from artificially generated electrical current.

The HO-3 is an "all-risk" policy. In this format, instead of enumerating the perils insured against, it insures against all perils except those listed as uninsured risks. The HO-6 condominium owner's policy covers the condominium unit and personal property in the same basic fashion as the HO-2 coverage. All-risk coverage is also available for the condominium owner.

Consistent with the concept of providing homeowners with a package of insurance, the HO policies provide other coverages that are a natural part of a full package of protection for homeowners. Be warned that the specifics of coverage vary from company to company. The policies themselves must be reviewed to determine that they provide adequate coverage.

16.04(a) Personal Property Coverage

Personal property coverage extends insurance to the homeowner's personal effects—that is, furniture, stereo equipment, color TV, clothes, and so forth. The policy coverage on valuables such as jewelry, furs, silverware, and so forth is very low. The insurance agent should be consulted for a special endorsement covering valuables. Sophisticated homeowners have inventoried and photographed these items for use in claiming loss and to help the insurer recover the stolen articles. An appraisal is a requirement to recovery of insurance on valuables such as furs, jewelry, antiques, fine paintings, etc. An appraisal will also help the insured make a claim if the property is stolen.

Scheduling of personal property removes the restrictions caused by the formula coverage built into the policy for personal property. Typically, unscheduled personal property is covered to the extent of 50 percent of the coverage on the building. Therefore a policy with $500,000 in coverage on the building would provide $250,000 of coverage for unscheduled personal property. Those formulas are inapplicable to scheduled personal property, which has its own value statement unrelated to the amount of coverage on the building.

16.04(b) Liability Coverage

In addition to providing coverage for the building and its contents, the homeowners' policies provide liability coverage for bodily injury and property damage to others arising out of the insured's negligence. This coverage applies to accidents occurring both on and off the insured premises and extends to damages caused by members of the insured's family who live with the insured and the insured's pets. Typically, the coverage is for a low amount. It can be increased by endorsement. Many insureds, both homeowners and businesses, have excess or umbrella coverages that provide a layer of liability protection after the lower limits of the primary coverage are exhausted. This coverage is typically available at a lower cost because the chance of loss at this level is less than at the lower levels of coverage.

16.04(c) Medical Payments

The liability insurance protects the insured for damages that it causes to someone else. Medical payment coverage defrays the cost of injuries that occur through no one's fault, events that are purely accidental. This coverage, usually $5,000 per person and $25,000 per accident on a homeowner's policy, is available for injuries occurring to anyone other than the insured and the insured's family.

16.05 Other Insurance

The popularity of certain forms of coverage varies from region to region. For example, in the Midwest, earthquake coverage is cheap but practically never purchased. In California, it is popular, and its price varies depending upon the type of structure and locale.

In making the decision as to which coverage is appropriate, it is good to note that the disparity in price between the premiums for the least comprehensive and most comprehensive policies is relatively minor. The extra coverage is usually well worth the few extra dollars spent. Be watchful also to increase coverage as the value of property increases. For example, if the property has been rehabbed or improved by a room addition, the policy should be appropriately endorsed to increase the level of coverage. Similarly, as inflation increases the value of the property, coverage should be increased. These increases in the amount of insurance are necessary to avoid the operation of the coinsurance clause discussed in a subsequent section.

Some property is in slum areas where insurance is not ordinarily available. A federal program, the FAIR plan, exists to provide coverage for these properties. Flood insurance is available in flood-prone areas. Federal National Mortgage Association and federal lenders in general require flood insurance in such areas.

16.06 Rent Loss and Business Interruption

Since the policy covers fire damage to the building, it does not cover loss of rents when a rental building is rendered untenantable by fire, nor does it cover loss of profits when operation of a business is interrupted by fire. Rent loss insurance is obtained by landlords to protect against loss of rents resulting from a casualty loss to the building where the leases allow rent to abate in the event of a casualty. Business interruption insurance provides a business owner, including a business owner who is a tenant, with protection against the obligation to pay fixed costs even though the premises are closed as a result of the casualty and therefore not producing any revenue to pay those expenses. Both forms of insurance can be covered by riders attached to a casualty policy or by separate insurance such as rent insurance and business interruption insurance.

16.07 When Protection Attaches

It often takes some time for a formal policy of insurance to be prepared and forwarded to the insurer. Hence, oral coverage is perfectly valid, pending the issuance of the policy. This gives the insured the coverage of the standard policy, subject to its terms and conditions. *Bersani v. General Accident, Fire & Life Assur. Corp.,* 330 N.E.2d 68 (N.Y. 1975). Oral coverage is usually confirmed by a certificate of insurance or binder.

While oral assurance that coverage is in place may be valid and enforceable, it is unwise to leave something as important as insurance to chance. Insurance is complex in that there are many different coverages included in any package of coverage, each with its own policy limit or amount and applicable deductible amount. Indeed, even having certificates of insurance is not absolute assurance that the insurer is absolutely bound to cover the risks.

16.08 Description of the Property Insured

The property insured should be accurately described in the policy, and all policies applying to the same property should contain identical descriptions. The street address of the property is often used in insurance policies. There has been a tendency in recent times, however, to insist on the insertion of a full legal description so that there will be no dispute as to the property covered. This is particularly true with respect to houses recently constructed, which often do not have a street address at the time the policy is written.

16.09 Insurable Interest

The insured must have some insurable interest in the property. Otherwise the policy is void. Persons having an insurable interest include both buyer and seller in a contract for the sale of land, mortgagor, mortgagee, part owner, trustee, receiver, and life tenant.

16.10 Interest Covered by Policy

Insurance policies are generally "interest policies." They protect only the party insured and cover only the financial loss suffered by the insured, which can never be more than the value of the insured's interest in the property and which may be less than the actual damage to the building.

> **EXAMPLE:** A bachelor buys a home and takes out a policy in his name. He then marries and has the home placed in joint tenancy. He now owns only a half interest in the home and could collect no more than half of any loss. Suppose further that a loss occurs after the former bachelor's death. Here, his entire interest in the property has passed to his wife, but she has no insurance whatever.

Some homeowners' policies cover the named insured "and relatives living on the premises."

16.11 Acts of the Party Insured
Where the party insured causes the loss, as when the insured commits arson to collect the insurance, the insurance company is not liable. Courts hold that this is an "act of the assured," which invalidates the entire policy. *Lovall v. Rowan Mutual Fire Ins. Co.,* 302 N.C. 150, 274 S.E.2d 170 (1981); *Klemens v. Badger Mut. Ins. Co.,* 99 N.W.2d 865 (Wis. 1959); 10A Couch, Insurance Sec. 42.680.

16.12 Unoccupancy Clause
The policy typically provides that the insurer shall not be liable while the building is vacant or unoccupied for a period of thirty consecutive days. The words *vacant* and *unoccupied* are not synonymous. *Vacant* means without inanimate *objects; unoccupied* means without animate occupants. A dwelling is unoccupied when it has ceased to be a customary place of habitation or abode and no one is living in it. Thus, if furniture remains in the building, it is not vacant, but if the owner has left the dwelling with the intention of permanently residing elsewhere, the building is unoccupied, and the insurance may become void. *Vandalism coverage* usually ceases if the building is unoccupied for thirty days.

Because the danger of vandalism has greatly increased in recent times, insurance companies are enforcing this clause. This requires that the owner obtain an endorsement waiving the clause or have someone stay in the property if a lengthy absence is planned.

16.13 Progressive Damage
In some situations, damage occurs over time and is not at all visible when it begins. This creates two problems for the insured. Most policies and statutes of limitations require that suit be brought within a stated period of time. If the owner does not know that the damage has begun, how can it make a claim or bring a suit against the insurer within the required time limit? Further, many people change insurance companies from time to time. How can any insured know which of the several insurers is responsible for the loss?

Some courts have held that the insured has the benefit of the so-called "delayed discovery rule," which allows the insured to bring suit under the policy within one year of the discovery of the loss. The court went on to hold that the insurance company that insured the risk at the time of the first manifestation of the damage should pay the loss. *Prudential-EMI Commercial Ins. Co. v. Superior Court,* 798 P.2d 1230 (Cal. 1990).

16.14 Increase of Hazard
The policy provides that the company shall not be liable for any loss occurring if the hazard is increased by any means within the control or knowledge of the insured. The operation of this clause is restricted to physical changes in the building or in the use or occupancy of the premises. Any alteration or change in the building or in the use of the property that will increase the risk of loss violates this clause if the change is of a more or less permanent nature. M.T. Bruner, Annotation, *Casual or Temporary Repairs, and the Like, as Constituting Increase of Hazard so as to Avoid Fire or Other Property Damage Insurance,* 28 A.L.R.2d 751, 762 (1953).

> **EXAMPLE:** The following operations increase the hazard and invalidate the insurance: (1) Tenant began operating a still; (2) Owner turned off a sprinkler system; (3) Owner brought fireworks on the premises; and (4) Owner began use of a room as a tin shop.

Merely doing something that involves risk, that is a more or less normal and expected routine operation, is not considered an increase of hazard that invalidates the hazard insurance policy. For example, coverage is not invalidated by the owner's use of a torch to burn off old paint preparatory to repainting. 28 A.L.R.2d 762, at 771 *supra.* Also, the increase of the hazard must contribute to or cause the loss. *Northern Assurance Co. v. Spencer,* 246 F. Supp. 730 (W.D. N.C. 1965).

16.15 Double Insurance

Unless a policy endorsement provides otherwise, the insured may procure additional insurance. However, the liability of each company is limited to the proportion of the loss that its insurance bears to the total insurance covering the property. For example, if the same property is insured by two companies through two policies of $5,000 each, and if a loss of $2,000 occurs, the maximum liability of each company would be $1,000. To guard against coverage disputes, the insured should check to see that all portions of all policies covering the same property read exactly alike.

16.16 Amount Recoverable

When insurance is bought, the insured is concerned with two things. First, what hazards or risks are covered? Second, what amount will the insurance company pay if a loss occurs? The premium is based upon many factors, but it is primarily determined by the combination of these factors.

While it is the amount of coverage that primarily sets the maximum limit on a claim, aside from the amount of coverage purchased, the amount that the insurance company will pay is determined by whether the policy calls for the loss to be measured by the *actual cash value method* or the *replacement cost method*. Under the still, but infrequently, used 1943 New York standard policy, the measure of loss is the "actual cash value of the property at the time of loss," but not more than the cost to replace or repair the damaged property. Thus, if the actual cash value of the loss was $1,000, but the cost to replace was $700, the insurance company would pay $700, not $1,000.

While the term *actual cash value* is easy to say, its meaning is not always easy to determine. The courts have found three different ways to apply this term as a measure of loss. Some courts hold that actual cash value is determined by subtracting the fair market value of the property after the loss from the fair market value of the property before the loss. Other courts have adopted the cost of repair or replacement less depreciation formula. Yet other courts use the broad evidentiary rule that takes all factors into consideration (i.e., obsolescence, utility of buildings, depreciation, market value, etc.). Cozen, *Measure and Proof of Loss to Buildings and Structures Under Standard Fire Insurance Policies—The Alternatives and Practical Approaches,* 12 Forum 647 (1977); Dykes, *"Actual Cash Value": The Magic Words—What Do They Mean?,* 16 Forum 397 (1981); Wendy Evans Lehmann, Annotation, *Depreciation as Factor in Determining Actual Cash Value for Partial Loss Under Insurance Policy,* 8 A.L.R.4th 533 (1981).

Replacement cost insurance can be obtained by adding an endorsement or rider to the standard fire policy. Today's package policies typically provide replacement cost insurance without the need for a special endorsement. However such insurance is obtained, under replacement cost coverage, the insured is paid the actual cost of replacing or restoring the damaged property. Dag E. Ytreberg, Annotation, *Construction and Effect of Provision of Property Insurance Policy Permitting Recovery of Replacement Cost of Property in Excess of Actual Cash Value,* 66 A.L.R.3d 885 (1975). This method eliminates the guesswork and argument involved in agreeing upon the application of the actual cash value standard. Most lenders require replacement cost coverage.

The replacement cost coverage of the homeowner's policy is conditioned upon the property being insured for 80 percent of its replacement cost. This provision and the coinsurance clause discussed later require the insured to be watchful of the amount of insurance purchased so as always to have the required percentage of coverage. Some newer forms of homeowners' policies automatically increase the amount of insurance to adjust for increases in value caused by inflation, but not for improvements made to the property. Insureds are well advised to be watchful at the time of their annual renewals so that the details of the insurance coverage are carefully attended to and adequate insurance is in place before a loss occurs.

The amount of coverage purchased is also important because other coverages (i.e., liability, personal property, and medical payments), are set at percentages of the building coverage. The insured should compare its needs for these coverages to the amounts set by the application of these formulas. Most notably, an inventory of personal property should be made and compared to the amount of personal property insurance to determine whether the amount of insurance is sufficient.

16.17 Coinsurance Clause

Very few fires or other casualties cause a total destruction of the property. Insureds are aware of this fact. If it were not for the coinsurance clause, insureds would consistently underinsure, thereby taking or retaining part of the risk of total loss while passing the first layer of loss, where most losses will fall, to the insurer. To prevent this strategy, and to encourage insurance to the full value of the property, insurance companies have added the coinsurance clause. This provision requires the owner to keep the property insured to a prescribed level, often 80 percent of the replacement value, if insurance benefits are to be paid in full. The customary use of the 80 percent coinsurance factor stems from the fact that generally only 80 percent of a building's value is destructible. The masonry, foundation, underground utilities, and the like will remain even after a catastrophe. If the owner insures for less than the stated percentage, the coinsurance clause operates to reduce the amount of loss payable to the insured.

> **EXAMPLE:** Assume an 80 percent coinsurance clause, a building worth $10,000, and insurance in the amount of $4,000. The most the insurance company will pay is 50 percent of any loss. The same formula applies to rent loss coverage.

Typically, the insurance value of new buildings is easily determined. The older the building gets, however, the easier it is to inadvertently fall into a coinsurance problem. To avoid this, some insurance companies have adopted the use of *automatic increase endorsements* or the *agreed amount clause*. Through the latter device, the insurer agrees that the amount of insurance coverage satisfies the coinsurance requirement. Without these provisions, the owner should obtain a replacement cost appraisal from a real estate appraiser or from the insurance company, to be sure that the coverage meets the 80 percent requirement.

16.18 Mortgage Interests

Both the mortgagor and the mortgagee have an insurable interest. Both interests may be, and usually are, covered in one policy. But each may take out a separate policy. This right is of value to the mortgagee when the mortgagor has defaulted in its mortgage payments and declines to take out insurance since it feels that it will lose the property anyway through foreclosure. If the mortgagee obtains its own insurance with its own funds and a loss occurs, the mortgagor is not entitled to the insurance proceeds. If the insurer pays off the mortgage in such case, it is entitled to an assignment thereof and may foreclose. Of course the mortgagee's recovery is limited to the balance due on the debt, for that is the measure of its interest in the property.

On the other hand, in the absence of any clause in the mortgage requiring the mortgagor to insure for the mortgagee's benefit, the mortgagee is not entitled to insurance money paid under a policy obtained by the mortgagor in its own name and at its own expense. L.S. Tellier, Annotation, *Right of Holder of Mortgage or Lien to Proceeds of Property Insurance Payable to Owner Not Bound to Carry Insurance for Former's Benefit*, 9 A.L.R.2d 299 (1950). Most mortgage forms require the mortgagor to keep the buildings insured for the benefit of the mortgagee, and if a loss occurs in such case, the mortgagee is entitled to have the insurance proceeds applied in reduction or payment of the mortgage debt. *Sureck v. U.S. Fidelity & Guaranty Co.,* 353 F. Supp. 807 (1973). Where a mortgage containing a covenant to insure is assigned, the assignee obtains a right to the insurance proceeds. *Kintzel v. Wheatland Mutual Ins. Ass'n,* 203 N.W.2d 799 (Iowa 1973). An extended discussion of this subject can be found in Patrick A. Randolph, Jr., *A Mortgagee's Interest in Casualty Loss Proceeds: Evolving Rules and Risks*, 32 Real Prop. Prob. & Tr. L.J. 1 (1997).

16.18(a) The Mortgage Clause

It had been customary for the mortgagor to take out insurance in its own name and, with the insurer's consent, assign the policy to the mortgagee. This did not adequately protect the mortgagee. It simply stood in the mortgagor's shoes, and if the mortgagor violated the conditions of the policy so that it became void, the mortgagee was unable to collect the insurance. For example, if the mortgagor committed arson, the policy became void. The same result followed where the *open mortgage clause* was used. This clause simply stated that loss, if any, was payable to the mortgagee *as its interest shall appear,* which still left the mortgagee's insurance subject to be destroyed by the ignorance, carelessness, or fraud of the mortgagor. *Central Nat'l Ins. Co. v. Manufacturer's Acceptance Corp.,* 544 S.W.2d 362 (Tenn. 1976). Hence the mortgagee loss clause, also known as the New York, standard, or union loss clause, was developed. S*yndicate Ins. Co. v. Bohn,* 65 F. 165 (8th Cir. 1894). This clause, now in general use, provides that the insurance shall not be invalidated by acts of the mortgagor. Under this clause, if the mortgagor does any act that would ordinarily make the policy void, for example, commits arson or brings dynamite on the premises, *such act merely makes the policy void as to the mortgagor, but the insurance remains in force for the benefit of the mortgagee. City-Wide Knitwear Processing Co., Inc. v. Safeco Ins. Co.,* 366 N.Y.S.2d 81 (1973). When such a clause is used, there are really two separate contracts, one between the insurer and the mortgagor and the other between the insurer and the mortgagee, and most matters that would invalidate the first of these contracts leave the second intact and in full force.

Since the standard mortgage clause is a separate contract between the mortgagee and the insurer giving the lender coverage that is separate from the owner insured's, it follows that many acts that invalidate the owner's coverage do not affect the lender's coverage. Thus, the mortgagee's protection continues even where

1. The policy is canceled without the mortgagee's consent. *Mutual Creamery Ins. Co. v. Iowa Nat'l. Ins. Co.,* 294 F. Supp. 337 (D. Minn. 1969). Do not confuse cancellation with expiration and nonrenewal. If the policy expires, the mortgagee is not entitled to any special notice, and the mortgagee's protection ends. Allan E. Karpela, Annotation, *Right of Mortgage to Notice by Insurer of Expiration of Fire Insurance Policy*, 60 A.L.R.3d 164 (1974).

2. The mortgagor increases the hazard in the use of the property without the mortgagee's knowledge, for example, by storing flammable substances.

3. The mortgagor is negligent or intentionally damages the insured property. This is very important to the lending industry at a time when arson is a national problem.

   EXAMPLE: John Smith takes out fire insurance with ABC Co. on a home he occupies. He mortgages the home to XYZ Mortgage Co. and the standard mortgage clause is attached to the fire policy. Needing money desperately, John Smith sets fire to his home. It is destroyed. This act of John Smith precludes him from collecting on the insurance if the arson can be proved. But, XYZ Mortgage Co. will collect insurance up to the amount remaining due on the mortgage. Its separate contract (the mortgagee loss clause) is not affected by Smith's acts.

There are limits on the protection afforded by the mortgagee loss clause. The mortgagee must notify the insurer of any change in ownership of the property that comes to the knowledge of the mortgagee. The mortgagee is also bound by the coinsurance clause and any limitation periods in the policy upon the time in which a suit on the policy may be brought. *Greater Providence Trust Co. v. Nationwide Ins. Co.,* 355 A.2d 718 (R.I. 1976).

Since the mortgage clause is a separate and independent contract of insurance, the name of the mortgagee as a party insured must be stated in the mortgage clause. *Pacific Ins. Co. v. R.L. Kimsey Cotton Co.,* 151 S.E.2d 541 (Ga. 1966). If the mortgage is released and a new mortgage placed on the property, then a new mortgagee clause must be issued even though the mortgage runs to the same mortgagee that was covered by the previous mortgage clause. *Attleborough Sav. Bank v. Security Ins. Co.,* 46 N.E. 390 (Mass. 1897).

The homeowner's policy forms now include the mortgage loss clause in the body of the policy. It runs in favor of the mortgagee "named in this policy." On the cover page of the policy is a place for the insertion of the name of the mortgagee. It is important that this blank be filled in. Unless this is done, the mortgagee has no independent coverage. *Pac. Ins. Co. v. R.L. Kimsey Co.,* 151 S.E.2d 541 (Ga. 1966). This could be fatal—for example, if the landowner commits arson. The insurance policy becomes void and a mortgagee not named has no coverage. This point must be stressed because people do change insurance agents from time to time. The new agent may fail to fill in the blank because it has not been told about the mortgage.

16.18(a)(1) The Mortgage Clause— Foreclosure

The mortgagee loss clause continues to protect the lender after foreclosure. *Northwestern Nat'l. Ins. Co. v. Mildenberger,* 359 S.W.2d 380 (Mo. App. 1962). *But see Consolidated Mortgage Corp. v. American Sec. Ins. Co.,* 244 N.W.2d 434 (Mich. App. 1976), which requires notice to the insurer of the foreclosure. The mortgagee that takes a deed in lieu of foreclosure also has continued protection. *Union Central Life Ins. Co. v. Franklin County Farmers Mutual Ins. Ass'n,* 270 N.W. 398 (Iowa 1936). *But see Insurance Co. v. Citizens Ins. Co.,* 425 F.2d 1180 (7th Cir. 1970). These statements must be taken with a grain of salt.

A serious problem exists as to the rights of the mortgagee after the foreclosure sale. In most cases, the mortgagee is the highest bidder at the foreclosure sale, and usually bids an amount close to the amount of its mortgage debt. In a number of cases the courts have stated that this amounts to a satisfaction or payment of the mortgage debt in the amount of the foreclosure sale price. The thinking here is that if a third party had been the successful bidder, its cash money would have gone to the mortgagee in reduction of the mortgage debt, and the result should be the same where the mortgagee "bids its mortgage" at the foreclosure sale. The consequence is that if a fire occurs after the foreclosure sale, the mortgagee recovers, at a maximum, the difference between the foreclosure sale price and the amount due on the mortgage debt, which is usually a trifling amount. *Northwestern Nat'l. Ins. Co. v. Mildenberger,* 359 S.W.2d. 380 (Mo. App. 1962). *Whitestone Sav. & Loan Ass'n v. Allstate Ins. Co.,* 270 N.E.2d 694 (N.Y. 1971). Other courts say that the mortgagee should be allowed full recovery where a mortgagee loss clause exists. *Trustees of Schools v. St. Paul Fire & Marine Ins. Co.,* 129 N.E. 567 (Ill. 1920); *City v. Maynur,* 329 N.E.2d 312 (Ill. 1975).

The lesson is obvious. The mortgagee should obtain a new policy or a rider to the existing policy the moment it has made the successful bid at the foreclosure sale.

16.19 Contracts for the Sale of Land

When a landowner takes out insurance and thereafter contracts to sell the land to a purchaser, the sensible course is to have the insurance endorsed to cover both parties as their interests may appear. Then, in case of serious loss, the company will pay the seller the balance due on the contract, and the balance will be paid to the buyer.

When a policy taken out by the buyer is payable to the seller and a fire occurs and the company pays the unpaid balance of the purchase price to the seller in satisfaction of the insurance claim, all rights of the seller in the property are extinguished, and the company is not entitled to any assignment of the contract. *Fields v. Western Millers Mutual Fire Ins. Co.,* 37 N.Y.S.2d 757 (1942). The buyer is entitled to a deed to the land since the insurance money has paid the purchase price. *Dysart v. Colonial Fire Underwriters,* 254 P. 240 (Wash. 1927).

When the buyer takes out a policy with loss payable to the buyer and seller as their interests may appear, and thereafter the seller declares the contract forfeited because of the buyer's default in its payments, the seller is still covered by such insurance. *Aetna Ins. Co. v. Robinson,* 10 N.E.2d 601 (Ind. 1937). A mere default in the buyer's payments does not terminate the buyer's insurance. The buyer remains covered until the seller declares a forfeiture of the contract.

Suppose the contract of sale (as is customary in installment contracts) requires the buyer to take out insurance for the benefit of the seller and buyer, but the buyer takes out insurance in its own name only. If a loss occurs, the courts will require the buyer to carry out its contract by forcing the buyer to apply its insurance money in payment of the contract price due to the seller. *American Equitable Assurance Co. v. Newman,* 313 P.2d 1023 (Mont. 1957); F.M. English, Annotation, *Rights of Vendor and Purchaser as Between Themselves in Insurance Proceeds,* 64 A.L.R.2d 1416 (1959).

It now seems clear that where a landowner has entered into a contract of sale and a fire occurs after the buyer has substantially reduced the balance due, the seller may nevertheless collect for the full amount of the loss.

> **EXAMPLE:** *A* took out a fire insurance policy and thereafter contracted to sell the land to *B.* When the contract had been paid down to $16,000, a fire loss occurred. *A* was allowed to collect $46,750 in fire insurance. *First Nat'l Bank v. Boston Ins. Co.,* 160 N.E.2d 802 (Ill. 1959); *Edlin v. Security Ins. Co.,* 269 F.2d 159 (7th Cir. 1959).

Although a contract-of-sale endorsement can be obtained to add the purchaser as an insured, no satisfactory standard form endorsement for the homeowner's policy exists to protect the installment contract seller.

> **EXAMPLE:** Seller enters into an installment contract to sell a home to Buyer. The existing homeowner's policy was written to insure Seller. A new policy is written to insure the Buyer, but with an endorsement making loss payable to Buyer and Seller, as their interests may appear. Buyer commits arson and the building is totally destroyed. Seller may be unable to collect on the insurance. *Langhome v. Capitol Fire Ins. Co.,* 44 F. Supp. 739 (D. Minn. 1942).

For proper protection, a *manuscript endorsement* should be used. This is a tailor-made endorsement used when no adequate printed form is available. It should state that no acts done or suffered by the buyer will in any way affect or impair the coverage to the seller.

16.20   Assignment   Assignment of the policy does not render the policy void, but the assignment itself is not valid except with the written consent of the insurance company. For this reason, when the policy is assigned in connection with a sale, a popular practice in the past that is rarely used today, the seller cannot collect on the policy for a subsequent loss, since after the sale it has no insurable interest in the property. Nor could the buyer collect if the assignment had not been consented to by the company. In other words, hazard insurance does not "run with the land." It must be assigned to the buyer for the buyer's protection. *Eastway Constr. v. New York Property Underwriting Ass'n,* 382 N.Y.S.2d 949 (1976). The right to the insurance proceeds is assignable after loss. *Travelers Indemnity Co. v. Isreal,* 354 F.2d 488 (2nd Cir. 1965).

As a practical matter, the problem of assignment has become less significant in recent years. Frequently, the seller's policy is canceled upon closing. Similarly, the buyer must tailor its protection and seek its own coverage, possibly written by the buyer's regular insurance agent.

16.21 Liability Insurance

A building owner and lessee must carry liability insurance to protect them against loss or injury caused to someone as a result of their involvement with the real estate.

EXAMPLE: A customer who slips on the threshold and breaks a leg will sue the building owner and the tenant who runs the store.

The homeowner's policy automatically includes liability insurance.

Obviously, an injured party will sue everyone involved with the property. It is best to have coverage if for nothing more than protection against the costs of defending cases of this type.

16.21(a) Liability Insurance for Contractors

A liability policy issued to a general contractor is likely to contain exclusions colloquially referred to as "x," "c," and "u." The "x" exclusion excludes liability for blasting. The "c" exclusion excludes liability for collapse of building. The "u" exclusion excludes liability for damage to underground facilities such as conduits and sewers. Coverage can be obtained to fill all of these voids in insurance protection, but appropriate endorsements must be identified and requested.

Completed operations insurance covers liability for a completed job.

EXAMPLE: A contractor completes a bridge and later it collapses, causing bodily injury and property damage.

In general, a mortgage lender wants to see that all proper insurance is obtained.

EXAMPLE: Lender is lending money on a large construction loan, with Contractor acting as general contractor. A bridge built by Contractor in another state collapses. With no insurance coverage, Contractor goes broke. A new contractor must be found and costs go up astronomically.

16.21(b) Builder's Risk Insurance

Builder's risk insurance comprises fire and extended coverage insurance for a building under construction. In its natural state, the amount of coverage under this form of policy increases as the building is completed. Today, a completed value form is available from the very outset of construction. This form eliminates the need to report construction progress. Also, in its natural state, builder's risk insurance will not cover an occupied project. An endorsement can be obtained, either at the outset of the job or at completion, to give this coverage.

16.21(c) Business Interruption Insurance

The ordinary fire policy covers damage to the building caused by fire. It does not cover loss of business profit. Business interruption insurance is required to protect from loss of income and continuing expenses when a business property is destroyed or damaged. There are two kinds of business interruption insurance. The "gross earnings" form pays an amount roughly equal to the gross earnings lost while business was interrupted. This coverage puts the insured business in the place it would have been if the business continued. It pays lost profits only to the extent that profits would have been earned. If losses would have been sustained, no payment is made under the insurance policy. Proving the amount of loss under this form is fairly complicated. Another form of business interruption insurance is the valued form under which the insurer and the insured agree at the time the policy is issued on the duration and amount of coverage.

EXAMPLE: An insured obtains a policy that pays $1,000 per week for a period of not more than six months while its plant is shut down by fire damage. There is a fair amount of guesswork in this type of coverage.

REFERENCE: Alan G. Miller, *Types of Business Interruption Insurance Coverage in Business Interruption Insurance: A Primer* (1987).

16.22 Public Insurance Adjuster

Some insureds who have suffered a loss immediately turn to a public insurance adjuster for expert help in gathering the evidence of the extent of loss and prosecuting the claim. For a fee of usually ten percent of the recovery from the insurance company, the adjuster will prepare inventories of damaged property, determine the extent of seen and unseen damage, calculate the cost of repair and replacement, and the like. Adjusters also have access to a group of support personnel, expert engineers, architects, appraisers, and others who aid in determining the loss.

Public adjusters also offer other valuable services where a fire occurs. The policy requires the owner to board up windows and take other steps to minimize loss. The insured is often in a state of shock, devastated by the casualty. It has no idea how to go make its claim under the insurance policy. The public adjuster is an expert in this area. The insurance company has its own adjuster. Its job is to minimize the amount the company pays. Often, the public adjuster and the insurance company's adjuster have dealt with each other before and know how to deal with the casualty loss that confronts them.

CHAPTER 17

Land Acquisition
and Assembly

17.01 In General

Before land can be developed, it must be acquired. While the suggestions made in the chapters on contracts of sale and land development are, of course, applicable to the process of land acquisition, the mechanics of land acquisition and assembly call for special expertise.

17.02 Precautions Prior to Undertaking Assembly

Before undertaking a land assembly, the developer obtains a title commitment to get an idea of the ownerships involved and possible restrictions and the like that may prohibit or impair the developer's ability to carry out the development concept. Obviously, it is easier to assemble three or four ownerships than thirty or forty ownerships. It is also crucial that the developer have a good understanding of the developmental process and obtain some comfort that the project can be built under local zoning and planning laws, or at least know whether those local laws and ordinances need to be changed to accommodate the development.

17.03 Gaps and Gores

It is often necessary to acquire and assemble the lands of several adjoining landowners to accommodate the entire development, whether that development be residential, commercial or industrial. Here the danger is that the legal descriptions used for the several parcels may leave small gaps between the parcels.

> **EXAMPLE:** Buyer proposes to acquire the Northwest Quarter of Section 10 in a government township. He assumes that it contains exactly 160 acres, which it theoretically should contain. Actually, of course, owing to inaccuracies in surveying, there is no such thing as a perfect quarter section, and it happens that this quarter section contains 161 acres. Suppose, then, that Buyer acquires from Seller 1 the "east eighty acres" of the quarter section and gets a deed from Seller 2 to the "west eighty acres" of the quarter section. This leaves a one-acre strip between the two eighty-acre tracts. Buyer thus does not acquire title to this strip.

These small strips between parcels are called *gores.*

The more likely scenario is the buyer's acquisition of several parcels, each having its own long metes-and-bounds legal description. The developer will want to have surveys of each of these parcels and a separate survey of the whole tract showing each of the separate parcels on that larger survey. Where one seller owns all of the parcels being acquired, the surveyor can be asked to furnish a *perimeter description*. This is a description of the entire tract being acquired by metes and bounds. If gaps or gores are revealed, the buyer can report the title as unmarketable.

What is typically done in these situations is to obtain an endorsement to the owner's title policy ensuring that all of the several parcels are contiguous to one another at what appear to be their common boundaries.

17.04   Nominees   Land is often acquired in the name of a nominee, often a skilled negotiator from a local real estate firm. This is done because asking prices soar when it becomes known that some well-known company is acquiring land in the area. The nominee need not disclose that it is acting for an undisclosed principal. Case Note, *Specific Performance—Contracts for Sale of Land—Undisclosed Principal as Plaintiff*, 32 Iowa L. Rev. 790 (1947). But, if the seller inquires, the nominee must not misrepresent the identity of the purchaser, for if it does, the seller has the right to terminate the contract, because a material misrepresentation has been made. Friedman, *Contracts and Conveyances of Real Property* § 2.2 (3d ed. 1975); H.A. Wood, Annotation, *Concealment of Fact that One of Parties to Land Contract Was Acting for Third Person, or Misrepresentation as to Identity of Party for Whom He Was Acting as Reason for Denying Specific Performance, or for Rescission of Contract*, 121 A.L.R. 1162 (1939); Annotation, *Purchaser's Misrepresentations as to Intended Use of Real Property as Ground for Vendor's Equitable Relief from Contract and Deed*, 35 A.L.R.3rd 1369, 1374 (1971). Indeed, if such misrepresentation is made, the seller can have its deed set aside even after the deal has been closed, so long as the seller acts promptly on learning of the misrepresentation. The nominee must refrain from misrepresenting the use to which the property will be put. 35 A.L.R.2d 1369, *supra*.

> **EXAMPLE:** Nominee went to Seller and persuaded Seller to sell a vacant lot adjoining Seller's home. Nominee stated that it planned to build a house. When it later developed that Nominee was buying on behalf of a church, the deed was set aside. *Keyerleber v. Euclid Congregation*, 143 N.E.2d 313 (Ohio 1957); W.E. Shipley, Annotation, *Concealment, Misrepresentation or Mistake as Regards Identity of Person for Whom Property Is Purchased as Ground for Cancellation of Deed*, 6 A.L.R.2d 812 (1948).

This rule has special force where the seller retains some land and the buyer intends to devote the acquired land to some offensive use, such as a junkyard, cemetery, or bar. 35 A.L.R.3d 1369, 1370, *supra*. If bad blood or previous dealings lead a buyer to believe that the seller will not sell to him or her, it is useless to hire a nominee. The seller can have the deal set aside. 6 A.L.R.2d 812, *supra*; 35 A.L.R.3rd 1369, 1374, *supra*.

There seems to be some advantage in having the developer form a straw corporation or other entity with some nondescript name to acquire the land. This would be a wholly owned subsidiary of the developer. The subsidiary could then hire the nominee, who, if asked, or even if not asked, can truthfully state, "I'm working for Real Estate Associates, Inc."

Where it is decided to attempt a secret assembly, some developers use a different nominee, lawyer, and real estate broker for each acquisition. Obviously, a nominee who has no judgments or other liens against it should be used. Often an unmarried person is employed, for then no spouse's rights questions arise.

At times, the nominee will request that its employer sign an indemnity agreement protecting the nominee against liability by reason of its ownership of the land. Even with indemnities, nominees are increasingly reluctant to take title to or control a parcel of land. Landownership brings with it liability. For example, the mere ownership of land may expose the nominee to liability for the cleanup of hazardous waste.

17.04(a)   Written Authority   Because an agent's authority to buy land must be in writing in some states, there should be a written contract of employment.

17.04(b)   Trust Declaration by Nominees   The nominee routinely signs a brief trust agreement reciting that it is acquiring the land and will hold it in trust for the developer. This is acknowledged, just as a deed is acknowledged, but it is not recorded. The trust declaration is an indispensable document—for example, if the nominee dies while the ownership of the land stands in its name. It is especially important in land assemblies that may take a long period of time. Some developers also require the nominee to sign an unrecorded quitclaim deed simultaneously with the acquisition of the land.

17.05 Escrows A seller who senses that it is not dealing with the real purchaser may become uneasy. To quiet these fears, the deal should be closed in escrow.

> **EXAMPLE:** Nominee tenders a contract of sale to Seller, with a provision that the entire purchase price will be held by ABC Bank under an escrow agreement providing that Seller gets the entire purchase price or gets ownership of the land back just as it was before the contract was signed.

17.06 Subdivision Trusts In Arizona, extensive use is made of the *subdivision trust.*

> **EXAMPLE:** Seller enters into a contract to sell vacant land to Buyer for $100,000. Buyer pays $20,000 down. Seller now makes a deed of the land to ABC Title Co. in trust. Seller is the first beneficiary of the trust and Buyer is the second beneficiary. The trustee files a plat of subdivision. Buyer engages in sales of lots. Lot buyers make their payments to ABC Title Co., which remits to Seller and Buyer according to a schedule with a minimum amount due periodically. The lot buyers receive their deeds from ABC Title Co. Ultimately, Seller is paid the balance of the purchase price. If sales collapse, and Buyer cannot meet the schedule of payments, Seller can declare a forfeiture of Purchaser's interest. Thereupon, ABC Title Co. deeds the unsold lots to Seller. George Read Carlock, *The Subdivision Trust—A Useful Device in Real Estate Transactions,* 5 Ariz. L. Rev. 2 (1963).

17.07 Land Trusts The land trust is an ideal vehicle for land assemblies. It enables the developer to acquire the individual parcels in the name of a trust company.

17.08 Holding Agreements In California and Nevada, a device somewhat similar to the land trust is used, called a *holding agreement.*

17.09 Purchase Money Mortgage Often, the developer who is purchasing a development parcel will arrange the purchase with the seller taking back a purchase money mortgage. Any such transaction must have special provisions for the developer's benefit. First, the purchase money mortgage must have a clause that requires the seller/mortgagee to join in the plat of subdivision and execute necessary consents and governmental documentation for the platting and sale of the property. Platting statutes require that mortgagees join in the execution of the subdivision plat. Otherwise, foreclosure of the prior mortgage will extinguish the streets and other public areas dedicated on the plat.

Another necessary clause requires the mortgagee to give partial releases as lots or parcels are sold. This is necessary to clear title for the buyer and mortgagee. If the developer plans to put a construction mortgage on the property, the purchase money mortgage must contain a clause whereby the seller/mortgagee subordinates the purchase money mortgage to the construction mortgage. This is done in anticipation that the construction lender will insist upon a first mortgage to secure the construction loan. A great deal of caution must be used in drafting this clause. If it is not complete and precise in its terms, it may be unenforceable. *See* Robert Kratovil & Raymond J. Werner, *Modern Mortgage Law and Practice,* Ch. 30 (2d ed. 1981).

Of course, standards should be included in all of these clauses. The seller/mortgagee should not be obligated to execute just any document that the purchaser/mortgagor tenders.

Rather, the documents tendered by the purchaser/mortgagor should conform to standards that had been previously agreed upon between the parties. The subdivision plat must be for a particular type of development in which the seller/mortgagee has confidence. The partial release clause should set out partial release prices or a formula for the giving of such releases. The seller should also guard against the release of noncontiguous parcels lest the seller/mortgagee be left with an unsalable checkerboard of land as security for the mortgage.

If there are barns or other buildings on the land being sold, the contract and mortgage should give the developer the right to demolish them. A mortgagee can block demolition of buildings on mortgaged land unless the mortgage provides to the contrary.

17.10 Options Options are often used in land acquisitions.

> **EXAMPLE:** Buyer plans a site that requires assembly of ten separately owned tracts of land. Buyer hires agents who procure options on all ten tracts of land. If Buyer is unable to obtain options on all ten tracts, Buyer allows all options to lapse. If all ten options are procured, Buyer exercises all options.

Options are fragile interests and are subject to various defenses. The law in this area is a bit tricky and should be carefully considered when dealing with an option agreement. Gregory G. Gosfield, *A Primer on Real Estate Options*, 35 Real Prop., Prob. & Tr. J. 129 (2000). One of those defenses is the ancient rule against perpetuities, which provides that any interest in real estate must vest during lives in being at the time of the transfer plus twenty-one years. An Indiana court recently invalidated a right of first refusal given in a real estate contract where there was no time limit placed on the purchaser's right. *Buck v. Banks*, 668 N.E.2d 1259 (Ind. App. 1996). *Compare Pathmark Stores, Inc. v. 3821 Associates, L.P.*, 663 A.2d 1189 (Del. Ch. 1995) (that upheld an option with a thirty-year term in a commercial transaction). Other courts have held that the rule against perpetuities does not apply to commercial transactions. *Shaver v. Clanton*, 26 Cal. App. 4th 568, 31 Cal. Rptr. 2d 595 (1994); *Juliano & Sons Enterprises, Inc. v. Chevron, U.S.A., Inc.*, 250 N.J. Super. 148, 593 A.2d 814 (1991).

A right of first refusal is related to an option in that it gives to the holder the right to purchase the property if another party makes an offer to purchase. There are many mechanical issues to be worked out in the drafting of a right of first refusal, including the time allowed to the purchaser/optionee to exercise or lose its right, and the time after exercise of the right that the property must be acquired by the optionee. In some cases, the optionee must take the deal offered to the seller/optionor as offered, without any changes. In other cases, the optionee may have some flexibility with the general provisions of the agreement and is merely obligated to take up the economic terms of the transaction coming from the third party.

One of the trickier issues involves the optionor's receipt of an offer for a larger tract that includes the parcel to which the right of first refusal relates. The majority of courts allow the optionee to enjoin the sale of the tract that is covered by the right of first refusal. In a minority of jurisdictions, the holder of the right of first refusal may specifically enforce its right to compel the sale of the leased parcel to the holder. Jean A. Maess, Annotation, *Option to Purchase Real Property as Affected by Optionor's Receipt of Offer for, or Sale of, Larger Tract Which Includes the Optioned Parcel*, 34 A.L.R.4th 1217 (1984).

17.11 Taxes Assessors usually assess farmland considerably lower than subdivided land. This suggests that the development should proceed in stages, if this is possible. The developer will leave as much as possible in farmland or vacant until the developer is ready to go forward with the project or that phase of the project. And if the developer plans a commercial development, it will postpone platting until it is ready to build, for the tax assessor will assess commercial land higher than residential land or farmland.

17.12 Leasehold Acquisitions

Obviously, acquisition of a leasehold presents problems different from those involved in acquisition of outright ownership.

> **EXAMPLE:** Condominium Developer acquires a leasehold. It then discovers that local law does not permit condominium developments on leaseholds.

> **EXAMPLE:** Co-op Developer acquires a leasehold and erects a high-class apartment building. It encounters sales resistance. Prospective tenants point out that as the mortgage on the leasehold is reduced by payment, the equity of the apartment owner becomes so substantial that it becomes difficult to sell the apartment for cash, and mortgage financing on a co-op is virtually unobtainable. This makes it almost necessary for the ground lease to contain some provision for the landlord joining in the ground lessee's financing. Obviously, there is a problem here.

17.13 Contract Provisions

When land is assembled or acquired for development, the buyer/developer will typically enter into a contract that provides that the purchaser is not obligated to close until a laundry list of conditions are fulfilled. That list will include satisfying the purchaser that the condition of title is acceptable for the proposed development, including obtaining special endorsements from the title company to address special circumstances of the subject development, obtaining necessary financing, obtaining any necessary planning and zoning approvals or changes, and, in some cases, satisfying the purchaser that the project is economically feasible. If the developer's due diligence does not show that the property is acceptable and the project is likely to succeed, the developer will have the right to exercise its option to terminate the contract and receive its earnest money back.

CHAPTER 18

Co-Ownership—
Community Property

18.01 In General Once people decide to own property jointly, they must decide upon the form of their co-ownership. Should they form an artificial entity—that is, a corporation, partnership, limited liability company, or trust—or should they hold their property in their own names? If they choose the latter approach, should they own the property as joint tenants or tenants in common? If they are married, what of the impact of tenancy by the entireties, community property, or other laws dealing with marital rights? In determining what form of ownership to use, the parties must consider, among other things, the income tax and estate planning consequences of the various forms of ownership. These decisions are not easily made and are not entirely legal in nature. The law tells the parties the consequences of their actions; the parties must then choose which consequences they want.

A person can be the sole owner of a tract of land or may own the land with others. Where there are two or more co-owners they are known as *co-tenants*. There are different kinds of co-ownerships, or co-tenancies, as they are called. Persons may own the land as *joint tenants,* as *tenants by the entireties,* or as *tenants in common,* or in *community property.*

18.02 Joint Tenancy–Tenancy in Common Distinguished When a deed is made to two or more persons who are not husband and wife and nothing is said in the deed concerning the character of the tenancy created by the deed, the grantees acquire title as tenants in common. Under this form of co-ownership, on the death of either party, the interest in the real estate will go to the decedent's heirs, if he or she dies without leaving a will, or to the persons named in the will, if the decedent died with a will.

> **EXAMPLE:** Seller conveys land to Brother 1 and Brother 2. Since the deed is not in joint tenancy form, Brother 1 and Brother 2 are tenants in common. Brother 1, a widower, dies without a will, leaving Child 1 and Child 2 as his only children. Brother 2, Child 1, and Child 2 own the land as tenants in common, with Brother 2 owning one half and Child 1 and Child 2 owning each one fourth.

If, however, the deed runs to two or more persons as joint tenants, a different rule applies. While both joint tenants are alive, they are co-owners of the land, but as soon as one dies, the decedent's share passes automatically to the surviving joint tenant.

> **EXAMPLE:** In the previous example, if Brother 1 and Brother 2 held the property in joint tenancy, Brother 2 would have become the sole owner of the property upon the death of Brother 1. Child 1 and Child 2 would have no interest in the property.

Any number of persons may hold real estate in joint tenancy.

EXAMPLE: Seller makes a deed to *A*, *B*, *C*, and *D*, as joint tenants. *D* dies. *A*, *B*, and *C* now own the land as joint tenants. A dies. B and C own the land as joint tenants. *B* dies. *C* is now the sole owner.

18.02(a) Abolition of Survivorship

Some states have enacted laws that purport to abolish the joint tenant's right of survivorship, so that on the death of a joint tenant, the decedent's share goes to heirs or to the persons named in the will, just as if a tenancy in common had been created. *See* Ariz. Rev. Stat. § 33-43 1; Fla. Stat. Ann. § 689.15. However, even in these states, the right of survivorship is not absolutely prohibited. If the deed to the joint owners expressly states that upon the death of one owner the property shall go to the survivor, the right of survivorship will be enforced. *Chandler v. Kountze,* 130 S.W.2d 327 (Tex. 1939); W.W. Allen, Annotation, *Construction of Devise to Persons as Joint Tenants and Expressly to the Survivor of Them or to Them "With Right of Survivorship",* 69 A.L.R.2d 1058 (1960).

18.02(b) Joint Tenancy—Creation

To create a joint tenancy, a deed must state that the grantees are acquiring title as joint tenants. The actual language used varies somewhat from state to state, but it is best to use comprehensive language in creating a joint tenancy. W.W. Allen, Annotation, *What Constitutes a Devise or Bequest in Joint Tenancy Notwithstanding Statute Raising a Presumption Against,* 46 A.L.R.2d 523 (1956). A suitable clause would provide that the property is conveyed to *A* and *B* as joint tenants with the right of survivorship, and not as tenants in common or as tenants by the entirety, or as community property.

A deed to persons who are husband and wife poses special problems. It may create a tenancy by the entireties, Daniel H. White, Annotation, *Estate by Entireties as Affected by Statute Declaring Nature of Tenancy Under Grant or Devise to Two or More Persons*, 32 A.L.R.3d 570 (1970), or it may create community property interests in the grantees. If it does neither of these things and is not a joint tenancy deed, the husband and wife are tenants in common. An exception to this general rule is found in Wisconsin and New York where a deed to a husband and wife creates a joint tenancy unless the deed states otherwise.

A joint tenancy may also be created when the parties have ineffectively attempted to create a tenancy by the entireties.

Rather frequently we find a husband and wife helping a newly married son or daughter to buy a house. The couples may buy a two-apartment dwelling for their joint occupancy, each couple acquiring a one-half interest in the property. The old couple wants their half interest held in joint tenancy, but does not want the young couple to have any interest in the old couple's half. The young people feel the same about their half. Each couple wants its half to be in joint tenancy, so that when one of them dies the surviving spouse will own the entire half interest, but they want a tenancy in common as between the two half interests. To accomplish this, it is best to use two separate joint tenancy form deeds, one going to each couple. Before the land description in each deed, insert, "An undivided one-half interest in. . . ." Thus, each couple will have its own deed. If one of the owners dies, the surviving spouse will own a one-half interest in the property as the surviving joint tenant. The others continue to own their half as joint tenants. The two halves are as separate for this purpose as if they were separate tracts of land.

A similar problem results when friendly couples purchase property together.

EXAMPLE: John Jones and Mary Jones, his wife, and Henry Brown and Susan Brown, his wife, are friends. They decide to invest in real estate and buy a twelve-unit apartment building together. They take title as "John Jones and Mary Jones, as joint tenants as to an

undivided one-half interest, and Henry Brown and Susan Brown, as joint tenants as to an undivided one-half interest."

Of course, the parties should have a written agreement spelling out their respective rights and duties. This agreement should address upkeep and maintenance obligations, occupancy rights of the parties, rights to rents and profits of the property, debt service obligations, buy-out obligations, rights of first refusal, the right of one or more of the parties to cause the property to be sold or used to secure a loan, and the like.

In states that have abolished survivorship rights in joint tenancies, some special problems exist.

> **EXAMPLE:** In a state where the law states that the right of survivorship in joint tenancies is abolished, Seller makes a deed to Husband and Wife "as joint tenants with the right of survivorship and not as tenants in common." Husband dies. Wife takes all as the survivor. However, the cases are not in agreement as to the nature of the interest created by the deed. One line of cases says that a joint tenancy was created by agreement of the parties. It becomes an ordinary joint tenancy. In other states, it creates an estate for lives with the right of survivorship. Neither party can sever it by deed as can be done in an ordinary joint tenancy. It is an indestructible right of survivorship. *Anson v. Murphy,* 32 N.W.2d 271 (Neb. 1948); *Bernhard v. Bernhard,* 177 So. 2d 565 (Ala. 1965). Statutes of the type discussed will likely disappear in time. They cause difficulties with common, necessary joint tenancies, such as those in bank accounts.

18.02(b)(1)   The Four Unities

Not every deed that describes the grantees as joint tenants is sufficient to create a joint tenancy. In the creation of a joint tenancy, the four unities of time, title, interest, and possession must be present. That is, the joint tenants must have one and the same interest, acquired by one and the same deed, commencing at one and the same time, and they must hold by one and the same undivided possession.

> **EXAMPLE:** Owner owned a tract of land. Thereafter, he married and executed a deed to himself and his wife "as joint tenants." No joint tenancy was created by this deed. Owner and his wife did not acquire title at the same time or by the same conveyance, since Owner had owned the land long prior to the making of the deed. The unities of time and title were not present. The deed actually created a tenancy in common. Owner and his wife should have conveyed title to a third person, and this third person should have thereupon reconveyed the title to Owner and his wife as joint tenants. *Deslauriers v. Senesac,* 163 N.E. 327 (Ill. 1928).

Pointless technicalities like these are going out of fashion. Hence, in many states, laws have been passed under which a deed by a landowner to him- or herself and another as joint tenants creates a good joint tenancy. *See, e.g.,* Cal. Civ. Code § 83; Ill. Rev. Stat. Ch. 76, § b.

For reasons relating to community property, spousal rights, and homestead, the landowner's spouse should join in the deed. One often sees a landowner and his wife conveying to themselves as joint tenants, and the whole thing, though odd, is quite legal in most states. W.W. Allen, Annotation, *Character of Tenancy Created by Owner's Conveyance to Himself and Another, or to Another Alone, of an Undivided Interest,* 44 A.L.R.2d 595, 605 (1955).

When a deed reveals an intention to create a joint tenancy, but fails to for some technical reason, some modern courts tend to show little patience with the old technicalities and give the property to the survivor, even though a true joint tenancy has not been created.

> **EXAMPLE:** A husband who owned some land in his own individual name signed a deed conveying a half interest in this land to his wife, the deed stating that they were to hold the

land as joint tenants. In some states, this does not create a valid joint tenancy, for the four unities are lacking. Nevertheless, on the death of the husband, the court awarded the entire property to the surviving wife. *Runions v. Runions,* 207 S.W.2d 1016 (Tenn. 1948). There can be a right of survivorship even though the land is not owned in joint tenancy, which is something of a subtle distinction, but has the happy result of achieving what the parties wanted.

It is impossible to make a deed to *A* of a one-fourth interest in the land and to *B* of a three-fourths interest to hold as joint tenants. A deed creating joint tenancies must give the joint tenants equal shares as to the property conveyed in joint tenancy. This does not prevent a joint tenant from owning a different and distinct interest in the land.

> **EXAMPLE:** *X* conveys a half interest to *A* and a half interest to *A* and *B* as joint tenants. This is perfectly valid. *In re Galleto's Estate,* 171 P.2d 152 (Cal. App. 1946).

18.02(c) Severance of Joint Tenancy

There is nothing sacred about a joint tenancy. Either joint tenant has the right to break the joint tenancy. W.W. Allen, Annotation, *What Acts by One or More Joint Tenants Will Sever or Terminate the Tenancy,* 64 A.L.R.2d 918 (1959). Certain actions will break the joint tenancy and convert it into a tenancy in common, even against the wishes or without the knowledge of the other parties.

1. A conveyance by a joint tenant to a third party destroys the joint tenancy.

> **EXAMPLE:** *A* conveys to *B* and *C* in joint tenancy. *C* conveys half of the title to *D*. *D* thereafter conveys this interest back to *C*. *C* dies. *C*'s title passes to his heirs, not to *B*. The conveyance from *C to D* severed or terminated the joint tenancy. The joint tenancy was not revived by the reconveyance. At *C*'s death, *B* and *C* were holding title as tenants in common. *Szymczak v. Szymczak,* 138 N.E. 218 (Ill. 1923). It is not necessary that *B* be informed of the fact that *C* is breaking the joint tenancy. *Burke v. Stevens,* 70 Cal. Rptr. 87 (1968).

In some states, where a deed runs to *A* and *B* as joint tenants with the right of survivorship, neither joint tenant alone is permitted to sever the joint tenancy.

Where there are three or more joint tenants and only one makes a deed to a third party or to one of the other joint tenants, some highly technical problems are encountered.

> **EXAMPLE:** *A, B,* and *C* own land as joint tenants. *C* conveys his third to *D*. *A* and *B* continue to hold their two-thirds as joint tenants. *Morgan v. Catherwood,* 167 N.E. 618 (Ind. 1929); *Hammond v. McArthur,* 183 P.2d 1 (Cal. 1947).

> **EXAMPLE:** *A, B,* and *C* own land in joint tenancy. *A* conveys to *B* by quitclaim deed. *B* and *C* continue to own a two-thirds interest in the land in joint tenancy, and *B* owns a one-third interest as tenant in common. *Shelton v. Vance,* 234 P.2d 1012 (Cal. 1951); *Jackson v. O'Connell,* 177 N.E.2d 194 (Ill. 1961).

> **EXAMPLE:** *A, B,* and *C* own land in joint tenancy. *C* conveys one-twentieth of his interest to *X*. *A* and *B* continue to own their two-thirds in joint tenancy. *C* and *X* are tenants in common. *Giles v. Sheridan,* 137 N.W.2d 828 (Neb. 1965); Swenson & Degnan, *Severance of Joint Tenancies,* 38 Minn. L. Rev. 466, 472 (1954). This severance occurs notwithstanding the fact that the deed was not recorded. *Carmack v. Place,* 535 P.2d 197 (Colo. 1975).

2. An involuntary transfer of title will sever a joint tenancy.

> **EXAMPLE:** *A* and *B* hold title as joint tenants. *A* goes into bankruptcy. Under the old bankruptcy law, title to all of *A*'s property was automatically transferred to the bankruptcy trustee. This transfer severed the joint tenancy. *In re Victor,* 218 F. Supp. 218 (S.D. Ill.

1963). Whether the same result will follow under the new bankruptcy law is not entirely clear. Rather than transferring the debtor's property to the bankruptcy trustee, the new law creates a bankruptcy estate when the bankruptcy case has begun. 11 U.S.C. § 541.

The actions of creditors of one of the joint tenants can also sever the tenancy.

EXAMPLE: *A* and *B* hold title as joint tenants. Creditor obtains a judgment against *A,* and a sheriff's sale is held to obtain money to pay the judgment. Buyer purchases the property at the sheriff's sale and obtains a sheriff's deed. This severs the joint tenancy. Buyer and *B* now hold as tenants in common. However, the rendition of a judgment against one joint tenant and the making of a levy on his interest will not sever a joint tenancy. *Van Antwerp v. Horan,* 61 N.E.2d 358 (Ill. 1945); *Hammond v. McArthur,* 183 P.2d 1 (Cal. 1947); *Eder v. Rothamel,* 95 A.2d 860 (Md. 1953). It has even been held that a sheriff's sale under such a judgment does not sever the joint tenancy and that the joint tenancy is not severed until a sheriff's deed issues. If the joint tenant against whom the judgment was rendered dies before the sheriff's deed issues, the other joint tenant takes all the property free and clear of the judgment creditor's rights. *Jackson v. Lacey,* 97 N.E.2d 839 (Ill. 1951).

3. In title and intermediate states, a mortgage executed by one of the joint tenants severs the joint tenancy, notwithstanding the fact that the mortgage is subsequently paid and released by the mortgagee. W.W. Allen, Annotation, *What Acts by One or More of Joint Tenants Will Sever or Terminate the Tenancy,* 64 A.L.R.2d 918 (1959). *But see Harms v. Sprague,* 473 N.E.2d 930 (Ill. 1984).

    EXAMPLE: *A* and *B* hold title as joint tenants. *A* executes a mortgage on his half of the title and thereafter pays off the mortgage, which is released. Thereafter, *B* dies. *B's* half of the title passes to his heirs, not to *A. A's* mortgage severed the joint tenancy.

    A mortgage executed by both joint tenants does not sever the joint tenancy.

    EXAMPLE: *A* and *B* hold title as joint tenants. They both join in a mortgage. Thereafter, *A* dies. *B* takes title as the surviving joint tenant. 64 A.L.R.2d 918, 935. In a lien state, a mortgage signed by one joint tenant is extinguished as a lien against joint tenancy property upon the death of the joint tenant. *D.A.D., Inc., v. Moring,* 218 So. 2d 451 (Fla. App. 1969); *Harms v. Sprague,* 473 N.E.2d 930 (Ill. 1984).

4. A contract by one joint tenant to sell or convey his or her interest in the land to a third person will operate as a severance of the joint tenancy. *Naiburg v. Hendricksen,* 19 N.E.2d 348 (Ill. 1939); Sara L. Johnson, Annotation, *Contract of Sale or Granting of Option to Purchase, to Third Party by Both or All Joint Tenants or Tenants by Entirety as Serving or Terminating Tenancy,* 39 A.L.R. 4th 1068 (1985).

5. If one joint tenant files a partition suit against the other, and a partition decree is entered, the joint tenancy is severed. *Schuck v. Schuck,* 108 N.E.2d 905 (Ill. 1952); *Hammond v. McArthur,* 183 P.2d 1 (Cal. 1947).

6. A husband and wife own land in joint tenancy. One files a divorce suit against the other. A divorce decree is entered. It orders the land sold and the proceeds of sale divided between them. The joint tenancy is severed. *Baade v. Ratner,* 359 P.2d 877 (Kan. 1961). Indeed, if a husband and wife own land in joint tenancy and they enter into a separation agreement providing that the land will be sold when the divorce decree is entered and the proceeds of sale divided between them, this agreement will sever the joint tenancy. *Carson v. Ellis,* 348 P.2d 807 (Kan. 1960).

7. A simple, written, signed, and recorded declaration by one joint tenant that the tenancy has been severed has been held sufficient to terminate the joint tenancy, thereby converting it into a tenancy in common. *Hendrickson v. Minneapolis Fed. Sav. & Loan Ass'n.,* 161 N.W.2d 688 (Minn. 1968).

8. Any agreement between the joint tenants that shows an intention to treat the land as a tenancy in common will cause a severance. 64 A.L.R.2d 918, 941, *supra.*

9. In one or two states, the making of a lease by one joint tenant severs the joint tenancy. *Alexander v. Boyer,* 253 A.2d 359 (Md. 1969).

There are other events that do *not* break the joint tenancy as follows:

1. A will by the deceased joint tenants.

   EXAMPLE: *A* and *B* own land as joint tenants. *A* makes a will giving all his property to *C*. *A* dies. *B* takes all the joint tenancy property, and *C* gets no part of it. *A*'s will does not break a joint tenancy. *Eckardt v. Osborne,* 170 N.E. 774 (Ill. 1930); *Matter of Estate of Kokjohn,* 531 N.W.2d 99 (Iowa 1995).

2. A lien created against one of the joint tenants.

   EXAMPLE: *A* and *B* own land as joint tenants. A judgment lien, internal revenue lien, or other lien is filed against *A* only. *A* dies before he has lost his title through enforcement of the lien. *B* takes the entire title free and clear of the lien. In other words, if *A* is a joint tenant, a lien against him attaches not to the land but to *A*'s *interest in the land,* which is an interest that will be totally extinguished if *A* dies before *B* does, so long as the parties are joint tenants when *A* dies. One who has a lien on *A*'s interest ordinarily can have no greater rights than *A* has, and if *A*'s rights will be extinguished by his breach, so will the lien. Francis M. Dougherty, Annotation, *Judgment Lien or Levy of Execution on One Joint Tenant's Share or Interest as Severing Joint Tenancy,* 51 A.L.R. 4th 906 (1987).

3. A contract to sell the property that is executed by both joint tenants. *But see In re Baker's Estate,* 78 N.W.2d 863 (Iowa 1956), *criticized in* Robert Kratovil, *Joint Tenancies and "Creative Financing"—the Land Contract,* 5 U. Ark. Little Rock L.J. 475 (1982). *See* 39 A.L.R.4th 1068, *supra.* Law here is unclear.

4. An easement created by one joint tenant only.

   EXAMPLE: *A* and *B* own land as joint tenants. *A* alone signs an easement grant to *C,* and *A* dies before *B* does. *B* then owns the entire title free and clear of the easement.

5. Dower and curtesy of a spouse of a deceased joint tenant.

   EXAMPLE: If *A* and *B,* both married men, own land as joint tenants, and *A* dies first, his wife has no dower in the land because at *A*'s death, all his title to the land is extinguished, leaving nothing to which dower can attach.

6. Divorce. State laws differ on the subject of divorce.

   EXAMPLE: In some states, a divorce does not break a joint tenancy. Where no specific law exists, if *H* and *W* own land as joint tenants, are divorced, and if nothing is said in the divorce decree about the property, the joint tenancy is unbroken. Suppose that *H* thereafter marries another person, *X. H* dies before *W* does. *W,* the former wife of *H,* takes the entire property, and *X* takes nothing. *H* could have prevented this by breaking the joint tenancy by deed. On the other hand, in some states, the entry of a divorce decree automatically converts the joint tenancy into a tenancy in common. This is by virtue of special laws.

7. The making of a lease by one of two joint tenants does not sever the joint tenancy. *Tindall v. Yeats,* 64 N.E.2d 903 (Ill. 1946). *See* Note, 7 Baylor L. Rev. 97 (1955); Comment, 25 Cal. L. Rev. 203 (1937).

8. One joint tenant files a partition suit against the other, but one of them dies before a partition decree is entered. The survivor takes all as surviving joint tenant. 64 A.L.R.2d 918, *supra.*

9. A deed by one joint tenant to him- or herself does not sever the joint tenancy because it is nothing but an empty ceremony. *Clark v. Carter,* 70 Cal. Rptr. 923 (1968), and the contrary has also been held. *Minonk State Bank v. Grassman,* 432 N.E.2d 386 (Ill. 1982). *See* Wendy Evans Lehmann, Annotation, *Severance or Termination of Joint Tenancy by Conveyance of Divided Interest Directly to Self,* 7 A.L.R.4th 1268 (1981).

10. Where one of two joint tenants grants a life estate to another this does not sever the joint tenancy. *Hammond v. McArthur,* 183 P.2d 1 (Cal. 1947).

11. The mere granting of an option to purchase one joint tenant does not sever the joint tenancy. *Alexander v. Boyer,* 253 A.2d 359 (Md. 1969).

REFERENCE: *Severing Joint Property Interests,* 16 Real Prop., Prob. & Tr. J. 435 (1981).

18.02(d) Disadvantages of a Joint Tenancy

Rather frequently, when title is held in joint tenancy by a husband and wife and one of them dies, the survivor, impressed with the simplicity of transfer of ownership on the death of a joint tenant, ponders the advisability of creating a new joint tenancy in which the surviving spouse will be joint tenant with one or more of the children of the surviving spouse. This estate planning technique has certain disadvantages. Such a deed cannot be unmade. All of the grantees must convey the property as the surviving spouse may wish. That may not be possible. Suppose that the surviving spouse and the child named as joint tenant quarrel, a not uncommon situation. Indeed, the mere fact that the parties share ownership of the real estate seems to trigger quarrels. The child may file a partition suit and put the property up for sale. Thus, the surviving spouse would be without a place to live. Judgments may be rendered against the child, and creditors may force the property to an execution sale.

Many lawyers counsel the surviving joint tenant to avoid setting up a joint tenancy such as this. Where a will or revocable trust is made, the estate plan can always be changed. No child would have a right in the property until the landowner dies. The fact remains that when there is a will rather than a deed, there is much less likelihood of family quarrels.

18.02(e) Joint Tenancy—Creditors' Rights

A judgment or other lien creditor against one joint tenant's interest is in a somewhat fragile position. If the lien is not transformed into ownership, as, for example, by an execution sale, before the death of the debtor joint tenant, the interest of the lienor is cut off. The deceased joint tenant's interest vests in the surviving joint tenant free of the lien. To an opposite effect, if the other joint tenants die before the debtor joint tenant, the lien will spread to the entire fee interest that vests in the surviving debtor joint tenant upon the death of the other joint tenant.

EXAMPLE: *A* and *B* own Blackacre as joint tenants. Creditor obtains a judgment lien against *A.* The following results are possible: (1) if *A* dies before levy and execution sale, Creditor's lien is extinguished and *B* acquires Blackacre free of Creditor's lien; (2) if *B* dies before levy and execution sale, *A* owns a 100 percent interest in Blackacre, which is entirely subject to Creditor's lien; (3) if Creditor levies, executes, and purchases at the execution sale, the joint tenancy is severed and Creditor and *B* own undivided one-half interests in Blackacre.

18.03 Tenancy by the Entireties—In General

In many states, a form of joint tenancy, known as tenancy by the entireties, exists. This tenancy exists only where the co-owners are husband and wife and is based upon the common-law notion that they are one person, and each are holders of the entire estate. In many states, no special words are necessary to create a tenancy by the entireties.

EXAMPLE: In a tenancy-by-the-entireties state, *X* makes a deed to *H* and *W,* husband and wife. Nothing is said as to the character of their co-ownership. They are tenants by the entireties.

In some tenancy-by-the-entireties states, laws have been passed stating that the deed must expressly show that the grantees are husband and wife and an intention to create a tenancy by the entireties. 765 ILCS 1005/1c.

Tenancy by the entireties resembles joint tenancy in that upon the death of either husband or wife, the survivor automatically acquires title to the entire property, including the share of the deceased spouse. Tenancy by the entireties differs from joint tenancy in that neither spouse has the power to defeat or sever the tenancy by a deed or mortgage to a stranger made without the signature of the other spouse. *Hoffman v. Newell,* 60 S.W.2d 607 (Ky. App. 1932).

> **EXAMPLE:** A deed is made to a husband and wife. Nothing is stated in the deed as to the character of their tenancy. Thereafter, the husband makes a deed that purports to convey his interest in the land to *X*. The wife does not join in this deed. The husband dies. The wife now has full title to all the land. *X* has nothing.

However, a deed by both husband and wife will, of course, give the grantee good title.

As long as the marriage exists neither spouse may partition the estate by the entireties. *Lawrence v. Lawrence,* 190 A.2d 206 (N.J. App. 1963).

> **EXAMPLE:** *A* and *B* hold property as tenants in common. If they disagree upon the disposition of the property, they can ask the court either to physically divide the property between them (this is called partition in kind) or sell the property and divide the proceeds. This relief is not available to tenants by the entireties.

> **EXAMPLE:** Where *H* and *W* hold property as tenants by the entireties and *W* sues *H* for divorce, *H* can ask the court, but only if a divorce is allowed, to divide the property or sell it and divide the proceeds. *Bastians v. Bastians,* 321 N.Y.S.2d 480 (1971).

Tenancy by the entireties is not recognized in community property states.

18.03(a) Creation of Tenancy by the Entireties

In the states where tenancies by the entireties are recognized, there is much difference of opinion as to the legal effect of a deed to a husband and wife that describes the grantees as joint tenants. In some states, such a deed creates a joint tenancy, rather than a tenancy by the entireties. *Witzel v. Witzel,* 386 P.2d 103 (Wyo. 1963). But in most of the states that recognize tenancy by the entireties, such deeds are held to create a tenancy by the entireties. *Hoag v. Hoag,* 99 N.E. 521 (Mass. 1912). If a joint tenancy is desired, the deed should always state that the grantees are "joint tenants and not tenants in common or tenants by the entireties." This should avoid litigation over the issue.

However, when a deed to a husband and wife describes them "as tenants in common," such a deed is almost universally regarded as creating a good tenancy in common rather than a tenancy by the entireties.

For the creation of a tenancy by the entireties, it is necessary that the grantees be husband and wife. If they are not husband and wife, even express language in the deed declaring an intention to create a tenancy by the entireties will not create such a tenancy.

In many states, a landowner who marries is permitted to give a deed to the landowner and the spouse as tenants by the entireties. The more traditional format used to accomplish this end is for the landowner and spouse to deed the property to a nominee who in turn deeds the property back to the landowner and the new spouse.

18.03(b) Defective Tenancy by the Entireties as Creating a Joint Tenancy

Tenancy by the entireties exists only as between husband and wife. A deed to parties who are not husband and wife creates some other kind of tenancy even though a tenancy by the entireties is specified. Wendy Evans Lehmann, Annotation, *Estate Created by Deed to Persons as Husband and Wife but Not Legally Married*, 9 A.L.R.4th 1189 (1981).

> **EXAMPLE:** A deed to *A* and *B,* who claimed to be, but were not, husband and wife, recited that it was made to them as tenants by the entireties and not as tenants in common. Since this revealed a general intention to create survivorship rights, but could not create a tenancy by the entireties, the parties not being husband and wife, the court held that a joint tenancy was created. Donald Kepner, *The Effect of an Attempted Creation of an Estate by the Entirety in Unmarried Persons,* 6 Rutgers L. Rev. 550 (1952); Theodore A. Fitzgerald, *Real Property—Tenancies by the Entirety—Joint Tenancy—Deed Purporting to Convey Property by the Entireties to Man and Woman Not Legally Married Created a Joint Tenancy,* 37 Notre D. Law 441 (1962); Arnold T. Burns, *Real Property: Co-ownership by Husband and Wife: Creation of a Tenancy by the Entirety by a Conveyance to Three or More, Two of Whom Are Husband and Wife*, 37 Cornell L.Q. 316 (1952).

> **EXAMPLE:** In states that do not recognize tenancy by the entireties, a deed to husband and wife "as tenants by the entireties" creates a joint tenancy. *In re Ray's Will,* 205 N.W. 917 (Wis. 1925); R.P. Davis, Annotation, *Creation of Right of Survivorship by Instrument Ineffective to Create Estate by Entireties or Joint Tenancy,* 1 A.L.R.2d 247 (1948).

> **EXAMPLE:** A deed to two sisters "as tenants by the entireties" has been held to create a joint tenancy. *In re Richardson's Estate,* 282 N.W. 585 (Wis. 1938). Likewise this was true where the deed was to two brothers. *Penn. Bank & Tr. Co. v. Thompson,* 247 A.2d 771 (Pa. 1968).

However, in most states, a deed to two people, describing them as tenants by the entireties or as husband and wife, creates only a tenancy in common if they are, in fact, not married. *Pierce v. Hall,* 355 P.2d 259 (Or. 1960); 9 A.L.R.4th 1189, *supra.*

> **EXAMPLE:** A deed was made to Charles Smith and Julia Smith, *husband and wife.* Actually, they were not married. Julia died. Charles, describing himself as a "surviving spouse," made a deed to a purchaser. Then, three sisters of Julia appeared and claimed her half of the property as her heirs. They succeeded. Only a tenancy in common existed and Charles was not even an heir. *Thurmond v. McGrath,* 334 N.Y.S.2d 917 (1972).

18.03(c)   Tenancy by the Entireties—Deeds Between Spouses

Suppose a husband or wife owns land in his or her own name, or they own land as tenants in common. They wish to put the land in their names as tenants by entireties. The traditional way of accomplishing this is to have the husband and wife join in a deed to a nominee, and such nominee then deeds the land back to the husband and wife as tenants by the entireties. Just as in the case of joint tenancies, the old rule is as follows: In order to have good tenancy by the entireties, the husband and wife must acquire title by the same deed, and the dummy conveyance satisfies this requirement.

Just as in the case of joint tenancies, recent laws and court decisions allow a husband or wife to create a tenancy by the entireties without deeding out to a dummy. In these states, if the husband owns land and wishes to create a tenancy by the entireties with his wife, he makes out a deed running to himself and his wife "as tenants by the entireties, and not as joint tenants or as tenants in common." Oval A. Phipps, *Tenancy by Entireties,* 25 Temple L.Q. 24, 43 (1952); W.H. Allen, Annotation, *Character of Tenancy Created by Owner's Conveyance to Himself and Another, or to Another Alone of Undivided Interest*, 44 A.L.R.2d 595, 598 (1955). For reasons relating to dower and homestead, the wife should join in this deed as co-grantor.

In a few other states, it has been held that it is still necessary, if a good tenancy by the entireties is to be created, that the husband landowner and his wife join in a deed to a third person, who thereupon conveys to the husband and wife. This practice should be followed unless it is clear that the state has abolished the need for a third-party conveyance.

When land is held in tenancy by the entireties, a deed by the husband to the wife gives her good title even though she does not join in the deed to herself. The same is true of a deed by the wife to the husband. W.E. Shipley, Annotation, *Validity and Effect of Conveyance by One Spouse to Other of Grantor's Interest in Property Held as Estate by Entireties*, 8 A.L.R.2d 634.

18.03(d)   Tenancy by the Entireties—Deeds, Mortgages, Leases, Rents, and Brokers' Listings

As a rule, a deed or mortgage of property owned in tenancy by the entireties must be signed by both husband and wife. In most states, when a tenancy by the entirety exists, a deed to a stranger signed by the husband or wife alone is void. Oval A. Phipps, *Tenancy by Entireties,* 25 Temple L.Q. 24, 46 (1952). In a few states, the deed is given some effect, but the effect varies from state to state. It may grant a share of the rents or may be operative if the grantor survives the other spouse. In any event, in all states, the deed becomes void if the spouse who did not join in the deed survives the spouse who conveyed.

Both parties should sign any lease. In many tenancy-by-the-entireties states, husband and wife have equal rights to rents and possession, and any lease must be signed by both. Oval A. Phipps, *Tenancy by Entireties,* 25 Temple L.Q. 26, 46, (1952).

Certainly this is the impact of new laws designed to equalize the rights of the wife and those of the husband. Mich. Stat. Ann. § 26.210(1).

If the husband alone lists property with a real estate broker for sale, he will be liable for a commission if the broker finds a buyer. It is no defense that the wife failed to sign. *Taub v. Shampanier*, 112 A. 322 (N.J. 1921).

18.03(e)   Tenancy by the Entireties—Creditor's Rights

In most tenancy-by-the-entireties states, a judgment creditor of either husband or wife alone can acquire no rights by a sheriff's sale of the land. Since neither husband nor wife alone can make a voluntary sale of his or her interest in the land, an involuntary or forced sale of the interest of either husband or wife alone cannot be valid. J.H. Cooper, Annotation, *Interest of Spouse in Estate by Entireties Subject to Satisfaction of His or Her Individual Debt*, 75 A.L.R.2d 1175 (1961). In a few states, a husband's interest can be sold by the sheriff under a judgment against the husband alone, but the sheriff's deed will automatically become void if the wife survives the husband. The wife then remains the sole owner, free of the judgment. Oval A. Phipps, *Tenancy by Entireties,* 25 Temple L.Q. 24, 39 (1952); 75 A.L.R.2d 1183, *supra.*

Of course, if the judgment is against both husband and wife, the land may be sold by the sheriff, provided it is not their homestead.

As stated, in most of the tenancy-by-entireties states, the rents of the land belong to the husband and wife jointly. Therefore, a creditor of either the husband or wife alone cannot reach the rents, income, or crops of the land. There are some exceptions to this rule. Oval A. Phipps, *Tenancy by Entireties,* 25 Temple L.Q. 24, 39 (1952). *See* S.A. Yeaguy, *Constitutional Law—Right to Privacy of Husband and Wife Who Permit Third Party to Observe Their Sexual Activities to Waive Right of Marital Privacy*, 8 Rut.-Cam. L.J. 707, 714 (1977); Solomon Bienenfeld, *Creditors Versus Tenancies by the Entirety*, 1 Wayne L. Rev. 105 (1955).

18.03(f)   Tenancy by the Entireties—Divorce

A divorce converts a tenancy by the entireties into a tenancy in common. Some states, however, have an opposite rule, which holds that divorce changes a tenancy by the entireties into a joint tenancy with the right of survivorship. *Shepherd v. Shepherd,* 336 So. 2d 497 (Miss. 1976).

18.04 Murder—Joint Tenancies and Tenancies by the Entireties

When one joint tenant or tenant by the entireties murders the co-tenant and later is convicted of such murder in a court trial, one of three results is possible:

1. The murderer will, despite the crime, take the entire property by virtue of the right of survivorship. This is a bad rule that is certainly doomed to disappear.

2. The murderer, because of the crime, loses all interest in the property, and the heirs of the murdered co-owner take the entire property. *Vesey v. Vesey,* 54 N.W.2d 385 (Minn. 1952); *In re King's Estate,* 52 N.W.2d 885 (Wis. 1952).

3. The murder is regarded, in legal effect, as converting the tenancy into a tenancy in common, so that the murderer retains a half interest, and the heirs of the murdered co-tenant take the other half. This rule is followed in most states. *Abbey v. Lord,* 336 P.2d 226 (Cal. 1959); *Bradley v. Fox,* 129 N.E.2d 699 (Ill. 1955); Case Notes, *Property—Murder by Joint Tenants Extinguishes Right of Survivorship*, 5 DePaul L. Rev. 316 (1956).

Of course, if, in the murder trial, the killer is acquitted—on the ground of self-defense, for example—the killing is not murder but justifiable homicide, and the survivor will take the entire property even though he or she caused the death of his or her co-tenant.

18.05 Contracts of Sale—Joint Tenancies and Tenancies by the Entireties

A contract to sell property owned in tenancy by the entireties should be signed by both husband and wife. If it is not, the buyer will be unable to obtain specific performance, though the seller who signed might be liable for damages. *Cartwright v. Glacosa,* 390 S.W.2d 204 (Tenn. 1965).

In tenancy-by-the-entireties states, when a landowner signs a contract to sell land to a husband and wife, the buyers hold the contract interest as tenants by the entireties, so that if either dies, the deal is closed; the seller's deed should be made to the survivor. *Comfort v. Robinson,* 118 N.W. 943 (Mich. 1908); Michael S. DiSabatino, Annotation, *Proceeds or Derivatives of Real Property Held by Entirety as Themselves Held by Entirety,* 22 A.L.R.4th 459 (1983). If the state does not recognize tenancy by the entireties or community property, a contract to sell land to *H* and *W,* who are husband and wife, creates a tenancy in common in the contract interest. If *H* dies, his contract interest passes to his heirs or devisees, and the seller must not make the deed to *W* alone. Obviously when an installment contract is involved, it may take years to pay the purchase price, and the death of one of the buyers is a real possibility.

To avoid the endless complications of tenancy in common or necessity of probate, buyers may agree to buy the land "as joint tenants with the right of survivorship, and not as tenants in common nor by the entireties nor as community property."

Of course, if land is owned in joint tenancy, all owners must join as sellers in any contract to sell the land.

Where a husband and wife enter into a contract to sell their land, and one of them dies before the purchase price is fully paid, questions arise as to who gets the balance of the purchase price, the surviving spouse or the estate of the decedent. Where the sellers held the land in joint tenancy or tenancy by the entireties, some courts hold that the right to the money goes to the survivor just as though there were a right of survivorship as to the contract price. *Watson v. Watson,* 126 N.E.2d 220 (Ill. 1955); *Hewitt v. Biege,* 327 P.2d 872 (Kan. 1958); *DeYoung v. Mesler,* 130 N.W.2d 38 (Mich. 1964). *In re Maguire's Estate,* 296 N.Y.S. 528 (1937); Robert Kratovil, *Joint Tenancies and Creative Financing,* 5 U. Ark. Little Rock L.J. 475 (1982).

EXAMPLE: *H* and *W,* joint tenants, enter into a contract to sell their land to *X.* After a few payments are made on the contract, *H* dies, leaving a will giving all his property to children by a former marriage. *W* will get the entire remainder of the purchase price.

There are cases taking a contrary view.

> **EXAMPLE:** *H* and *W,* joint tenants, entered into a contract to sell land. *H* dies. His heirs got his share of the sale price. In a few states, sale proceeds are treated as though held in tenancy in common. *Register of Wills v. Madine,* 219 A.2d 245 (Md. 1966). *In re Baker's Estate,* 78 N.W.2d 863 (Iowa 1956); *Buford v. Dahlke,* 62 N.W.2d 252 (Neb. 1954).

> **EXAMPLE:** *H* and *W,* tenants by the entireties, entered into a contract to sell land. *H* died. His heirs got his share of the purchase price. *Panushka v. Panushka,* 349 P.2d 450 (Or. 1960); Note, *Real Property—Estate by Entirety—Equitable Conversion Converts Ownership of Proceeds to Tenancy in Common Absent of Contrary Intent,* 14 Vand. L. Rev. 687 (1961). This result is dictated by the rule in some tenancy-by-the-entireties states that do not recognize this type of tenancy in money or *personal property.*

Once again, the sellers can take the uncertainty out of this eventuality by agreeing in advance as to the disposition of these proceeds. Of course, once the money has been paid by the buyer to the sellers, the cash money, even if held intact by the sellers in a joint safe-deposit box, is owned by them in tenancy in common. *Ill. Public Aid Commission. v. Stille,* 153 N.E.2d 59 (Ill. 1958).

Suppose that the sellers are tenants by the entireties. They give a deed to the buyer and take back a purchase money mortgage. Some states hold that the mortgage is owned as tenants by the entireties. *Ciconte v. Barba,* 161 A. 925 (Del. 1932). Others hold that the mortgage is owned in tenancy in common. W.H. Allen, Annotation, *Estates by Entirety in Personal Property,* 64 A.L.R.2d 8 (1959); Michael A. DiSabatino, Annotation, *Proceeds or Derivatives of Real Property Held by Entirety as Themselves Held by Entirety,* 22 A.L.R.4th 459 (1983). The problem extends even to condemnation awards.

> **EXAMPLE:** *H* and *W* owned land in tenancy by the entireties. The city condemned the land and deposited $100,000 as a condemnation award. *H* died. *W* takes the entire award as the surviving tenant by the entireties. *H*'s other heirs take nothing. *Smith v. Tipping,* 211 N.E.2d 231 (Mass. 1965); *In re Idlewild Airport,* 85 N.Y.S.2d 617 (1948).

Community property states present special problems.

> **EXAMPLE:** In a community property state, *H* and *W,* joint tenants, entered into a contract to sell land. The proceeds of sale are community property. *Smith v. Tang,* 412 P.2d 697 (Ariz. 1966).

The problem also exists with respect to the proceeds of fire insurance policies. The better rule is that the money goes to the survivor. Had the parties been asked about this when they received their deed, virtually all would have been astonished to hear any question raised as to the right of the survivor to get the money. This intention ought to be controlling. The contract should read that the price is payable to the sellers as joint tenants with the right of survivorship and not as tenants in common, as tenants by the entireties, or as community property.

Suppose that a contract of sale names the buyers as joint tenants. Their rights *as between themselves* are established as soon as the contract is signed.

> **EXAMPLE:** Seller contracts to sell a home to Husband and Wife, as joint tenants. Husband persuades Seller to make the deed run to Husband only. Wife discovers this. She is entitled to a court order reforming the deed to run to Husband and Wife as joint tenants. *Remus v. Schwass,* 406 Ill. 63, 92 N.E.2d 127 (1950).

18.06   Tenancy in Common

Co-owners who are not joint tenants, tenants by the entireties, or owners of community property are tenants in common. While the presumption is that co-tenants have equal interests, *Asante v. Abban,* 568 A.2d 146 (N.J. Super. 1989), their shares need not be equal. For example, one co-owner may have an undivided one-tenth interest and the other the remaining undivided nine-tenths interest. They need not have acquired their titles at the same time nor by the same instrument.

Tenants in common are entitled to share the possession and rents of the property according to their shares in the property. Except for their sharing of possession and rents, however, the situation is almost as if each tenant in common owned a separate piece of real estate. Each tenant in common may convey or mortgage its share, and the share of each tenant in common is subject to the lien of judgments against it.

Upon the death of a tenant in common, its share goes to the heirs or the parties named in the will. Also, only the decedent's share of the property is included in the estate.

18.07   Partition

If tenants in common, or joint tenants, for that matter, wish to terminate their joint possession of the land, any of the co-tenants may file a suit to partition the real estate. The court will appoint commissioners to divide the land into separate tracts according to the shares of the co-tenants, so that each will become the sole owner of the tract set aside for it. If the land cannot be divided in this manner, the court will order the land sold and will divide the proceeds of the sale among the co-tenants according to their respective interests.

> **EXAMPLE:** *A* dies owning a tract of land improved with a single-family dwelling, leaving no widow and no will, but leaving as his heirs a son, *B,* and two grandchildren, *C* and *D,* who are children of a deceased son, *E. B* owns one-half of the title, and *C* and *D* own one-fourth each. *B* files a partition suit against *C* and *D.* The court finds, as it must, that the land cannot be divided among the three tenants in common. It orders the land sold at public auction, whereupon the same is sold to *F,* the highest bidder, for $100,000. *B* receives $50,000 from the proceeds of the sale, and *C* and *D* each receive $25,000.

Partition can, of course, be accomplished by the voluntary action of all co-owners without the necessity of court proceedings. Frequently, this is impossible, since many co-ownerships involve minor heirs, who cannot participate in voluntary partition. As a rule, community property and land held in tenancy by the entireties are not subject to partition during the continuance of the marriage. *Stanley v. Mueller,* 350 P.2d 880 (Or. 1960); *Lawrence v. Lawrence,* 190 A.2d 206 (N.J. 1963).

18.08   Rights and Obligations of Co-Owners

Co-owners must, as a rule, contribute ratably toward payment of taxes, special assessments, mortgages, and repairs of the property. E.H. Schopler, Annotation, *Contribution, Subrogation and Similar Rights, as Between Cotenants, Where One Pays the Other's Share of Sum Owing on Mortgage or Other Lien*, 48 A.L.R.2d 1305 (1956). If one co-owner, through refusal of the other co-owners to contribute, is compelled to pay more than its share of the necessary expenses, it thereby acquires a lien analogous to a mortgage lien on the shares of the other co-owners, and it may foreclose such lien if the other co-owners persist in their refusal to contribute. *Calcagni v. Cirino,* 14 A.2d 803 (R.I. 1940). But one co-owner cannot purchase the property at a mortgage foreclosure sale or tax sale of the land and thus acquire a title that would enable him or her to oust the other co-owners. The title thus acquired is acquired for the benefit of all co-owners if they seasonably contribute their respective proportions of the expense incurred by the tenant who purchased the outstanding title. *Laura v. Christian,* 537 P.2d 1389 (N.M. 1975).

If one co-owner collects all the rents but does not occupy the land, it must account to the other co-owners for their share of the rents. *Thompson v. Flynn,* 58 P.2d 769 (Mont. 1936). A few states have laws making a co-owner liable to the other co-owners for rent where it alone occupies the land, collecting no rent therefrom. *Hazard v. Albro,* 20 A. 834 (R.I. 1890). But, in many states, a co-owner who personally occupies the premises and does not rent them out is not liable to the other co-owners for the rental value of the premises unless it has agreed to pay them rent or has forcibly kept them out of possession. *Burk v. Burk,* 22 So. 2d 609 (Ala. 1945). But, a co-owner who exclusively possesses the premises must bear the entire burden of taxes, repairs, and mortgage interest payments. *Clute v. Clute,* 90 N.E. 988 (N.Y. 1910). Often, the details of the co-tenancy arrangement are set out in a co-tenancy agreement. Harris, *How to Draft an Effective Residential Co-Tenancy Agreement,* 7 No. 2 Pract. Real Est. Law. 25 (Mar. 1991).

18.09 Grants by One Co-Tenant

A mortgage signed by only one of the co-owners does not bind the others. It creates a lien only on the interest of the co-tenant who signs. *Rostan v. Huggins,* 5 S.E.2d 162 (N.C. 1939). Likewise, a judgment, federal lien, or other lien against one of the co-owners creates no lien on the shares of the others. The lessee of one co-tenant becomes, for the term of the lease, a co-tenant of the nonjoining owners. *Garland v. Holston Oil Co.,* 386 S.W.2d 914 (Tenn. 1965). The actions of the nonjoining co-tenants may amount to a ratification, thereby estopping them from denying the validity of the lease even as against their interest.

> **EXAMPLE:** *H* and *W* owned recreational property. *H* leased the property to *T. W* knew of lease renewals and received some rent payments. The court held that *W* acquiesced in *H*'s leasing of the property and was estopped from denying the validity of the lease. *Gleason v. Tompkins,* 375 N.Y.S.2d 247 (1976).

18.10 Bankruptcy of Co-Tenant

Where land is owned by two or more persons in any kind of co-tenancy and one of the co-tenants goes bankrupt, the bankruptcy court has the power to sell all of the property. 11 U.S.C. § 363(h). The obvious reason is that it is almost impossible to sell a fractional interest in property. Because of this eventuality, great care must be used in selecting co-owners.

18.11 Federal Tax Liens

Where two or more persons own land as co-tenants and a federal lien (e.g., for unpaid income tax) is filed against one co-tenant, the federal government may force a sale of the entire property. *United States v. Rodgers,* 103 S. Ct. 2132 (1983). The nondelinquent spouse is entitled to so much of the sale proceeds as represents complete compensation for the loss of its interest, the government will receive the amount of the tax delinquency, and the balance, if any, will be distributed to the delinquent taxpayer and others having an interest in the property. Again, this is evidence that one must use care in choosing investment partners. However, in most states where tenancy by the entireties is recognized, and a creditor of one spouse cannot reach any share of the property, the federal lien does not attach at all if it is against only one spouse. Plumb, *Federal Tax Liens* 37 (3d ed. 1972).

18.12 Community Property—In General

The community property system is of Spanish origin and obtains in states that were subject to Spanish influence, namely, Arizona, California, Idaho, Louisiana, Nevada, New Mexico, Texas, and Washington. The law of these states recognizes two kinds of property that may belong to the spouses in case of marriage—*separate property* and *community property.* The separate property of either the husband or the wife is what he or she owned at the time of marriage and what he or she acquired during marriage by inheritance, will, or gift. The separate property of each spouse is wholly free from all interest or claim on the part of the other and is entirely under the management and control of the spouse to whom it belongs. All other property is community property.

18.12(a)   Theory of Community Property

It is the theory in these states that the husband and wife should share equally in property acquired by their joint efforts during marriage. Thus, the husband is as much entitled to share equally in acquisitions by the wife through her industry as she is entitled to share equally in acquisitions by the husband, and each spouse owns one-half of all that is earned or gained, even though one earned or gained more than the other or the other actually earned or gained nothing. *See* Cal. Civ. Code § 5105.

18.12(b)   Property Acquired During the Marriage

Property purchased with separate funds is the separate property of the purchaser, whereas property purchased with community funds is community property. Property acquired by purchase during the marriage is ordinarily presumed to vest in the husband and wife as community property, regardless of whether the deed is made to the husband, wife, or both. Under the community property system, the ownership of property does not depend upon the question of who happens to be named as grantee in the deed.

In California prior to January 1, 1975, and in New Mexico prior to July 1, 1973, it was provided that real estate conveyed to a married woman in her separate name was presumed to be her separate property. So far as the husband and wife are concerned, this presumption can be destroyed by proof that the property was purchased with community funds and that the placing of title in the wife's name was not done with the intention of making a gift to her. Such property is community property. But, the presumption that the property is the separate property of the wife and can be sold or mortgaged without the husband's signature is conclusive in favor of purchasers and mortgagees dealing with the wife in good faith and for a valuable consideration. *Fulkerson v. Stiles,* 105 P. 966 (Cal. 1909).

In most community property states, a husband and wife may, by agreement, change the status of property from separate to community property or from community to separate property. Income tax returns are often received as evidence of such agreements.

A deed by the husband to the wife raises a presumption that this was intended to convert the land into her separate property. But this presumption can be rebutted. 41 C.J.S. *Husband & Wife* § 491(c). In some states, a deed to husband and wife as joint tenants makes the property they hold in ordinary joint tenancy the separate property of each. *Collier v. Collier,* 242 P.2d 537 (Ariz. 1952); *Siberell v. Siberell,* 7 P.2d 1003 (Cal. 1932). However, oral evidence can be admitted in court to show that the husband and wife really intended this to be community property, and such intention will prevail. *Gudelj v. Gudelj,* 259 P.2d 656 (Cal. 1953). Rather than leaving the matter of the vagaries of proof of oral statements, the deed should state the mode of ownership that was intended. In Nevada, the grantor can deed the land to husband and wife "as community property with the right of survivorship." Mennell, *Survivorship Rights in Community Property,* 11 Comm. Prop. J. 5 (1984).

It is difficult to present briefly an accurate picture of the law in community property states relative to joint tenancies. The law is complex and some standard treatise should be consulted. Baxter, *Marital Property* § 18.5 (1973); Terrence R. Kamm, *Clouded Title in Community Property States: New Mexico Takes a New Step*, 21 Nat. Resources J. 593 (1981). Only one thing seems clear, namely, the fact that the deed runs to the husband and wife as joint tenants will not prevent a court from holding that the land is held as community property. In states other than California, the claim of community ownership seems to be favored despite the joint tenancy form of the deed.

A husband may transfer his interest in community property to his wife and it will become her separate property. A like result occurs where the land is purchased with community property and the husband directs that the land be conveyed to the wife. A gift made to both spouses is community property.

18.12(c) Deeds and Mortgages of Community Property

It is desirable and customary in most states for the husband and wife to join in any deed of any kind of land. And their joining is legally necessary where the land conveyed is occupied by the parties as their home. In most community property states that require the wife's consent to a deed or mortgage of community property, the wife's signature is also needed for a valid contract to convey community property. *Rundle v. Winters,* 298 P. 929 (Ariz. 1931); *Elliott v. Craig,* 260 P. 433 (Idaho 1927); *Adams v. Blumenshine,* 204 P. 66 (N.M. 1922); *Chapman v. Hill,* 137 P. 1041 (Wash. 1914). The wife should also join in all but short-term leases of community property. *Bowman v. Hardgrove,* 93 P.2d 303 (Wash. 1939).

The aspects of the community property system that give sole control to the husband are invalid on constitutional grounds. The battle is being fought both in the state legislature and the courthouse. *See Kirchberg v. Feenstra,* 450 U.S. 455 (1981); *Powell on Real Property* § 626(2); 15A Am. Jur. 2d *Community Prop.* § 78.

18.12(d) Wills and Descent of Community Property

The descent of community property when there is no will varies from state to state. It must be remembered in this connection that, regardless of the legal title, each spouse owns one-half of the community property. In some community property states, in the absence of a will that specifies another disposition of the property, the surviving spouse succeeds to the decedent's share of the community property. In other states, the decedent's share goes in whole or in part to his or her descendants. All community property states recognize the right to make a will by the first spouse to die.

CHAPTER 19
Rights of Spouses and Unmarried Cohabitants

19.01 Dower and Curtesy—In General

Dower and curtesy are aspects of the property relationship between a husband and wife. While these rights still exist in a minority of states today, of far more significance is modern estate planning that implements the intentions of the decedent while achieving estate tax advantages at the same time, and statutory replacements for dower and curtesy, which give the surviving spouse the power to elect to receive a share of the deceased spouse's estate, which, of course, will include both real and personal property. Nonetheless, dower and curtesy are still part of the fabric of the law relating to marital property in some states. *Powell on Real Property* § 213; Joslyn, *Surviving Spouse's Right to Share in Deceased Spouse's Estate,* ACPC Study No. 10 (1985).

19.01(a) Dower

The right of dower originated in early times when a man's wealth consisted largely of real estate. Dower gives the widow a life estate in one-third of the lands owned by the husband during the marriage to provide her with a means of support after her husband's death. The requirements of dower are as follows: (1) a valid marriage, (2) the ownership of real estate by the husband during the marriage, and (3) the death of the husband before the wife. During her husband's lifetime, the wife's rights consist merely of the possibility that she may become entitled to her dower. Until his death, the wife's dower is said to be *inchoate*. It is not such an interest that the wife can convey to a stranger, nor can it be sold at a forced sale to pay the wife's debts. The right can be released, however, as where the wife joins in her husband's deed of the property to a third party.

Should the wife predecease her husband, even this incipient right is automatically extinguished. Thus, if her husband has previously conveyed his land without obtaining her signature on the deed, the grantee's title becomes perfected upon the wife's death before her husband's. It is as though her dower had never existed.

On the husband's death, her dower becomes *consummate*. It has ripened into something that she is certain to own. If the husband conveys his land without his wife joining in the deed, and the wife survives her husband, she then becomes entitled to her dower. If the husband is indebted at the time of his death, the widow's dower rights are superior to any claims of his creditors to the land. This is one of the important characteristics of dower.

In many states, the surviving spouse can elect an intestate share in the estate of the decedent, typically a more valuable interest than the life estate given by dower. If such an alternative is available, the full ownership election of the intestate share is the likely choice.

19.01(a)(1) Joint Tenancy and Dower

Although a widow has dower in lands owned by her husband in tenancy in common with others, there is no dower in a joint tenancy.

> **EXAMPLE:** Two men, *A* and *B,* hold title in joint tenancy. *A* is married to *C,* and *B* is married to *D. A* conveys to *X. A*'s wife, *C,* does not join in the deed. Ordinarily, when a wife does not join in her husband's deed, her dower remains outstanding, but here no dower remains outstanding in *C* because *A* held title as a joint tenant. However, *A*'s conveyance breaks the joint tenancy, and *B* and *X* now hold title as tenants in common, and their wives have dower in the real estate. *Johnston v. Muntz,* 4 N.E.2d 826 (Ill. 1936).

19.01(a)(2) Mortgages and Other Liens

When a wife fails to join with her husband in the execution of a mortgage on the husband's land, any title acquired through foreclosure of such mortgage will be subject to the wife's dower. *Thomas v. Thomas,* 18 So. 2d 544 (Ala. 1944). An opposite result occurs where the mortgage provides the purchase money for the property mortgaged. *Frederick v. Emig,* 57 N.E. 883 (Ill. 1900). The same results follow in some states that have substituted some ownership share for dower, but require the wife to join in any deed in order to release her ownership share. Likewise, the same result follows in many states where the husband has curtesy, dower, or an ownership share in the wife's real estate and fails to join in her mortgage. Obviously, where land is owned by either husband or wife, it will usually be necessary for the spouse to join in any mortgage on the land.

Dower is subject to any liens or encumbrances to which the land was subject at the time of the marriage or at the time the husband acquired title.

> **EXAMPLE:** *A* buys a tract of land on which there is a mortgage. On foreclosure of this mortgage, the dower of *A*'s wife will be extinguished.

19.01(a)(3) Leaseholds

The leasehold interest of a tenant under a lease is personal property and, since dower is a right that attaches to real estate only, a tenant's wife has no dower in the leasehold. W.R. Habeeb, Annotation, *Lessee's Interest in Mineral Lease as Subject to Dower*, 173 A.L.R. 1260 (1948). Ordinarily, a tenant may assign a leasehold without the spouse's signature when no homestead rights are involved.

19.01(a)(4) Contract for Sale of Land

If a husband signs a contract for the sale of land, but his wife does not, she cannot be compelled to join in the deed to the buyer, and her dower will remain outstanding. Obviously, any prudent buyer will insist that the wife sign the contract.

19.01(a)(5) Release of Dower

The widow is entitled to have dower assigned out of any land conveyed, mortgaged, or leased by her husband during the marriage without her signature. Hence it is important that the landowner's wife release her dower by joining with him in any deed, mortgage, or lease of his land.

19.01(a)(6) Dower—Election

Many states give the widow, at her husband's death, a right to elect between her dower or some ownership (fee simple) share of the land.

19.01(b) Curtesy

In some states, a widower has a life estate known as *curtesy* in the lands owned by his wife during their marriage. George L. Haskins, *Curtesy in the United States*, 100 U. Pa. L. Rev. 196 (1951). It is somewhat analogous to the widow's dower, but there are these following points of difference:

1. In some curtesy states, a child must be born to the couple for this interest in land to arise. Most states have abolished this requirement.

2. The widower's curtesy, according to the old English law, was a life estate in all the land owned by the wife during the marriage, as contrasted with the one-third allowed the widow as her dower. In most of the curtesy states, however, the husband's share has been reduced by modern laws to some fraction, such as one-third.

In some states, the husband is given dower instead of curtesy. Whenever a husband has dower or curtesy, he should join in the wife's deed, mortgage, or contract of sale of her property. However, in some states, a deed given by the wife conveying her own land bars the husband's curtesy, even if he does not join in the deed.

In a number of states, a surviving husband is given a share in fee simple of the wife's lands in lieu of curtesy. In some of these states, for example, the widower's share is limited to the land that the wife owned at her death. He has no claim whatever upon land conveyed by her in her lifetime without his signature. In still other states that give the widower an ownership share in lieu of curtesy, the widower is entitled to his ownership share in any land conveyed by the wife in her lifetime without his signature.

Many states that give a widower curtesy or dower allow him, at the wife's death, to choose an ownership share instead.

19.01(c) Divorce

Divorce terminates dower, curtesy, and their statutory substitutes. Some state laws provide, however, that a divorce bars only the dower or curtesy of the spouse for whose fault the divorce was obtained. No-fault divorce laws and similar measures enacted in many states, such as the Uniform Marriage and Divorce Act, allow an equitable division of property on divorce without regard to marital fault. This eliminates the false adultery and cruelty charges that formerly characterized divorce. *Kujawinski v. Kujawinski,* 71 Ill. 2d 563, 376 N.E.2d 1382 (1978). As to real estate owned separately by one of the spouses, such as land owned by the spouse before marriage, that spouse may sell and convey the land before divorce without obtaining the signature of the other spouse. *Id.* This rule applies as soon as divorce proceedings have been filed. *Cady v. Cady,* 581 P.2d 358 (Kan. 1978). Of course, this does not apply to the marital home. In all states having homestead laws, such a deed requires both signatures. *See* Michael W. Kalcheim, *Intention Controls: The Theory of Transmutation—The Effect of Placing Property Which Was Initially Nonmarital into Joint Tenancy: The Theory of Commingling*, 68 Ill. B.J. 320, 698 (1980).

19.02 Marital Property Rights

The trend today is for dower and curtesy laws to be replaced with statutes that give the surviving spouse a statutory share of all of the assets of the deceased spouse. An even more far-reaching trend is embodied in the Uniform Marital Property Act (UMPA). This act gives each spouse an immediate ownership interest in marital property similar to a community property interest. Walter Wadlington, *Uniform Marital Property Act Symposium—Forward*, 21 Hous. L. Rev. 595 (1984).

19.03 Homestead

When a family owns and occupies a tract of land as its home, in many states that portion of the tract that does not exceed in area or value the limit fixed by law for homesteads is the family homestead, and certain rights, called homestead rights, are created. These homestead rights may, of course, extend to the entire tract if it is within the area and value limits fixed by law.

There are three principal motives behind the various state homestead laws. One is the protection of the family against being evicted from their home by enforcement of the claims of creditors. The homestead portion of the tract of land is protected against sheriff's sales following a judgment against the landowner.

The second object of the homestead laws is to protect the wife against the husband. The lawmakers thought it would be a good idea if the husband were not allowed to sell his own home if the wife was opposed to the idea. Evidently, the theory was that the old home should not be disposed of until a new home suitable for the family had been provided. To accomplish this, the lawmakers provided that the husband could not convey good title to his own home unless his wife signed the deed. It is therefore necessary that both husband and wife join in any deed or mortgage of homestead property, except, of course, a purchase money mortgage.

As a final protection of the wife against the husband and his creditors, the homestead laws provided some protection for the widow after the death of her husband. This was necessary because dower did not afford the widow adequate protection. Dower did not give the widow any right to the occupation of any real estate until a particular tract of land has been set apart or assigned to her as dower. Immediately upon the husband's death, the widow might be subject to eviction from the home. Protection was afforded by the laws providing for the widow's homestead. Even a husband who has quarreled bitterly with his wife cannot legally deprive her of this protection. A final development in this direction was the *probate homestead,* which created a home for the widow in land that the husband had never occupied as his home. In this regard, the widow's rights are superior to the rights of any creditor of the deceased husband. Land so occupied by the widow cannot be sold to pay the deceased husband's debts.

For a valid deed or mortgage of the homestead, it is necessary that both husband and wife join in the same deed or mortgage. The wife is thus protected against the improvidence of the husband. In some states, it is necessary that the deed or mortgage of the homestead contain a clause expressly releasing or waiving all homestead rights, and, in many states, a deed or mortgage of the homestead land must be acknowledged in order to be valid.

19.04 Unmarried Cohabitants

The number of instances where individuals have established housekeeping units without the benefit of formal marriage has continued to increase. This may cause problems.

> **EXAMPLE:** *A,* a single man, and *B,* a single woman, buy a house. The deed simply runs to them as *A* and *B*. Both sign the mortgage required for part of the purchase price. Both contribute to the cash payment, since both have jobs. There is no contract between them. *A* dies. *B* is a stranger and inherits nothing from *A*. Still, *B* must continue making payments on the mortgage to prevent foreclosure.

Of course, the parties can quite simply solve this problem.

> **EXAMPLE:** In states where joint tenancy is recognized, *A* and *B* can have the deed run to them as joint tenants.

Except in those jurisdictions that still recognize common-law marriage, dower, curtesy, spouse's rights statutes, and the law relating to distribution of property upon divorce are inapplicable to unmarried cohabitants. *Hewitt v. Hewitt,* 394 N.E.2d 1204 (Ill. 1979). *But see* Gregory G. Sarno, Annotation, *Rights in Decedent's Estate as Between Lawful and Putative Spouse,* 81 A.L.R.3d 6 (1977); Scott F. Sullen, *Rights of Putative Spouse Under Section 305 of the Illinois Marriage and Dissolution of Marriage Act,* Comment, 1978 So. Ill. U. L.J. 423 (1978); Joel E. Smith, Annotation, *Property Rights Arising from the Relationship of Couple Cohabiting Without Marriage,* 3 A.L.R.4th 13 (1981).

Various reasons have been given by courts in the various states in refusing to recognize property rights in unmarried couples. The most extreme of these is the courts' refusal to enforce contracts relating to property rights of unmarried persons who live together. These attitudes must change. The social reality is that such living arrangements are common and the courts and legislatures must adapt.

Some courts make a distinction between cases involving parties who honestly thought they were married and those who knew full well that they were not married. Alvin E.

Evans, *Property Interests Arising from Quasi-Marital Relationships,* 9 Cornell L. Rev. 246 (1924).

> **EXAMPLE:** *M,* thinking his divorce from *F* was final, engaged in a marriage ceremony with *W.* Both *M* and *W* intended to marry and otherwise complied with all formal requirements. The failure of *M* to be finally divorced from *F,* however, rendered the marriage of *M* to *W* a nullity. This is a *putative* marriage and *M* and *W* are putative husband and wife. The courts will treat their property as if they were husband and wife.

> **EXAMPLE:** *M* and *W* decide to live together without the benefit of any formal marriage. Some courts refuse to recognize property rights by either in the property of the other.

There are various grounds for awarding property rights to the parties of a nonmarital relationship. Primary among them is the *express agreement.* The parties may expressly agree to pool their assets and share in their accumulations, enter into a partnership or joint venture agreement, or exchange property for services. An express agreement is certainly the preferable course of action, since it is are almost always enforced by the courts if sexual conduct is not mentioned in the contract. Unfortunately, most cohabitants do not have the foresight to enter into such agreements. This is folly, especially where substantial assets are involved.

It is preferable that such agreements be in writing. The intent of the parties and the terms of the agreement are more easily proved. Oral agreements are nonetheless enforceable. While these agreements have been subject to the defense of illegality as encouraging immorality, they will only be declared invalid where sexual services are the principal consideration. Courts frequently hold, however, that if the woman makes a financial contribution, she will be protected.

> **EXAMPLE:** *M* and *W* lived together for seven years. All property acquired during this period was taken in *M*'s name. At the outset of the relationship, *M* and *W* orally agreed that while the parties lived together they would combine their efforts and earnings and would share equally in all accumulations as a result of their individual or combined efforts. *W* also agreed to render services as companion and homemaker. *M* agreed to provide for *W*'s financial support and needs for the rest of her life. *W* gave up a lucrative singing career to devote her time to her household responsibilities. During the period of cohabitation, and as a result of their efforts and earnings, *M* and *W* acquired substantial property in *M*'s name. The relationship then came to an end. The court allowed the enforcement of this oral contract even though sexual relations may have been involved. *Marvin v. Marvin,* 557 P.2d 106 (Cal. 1976).

There are other grounds for awarding property to the parties to a nonmarital relationship. The courts may struggle to find some sort of partnership, trust, or gift as grounds for allocating property rights between the parties. These courts try to allow the bargain of the parties to be enforced rather than allow one of the parties to be deprived of what was jointly accumulated. *Latham v. Latham,* 547 P.2d 144 (Or. 1976). Modern courts will try to enforce the reasonable expectations of the parties. *Carlson v. Olson,* 256 N.W.2d 249 (Minn. 1977). The decisions go so far as to order specific performance of an oral promise to convey real estate. *Tyranski v. Piggins,* 205 N.W.2d 595 (Mich. App. 1973).

Older decisions that deny protection to the unmarried woman no longer appear to be valid. The courts should be free to inquire into the conduct of the parties to determine whether their conduct demonstrates an implied contract or implied agreement of partnership or some sort of trust. Also, the older barrier against recovery for the reasonable value of services rendered may well be removed. *Marvin v. Marvin,* 557 P.2d 106 (Cal. 1976).

Unmarried cohabitants are vulnerable where a zoning ordinance forbids occupancy of homes by unrelated persons. Although these ordinances were aimed at communes, they have been used against unmarried cohabitants.

19.05 Homosexual Cohabitants

No dependable statement can be made regarding the property rights of cohabiting homosexuals. Arguably, express agreements between them relating to their property rights should be enforced. Public policy, however, may stand in the way. *Jones v. Daly*, 176 Cal. Rptr. 130 (1981); Baxter, *Marital Property* 185 § 35.15 (pocket part 1980).

REFERENCES: The authorities on the rights of unmarried cohabitants are many. Baxter, *Marital Property* 185 § 35.15 (pocket part 1980); Carol S. Burch, *Property Rights of De Facto Spouses Including Thoughts on the Value of Homemakers' Services,* 10 Fam. L.Q. 101 (1976); Alvin E. Evans, *Property Interests Arising from Quasi-Marital Relationships,* 9 Cornell L. Rev. 246 (1924); Kaminski, *Joint Tenancy and a Residential Mortgage: An Unmarried Couple's Estate Tax Problem,* 69 Ill. B.J. 706 (1981); Robert C. Angermeier, *Property Rights Between Unmarried Cohabitants,* 50 Ind. L.J. 389 (1975); Joel E. Smith, Annotation, *Property Rights Arising from the Relationship of Unmarrieds,* 3 A.L.R.4th 13.

CHAPTER 20
Real Estate Finance— Mortgages

20.01 Mortgage Defined   A mortgage is a conveyance or transfer of real property given to secure the payment of a debt. This definition reveals that a mortgage has two elements. First, like a deed, a mortgage is a conveyance of land. However, the intention is not, as in the case of a deed, to absolutely and unconditionally transfer ownership of the property, but to provide security for the payment of a debt.

20.02 History of Mortgage Law   The history of mortgage law is the history of hundreds of years of struggle for advantage between borrowers and lenders. The law books reflect the constantly shifting fortunes of this war. Occasionally, the battle has gone in favor of the lenders. Then, somewhat recently, consumerism has resulted in court decisions and new laws favorable to the borrowers. The playing field may have leveled somewhat during the real estate recession of the late 1980s and early 1990s. The current situation seems to reflect a crosscurrent of legislation and judicial decisions, some pro consumer and some pro business or lender. Perhaps balance is being reached on many fronts where pitched battles had been waged.

To understand how the modern mortgage developed out of centuries of struggle is to take a long step toward understanding modern mortgage law. Much of our mortgage law comes to us from England. In that country, mortgage arrangements of various kinds existed even in the Anglo-Saxon times before the conquest of England by William the Conqueror in 1066. It will suffice for our purposes to begin with the mortgage of the fourteenth century. This document was a simple deed of the land, running from the borrower (mortgagor) to the lender (mortgagee). All of the ceremonies needed for a full transfer of ownership took place when the mortgage was made. The mortgagee became the owner of the land just as if a sale had taken place. That ownership was subject to two qualifications. First, the mortgagee, as owner, could oust the mortgagor, take immediate possession of the property, and collect the rents. The rents so collected had to be applied on the mortgage debt. For this reason, the mortgagee often permitted the mortgagor to remain in possession. Second, the mortgage described the debt it secured and stated a date of payment, known as the *law day*. The mortgage gave the mortgagor the right to pay the debt on the law day. If the debt was so paid, the mortgage provided that it thereby became void. This provision was known as the *defeasance clause,* for payment of the debt on the law day defeated the mortgage and put ownership back in the mortgagor.

In early times, the courts enforced the mortgage as it was written. Foreclosure proceedings did not exist. Failure to pay the mortgage debt when due, a *default,* automatically extinguished all of the mortgagor's interest in the land.

20.03   The Equity of Redemption

For many years, no one dreamed of questioning this scheme of things. Then, slowly at first, and later in greater numbers, borrowers who had lost their property through default began to seek the assistance of the king. A typical petition by a borrower would state that the money was borrowed, that the mortgage was made, that the borrower defaulted in payment, and the land was lost as a result. The petition would continue with the statement that the borrower had the necessary funds and offered to pay the mortgage debt in full, with interest. The petition would then ask that the king order the mortgagee, who now owned the land, to accept the offered money and convey the land back to the borrower.

The king had little time or inclination to tend to these petitions personally, and so he habitually referred them to a high official, the lord chancellor. Since the king was the fountain of all justice, it was the chancellor's duty to dispose of these petitions justly and equitably, according to good conscience. In cases of hardship or accident, for example, where the mortgagor had been robbed while on the way to pay the debt, the chancellor would order the mortgagee to accept payment of the debt from the borrower and to convey the land back to the borrower. A mortgagee who refused to do as told was sent to jail.

In time, by about the year 1625, what had begun as a matter of grace on the part of the king had developed into the purest routine. Borrowers filed their petitions directly with the chancellor, who was now functioning as the judge of a court, and, with regularity, the order was issued commanding the mortgagee to reconvey. Thus, a new and very important right was born, the right of the mortgagor to pay the debt even after default and to recover his property. This right came to be known as the *equitable right of redemption,* or the *equity of redemption.* Later, the courts held that the mortgagor could sell the equitable right of redemption, that the right of redemption could be disposed of at will, and that if the owner of the equity of redemption died leaving no will, the right could be exercised by the heirs. As a result of these developments, the mortgagor, even after default, retained very important rights in the land.

20.03(a)   Waiver of Right of Redemption

The mortgagees reacted to the development of the equitable right of redemption by inserting clauses reciting that the mortgagor waived and surrendered all of the equitable right of redemption. The courts, however, nipped this idea in the bud by holding that all such clauses were void. This result was based upon the courts' feeling that it was their duty to protect the needy borrower who would sign anything at the time the mortgage was made. This rule flourished and exists in full vigor today. Any provision in the mortgage purporting to terminate the mortgagor's ownership in case of failure to make payments when due is against public policy and is void. *Once a mortgage, always a mortgage.* It cannot be converted into an outright deed by the mere default of the mortgagor. No matter how the mortgage seeks to disguise an attempted waiver of the equitable right of redemption, the courts will strike it down.

> **EXAMPLE:** At the time the mortgage was made, the mortgagor signed a deed conveying the property to the mortgagee. The mortgagor then delivered the deed to a third person in escrow with directions to deliver the deed to the mortgagee in case of default in the mortgage payments. This deed and escrow were held invalid as an attempted waiver of the equitable right of redemption. *Plummer v. Ilse,* 82 P. 1009 (Wash. 1905); *Hamud v. Hawthorne,* 338 P.2d 387 (Cal. 1959).

20.03(b)   Clogging the Equity

Other means were invented to hamper the exercise of the equitable right of redemption. Instead of waiving the right of redemption, mortgagors executed documents that limited the way the right of redemption could be exercised. Courts would not allow arrangements where the right of redemption could be exercised only for a certain period after law day or only by the mortgagor itself. The courts will also use their powers to invalidate any agreement whereby the mortgagee oppresses or takes unconscionable advantage of the mortgagor. 55 Am. Jur. 2d *Mortgages* § 514; 59 C.J.S. *Mortgages* § 113.

> **EXAMPLE:** Owner mortgaged Lot 1 to Lender. Lender demanded and received from Owner an option to buy Owner's Lot 2. When Lender sought to exercise this option, Owner resisted, and litigation ensued. The court held the option void. *Humble Oil & Refining Co. v. Doerr,* 303 A.2d 898 (N.J. 1973). While a mortgagee is entitled to payment of the mortgage debt, the mortgagee cannot take advantage of the mortgagor by compelling the granting of "collateral advantages."

This theory has somewhat impeded the use of forms of mortgages that became very popular during the 1980s. Shared-appreciation and convertible mortgages have features that in theory run afoul of this legal principal. Under the shared-appreciation mortgage, the lender is to receive a portion of the appreciation of the property standing as security for the loan in the event of a sale of the property, or after a certain period of time. Under the convertible mortgage, the lender has the right, to be exercised under certain conditions, to convert the outstanding mortgage to an ownership interest in the property. If the clogging theory is applicable to these forms of loan transactions, the theory would be that the lender wrongfully has exacted some form of collateral advantage in addition to the interest specified in the loan, and has made the transaction something other than a loan that can be repaid, thereby returning the borrower to the position it was in before the loan was made.

This ancient rule should not find application in transactions negotiated at arm's length between sophisticated parties represented by attorneys and other advisors. The old law should not rise up to frustrate the bargained-for expectations of well-advised parties. Some state legislatures have addressed this problem by abrogating the clogging rule in certain loan transactions. Lawrence G. Preble & David A. Cartwright, *Clogging the Equity of Redemption: Old Wine in New Bottles,* Prob. & Prop. 7 (Nov./Dec. 1987); Lawrence G. Preble & David A. Cartwright, *Convertible and Share Appreciation Loans: Unclogging the Equity of Redemption,* 20 Real Prop. Prob. & Tr. L.J. 821 (1985); Howard Kane, *The Mortgagee's Option to Purchase Mortgaged Property, Financing Real Estate During the Inflationary 80s,* A.B.A. Section of Real Prop., Prob. & T.L. (B. Strum, ed. 1982); *MacArthur v. North Palm Beach Utilities, Inc.,* 202 So. 2d 181 (Fla. 1967); *Griffin v. The Marine Co.,* 52 Ill. 130 (1869); *Blackwell Ford, Inc. v. Calhoun,* 555 N.W.2d 856 (Mich. App. 1996); *Smith v. Smith,* 135 A. 25 (N.H. 1926); *Coursey v. Fairchild,* 436 P.2d 35 (Okla. 1967); *Hopping v. Baldridge,* 266 P. 469 (Okla. 1928); John C. Murray, *Clogging Revisited,* 33 Real Prop. Prob. & Tr. L.J. 279 (1998).

20.04 Development of Foreclosure

The efforts of the courts to rescue the mortgagor in turn placed the mortgagee at a disadvantage. The mortgagee, it is true, became the owner of the land when the mortgagor defaulted, but the mortgagee could not be certain it would remain the owner because the mortgagor might redeem. To remedy this situation, a new practice sprang up. Immediately upon default in payment of the mortgage debt, the mortgagee would file a petition in court, and the judge would enter a decree allowing the mortgagor additional time, usually six months or a year, to pay the debt. If the mortgagor failed to make the payment within this time, the decree provided that the equitable right of redemption was barred and foreclosed. Thereafter, the mortgagor could not redeem the property. Thus developed the *foreclosure suit,* a suit to bar or terminate the equitable right of redemption.

The method of foreclosure just described is known as *strict foreclosure*. It is still used in Connecticut and Vermont and occasionally elsewhere.

The next development was foreclosure through public sale. The idea emerged that in mortgage foreclosures, justice would best be served by offering the land for sale at public auction. If the property sold for more than the mortgage debt, the mortgagee would be paid in full and the surplus proceeds of the sale would be paid to the mortgagor. This method of *foreclosure by sale* is the most common method of foreclosure in the United States today. This development constituted another major victory for the mortgagor. As the practice of foreclosure by sale grew more common, the view emerged that the mortgage, despite its superficial similarity to a deed, was really not a deed of conveyance but only a *lien* on the land—that is, merely a means of bringing about a public sale to raise money for the payment of the mortgage debt.

20.05 The Institutionalization of Mortgage Law

Mortgage lending has also progressed from pre–World War I days, when the majority of mortgage lenders were individuals, to a time when lenders were primarily local lending or banking institutions, to today, when mortgages are mostly originated and sold in the secondary mortgage market or on Wall Street to investors who are virtually anonymous ultimate investors, isolated from the borrower. This evolution has taken mortgage processing from an individual-to-individual context to a context where the borrower deals with a skilled professional investor who is represented by a loan servicer.

Thus, mortgage lending has become institutionalized, federalized, and securitized with the holders of the beneficial interest in the mortgages being diverse pools of investors, such as pension funds, 401(k)-like plans, and individuals.

20.06 Federalization of Mortgage Law

The federalization of mortgage law has been accomplished by direct federal legislation, such as the Real Estate Settlement Procedures Act, the Equal Credit Opportunity Act, and so forth, and by the involvement of the U.S. Department of Housing and Urban Development (HUD), largely through the Federal Housing Administration (FHA). Under the HUD system, a home buyer makes a small down payment and obtains a mortgage loan for the balance of the purchase price. The loan is made by a bank, savings and loan association, mortgage originator, or other loan originator. The Comptroller of the Currency and the Office of Thrift Supervision, which regulate banks and federal savings and loan associations, have also had an impact on lending practices of those lenders, as have the federally related instrumentalities of the secondary market, and the requirements of the investment bankers that need uniform investment grade obligations to allow investors to have a high degree of uniformity and security for their investments, thus locking in the expected returns on their invested capital.

All of these programs have their own sets of standards and regulations, which have played a large role in shaping underwriting requirements, the terms of loan documents, and foreclosure practices to align mortgage practices with the goals of the ultimate investors.

20.07 Secondary Mortgage Market

The mortgage industry is divided into two markets: the primary market of loan originators or conduit lenders and the secondary market of investors that purchase the loans from the originators, holding them in a loan portfolio for a long-term investment. This secondary market has several benefits, both for the investors and the housing industry. First, it provides liquidity in that an investor in a mortgage security has a ready market for the sale of that asset. Second, it tends to moderate dips in the flow of mortgage capital, allowing lenders to sell portfolios of loans to replenish their supply of funds. Third, it moves capital from one area of the country to another. And fourth, it permits investor portfolio diversification. Indeed, in the most streamlined example, the ultimate lender does not need an origination staff. Rather, it can simply purchase interests in a variety of loan portfolios, diversifying its investments and eliminating a great deal of overhead.

One of the principal participants in the secondary mortgage market is the Federal National Mortgage Company (FNMA) or Fannie Mae. FNMA was begun in 1938 as a corporation wholly owned by the federal government. In 1968, FNMA was split into two separate corporations. One, the Government National Mortgage Association (GNMA) or Ginnie Mae, continues to be wholly owned by the federal government. The other, FNMA, became a privately owned, federally chartered, New York Stock Exchange corporation subject to federal regulation. FNMA is the largest supplier of mortgage funds for homes and apartments, purchasing these loans from the originator, thereby giving the lender funds to lend again. FNMA has long specialized in buying FHA-insured or Veterans' Administration (VA) guaranteed loans, but it also buys large quantities of conventional loans that are not backed by the government. FNMA either holds the mortgages in its own portfolio or sells them to investors. All the while, the loan is typically being serviced by the originating lender or some other entity.

GNMA is organized a bit differently. It is still a government agency, but it buys pools of mortgages and holds them as security for certificates that are issued to investors.

> **EXAMPLE:** Mortgage Banker has originated a volume of mortgages that are sold to GNMA. GNMA gets the funds to make this purchase by selling mortgage-backed securities that may be purchased by investors with a minimal investment.

The pools are made up of FHA and VA mortgages, and the investors' security lies both in the mortgages backing the pool and the full faith and credit of the U.S. Treasury that guarantees payment. Every month, the investors receive a check that represents one month's interest on the remaining balance plus repaid and prepaid principal. These securities are held primarily by large investors, such as banks, savings and loan associations, credit unions, and pension funds. Billions of dollars of such securities have been issued.

The Federal Home Loan Mortgage Corporation (FHLMC), or Freddie Mac, buys conventional, non-government-insured mortgages in the secondary market. These mortgages are also placed in pools, and certificates backed by these pools are sold to investors who ultimately receive the payments made by the mortgagors.

20.08 Title and Lien Theories

The relatively recent view that the mortgage is not really a conveyance of land but only a lien, has reached its fullest development in the agricultural and Western states. Certain states, called *title theory states,* still take the older view that a mortgage gives the mortgagee some sort of legal title to the land. *Conference Center, Ltd. v. TRC,* 455 A.2d 857 (Conn. 1983). In other states, called *lien theory states,* the view that the mortgagee has the legal title is entirely superseded by the view that the mortgagee has merely a lien to secure its debt. Some states take a position midway between these two views. These are called *intermediate states.*

It is not possible, however, to draw any hard and fast line between these groups of states, since vestiges of title theory will be found in lien theory states, and many title theory states have adopted rules developed by lien theory courts. The differences in point of view are of importance in determining the mortgagee's rights with respect to possession and rents of the mortgaged property.

20.09 Types of Mortgages

There are several different types of mortgage instruments. Those commonly encountered are regular mortgages, deeds of trust, equitable mortgages, and deeds absolute given as security for debts.

20.09(a) Regular Mortgages

A mortgage is, in form, a deed or conveyance of the land by the borrower to the lender. The mortgage describes the debt and includes a provision to the effect that the mortgage shall be void on full payment of such debt.

20.09(b) Deeds of Trust

The regular mortgage involves only two parties, the borrower and the lender. In the trust deed or deed of trust, the borrower conveys the land, not to the lender, but to a third party, a trustee, in trust for the benefit of the holder of the note or notes that represent the mortgage debt.

The deed of trust form of mortgage has the advantage that, in a number of states, it can be foreclosed by trustee's sale under the power-of-sale clause without any court proceedings. The power-of-sale trust deed is used in Alabama, Alaska, Arizona, California, Colorado, District of Columbia, Mississippi, Missouri, Montana, Nebraska, Nevada, New Mexico, North Carolina, Oregon, South Carolina, Tennessee, Texas, Virginia, Washington, and West Virginia.

20.09(c) Equitable Mortgages

As a general rule, any writing by which the parties show their intention that real estate be held as security for the payment of a debt will constitute an equitable mortgage. If the arrangement is determined to be an equitable mortgage, it must be foreclosed in a court of equity.

> **EXAMPLE:** A landowner borrowed money from a mortgagee giving a promissory note to evidence the debt. On this note, the borrower placed the following recital: "This note is secured by a real estate mortgage on . . ." (here followed a description of the land). No separate mortgage was executed. The court held that the note itself, with the quoted language, constituted an equitable mortgage on the land, for it clearly expressed an intention that the land should stand as security for the debt. *Trustees of Zion Methodist Church v. Smith,* 81 N.E.2d 649 (Ill. App. 1948).

An instrument intended as a regular mortgage, but which contains some defect, may also operate as an equitable mortgage.

> **EXAMPLE:** When, through inadvertence, a trust deed altogether omitted the name of a trustee, it was obviously ineffective to transfer title or create a power of sale in anyone since it lacked a grantee. However, it was sustained as an equitable mortgage, which could be foreclosed by means of a foreclosure suit. *Gen. Glass Corp. v. Mast Constr. Co.,* 766 P.2d 429 (Utah App. 1988); *Dulany v. Willis,* 29 S.E. 324 (Va. App. 1898).

20.09(d) Deeds Absolute Given as a Security

Often a landowner borrows money and gives as security an absolute deed to the land. The deed looks absolute on its face, just as any other deed that is used in an ordinary land sale. On its face, the transaction looks like a sale of the land. Nevertheless, the courts treat such a deed as a mortgage where the evidence shows that the deed was really intended only as a security for a debt. This action of the court is called *recharacterization* of the deed that was absolute on its face into an equitable mortgage.

> **EXAMPLE:** Owner owns a home, which is already mortgaged to a bank. Owner needs money for medical expenses and goes to Brother for a loan of $1,000. Brother loans Owner the money but insists that Owner sign a simple promissory note and give a quitclaim deed to the home. It is agreed orally that if the debt is paid when due, Brother will quitclaim the prop-

erty back to Owner. Owner fails to pay the debt. Brother is not the owner of the land. Brother merely holds a mortgage on it, which must be foreclosed.

A deed such as that described in the previous example is regarded by the courts as an attempt to "waive the equitable right of redemption." The courts often use the maxim, "Once a mortgage, always a mortgage." It cannot be converted into a conveyance of absolute ownership by mere default. Hence, it becomes necessary for the courts to go back to the very beginning of the transaction. The task is a simple one. Either the deed was intended as an absolute *transfer of ownership* (as in a land sale), or it was intended merely to provide *security to a lender.* The court will hear the evidence regarding the transaction and determine the intent of the parties. Was the deed intended to transfer absolute ownership or was it merely intended to provide security for the lender? Roger A. Cunningham & Saul Tischler, *Disguised Real Estate Security Transactions as Mortgages in Substance,* 26 Rutgers L. Rev. 1 (1972).

The following circumstances are usually considered:

1. *Adequacy of consideration.* If owner conveys land worth $10,000 and receives only $5,000, the indication is that the transaction is a mortgage. Normally, land will sell for its full value.

2. *Prior negotiations between the parties.* When the owner applies to a lender for a loan and the transaction is consummated by the owner giving the lender a deed to the land, this tends to show that the transaction is a mortgage. It is as if the lender had said: "I will lend you the money, but give me a deed as security." If it appears that the lender rejected the application for a loan, this tends to show that the transaction is a sale. It is as if the lender had said: "I will not loan you any money, but I am willing to buy your land."

3. *Subsequent conduct of the parties.* If the owner receives money from the lender and gives the lender a deed to the land, but the owner remains in possession, paying taxes, insurance premiums, and so on, this tends to show that the transaction is a mortgage, for in a normal land sale the buyer takes possession.

If the court construes the transaction to be a deed given as security for a debt, the mask of the sale transaction is stripped away and the mortgage aspects of the transaction are exposed. This means that the grantor/borrower has redemption rights according to state law. The borrower may repay the debt and demand reconveyance of the property just as in the case of an ordinary mortgage. *Sannerud v. Brantz,* 928 P.2d 477 (Wyo. 1996). If the debt is not paid, the grantee/lender must foreclose just as if a regular mortgage had been made.

The return going to the lender/grantee is also measured against the usury laws to determine whether the charges assessed against the borrower resulted in a greater return than authorized by law. *Schulte v. Franklin,* 633 P.2d 1151 (Kan. App. 1981). A return greater than the usury laws permit tends to stamp the transaction as a disguised loan.

Another result of a deed being recharacterized as a security device lies in the fact that truth-in-lending requirements may be applicable. If the proper disclosures were not made, the truth-in-lending penalty provisions may be invoked against the lender. *Long v. Storms,* 622 P.2d 731 (Or. App. 1981).

20.10   Vendor's Lien Reserved by Deed

In some instances, in lieu of taking back a mortgage from the buyer, the seller will expressly reserve in the deed to the buyer a lien on the land to secure payment of the balance of the purchase price. Such a lien is called a *vendor's lien*. It is really a mortgage.

EXAMPLE: *A,* a landowner, conveyed land to *B* by a warranty deed that warranted that title was free from all encumbrances excepting three certain notes executed by *B,* for which a vendor's lien was retained until said notes and the interest thereon should be fully paid. The court held that this clause created a lien on the land. Such a lien is regarded as partaking of the nature of an equitable mortgage. This device is governed by the same rules as a mortgage and may be foreclosed as such. *Crabtree v. Davis,* 186 So. 734 (Ala. 1939); *Lusk v. Mintz,* 625 S.W.2d 774 (Tex. App. 1981).

Such a lien enjoys priority over subsequent liens and encumbrances and, like a purchase money mortgage, has priority over prior judgments against the purchaser. The grantee under such a deed does not become personally liable for the purchase money unless the grantee executed a promissory note, as in the previous example, or otherwise obligated itself personally to pay the debt. And, a purchaser from such grantee does not become personally liable to the holder of the vendor's lien, unless by the deed the purchaser assumes and agrees to pay the unpaid balance of the debt. The debt may be assigned, and the assignee will have the right to foreclose the lien.

20.11   Purchase Money Mortgages

Purchase money mortgages taken back by sellers provide a major form of real property financing in periods of tight credit. In such times, this form of financing vehicle provides the basis of most forms of creative financing that allows property to be sold. In today's world of mortgage finance, purchase money financing is typically given by a third party to finance the home purchase.

Purchase money financing is afforded priority against liens that would otherwise attach to the property immediately upon acquisition. For example, if a home buyer who has a judgment outstanding that would attach to the home buyer's property purchases a home and gives a purchase money mortgage, the judgment lien will be junior to the mortgage. *Guffey v. Creutzinger,* 984 S.W.2d 219 (Tenn. App. 1998).

20.12   Current Mortgage Terms

The previous discussion deals with the legal form of the mortgage. The mortgage terms are the business terms of the deal between the lender and the borrower and are of greater concern to the parties than the legal form that the mortgage document may take. In the relatively recent past, mortgages were generally flat-rate amortizing loans with payment schedules designed to cause the repayment of the loan on a predetermined schedule. Such is not always the case today. Loans have more sophisticated business terms to meet the needs of both the borrower and the lender.

Variable-rate loans allow the borrower and the lender to share the risks and get the benefits of interest rate movements. Shared-appreciation or convertible loans allow the lender to enjoy some of the appreciation that it helps the borrower obtain, while giving the lender the benefit of a lower interest rate. Reverse mortgages allow elderly persons to realize some of the value of their home without selling it.

These types of mortgage loans are no longer new. What we see now is the maturation of the loan terms and the litigation over the implementation of the loan terms. All of these loan forms have one thing in common. They were born out of the economic conditions of the time. As those economic conditions change, so will the terms of mortgage loans.

20.13   Variable Rate Loans—In General

Any discussion of loan terms other than the terms of a flat-rate amortized mortgage loan must be preceded by a discussion of the economic conditions that made variable-rate loans necessary. While such loans are now ordinary, this was not always the case, at least with respect to residential loans. In the period from the beginning of the first Roosevelt administration and ending in the early 1970s, interest rates fluctuated very little and inflation was very modest. Then, in the 1970s, interest rates began to soar and fluctuate. The financial institutions were very badly hurt. Lenders found their portfolios full of thirty-year fixed rate mortgages paying low rates, as compared with the lenders' cost of funds. With this negative spread, many institutions became insolvent.

The problem was too big for the states to handle. The federal government stepped in and the Garn-St.Germaine Depository Institution Deregulation Act, which included the Alternative Mortgage Transaction Parity Act of 1982, was enacted by Congress. 12 U.S.C. § 3801, *et seq.* Under this law, all home lenders were given the power to make home loans with fluctuating interest rates or that share in the appreciation of the property that secures the loan. These loans may be insured under FHA programs. 12 U.S.C. § 1715z–16. The lender is required to select some "index" that is regularly published, such as the rate of interest on treasury bills that the federal government regularly issues. Such interest rates are published in *The Wall Street Journal* and other financial media. The interest rate charged on the loan will then be set at some margin (say 2 or 3 percent) above the index and fluctuate over time. To make this type of loan attractive to borrowers, the interest rate in the early part of the loan term is usually fixed at a rate slightly lower than the rate charged on the flat-rate mortgages. This is a teaser rate.

Because the interest rate on these loans is periodically adjusted, these mortgages, at least in the residential setting, are called *adjustable-rate mortgages* (ARMs).

Borrowers should not assume that variable-rate loans are the only type of loan available. Many lenders continue to make fixed-rate loans, but borrowers are now put to the task of evaluating the benefits and detriments of each in making the decision of which form of loan to accept. Furthermore, if the borrower decides to accept an ARM loan, it should be understood that all ARM loans are not the same.

Borrowers should shop and analyze the differences between ARMs offered by various lenders, inquiring about many factors, such as the following:

1. How are interest rate adjustments put into effect? Does the monthly payment change, the principal amount of the loan change, or the maturity of the loan change?

2. Will the interest rate move up and down according to some index, such as the interest paid on treasury notes?

3. How frequently will rates change? Daily as the index changes? Every month? Every six months? Every year? Every five years?

4. Are there minimum and maximum limits on interest rate movements?

5. What period of notice must be given to the borrower before a change will be allowed?

6. Are the borrowers charged a fee upon adjustment of the interest rates or refinancing with the same lender?

7. Must the lender offer to refinance at the conclusion of each adjustment period?

8. What index is used to determine the extent of any rate change?

9. Over what period is the loan amortized?

10. Is the loan prepayable at any time? If so, the borrower is free to take advantage of other financing that may become available.

11. What happens if the selected index pushes the monthly payments so high that all of the payment must be allocated to interest, even leaving some accrued interest unpaid, thus forcing the interest to accumulate?

12. Are the mortgages acceptable to the secondary market?

13. Is a fixed-rate loan available? If so, compare the projected payments on the fixed-rate loan to the projected payments on the variable-rate loan. Of course, some assumptions will have to be made to make this comparison, and assumptions of economic expectations are often wrong, but some comparison is needed if an informed decision is to be made.

14. Is it possible that reasonably foreseeable increases in interest rates will cause the periodic payments to increase to such a level that will be only burdensome to the borrower?

15. How long does the borrower intend to keep the property?

20.13(a) Risks in Adjustable-Rate Mortgages

It is obvious that the ARM creates risks not present in the fixed-rate mortgages. These risks include (1) the inability of the borrower to handle payment increases, where an increase in the market interest rate compels an increase in the size of the monthly payment, and (2) the erosion of the equity due to negative amortization. These risks can be minimized for the borrower by the inclusion in the mortgage of a stated maximum on the permitted increase in interest.

These loans must be looked at very carefully by borrowers. In standard mortgages, every payment goes to reduce the loan balance and increase the borrower's equity. The addition of amounts to principal in an ARM can have a long-term impact on the borrower's financial planning and should not be taken lightly. Borrowers must carefully study these loans and shop for alternatives.

20.13(b) Rollover Mortgage

In the renegotiable-rate loan, or rollover, the interest rate is set for a period of time, say three, five, or seven years, at which time the loan matures or is due and payable in full. In spite of the shorter loan term, the monthly payments are based upon a longer maturity, often thirty years. Thus, at maturity, a significant unpaid principal balance must be repaid or refinanced. At that point, the loan is renegotiated in that the borrower may seek to finance the unpaid balance with the current lender, or a new lender.

20.13(c) Rate, Adjustment Period, and Margin

Prevailing interest rates change from time to time. To reflect these changes, adjustable-rate loan documents establish a mechanism for implementing changes in the loan rate. The note will typically establish an adjustment period. With most residential ARMs, the interest rate and monthly payments change on an anniversary date. In commercial loans, the interest rate usually changes simultaneously with changes in the index. The period between one rate change and the next is called the *adjustment period*. A loan with an adjustment period of one year is called a *one-year ARM,* and the interest rate can change once every year. All lenders tie ARM interest rate changes to changes in an *index rate*. These indexes usually go up and down with the general movement of interest rates. If the index rate moves up, so does the mortgage rate in most circumstances, and the mortgagor will have to make higher monthly payments. On the other hand, if the index rate goes down, the mortgagor's monthly payment will go down.

To determine the interest rate on an ARM, lenders add to the index rate two or three percentage points, called the *margin*. The amount of the margin can differ from one lender to another, and from index to index, with some margins being smaller when the index is closer to current mortgage interest rates. The margin is usually constant over the life of the loan.

20.13(d) The Index

The ARM interest rate changes periodically as some specified index changes, and monthly payments go up or down accordingly. Various indexes can be used.

From the lender's point of view, the index should reflect the lender's cost of funds—that is, the index should move up and down as the lender's cost of funds increases and decreases. From the borrower's point of view, an index that could move up so fast as to outstrip the borrower's ability to pay the loan should be avoided. Both borrowers and lenders are concerned with the volatility of the index. Does it quickly respond to changes in short-term interest rates or does it reflect long-term interest rate trends?

The indexes currently in greatest use are those based on the yield afforded by U.S. Treasury securities. Treasury bills are short-term U.S. Government debt instruments maturing in three, six, or twelve months. They are sold at a discount rather than at face or par value.

> **EXAMPLE:** An auction price of three-month treasury bills may be $96.562 per $100 of face value, giving an investor an effective yield of 14.28 percent.

Treasury notes and bonds are longer maturity debt instruments of the U.S. Government, which pay the investor a fixed amount of interest on a semiannual basis. These instruments may be sold either at a discount or a premium thereby yielding the investor more or less than the stated interest.

> **EXAMPLE:** The U.S. Treasury auctions a two-year note with a stated interest rate of 8.5 percent at $99.802 per $100 of par value. The effective annual yield to the investor is 8.61 percent.

If the index is based upon short-term rates such as one-year U.S. Treasury notes, it will move up and down faster than if it is based on long-term rates. Conversely, an index based upon longer maturity securities, such as three- or five-year U.S. Treasury notes, is slow moving and will not rise or fall as quickly as market rates may move.

Other indexes from the simple to the exotic are available.

20.13(e)   Limits on Interest Rate Movement—"Caps" and "Floors"

If interest rates were to rise 5 percent per year, the ARM borrower would quickly lose the property unless the mortgage limited the amount that the interest rate could increase. This is called a cap. An interest rate cap places a limit on the amount an interest rate can increase. ARMs with caps may command higher rates than ARMs without caps. Interest rate caps come in two versions: (1) *periodic caps,* which limit the interest rate increase from one adjustment period to the next; and (2) *overall caps,* which limit the interest rate increase over the life of the loan. The borrower wants both caps. Residential ARM loans must have a cap on the maximum interest rate, which may be charged over the life of the loan. 12 U.S.C. § 3806(a).

To the same effect, interest rates may decrease. Commercial lenders often want some floor below which the rate will not go, even if the movement in the index would otherwise dictate a lower loan interest rate.

20.13(f) Payment Caps

Some ARMs include payment caps that limit the monthly payment increase at the time of each adjustment, usually to a percentage of the previous payment. Ideally, for the borrower, the mortgage will have a cap on both interest and monthly payments. If the mortgage contains only a payment cap, negative amortization may result.

20.13(g)   Frequency of Interest Rate Movement

Depending upon the type of loan and its documentation, the interest rate may fluctuate simultaneously with interest rate index changes or only after a stated period, for example, six months or two years. In commercial mortgages, particularly construction loans, the loan rate often moves as the index rate moves. As can be guessed, the frequency of adjustment may be high in these types of loans. In residential loans, most lenders have programs that call for adjustments in the interest rate at intervals of six months or longer.

20.13(h)   Negative Amortization

ARM loan formats may involve negative amortization. In the fixed rate loan, each monthly payment consists of two parts. One part is allocated to the interest due for the month. The remainder is allocated to reduce the principal. Suppose, in an ARM, the interest moves up and down as interest rates on one-year treasury notes move up and down. The interest rate on treasury bills may swing sharply upward. If the monthly payment is fixed, the entire payment may be insufficient to pay the interest. The unpaid portion of the interest is added to the principal and with each monthly payment, the amount of the mortgage debt increases. This is negative amortization because the principal grows instead of being reduced.

This creates the following issues that must be resolved: (1) the loan-to-value ratio may increase, making the loan riskier from the lender's standpoint, and (2) the increased principal may not have the same priority over intervening lien claimants as the original principal.

20.13(i)   Term of Loans

Federal regulations limit most loans to a maximum of forty years. Thus, negative amortization can be avoided by "stretching" the term of the loan, leaving the monthly payments the same as the interest rate goes up, but requiring the full payment within forty years. A borrower must fully understand the treatment of negative amortization.

20.13(j)   Prepayment

An ARM mortgage often provides for prepayment without penalty or allows prepayment on payment adjustment dates. In any case, prepayment penalties are negotiable.

20.13(k)   Conversion

Many ARM mortgages provide that, at some point, the mortgage becomes convertible into a fixed-rate mortgage calling for interest at the current market rate for a fixed-rate mortgage. In other, more sophisticated, commercial loans, the borrower is given the option to switch indices at certain intervals. A conversion fee is often charged. Some commercial loans allow the borrower the option of converting to another index at some point during the loan term.

20.13(l)   Future Advance Problems

Because the ARM secures a debt that may increase in the future by negative amortization, a future advance problem may be present. Some states have enacted legislation that gives the increased principal the same priority as the original principal advance. Title insurance companies offer endorsements to their policies insuring the priority of these future additions to principal.

20.13(m)   Effect of Variable-Rate Clauses on Parties Secondarily Liable

Frequently, mortgage transactions involve parties that are secondarily liable, with the borrower being primarily liable for payment of the debt. For example, in major transactions, it is not uncommon to have guarantors for the borrower's obligation to pay the debt and to otherwise comply with the obligations of the loan documents. Endorsers and assignors may also have secondary liability. Under traditional theories, an alteration of the obligation between the principal and the creditor will discharge the obligation of the secondarily liable parties. This should present no great difficulty in the variable-rate mortgage context since careful draftsmanship, even where the increase in the interest rate is optional, can continue the obligation of these parties notwithstanding the increase in the burden upon the primary debtor.

20.14   Graduated Payment Mortgage

The graduated payment mortgage (GPM) is characterized by lower payments during the initial period of the loan and higher payments in later periods. Theoretically, as the borrower's revenue increases, or cash flow demands decrease, payments increase. The payment graduation schedule and the interest rate are set at the outset of the transaction. While payments on this mortgage are lower during the initial years, the periodic payments level off at a higher plateau than for a comparable level payment mortgage. The total amount paid on this type of mortgage exceeds the amount that would be paid on a level payment mortgage of the same amount for the same period of time.

> **EXAMPLE:** A borrower under a thirty-year, 8.5 percent, $30,000 GPM, with payments increasing by 5 percent per year for the first five years with level payments thereafter, would make monthly payments of $190.83 during the first year, $200.37 during the second year, $210.39 during the third year, $220.91 during the fourth year, $231.96 during the fifth year, and $243.56 thereafter. A level payment mortgage of the same amount would have monthly

payments of $230.68. If both the GPM and the level payment mortgages run to maturity, the borrower under the GPM plan will make principal and interest payments totalling $85,724.28; the borrower under the level payment plan will make principal and interest payments totaling $83,044.80, $2,679.48 less than under the GPM plan.

The increase in periodic payments in the years after the loan is originated can cause strains upon the ability of the borrower to make payments if expected increases in revenue do not occur or if inflation in other areas of the economy causes unexpected strains on the borrower's income stream.

A feature of this type of financing device is that initial payments are not of sufficient size to fully pay the interest that accrues during any month. To the extent that the initial payment is insufficient in this regard, additional principal is created. Thus, in the early stages of the payment schedule, the debt increases rather than decreases, and *negative amortization* occurs. This type of loan may qualify for FHA insurance. 12 U.S.C. § 1715z-10.

If the value of the property does not increase at an acceptable pace, the negative amortization feature of a GPM can cause the borrower an out-of-pocket expense upon the sale of the property. Frequently, these mortgages are low down payment loans, and the "thin equity" of the borrower is made even thinner by operation of negative amortization. Selling costs can quickly erode whatever equity exists.

The principal advantage of negative amortization in a GPM is to allow borrowers to qualify with a lower annual income than would be the case with the same size of fixed-rate loan. The key to the success of this program is the increase in the borrower's income level so that the higher future payments can indeed be made.

The mortgage and note should state that the size of the monthly payment increases periodically and should contain a provision such as, "From time to time, deferred interest shall be added to the principal balance outstanding on this loan." This statement is made necessary by state laws requiring the character of the debt or mortgage to be reflected in the recorded documents. Other state laws require that the mortgage state the maximum amount to be advanced or secured. Careful draftsmanship can solve these problems.

20.14(a) GPM— Usury Problems

The GPM may cause usury problems. If state law or policy forbids interest on interest and thus interest is treated not as being on an increased principal amount but rather as additional interest, the effective rate of interest will be increased and state usury laws could be violated. W.A.E., Annotation, *Validity of Agreement to Pay Interest on Interest*, 37 A.L.R. 325, 345 (1925), *supp. by* 76 A.L.R. 1484, 1487 (1932).

> **EXAMPLE:** The GPM is made at 10 percent, the maximum allowable interest rate. If state law will not recognize the concept of increasing the principal and charging interest on the increased principal, the effective rate of interest will be increased above 10 percent, and the usury law will be violated, absent, of course, any federal preemptive law applying to the situation.

20.15 Discounts and Buy-Downs

A builder/seller often arranges financing for its buyers. As a sales gimmick, the developer will arrange to pay funds to a mortgage lender over a period, often three years, and in return the lender will finance the buyer at below-market interest rates for these three years. Of course, this device is only attractive and necessary when interest rates are high.

20.16 Reverse Mortgages

The reverse mortgage is designed to allow an elderly homeowner to convert home equity into a cash flow that can be used to pay normal living expenses. Many elderly persons prefer to live out their lives in the home they have occupied for many years. In one version of this loan, the lender purchases an annuity with the proceeds of the loan. It is a strange sort of mortgage, in which the lender makes payments to the borrower. Of course, sooner or later, the loan falls due and if the mortgagor is still alive, there must be a refinancing. This form of mortgage is the least used form of the ARM category.

This form of mortgage derives its name from the fact that the lender at times purchases an annuity for the borrower, and mortgage payments are made by the lender to the borrower, just the reverse of the typical mortgage.

This mortgage requires the borrower to guess his or her life expectancy and hopes the borrower does not outlive the maturity of the mortgage. Refinancing is very difficult for elderly people.

> References on this form of mortgage can be found in the following authorities: Celeste M. Hammond, *Reverse Mortgages: A Financial Planning Device for the Elderly*, Elder Law J. 75 (1993); Comm'n on Legal Problems of the Elderly, A.B.A., *Attorney's Guide to Home Equity Conversion* (1986); Scholen, *A Financial Guide to Reverse Mortgages* (5th ed. 1990); Belling & Scholen, *Counselor Training and Reference Manual, Home Equity Conversion Mortgage Insurance Demonstration*, A.A.R.P. (1990); 24 C.F.R. §§ 200 & 206.

20.17 Shared Appreciation Mortgages

Inflation may greatly enhance the return to developers and project owners while decreasing the economic return to the lender that has financed the equity build-up. Traditional permanent lenders altered their investment philosophy by seeking out investment devices that allow the lender to participate in this growth in property value. Examples include the outright purchase of a property, the purchase of a part interest in the property, short-term loans, contingent interest loans, indexed interest, and shared appreciation mortgages (SAMs). While these loans are not popular at this time, they were very popular in the 1970s and 1980s, when property values were appreciating greatly. Some lenders may revert to these forms of mortgages as real estate appreciates from the recessionary levels of the late 1980s and early 1990s.

In the SAM, the lender, as an inflation hedge, obtains a share of the appreciation of the property that is security for the debt. This is done in one of two general formats. In one, the lender finances the property, usually at below-market rates and, at the same time, takes an ownership interest in the property. In the other format, the borrower promises to pay the lender *contingent interest*—that is, interest that is payable only out of appreciation in the value of the property or, in the case of income property, out of the proceeds from the operation of the property. These types of mortgage loans are eligible for FHA insurance. 12 U.S.C. § 1715z-18.

Where the contingent interest format is used, the lender must be careful in defining the income that is subject to the contingent interest application and establish a system to carefully monitor the income to determine that the proper amount of contingent interest is in fact being paid.

20.17(a) SAM— Refinance Provisions

Some SAMs require a sale or refinance after a period of years, often five or ten years, to "buy out" the lender's position. How is the value to be determined if the property is not sold? How are improvements to be factored into the valuation? How is the lender to be paid its share of the appreciated value of the property—by a cash payment or by addition to the loan principal? If the latter method is chosen, will the borrower be able to meet the debt service requirements of the larger loan?

20.17(b) SAM— Ownership Considerations

The SAM program presents certain ownership-related issues that must be addressed Owners have liability for the operation of the property, different insurance needs, concern that their partner is fairly accounting for the property's revenues, and so on. The lender is also in a somewhat dangerous position, because of the potential that junior lien claimants may contend that the quasi-equity position of the lender destroys any priority rights available to the lender upon foreclosure as against the junior lien claimant.

> **EXAMPLE:** Buyer and Lender enter into a transaction where Lender finances the acquisition of a property and certain rehabilitation improvements. Through the shared equity device, these improvements will work to the Lender's benefit in that the value of the property will be increased. Even though the law of the state where this loan is made allows a true "lender" priority interest in this regard against mechanic's lien claimants, that priority protection is not available to an owner. If the loan goes into default, mechanic's lien claims arising out of the improvements will be alleged to be prior to the owner/lender's interest.

20.18 Deferred Interest Mortgage

In the deferred interest mortgage (DIM), early payments, if any are called for, not only fail to contribute to the amortization of principal, but also fail to cover all of the accrued interest. This results in negative amortization and possibly interest on interest.

20.19 Interest-Only Mortgage

Under the interest-only mortgage, payments do not contribute to the amortization of principal but only pay accrued interest. Either the mortgage is payable at a stated date, perhaps three to five years from its creation, or principal amortization is deferred until a later date.

20.20 Balloon Loans

Balloon loans have a maturity that comes before the periodic payments have resulted in the full payment of the principal and other sums due. When the balloon loan does mature, the loan is either renegotiated, refinanced, or paid off. This is really a form of ARM, giving the lender the chance to adjust the interest rate to current market conditions every maturity date.

Balloon loans pose dangers to borrowers. The expectation is that when a balloon loan comes due, new financing will be available at reasonable rates. This is a pure guess. New financing may be unavailable or may command high interest rates. The real estate recession has demonstrated the consequences of the maturity date arriving at a time when financing was not available at all or, if available, only to the prime properties and borrowers. Much balloon financing takes place when a seller takes back a second mortgage upon the sale of property.

20.21 Interest on Interest

The negative amortization feature of an ARM and GPM involves the legal problem of charging interest on interest.

> **EXAMPLE:** To the extent that any monthly payment does not fully pay the interest due on the principal for that month, an addition to the principal is made. Interest for the next month is then charged on the new principal balance, which includes the amount added after the application of the last payment.

This practice is prohibited as being against the public policy of many states. *See generally* 37 A.L.R. 325, 332, *supp. by* 76 A.L.R. 1484, 1485, *supra*.

This should not be confused with the allowable process of settling an overdue debt by an agreement that capitalizes past due interest and charges interest on the new principal amount including that past due interest. *Hamilton v. Stephenson,* 55 S.E. 577 (Va. App. 1906); 37 A.L.R. 325, 328, *supp. by* 76 A.L.R. 1484, 1485, *supra*.

> **EXAMPLE:** *A* loaned *B* $10,000 for one year with interest at 10 percent per annum. At the end of the year, *B* owed *A* $11,000, the $10,000 principal originally advanced, and $1,000 in interest. *B* was unable to pay at that time, but, if given the chance, had a reasonable opportunity of fully repaying the debt upon the successful conclusion of a business transaction. *A* and *B* agreed, and a new note was executed for the $11,000 debt (the $11,000 being the

principal on the new obligation, the amount upon which interest would be charged) with interest at 10 percent per year.

This device is perfectly valid. It is distinguished from the graduated payment mortgage system, which, at the outset, creates a program for automatically increasing the principal each month by the amount of unpaid interest and charging interest for that month on the increased principal amount.

ARMs, GPMs, and RAMs may run afoul with this prohibition, but it is becoming less of a problem as states have enacted statutes to facilitate the making of such mortgages. These statutes generally exempt ARMs, GPMs, and RAMs from the interest on interest prohibition. Title insurance endorsements may be obtained to protect against the invalidity or unenforceability of the mortgage lien or loss of priority resulting from interest on interest provisions in the mortgage.

**20.22
Intervening Liens**

While it is a simple task for the borrower and lender to allow the property to stand as security for additional debt created by negative amortization, the retention of priority over other lien claimants for that additional debt is another matter. This is especially a problem where negative amortization is used. As long as the "advances" or additions to principal caused by the negative amortization are obligatory on the part of the lender, the priority of the ARM will be preserved against intervening lien claimants. Robert Kratovil & Raymond J. Werner, *Modern Mortgage Law and Practice*, § 11.02 (2d ed. 1981). However, since under some loan programs, the lender may have the option of increasing the interest rate, the priority for all negative amortizations cannot be upheld under the obligatory advance theory.

In addition, the right of the lender to increase the mortgage debt as the index moves up poses a possible future advance problem, not only where negative amortization operates to increase the principal of the mortgage debt, but also where there is an increase in the interest rate. No reliable body of law has as yet been developed in this area. Among the liens that may intervene between the recording of the mortgage and the increase in the mortgage debt are second mortgages, judgment liens, mechanic's liens, and federal tax liens. The simple solution, wherever title insurance is available, is for the lender to insist on a title insurance endorsement to protect against the loss of priority to these intervening lienholders. Sophisticated lenders require this endorsement on all negative amortization mortgages. Of course, it is naive to assume that the title insurer will give the endorsement if the law of the state involved does not allow the title insurer to feel protected against the risk.

20.23   Usury

An adjustable mortgage may become usurious if the index carries the rate over the usury limit. *Kin-Ark Corp. v. Boyles,* 593 F.2d 361 (10th Cir. 1979). Another court has held that usury is not present even though the variable rate provisions at times carry the loan rate above the legal maximum, if the parties contracted in good faith and without the intent to avoid usury laws. *McConnell v. Merrill, Lynch Pierce, Fenner & Smith, Inc.,* 146 Cal. Rptr. 371 (1978). *See generally* Raymond J. Werner, *Usury and the Variable-Rate Mortgage, 5* Real Est. L.J. 155 (1976). This is the better view.

Absent an exemption or preemption, the lender must include a provision in the loan documents that the interest rate will not increase to a level above the maximum rate allowed by law. Indeed, this is a typical loan document provision in jurisdictions that allow it.

20.24   Disclosures

Certain disclosures must be made to applicants for ARM loans. Savings and loan associations or thrifts are required to provide the borrower with a booklet that explains adjustable-rate mortgages and gives certain information regarding the loan terms, such as the identity of the index, the frequency of adjustment of the interest rate, and a historical example illustrating a $10,000 loan.

20.25 Application and Commitment

A mortgage transaction usually begins with an application for a loan. The application serves a double purpose, in that it is a source of information on which the lender will base its decision to make the loan, and it defines the terms of the loan contract. The application is usually made on the mortgagee's preprinted form and signed by the prospective borrower. After investigating the prospective borrower's financial circumstances and appraising the real estate, the lender may write the applicant a letter stating that the loan application has been accepted. This letter is sometimes referred to as a *commitment* and will usually result in a contract for the making of a mortgage loan.

Technically, the application is an *offer* by the mortgagor to give a mortgage and note on the terms specified in the application. The commitment is an *acceptance* of the offer, *Burns v. Washington Sav.,* 171 So. 2d 322 (Miss. 1965), which, under basic contract law, creates a contract. If the commitment makes any changes in the terms of the application, it is technically a *counteroffer.* There is no contract in this instance unless the applicant agrees to the new terms, which it may do by writing the word "accepted" and signing the commitment. To the lawyer, this is the typical "offer and acceptance" process.

Since the application and commitment define the terms on which the loan is to be made and constitute a contract that neither party can change or add to without the other's consent, the application should state the terms in detail. Indeed, a failure to include essential terms will lead a court to hold that no binding contract came into existence. *Calosso v. First Nat'l Bank,* 143 So. 2d 343 (Fla. 1962). All contracts must be complete and certain. The mortgagee will, of course, want to see to it that the offer and acceptance contain various other terms that may or may not be essential to the formation of a contract. Included among these other terms is the agreement of the borrower to sign a note and mortgage in a certain specified form; the borrower's agreement to furnish evidence of title and survey at its expense; the borrower's agreement to sign chattel security documents and to sign an assignment of leases and rents; provisions for deducting title and other charges from the proceeds of the loan; provisions regarding the form of insurance coverages to be obtained by the borrower.

The foregoing description of the application and commitment procedure has been modified in the residential setting. The great diversity in loan terms offered by residential lenders has made it almost impossible for the applicant to do anything but furnish personal information in the loan application. A discussion ensues or a computer prints out a variety of available mortgage plans. Some plan is agreed upon, and the lender prepares a commitment outlining the plan and listing the various deductions from the loan amount that will be required to defray loan expenses, such as appraisal fees. About this time, the lender will furnish the prospective borrower a Truth-in-Lending statement and a Federal Reserve Bank pamphlet describing the new forms of mortgages. If the borrower is satisfied, the commitment is accepted, and a loan contract is created. The commitment, of course, is conditioned on satisfactory appraisal, satisfactory title, and so on. Today, this is often done in a matter of hours and confirmed in a few days.

Computerized networks allow the borrower to shop for residential loans in the real estate broker's office and provide application-type information through a computerized system. If the property appraises out and the title proves to be clear, the commitment becomes firm. This is all part of the process that is evolving in making the real estate broker the "one-stop shop" place to order all of the services that are involved in the home purchase. Those services include the loan, title insurance, survey, appraisal, flood certification, pest inspection, and insurance. While some brokers provide some or all of these services, it is clear that the home-buying process is becoming easier, more streamlined, and more centralized. In the end, this will shorten the time for the closing, but it will also reduce, somewhat, the extent of competition in the industries related to the home-buying process.

The residential commitment will either tie the mortgagee's interest rate to an agreed rate or to the market rate at the time of closing. All commitments have time limits. If the time expires before the deal is closed, the process goes back to square one. A higher interest rate may be charged. If the borrower is willing to proceed, the terms of the revised loan commitment must be accepted in writing.

Reg. B, as the federal regulation is called, requires the lender to notify the applicant of the action taken on the application and, if refused, why credit was refused the applicant.

The requirements of a residential loan commitment should look ahead to the possibility or probability that the loan will be sold in the secondary market. It should require, for example, those things that FNMA and FHLMC will require. This is typical today.

Application and commitment procedures vary depending upon whether the loan is a residential or commercial loan. In the commercial transaction, the developer's loan application is often merely a sales pitch describing the proposed project. It is too skimpy to be regarded as a legal document. If the bank is interested in the project, its loan committee will set out the terms on which it is prepared to make the loan in the form of a "commitment." There is some bargaining before a commitment acceptable to both parties is agreed upon. By the borrower's acceptance of the commitment, a loan contract comes into existence. This acceptance ought to contain a promise by the borrower to perform its part of the bargain.

This entire aspect of the mortgage business is not well understood, even by sophisticated lawyers. A good, binding loan contract is needed if the mortgage lien is to maintain its priority as an "obligatory advance" mortgage. Illustrative of the lack of understanding of this procedure in the mortgage business, not too many years ago residential lenders were giving *oral commitments*. Indeed, this still happens. A mortgage loan comes under the Statute of Frauds. Everything must be in writing.

The borrower is particularly interested in the duration of the commitment and the interest rate. Interest rates can be volatile. If borrower gets a forty-five-day commitment at 10 percent interest, the commitment may expire without completion of closing. Slow production of the appraisal is a constant complaint, but that is becoming less of a problem today as lenders begin to rely upon computer data banks of sales of comparable properties. Even if the commitment expires, the lender may still be willing to make the loan, but at a higher interest rate. If this occurs, the monthly payments may be increased beyond the borrowing power of a marginal borrower. A borrower may wish to insist on a longer term commitment. Lenders are reluctant to commit to a fixed interest rate for too long. Rate movement creates risks for the borrower and lender.

In a commercial loan, the commitment will describe the leases and the lender will check them before closing. The commitment will call for an assignment of the leases and rents, requirements as to guarantees by third parties, survey and chattel lien searches, etc. In a construction loan, the commitment contains a wealth of detail regarding disbursement of the loan proceeds.

Commercial loan commitments are typically conditional. That is, the borrower is usually obligated to satisfy several conditions before the lender is obligated to fund the loan. The nature of these conditions varies with the type of loan, the property securing the loan, the borrower, and the economic climate.

Whatever the loan type, the commitment conditions usually fall within several categories. Some, such as the submission of the borrower's financial statements, operating statements, and appraisals for the property, go to the creditworthiness of the borrower and the value of the property. Others, such as requirements for the submission of title evidence, U.C.C. searches, and a survey, go the definition of the legal interest conveyed to the lender as security and the verification of the use of the loan proceeds. It is important that the commitment expressly allow the lender to avoid funding if the submitted materials disclose matters that are not acceptable to the lender or reveal an adverse change in the condition of the borrower.

The borrower will be held to the task of fulfilling those conditions on time or the commitment fee may be forfeited, since the lender is not under an obligation to extend the commitment to allow the borrower extra time to satisfy the conditions. *Penthouse Int', Ltd. v. Dominion Fed. Sav. & Loan Ass'n,* 855 F.2d 963 (2d Cir. 1988); *Brighton Dev. Corp. v. Barnett Bank of South Florida,* 513 So. 2d 1103 (Fla. App. 1987).

20.25(a)
Commitment Fees

Quite commonly, in larger loans, the borrower pays a commitment fee, which is refundable only if the borrower performs its part of the bargain and the lender defaults.

> **EXAMPLE:** *B* procured a commitment from *L* for a mortgage loan on a shopping center. The commitment was contingent upon *B*'s procuring eight leases with major tenants. *B* paid *L* a commitment fee. *B* was able to procure only six leases. *L* could keep the fee. *Boston Road Shopping Center v. Teachers Ins. & Annuity Ass'n of Am.,* 182 N.E.2d 116 (1962). *Accord, First Nat'l Bank v. Atlantic Tele-Network Co.,* 946 F.2d 516 (7th Cir. 1991); *White Lakes Shopping Ctr, Inc. v. Jefferson Standard Life Ins. Co.,* 490 P.2d 609 (Kan. 1971); Sonya A. Soehnel, Annotation, *Enforceability of Provision in Loan Commitment Agreement Authorizing Lender to Charge Standby Fee, Commitment Fee or Similar Deposit,* 93 A.L.R.3d 1156 (1979).

20.25(b) Damages

A lender will be liable to the borrower for damages if the lender breaches the commitment. *St. Paul at Chase Corp. v. Manufacturer's Life Ins. Co.,* 278 A.2d 12 (Md. 1971); *Liben v. Nassau Sav. & Loan Ass'n,* 337 N.Y.S.2d 310 (1972); L.S.E., Annotation, *Measure of Damages for Breach of Contract to Lend Money,* 36 A.L.R.. 1408 (1925); Debra T. Landis, Annotation, *Measure and Elements of Damages for Breach of Contract to Lend Money,* 4 A.L.R.4th 682 (1981).

> **EXAMPLE:** Lender commits to loan Borrower $1,000,000 at 12 percent interest. Lender refuses to make the loan when the time for funding arrives. Borrower obtains a loan from Banker at 14 percent interest. Lender is liable to Borrower for the 2 percent interest differential. *Lester v. Resolution Trust Corp.,* 125 Bankr. Rptr. 528 (N.D. Ill. 1991); *Pipkin v. Thomas & Hill, Inc.,* 258 S.E.2d 778 (N.C. 1979).

Some further examples may help to illustrate how this problem is being handled by the courts.

> **EXAMPLE:** Buyer applied to Lender for a mortgage and was given a commitment at an interest rate of 6 percent. At closing, Buyer was told by Lender that interest rates had risen and he would have to pay 7.25 percent. Buyer had no place to live so he closed the deal at 7.25 percent. He filed suit and the court ordered Lender to reduce the rate to 6 percent. *Leben v. Nassau Sav. & Loan Ass'n,* 337 N.Y.S.2d 310 (1972).

If the lender wishes to protect itself against rising interest rates, the commitment should so provide. This is often handled by lenders not setting the rate until a date close to the closing, or allowing the borrower to lock-in a rate by the payment of a fee. The risk of changes in the prevailing interest rate must be borne by one or the other of the parties. Borrowers are well-advised to carefully attend to this detail.

Even when the documents make the rights of the parties clear, the lender must be careful that its conduct does not detract from its ability to enforce its loan documents as written.

> **EXAMPLE:** Borrower signed a note containing a variable interest rate clause. Borrower asked Lender's officer about a variable interest rate and was told that Lender "probably" would not raise its rates. In less than a year, Lender raised the interest rate. The court refused to permit Lender to foreclose and awarded damages to Borrower. *Peoples Trust & Sav. Bank v. Humphrey,* 451 N.E.2d 1104 (Ind. App. 1983).

While the lender may be liable for the borrower's damages incurred as a result of the lender's breach of the commitment, punitive damages are generally not recoverable for breach of contract, and damages are generally limited to those necessary to compensate the borrower for the lender's breach. *Mortgage Finance, Inc. v. Podelski,* 742 P.2d 900 (Colo. 1987).

Liability for breach of a loan commitment goes both ways. The borrower may be liable to the lender for the failure to honor the commitment when the borrower breaches the commitment to take advantage of falling interest rates. *New England Mut. Life Ins. Co. v. Stuzin,* 1990 W.L. 150065 (D. Mass. 1990). *See also First Nat'l Bank of Chicago v. Atlantic Tele-Network Co.,* 946 F.2d 516 (7th Cir. 1991) (awarding the lender its fees as a result of the borrower's breach of the commitment); *Teachers Ins. & Annuity Ass'n of Am. v. Butler,* 626 F. Supp. 1229 (S.D. N.Y. 1986) (where the lender was awarded the difference between the rate contracted for in the loan commitment and the rate of interest at the time of the breach for the life of the loan, but discounted to present value).

20.25(c) Specific Performance

As an alternative to damages, especially in large loans, the borrower may sue the lender for specific performance. *Vanderventer v. Dale Constr. Co.,* 334 P.2d 183 (Or. 1975); John C. Williams, Annotation, *Specific Performance of Agreement to Lend or Borrow Money,* 82 A.L.R.3d 1116 (1978).

> **EXAMPLE:** Owner obtains a construction loan from Lender 1 to build an office building. Lender 1 makes the loan in reliance on Lender 2's commitment to make a permanent loan when the building is completed, thereby paying off Lender 1's mortgage. When the building is completed, the mortgage market and office building market are in a recession. Funds are simply unobtainable elsewhere. Specific performance can be used to force Lender 2 to honor the commitment.

20.25(d) Credit Information

Credit information must be provided and obtained in accordance with the terms of the Fair Credit Reporting Act, 15 U.S.C.A. § 1681. This law protects the borrower against inaccurate credit reports. The Federal Home Loan Bank Board (FHLBB) Fair Lending Regulations and Guidelines, 12 C.F.R. § 528, protect borrowers against unfair credit practices, such as a refusal to lend on a home simply because of its age. The Equal Credit Opportunity Act, 15 U.S.C.A. § 1691, makes credit available with fairness, impartiality, and without discrimination on the basis of race, color, religion, national origin, sex, marital status, or age. While marital status inquiries are not absolutely prohibited, 12 C.F.R. § 202.5(c)(1), only the terms "married," "unmarried," or "separated" may be used. 12 C.F.R. § 202.6(d)(1). The thought is that other inquiry is not directed toward an applicant's creditworthiness.

The creditor cannot discount the income of an applicant or an applicant's spouse solely because it is derived from part-time employment, but the probable continuity of such income may be considered. 12 C.F.R. § 202.5(c). Inquiries into the birth control practices and the child-bearing intentions of the applicant are forbidden. 12 C.F.R. § 202(d)(4). A lender may be fined for violating this law and a wrongfully rejected applicant may sue for damages.

The Act does not prohibit a lender from establishing valid credit criteria. The lender may, for example, inquire into the fact that the applicant has taken bankruptcy or lacks U.S. citizenship. *Nguyen v. Montgomery Ward & Co., Inc.,* 513 F. Supp. 1039 (N. Dist. Tex., 1981).

20.25(e)   Denial of Loan Application

A lender must advise a loan applicant of the denial of the application and give the applicant a statement of the reasons for the denial. 15 U.S.C. § 1691.

20.25(f)   False Applications

Borrowers are tempted to falsify their loan applications in order to get a loan or to get the loan at more favorable terms.

> **EXAMPLE:** A borrower states that it is making a 20 percent down payment when really the seller is receiving 10 percent in cash and taking back a second mortgage for 10 percent of the purchase price. Some buyers and sellers go so far as to have two sets of documents, one stating the form of the transaction as the lender wants to see it and the other stating the form that the transaction really takes.

> **EXAMPLE:** A borrower will state its intent to occupy the property when it has no real intent of living there.

These kinds of false statements are violations of state law and, if a federal instrumentality is involved, federal law. *See, e.g.,* 18 U.S.C. §§ 1010–1014; Ill. Rev. Stat. Ch. 38, § 17-1(C).

20.25(g)   Truth in Lending

The Federal Truth-in-Lending Act, 15 U.S.C. §§ 1601, *et seq.,* was enacted to give the consumer a disclosure of various credit terms to enable him or her to shop several lenders to obtain the best deal possible. The required disclosures include the annual percentage rate; the number, amount, and due dates of scheduled payments; the amount of any balloon payments; the conditions of refinancing; the amount of the late payment charge; a description of any security interest; whether after-acquired property will be subject to the security interest; a description of any prepayment penalty; and the amount of any escrow account required for the payment of taxes, insurance, and the like. 12 C.F.R. § 226.8. Special disclosures are also needed of the provisions of a variable rate or graduated payment mortgage.

Of course, all of the consumer or residential loans that are ARMs, SAMs, and the like must comply with additional and more complicated truth-in-lending disclosure requirements. 15 U.S.C. §§ 1601, *et seq.* The more complex the loan, the more extensive the disclosures must be. *See, e.g.,* 15 U.S.C. §§ 1637 & 1647 (which deal with variable-rate, balloon, negative amortization, and home equity loans). *See also* 12 C.F.R. § 226.5b (regarding home equity loans); 12 C.F.R. §§ 226.18, 19 & 20(c) (regarding variable-rate loans).

20.25(h)   Flood Insurance

The lender must determine whether the property is located in an area designated by the federal government as flood prone. If the community participates in the federal government flood program, flood controls on development (state and federal) will be in force and flood insurance will be available. Ordinary insurance does not cover flooding. It is risky to build or buy in such areas without obtaining flood insurance.

Most municipalities and counties base their flood plain development plans on the state's model ordinance for cities. The ordinance defines minimum state and federal guidelines for land-use planning and development in designated flood hazard areas. The ordinance provides the following:

1. Buildings may be constructed on permanent landfill in layers no greater than one foot deep before compaction.
2. The lowest floor (including basement) must be at or above the flood protection elevation (the elevation of the base flood plain plus one foot at any given location in a flood hazard area).
3. Landfill must be protected against erosion during flooding by vegetative cover and other erosion-protection implements.
4. Landfill must not adversely affect the flow of surface drainage from or onto neighboring properties.
5. Buildings may be elevated on crawl space, walls, stilts, piles, or other foundations.
6. Structural walls must have permanent openings (windows, doors) no more than one foot above the level of the lot.
7. Foundation and supports must be anchored and aligned in relation to flood flows and adjoining structures so as to minimize exposure to known hydrodynamic forces, such as current, waves, ice, and floating debris.
8. Areas below the flood protection elevation must be constructed of materials resistant to flood damage.
9. Electrical, heating, ventilation, plumbing, and air-conditioning systems, and utility meters must be placed at flood protection elevation.
10. Water and sewer pipes, electrical and telephone lines, and submersible pumps also must be placed at flood protection elevation.

20.26 Mortgage Forms and Practice

In the field of residential mortgage, both homes and apartments, mortgage loans are typically made on the FNMA/FHLMC uniform instruments. The diversity of forms that was prevalent several years ago has vanished. Moreover, the details of mortgage practice are set forth in the detailed servicer's guides—for example, those of FHLMC and FNMA. Through the use of these guides, standardized mortgages are originated for sale in the secondary market. This is the model that has been adopted in the capital markets as funds are raised for vast pools of residential and commercial mortgages.

To a very great extent, lenders today choose to use the FNMA/FHLMC form of mortgage and note, or some other form that has been approved by the conduit lending industry. This is done so that the loan may be immediately sold or placed into the secondary market or be available for sale in the future.

20.27 The Mortgage Note

At the loan closing, the borrower executes a number of loan documents, each having its own function. Chief among those documents is the mortgage note, the document that evidences the borrower's obligation to pay the loan amount. The note also sets out the economic terms of the debtor/creditor relationship, including the interest rate, the repayment timetable, and the nature of any personal liability that the borrower may have for the repayment of the debt obligation.

20.27(a) The Mortgage Note— Negotiability

If a note is drawn to meet certain technical requirements, it can obtain the legal status of negotiability. This means that it can pass from the original creditor to a holder in due course. While the debtor may have had some defenses against the original creditor, those defenses will not work against the holder in due course.

A problem is posed by the new mortgages where interest rates vary from time to time as selected indexes move up and down. It seems doubtful that those mortgage notes are negotiable, unless the state's law that controls the transaction has been amended to conform with a change in Article 3 of the Uniform Commercial Code to make these notes negotiable. *A. Alport & Son, Inc., v. Hotel Evans, Inc.,* 317 N.Y.S.2d 937 (1970). Many lenders are no longer concerned that the note be negotiable, being more concerned with the warranties and covenants made by the originating lender prior to placing the loan in the secondary market or securitized pool of loans. Tillman & Johnson, *Lender Litigation: Variable Interest Rates and Negotiability,* 27 Am. Bus. L.J. 121 (1989).

The negotiability concept has an interesting, if not forgotten, impact on the payment of the mortgage debt. Since the holder of a negotiable instrument takes free of the defenses that would be available against the original or prior payee or holder, and the note is transferred to a new holder in due course by transferring the physical note itself, any payment on the note should be accompanied by the exhibition of the note for the endorsement of the payment thereon. This rule applies to both the partial and final payment of a negotiable instrument. If the note has been assigned and the borrower makes the payment to the assignor, the assignee may demand that the full payment be made to the assignee. Dale A. Whitman, *Reforming the Law: The Payment Rule as a Paradigm,* 1998 B.Y.U. L. Rev. 1169 (1998). Of course, borrowers large and small, from the most unsophisticated consumers to the most sophisticated commercial entities do not require the production of the notes before making the payment. Real estate commerce would come to a screeching halt if this was done. Nonetheless, this rule would require the borrower to pay the assignee the payment made to the assignor after the assignment.

The rule is otherwise if the note secured by the mortgage is not a negotiable instrument. In that case, payment to the assignee is effective, unless the borrower had prior notice of the assignment of the note. Restatement (Third) of Property (Mortgages) § 5.5 (1997).

20.28 Parties to the Mortgage

The borrower is known as the mortgagor. The lender is known as the mortgagee. In general, the requirements relative to the grantor and grantee in a deed are applicable to the mortgagor and mortgagee in a mortgage. It is important that the names of the parties be given accurately and fully in the mortgage. The marital status of the mortgagor, as bachelor, spinster, or widower, should be recited. The same considerations that require the grantor's spouse to join in a deed require the mortgagor's spouse to join in a mortgage. A mortgage by a minor or an insane person is subject to the same objections that exist in the case of deeds. A mortgage by a corporation must be authorized by proper corporate resolutions, which should show that the money is being borrowed for proper corporate purposes.

20.29 Private Mortgage Insurance

As a result, private insurance companies have been formed to supplement governmental programs and furnish mortgage insurance for a premium paid by the borrower. Financial problems have affected this industry and, as with other forms of insurance, insureds must be concerned with the financial standing of their insurer. The secondary market (FNMA and FHLMC) has introduced requirements of such insurance in their lending guides.

20.30 Foreclosure Provisions and Power of Sale

Foreclosure provisions are usually included in the mortgage, and, in states permitting foreclosure by exercise of power of sale, the power of sale is fully set forth in the mortgage.

20.31 Waiver of Homestead and Dower

In some states, a mortgage on homestead land must include a clause releasing and waiving homestead rights. Similarly, a mortgage signed by the spouse of the mortgagor should contain a clause stating that the spouse thereby waives all dower and other spousal rights as against the mortgagee.

20.32 Execution

The mortgagor and spouse should sign the mortgage. Some states require that the word "SEAL" appear after their signatures. A corporation should always affix its corporate seal. In some states, witnesses are required. The mortgage should also be acknowledged and delivered to the mortgagee.

20.33 Recording

As a practical matter, a mortgage must be recorded, since an unrecorded mortgage is ineffective as to subsequent purchasers, mortgagees, and, in some states, judgment creditors who are ignorant of the existence of the mortgage. It is important that the mortgage be filed or recorded as soon after its execution as possible.

As a general rule, the priority of successive liens often is determined by priority of recording, the first mortgage recorded being a first lien on the land, the second mortgage recorded being a second lien, and so on. The importance of early recording thus becomes obvious, since foreclosure of a first mortgage will extinguish all junior liens, such as second mortgages.

In states that have mortgage taxes, the recorder will want proof that the tax was paid.

20.33(a) Master Mortgage

To save recording expenses, mortgagees sometimes use a *master mortgage*. A master mortgage is the lender's usual form of mortgage with none of the blanks filled in, or as executed and recorded in connection with a prior transaction. Thereafter, each mortgage recorded by the mortgagee simply refers to the book and page of the recorded master mortgage for the fine-print provisions, enabling the mortgagee to get all the necessary recordable data of each mortgage in a one-page document. Laws permitting this have been enacted in many states. Of course, the mortgagor executes the entire mortgage document, with only a part of the mortgage being recorded.

20.34 Debt— In General

For a mortgage to exist, there must be a debt for the mortgage to secure. Without the debt there is nothing to secure, and the mortgage has no effect. Ordinarily, the debt takes the form of an obligation to pay money, such as a promissory note or a bond, which may or may not be negotiable. This is not necessarily so, however, and the debt may be in the form of any contractual relation.

The mortgage lien is measured by the amount of the mortgage debt. Thus, if a mortgage recites a debt of $10,000, but actually only $5,000 is advanced, the mortgage only stands as security for a $5,000 debt. Likewise, the mortgage lien diminishes as the mortgage debt is reduced by payment. Thus, if a mortgage of $10,000 is paid down to $5,000, the mortgage lien is reduced accordingly, and if the mortgagee thereafter loans the mortgagor additional funds, these additional funds are not secured by the mortgage unless the mortgage contains a clause covering future advances.

20.34(a) Debt— History of Debt Payment Structure of Home Loans

Prior to the Great Depression, first mortgages on homes were usually payable in five years, with one principal note and ten interest coupons due semiannually. When the maturity date arrived, quite commonly the mortgagor made a nominal payment on principal, and the balance was extended. The extension agreement was recorded. The parties were not greatly concerned about ultimate repayment of the principal. Second mortgages were common.

They were used where the purchaser of the home lacked funds to make the required down payment. Many second mortgages were sold to individuals, who were eager investors because of the higher returns generally associated with second mortgages.

Following the crash of 1929, many mortgages went into foreclosure. Banks closed. Mortgage funds dried up. The Roosevelt administration put the FHA insurance program in place. With the FHA insurance, mortgage lenders could once more loan money safely on homes. The FHA insisted that the mortgage be amortized. Monthly payments were made, so that a constant reduction of the portion devoted to interest assured ultimate repayment of the principal. To be sure, few mortgages ran their full term, since homes sell before the loan amortizes the mortgage debt, at each sale the existing mortgage was commonly repaid through funds obtained by the purchaser on a new mortgage.

20.34(b)   Debt— Priority of Lien

Any discussion of mortgage debt inevitably involves questions of priority of the mortgage lien. Often, there will be two or more liens against the same property.

> **EXAMPLE:** Owner mortgages his property to Lender 1 in 1991 and then mortgages the same property to Lender 2 in 1992. If both mortgages are valid and both are properly and timely recorded, Lender 1's mortgage is a first lien, and, if Lender 1 is compelled to enforce it by foreclosure, Lender 1 will extinguish Lender 2's mortgage, which is a subordinate or inferior lien. Of course, Lender 2 has the right to pay Lender 1's mortgage to prevent this extinguishment and to foreclose for the amounts due on both mortgages. It is said, in such circumstances, that Lender 1 enjoys priority of lien. Lender 2's lien is subject to Lender 1's.

The same situation exists when the liens are of different kinds.

> **EXAMPLE:** Lender acquires a mortgage lien on the property in 1991. Creditor acquires a judgment lien on the same property in 1992. Mechanic acquires a mechanic's lien on the property in 1993. Normally, these liens have priority according to the time they attach to the land. First in time is first in right. There are, however, many exceptions to the rule.

20.34(c)   Debt— Description of Debt

A mortgage must in some way describe and identify the debt that it is intended to secure. T.C. Williams, *Omission of Amount of Debt in Mortgage or in Record Thereof (Including General Description Without Stating Amount) as Affecting Validity of Mortgage, Its Operation as Notice, or Its Coverage with Respect to Debts Secured*, 145 A.L.R. 369 (1943); Wayne F. Foster, Annotation, *Recorded Real Property Instrument as Charging Third Party with Constructive Notice of Provisions of Extrinsic Instrument Referred to Therein*, 89 A.L.R.3d 901, 937–39 (1979). The character and amount of the debt must be defined with reasonable certainty in order to preclude the parties from substituting debts other than those described. *Bowen v. Ratcliff,* 39 N.E. 860 (Ind. 1895). Otherwise, in some states, subsequent mortgagees, purchasers, or judgment creditors will acquire rights superior to those of the mortgage. 2 M. Merrill, *Merrill on Notice* § 1090 (1952); 5 Herbert Thorndike Tiffany, *Tiffany on Real Property* § 1407 (3d ed. 1939).

> **EXAMPLE:** Owner borrows $10,000 from Lender and gives Lender a promissory note as evidence of the debt and by which Owner agrees to repay the debt. To secure the loan, Owner gives Lender a mortgage, but the mortgage does not recite the amount of the loan. The mortgage is recorded. Thereafter, Creditor obtains a judgment against Owner. Creditor's judgment is a prior lien, coming in ahead of Lender's mortgage. *Bullock v. Battenhousen,* 108 Ill. 28 (Ill.1883). *See also Flexter v. Woomer,* 197 N.E.2d 161 (Ill. 1964).

The mortgage need not state the maturity date of the debt. 1 *Jones on Mortgages* 549, 559 (8th ed. 1928). *Contra Sullivan v. Ladden,* 125 A. 250 (Conn. 1924). However, it is advisable that it do so. Similarly, the mortgage need not state the interest rate. *Metropolitan Life Ins. Co. v. Kobbeman,* 260 Ill. App. 508 (1931).

Where the note provides for future advances, the mortgage should state the maximum amount of future advances that the mortgage will secure. *Northridge Bank v. Lakeshore Commercial Fin. Corp.,* 365 N.E.2d 382 (Ill. 1977).

Where future advances are secured by the mortgage, special title insurance endorsements must be obtained. The typical ALTA loan policy does not cover advances made by the lender after the policy date unless those endorsements are obtained.

20.34(d)   Debt— Terms of Repayment

Most mortgage financing of homes is governed today by some form of federal regulation that supersedes state regulation. The secondary market and securitization industry impose their own regulations and requirements on debt terms. FNMA, for example, wants the monthly payment to be payable on the first day of each month. In short, the old pre-Depression mortgages, drafted to suit the needs of particular institutions, have all but disappeared in the home loan field.

20.35   Description of the Mortgaged Property

An accurate description of the mortgaged land is of great importance. Even greater care must be exercised in this regard than in the case of deeds, since a purchaser usually goes into the possession of the land conveyed by the deed and thereby gives all the world notice of its rights. A mortgagee rarely goes into possession and therefore depends entirely on the recording of the mortgage to give subsequent purchasers and mortgagees notice of its rights.

When a mortgage is foreclosed, the mortgagee should be in a position to take over the mortgaged building as a functioning and operating unit. This is something to be considered at the time the mortgage is made. For example, if the building contains personal property necessary for its proper functioning, such as furniture in a furnished apartment building, some arrangement must be made to enable the mortgagee to take over these items in the event the mortgage is foreclosed. To accomplish this, it may be necessary to have the mortgagor execute a security agreement and related financing statement under the Uniform Commercial Code, thereby encumbering such personal property; for a real estate mortgage, although it covers fixtures, will not cover personal property, unless it also contains special language granting a security interest in the fixtures.

In the package method of financing, the home loan also finances the purchase of equipment, such as stoves, refrigerators, dishwashers, or washing machines, which are essential to the livability of the property. Following the legal description in the mortgage is a clause containing a general catchall enumeration of the common items and a provision reciting that all such items are fixtures and therefore part of the real estate. The package mortgage attempts to make specific articles fixtures by means of an agreement between the mortgagor and mortgagee, even though, in the absence of such agreement, the articles would be chattels. The practical advantages of this course are obvious. Installation of such equipment by the builder makes the house more salable. Moreover, it enables the prospective home buyer to finance the initial purchase of such equipment at a lower interest rate and over a longer term than if the purchases were made separately from a department store. Robert Kratovil, *Fixtures and the Real Estate Mortgage,* 97 U. Penn. L. Rev. 180, 210 (1948); 6 Kan. L. Rev. 66 (1957).

When the article is actually removed from the mortgaged premises and then sold to a bona fide purchaser, it is then, to all appearances, a chattel, and, in some states, such a purchaser will acquire good title to the article. If this were not the law, any purchaser of chattels would incur the risk of losing them if it should later develop that they were wrongfully removed from mortgaged land. In other states, the real estate mortgagee is permitted to reclaim such articles, even when it finds them in the possession of an innocent purchaser. Generally, a purchaser of such articles who buys them while they are still installed on the mortgaged land will not be protected. *First Mortgage Bond Co. v. London,* 244 N.W. 203 (Mich. 1932); *Dorr v. Dudderar, 88* Ill. 107 (1878).

Since it is by no means certain that, even with elaborate fine-print clauses, the real estate mortgage alone will afford the mortgagee protection against the removal of readily removable articles, mortgagees in commercial loan transactions insist upon a separate security agreement and financing statement under the Uniform Commercial Code. In other words, where chattels form a substantial part of the mortgage security, the mortgagor will give the mortgagee a security agreement, and both will execute a financing statement that will be filed with the appropriate chattel filings under the Uniform Commercial Code.

20.36   Interest   The mortgage should state the rate and time of payment of interest, though failure to do so will not invalidate the mortgage.

20.37(a)   Interest—Usury   At one time, most states had laws applicable to real estate secured loan transactions fixing the maximum rate of interest lenders may charge. Many states still have usury laws that are applicable to many forms of loan transactions. These laws, which find their origins in Old Testament times, were designed to protect the needy but unsophisticated borrower from crafty and knowledgeable lenders. Time and upward pressure of interest rates brought many exceptions to these laws.

There is no reason to protect knowledgeable and sophisticated borrowers, so exceptions were made for loans to corporations and businesses. There is likewise no need to protect the public from well-regulated, responsible financial institutions, so loans made by such lenders, such as banks, were exempted from the usury laws of some states. As market interest rates pushed upward against antiquated usury ceilings, state legislatures reacted by legislating higher interest rate limits or floating maximum rates that are set periodically by reference to various economic indicators.

The national mortgage market was a confusing hodgepodge of usury laws and exemptions. Mortgage funds in states with below-market limits on interest rates flowed to other states where higher yields were available. This artificial disruption of the availability of funds was harmful to potential home buyers in states with low interest rate ceilings and frustrated national housing programs and policies.

Finally, in 1980, the federal government reacted by preempting state usury laws to the extent that they apply to most first mortgages on residential real property. 12 U.S.C. § 1735F-7; 12 C.F.R. § 590. The institutions so preempted include all federally regulated institutions that lend on residential properties, so that virtually all home loans are preempted. There is no usury limit on these loans.

The federal law gave the states the right to choose to remain under state law. Some states have rejected the federal law, in whole or in part. A state may also limit certain charges (e.g., "points") on residential loans.

20.37(b)   Exceptions to the Federal Preemption   The federal statute that preempts state usury laws has no application to some state aspects of finance charges, such as late charges, prepayment charges, and attorneys' fees. It applies only to first mortgages, not second mortgages. It also applies to first liens on stock in a residential cooperative and to first liens on mobile homes. A simple assumption of an old mortgage is not affected by the federal law. Since the law covers federally insured lenders, it affects nearly all state banks and state-chartered thrift institutions.

20.38 Escrows   A subject of much litigation, legislation, and writing is the so-called *mortgage escrow* or *impound* that lenders establish to ensure payment of taxes and insurance premiums. For many years, this device was an effective and virtually unchallenged tool, which lenders used to ensure that necessary payments were made. In the context of residential loans, consumer groups took to the courtroom and statehouse to correct abuses that may have crept into the use of this device. The attack has been primarily aimed at attempting to force the lender to limit the size of or pay interest on the impounded amount. The judicial response has been almost universally that the lender does not have to pay interest absent a statute, regulation, or mortgage provision to the contrary. *Sears v. First Fed. Sav. & Loan Ass'n,* 275 N.E.2d 300 (Ill. 1971); *Tierney v. Whitestone Sav. & Loan Ass'n,* 373 N.Y.S.2d 724 (N.Y. 1974). *Contra Derentco, Inc. v. Benjamin Franklin Fed. Sav. & Loan Ass'n,* 577 P.2d 477 (Or. 1978). Ferdinand S. Tinio, Annotation, *Rights in Funds Representing "Escrow" Payments Made by Mortgagor in Advance to Cover Taxes or Insurance,* 50 A.L.R.3d 697 (1973). Borrowers then addressed their pleas to legislatures and found that the response was more favorable to the borrowers' situation. Perhaps the most significant factor in the ability of the legislature to respond was the fact that, as opposed to the courts that were called upon to act in the face of the contract binding upon the mortgagor and mortgagee, the legislation enacted takes prospective effect only, operating on transactions entered into after its effective date.

States have enacted various types of laws relating to such escrow accounts. Some laws require that lenders pay interest on the funds. *See* Cal. Civ. Code § 2943. Others limit the size of the impound, or provide that the borrower be allowed the option of pledging an interest-bearing savings account in lieu of the monthly escrow payment. 765 ILCS 910/1, *et seq.* The Real Estate Settlement Procedures Act falls into the category of those laws that limit the size of accounts held by lenders in connection with federally related mortgage loans. 12 U.S.C. § 2609.

Some creditors of borrowers have attempted without success to garnishee monies paid into these funds by borrowers. Robert Kratovil & Raymond J. Werner, *Modern Mortgage Law and Practice* § 25.34 (2d ed. 1981).

20.39 Real Estate Taxes   Especially in connection with parcels having an irregular shape, some question may arise as to whether the mortgaged land is identical with the land covered by a real estate tax. This is due to the fact that tax authorities attempt to shorten the description. A competent person must determine that the two descriptions cover the identical tract of land. Federal lenders want such proof. An endorsement can be obtained from the title company ensuring the identity of the land insured under the policy is the land covered by a tax parcel number and that no other tax numbers apply to the legal description of the mortgage.

Most mortgage companies contract with a tax service company. This company receives the tax bills and arranges for their payment. The contract for this service should make the service liable for any errors and fix a time limit for reimbursement. Many complaints have been made about errors by tax servicers. In this connection, it should be noted that many statutes allow the tax bill to be sent to the lenders, rather than the landowner. 35 ILCS 200/9-85; 35 ILCS 200/9-260; 35 ILCS 200/12-10.

20.40 Leases Antedating Mortgage   It is important to distinguish between the rights of a tenant under a lease made prior to the mortgage and those of a tenant under a lease made subsequent to the mortgage. When the lease is made subsequent to the mortgage, the mortgagee can, by foreclosing its mortgage, extinguish the rights of the tenant under the lease. When the lease antedates the mortgage, the mortgagee must respect the tenant's rights, and, regardless of foreclosure, the tenant cannot be evicted prior to the expiration of the lease, unless, of course, the tenant fails to pay its rent or has subordinated its interest to the mortgage. Here again, we have an application of the rule that "prior in time is prior in right."

Again, in title or intermediate theory states, if the lease antedates the mortgage, then immediately upon the mortgagor's default, the mortgagee may serve a demand upon the tenant that the tenant pay all rents to the mortgagee. Thereafter, the tenant must pay all rents to the mortgagee. *King v. Housatonic R.R. Co.,* 45 Conn. 226; L.R.A. (1915C) 200. Of course, the tenant may continue to pay rents to the mortgagor until such demand has been served upon it. In lien theory states, the mortgagee ordinarily is not entitled to make such a demand on the tenant. L.R.A. (1915C) 200.

20.41 Leases Subsequent to Mortgage

Obviously, a mortgagor cannot make any leases that will give the tenant greater rights than the mortgagor possesses. Most important, where the lease is subsequent to the mortgage, it is inferior to the mortgage, and the mortgagee can extinguish the lease if and when it forecloses the mortgage. Likewise, in title and intermediate states, the mortgagor has no right, absent statutory provisions to the contrary, to retain possession after default. Tenants who occupy by virtue of leases made after the making of the mortgage also have no right to retain possession of the premises after the mortgagor's default, and the mortgagee may evict such tenants. To avoid eviction, the tenant, upon the mortgagee's demand for possession, may agree to pay rent to the mortgagee, and the mortgagor will have no right to collect further rent from such tenant. *West Side Trust & Sav. Bank v. Lopoten,* 358 Ill. 631, 193 N.E. 462 (1934); *Del-New Co. v. James,* 111 N.J.L. 157, 167 A. 747 (1933); *Anderson v. Robbins,* 82 Maine 422, 19 A. 910 (1890). One disadvantage of this course of action is that it automatically terminates the lease, and the tenant becomes a tenant either from month to month or from year to year. *New York Life Ins. Co. v. Simplex Products Corp.,* 135 Ohio St. 501, 21 N.E.2d 585 (1939). *Gartside v. Outley*, 58 Ill. 210 (1871). If the lease is one favorable to the landlord, the mortgagee will prefer to have a receiver appointed, since in many states the receiver can hold the tenant to its lease.

In lien theory states, in the absence of a provision in the mortgage, the mortgagee is not entitled to collect rents even under leases made after the making of the mortgage. When the lease is favorable to the landlord, a mortgagee will attempt to preserve the lease, even though it wishes to consummate foreclosure of the mortgage. In some states, for example, a mortgagee may, if it elects, leave unaffected by the foreclosure a lease that was executed subsequent to the mortgage, and the mortgagee, on acquiring title by foreclosure, may hold the tenant on such lease. 109 A.L.R. 457. In other states, completion of the foreclosure automatically wipes out any lease made after the mortgage and thus relieves the tenant of further liability. 109 A.L.R. 455. In these states, there is nothing that the mortgagee can do to keep the lease alive after foreclosure.

Many lawyers feel that an express provision in the lease that it will survive foreclosure if the mortgagee desires will be valid, even as to a junior lease. Alternatively, the tenant and mortgagee might enter into a separate agreement that they will execute a new lease on the old terms if the old lease is extinguished by foreclosure. Or, as a further alternative, the mortgagee and lessee may sign a subordination under which the lease is made prior and superior to the mortgage. Bear in mind that many mortgage loans today are made in reliance on the financial strength and power of the tenant to draw other tenants and users to the property. A loss of such a tenant could be disastrous.

20.42 Possession and Rents

The difference in viewpoint between title theory and lien theory states is of greatest importance with respect to the mortgagee's right to the possession and rents of the mortgaged property. To illustrate the significance of this statement, let us list, in chronological order, some important dates in a defaulted mortgage transaction: (1) the date the mortgage is signed by the mortgagor; (2) the date the mortgagor defaults; (3) the date the mortgagee files its foreclosure suit; (4) the date of the foreclosure sale; and (5) the date the statutory redemption period expires and the mortgagee or some other party receives the deed under which it becomes the owner of the mortgaged property.

Let us first make broad generalizations and then list the particular points of difference that exist. In general, the title theory states regard the mortgage as retaining some of its early character; that is, they view it as a conveyance of the land, so that immediately on the signing of the mortgage, the mortgagee has the right to take possession of the property and collect the rents. On the other hand, lien theory states regard the mortgage as merely creating the right to acquire the land through foreclosure so that the mortgagor remains the full owner of the land with the right to possession and rents until the statutory redemption period has expired and the foreclosure deed has issued to the mortgagee. In other words, at its most extreme, this difference in point of view represents to the mortgagee the difference between dates (1) and (5) in the previous list, so far as the right to possession and rents is concerned. In title states, therefore, rents are a more readily realizable part of the mortgagee's security. In lien states, this is not the case.

Now let us analyze the situation in somewhat greater detail, from the point of view just expressed.

1. In a number of title theory states (e.g., Alabama, Maryland, and Tennessee), the mortgagee, immediately upon execution of the mortgage, has the right to take possession and collect the rents of the mortgaged property. *Darling Shop of Birmingham, Inc. v. Nelson Realty Co.,* 79 So. 2d 793 (Ala. 1953). The right exists even though the mortgage is silent on this point. There are two exceptions: (1) in recent times, laws have been passed in some title states giving the mortgagor the right of possession until default occurs; and (2) many mortgage forms used in title states give the mortgagor the right of possession until default.

2. In intermediate theory states (e.g., New Jersey, North Carolina, and Ohio), the mortgagor has the right of possession until the borrower defaults, but after default, the mortgagee has the right to take possession.

3. In lien theory states, in the absence of a contrary provision in the mortgage, the mortgagor is entitled to possession and rents at least until the foreclosure sale.

4. In some lien theory states, either by express provision in the mortgage or by a separate assignment of rents given at the time the mortgage is made, the mortgagor may give the mortgagee the right to take possession and collect rents as soon as a default occurs. Such provisions are valid. *Penn Mut. Life Ins. Co. v. Katz,* 297 N.W. 899 (Neb. 1941); Kinnison *v. Guaranty Liquidating Corp.,* 115 P.2d 450 (Cal. 1941); *Dick & Reuteman Co. v. Jem Realty Co.,* 274 N.W. 416 (Wis. 1937). However, some of these lien theory states make special rules as to owner-occupied homes. In New York, for example, a homeowner cannot be compelled to pay rent pending foreclosure. *Holmes v. Gravenhorst,* 188 N.E. 285 (N.Y. 1933).

5. In other lien theory states, the provisions described previously are considered void as against public policy. *Rives v. Mincks Hotel Co.,* 30 P.2d 911 (Okla. 1934); *Hart v. Bingman,* 43 P.2d 447 (Okla. 1935). Notice that it is the provision binding the mortgagor to give up possession at some future time when default occurs that is held void. The same agreement made after default is valid. The mortgagee is then called a *mortgagee in possession*.

6. In all states, if the mortgagor, after defaulting in its mortgage payments, voluntarily turns over possession to the mortgagee, the mortgagee has the legal right to remain in possession.

7. Whenever a mortgagee takes possession before it has acquired ownership of the property by foreclosure, the rents it collects must be applied in reduction of the mortgage debt once prop-

erty expenses are paid. A mortgagee does not become the owner of the property by taking possession. Foreclosure is still necessary.

8. Whenever a mortgagee has the right to possession and fails to exercise that right, allowing the mortgagor to remain in possession and to collect rents, the rents so collected belong to the mortgagor.

9. In many states, there is a statutory period of redemption. No general rule can be laid down as to the right of possession during this period, for each state has its own rule.

20.42(a)   Practical Aspects of the Problem

A mortgage lender seeks a regular return on a safe investment and does not wish to assume the responsibilities of management. A lender is most unlikely to make a loan that will require it to go into immediate possession of the land, and this right is, therefore, seldom exercised. On the mortgagor's default, however, it is imperative that prompt action be taken to seize the rents so that they will not be diverted to the mortgagor's use and not applied to property expenses and the mortgage debt. An eviction suit to enforce the mortgagee's right to possession is often a long, drawn-out affair, especially when the mortgagor is interposing all the legal obstacles available to it. However, if the mortgagee files a foreclosure suit, it might be able to have a receiver appointed. This is often the preferred course.

Courts differ as to the grounds for appointment of a receiver. Some say it is enough that the property is inadequate security for the mortgage debt. Other courts require a showing that the security is inadequate and that the mortgagor is insolvent. Still others appoint a receiver only when the property is in danger of destruction. W.A.E., Annotation, *Right of Mortgagee to Receiver*, 26 A.L.R. 33 (1923).

It is important to distinguish between possession problems related to a home and rent problems relating to commercial properties, such as multifamily properties, office buildings, and shopping centers. The lender who lends on the security of a shopping center makes its loan in reliance on the cash flow coming from rentals paid by high-credit tenants. If the project runs into trouble, the lender wants to step in at the earliest possible time to collect the rents and manage the property. To give the lender these powers, the mortgagor, at the time the mortgage is executed, also makes an assignment of leases and rents. Notice of this assignment may be given to existing tenants. The assignment is recorded, thus giving notice to subsequent tenants.

The assignment does not give the lender the right to begin collecting rents the moment the assignment is made. Usually, the assignment is absolute in form, but gives the borrower a license to collect the rents until a default occurs. This suits the lender just fine. The lender does not wish to step into the picture while things are going smoothly. But it does want the right to step in when the project runs into trouble. Thus, the lender's right to collect rents ripens when the assignment is *activated*. The mechanics of activation need not be discussed here. *See* Robert Kratovil & Raymond J. Werner, *Modern Mortgage Law and Practice,* 276 (2d ed. 1981).

Let us look, for example, at a fifteen-year lease of space in a shopping center. Certainly, this lease gives the landowner important rights, such as the right to collect rents for the duration of the lease term. These rights can be transferred to others. Suppose the landowner makes a mortgage on its shopping center to a lender. Simultaneously, the landowner assigns the rights under the lease to the lender. Now the lender has two sets of rights, the right to foreclose the mortgage and acquire the shopping center if default occurs and the right to collect the rents that have been assigned. In a regional shopping center, the rents accruing on the numerous leases amount to a huge sum of money.

Let us look, then, at the way in which such an assignment affects the lender's right to rents.

1. In most lien theory states, an assignment of rents enables the mortgagee to reach the rents accruing prior to foreclosure sale and to treat them as part of the security for its debt. This gives the mortgagee in a lien theory state virtually as favorable a position with regard to rents as the mortgagee has in title and intermediate states.

2. Since the assignment does not contemplate that the mortgagee will begin collecting rents immediately upon the signing of the assignment, but only after a default occurs, the assignment is inoperative until it is activated by some action of the mortgagee. *Ivor B. Clark Co. v. Hogan, 296* F. Supp. 398 (S.D. N.Y. 1968); 2 Garrard Glenn, *Mortgages,* 940 (1943); 59 C.J.S. *Mortgages* § 317. Rents collected by the mortgagor before the assignment is activated belong to the mortgagor. *Sullivan v. Rosson,* 223 N.Y. 217, 119 N.E. 405 (1918).

3. Everywhere, the assignment is properly activated if, after default and pursuant to the assignment, the mortgagor consents to collection of the rent and the tenants begin paying rent to the mortgagee.

4. In title and intermediate theory states, the assignment is activated on default by the mortgagee's serving notice on the tenants to pay rent to the mortgagee. The mortgagor's consent is unnecessary. *Randal v. Jersey Mortgage Inv. Co.,* 306 Pa. 1, 158 A. 865 (1932); *Grannis-Blair Audit Co. v. Maddux,* 167 Tenn. 297, 69 S.W.2d 238 (1934). Frequently, however, the mortgagor and mortgagee make conflicting demands upon the tenants, and the issue must be resolved by a court, which may prefer to appoint a receiver. Robert K. Lifton, *Real Estate in Trouble: Lender's Remedies Need an Overhaul,* 31 Bus. Law. 1927, 1932 (1976). Where the mortgagee is a substantial financial institution, it can usually overcome the tenant's fears about being liable for rent to the landlord by offering the tenant an indemnity agreement.

5. In some lien theory states, the assignment can be activated in the same manner as in title theory states. *Kinnison v. Guaranty Liquidating Corp.,* 115 P.2d 450 (Cal 1941).

6. In other lien theory states, as has been stated, the assignment can be activated only by the mortgagee's filing a foreclosure suit and applying for the appointment of a receiver, *Dick & Reuteman Co. v. Jem Realty Co.,* 274 N.W. 416 (Wis. 1937); *Hall v. Goldsworthy,* 14 P.2d 659 (Kan. 1932); *State C. & Hall v. Goldsworthy,* 14 P.2d 659 (Kan. 1932), or obtaining possession of the property. *Lincoln Crest Realty, Inc. v. Standard Apartment Dev.,* 211 N.W.2d 501 (Wis. 1973). Of course, these same steps will serve to activate an assignment in a title or intermediate state.

7. Rents collected by the mortgagee under an activated assignment may be applied to taxes, repairs, insurance, and, in most states, the mortgage debt.

8. Whenever a mortgagee acts under an activated assignment, it does not destroy existing leases, as sometimes occurs when a mortgagee takes possession under its mortgage. An assignment preserves valuable leases.

9. A mortgagee acting under an assignment is accountable to the mortgagor only for rents actually collected.

10. When a mortgagee who holds an assignment of rents sells and assigns its mortgage, it should also assign the assignment of rents to the assignee of the mortgage.

The bankruptcy courts have become the battlefield for the contest over rents of income-producing property when the borrower goes into default. In *Butner v. United States,* 440 U.S. 48 (1979), the U.S. Supreme Court held that the secured creditor's right to the rents and profits of the property is to be determined under applicable nonbankruptcy state law. This is easy to say but difficult to analyze.

Many bankruptcy courts hold that even where the assignment of leases and rents is in a separate document and is absolute in form, giving the borrower only a license until default to collect and apply the rents, the interest of the lender has not been sufficiently perfected. *Saline State Bank v. Mahloch,* 834 F.2d 690 (8th Cir. 1987). These courts require that the lender take additional steps to perfect its rights in the rents. *In re Raleigh/Spring Forest Apartment Assoc.,* 118 B.R. 42 (Bankr. E.D. N.C. 1990). Some require that the lender go so far as to actually have a receiver appointed or to be in possession of the property collecting rents as the mortgagee in possession prior to the filing of the bankruptcy. *Comerica Bank-Illinois v. Harris Bank Hinsdale, as Trustee*, 673 N.E.2d 380 (Ill. App. 1996); *In re 1726 Washington, D.C. Partners*, 120 B.R. 1 (Bankr. D.C. 1990); *In re Gelwicks*, 81 B.R. 445 (Bankr. N.D. Ill. 1987). Other courts have allowed the absolute nature of the assignment of rents to control. *In re Galvin*, 120 B.R. 767 (Bankr. Vt. 1990).

Whatever the local courts may hold, it is usually in the lender's best interest to take prompt action to enforce its right to rents when the borrower defaults. Too often the lender allows the borrower to continue to take the income stream of the property, diverting it to other uses while the borrower decides what to do. Negotiations drag on while the lender gets nothing and perhaps prejudices its position. While the lender must be careful to act in good faith and within the provisions of the loan documents, delay usually hurts more than helps the lender. Patrick A. Randolph, Jr., *Recognizing Lenders' Rents Interests in Bankruptcy*, 27 Real Prop. Prob. & Tr. L.J. 281 (1992); Patrick A. Randolph, Jr., *When Should Bankruptcy Courts Recognize Lenders' Rents Interests?*, 23 U.C. Davis L. Rev. 833 (1990); Sutin, *Assignment of Leases and Rents in Mortgage Financing with Form*, 6#6 Pract. R.E. Lawyer 23 (Nov. 1990).

With respect to the language of the assignment, some suggestions might be pertinent:

1. It should be a document separate from the mortgage. *Harris v. Lester*, 54 N.Y.S. 864 (1898); *Franzen v. G.R. Kinney Co.*, 259 N.W. 850 (Wis. 1935); Note, 50 Harv. L. Rev. 1322 (1937). After all, foreclosure of the mortgage extinguishes the mortgage. And, there are decisions holding that the assignment of rents clause in the mortgage is meaningless. *Myers v. Brown*, 92 N.J. Eq. 348, 112 A. 844, *aff'd* 115 A.2d 926 (1921). It should assign the mortgagor's interest in the reversion and all existing leases and the interest of the mortgagor, or its assignee, in leases that may be executed in the future by the mortgagor or its assignees. Existing leases of any importance should be specifically set forth in the assignment. The assignment should merely give the mortgagor the privilege of collecting rent until default. Careful draftsmanship is very important. The courts make the distinction between a pledge of the rents as additional security and an absolute assignment effective in operation upon default. *In re Ventura-Louise Properties*, 490 F.2d 1141 (9th Cir. 1974).

   A typical clause would provide that notwithstanding anything set forth in the assignment, the assignment is a present assignment of rents with the understanding that the borrower has permission to collect the rents and revenues of the property and manage the property the same as if the assignment had not been given. This permission or license lasts only so long as the borrower shall not be in default with respect to the payment of principal or interest, or in the performance of any other obligation to be performed under the loan documents. The permission given to the borrower terminates automatically on the occurrence of default in the payment or performance of the borrower under the loan documents. In some states, the courts have held, quite erroneously, that such an assignment is not entitled to be recorded. B. Glenn, Annotation, *Business Interruption or Use and Occupancy Insurance*, 83 A.L.R.2d 885 (1962). In these states, the mortgage should make specific reference to the accompanying assignment of rents and, for greater safety, state that all of the terms thereof are incorporated in the mortgage.

2. The mortgage and the assignment of rents should be completely consistent in their provisions. While this is rather obvious, it is not always the case in practice. In addition, the assignment of rents in both the separate document and the mortgage should allow the mortgagee to enforce its rights under the assignment without necessarily enforcing its rights under the mortgage. In this way, if the law otherwise allows, the lender may be able to obtain the rents and profits of the property without foreclosure.

3. The assignment should include the right to use and possession of furniture, appliances, and so forth. While such a provision will be helpful, neither a rent assignment nor the appointment of a receiver is a substitute for a security agreement and financing statement under the

Uniform Commercial Code. If there is valuable personal property on the mortgaged premises, for example, a hotel, the mortgagee may not have the legal right to the possession of such personal property unless it has a perfected personal property security interest.

4. The assignment should include the right to operate the business and to take possession of books and records, stationery, promotional material, and so forth.

5. The assignment should confer the right to apply rents to the payments on furniture bought on credit, to insurance premiums on personal property, and other property expenses. If the lender takes the rents and revenues of the property and does not apply them to property expenses, the property will deteriorate.

6. The assignee should be given the right to apply rents to the mortgage debt. Otherwise, some states limit application of rents collected to taxes and maintenance. *Western Loan & Bldg. Co. v. Mifflin,* 297 P. 743 (Wash. 1931).

7. The document should provide that the assignee shall not be accountable for more monies than it actually receives from the mortgaged premises, nor shall it be liable for failure to collect rents. The assignment should allow the lender to take certain actions, such as the enforcement of the owner's rights against defaulting tenants or performing the landlord's obligations under the leases, but not obligate the lender to take those actions. The last thing a lender wants in a defaulted loan situation is liability to the borrower for the failure to take actions or exercise the rights that the assignment gave to the lender.

8. In commercial properties, the document should forbid any cancellation or modification of leases by the landowner and should also forbid any prepayment of rent except the normal prepayment of monthly rent on the first of the month. Obviously, such a provision is not appropriate in multifamily properties. In any type of property, the mortgagee may wish to approve the form of lease. If so, the assignment should so provide.

9. Authority should be given to the assignee to sign the name of the mortgagor on all papers and documents in connection with the operation and management of the premises.

10. The assignment should provide that any assignee of the assignment shall have all the powers of the original lender.

11. It should contain a recital that (1) all rents due to date have been collected and no concessions granted and (2) no rents have been collected in advance.

12. It should provide that the assignee may execute new leases, including leases that extend beyond the redemption period.

13. Compliance with the UCC filing requirements is not necessary. *In re Bristol Assoc., Inc.,* 505 F.2d 1056 (3rd Cir. 1974). *In re Remcor, Inc.,* 186 B.R. 629, 635 (Bankr. W.D. Pa. 1995).

Of course neither an assignment of rents nor any other device can make a good lease out of a bad one.

EXAMPLE: A shopping center lease to a department store provides that if 5 percent or more of the parking lot is condemned, the tenant may terminate the lease. This is a key lease, providing revenue for retirement of the mortgage and shopping traffic to support the business of the other stores. From the lender's perspective, this provision should be amended, because if 5 percent or more of the parking lot is condemned, for example, for a street widening, and the tenant terminates the lease, sales at the other stores will dry up, and the mortgage will go into default.

If the lease provides for a security deposit by the tenant with the landlord, an assignment of leases and rents standing alone gives the mortgagee no right to the security deposit. *Anuzis v. Gotowtt,* 248 Ill. App. 536 (1928); *Keusch v. Morrison,* 240 App. Div. 112, 269 N.Y.S. 169 (1934); 52 C.J.S. *Landlord and Tenant* § 473. Specific language should be included in the assignment transferring all rights in security deposits.

20.42(b)   Assignment of Leases and Rents—Prepayment of Rent—Rent Reduction—Lease Cancellation

A problem of considerable importance is the extent to which a receiver or a mortgagee entering into possession is bound by rent reductions, prepayments of rents, and lease cancellations effected by the mortgagor for a cash consideration. Such agreements are standard devices by which hard-pressed mortgagors pocket the future earning capacity of the property and deliver to the mortgagee the economically empty shell of the mortgaged asset. Again, differences exist between title theory and lien theory states. The following are some of the applicable rules:

1. In title and intermediate theory states, when the lease is made subsequent to the mortgage, the mortgagee is not bound by advance rent payments made by the tenant to the mortgagor, and upon appointment of a receiver or the mortgagee's taking possession of the land, the tenant will nevertheless have to pay rent thereafter to such receiver or mortgagee, even though the tenant has already paid its rent in advance to the mortgagor. This rule follows from the rule that recording of the mortgage and assignment of leases and rents gives all the world, including subsequent tenants, notice of the mortgagee's rights, and these rights include the right to take possession on default. This rule is of special importance to a tenant who pays a large sum of money for the privilege of receiving a lease, for example, a tenant in a cooperative apartment, a tenant of commercial space who pays a large "bonus" for receiving its lease, or a tenant who plans to make substantial investments in alterations in reliance on its lease.

2. In title and intermediate theory states, if the lease antedates the mortgage, recording of the mortgage does not give the tenant notice of the mortgagee's rights, for recording of the mortgage gives notice only to those persons who acquire rights in the property after recording of the document. The question therefore arises if the tenant, acting in good faith and in ignorance of the mortgage, prepays its rent to the mortgagor, and the mortgagor thereafter defaults, is this prepayment binding on the mortgagee, or must the tenant pay its rent again to the mortgagee? Some cases hold for the mortgagee and some for the tenant. Annotation, 1916 D Ann. Cas. 200; 55 L.R.A. (N.S.) 233; 2 Leonard A. Jones, *Jones on Mortgages,* 362 (8th ed. 1928). Arguably the best rule is that no abnormal prepayment of rent is good against the mortgagee. 2 Garrard Glenn, *Mortgages,* 952 (1943). The mortgagee can protect itself at the time the mortgage is signed by procuring an assignment of all existing leases and giving tenants notice at that time of their rights under the assignment.

3. In many lien theory states, the mortgagee is bound by advance payments of rents made in good faith by the tenant to the mortgagor, and when the mortgagee's receiver takes possession, it will find itself unable to collect any rents from the tenant. *Smith v. Cushatt,* 199 Iowa 690, 202 N.W. 548 (1925); *Kelley/Lehr & Assoc., Inc. v. O'Brien,* 551 N.E. 2d 419 (Ill. App. 1990). *Ottman v. Cheney,* 204 Wis. 56, 234 N.W. 325 (1931).

4. But even in lien theory states, following the rule stated in No. 3, if, at the time the mortgage is made, the mortgagee obtains from the mortgagor an assignment of rents and leases and notifies the tenants thereof, the mortgagee will not be bound by any advance payments of rent made by the tenant to the mortgagor. Also, no rent reduction granted by the mortgagor after the tenant has notice of this assignment will be effective. *Franzen v. G.R. Kinney Co.,* 218 Wis. 53, 259 N.W. 850 (1935).

5. Where, at the time of making the mortgage, the mortgagor, by a separate instrument, assigns an existing lease to the mortgagee, and the lessee is notified of the assignment, the tenant and mortgagor cannot thereafter cancel the lease or reduce the rent so far as the mortgagee is concerned. On the mortgagee's taking possession, or on the appointment of a receiver, the tenant can be held to its lease. *Metropolitan Life Ins. Co. v. W.T. Grant Co.,* 321 Ill. App. 487, 53 N.E.2d 255 (1944); *Mercantile & Theatres Properties v. Stanley Co.,* 346 Pa. 343, 30 A.2d 136 (1943); *Franzen v. G.R. Kinney Co.,* 218 Wis. 53, 259 N.W. 850 (1935); *Darling Shop of Birmingham v. Nelson Realty Co.,* 262 Ala. 495, 79 So. 2d 793 (1954). If there is no assignment of rents, and the lease is prior to the mortgage, a cancellation of the lease made by the mortgagor and lessee may be *valid. Metropolitan Life Ins. Co. v. W.T. Grant Co.,* 321 Ill. App. 487, 53 N.E.2d 255 (1944).

6. The courts are less likely to be sympathetic toward advance payments of rent made pursuant to a conspiracy entered into between the mortgagor and the tenant in an effort to deprive the mortgagee of the rents. *Boteler v. Leber,* 112 N.J. E.Q. 441, 164 A. 572 (1933).

7. The courts are also very unsympathetic toward last-minute rent reductions granted by the mortgagor to the tenant on the eve of foreclosure. *First Nat'l. Bank v. Gordon,* 287 Ill. App. 83, 4 N.E.2d 504 (1936).

8. In an effort to attract mortgage money to the state, various states that previously held views hostile to the mortgagee's right to rents (e.g., Minnesota, Oregon, and Washington), have enacted laws validating the assignment of leases and rents. Each such statute must be examined to determine what qualifications it has attached to the mortgagee's rights. The Minnesota statute followed the suggestions expressed in Note, *Proposed Changes in Minnesota Mortgage Law,* 50 Minn. L. Rev. 331 (1965). *See also In re Federal Shopping Way Inc.,* 457 F.2d 176 (9th Cir. 1972) (discussing Oregon and Washington statutes).

Recent securitized lending transactions call for "lock-box" arrangements under which tenants are notified to pay their rent directly to the lender, with the lender then giving to the borrower any amounts by which regularly scheduled rental payments exceed debt service. Since the tenants are under notice that the rent should be paid to the lender through the lock-box, the risk to the lender that advance rental payments will be made to the borrower is greatly reduced.

**20.43 Acceleration—
Default—Curing**

The mortgage and mortgage note usually provide that in case of any default, the entire principal sum shall become immediately due and payable. This clause is known as the *acceleration clause.* If it is not present, the lender must file separate foreclosure suits as each installment of the mortgage debt falls due and is not paid. Obviously, the acceleration clause is one of the most important provisions of the mortgage.

There are two kinds of acceleration clauses, automatic and optional. The theory of the automatic clause is that the happening of the event, all by itself and without any action on the part of the lender, advances the maturity of the debt. The optional clause, as its name implies, merely allows the lender to call the debt due. The latter form is preferable because it obviates problems caused by accidental or minor defaults while it gives the lender the ability to protect its interest.

We usually think of acceleration in terms of payment-type defaults, but mortgages allow acceleration in the event of nonmonetary defaults. Courts have enforced these clauses, allowing a lender to accelerate because the borrower has failed to perform the nonmonetary obligations imposed upon it under the mortgage. Examples include the mortgagor's failure to keep a building in repair, or failure to keep insurance in force.

The operation of the acceleration clause upon the borrower's default may bring about a harsh result. Some courts, even when confronted with minor deviations caused by the borrower's mistake or inadvertence, find themselves powerless to avoid the strict application of the mortgage provisions. Other courts, finding themselves not so hamstrung, get around the strict application of the language of the loan documents, either by holding its operation to be unconscionable in the given instance or by deeming some act of the mortgagee to have negated the impact of the language. *Continental Bank v. Eastern Ill. Co.,* 37 Ill. App. 3d 148, 334 N.E.2d 102 (1975); Robert R. Rosenthal, *The Role of Courts of Equity in Preventing Acceleration Predicated upon a Mortgagor's Inadvertent Default,* 22 Syracuse L. Rev. 897 (1971).

EXAMPLE: Where an acceleration is declared only because of the mortgagor's failure to pay real estate taxes, the courts will allow the mortgagor to cure this default before foreclosure. *Kaminski v. Longon Pub Inc.,* 301 A.2d 769 (N.J. 1973); G.S.G., Annotation, *Time Within*

Which Taxes May Be Paid to Prevent Operation of Acceleration Clause in Mortgage, 31 A.L.R. 731 (1924).

> **EXAMPLE:** Acceptance of past-due interest payments may operate as a waiver of the mortgagor's right to accelerate upon a prior default. E.J. Spires, Annotation, *Acceptance of Past Due Interest as Waiver of Acceleration Clause in Mortgage or Note,* 97 A.L.R.2d 997 (1964). Acceptance of late payments will not, however, prevent the lender from accelerating the balance due and otherwise enforcing its rights if the borrower defaults in the performance of its other obligations, such as the payment of real estate taxes. *Alderman v. Davidson,* 933 P.2d 365 (Or. 1997).

It is clear that consumerist, proborrower judicial attitudes have no use for the older decisions. Courts will set accelerations aside when the lender's actions are unconscionable. *Fed. Home Loan Corp. v. Taylor,* 318 So. 2d 203 (Fla. App. 1976); *Miller v. Pac. First Fed. Sav. & Loan Ass'n,* 545 P.2d 546 (Wash. 1976); *Streets v. MGIC Mortgage. Corp.,* 378 N.E.2d 915 (Ind. App. 1978). In other instances, courts have refused to follow the letter of the acceleration clause.

For example, a mortgage and note may provide that, in case of default, the mortgagee could declare an acceleration "without notice to the mortgagor." The court set aside an acceleration declared without notice to the mortgagor. *White v. Turbidy,* 183 S.E.2d 363 (Ga. 1971). This is contrary to earlier decisions on this point. There is, however, a strong trend of statutes and case law to require such a notice. In effect, this gives the mortgagor an opportunity to cure defaults. A mortgagor must be given notice of an intended acceleration and a reasonable time to cure defaults. *Haase v. Blank,* 187 N.W. 669 (Wis. 1922). Some states allow the foreclosure complaint to stand as notice of the mortgagee's election to accelerate, *Home Fed. Sav. & Loan Ass'n v. LaSalle Nat'l Bank,* 264 N.E.2d 704 (Ill. 1970), but better practice is to give formal notice. Such notice is required by statute when foreclosure is by power of sale, *Crow v. Heath,* 516 S.W.2d 225 (Tex. App. 1974). *Contra S & G Inv., Inc. v. Home Fed. Sav. & Loan Ass'n,* 505 F.2d 370 (D.C. Cir. 1974).

> **EXAMPLE:** A mortgagee had been in the habit of accepting tardy payments. The court held that it could not accelerate without giving the mortgagor a reasonable opportunity to pay. *Stinemeyer v. Wesco Farms, Inc.,* 487 P.2d 65 (Or. 1971).

Legislatures in California, Colorado, Illinois, Minnesota, New York, Oregon, and other states have passed laws that, within defined time limits, give the borrower the right to cure defaults by paying the sums necessary to make the mortgagee whole. Lenders operating under the federal usury preemption are required to give the borrower at least thirty days notice of intention to accelerate. *Quiller v. Barclays Am. Credit,* 727 F.2d 1067, 764 F.2d 1400, 1404 (11th Cir. 1984).

One important question relates to the problem of the mortgagee's rights under Chapter 13 of the Bankruptcy Code, a provision very commonly used by individuals who hope to get back on their feet and ultimately take care of their debts. First of all, the mere filing of the bankruptcy petition operates as a "stay" or prohibition against further prosecution of the foreclosure. At this point, can the bankruptcy judge "unaccelerate" the mortgage debt? The decisions are in total confusion. Some say that the bankruptcy court cannot "deaccelerate" at all. Others say the bankruptcy court can "deaccelerate" at any time before judgment of foreclosure has been entered. David J. Oliveiri, Annotation, *Right of Debtor to "De-Acceleration" of Residential Mortgage Indebtedness Under Chapter 13 of the Bankruptcy Code,* 67 A.L.R. Fed. 238 (1984). Other decisions say the court can deaccelerate at any time before foreclosure sale. 67 A.L.R. Fed. 217, *supra*. Others say the court can deaccelerate after sale and during the redemption period. 67 A.L.R. Fed. 217, 240, *supra*. All agree that there can be no deacceleration after ownership has vested in the foreclosure purchaser. 67 A.L.R. Fed. 236.

20.43(a)
Acceleration—
Late Payment

If the mortgage specifies a period after which a "late payment" charge is imposed, a payment made before that period expires is timely and prevents acceleration. *Baypoint Mortgage v. Crest Trust,* 214 Cal. Rptr. 531 (Cal. App. 1985).

20.44 Assignment
of Mortgage

In the past, mortgage loans were originated by a lender and kept in that lender's portfolio until final payment and release. That is not the case today. Most loans are sold into the secondary market or securitized with financial institutions or others taking ultimate ownership of the loans as an investment. Indeed, many of these secondary market transactions involve investors who acquire a fractional interest in a loan or pool of loans.

The manner in which the transfer may be accomplished depends upon whether the mortgage in question is a deed of trust or a regular mortgage. A deed of trust is usually given to secure a negotiable note that passes from hand to hand, very much as money. Such a note may be payable to the bearer. In that case, merely handing the note to the purchaser will be sufficient to transfer title to the note. Endorsement is unnecessary. If the note is payable to the order of a named entity, that person must endorse the note over to the purchaser. In the case of a deed of trust securing negotiable notes, a sale of the mortgage is affected by properly transferring the notes by delivery or endorsement, depending on the character of the note.

In the case of a regular mortgage, it is necessary to execute an assignment, which is a brief form reciting that the mortgagee, the assignor, transfers and assigns the mortgage and mortgage note to the purchaser, the assignee. The mortgage is identified by a recital of the names of the parties to the mortgage, its date, the recording date, the recording information, and so on. The assignment should be signed by the mortgagee, acknowledged, delivered to the assignee, and recorded. The mortgage note, too, should be endorsed or delivered to the assignee along with the original mortgage. In today's financial world, the frequency of assignment of mortgages is clogging recorders' offices across the country. The recording cost and paper handling mechanics cause some lenders to simply not record the assignment and run the risk that something irregular will happen.

A project is underway to help address this issue. A group of the largest secondary mortgage market members has formed the Mortgage Electronic Registration System (MERS) to facilitate mortgage assignments. With MERS in place, the mortgage will be assigned of record to MERS who will then keep track of the owner of the beneficial interest in the mortgage and the note that the mortgage secures. Transfers of those interests will be done on MERS accounting records and not in the public records.

The mortgage cannot be assigned except in connection with a sale of the mortgage debt. The reason for this is that the mortgage is incidental to and exists only for the purpose of securing payment of the debt. A person who does not own the mortgage debt can have no reason for obtaining the mortgage, and any attempt to assign the mortgage without a transfer of the debt is a nullity. *Commercial Products Corp. v. Briegel,* 242 N.E.2d 317 (Ill. App. 1968). The assignee of the mortgage must insist on receiving the mortgage note, since if the mortgagee has already transferred the mortgage note to someone else, it can no longer make a valid assignment of the mortgage.

On the other hand, whatever is sufficient to transfer the mortgage debt will transfer a mortgage given to secure it. This is because the debt secured by the mortgage is the principal thing and the mortgage is a mere security for its payment. Thus, if a regular mortgage secures a note, its transfer without an assignment of the mortgage will give the transferee the right to foreclose the mortgage. As a practical matter, for the assignee's protection, it is necessary to obtain an assignment of the mortgage. The reason for this is that in the case of a deed of trust securing negotiable notes, everyone is supposed to know that it is likely that the notes will be sold. However, in the case of a regular mortgage securing a note payable to the mortgagee, unless an assignment of the mortgage is filed in the recorder's office, subsequent purchasers or mortgagees of the mortgaged premises are entitled to assume that the mortgagee continues to hold the mortgage note.

> **EXAMPLE:** Owner executed a regular mortgage to Lender 1 to secure a note payable to Lender's order. Lender 1 endorsed the note to Assignee but no assignment of the mortgage was recorded. Thereafter, Owner sold the mortgaged land to Lender 1, and Lender 1 entered a satisfaction of the mortgage on the public records. Lender 1 then mortgaged the land to Lender 2. It was held that Lender 2's mortgage was a first mortgage on the land, since when Lender 2 took the mortgage on the land, the earlier mortgage appeared from the public records to have been released by the apparent owner thereof. *Bowling v. Cook,* 39 Iowa 200 (1874).

When the mortgage secures a nonnegotiable note, a purchaser of the mortgage takes it subject to all defenses to which it was liable in the hands of the original mortgagee. *Holly Hill Acres, Ltd. v. Charter Bank,* 314 So. 2d 209 (Fla. App. 1975). This means that if the original mortgagee has been guilty of fraud or some other conduct that would make it impossible for it to foreclose the mortgage, any person to whom it sells the mortgage will also be unable to foreclose.

> **EXAMPLE:** Owner mortgages its land to Lender to secure a nonnegotiable note for $5,000, but Lender never pays out the money to Owner. Lender sells the mortgage to Assignee. Assignee will be unable to foreclose the mortgage.

In time, American mortgage bankers began the experiment of having the mortgage secure a negotiable note. The experiment proved highly successful. In all states except Illinois, Minnesota, and Ohio, it is now the rule that *a holder in due course* of the negotiable note secured by a mortgage, that is, one who buys the note and mortgage in good faith before the debt is overdue and without knowledge of any infirmities, takes the mortgage as well as the note, free from defenses that would have been available to the mortgagor against the original mortgagee. The theory is that negotiable notes, like money, should pass freely from hand to hand, without the necessity of any inquiry by purchasers as to the possible invalidity of the paper. And, since the mortgage is security for the note, it should enjoy the same protection that the law accords to the note.

> **EXAMPLE:** Owner gave Lender a mortgage securing a negotiable note for $50,000 but never received any money from Lender. Lender sold the note and mortgage to Assignee before the due date of the note. Assignee can foreclose the mortgage even though Owner never received the mortgage money. As an innocent purchaser of a negotiable note, Assignee is protected against any defenses that existed between Owner and Lender.

A purchaser of a mortgage can also be protected against unknown infirmities existing as between the mortgagor and the original mortgagee by insisting that it be furnished a statement signed by the mortgagor stating that the mortgagor has no defenses to the enforcement of the mortgage. This document is variously called a *waiver of defenses, estoppel certificate, no set-off certificate,* or *declaration of no defenses.* Under standard mortgage practice, it is addressed to "all whom it may concern" and is signed by the mortgagor at the time the mortgage is signed.

The practical effect of a waiver of defenses is to give the assignee a legally enforceable mortgage even though the mortgage does not secure a negotiable note and the mortgagee could not have successfully foreclosed. For example, if the mortgagee had paid out no money or had received payment in full, it could not foreclose. But an assignee who receives a waiver of defenses can foreclose, since the assignee received the mortgagor's written assurance that the mortgage is valid and enforceable. 59 C.J.S. *Mortgages* § 531.

> **EXAMPLE:** Owner gave Lender a mortgage securing a note for $50,000, but never received any money from Lender. Lender sold the note and mortgage to Assignee before the due date of the note. Lender also delivered to Assignee a waiver of defenses signed by Owner. Assignee can foreclose the mortgage even though Owner never received the mortgage money. As an innocent purchaser relying on a waiver of defenses, Assignee is protected against any defenses that existed between Owner and Lender.

Before purchasing a mortgage, one should always check the public records for any prior recorded assignment of the mortgage, since, in many states, where there are two or more assignments of the mortgage by the mortgagee, the first recorded assignment prevails. The assignee should also obtain the mortgagee's evidence of title, assignment of chattel security agreements, if any, and other such papers.

The assignee of a mortgage may foreclose for the full amount due on the mortgage even though he or she purchased at a discount. 2 Leonard A. Jones, *Jones on Mortgages* § 997 (8th ed. 1928).

20.44(a) Notice of Assignment

The purchaser of a note secured by either a regular mortgage or deed of trust should always give personal notice to the mortgagor that it has purchased such note. If it fails to do so, and the mortgagor afterward in good faith makes a payment to the original mortgagee, this payment will reduce the mortgage debt accordingly. *Sixty St. Francis St. v. Am. Sav. & Loan Ass'n,* 554 So. 2d 1003 (Ala. 1989). This rule is adopted by the Restatement (Third) of the Law of Property: Mortgages § 6.1. Dale A. Whitman, *Mortgage Drafting: Lessons from the Restatement of Mortgages*, 33 Real Prop. Prob. & Tr. L.J. 415 (1998). Further, the rule is otherwise where the mortgage note is negotiable. U.C.C. § 3-603(1). In some states, even where the mortgage secures a negotiable note, the mortgagor may continue to make payments to the original lender until it receives notice of the assignment, *Napieralski v. Simon,* 64 N.E. 1042 (Ill. 1902).

The rule that payment to a prior holder of the note is not good against a subsequent holder of the note who took its interest before the payment and did not notify the borrower is absurd and should be changed. It simply does not follow the way real estate mortgage payments are handled in today's marketplace. Any rule that requires the production of the mortgage note each time a payment is made on the mortgage debt is out of touch with reality.

Whenever notice of assignment is necessary, the notice should be given personally to the mortgagor. Merely recording an assignment of the mortgage ordinarily will not suffice. The mortgagor should not be subject to the burden of making constant searches of the records to see if the mortgage has been assigned, especially since it requires little effort for the assignee to serve a personal notice on the mortgagor. J.S. & H.R. , Annotation, *Record-*

ing Laws as Applied to Assignment of Mortgages on Real Estate, 89 A.L.R. 171, 197 (1934). However, any purchaser of the property from the mortgagor is usually required to take notice of such a recorded assignment. *Erickson v. Kendall,* 191 P. 842 (Wash. 1920).

20.44(b)
Warehousing

There is usually a time lag between the date a mortgage is made to a home buyer by a mortgage banker and the date it is sold to a permanent investor. The period will be longer when a construction loan is involved, shorter when the loans are simply awaiting packaging and sale to an investor or sale to a permanent lender. At times, the mortgage banker has a commitment by a permanent lender to purchase the mortgage at a later date, say, when construction has been completed.

A mortgage banker borrows the money it takes to bridge the gap between the time it disburses the loan proceeds to the borrower and the time the loan is sold to the investor. The mortgage banker arranges a line of credit with a commercial bank. The bank arranges to "buy" the individual mortgages, and the mortgage banker agrees to "buy" them back at the appropriate time.

To show the world that the commercial bank is in the picture, the individual mortgage notes are transferred to the custody of the commercial bank or other institutional custodian. Some banks insist that an assignment of the mortgages be recorded. The reason is obvious. The bank cannot loan millions to the mortgage banker while leaving all the documents in the apparent custody and ownership of the mortgage banker. One risk, of course, is that the mortgage banker might sell the mortgages to a third party. *See generally Rucker v. State Exchange Bank,* 355 So. 2d 171 (Fla. App. 1978); *In re Staff Mtg. Corp.,* 625 F.2d 281 (9th Cir. 1980); Murdoch K. Goodwin, *Mortgage Warehousing, a Misnomer*, 104 U. Pa. L. Rev. 494 (1956); Michael T. Madison & Jeffrey R. Dwyer, *The Law of Real Estate Financing,* 11-4 (1981).

20.45   Payment

The loan documents must clearly set forth the payment schedule. This is typically done by a provision to the effect that the payments shall be of interest only, with the balance due on a set date, or by the statement that a specified sum, calculated outside of the loan documents pursuant to an agreed amortization schedule, be paid on a monthly basis. In the worst of circumstances, an inadequate statement of the manner in which the loan is to be repaid could invalidate the mortgage. *In re Boyd*, 185 B.R. 529 (Bankr. E.D. Mich. 1995).

Payment has the effect of extinguishing the mortgage lien to the extent of the principal payments that are made. When the mortgage is paid in full, the lien is automatically extinguished in full. *Am. Nat'l Ins. Co. v. Murray*, 383 F.2d 81 (5th Cir. 1967). While this may be the legal result, it is customary to record a release, satisfaction, or discharge of the mortgage in order to clear the public records in the recorder's office.

Almost all jurisdictions require the lender to deliver a release to the borrower shortly after the final payment of the mortgage loan has been made. The borrower can then record the release or satisfaction to clear the record title of the mortgage encumbrance. Frequently, however, the release is not delivered to the borrower and the public records remain cluttered with mortgages that have in fact been paid, but not released of record. To address this problem, title insurance companies will insure over the paid mortgage upon the receipt of evidence that the prior mortgage has in fact been paid.

20.45(a)   Payment
to Agent

A mortgagor, before making payment to an agent of the mortgagee, should ascertain the agent's authority by inquiring of the mortgagee or by requiring the agent to produce a power of attorney from the mortgagee. *Coxe v. Kriebel*, 185 A. 770 (Pa. 1936).

20.45(b) Payment— Joint Mortgagees or Joint Sellers

Where a husband and wife own land jointly, sell it, and take back an installment contract or purchase money mortgage, payment to either party is good payment. 70 C.J.S. *Payment* § 4, 59; C.J.S. *Mortgages* § 446. The party receiving payment can give a release of the mortgage. One would think that the buyer would feel more comfortable if this is spelled out in the documents. Of course, if the check is made payable to both, a different problem arises, namely, whether one party can endorse the other party's name. Again, the documents should cover this.

20.45(c) Prepayment of Mortgage Debt

In the absence of an agreement to the contrary, the mortgagee has a contractual right to have the loan principal earning the agreed-upon interest rate for the loan term. *Dugan v. Grzybowski,* 332 A.2d 97 (Conn. 1973). Stated otherwise, unless the loan documents allow the borrower to prepay the loan, the borrower may not prepay without the lender's consent. *Metropolitan Life Ins. Co. v. Promenade Towers Mut. Housing Corp.,* 581 A.2d 846 (Md. App. 1990); *Young v. Sodaro,* 456 S.E.2d 31 (W.Va. 1995). Courts enforce these so-called "lock-in" provisions in loans, which either do not permit or expressly prevent the borrower from prepaying the debt. *Trident Ctr. v. Connecticut Gen. Life Ins. Co.,* 847 F.2d 564 (9th Cir. 1988). Dale A. Whitman, *Mortgage Prepayment Clauses: An Economic and Legal Analysis,* 40 U.C.L.A. L. Rev. 851, 866 (1993). In fact, if the loan is not prepayable, the borrower has no right to make a prepayment before maturity, even with the payment of all interest to maturity. *Peter Fuller Enter. Inc. v. Manchester Sav. Bank,* 152 A.2d 179 (N.H. 1959). It should be noted, however, that some recent cases have taken the minority view that the borrower may prepay the loan unless the loan documents expressly prohibit prepayment. *Hatcher v. Rose,* 329 N.C. 626, 407 S.E.2d 172 (1991); *Mahoney v. Furches,* 503 Pa. 60, 468 A.2d 458 (1983); *Citicorp Mortgage, Inc. v. Morrisville Hampton Village Realty Ltd. Partnership,* 443 Pa. Super. 595, 662 A.2d 1120 (1995).

Loans may be made prepayable by the simple provision that the loan is "payable on or before" a given date. *Fortson v. Burns,* 479 S.W.2d 722 (Tex. App. 1972). Alternatively, the loan documents may provide that the periodic payment be "not less than" a certain amount, or that the payment be of a stated amount "or more." *Peters v. Fenner,* 199 N.W.2d 795 (Minn. 1972). Even the term "if not sooner paid," *Latimer v. Grundy County Nat'l Bank,* 239 Ill. App. 3d 1000; 607 N.E.2d 294 (1993), will result in the loan being prepayable. Today, most loan documents, even in simple residential settings, specifically address the prepayment issue, if with nothing more than the simple statement, "The principal may be repaid in whole or in part at any time without penalty." Again, however, lenders may want to control even permitted repayments by allowing them to be made only when regularly scheduled payments are to be made or limiting the size of partial prepayments.

Bankruptcy courts strike down prepayment formulas that do not bear a reasonable relationship to the lender's actual or probable loss resulting from the prepayment. *In re Imperial Coronado Partners, Ltd.,* 96 B.R. 997 (Bankr. 9th Cir. 1988). Similarly, yield maintenance clauses that do not discount the loss of interest to its present value will not be enforced in bankruptcy. *In re Skyler Ridge,* 80 B.R. 500 (Bankr. C.D. Cal., 1987).

Various forms of limitations on prepayment penalties have found their way into the fabric of mortgage law. In some states prepayment penalties on consumer or residential loans may be exacted only during the initial years of the loan term. Alternatively, in other states, if the interest exceeds a certain rate, prepayment penalties are absolutely forbidden. In yet other states, the presumption has changed to the effect that the mortgage debt is prepayable unless the loan documents specify otherwise.

Where a mortgagor takes advantage of a mortgage provision that allows prepayments on any monthly payment date and suddenly becomes pinched for ready cash, the mortgagor may contend that it has the right to skip payments until the prepaid amount is exhausted. This contention will not prevail. In effect, the prepayments are applied against the last payments falling due. *Smith v. Renz,* 265 P.2d 160 (Cal. 1954). Some recent cases hold, however, that where the mortgagor has been making prepayments, it will not be in default until these prepayments have been exhausted by application to current payments. *Bradford v. Thompson,* 470 S.W.2d 633 (Tex. 1971).

20.45(d)   Payment— Late Charges

A late charge is, as the name implies, a customary charge made by the lender for the expense involved in processing and pursuing late payments. Gary D. Spivey, Annotation, *Validity and Construction of Provision Imposing "Late Charge" or Similar Exaction for Delay in Making Periodic Payments on Note, Mortgage or Installment Sale Contract,* 63 A.L.R.3d 50 (1975). If reasonable, it is valid and devoid of the taint of usury. The lending community was faced with a surprising development recently when a New Jersey court held that late charges and default interest charges, two very typical loan provisions, could be unenforceable penalties. *MetLife Capital Fin. Corp. v. Washington Ave. Assoc.,* 313 N.J. Super. 525, 713 A.2d 527 (1998). *See also, Ridgley v. Topa Thrift and Loan Ass'n,* 17 Cal. 4th 970, 953 P.2d 484 (1998). Fortunately, this case was later overturned. *MetLife Capital Fin. Corp. v. Washington Ave. Assoc.,* 159 N.J. 484, 732 A.2d 493 (1999). The lesson of this case, however, as stated by the higher court, is that such charges must be reasonable.

The late charge is, however, only to be imposed once, when the payment is late. 12 C.F.R. § 560.33.

It is important to scrutinize late payment penalty provisions. They may be so worded as to be inapplicable to certain types of payments, such as the final balloon payment due at maturity. *Sterling v. Goodman,* 719 P.2d 1262 (Nev. 1986). Where the late charge is applicable to the "aggregate monthly payment," the late charge percent is levied on the full amount of the payment, including principal, interest, taxes, and insurance. *Baker v. America's Mortgage Servicing, Inc.,* 58 F.3d 321 (7th Cir. 1995).

It is also important that the parties come to some agreement on what is payment. Unless the parties agree otherwise, if a course of dealing is established that the use of the mails is an acceptable way to transmit mortgage payments, as it typically is, the payment will be deemed to have been made when it is deposited, properly addressed and stamped, into the mail. 60 Am. Jur. 2d *Payment* §18. If the payment is then received after the payment date, or the grace period within which the payment is to be made, the payment will be deemed to have been timely made. For this reason, many loan documents expressly require the payment to be received within the time period.

20.45(e)   Payment— Default Interest

Loan documents often provide that, in addition to late charges, the lender will be allowed to charge interest at a higher rate, the default rate interest, if the loan is in default. These clauses are enforceable and need not satisfy any special requirements that would be imposed in the case of liquidated damages. *TMG Life Ins. Co. v. Ashner,* 898 P.2d 1145 (Kan. App. 1995). Lenders do typically provide, however, that in no event will the interest exceed the maximum permitted by law. In this way, if the default interest rate provision increased the rate to a level above that allowed by the usury law, the lower rate set by the usury law would limit the rate of interest to be charged in the case of a default.

20.45(f)   Payment— When a final payment has been made on a mortgage, the landowner should insist on re-
Final Payment ceiving a receipt stating that payment in full has been made. The landowner should also insist on receiving a release in recordable form satisfying the mortgage of record; the
canceled mortgage and note; all evidence of title and other loan documents held by the
lender; and an endorsement from the hazard insurance company stating that the mortgage
loss clause (giving the name of the lender as an additional party insured) has been released.
This last requirement is quite important. Lacking this endorsement, the insurance company
will make any check for loss payable to the mortgagee as well as the landowner. The owner
then must go through the bother of obtaining the old lender's endorsement on the check, a
task that may take some time.

20.46   Limitations In all states, a promissory note ceases to be enforceable after a certain time if no payments
are made. Such a note is said to be barred by the limitations period. The applicable limitations period varies from state to state. In most states, the fact that the mortgage note is
barred by limitations only prevents the obtaining of a personal judgment on the note and
does not prevent foreclosure of the mortgage. But, in other states, the mortgage is automatically barred from being foreclosed whenever the mortgage note is barred.

In many states, if a period of twenty years elapses after the maturity date of the mortgage note, the mortgage is presumed to be paid. The mortgagee, however, may overcome
this presumption by proving that the mortgage has not been paid, but has been kept alive by
partial payments of principal or interest thereon. Since this rule makes it dangerous to disregard even an old recorded mortgage, some states go further and provide by law that after
a stated period of time, the mortgage becomes void. The period varies from state to state.
In Michigan, it is thirty years; in Kentucky, fifteen years.

20.47   Extension Where the mortgagor and mortgagee agree to extend the maturity date of the mortgage note,
Agreements and the priority of the mortgage over those who took their interest between the recordation of the
Modifications mortgage and the execution of the extension agreement remains undisturbed. The same is
true when the earlier note is replaced by another bearing a later maturity date. A different result follows, however, where in addition to merely extending the maturity date, the extension
works a prejudice against the interests of the intervening interest holders.

> **EXAMPLE:** As a result of an economic downturn, Mortgagor's business activity and profits
> are sharply reduced. To cope with this problem, Mortgagor and Mortgagee agree to alter the
> payoff schedule on the mortgage covering Mortgagor's plant. It is agreed that principal pay-
> ments would be deferred for eighteen months, Mortgagor only being required to pay interest
> for that period. The ultimate maturity date is thereby extended eighteen months. Priority over
> junior mortgagees should remain the same. This is a valid extension.

> **EXAMPLE:** Mortgagor and Mortgagee agree to extend the maturity date and increase the in-
> terest rate. This agreement results in a split priority for the mortgage over junior lienors. To
> the extent of the unpaid principal and original interest, the mortgage is senior; to the extent of
> the increased interest, the priority will date from the modification date. This agreement results
> in a highly unusual priority problem: (1) the original mortgage principal and interest will have
> a first lien; (2) the second mortgage will take second place, subject only to (1) above; and (3)
> the increased interest will have a third lien on the property. *Lennar Northeast Partners v.
> Buice Revocable Living Trust,* 57 Cal. Rptr. 435 (1996); *Bowen v. Am. Arlington Bank,* 325
> So. 2d 31 (Fla. App. 1976).

A question arises whether the first mortgagee can overcome this handicap by language
inserted in the first mortgage. No case has been discovered indicating that this can be done.

Probably it is impossible. The granting of the extension is like an "optional advance." Robert Kratovil and Raymond J. Werner, *Mortgage Extensions and Modifications,* 8 Creighton L. Rev. 595 (1975).

Where the mortgagor defaults because of circumstances beyond the mortgagor's control, it may enter into a forbearance agreement wherein mortgage payments may be altered or suspended for a specified period. Also, the lender may approve a modification of the amortization provisions by recasting the balance due over the original term of the mortgage or an extended term. Recent cases have held that the HUD-insured mortgagees must seek to aid the distressed debtor and, absent such efforts, foreclosure is not allowed. *FNMA v. Ricks,* 372 N.Y.S.2d 485 (1975). Where the mortgage has been assigned to FNMA or FHLMC, these institutions must consent to any modification.

20.48   Release, Satisfaction, or Discharge of Mortgage

Although the payment of the mortgage debt discharges the mortgage, it nevertheless remains on the public records as a cloud upon the title until it has been released. The common method of releasing a mortgage or deed of trust is by execution, acknowledgment, delivery, and recording of a *release deed,* also variously called *satisfaction, discharge,* or *deed of reconveyance,* executed under seal by the trustee or mortgagee.

These formalities are necessary even though full payment has the effect of extinguishing the lien of the mortgage. Payment is not revealed by the public records, and without the recordation of a properly executed satisfaction or release deed, the mortgage remains a defect in title.

20.48(a)   Partial Release

When a mortgage conveys several distinct tracts of land, payment of a specified portion of the debt may entitle the mortgagor to a release of the mortgage as to a certain part of the land. Such a release is known as a partial release. In the absence of a provision in the loan documents to this effect, the mortgagor is not entitled to a release of the mortgage, except upon full payment of the mortgage debt. When a blanket mortgage is placed on an entire subdivision, a partial release provision is indispensable, since otherwise the developer could not furnish lot purchasers with clear title to their lots.

Typically, the release clause will contain a partial release formula or a schedule showing what lots may be released and the amount of payment for the lot or lots released. This must be set forth in accurate detail. *White Point Co. v. Herrington,* 73 Cal. Rptr. 885 (1968).

Unless the mortgage provides otherwise, the mortgagor can legally insist on a partial release even if the mortgagor is in default in its obligations under the loan documents. J.R. Kemper, Annotation, *Construction of Provision in Real Estate Mortgage and Contract, or Other Security Instrument for Release of Separate Parcels of Land as Payments Are Made,* 41 A.L.R.3d 7 (1972); 59 C.J.S. *Mortgages* § 759. Hence, it is best for the mortgagee to insist on a clause preventing this result.

20.49   Deed by Mortgagor to Mortgagee

Earlier, the deed absolute problem was described. There is a second type of deed absolute problem. At times, a mortgagor will find that it is unable to pay the mortgage debt. In this event, the mortgagee may, of course, foreclose the mortgage. Foreclosure, however, usually costs the mortgagee time and money. It may wish to make some arrangement with the mortgagor for acquiring ownership of the land without the necessity of foreclosure. This is accomplished by means of an agreement between mortgagor and mortgagee whereby the mortgagor agrees to sell the land to the mortgagee for a small sum of money, and the mortgagee, in return, agrees to cancel the mortgage debt. The mortgagor thereupon gives the mortgagee a deed, and the mortgagee cancels the notes and releases the mortgage. The courts are inclined to be suspicious of such transactions, since the mortgagee is in a position to exert pressure on the mortgagor. To give validity to such a sale by the mortgagor, it must appear that the conduct of the mortgagee was, in all things, fair and frank and that it paid for the property what it was worth, and that it did not coerce the mortgagor into signing the deed. To protect itself, a mortgagee entering into such a transaction should take the following precautions:

1. It should examine the title to the land to make sure that no other liens, such as judgments or junior mortgages, attached to the land after the date of the mortgage.

2. A written contract should be entered into between the mortgagor and mortgagee. This contract should show that it was the mortgagor, not the mortgagee, who proposed the transaction. This renders it difficult for any court to hold that the mortgagor was coerced, since the agreement itself shows that the mortgagor took the initiative in the transaction. The contract should also provide that the deed is given in full satisfaction of the mortgage debt. *Rooker v. Fidelity Trust Co.,* 109 N.E. 766 (Ind. 1915). In some states, the same result is accomplished by putting a clause in the deed or in a separate affidavit.

3. The mortgage should be released and the mortgage and mortgage note canceled. If the mortgage debt is not canceled, courts tend to regard the deed as merely additional security for the debt rather than an outright sale of the mortgagor's equity. W.W. Allen, *Deed from Mortgagor or Privy to Mortgage Holder as Extinguishing Equity of Redemption,* 129 A.L.R. 1435, 1495 (1940).

4. The mortgagee should not enter into any contract to resell or reconvey the land to the mortgagor, though it may safely give the mortgagor an option to repurchase the premises. 129 A.L.R. 1435, 1473, *supra.*

A mortgagee in a HUD mortgage may acquire the security from a mortgagor by a deed in lieu transaction, if the following conditions are met: (1) the mortgage must be in default at the time the deed in lieu is executed and delivered; (2) The credit instrument must be canceled or surrendered to the mortgagor and the mortgage must be satisfied of record; and (3) the mortgagor must give a warranty deed and convey good marketable title. 24 C.F.R. § 203.357(4).

The problem is in determining whether the deed was actually given with the intention to transfer the absolute ownership of the land or was given primarily as additional security, without the intention of extinguishing the mortgage.

20.50 Refinancing Landowners tend to refinance their mortgages when interest rates drop more than two percent. This is possible if the mortgage documents permit prepayment. An alternative is to negotiate with the existing mortgagee. It may rather reduce the interest than lose a customer. Such modification may not be possible where the mortgage has been sold in the secondary market.

CHAPTER 21

Real Estate Finance—
Commercial Mortgage and
Loan Document Provisions

21.01 Due-on-Sale Clause—Background

This clause should be put into historical context. Mortgage lending that took place prior to the Great Depression was essentially balloon-note financing based on a bricks-and-mortar appraisal of the property. In the depth of the Depression, mortgage lending ground to a halt. After President Roosevelt took office in 1933, there was a modest revival of home mortgage lending sparked by the introduction of FHA mortgage insurance and the creation of the federal savings and loan associations.

A new concept, the amortized loan made to a creditworthy borrower, then found its way into mortgage lending. The borrower would have to "qualify" financially for the loan. As a corollary, the lender wanted to prevent the subsequent conveyance of the property, still encumbered by the mortgage, into the hands of an owner who was not creditworthy and who might allow the property to run down. Toward that end, lenders began to insert the due-on-sale clause into their mortgages. Even the FHA used the clause.

Attention focused on this clause during the economic and financial turmoil of the early 1970s. Inflation roared out of control. Interest rates soared. The federal government stepped in, virtually abolishing state usury laws in residential lending and allowed variable interest rate mortgages that permit a lender to charge a rate of interest that fluctuates over the loan term as the rate paid by the lender for its funds changes. The federal government vastly increased the availability of mortgage funds by creating the GNMA, FNMA, and FHLMC to issue and sell securities backed by pools of mortgages.

Ultimately, the federal government had to step in to regulate the effectiveness of the due-on-sale clause, which was being invalidated and emasculated by state statutes and decisions. A typical example shows the effect of a due-on-sale clause upon the sale of property and the returns available to lenders.

> **EXAMPLE:** Owner mortgaged his home to Lender in 1969 for $50,000 at 8 percent interest. The mortgage contains a due-on-sale clause reading as follows:
>
> > In case of a transfer of the mortgaged premises without the written consent of Lender, the entire principal of the mortgage debt shall, at the election of the mortgagee, become immediately due and payable.
>
> In 1978, the mortgage was paid down to $45,000. Owner sold the home to Buyer for $70,000. Ordinarily, the existing mortgage would be paid off when the home sold. The buyer would get a new mortgage on terms that suit it. But the new mortgages made in 1978 carry an interest rate of 15 percent. Both Owner and Buyer would be better off if they allow the old mortgage to remain, for the then amount of the debt will bear interest at only 8 percent rather than the prevailing rate of 15 percent. As a result, the sale is arranged as an installment sale. Owner sells its equity for cash, with the balance payable in installments. If Lender threatens to invoke

the due-on-sale clause and thus accelerate the mortgage debt, the answer will be, "No deed was made. Therefore, this is not a transfer." Creative financing was born.

If the clause worked to allow the lender to accelerate the debt, the lender would receive the loan balance which could be reloaned at current rates, thereby changing an 8 percent loan into a 15 percent loan. Multiply this by thousands of transactions and it is apparent why this clause is so significant to the lending industry. On the other hand, if the effect of the clause is thwarted, the property owner can make the sale more attractive, because the sale involves not only the property, it also effectively involves the making of a below-market rate loan. The property owner effectively makes an 8 percent loan on the remaining balance of the loan when the market would charge 15 percent. John P. Ludington, Annotation, *Validity and Enforceability of Due on Sale Real Estate Mortgage Provisions*, 61 A.L.R.4th 1070 (1988).

21.01(a)   Due-on-Sale Clause—Creative Financing

Not all mortgages contained due-on-sale clauses. While the savings and loan industry made use of these clauses, mortgage forms used by many insurance companies, banks, and FHA lenders did not contain this term. This set the stage for many "creative financing" transactions, especially when market interest rates were high and mortgage credit was generally unavailable. A seller eager to dispose of property sold it subject to the existing mortgage, with the balance of the sale price to be paid in cash and a second mortgage back to the seller.

Even if the existing mortgage contained a due-on-sale clause, buyer and seller were left with some options. Many deals were closed secretly in the hope that the lender would not discover the transaction. Lenders became vigilant, watching more carefully the names of the payees on checks given to make the periodic mortgage payments and the names of the insured on the casualty insurance policies covering the mortgaged property for indications that a sale had taken place secretly. It was easier to keep the sale a secret when the seller and buyer entered into an unrecorded installment contract for the balance of the sale price over the balance of the mortgage.

Other borrowers simply defied the lender to enforce the due-on-sale clause. Some lenders took up the challenge and litigation followed. Some state courts refused to enforce the clause where the buyer was creditworthy; others sustained the use of the clause, even where the lender was using it as a device to increase the interest rate. While these battles were raging in the marketplace and the courtroom, states began to enact legislation, and a crazy-quilt pattern of laws resulted. The controversy continued. Federal associations challenged state laws and court decisions that seemed to limit their use of the due-on-sale clause. Mark Roszkowski, *Drafting Around Mortgage Due-on-Sale Clauses: The Danger of Playing Hide-and-Seek,* 21 Real Prop. Prob. & Tr. J. 23 (1986).

21.01(b)   Due-on-Sale Clause—Federal Preemption—The Garn-St. Germain Act

Some lenders are organized under state law, others under federal law. To a considerable but poorly defined extent, federal lenders are governed by federal law. Federal banks and thrifts are largely governed by federal laws and federal regulations. For many years, they have used and enforced the due-on-sale clause. Federal regulations have long provided that enforcement of this clause is a federal matter. Nevertheless, beginning in 1976, California and other states took the position that the clause could not be enforced by either federal or state institutions where the buyer of the mortgaged property was creditworthy.

The U.S. Supreme Court ultimately decided that *federal* savings and loan associations invoking the due-on-sale clause were immune from state regulation or state court interference. *Fidelity Fed. Sav. & Loan Ass'n v. de la Cuesta,* 458 U.S. 141, 102 S. Ct. 3014, 73 L. Ed.2d

664 (1982). Of the many articles previously written on the subject, only a few had anticipated this result. *See* Robert Kratovil, *A New Dilemma for Thrift Institutions: Judicial Emasculation of the Due-on-Sale Clause,* 12 J. Marshall J. of Prac. & Proc. 299 (1979); Robert Kratovil, *Epilogue: Wellenkamp v. Bank of America,* 15 J. Marshall L. Rev. 435 (1982).

In September 1982, Congress enacted the Garn-St. Germain Act. While this act has been criticized for the contributing effect it has had on the thrift crisis, it dealt with several lender-related topics including the due-on-sale clause. The Supreme Court's decision that neither state laws nor state court decisions can limit a federal savings and loan association's enforcement of the due-on-sale clauses in their mortgages gave the federal associations a competitive advantage over state associations. Congress therefore enacted a law allowing all lenders, state and federal, to exercise the due-on-sale clauses in their mortgage documents regardless of the buyer's creditworthiness. In effect, this permits the lender to demand increased interest as the price of consenting to the sale. 12 U.S.C.A. § 1701j(3).

In matters of national interest, Congress has the power to overrule state laws and court decisions. This is called *preemption.* Garn-St. Germain is an instance of federal preemption.

21.01(c)   Due-on-Sale Clause—Federal and Other Limits on Triggering Events

Where the mortgaged property consists of fewer than five residential units, the Garn-St. Germain Act limits the lender's right to invoke, or "trigger," the due-on-sale clause. No matter what the mortgage may provide, acceleration will not be allowed under the due-on-sale clause in the event of any of the following:

1. The creation of a junior lien or encumbrance that does not relate to the transfer of the right to occupy the property.
2. The creation of a purchase money security interest for household appliances.
3. A transfer by devise, descent, or operation of law upon the death of a joint tenant or tenant by the entirety.
4. The granting of a leasehold interest of three years or less that does not involve an option to purchase.
5. A transfer to a relative resulting from the death of the borrower.
6. A transfer to a spouse or child of the borrower.
7. A transfer resulting from a divorce or legal separation by which the spouse of the borrower becomes an owner of the property.
8. A transfer to an inter vivos trust in which the borrower is and remains a beneficiary and that does not relate to a transfer of rights of occupancy.
9. Any other transfer or disposition described in regulations prescribed by the Federal Home Loan Bank Board. 12 U.S.C.A. § 1701j(3).

The Garn-St. Germain Act provided for a window period, which began on the date that a state law or court decision prohibited the unrestricted exercise of a due-on-sale clause upon outright transfers of property and ended on October 15, 1982. For states that have enacted window-period laws regulating due-on-sale clauses, loans made by lenders other than federal thrifts during this period are subject to the state law regulation of the due-on-sale clause. Only Arizona, Michigan, Minnesota, New Mexico, and Utah have enacted such laws.

21.01(d)   Due-on-Sale Clause—Installment Contract

An installment contract may contain a due-on-sale clause.

EXAMPLE: Vendor enters into an installment contract to sell property to Purchaser for $100,000, payable in $10,000 cash, and the balance of $90,000 payable in monthly installments over a ten-year period. The contract provides that if Purchaser assigns the contract interest without Vendor's written consent, Vendor may declare the entire balance immediately due and payable. Probably, the Garn-St. Germain Act applies to this clause. Grant S. Nelson & Dale A. Whitman, *Congressional Preemption of Mortgage Due-on-Sale: An Analysis of Garn St. Germain Act,* 35 Hastings L.J. 241, 266 (1983).

21.01(e) Due-on-Sale Clause—The Clause

Controversies often center upon the events that trigger the operation of the due-on-sale clause. The resolution of any such dispute is obviously tied to the language of the clause itself. As with many other mortgage clauses, the early mortgage provisions were rather simple. For example, an early form of this clause may read

In case of a sale of the mortgaged premises without the written consent of the mortgagee, the entire principal of the mortgage debt shall, at the election of the mortgagee, become immediately due and payable.

Experience with the earlier simplified clauses has led to today's provisions that are well drafted from the lender's point of view and cover a broad spectrum of actions that will trigger its operation. The courts have given some guidance into the application of these clauses, and some common patterns have begun to emerge.

21.01(f) Due-on-Sale Clause—Events Causing the Clause to Be Invoked

From a simple perspective, the mere entry into a contract to sell the encumbered property may trigger the clause. *Baltimore Life Ins. Co. v. Harn,* 15 Ariz. App. 78, 486 P.2d 190 (1971). If however, the contract is an installment contract for the sale of the property, the result may be opposite. *Krause v. Columbia Sav. & Loan Ass'n,* 631 P.2d 1158 (Colo. Ct. App. 1981). *But see Fidelity Fed. Sav. & Loan Ass'n v. Grieme,* 112 Ill. App. 3rd 1014, 446 N.E.2d 292 (1983). Federal law does not prohibit the triggering of the clause when the landowner contracts to sell the land on the installment method. Indeed, the language of the Garn-St. Germain Act leans toward permitting the clause to be invoked. Much of the debate in the state courts turns on the meaning of the word "sale." Does it mean only a cash sale, or does it also include a credit sale on the installment basis? Most of the decisions treat an installment sale as a sale, as that term is generally used in the due-on-sale clause. Eunice A. Eichelberger, Annotation, *What Transfers Justify Acceleration Under "Due on Sale" Clause of Real Estate Mortgage,* 22 A.L.R.4th 1266 (1981).

21.01(g) Due-on-Sale Clause—Junior Mortgages Causing the Clause to Be Invoked

Some clauses are drafted broadly enough to prohibit further encumbrance of the property while the mortgage is in place. If so drafted, the clause would include a second mortgage as an event that triggers the operation of the clause. This is a common provision in large-scale mortgages. The theory is that revenue from a mortgaged property will be diverted to the payment of the junior mortgage, and cash flow will not be sufficient to also support the first mortgage.

Federal law now prohibits the application of a due-on-sale clause to the placement of a junior mortgage only on *residential* property. This was needed to allow the home equity lending industry to thrive as it has in the recent past. Thus, the law seems to have responded well to today's economics. A homeowner is free to put a second mortgage on the home, and a life insurance company is free to accelerate a commercial mortgage if the developer places a second mortgage on the mortgaged property.

Some courts have held that the foreclosure of a junior mortgage does not trigger the due-on-sale clause. *Yelen v. Bankers Trust Co.,* 476 So. 2d 767 (Fla. Dist. Ct. App. 1985);

Barr Dev., Inc. v. Utah Mortgage Loan Corp., 106 Idaho 46, 675 P.2d 25 (1985); *In re Ruepp,* 71 N.C. App. 146, 321 S.E. 517 (1984).

21.01(h)   Due-on-Sale Clause—Partnership and Corporate Transactions Causing the Clause to Be Invoked

Transactions taking place within the ownership entity may trigger the clause. These transactions should be viewed with two thoughts in mind. The first is a transaction motivated by factors completely unrelated to the transfer of property rights, such as a corporate merger, which is merely complicated by the presence of a mortgage on corporate property that contains a due-on-sale clause drafted broadly enough to cause the acceleration of the mortgage debt upon the closing of the corporate transaction. The second is the transaction being structured as a corporate restructuring to get around a narrowly drawn due-on-sale clause. For example, the transaction may be structured as a sale of the stock of the corporate owner of the property so that the property can effectively be transferred without the acceleration of the mortgage debt.

The form of the clause is crucial to the ability of the lender to accelerate the debt in these instances.

> **EXAMPLE:** Two partners withdrew from the partnership that owned property encumbered by a mortgage which contained a due-on-sale clause, and the partnership contracted to sell the property to the remaining partners. The court held this did not trigger the acceleration of the debt. *Hodge v. DMNS Co.,* 652 S.W.2d 762 (Tenn. Ct. App. 1982).

> **EXAMPLE:** The sale of the stock of the borrower did not trigger the due-on-sale clause in *Gasparre v. 88-36 Elmhurst Ave. Realty Corp.,* 119 Misc. 2d 628, 464 N.Y.S.2d 106 (1983). *But see United States v. Med O Farm, Inc.,* 701 F.2d 88 (9th Cir. 1983). Similarly, the clause was not triggered by the transfer of the property by the corporate borrower to its principal shareholder. *Fidelity Land Dev. Corp. v. Rieder & Sons Bldg. & Dev. Co.,* 151 N.J. Super. 502, 377 A.2d 691 (N.J. 1977).

21.01(i)   Due-on-Sale Clause—Drafting the Clause in the Commercial Loan Transaction

In the commercial setting, the drafter of the due-on-sale clause should consider the following:

1. Listing the types of transfers that will be permitted and the types of transactions that will be prohibited. For example, will the owner be allowed to transfer the property by merger, consolidation, reorganization, or other type of corporate transaction that incidentally causes the property to be vested in a new entity within the same corporate family as the former owner? Similarly, will the owner be allowed to transfer the property to trusts, partnerships, and other entities for estate planning purposes? If such transactions are to be allowed, will any limits be imposed, such as the requirement that the borrower retain at least a 51 percent interest in the new ownership entity, or that certain key individuals continue to be involved as the chief executive officer of the ownership entity?

2. Requiring that the loan be paid down to a certain percentage of the sale price or original loan balance.

3. Requiring that the loan not be in default at the time of transfer.

4. Requiring that the lender be reimbursed for its attorneys' fees and expenses, be paid a fee, and be authorized to change the interest rate, amortization, or other key loan terms, if the transfer is not to trigger acceleration.

5. Allowing the lender to increase the interest rate as a condition to consenting to a transfer of the property. While this may be allowed without the clause so providing, setting this out in the loan documents clarifies the possible rights of the parties when the property is transferred. *Tierce v. APS Co.,* 382 So. 2d 485 (Ala. 1980); *Century Fed. Sav. & Loan Ass'n v. Van Glahn,* 144 N.J. Super. 48, 364 A.2d 558 (1976).

6. Addressing whether the borrower is to be released from liability and whether the new owner must assume the loan obligations, if the transfer is not to trigger acceleration.

21.01(j) Due-on-Sale Clause—Relationship with Prepayment Penalty Clause

If the lender may resort to the due-on-sale clause and accelerate the payment of the balance of the loan, may the lender also enforce the prepayment penalty clause and receive the premium due on the early payment of the loan? The prevailing law seems to be that the lender may collect the prepayment penalty, if the loan documents expressly give the lender that right upon acceleration in such circumstances.

21.02 Personal Liability— Nonrecourse Loans

The borrower need not be personally liable for the payment of the mortgage debt. The parties are at liberty to make any agreement they wish concerning personal liability. The requirement that the mortgage secure a debt is not a requirement that the borrower be personally liable for the payment of the debt. The borrower and lender may agree that the loan will be nonrecourse, in that the mortgagee will look only to the real estate as security for repayment of the loan, and not pursue the borrower individually. *City of Joliet v. Alexander*, 194 Ill. 457, 62 N.E. 861 (1902); *Bedian v. Cohn*, 10 Ill. App. 2d 116, 134 N.E.2d 532 (1956); *Gagne v. Hoban,* 280 Minn. 475, 159 N.W.2d 896 (1968). In such case, the mortgagee cannot obtain a personal judgment or deficiency decree against the mortgagor should the mortgaged land prove insufficient in value to satisfy the mortgage debt.

Indeed, most commercial mortgage loans are said to be nonrecourse, but in reality expressly make the borrower liable for the repayment of the debt under certain circumstances. The list of factual situations to which these "nonrecourse carveouts" apply is long and includes the following: the failure of the borrower to apply the rents and revenues of the property to the property expenses and debt service; commission of waste to the property, including the failure to pay real estate taxes; the failure to obtain proper insurance for the property; the misapplication of insurance or condemnation proceeds or security deposits; fraud or misrepresentation in the loan application process; allowing the property to become environmentally contaminated; removal of essential personal property from the security; failure to keep the property free from mechanics' liens; and filing a bankruptcy proceeding.

The "waste" carveout has been the subject of some interesting litigation. Lenders have successfully contended that the failure to pay real estate taxes constitutes waste. As a result, a borrower may be liable under an exception to the nonrecourse exculpation applicable to the borrower's commission of waste. *Travelers Ins. Co. v. 633 Third Assocs.*, 14 F.3d 114 (2d Cir. 1994).

Sophisticated clauses differentiate between those instances that create personal liability for the damages suffered by the lender as a result of the borrower's action, as in the case of environmental matters, and complete personal liability for the repayment of the debt, as in the case of fraud or misrepresentation in the loan application process. Indeed, some lenders insert *in terrorem* recourse clauses that make the loan fully recourse if the borrower asserts unwarranted defenses in an action to enforce the lender's rights or if the borrower files for bankruptcy relief. *First Nationwide Bank v. Brookhaven Realty Assocs.*, 637 N.Y.S.2d 418 (N.Y. 1996); *F.D.I.C. v. Prince George Corp.*, 58 F.3d 1041 (4th Cir. 1995).

Nonrecourse clauses may not be completely protective of the borrower's monetary liability. For example, where a borrower sets funds aside to pay real estate taxes or retains the security deposits posted by the tenants, a court may hold that these funds must be turned over to the lender. *Homecorp v. Secor Bank*, 659 So. 2d 15 (Ala. 1994). Similarly, if the borrower does not exactly comply with the provisions of the nonrecourse language, then the borrower may find itself liable to the lender. For example, if the loan documents provide that the borrower is not liable for the repayment of the debt, but is liable for rents collected after default, and the borrower does not pay such rents over to the lender, the borrower is liable to the lender for the misappropriated rents. *Prudential Ins. Co. of Am. v. Science Park Ltd. Partnership*, 106 Ohio App. 3d 823, 667 N.E.2d 437 (1995).

It must be kept in mind that the nature of the borrower's liability and the extent of the guarantee by responsible parties that participate in the borrower go hand in hand. Indeed, if the property is held in a single-asset entity whose sole asset is the property that is encumbered by the loan, the liability of that entity may be of no consequence. Indeed, to fully protect itself, the lender may want to have recourse against a creditworthy individual or entity. If such is to be the case, the lender should make sure that the guarantee liability at least matches or is broader than the liability of the borrower under the note and mortgage.

21.03 Guarantees Many notes and mortgages are signed by corporations or other business entities that may not have adequate capital to fully honor the payment and performance obligations of the loan documents. In such cases, the lender will typically have the debt guaranteed personally by the principals of the borrower. Prior to making the loan, the lender should obtain dependable financial statements and analyze them carefully. Only with properly analyzed financial information in hand can the lender determine who should be ultimately liable for the payment of the mortgage loan and the performance of the borrower's obligations.

Guarantees create fragile relationships between the guarantor and the lender. Actions of the lender that alter the debtor-creditor relationship without the guarantor's agreement will impair the effectiveness of the guarantor.

> **EXAMPLE:** ABC Corp. mortgages its land to Lender and signs the customary mortgage note. Guarantor, a shareholder, signs a guarantee. Later, the loan gets into trouble and the borrower and Lender recast the loan, reducing the monthly payments and extending the date of final maturity. This discharges Guarantor's liability unless it consents to the loan modification. Hence, the guarantee must contain an agreement by Guarantor that the modification of the loan will not affect Guarantor's liability.

Experience shows that guarantees are often effective. The guarantee, being a personal liability, appears on the guarantor's financial statements. If the loan goes into default, this is a black mark that will affect the guarantor's ability to obtain credit. The guarantor will struggle to prevent this. If there is a loan workout, the guarantor will often come up with a financial contribution in order to procure a release of the guarantee.

As is the case with many areas of mortgage law, the law relating to guarantees has bankruptcy issues. Where the guarantor goes into bankruptcy, payments made on the guaranteed debt may be recovered by the guarantor's bankruptcy trustee. *Levit v. Ingersol Rand Fin. Corp. (In re Deprizio Constr. Co.)*, 874 F.2d 1186 (7th Cir. 1989). This is the case because the guarantor is a conditional creditor of the borrower. The guarantor will automatically come into a debtor-creditor relationship with the borrower, if the guarantor honors the guarantee. As a result, guarantees typically provide that the guarantor's obligation will be reinstated to the extent that any payments made by the borrower to the lender must be given back by order of the bankruptcy court. David I. Katzen, *DePrizio and Bankruptcy Code Section 550: Extended Preference Exposure via Insider Guarantees, and Other Perils of Initial Transferee Liability,* 45 Bus. Law. 511 (1990).

Issues may also arise when the guarantee is made. For example, if the guarantee is made by one member of a family of corporations for the benefit of a parent, subsidiary, or sister company, the guarantee itself may be subject to state fraudulent conveyance laws, the fraudulent conveyance provisions of the Bankruptcy Code, or state corporate law. Of prime importance is the fraudulent transfer concept that arises when an obligation is incurred for less than reasonably equivalent value. If such is the case, the obligation may be set aside if the guarantor was insolvent at the time the guarantee was made, or became insolvent as a result of the making of the guarantee, or engaged in business or a transaction for which the guarantor had unreasonably small capital, or intended or believed that it would incur debts that would be beyond the guarantor's ability to pay as they matured. 11 U.S.C.S. § 548; 740 ILCS 160/5(a)(1).

Recently, guarantees have been used to lessen the likelihood that the borrower will file a bankruptcy proceeding if the loan falls into default and the lender commences the enforcement of its remedies. *See F.D.I.C. v. Prince George Corp.* 58 F.3d 1041 (3rd Cir. 1995) (upholding such clause in the nonrecourse provisions of a loan document). Typically, the guarantor is a principal of the borrower, having the ability to control the borrower's business decisions. If the guarantee makes the guarantor fully liable for the repayment of the mortgage debt if the borrower makes a bankruptcy filing, or a bankruptcy filing is made against the borrower and not dismissed within a limited amount of time, the guarantor will be very cautious about entering into the bankruptcy arena.

As is the case with recourse liability under the loan documents themselves, guarantees often provide for limitations on the liability of the guarantor. For example, the guarantee may limit the dollar amount of the guarantor's liability, thereby providing a cushion of credit enhancement if the property that secures the loan and the other avenues of recovery for the lender do not provide sufficient recovery. *See TMG Life Ins. Co. v. Ashner*, 21 Kan. App. 2d 234; 898 P.2d 1145 (Kan. App. 1995) (where the guaranty was limited to "one-third of the amount of the loan from time to time outstanding"). Another approach is to have the guarantor liable only for certain losses of the lender, such as losses resulting from the failure of the borrower to pay real estate taxes, or the application of the rents and revenues of the property to other than property expenses.

21.04 Future Advances— Obligatory Advances

A mortgage debt is not always created at the same instant that the mortgage is signed. The mortgagor in commercial loans and in home equity loans will frequently receive the loan proceeds some time after the signing and recording of the mortgage. The question that arises in these future advance situations is whether the mortgage has priority over junior mortgages, judgments, and other liens that may attach to the land after the mortgage at issue was executed and recorded, but before the money is paid out. The problem usually arises in three situations:

> **EXAMPLE:** An ordinary mortgage loan is applied for. The mortgage is executed and recorded. Payment of the mortgage money to the mortgagor is delayed pending the completion of a title search. A judgment or other lien attaches to the land after the recording of the mortgage. Thereafter, the mortgagee's title search is completed, but since the search covers only the date of the recording of the mortgage, the mortgagee is unaware of the judgment. Thereafter, the mortgagee pays out the mortgage money to the mortgagor.

> **EXAMPLE:** A line-of-credit mortgage loan document is executed and recorded with some of the loan proceeds being advanced immediately. The mortgage provides for additional advances up to a stated maximum amount and allows the borrower to repay the loan and obtain additional advances as the borrower's cash flow demands necessitate. While these advances, repayments, and additional advances are being made, a judgment or other lien attaches to the land.

> **EXAMPLE:** A construction loan is involved. The mortgage disburses the mortgage money as the building goes up, and before construction is completed, other liens attach to the land.

Where a mortgagee is obligated by contract with the mortgagor to advance funds to be secured by the mortgage, the mortgage will be a valid lien from the time of its recording, as against all subsequent encumbrances, even though some or all of the mortgage money is paid to the mortgagor after such subsequent encumbrances have attached to the mortgaged land. This holds true even though the mortgagee is actually aware of the existence of the subsequent encumbrances at the time it pays out the mortgage money. N.M. Moldoff, *Priority Between Mechanics' Liens and Advances Made Under Previously Executed Mortgage*, 80 A.L.R.2d 176, 191, 196, 199, 217, 219 (1961). Such advances are obligatory advances. Because of the mortgagee's obligation to pay out the money, the mortgage debt is regarded as being in existence from the time of the contract.

The obligation is usually created in one of two ways: (1) where the mortgagor has made written application for a mortgage loan and the mortgagee is contractually obligated to go through with the transaction and (2) where a revolving or construction loan is involved, the obligation is usually created by a loan agreement entered into between mortgagor and mortgagee. This agreement obligates the mortgagee to disburse the mortgage funds, if the borrower satisfies the conditions of disbursement. *See* Robert Kratovil & Raymond J. Werner, *Mortgages for Construction and the Lien Priorities Problem—The "Unobligatory" Advance,* 41 Tenn. L. Rev. 311 (1974).

In addition, in all states, expenditures made by the mortgagee to preserve the mortgage lien, such as payments made by the mortgagee on delinquent real estate taxes that the mortgagor has failed to pay, are considered obligatory expenses, and the mortgagee has the same lien for such advances as it has for the original debt. Some states give the mortgagee the same priority for advances made to protect the security for the loan, such as repairing a hole in the roof to protect against water infiltration into the structure.

21.04(a)   Future Advances—Optional Advances

Suppose that the mortgage documents do not absolutely bind the lender to fund additional mortgage debt. Advances under such a mortgage are called *optional advances*. Despite the fact that such a mortgage is duly recorded, it is by no means certain that it will have priority as a lien for all of the debt from the date of its recording as against all other liens attaching after that date. It will be argued that a mortgage is a conveyance to secure a debt and without a debt there is no mortgage. It must therefore follow that until the mortgage funds have actually been advanced to the mortgagor, no legal mortgage exists. In the case of obligatory advances, the courts dispose of the argument by saying that since the lender must loan the additional funds as it has contracted to do, for all practical purposes the debt exists at the time the obligation to make the loan was created. Since this obligation is normally created either by application and commitment or by a loan agreement, an obligatory advance mortgage is good against the whole world, including subsequent lienors, from the date the mortgage is recorded. As to mortgages where the lender has not entered into a binding contract to advance the additional funds, the problem is far more complex.

21.04(b)   Future Advances—Open-End Mortgages

The open-end mortgage provides that the mortgage secures not only the original note and debt, but also any additional advances that the mortgagee may choose to make to the mortgagor in the future. This means that if, in the future, the borrower wishes to obtain additional funds for the improvement of the property or for some other purpose, it can borrow this money from the mortgagee if the latter sees fit to lend it. The advantages are obvious. The expense of executing a new mortgage is obviated. The mortgagee's security is enhanced by the additions or repairs. Recourse to short-term high-rate consumer financing is eliminated. Clearly, the open-end mortgage is an optional advance mortgage. That is, the mortgagee is under no legal obligation to loan the additional funds. The problem here is one of intervening liens.

> **EXAMPLE:** Owner borrows $10,000 from Lender 1 on January 31 and gives Lender 1 a future advance type (open-end) mortgage. The mortgage is duly recorded. On July 1, Owner borrows $1,000 from Lender 2 and gives a junior mortgage on the land, which is duly recorded. On December 1, Owner borrows an additional $1,000 from Lender 1 under the future advance clause of the mortgage. Will this new advance enjoy equal priority with the original $10,000 advance over the junior mortgage of July 1, or will the July 1 mortgage enjoy priority over the new advance so that it is in effect a third mortgage on the property? In a majority of the states, the additional advance will enjoy priority over the intervening lien, the junior mortgage of July 1, unless Lender 1 has actual knowledge of the second mortgage when it gave Owner the advance. In Illinois, Michigan, Ohio, and Pennsylvania, a mortgagee must, before making an optional future advance, search the records for intervening liens. Record notice of intervening liens is enough to give the intervening lien priority over the additional advance. In these states, title companies make special, inexpensive title searches to cover mortgages that propose making additional advances. If the search reveals no intervening liens, the lender should be comforted in making the additional advance, especially if the title insurer endorses its loan policy to cover the additional advance.

A mortgage secures only the debt that is described. Hence, a mortgage designed to secure optional future advances should specifically so provide. The older decisions are somewhat liberal in this regard. Note, *The Open Ended Mortgage—Future Advances: A Survey*, 5 DePaul L. Rev. 76, 80 (1955). However, since the open-end mortgage has become popular, especially in the context of revolving credit loans, the notion that such mortgages should describe such future advances seems to be winning acceptance. At a minimum today, for safety's sake, the mortgage should specify the upper limit of the future advances to be made.

The future advances fall within the description of the debt contained in the mortgage.

> **EXAMPLE:** If the mortgage, by its terms, secures future advances made to multiple borrowers, an advance made to one but not all of the borrowers probably is not secured by the mortgage. *Capocasa v. First Nat'l Bank,* 36 Wis. 2d 714, 154 N.W.2d 271 (1967). Likewise, an advance made to a grantee of the mortgagors might not be secured by the mortgage unless the mortgage so provides. *Walker v. Whitemore,* 165 Ark. 276, 262 S.W. 678 (Ark. 1924).

The documents evidencing the future advance should refer to the mortgage, so that it is apparent that such advances were meant to be advances secured by the mortgage. If the mortgage makes no reference to future advances, any later document securing future advances must be executed and acknowledged like an original mortgage, recorded, and the title searches brought down to cover recording, for it is, in legal effect, a new mortgage on the property.

The distinction between optional and obligatory advances has been subject to criticism that it does not accommodate current forms of loan transactions. The law is beginning to change. In a number of states, subject to specified requirements, the priority of a mortgage dates from its recording regardless of when the loan is disbursed. 735 ILCS 5/15-1302. These new laws commonly require that the mortgage state the maximum amount to be advanced and that the priority only extend to advances made within a stated period of time, such as twenty years. *Fidelity Sav. Ass'n v. Witt,* 8 Kan. App. 2d 640, 665 P.2d 1108 (1983).

An interesting issue arises in the future advance context when the borrower is a partnership. Typically, the loan agreement is executed at a point in time, and later, some or all of the advances are made. Some courts would hold that only the partners at the time of the execution of the loan documents, and not later admitted partners, are liable for the repayment of the debt. *Citizens Bank of Mass. v. Parham-Woodman Medical Assocs.*, 874 F. Supp. 705 (E.D. Va. 1995).

21.05   Revolving Credit

The revolving credit mortgage has become very popular in both commercial and consumer settings. Many homeowners have seen their homes appreciate in value while their monthly payments have greatly reduced the amount remaining due on the first mortgage. Thus, a substantial equity has been created. Lenders have been heavily marketing home equity or line-of-credit loans. Many people are using this type of debt instead of their credit cards to take advantage of interest deductions for income tax purposes that are otherwise not available. Generally, a statute is needed to validate such liens. *See, e.g.,* 815 ILCS 205/4.1. The mortgage must be for a minimum amount ($5,000 in Illinois) and usually must state an upper limit. The interest rate typically floats, often using the prime rate as its index. Seven or ten years are common maturity dates. As the borrower draws on the line of credit, the debt increases and the line of credit or amount of available credit is reduced. As payments are made on the mortgage, the opposite occurs. The borrower draws on the credit line by writing checks. The statute must deal specifically with the priority this type of mortgage enjoys, since obviously the mortgage secures a number of liens accruing at the times that draws are made on the line of credit. At least one court has upheld the priority of the revolving credit loan over a junior lienor where the revolving credit lender made the required advances. *Goldome Realty Credit Corp. v. Hardwick,* 236 N.J. Super. 118, 564 A.2d 463 (1989).

Title companies issue policies insuring these mortgages. In Illinois, this form of title insurance does not protect against mechanic's liens. In other states, insurance does not protect against federal liens. Real estate taxes always enjoy a superior lien.

21.05(a)   Revolving Credit—State Institutions

Every state has either laws or court decisions that govern revolving credit loans. Since revolving credit loans are a type of future advance loan, they may be governed by a state law applying generally to future advance loans. In other states, there are specific statutes dealing with the priority of lien accorded to mortgages that secure future advances made on revolving credit loans.

21.05(b)   Revolving Credit—National Banks

National banks can make revolving credit mortgage loans. Richard P. Eckman & Andrew T. Semmelmen, *A Look at Home Equity Loans: Some Problems and Solutions*, 41 Bus. Law 1079 (1986). The U.S. Comptroller of the Currency has interpreted the law to preempt various state restrictions, including those on repayment of principal balances, balloon payments, and maximum limits on the total loan term. It is important to note that state law provisions not preempted include state-imposed usury ceilings, certain restrictions on second mortgages and non-purchase money adjustable-rate mortgages, homestead laws, and lien-priority, recording, and tax provisions. Further, the regulation provides that other applicable federal laws and regulations, including disclosure statutes and, presumably, consumer protection statutes, continue to apply to national banks making real estate loans.

21.05(c)   Revolving Credit—Title Insurance

The revolving credit mortgage in the form of a junior mortgage on a home is a new type of legal document in most states. There is practically no case law on the subject. The big unanswered question relates to the priority of the lien of the advances made. Without an endorsement, the loan policy will not cover advances made after the policy date. Special endorsements have been drafted to cover the priority of these advances.

21.05(d) Revolving Credit—Home Equity Loans

The home equity loan is a popular form of revolving credit loan found in the consumer setting. In this form of loan, a homeowner arranges for a line of credit with a lender. The loan is secured by the borrower's residence. The borrower can obtain loan advances up to a stated maximum amount, repay some or all of the loan balance, and make additional borrowings. These loans have various features and are typically due in five to seven years. The same issues applicable to revolving credit loans apply to these loans, except that many states have enacted legislation to help lenders who make revolving credit loans to consumers overcome problems, such as achieving priority for additional advances or providing that the lien of the mortgage will continue even if the loan is repaid in full but not released. This latter provision allows the borrower to make subsequent draws against the line of credit. These statutes also regulate the credit arrangement between the lender and the borrower, especially in consumer settings. *See, e.g.,* 815 ILCS 205/4.1.

Some special requirements must be met. The index that is used to set the interest rate as it varies over time must be publicly available and not under the lender's control. The lender may not stop making additional advances and require immediate payment, unless the borrower has committed a fraud or material misrepresentation in connection with the loan, fallen into default, or adversely affected the security. The lender may, however, prohibit additional loan advances if the value of the security declines to a level significantly below the original appraised value, or the lender reasonably believes that the borrower will not be able to repay the loan according to its terms as a result of a material adverse change in the borrower's financial condition.

21.05(d)(1) Revolving Credit—Home Equity Loans—Disclosures

The Home Equity Loan Consumer Protection Act of 1988 requires extensive disclosures to borrowers. The borrower must be given a brochure explaining the operation of the loan and certain other information including a statement of the conditions under which the lender may require immediate repayment, prohibit additional advances, or reduce the borrower's credit limit. Additional disclosures relate to the index to be used in computing the interest rate for the loan, together with a fifteen-year history of changes in the index. 15 U.S.C. § 1637.

21.06 Dragnet Clause

The dragnet clause is a special mortgage clause that secures additional indebtedness that the borrower may have to the lender.

EXAMPLE: A mortgage from Owner to Lender secures the promissory note of Owner for $10,000 and all other obligations of Owner to Lender. Here, Lender can buy up Owner's other obligations, perhaps at a steep discount, and enforce the mortgage for the face amount of all such debts in addition to the $10,000. Milton Roberts, *Debts Included in Provision of Mortgage Purporting to Cover All Future and Existing Debts (Dragnet Clause)—Modern Status*, 3 A.L.R.4th 690 (1981). Other courts hold that the obligations must be specifically identified to be included within the scope of the dragnet clause. *United Nations Bank v. Tellam*, 644 So. 2d 97 (Fla. App. 1994).

The courts are hostile to these mortgages and construe them strictly.

EXAMPLE: Husband and Wife give Lender a mortgage securing a note and all other obligations of Husband and Wife acquired by Lender. Lender bought a note signed by Husband only. The court held that this note was not secured by the mortgage. It was not an obligation of Husband and Wife. Milton Roberts, *Debts Included in Provision of Mortgage Purporting to Cover All Future and Existing Debts (Dragnet Clause)—Modern Status*, 3 A.L.R.4th 690 (1981).

For this type of clause to include other indebtedness, the second indebtedness must have been reasonably within the contemplation of the mortgagor and mortgagee at the time of the mortgage transaction. *Airline Commerce Bank v. Commercial Credit Corp.,* 531 S.W.2d 171 (Tex. 1975). Strict construction of these provisions protects those who subsequently acquire the property from additional debt being secured by these mortgages. This approach protects those who do not protect themselves at the time of the acquisition of the property.

21.07 Prepayment Penalties

Commercial loans typically have more elaborate prepayment clauses that may be heavily negotiated and are strongly influenced by the nature of the property, the borrower's business plans for it, and the lender's investment objectives. Some loan documents provide a sliding scale of prepayment penalties or premiums, often with the loan not being prepayable for the initial period of the loan term, with prepayment penalties declining in percent with each year thereafter. Other provisions require notice to the lender prior to prepayment. Still others allow only a portion of the loan to be prepaid in any one calendar year.

Many commercial loan documents contain a prepayment premium formula that evolved from the lender's attempt to match the yields on its investments with the lender's obligations to third parties on guaranteed investment contracts and other investment vehicles. George Lefcoe, *Yield Maintenance and Defeasance: Two Distinct Paths to Commercial Mortgage Prepayment,* 28 R.E. L.J. 202 (2000). Until rather recently, these formulas were fairly uniform and little doubt was cast upon their validity. The formulas determined the premium by multiplying (1) the difference between the loan interest rate and the yield as of the date of prepayment on U.S. Treasury obligations closest in maturity to the loan maturity with (2) the remaining balance on the loan with (3) the number of years or fraction thereof remaining in the loan term.

> **EXAMPLE:** A ten-year 10.25 percent loan with a remaining balance of $9,000,000 is paid off four years before its maturity. The loan documents contain a "yield maintenance" prepayment premium formula of the kind described earlier. At the time of payoff, the yield on U.S. Treasury notes maturing in four years is 7.45 percent. The yield maintenance prepayment premium would be calculated as follows.
>
> 10.25% − 7.45% = 2.80% the interest rate differential
>
> $$\begin{array}{r} \$9,000,000 \\ \underline{\times\ 2.80\%} \\ \$\ \ 252,000 \\ \underline{\times\ 4\ \text{years}} \\ \$1,008,000 \end{array}$$

Some bankruptcy courts have avoided this type of clause because it gave a possible windfall to the lender. The courts based their decision on the fact that the interest rate differential was not tied to the lender's actual rate of return upon the reinvestment of the funds received on loan repayment and was not a reasonable estimate of the damage to be suffered by the lender as a result of the repayment. Further, the formula failed to reduce the premium to its present value. *In re Skyler Ridge,* 80 B.R. 500 (Bankr. C.D. Cal. 1987) *In re Kroh Bros. Dev.,* 88 B.R. 997 (Bankr. W.D. Mo. 1988). *But see TMG Life Ins. Co. v. Ashner,* 21 Kan. App. 2d 234, 898 P.2d 1145 (1995), which rejects as incorrect *Kroh Bro.,* a case decided under Kansas law. In reaction to these cases, lenders have modified their yield maintenance clauses to address the courts' concerns. It should be pointed out, however, that prepayment premium or loss of yield clauses are not per se invalid. *See (Equitable Life Assurance Soc. v. United Merchants & Mfrs.) In re United Merchants & Mfrs, Inc.,* 674 F.2d

134 (2d Cir. 1982); *(Home Fed. Sav. & Loan Assoc. v. Imperial Coronado Partners, Ltd.) In re Imperial Coronado Partners, Ltd.,* 96 B.R. 997 (9th Cir. 1989). Indeed, the prepayment premium will not generally fall to the claim that it is unconscionable, even when the amount of the penalty is high as compared to the debt. *West Raleigh Group v. Massachusetts. Life Ins. Co.,* 809 F. Supp. 384 (E.D. N.C. 1992). *See generally* Chester L. Fisher III, *Make-Whole Prepayment Premiums Under Attack,* 45 Bus. Law. 15 (1989); Debra P. Stark, *Prepayment Charges in Jeopardy; The Unhappy and Uncertain Legacy of In re Skyler Ridge,* 24 Real Prop. Prob. & Tr. J. 191 (1989). *See also In re Hidden Lake Ltd. Partnership,* 2000 W.L. 518201 (Bankr. S.D. Ohio) (upholding the yield maintenance clause as a liquidated damages provision).

21.07(a)   Prepayment Penalties—Default and Acceleration

An interesting issue has developed where the borrower defaults and the lender accelerates the payment of the entire debt as a result. If the loan documents provide for a prepayment penalty or premium, will the lender be able to add that prepayment penalty amount to the debt to be paid? Many courts have held that the lender will not be allowed to require the payment of the prepayment penalty as part of the accelerated loan balance, unless the loan documents expressly give the lender the right to collect the prepayment premium in the event of default and acceleration. *Parker Plaza West Partners v. UNUM Pension & Ins. Co,* 941 F.2d 349 (5th Cir. 1991); *In re LHD Realty Corp.,* 726 F.2d 327 (7th Cir. 1984); *Tan v. California Fed. Sav. & Loan Ass'n,* 140 Cal. App. 3d 800, 189 Cal. Rptr. 775 (1983); *Slevin Container Corp. v. Provident Fed. Sav. & Loan Ass'n,* 98 Ill. App. 3d 646, 424 N.E.2d 939 (Ill. App. 1981); *McCarthy v. Louisiana Timeshare Venture,* 426 So. 2d 1342 (La. App. 1982); *3C Assoc. v. IC & IP Realty Co.,* 524 N.Y.S.2d 701 (1988); *Am. Fed. Sav. & Loan Ass'n v. Mid-America Serv. Corp.,* 329 N.W.2d 124 (S.D. 1983); *McCausland v. Bankers Life Ins. Co. of Nebraska,* 110 Wash. 2d 716, 757 P.2d 941 (1988); *Rogers v. Rainier Nat'l Bank,* 111 Wash. 2d 232, 757 P.2d 976 (Wash. 1988).

The same result follows if the loan is prepaid as a result of events out of the control of the borrower or lender.

> **EXAMPLE:** Property securing a loan is condemned and the award applied to the payment of the debt. The lender could not enforce the prepayment penalty clause. *Village of Rosemont v. Maywood-Proviso State Bank,* 149 Ill. App. 3d 1087, 501 N.E.2d 859 (Ill. App. 1986). If, however, the prepayment penalty clause expressly provided that the penalty could be imposed in the event of acceleration or condemnation, the provision would be enforced. *Connecticut Gen. Life Ins. Co. v. Schaumberg Hotel Owner Ltd. Partnership,* 97 B.R. 943 (Bankr. N.D. Ill. 1989).

It may be argued that the prepayment penalty cannot be imposed where the prepayment was not voluntary. Most courts do not agree and hold that the prepayment penalty is enforceable if the loan documents provide for the payment of the penalty in involuntary situations; whether the prepayment is caused by the voluntary act of the borrower, forces not under the borrower's control, or acceleration by the lender, the lender's right to receive the penalty will be enforced. *Golden Forest Properties, Inc. v. Columbia Sav. & Loan Ass'n,* 202 Cal. App. 3d 193, 248 Cal. Rptr. 316 (1988); *Pacific Trust Co. v. Fidelity Fed. Sav. & Loan Ass'n,* 229 Cal. Rptr. 269 (1986); *Camelot, Ltd. v. Union Mut. Life Ins. Co.,* 154 Ariz. 330, 742 P.2d 831 (1987).

All of this creates the following problem. If the borrower voluntarily prepays a loan that has a prepayment penalty provision, say upon a sale of the property securing the loan, the lender will be entitled to collect the prepayment penalty. But, a borrower wanting to sell the property may intentionally default. If the lender accelerates, the borrower may assert that because the loan documents do not expressly require the payment of the prepayment penalty in the event of prepayments resulting from acceleration, the lender is not entitled to the prepayment premium. In these circumstances, courts will consider the borrower's conduct and may allow the lender to collect the premium. *Florida Nat'l Bank v. BankAtlantic,* 557 So. 2d 596 (Fla. App. 1990). *But see First Nat'l Bank v. Equitable Assurance Soc'y,* 157 Ill. App. 3d 408, 501 N.E.2d 518 (Ill. App. 1987); *First Indiana Fed. Sav. Bank v. Maryland Dev. Co., Inc.,* 509 N.E.2d 253 (Ill. App. 1987). *See* Debra P. Stark, *New Developments in Enforcing Prepayment Charges After an Acceleration of a Mortgage Loan,* 26 Real Prop. Prob. & Tr. J. 213 (1991).

21.08   Bankruptcy Protective Devices— In General

Because of the losses that lenders suffered during the 1980s and early 1990s as a result of the delays resulting from a defaulted borrower's bankruptcy, lenders are now generally interested in bankruptcy proofing their loan documents so as to avoid those delays and the resulting losses. Devices used by lenders have taken many forms, ranging from requirements for the structure of the borrowing entities to new provisions in the loan documents used in today's transactions.

21.08(a)   Bankruptcy Protective Devices— Waiver of Automatic Stay

While the borrower cannot waive its right to file bankruptcy, *United States v. Royal Bus. Funds Corp.,* 724 F.2d 12 (2d Cir. 1983), many lenders have attempted to achieve a measure of protection from the lengthy delays that the automatic stay may cause by inserting a clause in their loan documents by which the borrower waives the protections of the automatic stay, or agrees not to contest the lender's efforts to obtain relief from the stay. While there is some doubt that these clauses will be effective in any event, or in all jurisdictions, it is generally felt that this type of clause will not be effective when it is contained in the original loan documents. A consent to the lifting of the automatic stay contained in a workout agreement will be enforced in some jurisdictions. *In re Citadel Properties, Inc.,* 86 B.R. 275 (Bankr. M.D. Fla. 1988).

21.08(b)   Bankruptcy Protective Devices— Bankruptcy-Remote Entities

Lenders seem to be more comfortable with a borrower structure that makes bankruptcy unlikely, rather than a covenant by the borrower that a bankruptcy will not be filed, or if filed, the borrower will take certain actions.

One such device is the single-purpose entity. Some lenders require all of their borrowers to be single-purpose entities owning only the property that secures the loan and having debt that relates only to the business enterprise of owning and operating that property. If such is the case, the borrower should only have trade debt and the debt to the lender, assuming that junior financing is prohibited. In addition, the single-purpose entity should carry on its activities as a separate and distinct entity from its affiliates, the other entities that have been organized by the same developer or principal. If this is not done, the possibility exists that all of the related entities will be consolidated for bankruptcy purposes, a result that would negate the protections afforded by requiring the single-purpose entity.

> **EXAMPLE:** Several single-purpose entities are organized by a developer to own and operate various real estate properties, as is required by the lenders of those projects. The developer, however, disregards the separateness of those entities and treats them all as one, with one checking account into which the funds from all of the projects are commingled, without making the proper filings each year with the corporate authorities of the states in which the entities were organized. In effect, the developer runs all of the entities as extensions of a single business. The possibility exists that if one or more of these entities fails, there would be

a substantial consolidation of the assets and liabilities of all of the affiliate entities, thereby negating the separate treatment that the lenders sought by requiring single-purpose borrowing entities.

Another form of bankruptcy-remote entity prevents the decision makers from taking bankruptcy. Through this device, the decision to file a voluntary bankruptcy can be made only with the approval of an individual who is under the lender's control or, at least, not under the promoter of the borrower's control. Alternatively, the lender may require that the corporate documents require a supermajority vote on any resolution that authorizes a bankruptcy filing. There is a considerable body of thought that this type of device exposes the lender's decision maker to liability if it responds as the lender would like rather than in the best interest of the borrower and the borrower's creditors. *In re Kingston Square Assoc.*, 214 B.R. 713 (Bankr. S.D. N.Y., 1997). Gregory Varallo & Jesse A. Finklestien, *Fiduciary Obligations of Directors of the Financially Troubled Company*, 48 Bus. Law. 239 (1992).

The springing guarantee is another bankruptcy-proofing device. Under this form of guarantee, the principal of the borrower is liable if the borrower files for bankruptcy protections.

21.09 Securitized Loans

Many loans today are made to be part of a securitized loan pool. That is to say that the ultimate holder of the loan will not be the typical bank, thrift, or life company that we came to know as the lender of the 1970s and 1980s. Securitized loans will be pooled and interests in the pool sold in the securities market. To the borrower, there are benefits and burdens that go hand in hand with this form of loan. Notably, the interest rate charged to the borrower will be less than would be paid if the loan was obtained through traditional sources. To get this lower interest rate, the borrower will give up some flexibility and the ability to deal with its "banker." Once the loans are sold or securitized, loan modifications will be difficult to obtain.

To be suitable for these securities pools, certain characteristics must be present. Principal among the characteristics of securitized loans is the prevention of prepayment. The securities buyers want the return virtually guaranteed, or compensation if the funds are at risk of not being invested at the expected return for the loan term. This is understandable, because the investor is often a pension fund that must have a high degree of assurance that the return on its investment will be achieved. The benefits that the fund is to pay to its members depends on this return. As with the secondary market, to the extent that the loans are made on standardized forms, they will be more attractive for consideration as securities. Joseph Philip Forte, *A Capital Markets Mortgage: A Ratable Model for Main Street and Wall Street*, 31 Real Prop. Prob & Tr. J. 489 (1996).

Securitized loan documents contain special provisions that require that the property be owned by a single purpose entity; give the lender the right to securitize the loan and require the borrower to cooperate by allowing inspections of the property by prospective purchasers and their representatives; require the borrower to give estoppels to participants and purchasers; require the borrower to give updated financial information, which may be distributed to prospective purchasers of securities interests in the loan; give loan purchasers and participants the right to rely upon and obtain the benefits of legal opinions, indemnities, and affidavits included in the loan documents; require that rents be paid to a lock-box arrangement with the servicer so as to prevent to the extent possible any interruption in the cash flow to the ultimate investor in the loans; and allow the transfer of the property to be conditioned upon the approval of the agency that rates the securities or the continuation of the rating of the securities.

21.10   Cross-Collateralization/ Cross-Default

The cross-default/cross-collateralization provisions of real estate loan documents are quite complex in themselves and involve many other provisions and concepts of loan documentation. In broad generalities, these provisions contain the borrower's agreement that a default under any of a group of loans is a default under all of the loans in the group, and that the property securing any one of those loans secures all of the loans. *Parsons v. Biscayne Valley Investors Ltd.,* 23 Kan. App.2d 718, 935 P.2d 218 (1997). Of necessity, the provisions must identify the loans in question and the properties securing each of the loans.

While for certainty in drafting, the properties in question should be identified, the legal descriptions of all of the properties are not needed. A typical style is for each of the sets of loan documents to contain the legal description of the individual parcel of property that is the subject matter of the individual loan and state that the property also secures each of several other loans that are described by reference to an exhibit that contains a schedule of the information about each of the other loans. This provision encumbers the property described in the loan documents as security for the other loans in much the same way that such property is agreed to stand as security for a promissory note or any other credit obligation.

The drafting of the documents to implement a cross-default/cross-collateralization loan frequently involves many legal issues that bear upon the enforcement of multiple loan and security agreements. The complexity of the process is often exaggerated when properties are located in different states and when the requirements of state-by-state mortgage tax issues and title insurance regulations are added to the mix.

A well-drawn cross-default clause will provide that a default under any of the documents relating to any of the loans shall entitle the lender to accelerate the maturity of any or all of the loans, including the loan to which the default relates. In addition to accelerating the loans, the lender should be expressly empowered to exercise any of the rights and remedies it may have against the borrower, or any of the properties standing as security for any of the loans, or any of the credit enhancements that may be available to the lender, such as guarantees and letters of credit. As is the case with acceleration, the lender should be entitled to exercise its enforcement rights and remedies against one or more of the properties that secure the loans.

As a complementary provision, any guarantee that is part of the loan document package should provide that the guarantor's liability is not affected by the fact that a default may have occurred with respect to one or more, but not all of the loans, and the lender may have accelerated one or more of the loan maturities by the operation of the cross-default clause, and the lender may be enforcing its rights against some but not all of the collateral.

The cross-collateralization clause is typically drafted from the perspective of the identification of the debt (i.e., the collective obligations under the loan at hand and the obligations under the other loans) that the property described in the documents for the loan at hand secures. The drafter of these documents must be careful to negate any notion that the debt is to be apportioned or allocated amongst the properties. The lender may have made loans of uneven loan-to-value ratios and may otherwise want to assure itself of complete flexibility in enforcing its rights amongst the properties, picking and choosing as it sees fit. Apportionment of the loan amounts amongst the properties would defeat the real leverage available to the lender under this scheme of loan documentation. The lender wants to be able to enforce its rights against all of the properties until the loan is paid in full. This is especially important where some of the properties have equity above the loan amount to offset the collateral deficiency that may be found with respect to other properties.

The flexibility that this clause gives to the lender must allow the lender to pick and choose among the various remedies available to it and to pick and choose the properties against which it will enforce its rights. Similarly, the lender wants to be free of any obligation to enforce its rights against any of the properties in any order or to enforce any of its remedies in any order of priority. In other words, the lender should be free to enforce its various rights, exercising its assignment of rents, seeking the appointment of a receiver, foreclosing, and enforcing the note and guarantee against the properties, the borrower and the guarantors, all in such order and combination as the lender deems appropriate at the time of the default.

Similarly, the lender's act of proceeding to enforce one or the other of its rights and remedies against the borrower and some or all of the property should not result in an election of the lender's remedies or prevent the lender from later seeking to enforce other remedies, or to enforce its remedies against other properties. Whether the lender chooses to proceed in such a fashion is irrelevant at the documentation stage. What is important is the preservation of the lender's rights to pursue the avenues of recovery that it deems best at the time.

On a related point, it is important to prevent the operation of the merger doctrine if the lender proceeds to judgment with respect to some but not all of the properties. The argument that the mortgage is merged into the foreclosure judgment must be negated so that a foreclosure of the cross-collateralized mortgage against one property will not prevent the foreclosure of that same mortgage against the other properties that continue to secure the loan. Similarly, the lender should not be limited in its ability to enforce its rights against the properties that it chooses because of the theory of marshaling of assets and the "inverse order of alienation."

Since the lender will have flexibility in enforcing its remedies and may pursue the properties in such order that the lender shall determine, the loan documents should give some guidance on how the proceeds of any foreclosure should be applied. In this regard, the provision should take the logical step of providing that the proceeds of the foreclosure of any mortgage should first be applied against the property to which the mortgage relates. Any surplus would be applied as the lender may determine.

21.10(a) Cross-Collateralization/Cross-Default—Release Provision

The release provision is probably the most complicated of all of the provisions of a cross-collateralized loan. Indeed, because of the cross-collateralization feature of the loan, the case can be made that none of the properties should be released until the entire loan is paid in full. Such an approach may be a bit unrealistic in that it is almost inevitable that events will transpire that cause the borrower to request the release of some of the property that secures the loan package. Some lenders take the position that they will deal with the request for a release when it is made. These lenders do not want to be bound by any predetermined formula that may bind them to give a partial release without taking into consideration factors that are not foreseen at the time the loan is made.

To accommodate the possibility of release, however, the loan documents frequently include a list of the conditions that must be fulfilled by the borrower if one or more, but less than all, of the loans are to be repaid in full and a partial release or satisfaction is to be given before the maturity date. Of course, the lender will insist that the loan not be in default. The lender would not allow the borrower to obtain the release of property that may contribute equity to the portfolio thereby depriving the lender of the benefits of the cross-collateralization provisions, just when those benefits are needed the most, at the time of default.

Often, the lender will require the payment of more than the full principal, interest, and other sums due with respect to a single loan as a condition to granting a release of some of the cross-collateralized property. By taking this approach, the lender gets more than a par payoff, thereby at least theoretically applying some of the borrower's equity in the released property to the loans in exchange for a payoff of less than all of the loans. The borrower is not harmed, because his or her overall account with the lender is reduced by the surplus in the payoff amount.

Finally, to ensure that the property remaining as security for the loans is adequate to carry the debt load that remains outstanding, the lender often will require that the property have a minimum debt service coverage ratio or loan-to-value ratio.

Release clauses in cross-collateralized loan documents can include many unusual provisions that are peculiar to the properties that secure the loan package and address the unique economics of those properties and the needs of the borrower and lender.

21.10(b)   Cross-Collateralization/Cross-Default—Multistate Transactions

The complexities of cross-collateralization are multiplied when the properties lie in different states. Some states allow nonjudicial foreclosure, while other states only allow foreclosure by judicial means. Even in states that allow nonjudicial foreclosures, the result may be different from state to state. In some states, the lender may not proceed to recover a deficiency if the foreclosure was by power of sale instead of a judicial proceeding. As a result, the lender could be prejudiced by proceeding to foreclose nonjudicially against a property in a state that has such antideficiency legislation and then proceeding judicially in another state that allows deficiency judgments.

Varying state laws on the subject of marshaling of assets and the enforcement of foreign judgments must be taken into consideration in structuring these transactions. In some cases, loans subject to one set of laws may be grouped into a separate cross-default/cross-collateral package from the rest to insulate the other loans from any possibility of being tainted by such limitations on the lender's recovery rights.

While the courts of one state will, as a general proposition, enforce the *in personam* decrees of sister states, *in rem* proceedings in one state will not generally be given effect against property in another state. As a result, lenders will want to bring separate foreclosure proceedings in the various jurisdictions in which the property is located. Case law and statutory law of some states may permit such action by allowing sequential or simultaneous foreclosures. *See, e.g., Eastern Ill. Trust & Sav. Bank v. Vickery*, 164 Ill. App. 3d 84, 517 N.E.2d 604 (1988) (which allows a foreclosure against Illinois property to be prosecuted after a prior foreclosure against property in another state); *Travelers Ins. Co. v. Holland Farms, Inc.*, 152 Ill. App. 3d 389, 504 N.E.2d 532 (1987) (which allows simultaneous foreclosure proceedings to proceed in two separate states).

Choice of law and choice of forum issues will always be sticky. While it can be stated generally that the law of the state where the property is located will govern the foreclosure, the remainder of the rights between the parties may be adjudicated pursuant to the laws of another state, either as a result of the law selected by the parties to govern their controversy or as a result of the application of choice of law rules. Beyond the identification of the body of law that may be applicable to the parties' dispute is the selection of the form for the adjudication of that dispute and the law relating to forum selection.

Multistate loan documents require the same analysis as any other agreement to determine that the provisions of those documents are enforceable under the law of the jurisdictions involved. Local counsel should be brought in early so that the deal structure takes in account special requirements that are dictated by state law.

21.10(c) Cross-Collateralization/ Cross-Default—Title Insurance Coverage

A cross-default/cross-collateralized loan transaction that is documented with several mortgages will typically be insured by several loan title insurance policies. Each of those policies will have the property-specific coverages and endorsements that would be obtained in a transaction that does not involve cross-default/cross-collateralization provisions. In the cross-default/cross-collateralized loan, four additional endorsements to the title insurance policies will usually be obtained by the lender.

The first of these is the so-called "tie-in" endorsement. This endorsement identifies the other loan policies and their amount, states that the land secures an indebtedness in the aggregate amount of the loans, and, in effect, increases the individual policy amount to the aggregate of the amount of all of the loans.

> **EXAMPLE:** If the policy related to one of three $1,000,000 loans that were cross-collateralized, the policy amount would be $1,000,000, but the tie-in endorsement would provide the lender with an aggregate of $3,000,000 of protection on each policy. This allows the lender to realize upon the equity in the property over and above the individual loan amount to secure itself against the under-collateralized companion loan. Of course, the lender's total protection would be limited to the aggregate of the insurance coverage or $3,000,000.

Two other endorsements go hand in hand in cross-default/cross-collateralized loan transactions. They are the "first loss" and "multiple foreclosure" endorsements. First loss coverage negates any requirement that the lender accelerate the maturity of the loans or pursue its rights against the other properties before the title company is required to pay its loss on any particular property. This coverage obviates the title company's argument that the lender may be fully secured by the other properties and should enforce its remedies against those properties before the lender insured's loss is determined.

The multiple foreclosure endorsement insures the lender against the risk that the mortgage may not be enforceable as a result of the foreclosure of one or more of the other mortgages that secures the cross-collateralized debt.

The "last dollar" endorsement is also utilized in these transactions, especially where several mortgages secure one debt obligation, but the amount of each of the mortgages, and thus the amount of each of the loan policies, is less than the amount of the total debt. Section 9(b) of the Conditions and Stipulation of a lender's title policy provides that payments of the principal of the indebtedness reduce the amount of insurance *pro tanto*. If the effect of this provision was not altered by the last dollar endorsement, a payment on the aggregate obligation could have the effect of reducing the coverage on each of the various loan policies, even if those payments resulted in the release of land not described in the policy at issue. The last dollar endorsement has the effect of deferring the application of such payments until the aggregate loan amount is reduced to the amount of insurance provided by such policy.

21.11 Licenses, Permits, and the Like as Collateral

Many loans involve property that has special value because of certain permits or licenses that relate to its operation. Examples include a liquor license for the beverage services in a hotel, a hotel franchise and reservations systems agreement, a certificate of need for a hospital or other health care facility, a gambling license for a casino, a permit to maintain an encroachment over or under a public street, and a Federal Communications Commission (FCC) license for a radio or television station. Because these licenses are issued to individuals who have been tested or screened by the issuing agency, they are not freely transferable, either by voluntary conveyance, or in the case of a loan transaction, by collateral transactions or foreclosure and the exercise of UCC enforcement rights. Indeed, many of the statutes and regulations under which these licenses are issued specifically preclude transfer of the license or permit.

While comfort letters, stock pledges, and UCC security agreements and financing statements may be used to get the best security possible, none of these devices are bullet proof. They all involve a degree of risk and trust that the issuer of the permit or license will look favorably upon the lender in the event of foreclosure and the enforcement of the lender's rights. The FCC takes the position that a broadcast license is not a property right that can be subject to a lien or pledge. *In re Merkley*, 94 F.C.C.2d 829 (1983), *aff'd* 776 F.2d 365 (D.C. Cir. 1985). The secured lender may, however, obtain a lien not on the license itself and the right to transfer the license, but on the proceeds realized from the sale or transfer of the license. *In re Ridgely Communication, Inc.*, 139 B.R. 374 (Bankr. D. Md. 1992); *In re Cheskey*, 9 F.C.C.R. 986 (1994). This distinction has expanded outside of the communication license arena. *Fed. Aviation Admin. v. Gull Air, Inc. (In re Gull Air, Inc.)*, 890 F.2d 1255 (1st Cir. 1989); *Freightliner Mkt. Dev. Corp. v. Silver Wheel Freight Lines, Inc.*, 823 F.2d 362 (9th Cir. 1987).

21.12 ERISA Because of the huge volume of mortgage loans originated and purchased by pension funds, and the investment of pension funds in realty assets, the Employee Retirement Income Security Act (ERISA), 29 U.S.C. § 1001, *et seq.*, creates compliance issues that must be addressed to avoid excise taxes and penalties, or worse yet, avoidance of the loan transaction. The first line of analysis is to determine whether ERISA plan assets are involved directly or indirectly in the transaction on either the lender's or borrower's side. This may not be as obvious as one would think. The plans themselves are not generally involved in the transactions. Rather, an insurance company, investment manager, bank trustee, or the like acting as a fiduciary and manager will likely be directly involved as a party. These fiduciaries are held to a high standard of conduct under ERISA and cannot engage in a "prohibited transaction." Such transactions include the sale, loan, or lease of property between the plan and a party in interest.

As a result, the analysis turns to the determination of who is a *party in interest,* a term that is broadly defined to include entities with a direct relationship with an ERISA plan and their affiliates. Caution is the watchword if involvement with ERISA is found.

21.13 Waiver of Right to Jury Trial Lenders have reacted to lender liability cases and the delays inherent with the judicial system by including loan document provisions that waive the right to a jury trial on behalf of both the lender and the borrower. These clauses are generally enforceable if they are clear in their meaning and conspicuously set out in the loan documents. *Lazere Fin. Corp. v. Reggie Packing Co. (In re Reggie Packing Co.)*, 671 F. Supp. 571 (N.D. Ill. 1987). *But see Bank South, N.A. v. Howard*, 264 Ga. 339, 444 S.E.2d 799 (1994). Lender will typically have this clause in all capital letters just before the signature lines of the loan documents. Debra T. Landis, Annotation, *Contractual Jury Trial Waivers in Federal Civil Cases*, 92 A.L.R. Fed. 688 (1989 Supp. 1998) .

21.14 Arbitration The use of arbitration clauses and other means of dispute resolution has come to loan documentation. The use of arbitration is related to the waiver of a right to a jury trial in that arbitration, by its very nature, does not involve a jury. In addition, arbitration cannot completely deal with the issues between the lender and the borrower when the loan falls into default. State law simply does not currently allow foreclosure to proceed through arbitration. Foreclosure must result from a court order, or as a result of the procedures set out in the local power of sale laws. That is not to say, however, that matters other than foreclosure cannot be arbitrated between the parties. These matters may include any claims of lender liability that the borrower may lodge against the lender.

While, in general, arbitration clauses are valid in loan documents, *Green v. Bank One LaGrange*, 266 Ill. App. 3d 344, 641 N.E.2d 1207 (1994), the lender is well advised to draft the provisions clearly, and highlight the provision so that the borrower must read it and perhaps initial it to acknowledge that the provision was read. *Bell v. Congress Mortgage Co., Inc.*, 30 Cal. Rptr.2d 205 (Cal. App. 1994).

21.15 Choice of Forum   A clause that typically accompanies the jury trial waiver clause contains the parties' agreement that matters between the borrower and the lender will be adjudicated in certain courts. These clauses will generally be enforced as long as the clause is clearly drafted and is not unreasonable under the circumstances. Also important, the jurisdiction must have some relationship to the transaction or the parties. *Hall v. Superior Court*, 150 Cal. App.3d 411, 197 Cal. Rptr. 757 (1983); *Credit Alliance Corp. v. Crook*, 567 F. Supp. 1462 (S.D. N.Y. 1983).

21.16 Antiwaiver Clause   Most loan documents provide that the lender's failure to assert its rights will not constitute a waiver of the lender's right to later require full and prompt performance of the borrower's obligations.

> **EXAMPLE:** The loan documents contain an antiwaiver clause. Borrower consistently makes its loan payments ten days after the due date. Lender accepts these late payments without objection. Lender then asserted that Borrower was in default for making the next late payment. Some courts will uphold the force of the antiwaiver clause in this situation. *Kirkham v. Hansen*, 583 A.2d 1026 (Me. 1990). Most courts, however, will require the lender to notify the borrower that late payments will no longer be tolerated as a condition to the lender's right to accelerate the loan balance and enforce the lender's remedies upon the borrower's subsequent late payments.

CHAPTER 22

Real Estate Finance—Sale Subject to Existing Mortgage

22.01 In General

Generally, when mortgaged land is sold, the mortgage is paid and released during the process of sale for the reason that the existing mortgage usually does not meet the financing requirements of the buyer. For example, if land is sold for $15,000 and there is an existing mortgage in the original principal amount of $13,000, which has been paid down to $6,000, the buyer will want a new mortgage of more than $6,000. Thus, it becomes necessary to retire the old mortgage in the process of closing the sale. It is possible, however, to sell mortgaged land without providing for retirement of the old mortgage. For example, where *A* owns land worth $15,000 on which there is a mortgage securing a debt of $5,000, the arrangement between seller and buyer can be that there will be a payment to the seller of the sale price ($15,000) less the amount of the mortgage debt ($5,000), in this case, $10,000.

The first focus of the parties' attention is on whether it is legally permissible for the seller to sell the property without paying off the old mortgage. The answer is that this can legally be done, except where the old mortgage contains an enforceable due-on-sale clause (see Chapter 21). If the sale can be accomplished without running afoul of the due-on-sale clause contained in the existing mortgage, the transaction must be properly structured so as to not result in any unexpected surprises for the parties.

22.02 Personal Liability of Seller to Lender After Sale

A typical mortgage transaction centers around two important documents, namely, a promissory note that creates the personal liability of the borrower and a mortgage that secures the note. If the owner sells the property to a buyer, the lender may not be involved. Its rights are not necessarily affected. The owner's personal liability to the lender will continue unless the lender agrees otherwise.

If the existing lender is willing to consider allowing the buyer to assume the existing loan thereby releasing the original borrower, the lender will typically underwrite the buyer's credit to ensure that the borrower has the ability to repay the balance remaining due under the old mortgage and reunderwrite the property to determine that the property generates adequate cash flow to pay property expenses and debt service and that the property has not deteriorated in value so that an acceptable loan-to-value ratio will be maintained. Assuming that the underwriting proves the transaction to be acceptable, the lender, borrower, and buyer will enter into a three-party agreement, which will contain any new terms (such as an increase in the interest rate), specify whether the seller will be relieved of liability (as is typical in residential loan assumptions), or continue to be liable, and obligate the buyer to pay the mortgage debt and perform the obligations of the borrower under the loan documents. These agreements are sometimes known as *assumption agreements* or *novation agreements*.

Certain distinctions must be kept in mind with respect to the personal liability of the buyer for the repayment of the mortgage debt. In the first place, regardless of whether the seller continues to be personally liable for the repayment of the debt, if the old mortgage is not paid off in the process of closing the sale, the old mortgage remains outstanding as a lien against the property, and if the payments on the mortgage are not made, the old mortgage can be foreclosed. The question then is whether in addition to foreclosing, the mortgagee can obtain a personal judgment against the buyer.

> **EXAMPLE:** The mortgage has a balance due of $80,000. The foreclosure sale price is $75,000. This is considered a part payment of the mortgage debt. Thus, the mortgage debt, after the foreclosure sale, is $80,000 minus $75,000, or $5,000. Can the mortgage lender obtain a judgment against the buyer for the $5,000 that remains unpaid? If the lender can, it can levy on the buyer's assets.

Not all transactions in which the property is sold subject to an existing mortgage involve an agreement with the existing lender with respect to the transaction. In such instances, the focus turns to the terms of the contract of sale and the deed.

> **EXAMPLE:** Owner owns property that has been mortgaged to Lender. The contract of sale and the deed to Buyer both recite that the property is sold subject to a mortgage to Lender, which Buyer does not assume or agree to pay. Here, the only relevant documents state unequivocally that Buyer does not assume liability for the mortgage debt. Buyer has no personal liability for that debt.

> **EXAMPLE:** If, in the previous example, both documents provided that Buyer assumed and agreed to pay the mortgage debt, Buyer becomes personally liable to Lender, even though Lender is not a party either to the contract of sale or the deed.

The theories differ from state to state. The majority rule is that the lender is the third-party beneficiary of a contract between the owner and the buyer. The buyer's liability to the lender attaches when the lender learns of the transaction and determines to hold the buyer liable. This is sort of a fiction in the law. The buyer and seller are not typically intending to benefit the lender. Rather, the seller who is personally liable to the lender is typically seeking protection against liability to that lender in the event that the buyer does not pay the mortgage debt. By having the buyer obligate itself to pay the mortgage debt, the seller, at least in legal theory, may pursue the buyer.

> **EXAMPLE:** If, in the prior example, the contract and deed simply stated that the property is being conveyed "subject to" the described mortgage, without the buyer expressly assuming and agreeing to pay the mortgage, in all but one or two states, the buyer would have no personal liability for the mortgage debt. *Pearce v. Desper,* 11 Ill. 2d 569, 144 N.E.2d 617 (Ill. 1957). Similarly, if neither the contract nor the deed says anything about the mortgage, the buyer would have no personal liability for the mortgage debt.

Much of this discussion is quite academic in a number of states. During the Great Depression, personal judgments in favor of mortgagees bankrupted many persons. This struck many legislatures as disgraceful. As a result, many states passed laws abolishing deficiency judgments in the context of a mortgage foreclosure.

In addition, there are factors today that diminish the importance of personal liability. Before a foreclosure is begun, the lender often attempts to work the situation out without foreclosure.

22.03   Protection of Buyer

There are some steps a buyer should take when entering into a "sale-subject-to" transaction.

First, the mortgage must be read very carefully. If it contains a due-on-sale clause, the conveyance of the property may entitle the existing mortgagee to foreclose and enforce the loan documents against both the land and the seller-original mortgagee. Some mortgages call for an automatic increase in the interest rate or the payment of a fixed sum when such a sale is made. In addition, if the violation of the due-on-sale clause is a default under the loan documents, the default interest provisions of the loan documents may cause the interest rate to increase, and the borrower may become liable for attorneys' fees incurred by the lender to enforce its rights under the loan documents.

Second, a careful buyer will seek an estoppel certificate from the existing mortgagee. This certificate will be given by the existing lender and will state the principal and interest balance due, whether the loan is in default, that there are no late charges or penalties due, and the balances in the tax and insurance impound or escrow accounts. Without this assurance from the lender, the buyer really has no assurance of the amount of the underlying debt and whether the loan is in default.

Third, title insurance is indispensable since the seller's state of title must be evidenced and the buyer must have assurance of that state of title. The contract should specify who pays for the title insurance and list the permitted title objections.

Fourth, if the seller's monthly payments include payments to a tax or insurance impound or escrow account, those accounts should be assigned to the buyer with the seller given an appropriate closing statement credit for the account balances.

In general, the contract should contain the other provisions that are customary in local real estate transactions. The buyer should also carefully review the existing mortgage because it will not be able to challenge the validity of the mortgage or any of its terms. *Pacific First Fed. Sav. & Loan Ass'n v. Lindberg,* 64 Or. App. 140667 P.2d 535 (Or. App. 1983).

22.04   Protection of Seller/Mortgagor

Where mortgaged land is sold without paying off the mortgage, it is necessary to provide carefully for the protection of the seller/mortgagor. As has been stated, the seller/mortgagor cannot get rid of its personal liability to the mortgagee merely by selling the mortgaged land. The seller will want an assumption or novation-type agreement whereby the lender accepts the buyer as the obligated party and relieves the seller from its obligations under the loan documents. In many ways, this transaction is like a new transaction, in that the lender must reunderwrite the loan or at least the new party to the transaction.

There are, however, other ways to structure the transaction, all with varying results.

> **EXAMPLE:** Owner owns property that has been mortgaged to Lender. Owner sells the property to Buyer. In the contract of sale and deed it is stated that the land is subject to the mortgage, which Buyer assumes and agrees to pay.

In a situation like this, the law creates a scheme of priorities, so far as personal liability is concerned. It is said that the buyer is primarily liable to the lender and the owner is secondarily liable to the lender. This is the first step in applying the law of subrogation. If the lender chooses to pursue the owner upon a default, and succeeds in collecting the balance of the mortgage debt from the owner, then the owner steps into the lender's shoes as mortgagee. The owner can then foreclose the mortgage against the buyer. This is because as between the owner and the buyer, the buyer should have paid the mortgage debt. The result would be the same if the deed merely stated that the land "is subject to" the described mortgage without adding words of assumption. Here, the courts say that use of the "subject-to clause" makes the land the primary fund for the payment of the mortgage.

All this is well and good, but it is better to have this and more in black and white. A carefully prepared document is needed, signed by the owner and the buyer when the sale to the buyer is made. It provides that if the owner is compelled by the lender to pay the mortgage debt, the owner is entitled to foreclose the mortgage against the buyer. But it goes further. It requires the buyer to pay the real estate taxes, keep up the insurance, keep the building in repair, and perform all of the other obligations of the borrower under the loan documents. If the buyer fails to perform those obligations, the owner may do so and add the amounts it expends to the mortgage. The owner is permitted to buy the mortgage at a discount and to enforce it for the full amount of the debt.

If the buyer is not to assume personal liability to the mortgagee for the mortgage debt, that ought to be spelled out clearly. Caution suggests the addition of a clause that the contract is only for the benefit of the parties thereto and not for the benefit of any third parties. This prevents the mortgagee from contending that one or more provisions of the sale contract were intended for the mortgagee's benefit.

22.05 Personal Liability of Buyer to Seller

If, in the previous example, the contract of sale and deed stated that the land is subject to a described mortgage, which the buyer assumes and agrees to pay, this promise would make the buyer personally liable to the lender when the lender learns of the transaction. But this promise runs to the owner, so the buyer also becomes personally liable to the owner.

What this means, in practical effect, is that if the lender and the buyer get together to work out a deed in lieu of foreclosure, it will also be necessary to get the owner into the deal. The lender will release the owner's personal liability to the lender, and the owner will release the buyer's personal liability to the owner.

CHAPTER 23

Real Estate Finance—
Purchase Money Mortgages

23.01 In General

The purchase money mortgage is a venerable device.

> **EXAMPLE:** Seller conveys property to Buyer for $100,000, Buyer paying $20,000 cash, and giving Seller a mortgage for the balance of $80,000. Notice that no outside lender is present in the transaction. Seller holds the mortgage and collects mortgage payments. The only cash involved is the $20,000 down payment. This is also called a "purchase money" or "take-back" mortgage.

Second mortgages given by commercial second mortgage lenders have terms and bear interest according to current market conditions. The traditional purchase money mortgage, in contrast, is given because the seller wants to sell the property. The seller will quote terms to facilitate the sale, often with interest well below market rates. Hence, many second mortgages are often purchase money mortgages.

> **EXAMPLE:** Seller is selling property to Buyer for $100,000. The existing mortgage has been paid down to $70,000. It has no due-on-sale clause. Thus, only $30,000 remains to be financed if Buyer takes subject to the existing mortgage. Buyer can pay $10,000 cash; Seller takes back a purchase money second mortgage of $20,000.

23.02 Legal Advantages of a Take-Back Mortgage

The take-back mortgage is a favorite of the law.

> **EXAMPLE:** Seller sells property to Buyer. Buyer is married to Wife, who is insane. Buyer needs a home for his children. Wife's signature would ordinarily be needed on any mortgage. Buyer gives a take-back mortgage to Seller. It is good without Wife's signature.

> **EXAMPLE:** Seller is selling property to Buyer. Buyer is in trouble with the IRS, which has filed an income tax lien against Buyer's assets for $10,000. Buyer is contesting this lien. Ordinarily, this lien would cloud Buyer's title. But, the purchase money mortgage to Seller has priority over the earlier IRS lien. *See Fleet Mortgage Corp. v. Stevenson,* 241 N.J. Super. 408, 575 A.2d 63 (1990).

In some states, the lien for taxes will attach to the buyer's interest and prime the lien of the purchase money mortgage. *Nelson v. Stoker,* 669 P.2d 390 (Utah 1983). While the traditional purchase money mortgage is given back to the seller, the law has evolved to give many of the protections that would otherwise be given to a traditional purchase money lender to the third-party purchase money lender. 59 C.J.S. *Mortgages* § 231(c).

23.03 Usury and the Purchase Money Mortgage

When the seller is also the lender, it is possible to structure the transaction so that the interest rates and debt levels are adjusted to give the seller an adjusted return. This juggling process gives rise to a usury problem.

> **EXAMPLE:** Seller sells property to Buyer for $100,000. Buyer pays $20,000 in cash and gives Seller a purchase money mortgage for $80,000. Obviously, the figures can be juggled. Seller can quote a price of $105,000, with a 10 percent interest rate, or a price of $100,000 with a 14 percent interest rate, having income tax consequences in mind. If the 14 percent rate exceeds the usury rate, it has nevertheless been held that there is no violation of the usury law. *Mandelino v. Fribourg*, 23 N.Y.2d 145, 242 N.E.2d 823 (1968), 20 Syracuse L. Rev. 762; 91 C.J.S. *Usury* § 18; 45 Am. Jur. 2d Interest & Usury § 126.

The philosophy here is that the parties can and do juggle the two components of the transaction, price, and interest rate, and the economic consequences to the buyer are the same. Bear in mind that this problem often arises on second mortgages and where the usury law may be different from that governing first mortgages.

23.04 Flexibility of Take-Back Mortgage

The take-back mortgage is as flexible as the parties wish to make it.

> **EXAMPLE:** Seller is selling Buyer a block of stores and taking back a purchase money mortgage, payable in monthly payments. The parties can agree that the monthly payments will fluctuate as cash flow fluctuates. And they can agree on a "balloon" maturity payment. The mortgage can also provide for lower payments during the first three years of the loan, as is commonly done where a "buy-down" exists.

23.05 Discounting the Take-Back Mortgage

The seller most often chooses to hold the take-back mortgage to maturity. After all, it is well secured. But if the seller needs to convert the take-back mortgage into funds, it will probably have to discount the mortgage balance.

> **EXAMPLE:** Seller sells property to Buyer for $100,000. Buyer pays $20,000 cash and gives Seller a purchase money mortgage for $80,000, bearing 12 percent interest. A year later, Seller needs money. Seller sells the mortgage to Mortgage Investor, who will only pay $67,000 for the mortgage. This gives Mortgage Investor a higher effective annual yield. This is the big disadvantage of the take-back mortgage. This may be an illiquid investment and those investors who buy individual mortgages want substantial returns and insist on this discount.

23.06 Hazard Insurance

Like any other mortgagee, the take-back mortgagee should insist that the standard mortgagee loss clause be attached to the fire insurance policy. The mortgagee may insist on holding the policy.

23.07 Due-on-Sale Clause

The due-on-sale clause has previously been discussed. Before any property can be sold without paying off the existing mortgage, such mortgage must be studied to see if it contains a due-on-sale clause. If it does, the mortgagee's consent to the transaction must be obtained unless the transaction falls into an exception to the due-on-sale clause. In any case, a seller selling with a take-back mortgage should insist that its mortgage contain a due-on-sale clause. The clause should be a broad form clause, covering such matters as installment contracts.

23.08 Balloon Notes

Perhaps the most popular device in the arsenal of creative financing draftsmen is the balloon note. The mortgage is drafted either calling for payments of interest only or with monthly payments as though the loan were to run for twenty or thirty years. But at the end of, say, three years, the entire debt falls due. This is the *balloon*. The philosophy is that over the short run, mortgage money will become more plentiful and interest rates will come down, or the borrower will be able to pay the debt.

The Depression experience with such notes was so bad that savings and loan associations were forbidden to use balloon notes. Some states, such as Florida, have statutes that forbid certain types of balloon notes. *O'Neil v. Lorain Nat'l Bank,* 369 So. 2d 378 (Fla. 1979). Regulation Z of the Federal Truth-in-Lending Act requires disclosure of the balloon. 12 C.F.R. § 226.5b.

The danger, of course, is that the borrower will be unable to borrow funds elsewhere to pay the balloon and the holder of the mortgage will be in a position to exact harsh terms for a renewal. Also, borrowers under balloon notes will have to go into the market to compete with other borrowers when the balloon comes due. It is uncertain what that market will be when those loans are sought. Alternatively, the borrower will approach the seller for an extension. The seller/lender will then have much more bargaining power. The seller/lender will not have the property to sell. There is no reason then for the seller to settle for a below-market interest rate. Moreover, the seller may not want to give the extension, at any rate.

23.09 Call Provisions

As an alternative to the balloon note, there is the call provision, which gives the mortgage holder the right to declare the entire debt due and to foreclose if alternative financing is available at reasonable terms and the borrower refuses to avail itself of it.

23.10 Deficiency Judgments

During the land sales boom of the 1920s, vacant land was sold at insane prices and huge purchase money mortgages were signed. When the Great Depression of 1929 began, thousands of mortgagors were subjected to large judgments obtained by the noteholders for a deficiency. These borrowers were forced into bankruptcy. As a reaction, many laws were enacted forbidding deficiency judgments in purchase money mortgages. Brainerd Curne & Mark Lieberman, *Purchase-Money Mortgages and State Laws: A Study in Conflict of Laws Methods*, 1960 Duke L.J. 1.

23.11 Form of Take-Back Mortgage Transaction

The take-back mortgage documents do not differ greatly from normal real estate mortgage transactions. There is a mortgage, a promissory note, and, where appropriate, an assignment of leases and rents; UCC financing statements and other typical loan documents are used. If the mortgage is a junior mortgage, as is often the case, the clauses needed in a junior mortgage are inserted.

Every purchase money mortgage ought to recite that it is a purchase money mortgage. And the deed to the buyer ought to recite that the grantor is taking back the mortgage as a purchase money mortgage. A purchase money mortgage, after all, enjoys priority over certain judgments, liens, dower, and homestead. The public records ought to reveal the true character of the mortgage so that the mortgagee is in a position to claim those benefits.

23.12 Truth-in-Lending

When the purchase money mortgagee-seller is the typical homeowner who is not in the business of buying and selling real estate, the federal truth-in-lending law and other disclosure-type statutes, such as RESPA, do not apply. 12 U.S.C.A. § 2603.

23.13 Co-Ownership Problems

Where a husband and wife own land as joint tenants or as tenants by the entireties, and they sell the land on an installment contract or take back a purchase money mortgage, questions arise as to the nature of their interest in the proceeds of sale.

> **EXAMPLE:** Husband and Wife own Lot 1 in joint tenancy. They enter into an installment contract to sell Lot 1 to Buyer. This contract creates a now "chose in action," namely, a right to receive the purchase money. The question that arises is this: Is this "chose in action" owned in joint tenancy or in tenancy in common? The same question arises where a purchase money mortgage is involved. The decisions are in wild conflict.

If a joint tenancy is the intended result, let the contract provide that the purchase price is payable to the husband and the wife as joint tenants with the right of survivorship and not as tenants in common or as community property. If a tenancy by the entireties is wanted, let the contract of sale, mortgage, and mortgage note read that the funds are payable to the husband and the wife as tenants by the entirety and not as joint tenants or as community property. Some states do not permit a tenancy by the entireties in personal property such as mortgages. 41 C.J.S. *Husband & Wife* § 35.

23.14 Payment— Joint Mortgagees or Joint Sellers

Where a husband and wife own land jointly, then sell it, and take back an installment contract or purchase money mortgage, the rule is that payment to either party is good payment. 70 C.J.S. *Payment* § 4; 59 C.J.S. *Mortgages* § 446. The party receiving payment can give a release of the mortgage. One would think that the buyer would feel more comfortable if this is spelled out in the documents. Of course, if the check is made payable to both, a different problem arises, namely, whether one party can endorse the other party's name. Again, the documents should cover this.

23.15 Contract Provisions

There are a number of legal problems involved in drafting a contract of sale where the seller is to take back a purchase money mortgage.

> **EXAMPLE:** The contract of sale calls for the seller to take back a mortgage of $30,000 but states no interest rate, manner of payment, or other terms or conditions. The contract cannot be enforced if either party chooses to resist enforcement. It is "incomplete." *Sweeting v. Campbell*, 8 Ill. 2d 54, 132 N.E.2d 523 (1956).

The contract of sale for a transaction including a purchase money mortgage should contain the usual provisions, including permitted title objections. It should also set forth (1) the specific form of mortgage and note to be used, since there is no such form as the "usual" form; (2) who pays the title insurance premium for the loan policy, recording fees, mortgage tax, if any, and other similar charges and fees; (3) whether the loan is prepayable, including any sliding scale of prepayment amounts if the seller is attempting to encourage prepayment; and (4) a list of any documents that the seller is to furnish, such as a statement by the first mortgagee as to balance due, no existing defaults, amounts in tax and insurance escrow, and documents required by local junior mortgage statutes.

CHAPTER 24

Real Estate Finance—
Junior Mortgages

24.01 In General There is generally no legal limit on the number of mortgages a landowner can place on his or her property. Ordinarily, these mortgages will be ranked according to time under the legal rule that *prior in time is prior in right*.

> **EXAMPLE:** Owner owns property and mortgages it to Lender 1 in 1978. The mortgage is duly recorded. In 1979, Owner mortgages the same property to Lender 2. The mortgage is duly recorded. The mortgage of 1978 is a *first lien* on the property. The mortgage of 1979 is a *second lien*. If both mortgages go into default, both will be foreclosed. But, foreclosure of the first lien wipes out the second lien. Lender 2 can prevent this by paying off Lender 1's lien. But, if this is not done, Lender 2's mortgage will be extinguished upon foreclosure by Lender 1. That is why Lender 2's mortgage is customarily referred to as a *junior lien*. Foreclosure of Lender 1's mortgage (the senior lien) extinguishes the junior lien.

As is evident, the risk involved in lending on a second or junior mortgage is greater than in lending on a first mortgage. For this reason, the interest rate is generally higher on a second mortgage. The usual rule governing all investments is that where the risk is greater, the return is higher. Conversely, where the return is high, suspicion is justified because the risk is greater. Also, customarily, the junior mortgage has a shorter maturity than a first mortgage. The philosophy is that risk is reduced by compelling retirement of the junior debt over a shorter span of time. Traditionally, a junior mortgage is made only when there is an equity over and above the first mortgage.

> **EXAMPLE:** Owner buys property in 1988 for $100,000, and borrows $80,000 from Lender 1 and gives Lender 1 a first mortgage on the home. In 1992, the property has risen to $150,000. Owner borrows $30,000 from Lender 2 and gives Lender 2 a second mortgage. The mortgage debts aggregate $110,000, but the combined loan-to-value ratio is 73 percent. This is safe, conservative lending.

That rule is being broken today by those lenders who are making over 100 percent loan-to-value ratio loans to consumers.

24.02 Form and Contents of Second Mortgage A second mortgage routinely contains clauses designed to project the lender against the first mortgage. Some typical clauses are as follows:

1. That the borrower will keep up the payments on the first mortgage and, if it fails to do so, the second mortgagee may make these payments, add the sums so paid to the second mortgage debt, declare an acceleration of the debt, and foreclose.

2. That the second mortgagee may, with the consent of the first mortgagee, buy the first mortgage at a discount and add the undiscounted balance due on the first mortgage to the second mortgage debt.

3. That the surplus proceeds of any foreclosure sale over and above the amount needed to pay the first mortgage debt are assigned to the second mortgagee. This is particularly helpful where a third party is the successful bidder at the foreclosure sale and bids more than enough to pay the first mortgage.

4. A covenant by the borrower reciting the total amount unpaid on the first mortgage and stating that no default exists under the first mortgage. Of course, the junior lender should not be content to rely upon the borrower's covenant. It should receive an estoppel certificate from the first mortgagee reciting the then current balance of interest and principal due, that there are no uncured defaults under the first mortgage, that the placing of the junior mortgage is not an event of default or a violation of the due-on-sale clause, and the balance in any escrow or impound funds.

5. That the borrower will forward to the second mortgagee any notices received by the borrower from the first mortgagee or any public body. This enables the second mortgagee to prevent foreclosure of the first mortgage in some cases. The second mortgagee can make the payments on the first mortgage. Or, if a public body is threatening action to close down the building for code violations, the second mortgagee can give the city assurances that all violations will be corrected.

6. That foreclosure of the first mortgage does not extinguish personal liability of the mortgagor on the note secured by the junior mortgage. 59 C.J.S. *Mortgages* § 523, 704.

Of course, any junior mortgagee will want other protections. On commercial property, the junior lender will demand an assignment of leases and rents. The junior lender will also insist on a title insurance policy that shows the first mortgage as the only prior lien. The junior lender will require the mortgagee loss clause of the fire insurance policy to also run for its benefit. The junior mortgagee has an equitable lien on insurance proceeds. *Arkansas Teacher Retirement Sys. v. Coronado Properties, Ltd.*, 33 Ark. App. 17, 801 S.W.2d 50 (1990). Either the first mortgagee or the junior mortgagor should provide the junior mortgagee each month with proof that the monthly first mortgage payment was made. The junior mortgagee should consider insisting on a due-on-sale clause in the mortgage. This is a necessity if the first mortgage contains such a clause. If the first mortgagee accelerates because of a sale of the property, the junior mortgagee will wish to do likewise. If the first mortgage is an ARM, it should be checked for caps on interest and monthly payments.

An analysis of the first mortgage provisions must be made to ensure that the junior mortgage contains provisions protective of the junior mortgage interest while, at the same time, not artificially causing defaults under either the first or junior mortgage. Inconsistent provisions may put the borrower into the position of complying with either one or the other mortgages and being in default under the other mortgage.

EXAMPLE: If both the first and second mortgages require the borrower to deposit tax and insurance impounds when making debt service payments, the borrower is faced with the obligation of either making double impound payments or being in default under one of the mortgages. This is to no one's advantage. The second or junior mortgage should provide that the borrower is obligated to maintain adequate tax and insurance impound accounts, except to the extent that the funds are held or paid to the first mortgagee. This ensures that, to the extent that the first mortgagee enforces its mortgage, taxes and insurance premiums will be paid. The junior mortgage should take into account the situation that may result if the first mortgage is repaid and the junior mortgage becomes the first mortgage after the tax and insurance impounds are released by the first mortgagee upon repayment of the first mortgage debt.

Similar analysis must be given to other provisions of the loan documents, such as the right to apply insurance proceeds to the debt or hold the proceeds during reconstruction, and the right to rents in the event of default.

24.03 Foreclosure Agreement with First Mortgagee

The second mortgagee may dicker with the first mortgagee and obtain a written agreement that the first mortgagee will give the second mortgagee a notice of any intended foreclosure of the first mortgage. These agreements are enforceable, even if the first mortgage is assigned to a third-party purchaser. *Miles Homes Div. of Insilco Corp. v. First State Bank*, 782 S.W.2d 798 (Mo. App. 1990). And, even without the first mortgagee's consent, the second mortgagee may, in some states, record a notice requesting that it be notified of any foreclosure. This is done routinely in California, for example, where a deed of trust with power of sale is the common mortgage instrument and foreclosure is by the trustee's exercise of the power of sale without any court proceedings.

24.04 Subordination Provisions

Second mortgages usually contain a clause that if it becomes necessary to refinance the first mortgage, the second mortgagee will subordinate its mortgage to the new first mortgage. Because of the technicalities involved in all subordinations, this clause must be set forth in detail. *See* Robert Kratovil & Raymond J. Werner, *Modern Mortgage Law and Practice,* Chs. 30 & 38 (2d ed. 1981).

> **EXAMPLE:** In 1985, Owner mortgaged property to Lender 1 for $100,000 with 11 percent interest. In 1991, Owner gave a second mortgage to Lender 2 for $20,000 with 16 percent interest. A clause was included that Lender 2 will subordinate to any refinancing mortgage paying off Lender 1's mortgage. in 1992, Owner gave a refinancing mortgage to Lender 3 bearing 16 percent interest. A dispute will surely arise. Lender 2 will argue that a "refinancing" should bear the same interest as the loan refinanced. Lender 2 will also argue that his mortgage is not subordinated to any commissions, points, attorney's fees, or title charges.

Subordinations are usually interpreted rather narrowly. Draft the clause broadly. *Shane v. Winter Hill Fed. Sav. & Loan Ass'n,* 397 Mass. 479, 492 N.E.2d 92 (Mass. 1986).

24.05 First Mortgage Provisions

Many first mortgages contain clauses dealing with second mortgage financing.

> **EXAMPLE:** Owner gives a first mortgage to Lender in 1982 on an office building. Almost certainly this mortgage will contain a clause providing that Owner will place no second mortgage on the property and that if this clause is violated, Lender may declare its mortgage debt due and foreclose. This is the "due-on-encumbrance" clause. Some states have laws covering this situation.

The philosophy here is that placing a second mortgage on the property has two adverse consequences to the first mortgage, namely, (1) it places an undue financial burden on the borrower, which may cause the borrower to default in the first mortgage payments; and (2) the second mortgagee may take action, such as foreclosing, that will destroy leases that could be valuable to the first mortgagee. Ominsky, *Why a Mortgagee Should Hesitate to Permit Junior Financing,* 1 Prac. Real Est. Law. Ma. 1985, at 83.

24.06 Statutes Governing Junior Mortgages

There are, of course, a variety of state laws governing junior mortgages.

> **EXAMPLE:** Some statutes define consumer loans (e.g., loans for home repairs) and declare the mortgage void if made by an unlicensed lender. The philosophy here is that the state has a duty to the small borrower to see that only reputable firms engage in second mortgage

lending. Small borrowers usually do not consult lawyers. The opportunity to charge exorbitant fees is present.

The law may also forbid banks or insurance companies to make second mortgages. *Juergens v. Cobe, 99* Ill. App. 156 (1900). Or the law may require a second mortgage to be so labeled in big print, so that any buyer of the paper will know he or she is buying a second lien. 815 ILCS 5/3.

A number of states have statutes invalidating certain junior mortgages.

EXAMPLE: The defendants became indebted to plaintiff's assignor for the purchase of an automobile secured by installment sale and security agreement and collaterally secured by real estate mortgage. At issue was whether the mortgage is good under the Secondary Mortgage Loan Act. It was held that a real property mortgage may not be taken as additional security under the Retail Installment Sales Act. A mortgage on real estate given by the retail installment buyer in connection with the financing of an automobile is null and void and will be ordered discharged of record. *Girard Acceptance Corp. v. Wallace,* 76 N.J. 434, 388 A.2d 582 (1978).

Similar consumer protection laws protect homeowners against sharp practices, such as kickbacks by building contractors to lenders. Some such laws declare the junior mortgage void. *First Nat'l Consumer Discount Co. v. Fuller,* 419 A.2d 940 (Del. 1980). Lawmakers generally regard the regulated first mortgage lenders as responsible parties, who can be trusted not to take advantage of borrowers. They tend to regard junior mortgage lenders as less responsible and impose more stringent regulation. Russell G. Donaldson, Annotation, *Construction and Application of Statutes Expressly Protecting Borrowers in Second Mortgage Transactions*, 43 A.L.R.4th 675.

24.07 Second Mortgage Companies

In many areas second mortgage companies are quite active. They are subject to licensing laws. *See, e.g., 205* ILCS 635/1-2, *et seq.* They will buy second mortgages, usually at a substantial discount. This means that a property seller who takes back a purchase money mortgage must be prepared to suffer a loss if he or she is forced to sell the purchase money junior mortgage. These mortgage companies also carry on an active business selling second mortgages to investors. A purchaser of a second mortgage from a mortgage company will ordinarily enter into a written agreement with the selling company under which it services the mortgage by collecting the payments, checking the property to see that the first mortgage payments, taxes, and insurance premiums are paid, and, in general, maintaining supervision of the loan, for which it receives a *service charge*.

24.08 Prepayment

It is customary in some areas for a second mortgage to carry a prepayment privilege clause that stipulates a penalty of some sort if the loan is prepaid, a not unlikely event. This produces a substantial return to the lender. Some second mortgages, especially purchase money mortgages, contain a clause requiring prepayment when regular bank financing is available. No prepayment penalty is charged. The terms of the financing are spelled out in detail. Some states (e.g., Georgia), permit junior mortgage lenders to use an add-on interest rate.

EXAMPLE: In an add-on loan, a borrower who borrows $100 has the interest (say 9 percent) added on immediately so that his or her monthly or weekly payments include payments on the principal of $109 rather than one of $100. Obviously, the yield to the lender is in excess of 9 percent.

These loans, it is evident, collect at the outset interest for the entire life of the loan. If the loan is prepaid, the portion of interest for the period from payment to maturity is technically unearned.

Some states (e.g., Georgia and Alabama), require the application of the Rule of 78s in such a case. This is a complex rule that provides for rebate of part of the unearned interest. *Winkle v. Grant Nat'l Bank,* 267 Ark. 123, 601 S.W.2d 559 (1980). It is not well adapted to long-term loans. Take the last example and suppose that the note has a prepayment privilege. Suppose that the borrower prepays on June 30, 1982. It is obvious that the $9.00 interest was intended to be spread over the entire year of 1982. Hence, that portion representing interest from July 1, 1982, to December 31, 1982, is unearned. Under this artificial rule, you divide the loan into 78 parts, allocating 12 parts to January, 11 to February, and so on, with 1 part allocated to December. You treat 12/78ths of the interest of $9.00 as being earned in January, an additional 11/78ths as being earned in February, and so on. If you add 12, 11, 10, 9, 8, 7, 6, 5, 4, 3, 2, and 1, you arrive at the sum of 78. Hence, the name of the rule.

In our case you would take July (6), August (5), September (4), October (3), November (2), December (1), and add them, which equals 21. Now take 21/78ths of the $9.00. This is the refund to which the prepaying debtor is entitled. The market has largely made interest charged pursuant to this formula unattractive to borrowers. It is not used often today.

24.09   Interest Rates

Local law concerning interest rates must be carefully analyzed where interest rates are concerned. State usury laws and the Uniform Consumer Credit Code come into play.

24.10   Rents

In large mortgages on commercial property, the first mortgagee may insist that any junior mortgage provide that all rents collected by the junior mortgagee shall be held in trust for the first mortgagee and applied on the first mortgage debt.

24.11   Open-End Senior Mortgage

While the danger does not appear to be great, there is at least a possibility that where there is an open-end senior mortgage, advances may be made under the senior mortgage that could prime the junior mortgage. It is therefore advisable for the junior mortgagee who finds such a first mortgage on the public records to notify the first mortgagee of the making of the second mortgage. This may protect the second mortgagee against such advances.

24.12   Condo Assessments

A common provision in condo declarations is that the lien of assessments shall be subordinate to institutional *first* mortgages. Of course, the lien of assessments, since it relates back to the recording of the condo declaration, will enjoy priority over the lien of a junior mortgage. *Washington Fed. Sav. & Loan v. Schneider,* 408 N.Y.S.2d 588 (1978).

24.13   Foreclosure of Senior Mortgage

Generally, the first mortgagee must name the junior mortgagee if the junior lien is to be extinguished by foreclosure of the first mortgage. When joined, the junior mortgagee typically reacts by seeking foreclosure of its mortgage. This assumes that the junior mortgage is in default. One way to ensure that the junior mortgage will be in default is to insert a covenant in the junior loan documents that the borrower will keep the senior loan free from default. In this way the junior lender will not find itself in the awkward position of not being able to foreclose when the senior lien is in foreclosure. The junior mortgagee will also want to sue the borrower for the repayment of the mortgage debt. In this way, if the junior lien claimant is not the successful bidder at the foreclosure sale, it can obtain the surplus over the amount of the first mortgage debt and pursue the borrower for a deficiency judgment if the second mortgage debt is not fully repaid. Indeed, the junior mortgagee is entitled to an accounting of the proceeds of the foreclosure sale of the first mortgage. *Arizona Motor Speedway, Inc. v. Hoppe*, 244 Neb. 316, 506 N.W.2d 699 (Neb. 1993).

The junior mortgagee is, however, really at risk to the first mortgage. In the absence of bad faith, the junior mortgagee is not entitled to damages for delay in the commencement of foreclosure by the first mortgagee. *Seppala Aho Constr. Co. v. Peterson,* 373 Mass. 316, 367 N.E.2d 613 (Mass. App. 1977). Further, some courts will not recognize a suit by one secured lender against the other for faulty use of the foreclosure process. *Berger v. First Fed. Sav. & Loan Ass'n,* 924 F.2d 400 (5th Cir. 1987).

The junior lender must be careful to enforce its rights if the prior mortgagee forecloses. If the junior mortgagee does not seek a deficiency judgment against the borrower in connection with the foreclosure of the first mortgage, any guarantors of the junior mortgage may be automatically released. *Bank of Oklahoma v. Welco*, 898 P.2d 172 (Okla. App. 1995).

One protection available to the junior lender is the revival of the junior mortgage if the borrower reacquires the mortgaged property after the foreclosure of the senior mortgage. *Old Republic Ins. Co. v. Currie*, 284 N.J. Super. 571, 665 A.2d 1153 (1995).

24.14 Wraparound Loans—In General

The wraparound loan or mortgage, sometimes known as the "all-inclusive deed of trust" is a special type of junior mortgage. The typical junior mortgage is one that is secured by land that is already subject to senior encumbrances. The face amount of the wraparound mortgage represents the total of the amounts then due on the senior mortgage and the new money advanced under the wraparound loan. This compares to the face amount of a typical junior mortgage, which is only the amount advanced under the junior mortgage.

Since the wraparound lender charges interest on the total debt stated in the wraparound mortgage (the total of the outstanding balances on prior mortgages plus the amount advanced under the wraparound mortgage), the wraparound loan has a yield far greater than the yield on an ordinary junior mortgage. Also, because the debts are aggregated in this fashion, the wraparound mortgagee collects payments sufficient to pay the payments due on the prior mortgages and the wraparound loan. The wraparound lender then makes the payments due on the prior mortgages.

> **EXAMPLE:** Owner mortgages a shopping center to Lender 1 for $5,000,000 at 8 percent interest. Over the course of years, the loan has been paid down to $4,000,000. Owner now would like to borrow an additional $5,000,000, and the present value of the shopping center will support such a loan. The going rate of interest is 13 percent. Owner gives Lender 2 a second mortgage in the amount of $9,000,000, but Lender 2 only advances $5,000,000. Owner pays 13 percent interest on the entire $9,000,000 debt as part of the debt service on the $9,000,000 debt. Lender 2 acts as an intermediate collection agent for the servicing of the first mortgage to Lender 1. In this way, Lender 2 deducts the amounts due Lender 1, including amortization of principal and the interest payment of 8 percent, and pays those monies to Lender 1. Lender 2 retains the 5 percent difference between the interest on the first mortgage and the interest payable on the wraparound. The result is a yield to Lender 2 of approximately 17 percent. Of course, prepayment of the first mortgage would reduce this yield on the wraparound loan to the stated rate.

Under some forms of the wraparound mortgage, the full amount stated as the debt is not advanced to the borrower at the time the loan is made. Rather, the wraparound loan funds will be advanced as payments are made to reduce the amount of the first mortgage. Eventually, the underlying mortgage is paid and the payments are then all directed to retire the wraparound.

For the life of the wraparound, there is the danger that other liens will attach to the property and assert priority. To meet this danger, the wraparound lender relies heavily on the theory of subrogation. This is a legal doctrine under which one who pays money on a senior lien is under certain circumstances entitled to claim the benefit of the priority enjoyed by the senior lien.

> **EXAMPLE:** At the time the mortgage to Lender 2 is executed, Owner and Lender 2 enter into an agreement providing that Lender 2 will be subrogated to Lender 1's prior lien position as to all payments made by Lender 2 to Lender 1. This is called "conventional" subrogation or subrogation by agreement. It is a technical concept, but is widely recognized. It gives Lender 2 all the priority that Lender 1's mortgage enjoys over intervening liens—that is, total priority.

Also, the mortgage to Lender 2 provides, as it invariably will, that all payments made by Lender 2 to Lender 1 shall be protected and secured by the mortgage to Lender 2 to the same extent as any previous disbursements and advances made by Lender 2. This is valid and binding. *Boone v. Clark,* 129 Ill. 466, 21 N.E. 850 (1889). This is the rule of tacking. Mortgagees often pay real estate taxes and insurance premiums under such covenants, and the courts hold that such payments give the mortgagee a lien equal in dignity to the mortgage debt. *Reisman v. Jacobs,* 107 Ga. App. 200, 129 S.E.2d 338 (1962).

The wraparound is used in residential financing as well as in commercial financing. In either case, the objective for the lender is an increased yield, while the benefit to the borrower is a lower overall financing cost than would be obtained through complete refinancing.

It often develops that the underlying loan is not prepayable, or has such a low interest rate that prepayment is undesirable. The borrower arranges a wraparound loan package that has higher than normal yield to the seller-lender, while allowing the buyer-borrower to pay a lower rate than if the property was refinanced.

> **EXAMPLE:** The rate on the underlying mortgage is 8 percent. Existing rates are 13 percent. The balance on the underlying mortgage is $50,000. The purchase price of the property is $100,000. The buyer can pay $20,000 down. Charging 11 percent, the seller finances the difference between the underlying loan balance and the down payment. The seller makes no actual advance of money, but sells the property, taking the down payment of $20,000 and obtaining a yield in excess of 15 percent, while the buyer, in effect, pays 2 percent below the market rate. The seller's yield is calculated as follows:

Interest on wraparound ($80,000.00 × 11%)		$8,800
Interest on underlying ($50,000.00 × 8%)		$4,000
Interest differential to wraparound lender		$4,800
$4,800 Interest differential	16%	
$30,000 Amount "advanced"		

The seller also gets the benefit of the use of the installment method of reporting gain for income tax purposes.

24.14(a)
Wraparound
Loans—Usury

Unless the borrower is exempt from usury laws (e.g., when the borrower is a corporation), or if the lender is exempt (e.g., when the lender is a bank), or the loan is exempt (e.g., when the loan is a business loan), the wraparound loan transaction may come within the prohibitions of state usury laws. If there is no local exemption, the question of usury may arise, especially if state law prohibits the lender from receiving more than the statutory maximum.

Beyond the statutory interest rate limitations, the common law prohibition against the exaction of unconscionable interest must be recognized and dealt with. While the stated interest rate is always under the statutory limit, the effective yield to the lender may increase the interest received by the lender on the funds actually advanced beyond the legal limit. This results from the lender's receipt of interest at the stated rate on the amount actually advanced, plus the spread between the stated interest and the interest remitted to the first lienholder. Comment, *The Wrap-Around Mortgage—A Critical Inquiry*, 21 U.C.L.A. L. Rev. 1529, 1532, *et seq.* (1974); Note, *Wrap-Around Financing: A Technique for Skirting the Usury Laws*, Duke L.J. 785 (1972).

24.14(b)
Wraparound Loans—
Documentation

For lenders who do not hold the original first-lien mortgage, certain borrower controls must be built into the wraparound mortgage documents to prevent possible deterioration of the wraparound loan's first-lien status or its high yield.

The most important wraparound mortgage "clause" is the cross-default provision. This is protective language, to the effect that a default on the senior mortgage is considered a default on the wraparound mortgage.

The wraparound contains covenants like those found in a second mortgage and like those in a first mortgage.

The borrower should not be allowed to prepay the first mortgage. This will protect a high wraparound yield. Sam M. Galowitz, *How to Use Wraparound Financing,* 5 Real Est. L.J. 107 (1976) (discusses mathematics involved); Francis Gunning, *The Wrap-Around Mortgage . . . Friend of UFO,* 2 Real Est. Rev. 35 (1972); Comment, The *Wrap-Around Mortgage: A Critical Inquiry,* 21 U.C.L.A. L. Rev. 1529 (1974); Robert Kratovil & Raymond J. Werner, *Modern Mortgage Law and Practice* §§ 24.11, *et seq.* (2d ed. 1981); Gordon & Meyer, *Foreclosing the Wraparound Mortgage: Practical Considerations and the Emergence of Texas Case Law,* 52 Tex. B.J. 1051 (1988); James L. Isham, *Validity and Effect of "Wraparound" Mortgages Whereby Purchaser Incorporates into Agreed Payments to Grantor Latter's Obligation on Initial Mortgage*, 36 A.L.R.4th 144.

CHAPTER 25

Real Estate Finance—
Commercial Financing Devices

25.01 Convertible Mortgages
A form of loan usually encountered in large-scale transactions in periods of anticipated appreciation of property values is the convertible mortgage. It starts out looking like the typical large-scale mortgage, but an option clause gives the mortgagee the privilege, at some future specified date, to convert the outstanding balance of the mortgage into a predetermined percentage of ownership of the property. While the loan may be at a lower interest rate, the lender may also have a provision for additional interest in the form of a participation in cash flow or operating results.

This type of provision is attractive to the borrower because it allows the borrower to retain all of the tax benefits associated with ownership until the lender exercises the conversion option. It is attractive to the lender because the lender exercises its option at a time when the property has proved itself to be viable and has increased in value. There is, however, some danger that a bankruptcy trustee might refuse to honor the conversion clause. Another danger is presented by the possibility that the arrangement be recharacterized as a partnership. For this reason, the loan documents should not give management rights to the lender.

As discussed above, the rule prohibiting clogs on the equity of redemption should not find application in transactions negotiated at arms' length between sophisticated parties represented by attorneys and other advisors. *Blackwell Ford, Inc. v. Calhoun*, 219 Mich. App. 203, 555 N.W.2d 856 (1996).

25.02 Participating Mortgage
In large mortgage transactions, the lender may wish to participate in the income or appreciation in the value of the property. The share of income to be paid over to the lender is stated in the mortgage or in a separate agreement. It is often described as "contingent cash flow participation." It presents many thorny legal problems. Among these problems are the possibility that the loan may be held to be usurious, unconscionable, a clog on the equity of redemption, or as creating joint venture between the borrower and the lender, totally recasting the nature of the lender's position.

To protect against such a result, the loan should be regularly documented and have a fixed maturity date. The interest rate should be clearly set out and be payable absolutely, without regard to the income or value of the property. Active and day-to-day property operation should be left to the borrower, perhaps with the requirement that the property be operated within mutually established guidelines. Losses should be borne by the borrower only. The tax consequences of the ownership and operation of the property should remain with the borrower and not be shifted, even partially, to the lender.

In addition, the laws relating to certain forms of lenders place limits upon or control the types of real estate investments they may make. *Legal Restrictions of Equity Participation Financings*, 20 Real Prop. Prob. & Tr. J. 1139 (1985).

25.03 Loan Participations

The mortgagee may sell a share of its mortgage to a third party. This is called a participation.

> **EXAMPLE:** Owner gives a mortgage to Lender for $100,000. Lender sells a 50 percent interest in the mortgage to Participant. Nothing is recorded as to this participation and no notice is given to Owner. There is a participation agreement between Lender and Participant, outlining Lender's rights and duties. As to the rest of the world, it is as if Lender remained the full owner of the mortgage.

The securitization industry works somewhat the same way in that the lender's interest is sold to various investors, such as pension funds, who seek passive investments with stable returns.

25.03(a) Participation Problems

Since the participation loan involves a transaction in which, in many cases, the originating lender will appear to be the absolute owner of the loan, opportunities for fraud abound. For example, if the promissory note and mortgage are made payable to the originating lender without revealing that others may hold an interest in the loan, the originating lender may sell or assign the loan to a holder in due course who will take the note free of the interest of the participants. In addition, some sellers of loan participations have submitted fraudulent appraisals or otherwise defrauded purchasers of participation interests in loans. While various precautions have been suggested, most are useless if the seller becomes insolvent.

The participation agreement should provide that the buyer is relying on the completeness and accuracy of the appraisals and other representations of the seller. The seller should also warrant that the loan documents are accurate and fully disclose all facts relevant to the loan. The agreement may give the buyer the right to compel the seller to repurchase the participation interest if the seller changes the terms of the loan, violates laws or regulations, or breaches any warranty or representation.

If the buyer wants extra protection, the participation agreement will provide that the seller's share of the mortgage is subordinated to the buyer's share. Indeed, often securitizations or participations have layers of recovery rights or priorities, sometimes called *tranches*. The holder of a higher level tranche may be entitled to priority of recovery, if the payments are inadequate to pay the holders of all tranches. In exchange for this benefit, the holders of the higher tranche will often receive a lesser share of the interest paid by the borrower, with a greater share of that interest going to the lower tranche that takes more of the risk.

In large loans, these protections are no substitute for the participant lender doing its own due diligence and loan underwriting, just as if the participant was originating the loan for its own account.

It is very important from the participant's perspective that the transaction be documented as a true sale of a participation interest and not as a loan by the participant to the originating lender. The parties should make their intentions clear. If the transaction is a loan by the participant to the lender, a debtor-creditor relationship exists between them rather than a co-ownership relationship. The difference is fundamental. If the transaction is a loan by the participant to the originating lender, the participant will have to perfect its security interest in the participation loan under Article 9 of the Uniform Commercial Code. This can only be done if the creditor/participant lender obtains possession of the note, an action that is rarely taken. *Zinker v. Ryan (In re Sprint Mortgage Bankers Corp.)*, 177 B.R. 4 (Bankr. E.D. N.Y. 1995). Without proper perfection of the participant lender's security interest, the creditor is exposed to the sale of the interest to a bona fide purchaser, or worse yet, the bankruptcy of the originating lender and the possibility of being a general creditor of the originating lender, a position far different from having a direct ownership interest in the loan.

If the transaction is properly structured as a sale of ownership interests in the loan, the participant will also have an ownership interest in the underlying collateral upon foreclosure. *Asset Restructuring Fund v. Liberty Nat'l Bank & Resolution Trust Corp.* 886 S.W.2d 548 (Tex. App. 1994).

25.04 Synthetic Leases

Synthetic leasing or off-balance-sheet financing has developed as a new form of financing in the 1990s. This device is unique because it is treated differently for accounting purposes than it is for income taxation purposes. From an accounting perspective, the transaction is treated as a lease and not as debt. The result of this accounting treatment is that the property is not shown as an asset on the user's balance sheet and depreciation of the asset is not charged as an expense against earnings. Tax treatment is quite different. The tenant is treated as the owner of the property and is entitled to take the depreciation of the property as an expense against taxable income, with monthly rent payments being treated as interest expense.

Transactions of this kind are quite complex and must be carefully structured to fit within the requirements of both the accounting standards and the Internal Revenue Code and regulations. If properly documented, the synthetic lease should be enforced according to its terms and not recharacterized. *Unocal Corp. v. Kaabipour,* 177 F.3d 755 (9th Cir. 1999). Financial Accounting Standard 13 sets the following four requirements that must be satisfied if this treatment is to be attained: (1) the property must not be automatically transferred to the tenant at the end of the term of the lease; (2) the term of the lease must be less than 75 percent of the useful life of the property; (3) the tenant may not be able to buy the property at a bargain purchase option price; and (4) the present value of the minimum lease payments must be less than 90 percent of the fair market value of the property determined as of the beginning of the term.

The first of these requirements can be satisfied by simply giving the tenant an option to purchase the property rather than providing for the automatic transfer of the property to the tenant. The option purchase price requirement can be satisfied by setting the price at the fair market value as determined by an appraiser at the outset of the lease or the unamortized debt and ownership equity. The payment structure usually is keyed to an interest-only arrangement. Therefore, this option purchase price should not be a bargain to the tenant. Since synthetic leases are generally for shorter terms of ten years or less, the useful life requirement is also easy to satisfy. The minimum lease payment test requires a bit of analysis and negotiation to satisfy. It will frequently entail the lessor retaining some risk if the property does not appreciate in value over the lease term.

The lease will typically give the tenant a termination right exercisable upon the payment of a contingent rent payment. Upon termination, the lessee will market the property using the sale proceeds to pay to the lessor any unpaid debt and equity investment, with any surplus going to the tenant. Nancy R Little, *Unraveling the Synthetic Lease*, Probate & Property 22 (Jan/Feb 1997); John C. Murray, *Off-Balance-Sheet Financing: Synthetic Leases*, 32 Real Prop. Prob. & Tr. J. 193 (1997).

Many of the benefits of ownership are retained by the user. The purchase option gives the user the ability to capture any appreciation in the value of the property. The lease will typically be triple net to the lessor, thereby giving the user operating control over the property.

25.05 Sale and Leaseback

This form of transaction typically involves a landowner in need of funds for use in its business. While the landowner cannot give up use of its business property, the landowner can give up ownership of the property. An investor is found to buy the property at its full value and lease the property back to the seller. Hence, the term "sale and leaseback." There are other frequently found characteristics of this form of transaction. The seller/lessee is usually a highly creditworthy retailer or industrial business. The lease is usually for a term of twenty to thirty years and the seller/lessee is usually given options to renew the lease and to purchase the property. The rental on the original lease term pays the buyer an amount equal to the purchase price plus a return higher than could be obtained on a conventional mortgage. The lessee is required to pay all real estate taxes, fire insurance, repairs, and other property expenses so that the rental is "triple net" to the lessor. There are some variations on the sale and leaseback pattern.

> **EXAMPLE:** XYZ Hamburgers, a chain, identifies a good location. ABC Realty Investment Trust buys the land, finances construction through an affiliate, and leases the location to XYZ Hamburgers.

The attraction of this type of transaction to the seller/lessee lies in the fact that it gets the full value of the property instead of the smaller amount that it could obtain on a mortgage, and it is under no obligation to repay this amount if it is willing to forego repurchase of the land. In other words, it is not saddled with a debt, as would be the case if it had made a mortgage on the land. Note, of course, the seller/lessee may have a continuing rental payment obligation. The advantage to the buyer is that foreclosure is not necessary if default is made in the rent payments, since the transaction is a sale and lease, not a mortgage.

Among the advantages to the lessee of such an arrangement are the following:

1. A tax advantage. In computing its income for tax purposes, the lessee deducts its rent payments under the lease. Were the transaction a mortgage, the only permitted deductions would be interest and depreciation. Also, if the building is not newly constructed, it may be that the current value and sale price are substantially less than the price paid when the seller/lessee bought the building. If such is the case, the sale to the investor represents an income tax loss to the seller/lessee. The seller/lessee must carefully analyze the income tax implications of a sale of the property because a gain could also be recognized, including the recapture of depreciation expenses taken by the seller/lessee.

2. By selling the property for its full value to the lessor, the lessee obtains much more cash than it could raise on a mortgage. Mortgagees do not typically loan up to 100 percent of the value of the property.

3. Existing mortgages, corporate charters, debenture agreements, or other documents binding on the lessee may place restrictions on the seller/lessee's right to borrow money. Since a lease is not a loan, the leaseback arrangement provides a method of getting around these restrictions. Caution should be exercised, however, in that these same documents may prohibit the sale of business assets without approvals.

The chief disadvantages to the lessee are as follows:

1. If the building goes up in value during the lease term, the investor, not the lessee, will reap the benefit of this increase once the lease expires.

2. The lessee has all of the burdens of ownership. The lease requires the lessee to pay taxes, insurance, and so on, but the lessee lacks the freedom of action that an owner enjoys. The lessee cannot tear down or remodel buildings as business needs dictate unless the investor consents. Likewise, to erect new buildings would be foolish, for they would belong to the landlord at the end of the lease period. Obviously, special arrangements must be made.

In the case of sale and leaseback transactions where the rent provision contains an escalator clause tied in some way to inflation, rentals have increased at times to a point where the transaction is no longer favorable to the tenant.

25.05(a)   Sale and Leaseback— Consequences of Transaction Being Set Aside

The sale and leaseback transaction is a very complex financing vehicle. It must be distinguished from a deed absolute to secure a debt. *In re Matter of Kassuba,* 562 F.2d 511 (7th Cir. 1977). Merely labeling a transaction a sale and leaseback will not make it immune from attack. Indeed, when the transaction is attacked, the courts will carefully analyze the relationship between the seller/lessee and the buyer/lessor to determine whether a sale really occurred or whether the transaction is really a mortgage. *Eurton v. Smith,* 357 So. 2d 324 (Ala. 1978).

If the transaction is found to be a mortgage, consequences befall both the seller/lessee and the buyer/lessor. The relationship of mortgagor-mortgagee with its requirement of foreclosure and redemption rights replaces the relationship of landlord and tenant with its quick possessory remedy of forcible entry and detainer. Usury laws may come into play as a standard for evaluating the fairness of the return to the buyer/lessor who has unexpectedly found itself in the role of lender. The income tax treatment that both parties had used and anticipated will not be available, and, indeed, past years' tax returns will have to be amended and tax liabilities changed beyond the parties' expectations. Egan, *Sale-Leasebacks: Protecting the Institutional Investor Against New Risks,* 6 Real Est. L.J. 199 (1978); Thomas C. Homburger & Brian P. Gallagher, *To Pay or Not to Pay: Claiming Damages for Recharacterization of Sale and Leaseback Transactions Under Owner's Title Insurance Policies*, 30 Real Prop. Prob. & Tr. J. 443 (1995).

As can be seen, the transaction is quite complex and should only be entered into after careful consultation with an experienced counsel and tax advisor. The consequences of a mistake can be awesome.

25.06   Senior Living Facilities

Senior living facilities have increased in number and significance as the population has aged and gained greater longevity. Like all real estate products, senior living facilities are financed. Loans secured by senior living facilities present special problems for lenders and their lawyers as they attempt to obtain the best security possible for the repayment of those loans. This is the case because both the state and federal governments have a role in regulating these facilities and reimbursing them for the cost of the care that they provide.

A new owner of a senior living facility will operate under the same provider agreement as the seller, 42 C.F.R. § 489.18(c), and therefore may be liable for the repayment of any Medicare or Medicaid overpayments made to the prior owner. 42 C.F.R. § 489.18(d). The lender is concerned that the income stream, whether from public or private sources, be maintained to provide the debt service for the loan. The unexpected action of the state or federal government to recover prior overpayments would likely have a drastic effect upon the ability of the borrower to repay the loan. On a related note, Medicare and Medicaid receivables are not assignable. The lender is unable to directly obtain the benefits that it would obtain if these receivables were ordinary rents.

In this regard, the lender is well advised to take a lesson from the cases that have interpreted whether an assignment of rents was effective to reach hotel revenues, or whether those revenues are general intangibles or other forms of collateral under the Uniform Commercial Code. There is no need for the lender to take the chance that the collateral documents are inadequate. The revenues of such a facility should be covered under both an expanded assignment of rents and UCC security agreements with related financing statements.

The operator must be properly licensed to be able to operate and receive reimbursements under state and federal programs. Even in the best of circumstances, obtaining the appropriate license and reimbursement number may take several months. The lender needs assurance that the borrower has, or will certainly be able to, obtain a license and provider number, and has the ability to make debt service and expense payments in the interim.

From an enforcement perspective, the lender must recognize that it or a third-party bidder at a foreclosure sale must be able to operate the facility and maintain the debt service in the event of the borrower's default. This is hard to achieve in the case where the license is not assignable. For this reason, the lender's ability to control management of the facility in the event of a default may be as important as the lender's ability to obtain a foreclosure decree. To achieve this, the lender will insist upon a collateral assignment of the management agreement, and the borrower is typically not allowed to change managers without the lender's approval.

In the majority of states, a facility may require a certificate of need if it is to operate. Through the certificate, the state focuses the development of health care facilities into areas where the need is the greatest. In most states, the certificate of need is not transferable. As a result, the lender must make sure that the borrower has the certificate, and the lender must be prepared to obtain the certificate if foreclosure or a deed in lieu ensues.

CHAPTER 26

Real Estate Finance—Miscellaneous Devices—Ground Leases— Sale and Leaseback

26.01 Ground Leases and Commercial Leases Distinguished—Legal and Financial Aspects—Mortgages of the Leasehold

There is no legal distinction between commercial leases and ground leases. Nevertheless, there are economic differences between them that have legal implications. A commercial lease is a lease of a building or part of a building such as a store to a tenant. If the tenant agrees in the lease to make improvements, as a rule, they are limited in scope. In a ground lease, the landowner leases the land only to a tenant who covenants in the lease to erect a building on the premises, or who otherwise takes fee simple ownership of the building by deed. The true ground lease is a net lease under which the tenant pays all expenses including taxes, insurance, and repairs. The landlord in a commercial lease and its mortgagee are concerned with the tenant's credit standing, since this is their assurance that the rent will be paid. This is the reason, for example, why shopping center developers and their lenders look to national chain stores as tenants.

Because the landlord and the mortgagee depend on the cash flow from triple-A tenants, the lease will forbid any assignment or sublease without the landlord's consent. In a ground lease, on the other hand, (1) the landlord looks for its security to the fact that the tenant will erect or own a valuable building on the property and will have to pay the rent in order to prevent loss of the investment in the building by the landlord's forfeiting the lease for non-payment of rent and (2) the tenant expects to borrow money to erect the building or finance its acquisition. This makes it necessary to draft the lease in such a fashion that the lessee's rights under the lease (the "leasehold estate") can be mortgaged without the landlord's permission. Since the mortgagee who forecloses will want the unhampered right to sell to anyone, the ground lease should not limit the lessee's right to assign without the landlord's consent. Also, the term of the lease should be long enough to make the mortgage on the leasehold a legal investment for banks, insurance companies, and other institutional investors. For example, a state law may provide that a mortgage on a leasehold is not a legal investment for banks or insurance companies unless the unexpired term of the lease exceeds twenty-one years. Some states have a fifty-year minimum.

To better enable the lessee to borrow money for the erection of the building, a ground lease may provide that the landlord will join in the mortgage without, however, incurring any personal liability by signing the mortgage note. Alternatively, the lease may provide that the landlord's title will become subordinate to the mortgage on the leasehold. The landlord who signs such a lease must understand that this weakens its legal position, since foreclosure of the mortgage will extinguish the landlord's ownership of the land. On the other hand, if the construction mortgage is only on the leasehold estate, foreclosure of the mortgage simply results in transfer of the tenant's leasehold interest to the mortgage lender, who then becomes the tenant paying rent to the landlord.

A mortgagee of the leasehold only should require that the lease contain a provision for notice to the mortgagee in case of default in payment of rent, so that the mortgage lender can step in and cure the defaults, thereby preventing a forfeiture of the lease, which would extinguish its mortgage.

There are two basic systems of ground rents, the Maryland system and the Pennsylvania system.

26.01(a) Ground Rents—The Maryland System

The chief characteristics of the Maryland ground rent leases are as follows: (1) the landowner leases the land to the lessee for a period of ninety-nine years; (2) there is a provision for the perpetual renewal of the lease from time to time as each ninety-nine-year period draws to a close, upon payment of a small sum of money called a *renewal fine;* (3) the lessee agrees to pay a certain sum of money (usually semiannually) as ground rent; and (4) the lease contains a provision that if the lessee defaults in making ground rent payments, the lessor may declare the lease void and evict the lessee. The lessee also agrees to pay the taxes on the property, and they are assessed to the lessee. The interest acquired by the lessee under the lease is regarded as personal property.

Prior to 1884, the ground rents reserved by such leases were not redeemable by the lessee unless expressly so stipulated in the lease, but in that year and by subsequent laws, it was provided that the lessee, in leases subsequently executed, could pay the lessor the value of the lessor's interest and thus redeem the rent and become the owner of the property. The original lease, and any assignments of that lease, must be executed, acknowledged, and recorded in the same manner as deeds. The leasehold estate is subject to the liens of judgments against the lessee.

In practical economic effect, the relation of the lessee to the property is that of the owner of the land subject to the payment of the annual rent and the taxes; the lessee's economic relation to the owner of the ground rent is much like that of a mortgagor paying interest on a debt where the principal never matures so long as the mortgagor pays the interest and taxes. The technical relation between the owner of the land and of the leasehold is that of landlord and tenant.

Such ground rents are bought and sold in the same way mortgages are bought and sold.

26.01(b) Ground Rents—Improved Property

A Maryland case, *Packard v. Corp. for Relief of Widows & Children of Clergy of Protestant Episcopal Church,* 77 Md. 240, 26 A. 411 (1893), describes the operation of the ground rent system in a sale of improved property.

> **EXAMPLE:** Landowner sold and conveyed land to Buyer for $4,500. Buyer immediately leased to Tenant for a consideration of $1,000 cash, and rent payable at $210, which capitalized at 6 percent equals $3,500. Thus, a margin of $1,000 was left to protect Buyer against loss in case he should be compelled to take the property back. It was held that this was not a mortgage, but was merely a ground rent.

The court pointed out that, in legal contemplation, this lease was not a mortgage, since, while the lessee had the privilege of redeeming, it was not obliged to do so. Thus, the relation of debtor and creditor, the distinguishing characteristic of mortgage transactions, is not present.

26.01(c) Ground Rents—The Pennsylvania System

In Pennsylvania, ground rents are created by a deed of the land that conveys the legal title to the grantee subject to the payment of rent to the grantor. *Jones v. Magruder,* 42 F. Supp. 193 (D. Md. 1941). A subsequent purchaser of the land must pay the stipulated rent, but the purchaser does not become personally liable therefor unless its deed provides that the grantee assumes and agrees to pay such rent. The grantee in the original deed remains liable for rents accruing even after the grantee's sale of the land. If default is made in payment of ground rent and the owner of the land obtains a judgment therefor, a sheriff's sale under this judgment wipes out all encumbrances and titles arising subsequent to the creation of the ground rent. Pennsylvania also has passed laws providing for the redemption of ground rents. *In re Crean's Estate,* 321 Pa. 216, 183 A. 915 (1936).

26.01(d) Ground Lease Financing

Today's ground lease financing is a relatively simple transaction.

> **EXAMPLE:** Builder builds an office building on land that it owns. Builder then enters into a contract of sale and lease with Tenant, the purchaser. The contract calls for the usual title search. When title shows clear title in Builder, Tenant receives a deed to the building and a long-term lease of the land. The lease may include an option to purchase the land. If the lease has no such option, the lease will provide that, at the end of the term, the building will become the property of the owner of the land. The lease is usually at a flat rental. The contract requires Tenant to execute a mortgage to ABC Co., the company financing the transaction. By means of the mortgage, Tenant mortgages the leasehold estate and the option to purchase. Builder joins in the mortgage or signs a separate document subjecting his ownership interest to the mortgage. This process is called "bringing the fee under the mortgage." *See* Robert Kratovil & Raymond J. Werner, *Modern Mortgage Law and Practice,* Ch. 30 (2d ed. 1981). The result is that if the mortgage is foreclosed, ABC Co. acquires full ownership of the land. Since Tenant initially acquired only a lease of the land, it is permitted to make a substantially smaller down payment. But, because Builder joins in the mortgage, the lender has total security.

Model provisions to be incorporated into ground leases to make them readily financable can be found in Subcommittee on Leasehold Encumbrances, Committee on Leasing, *Model Leasehold Encumbrance Provisions,* 15 Real Prop. Prob. & Tr. J. 395 (1980) and Committee Report of Committee on Leasing, *Ground Leases and Their Financing,* 4 Real Prop. Prob. & Tr. J. 437 (1969).

26.01(e) Modern Developments in Ground Leases

There have been two fairly recent developments in the area of ground rents and leases that have had some national attention.

Many homes in the area of Irvine, California, were developed largely through the device of ground leases. When a purchaser bought a home, it was just that, the purchase of the home that was constructed on the land of the developer who leased the land to the home buyer. The developer retained the land, and the land cost was not included in the price charged to the home buyer. The land was leased to the home buyer pursuant to a long-term lease, which was made at a fixed rent based upon then current economic conditions. Through this device, the home buyer had a lower initial cost because only the home was purchased. Monthly housing costs included not only monthly mortgage payments, but also monthly rental payments made back to the developer.

The area became quite affluent and desirable. The price of housing greatly increased, and homeowners naturally valued their homes and the lifestyle of the community. Then the leases began coming to an end. As the developer's successors began attempting to renegotiate the leases to what they believed were current values, homeowners realized that they were going to be paying significantly higher housing costs. Class action litigation ensued whereby the homeowners attempted to stop the landowner from terminating the rights of the homeowners and, at the same time, reduce the cost of renegotiating or buy out the landowner's interests. The matters were ultimately settled, but neither party obtained all that they had expected.

Ground leases are quite common in Hawaii. The land came to be owned by a few who held the land in trust, leasing it to those who built homes and otherwise improved it. Hawaii found this to be a system of land ownership that it wanted to change, and, for that reason, it enacted a statute that allowed the landowners' interest to be taken by the lessee by way of eminent domain proceedings. This law was challenged and upheld in the U.S. Supreme Court. *Hawaii Housing Authority v. Midkiff,* 467 U.S. 229, 104 S. Ct. 2321 (1984).

26.02   Sale and Management Agreement— "Earn Outs"

An owner of an existing commercial property (e.g., shopping center, office building) may, for a variety of reasons, choose to sell the asset. Yet, the seller may wish to have some further benefit from the property, for example, through a long-term (five years) management agreement. The buyer may be willing to agree to such an arrangement because the seller has general expertise in the field and intimate knowledge of the project, its tenants, and its legal and construction problems. Such an arrangement may be attractive to foreign investors who wish to avoid daily management problems. It may also be attractive to pension funds. Such funds are no longer content with mortgage investments, since the interest return dwindles in value as inflation continues.

The management agreement may be tailored so that the buyer sets financial goals for the project, and the seller's tenure as manager is contingent on achievement of these goals.

The contract of sale may provide for an adjustment in the sale price to take place after the closing of the deal. This adjustment may take place whether or not the seller retains a management position. It would be logical to use this "earn out" provision where the seller retains a management position and can control the economic destinies of the project. The adjustment will be in the form of the seller's participation in the earnings of the project based on economic achievements realized after the sale. The situation offers problems, since a seller retaining management control has an incentive to manipulate the project so as to reflect cash flow or rental achievements that will trigger the seller's participation in the earnings. This suggests that the buyer may need to have some control over the management operation, at least by way of audit of operating results. This, in turn, poses other problems. If the two parties share control, the deal begins to look like a partnership or joint venture (with the attendant liabilities) and the seller/manager looks less like an independent contractor.

A similar problem arises if the seller's share of the earnings is abnormally large. This again suggests joint venture. Also, a seller may be liable to the buyer on some fraud or securities law theories.

26.03   Pledge of Beneficial Interest

In states that recognize the validity of the land trust, there is a mode of financing that offers many advantages.

EXAMPLE: Owner owns Blackacre. Owner conveys it to XYZ Trust Co., as trustee, using typical land trust documentation. The trust agreement designates Owner as sole beneficiary. Under the land trust documentation, the beneficial interest is deemed personal property. Owner then wants to borrow money. He applies to ABC Bank for a loan. The loan is worked out as a pledge of the beneficial interest. Owner executes a collateral note to the bank. This is a lengthy promissory note well known to all bankers who lend money on corporate stock as collateral. Technically, it is a pledge of personal property. It contains provisions authorizing the bank, in the event of default, to declare an acceleration of the debt, to hold a pledgee's sale in its own offices, and to bid at its own sale. As security, Owner assigns the beneficial interest to the bank. This assignment is on a form furnished by the bank. It is lodged with XYZ Trust Co. Since the bank appears on the trust company's records as the purported owner of the beneficial interest, the trust company will not execute any deeds or mortgages or honor any further assignments of the beneficial interest without the bank's consent. The property is "locked up." In case of default, the bank holds a quick pledgee's sale under the Uniform Commercial Code and bids in the beneficial interest. It places Blackacre up for sale. It finds a purchaser. It directs XYZ Trust Co. to make a deed to the purchaser at the closing of this sale and this is done. Everything is accomplished quickly and inexpensively. Nothing relating to the loan appears on the public records.

There is one warning. This type of deal will not work where the landowner deeds the land into the trust and simultaneously pledges the beneficial interest. This is treated as an attempted waiver of the equitable right of redemption, and, under ancient principles of mortgage law, the whole transaction is deemed a real estate mortgage. Some of those who deal in real estate find it convenient to keep their real estate holdings in a land trust. Hence, this rule is no inconvenience.

Since many of the former benefits of holding real estate in a land trust, such as not having to pay transfer taxes on the sale of the beneficial interest and not having to report the sale price to the local assessor's office, thereby keeping the assessment low for real estate taxation purposes have been lost, land trusts are being used less frequently than in the past. As a result, this form of financing is being used less frequently.

26.04 Vendor's Lien Reserved by Deed

In some states, a seller, in lieu of taking back a mortgage from the buyer, expressly reserves in its deed to the buyer a lien on the land to secure payment of the balance of the purchase price. Such a lien is called a *vendor's lien.* It is really a mortgage.

EXAMPLE: Landowner conveyed to Buyer by a warranty deed, which warranted that title was free from all encumbrances excepting three certain notes executed by Buyer, for which a vendor's lien was retained until said notes and the interest thereon should be fully paid. The court held that this clause created a lien on the land.

Such a lien is regarded as an equitable mortgage. It is really a mortgage and is governed by the same rules as a mortgage and must be foreclosed as such. *Crabtree v. Davis,* 237 Ala. 264, 186 So. 734 (1939).

EXAMPLE: A promissory note was given by the buyer to the seller for part of the purchase price, and the deed recited that a purchase money lien was retained for the payment of the note. The court held that the fact that the payee of the note was not mentioned in the deed did not invalidate the deed. But under Kentucky law, the deed must recite the amount of purchase price remaining due if the lien is to be valid against subsequent creditors and purchasers of the property. *Campbell v. Salyer,* 290 Ky. 493, 161 S.W.2d 596 (1942).

A vendor's lien enjoys priority over subsequent liens and encumbrances, and, like a purchase money mortgage, has priority over prior judgments against the purchaser. The grantee under such a deed does not become personally liable for the purchase money, unless the grantee has signed a promissory note or otherwise obligated itself personally to pay the debt. And, a purchaser from such grantee does not become personally liable to the holder of the vendor's lien unless by the terms of the deed the purchaser assumes and agrees to pay the unpaid balance of the debt. The debt may be assigned, and the assignee will have the right to foreclose the lien.

26.05 Buy-Down

During times of high interest rates, developers have engaged in the practice of "buying down" the buyer's interest rate. The developer pays a lump sum or agrees to pay a stated sum to a lender who agrees to finance the buyer's purchase. If the developer is committing to pay instead of paying, a sum may be deposited with the lender's savings account deposits as security. The developer's money operates as an inducement to the lender to reduce the borrower's interest payments for a period of time, often one to three years.

Often, this is done on a sliding scale. The largest reduction in the buyer's interest rates occurs in the first year and the smallest in the third year. The obvious purpose here is to "hook" the buyer. Most people tend to think of their problems now, not three years from now.

At the end of the third year the mortgage payments move up to the market rate. Or, in some cases, there is a balloon at the end of the third year and the buyer must refinance. Some concern has been expressed about this practice. The ads in the newspapers tell the public that the interest rate is a comfortable 9.5 percent, for example. But in the fine print that follows we are told that this is for the first three years. Especially if there is a balloon, there is some concern that consumer-type litigation may result. In the consumer setting, the truth-in-lending documents must be reviewed carefully.

Some lenders offer individual buyers the opportunity of buying down the interest rate on their mortgages by increasing the origination points paid.

26.06 Sale and Leaseback   This form of transaction typically involves a landowner in need of funds for use in its business. While the landowner cannot give up use of its business property, the landowner can give up ownership of the property. An investor is found to buy the property at its full value and lease the property back to the seller. Hence, the term *sale and leaseback*. There are other frequently found characteristics of this form of transaction. The seller/lessee is usually a retailer or industrial concern, traditionally of high credit standing. The lease is usually for a term of twenty to thirty years and the seller/lessee is usually given options to renew the lease and to purchase the property. The rental on the original lease term pays the buyer an amount equal to the purchase price plus a return higher than could be obtained on a conventional mortgage. The lessee is required to pay all real estate taxes, fire insurance, repairs, and other property expenses so that the rental is "net" to the lessor. There are some variations on the sale and leaseback pattern.

> **EXAMPLE:** XYZ Hamburgers, a chain, spots a good location. ABC Realty Investment Trust buys the land, finances construction through an affiliate, and leases the location to XYZ Hamburgers.

The attraction of this type of transaction to the seller/lessee lies in the fact that it gets the full value of the property instead of the smaller amount that it could obtain on a mortgage, and the seller/lessee is under no obligation to repay this amount if it is willing to forego repurchase of the land. In other words, the seller/lessee is not saddled with a debt, as it would be if it had made a mortgage on the land. Note, of course, the seller/lessee may have a continuing rental payment obligation. The advantage to the buyer is that foreclosure is not necessary if default is made in the rent payments, since the transaction is a sale and lease, not a mortgage.

Among the advantages to the lessee of such an arrangement are the following:

1. A tax advantage. In computing its income for tax purposes, the lessee deducts its rent payments under the lease. Were the transaction a mortgage, the only permitted deductions would be interest and depreciation. Also, if the building is not newly constructed, it may be that the current value and sale price are substantially less than the price paid when the seller/lessee bought the building, and the sale to the investor represents an income tax loss to the seller/lessee.

2. By selling the property for its full value to the lessor, the lessee obtains much more cash money than it could raise on a mortgage, for no mortgagee will loan up to 100 percent of the value of the property.

3. Existing mortgages, corporate charters, debenture agreements, or other documents binding on the lessee may place restrictions on its right to borrow money. Since a lease is not a loan, the leaseback arrangement provides a method of getting around these restrictions.

The chief disadvantages to the lessee are as follows:

1. If the building goes up in value, the investor, not the lessee, will reap the benefit of this increase once the lease expires.

2. The lessee has all of the burdens of ownership, for the lease requires the lessee to pay taxes, insurance, and so on. But, the lessee lacks the freedom of action that an owner enjoys. The lessee cannot tear down or remodel buildings as business needs dictate unless the investor consents. Likewise, to erect new buildings would be foolish, for they would belong to the landlord at the end of the lease period. Obviously, special arrangements must be made.

In the case of a sale and leaseback where the rent provision contained an escalator clause tied in some way to the inflationary spiral, rentals have increased at times to a point where the transaction is no longer favorable to the tenant. Deals that looked bad for the investor in the late 1960s are now looking better.

26.07 Sale and Leaseback— Consequences of Transaction Being Set Aside

The sale and leaseback transaction is a very complex financing vehicle. It must be distinguished from a deed absolute to secure a debt. *In re Matter of Kassuba,* 562 F.2d 511 (7th Cir. 1977). Merely labeling a transaction a sale and leaseback will not make it immune from attack, and when the transaction is attacked, the courts will carefully analyze the relationship between the seller/lessee and the buyer/lessor to determine whether a sale really occurred or whether the transaction is really a mortgage. *Eurton v. Smith,* 357 So. 2d 324 (Ala. 1978). If the transaction is found to be a mortgage, consequences befall both the seller/lessee and the buyer/lessor. The relationship of mortgagor-mortgagee with its requirement of foreclosure and redemption rights replaces the relationship of landlord and tenant with its quick possessory remedy of forcible entry and detainer. Usury law may come into play as a standard for evaluating the fairness of the return to the buyer/lessor who has unexpectedly found itself in the role of lender. The income tax treatment that both parties had used and anticipated will not be available, and, indeed, past years' tax returns will have to be amended and tax liabilities changed beyond the parties' expectations.

As can be seen, the transaction is quite complex and should only be entered into after careful consultation with an experienced counsel and tax advisor. The consequences of a mistake can be awesome. Egan, *Sale-Leasebacks: Protecting the Institutional Investor Against New Risks,* 6 Real Est. L.J. 199 (1978); Thomas C. Homburger, *et al., Unresolved Questions in Sale-Leaseback Transactions,* A *New Look at Real Estate, Tax and Bankruptcy Law Issues,* 19 Real Prop., Prob. & Tr. J. 941 (1984).

CHAPTER 27

Real Estate Finance—
Foreclosure and Redemption

27.01 In General   After default, lenders will typically exhaust all possibility of working out the borrower's problems by granting an extension of time or moratorium on payment, agreeing to restructure the loan, allowing the sale of the property to a creditworthy buyer, or negotiating a deed in lieu of foreclosure. These alternatives are preferable to the lender than a foreclosure. If they fail and foreclosure becomes necessary, the foreclosure proceedings will be conducted according to local law. Even after foreclosure has begun, a workout is still possible until the foreclosure sale has taken place. Perhaps half of the states allow the owner a postforeclosure period of redemption, permitting the borrower to retain ownership of the property after the foreclosure sale until the applicable period has expired. The foreclosure and redemption process are determined largely by state law and are very technical.

27.02 Types of Foreclosures   While foreclosure procedure varies from state to state, the method of foreclosure generally falls within two categories. A common method involves a court proceeding filed by the mortgagee, called a *foreclosure suit*. In such suits, the court orders a public auction sale of the property, and the sale is held by an officer of the court. Foreclosure sales are, in some states, including Illinois, becoming more progressive. Ads are run not only in the legal notice section of the newspaper, but also in the real estate pages. Brokers and even real estate auction companies may be hired to sell the property. Up to the time of the foreclosure sale, the mortgagor, any junior mortgagee, or even the mortgagor's tenant may come in, pay off the mortgage, and stop the foreclosure. This is done through the exercise of the equitable right of redemption.

In states that have postforeclosure sale statutory right of redemption, the highest bidder at the foreclosure sale usually receives a certificate of sale reciting that it will be entitled to a deed if no redemption is made. In states that do not have a statutory redemption period after the foreclosure sale, the highest bidder receives a deed to the land, and this deed gives the buyer ownership of the mortgaged land, free and clear of the rights of the mortgagor. A summary of the foreclosure laws of the various states can be found in *Foreclosure Law and Related Remedies*: A State-by-State Digest, (Sidney A. Keyles, ed., 1995).

27.03 Redemption   There are two types of redemption rights held by the mortgagor, the equitable right of redemption and the statutory right of redemption. The equitable right of redemption is cut off by a sale under a foreclosure decree since that was the object of the foreclosure suit. Many states have codified the equitable right of redemption by statutorily prescribing the manner in which the redemption can be made. After the foreclosure sale, in many states, the statutory right of redemption remains. Laws providing for a statutory redemption give the mortgagor and other persons interested in the land, the right to redeem from the sale within a certain period. In some states, the equitable and statutory rights of redemption have been combined into one presale redemption right.

Most statutory redemption laws were passed in a time when America was predominantly agricultural and most mortgagors were farmers. When the weather was bad, crops failed, and foreclosures followed. It seemed logical to suppose that the next year might bring better weather and good crops. Hence, laws created the statutory redemption period, usually one year, and usually the law was so worded that the mortgagor had the right to possession during the redemption period. With exceptions for farmers and owner-occupied residential real estate, redemption periods have been shortened in many states so that the property will pass to the successful foreclosure sale bidder sooner rather than later. This stimulates bidding and protects against the deterioration of property that the defaulting owner may neglect.

Statutory redemption is usually accomplished by payment to the officer who made the sale of the amount of the foreclosure sale plus interest and costs. After redemption, the mortgagor holds the land free and clear of the mortgage.

At the expiration of the redemption period, if redemption has not been made, the purchaser at the foreclosure sale receives a deed from the officer who made the sale.

In a number of states, there is no statutory redemption after sale. Immediately after the foreclosure sale is held and confirmed, a deed is given to the purchaser. In states that do not permit redemption after the foreclosure sale, provision is often made to permit the mortgagor to effect a redemption or discharge of the mortgage prior to the foreclosure sale.

27.04 Deficiency Judgment

A mortgage foreclosure sale is regarded as a payment of the mortgage debt in an amount equal to the sale price. If the foreclosure judgment, or decree, finds that there is $5,000 due to the mortgagee on his or her mortgage, and the property is sold for $4,500, the mortgage debt is thereby reduced by $4,500, leaving a deficiency of $500 due the mortgagee. Since, by virtue of the promissory note that usually accompanies a mortgage, the mortgagor becomes personally liable to the mortgagee for the mortgage debt, the mortgagee is entitled to a personal judgment against the mortgagor for the amount of the deficiency. Of course, if the note limited the lender's recourse against the borrower, the lender may not be entitled to a deficiency judgment, or the amount of the judgment may be limited. Also, many states have passed laws limiting the mortgagee's right to a deficiency decree.

27.05 Foreclosure by Exercise of Power of Sale

In many states, mortgages may be foreclosed by exercise of a power of sale without resort to any court proceedings. If the mortgage is, in form, a deed of trust, a provision will be found conferring on the trustee the power to sell the land in the event of a default in the mortgage payments. If the instrument is a regular mortgage, the power of sale is conferred on the mortgagee. In Colorado, the power of sale must be exercised by an official known as the public trustee. In Minnesota, the sale is made by the sheriff or his or her deputy.

In states where this method of foreclosure is employed, the mortgage or deed of trust spells out the events of default that will give the trustee or mortgagee the power to cause the sale of the premises. The deed of trust and related power-of-sale foreclosure statute will set forth the notice of sale that must be given and the other formalities that must be complied with in making the sale. In some states, personal notice to the mortgagor is necessary, but, in others, advertisement is sufficient. *Chandler v. Orgain*, 302 S.W.2d 953 (Tex. Civ. App. 1957). Some state laws provide that a notice of default must be recorded and a stated period of time must elapse thereafter before the sale can be held. This gives the mortgagor a final opportunity to pay the debt.

At one time, concern was expressed over the validity of the power of sale in the aftermath of U.S. Supreme Court decisions, which held that prejudgment seizures of chattels violated the due process clause of the fourteenth amendment. *See, e.g., North Georgia Finishing, Inc. v. Di-Chem, Inc.*, 419 U.S. 601, 95 S. Ct. 719 (1975). The debate centered on whether power-of-sale foreclosures of real property were constitutional in the absence of prior notice and a hearing for the benefit of the defaulting mortgagor. This problem is largely resolved. Cases have upheld the nonjudicial power-of-sale foreclosure process. *Flagg Bros. v. Brooks*, 436 U.S. 149, 98 S. Ct. 1729; 28 De Paul L. Rev. 523; 27 Kan. L. Rev. 674 (1978). Also, consumer lobbies have succeeded in enacting amendments to the power-of-sale foreclosure laws of the various states. These new laws have been generally directed toward requiring that the borrower and other parties with an interest in the real estate be given a more effective notice of the impending foreclosure.

> **EXAMPLE:** Prior law in Texas merely required the posting of a notice of the foreclosure at three public places for three weeks prior to the sale. Obviously, this method is not the best practical method of notifying the debtor of the foreclosure sale. The amendment to that law requires the posting of such notices at the local courthouse and a certified mail notice to the debtor. Tex. Civ. St. Art. 3810.

Many states have also enacted foreclosure laws that require advertisement of the foreclosure sale beyond the legal notice in a legal publication so that the property is brought fairly into the market when the property has unique characteristics that affect its value. *Pizza v. Walter*, 694 A.2d 93 (Md. 1997).

27.05(a) Federal Foreclosures

When the federal government holds the mortgage that has fallen into default, it may resort to federal foreclosure laws that give it very strong powers. For several years, the federal government as mortgagee has been able to foreclose a defaulted mortgage that is secured by property that is not a one- to four-family residence by way of a special federal law that provides for foreclosure by power of sale. 12 U.S.C. § 3701, *et seq.* This procedure allows the federal government to foreclose by power of sale after a very short notice period. A similar expedited foreclosure by power of sale is available to the federal government in the case of loans secured by single-family properties. 12 U.S.C. § 3751, *et seq.* Debra Pogrund Stark, *Foreclosing the American Dream: An Evaluation of State and Federal Foreclosure Laws*, 51 Okla. L. Rev. 229 (1998); Patrick A. Randolph, Jr., *The New Federal Foreclosure Laws*, 49 Okla. L. Rev. 124 (1996).

27.06 Foreclosure by Other Methods

Other methods of foreclosure (e.g., strict foreclosure, foreclosure by entry and possession, and foreclosure by writ of entry) are allowed in a small number of states. These involve technical procedures that are only of local interest.

27.07 Foreclosure— Reinstatement, Cure, and Borrower Counseling

No matter what the method of foreclosure may be, lenders must always be mindful that courts protect consumers, and, in the single-family mortgage transaction, the borrower is the consumer. Evidence of the protection given to borrowers may be found in cases that have required lenders to ascertain the reasons for default and make a concerted effort to avoid foreclosure by voluntary forbearance or recasting the mortgage. *Fleet Real Estate Funding v. Smith*, 366 Pa. Super. 116, 530 A.2d 919 (1987); *Bankers Life Co. v. Denton*, 120 Ill. App. 3d 576, 458 N.E.2d 203 (1983); *Hamm v. Taylor*, 180 Conn. 491, 429 A.2d 946 (1981); *FNMA v. Ricks*, 372 N.Y.S.2d 485 (N.Y. 1975). While these cases may apply to a particular class of lenders (e.g., FHA and VA mortgagees) and have been undercut by subsequent proclamations by HUD, the decisions announce to lenders that conduct toward borrowers must be conscionable or foreclosure will not be allowed. Robert Kratovil, *Mortgage Law Today,* 13 John Marsh L. Rev. 251, 265 (1980).

> **EXAMPLE:** Borrower lost his job and fell four payments in arrears on his mortgage. Lender began foreclosure proceedings whereupon Borrower, once again employed, tendered the past due payments. Lender refused the tender because it did not include the attorney's fees incurred in beginning foreclosure. Foreclosure would not be allowed as Lender's conduct was unconscionable. *Brown v. Lynn,* 385 F. Supp. 986. (N.D. Ill.1974).

These decisions are reflections of not only the law but of also the "fireside equity" practiced by many judges when they sit in foreclosure courts. Frequently, foreclosure will not be allowed unless the borrower is at least three or four payments behind and good faith settlement negotiations have produced no results.

The FHA has a variety of rules relating to FHA-insured mortgages. The secondary market also has rules on this subject. In general, foreclosure of a first mortgage cannot, under FNMA rules, begin until at least three full monthly payments are past due. The FHA used to require that the mortgagor be given an opportunity to ask the FHA to take an assignment of the mortgage from the lender if it was shown that the default was caused by circumstances beyond the borrower's control and that the borrower has a reasonable chance to resume making regular mortgage payments within three years. If these conditions could be met, mortgage payments would have been reduced or suspended for up to thirty-six months. At the end of the grace period, the borrower would resume making regular payments.

The so-called HUD assignment program was terminated in 1996 and replaced with a program of loss mitigation under which the lender may allow forbearance for up to nine months, with an additional nine months to repay any arrearage that may have accumulated, mortgage modification, and refinances.

Some states have enacted statutes to provide relief to homeowners who have fallen into default because of economic factors beyond their control. These statutes may provide a moratorium, require the recasting of the loan, or require that the lender accept a cure payment to reinstate the loan. The pressure for these changes in the law increases and decreases as the economy goes through its normal business cycles.

27.08 Bankruptcy Stay

Bankruptcy proceedings are designed to collect the debtor's assets and then either liquidate the debtor's estate or restructure the debt payment schedules to allow the debtor to continue in business. Under either course of action, the bankruptcy trustee needs time to study the value of the debtor's assets and the extent of its liabilities. When the bankruptcy petition is filed, however, the debtor is usually in the midst of lawsuits and foreclosures caused by defaults on its loans and accounts. To give the bankruptcy trustee the time needed to inventory and evaluate the assets, the bankruptcy law provides that the filing of the bankruptcy stays or prohibits the commencement or continuation of any proceedings against the bankrupt, including the enforcement of liens against the debtor's property. 11 U.S.C. § 362(a). The stay stops foreclosures until the creditor successfully petitions the court to vacate or modify the stay.

27.09 Bankruptcy Problems in Foreclosure Sales

In a case that startled the legal profession, a federal court set aside a mortgage foreclosure sale on the grounds that it was a fraudulent transfer under the Bankruptcy Code (11 U.S.C. § 548) if it brought less than a "reasonably equivalent value" for the property. *Durrett v.*

Washington Nat'l Ins. Co., 621 F.2d 201 (5th Cir. 1980). The theory of the *Durrett* decision was applicable when (1) the foreclosure sale occurred within one year prior to the filing of the bankruptcy petition, (2) the foreclosure sale price was less than the "reasonably equivalent value" of the property, and (3) the debtor was insolvent at the time of the foreclosure sale. The direct threat of the *Durrett* case was removed with the Supreme Court's decision in *BFP v. Resolution Trust Corp.*, 511 U.S. 531, 114 S. Ct. 1757 (1994), which held that the amount bid at a regularly conducted, noncollusive foreclosure sale will be deemed to constitute reasonably equivalent value, thus not giving rise to a fraudulent transfer under the Bankruptcy Code. *See* Debra Pogrund Stark, *The Emperor Still Has Clothes: Fraudulent Conveyance Challenges After the BFP Decision*, 47 So. Car. L.R. 563 (1996).

**27.10 Bankruptcy—
Effect on
Redemption Rights**

The problem often arises that the mortgagor files bankruptcy during the redemption period. If the redemption period is before the foreclosure sale, the automatic stay operates to suspend further proceedings, thus preventing the sale. A different situation is presented in those jurisdictions that have postsale redemption rights. If the mortgagor files a bankruptcy after the foreclosure sale, but before the running of the redemption period, 11 U.S.C. § 108(b) extends the redemption period for sixty days from the commencement of the bankruptcy period if the period would have expired within that sixty-day period. *In re Tynan,* 773 F.2d 177 (7th Cir. 1985). Of course, if under state law there were more than sixty days to run in the redemption period, that longer period will be available to the mortgagor/debtor.

**27.11 Soldiers and
Sailors Civil Relief Act**

The Gulf War brought to new prominence the Soldiers and Sailors Civil Relief Act, 50 U.S.C. App. § 501, *et seq.* This law was originally enacted during the First World War and was reenacted during World War II. Left largely unchanged since then, the act caught some lenders unaware when a large number of borrowers were placed on active duty for Operation Desert Storm.

From the mortgage lenders' perspective, the act has two principal impacts. First, it caps interest rates on obligations incurred by noncareer service personnel prior to activation at 6 percent. The interest over 6 percent that would have otherwise accrued during active duty is simply forgiven, unless the lender can show that the borrower's ability to pay was not impaired by his or her being activated. Second, lenders cannot foreclose against active-duty service personnel while they are on active duty and for three months thereafter. 50 U.S.C. App. § 532; *Conroy v. Aniskoff,* 507 U.S. 511, 113 S. Ct. 1562 (1993).

**27.12 Fair Debt
Collection
Practices Act**

The Fair Debt Collection Practices Act, 15 U.S.C. § 1692, regulates the conduct of "debt collectors" in their collection of debts from "consumers." A debt collector is a party whose principal business is the collection of debts, or who regularly collects the debts owed to other parties. This term includes lawyers, but does not include a creditor who is collecting its own debts, unless it is pretending to be a third party. Even attorneys involved in litigation are not exempt from the coverage of the Act. *Heintz v. Jenkins,* 514 U.S. 291, 115 S. Ct. 1489, 131 L. Ed. 2d 395 (1995).

Where the Act is applicable, it regulates or prohibits many of the practices of debt collectors, including attempts to obtain information from third parties, communications with the debtor, harassing debt collection techniques, false or misleading statements, and the like. The Act also requires that certain warnings be given to the debtor and that the debt be validated by the debtor within thirty days after notice from the debt collector. Those attempting to foreclose mortgages made to consumers must comply with this law or be subject to its penalty provisions.

27.13   Mortgagee as Purchaser at Foreclosure Sale

For several reasons, the mortgagee is often the only bidder at the foreclosure sale. The mortgagee is allowed to bid up to the amount of the mortgage debt without producing any cash. The reason is obvious. If it were to pay cash, the officer holding the sale would have to hand the cash back to the mortgagee in payment of the mortgage debt, for, after all, the sale is held to raise money to pay the mortgagee. Again, in states that have redemption laws, the highest bidder will not get ownership or possession of the property until the redemption period is over, and then only if no redemption is made. Speculators, who are the chief bidders at public land sales, are unwilling to have their money tied up for long periods with such uncertainty as to ultimate ownership of the property.

Where the foreclosing creditor purchases the property at the foreclosure sale and, pursuant to a prior contract, sells the property to a third party for more than the foreclosed debt, the lender may not collect a deficiency judgment from the borrower. *Pearman v. West Point Nat'l Bank*, 887 S.W.2d 366 (Ky. Ct. App. 1994).

27.14   Mortgagee as Owner

Whenever and however the mortgagee becomes the owner of the property (either by foreclosure or deed in lieu of foreclosure), it must take all the precautions that an owner takes. Prior to foreclosure, the lender must obtain an environmental audit to determine whether ownership of the property exposes the purchasing lender to environmental liabilities.

Immediately upon the foreclosure sale, existing insurance policies must be endorsed to give protection to the mortgagee as an owner, or new policies must be obtained. Reliance on the old policy may be misplaced, since satisfaction of the debt by purchase at the foreclosure sale or in the deed in lieu transaction satisfies the mortgage debt and may simultaneously extinguish the lender's protection. *Whitestone Sav. & Loan Ass'n v. Allstate Ins. Co.*, 28 N.Y.2d 332, 270 N.E.2d 694 (N.Y. 1971). The necessity of other insurance such as liability, worker's compensation, dram shop, and so forth should be determined. Since foreclosure usually extinguishes any leases entered into after the mortgage, new arrangements should be entered into with the tenants. *Kage v. 1795 Dunn Road, Inc.*, 428 S.W.2d 735 (Mo. 1968). A new owner's title insurance policy should be obtained, and the currency and amount of real estate taxes and assessment payments should be examined. Inquiry should be made of the desirability of retaining or releasing the building manager. The building itself should be inspected for conditions potentially dangerous to tenants, compliance with local, state, and federal safety laws as they apply both to employees and others, and conditions that could damage the building or hinder its marketability.

27.15   Effect of Foreclosure on Junior Leases

The value of commercial property is often found in the cash flow that it produces. This is the case whether the property is industrial, residential, office, or retail in nature. This cash flow comes from tenants. There is often a struggle between the tenants and the mortgagee over priority. In commercial properties, the lender will typically want the leases to be junior to the lien of the mortgage. In this way, foreclosure of the mortgage will terminate the tenant's right to possession of the premises. *Dover Mobile Estates v. Fiber Form Products, Inc.*, 270 Cal. Rptr.183 (Cal. App. 1990).

The tenant typically cannot live with this, that is, allowing its business future in that location to depend upon whether or not the landlord defaults. The lender and tenant will typically enter into a subordination, nondisturbance, and attornment agreement under which the tenant acknowledges that its tenancy is junior to the lien of the mortgage. The tenant and the lender also agree that if the property is sold through foreclosure, and the tenant is not then in default under the lease, the tenant will attorn to the purchaser at the foreclosure sale and that purchaser will accept such attornment. The parties will go on as though the lease was an agreement between the tenant and the foreclosure sale purchaser.

Economically, under some circumstances, the foreclosing lender may be advantaged if it can terminate the leases, while under other economic circumstances, the lender may be advantaged if it preserves the leases. The result is dictated by the comparison of market rents to the rent set out in the lease.

> **EXAMPLE:** Tenant and Landlord entered into a fifteen-year lease with three five-year renewal options given to the Tenant. Rent starts at $9.00 per square foot and increases by $0.50 per square foot every five years during the base and renewal terms. Landlord defaults during the eighth lease year when the rent is $9.50 per square foot. Market conditions have changed. Space in the area is in high demand and rents at the time of the default are in the $12.00 per square foot range for comparable space. The lender is faced with the prospect of below market rents for this space for twenty-two years to come. If the lease is junior to the mortgage and there is no subordination, nondisturbance, and attornment agreement, the lender will try to extinguish the Tenant's lease through foreclosure. If, on the contrary, space in the area is not sought by competing tenants and rents have fallen, the lender will want to keep Tenant, even if Tenant's lease is junior to the lien of the mortgage.

Sometimes through oversight or as a result of intentional conduct, a junior tenant is not made a party to the foreclosure proceedings or is not notified of the power-of-sale foreclosure. While some courts hold that the foreclosure will terminate the rights of the junior tenant, *Director of Veterans Affairs v. Martin*, 135 Or. App. 416, 898 P.2d 230 (Or. App. 1995), other courts follow the majority rule to the contrary. *Como, Inc. v. Carson Square, Inc.*, 648 N.E.2d 1247 (Ind. App. 1995). If the junior tenant was not given notice of a power-of-sale foreclosure, the rights of a bona fide purchaser at the foreclosure sale may be protected by the language in the deed that all necessary parties were given adequate notice. *Homestead Sav. v. Darmiento*, 230 Cal. App. 3d 424, 281 Cal. Rptr. 367 (Cal. App. 1991).

27.16 Receivers   Often at the outset of the foreclosure, the lender will seek the appointment of a receiver for the property that collateralizes the loan. Although local law and the loan documents may allow the lender to become a "mortgagee in possession," the lender will most often seek the appointment of a receiver rather than take on the liabilities associated with the operation of the property. This is so because the lender typically will not have had adequate time to prepare for the operation of the property and will not want to expose itself to the liabilities associated with property operation, such as environmental liabilities, until it has had the opportunity to examine the property with experts, such as environmental auditors.

While the lender may have the ability under local law to designate the party that it wants to be the receiver, technically, the receiver is an officer of the court. As such, the receiver has responsibilities to both the lender and the borrower. Once appointed, the receiver manages and operates the property, subject to the controls imposed by the governing law and the order appointing the receiver. For example, governing law may provide that the receiver may not enter into a lease that will extend beyond the life of the receivership. The order of appointment may also prohibit the receiver from spending more than a stated amount of money on any one project without the prior approval of the court. If the receiver does not violate the constraints imposed by the order of appointment, the receiver will not be liable for mismanagement of the property, unless it acts in bad faith. *Resolution Trust Corp. v. Venus Plaza Assocs.*, 228 Mich. App. 357, 579 N.W.2d 99 (1998).

CHAPTER 28

Environmental Liabilities and Land Ownership

28.01   In General   Environmental matters continue to be of great concern in real estate transactions. Participants in the real estate industry are, however, becoming used to dealing with environmental issues with the result that properties that were once contaminated are being recycled and used for beneficial purposes. Indeed, many states have programs that encourage the cleanup of "brownfields" by providing financial assistance and a degree of immunity from liability to an owner who takes on one of these projects.

For many years, the real estate industry was rightly concerned with clean air laws, clean water laws, and other state and federal environmental legislation. These laws generally applied to the use of property and the facilities located on the property and expose successive owners, lenders, and tenants to liability for the acts of others. A learning curve developed with respect to the awareness of the requirements of the law, the liability implications of the law, and methods to react to the exposure presented by these laws. The impact of this learning curve and the maturation of thought and experience with environmental liabilities and exposures has enabled parties to participate in transactions involving land contaminated with toxic wastes. While deals are getting done, they take a bit longer to close and are more costly, but, importantly, deals are getting done.

28.02   CERCLA Liability   The cornerstone of environmental liability laws is the "Superfund" law, sometimes referred to as CERCLA, or the Comprehensive Environmental Response, Compensation, and Liability Act of 1980, which was amended by the Superfund Amendments and Reauthorization Act of 1986. 42 U.S.C. § 9607, *et seq.* This law, and many state laws that are modeled upon it, imposes liability for the costs of responding to, containing, and cleaning up, or remediating, any release of hazardous substances into the environment. 42 U.S.C. § 9607(a). A responsible party is also liable for any damage to natural resources that occurs as a result of the release. 42 U.S.C. § 9607(a). This liability is imposed on (1) owners and operators of the property or facility from which the release has occurred, (2) the parties who owned and operated the property or facility at the time of the release, (3) the generator of the hazardous substance, and (4) the transporter who took the hazardous substance from the site. 42 U.S.C. § 9607(a).

Property owners, buyers, lenders, and tenants are chiefly concerned with the aspect of this law that imposes liability on the owner and operator of the property from which the release occurred. Note that the law does not require that the owner or operator committed the act that allowed the release to occur. It is enough for the party to merely own the contaminated property. The liability extends not only to the cost of cleaning up the subject property but also includes the cost of cleaning up surrounding properties, which may become contaminated from the release on the subject property.

EXAMPLE: Prior Owner has dumped a toxic byproduct from its manufacturing operations into a pond at the rear of its plant. Prior Owner then sold the plant site to New Owner who intended to tear down the plant and build an automobile sales and repair facility. The toxins from the pond have leaked into the groundwater and a flume of contamination has migrated to an adjoining property. Both Prior Owner and New Owner are liable for the costs of cleaning up both the property on which the toxins were dumped and the adjoining site.

This liability is strict, joint, and several, and the government need not proceed against all potentially responsible parties, but rather may proceed against the party most likely to have the funds necessary to pay for the clean-up. Furthermore, the government need not be involved at all. If a private party conducted the clean-up, that private party may bring the suit for reimbursement. *Tanglewood East Homeowners v. Charles-Thomas, Inc.*, 849 F.2d 1568 (5th Cir. 1988).

28.02(a)
Environmental Audits

In responding to this potential liability, buyers, lenders, and tenants have sought out the services of a group of service providers who conduct due diligence reviews of the property and report to their clients the results of those reviews. While there is no accrediting body for these environmental professionals, they usually have engineering backgrounds. Over time, some nomenclature and broad standards have developed for the work of the environmental engineer. The so-called "Phase I" and "Phase II" audits are frequently referred to. Unfortunately, these terms do not have a uniform meaning.

Typically, a Phase I audit will not involve any testing and sampling, but will include initial due diligence work in an effort to determine whether any testing or sampling should be done. The Phase I audit will usually involve some or all of the following: an inspection of the site; interviews with on-site personnel; a review of on-site records; a review of available aerial photographs; a review of building and zoning department records; a review of the records of the federal and state environmental protection agencies relating to the subject property and surrounding properties; an inquiry of local utilities for a disclosure of whether any transformers located on the property contain PCBs; a visual inspection of neighboring properties; a review of the chain of title to the property going back fifty or one hundred years; and, perhaps, a limited sampling of materials that look like they could contain asbestos.

If the Phase I audit gives the environmental engineer reason to suspect that hazardous substances could be present at the property, the Phase II audit will be recommended. During this next level of review and evaluation, testing and sampling where indicated will be conducted. If this level of audit reveals the presence of contamination, the environmental engineer can be called upon to recommend a remediation plan and monitor the progress of clean-up and containment to determine whether the work is going as planned. *See* Janet M. Johnson, *For Real Estate Lawyers: A Practical Guide to Identifying and Managing Potential Environmental Hazards and Conditions Affecting Commercial Real Estate*, 32. Real Prop. Prob. & Tr. L.J. 619 (1998).

28.02(b)   Defenses—
Third-Party Defense

The Superfund law permits a potentially responsible party to assert a defense to liability when the contamination occurs as a result of the act or omission of a third party. This defense only applies where third parties are not employees or agents of the defendant or where the act or omission of the responsible third party does not occur in connection with a direct or indirect contractual relationship with the defendant. 42 U.S.C. § 9607(b). To take advantage of this defense, the potentially responsible party, or PRP as it is called in environmental jargon, must have exercised due care with respect to the hazardous substance and taken precautions against the foreseeable acts or omissions of third parties and the consequences that could have resulted from their acts or omissions. 42 U.S.C. § 9607(b)(3). Also, if the potentially responsible party transfers the contaminated property, a disclosure of all matters within its knowledge and that relate to the contamination must be made to the transferee or the defense is forfeited. 42 U.S.C. § 9601(35)(C).

From a real estate transactional context, a contractual relationship results from contracts, deeds, and other instruments that transfer title or possession of real estate. 42 U.S.C. § 9601(35)(A). Thus, contracts of sale, deeds, leases, and the like would create this contractual relationship and potentially disqualify the transferee from taking advantage of the third-party defense, unless the transferee can qualify for the so-called "innocent purchaser" defense.

28.02(b)(1) Defenses—Third Party—Innocent Purchaser

Under CERCLA, the concept of innocent purchaser relates to a set of statutory standards and not to an abstract concept of innocence. That is, a property owner will not escape CERCLA liability merely because the landowner was not involved in the act of contaminating the property.

> **EXAMPLE:** In *United States v. Monsanto Co.*, 858 F.2d 160 (4th Cir., 1988), Owner entered into an oral month-to-month lease with Chemical Co. At first, Chemical Co. stored raw materials and finished products on the leased property. Later, Chemical Co. began recycling chemical waste at the property. The Environmental Protection Agency ordered a clean-up of the property. The court held that the owners were liable regardless of their degree of participation in the waste disposal process.

Technically, an innocent purchaser is able to exclude documents of title from the "contractual relationship" qualification of the third-party defense to CERCLA liability. 42 U.S.C. § 9601(35)(A). Thus, merely because a potentially responsible party has taken title to the property by deed or is a tenant of the property, it is not disenabled from using the third-party defense. It is feared, however, that it may be difficult for potentially responsible parties to take advantage of this defense.

To qualify, the transferee must prove that at the time it acquired the property, it did not have any knowledge or reason to know that any hazardous substance was disposed of at the property. 42 U.S.C. § 9601(35)(A). This defense will only apply if the transferee, at the time that it acquired the property, made an appropriate inquiry into the previous ownership and uses of the property consistent with good commercial or customary practice in an effort to minimize liability. Many factors are considered in qualifying for this defense, including any specialized knowledge that the transferee may possess, the relationship of the purchase price to the value of the property in its uncontaminated state, commonly known or reasonably ascertainable information about the property, the obviousness of the presence or likely presence of contamination at the property, and the ability to detect the contamination by conducting an appropriate inspection. 42 U.S.C. § 9601(35)(B).

This is where the environmental audit comes into play. The problem is that the standards for taking advantage of the innocent purchaser defense are somewhat vague. Without a more explicit definition of these standards, purchasers are never sure that they have done enough to qualify. Indeed, many fear that they will be deemed to not qualify if previously existing contamination is found. They fear that the government will contend that their due diligence activities were not extensive enough if the property is found to be contaminated. Nonetheless, many parties involved in the real estate process have set out their minimum standards for environmental audits to be conducted before the property is acquired or the property is acceptable as security for a loan. *See* Federal Home Loan Bank Board, Office of Regulatory Activities, Thrift Bulletin 16 (Feb. 6, 1989); Federal National Mortgage Association, *Multifamily Guide,* § 501 (Aug. 1, 1988). *See also* Joseph Philip Forte, *Environmental Liability Risk Management,* Prob. & Prop. 57 (Jan.–Feb., 1989).

While these materials set out standards for environmental risk analysis and management, until the term "all appropriate inquiry" is defined by a court or by further legislation or regulation, it is uncertain whether those standards are adequate to qualify their user for the innocent landowner defense. Some states have begun to define the contours of the problem by outlining the nature of the steps that should be taken and the type of environmental audit that must be made to qualify for the defense under state laws. *See, e.g.,* 415 ILCS 5/22.2(j)(E), *et seq.*

28.03 Settlements—Innocent Purchaser—Brownfields Legislation

Under a related proposition, CERCLA allows certain parties to enter into so-called *de minimis* settlements of environmental liabilities in limited circumstances. 42 U.S.C. § 9622(g). One should not expect that these settlements will be available in all circumstances, and the availability of this procedure should not be looked upon as an inexpensive alternative to conducting appropriate due diligence prior to becoming involved with a parcel of land. Indeed, this settlement mechanism is not available to a party who purchased the property with actual or constructive knowledge that the property was used for the generation, transportation, storage, treatment, or disposal of any hazardous substance. The meaning of this language is unclear. Seemingly, it sets a lesser standard than that of the innocent purchaser defense. That should be the case since one provision, in theory, leads to a complete defense to liability and the other provision leads to a mechanism for achieving minimum cost settlements of environmental litigation. That is not, however, how the EPA interprets the statute. The EPA takes the position that even though the statutory language is different, the scope of the two provisions is substantially the same. *See* U.S. E.P.A., Guidance on Agreements with Prospective Purchasers of Contaminated Property and Model Prospective Purchaser Agreement, 60 Fed. Reg. 34792, (1995).

Similar programs are available under state laws that allow the purchaser to obtain a release from liability under the state law, if the purchaser agrees to complete a clean-up of the property under an agreement worked out with the state environmental agency. *See, e.g.,* 415 ILCS 5/22.2b-5/22.2l; 415 ILCS 5/58-5/58.14. The drawback of such an arrangement is that the extent of the clean-up likely will not be known at the time that the purchaser enters into the agreement to purchase the property and closes the transaction. Further, the state program will not generally preempt federal clean-up efforts or common lawsuits for damages resulting from the contamination. The federal EPA has taken the practical step of entering into memorandums of understanding with some states that have voluntary clean-up programs providing that the EPA will not pursue CERCLA claims against a landowner who has cleaned up a site pursuant to the state arrangement.

Under other programs, landowners may come forward to propose an arrangement for a state-supervised clean-up leading to the receipt of a no-further-remediation letter from the state. 415 ILCS 5/58, *et seq.* The degree of clean-up required will vary, depending upon whether the future use of the site is commercial or industrial, or residential.

As the Latin term *de minimis* implies, the settlement procedure only applies to situations where the settlement is small in proportion to the response costs. To qualify for this special settlement procedure, the potentially responsible party must have contributed only a minimal amount of hazardous substances or caused only a minimal amount of the toxic or hazardous effects of the release. Furthermore, the settling party must be the owner of the property, must not have conducted or permitted the generation, transportation, storage, treatment, or disposal of any hazardous substance at the property, and must not have contributed to the release or threat of release through any act or omission.

28.04   Lender Liability   Lenders must not become complacent and feel that the special protections of the CERCLA law enacted for their benefit have absolved them of environmental liabilities or losses merely because they are lenders. At a minimum, they are exposed to many risks, if not liabilities. If the property becomes contaminated, the borrower may be unable to repay the loan, and the property that was to secure the repayment of the loan will decline in value as a result of the contamination. In some states, the mortgage may lose its priority to a lien imposed to repay the state for clean-up costs.

CERCLA provides that a lender will not be an owner or operator of property if, without participating in the management of the property, it merely holds an indicia of ownership to protect its security interest. 42 U.S.C. § 9601(20)(A). This statutory provision contained its own self-defining exception. If the lender participated in the management of the property, it would be an operator of the facility and liable for clean-up costs, even though it holds a security interest in the property. Thus, lenders had to be cautious in their dealings with borrowers, especially in default situations. Where lenders, in pursuit of otherwise legitimate goals, exercised the powers given to them in their loan documents to take possession of the property, exercised management discretion, directed the borrower in the conduct of its business, and the like, they exposed themselves to environmental liabilities. *United States v. Mirabile,* 15 Envtl. L. Rptr. 20994 (E.D. Pa. 1985). Even participation in the financial management of the debtor exposed the secured lender to liability, if that participation effected hazardous waste disposal decisions. *United States v. Fleet Factors Corp.,* 901 F.2d 1550 (11th Cir. 1990).

The *Fleet Factors* decision caused extreme concern among lenders. They feared that the legitimate exercise of their rights under normal loan documents exposed them to environmental liabilities, in addition to leaving them with the potential of contaminated collateral property with the resultant loss in value. Lenders reacted by obtaining the adoption of the "Lender Liability Rule" by the Environmental Protection Agency to define the role that a lender may play without exposure to environmental liabilities. That rule was invalidated by the court. *Kelley v. E.P.A.,* 15 F.3d 1100 (D.C. Cir. 1994), *cert. denied sub non; Am. Bankers Assoc. v. Kelley,* 513 U.S. 1110, 115 S. Ct. 900 (1995).

As a result, CERCLA was revised to define the contours of a lender's safe involvement with a borrower and liability after foreclosure or other acquisition of the collateral. 42 U.S.C. § 9601(20)(E). The revised act expressly provides that to be liable as an owner or operator, a secured lender must actually participate in the management or operational affairs of the borrower and not merely have the ability to influence, or the unexercised right to control, the borrower's operations. For lender liability to result from lender action while the borrower is still in possession of the collateral, the lender must exercise decision-making control over environmental compliance matters so that the lender takes responsibility for the borrower's hazardous substance handling or disposal practices, or the lender must assume overall management of the borrower.

Lenders no longer have to fear that by merely including environmental compliance provisions in loan documents, monitoring and enforcing loan documents, making inspections of the collateral, requiring a response to a release or threatened release of a hazardous substance, providing financial or other advice to mitigate or prevent a borrower default, and taking other actions that responsible lenders normally take, they are exposed to environmental liabilities under federal law. To be exposed to liability, the lender must actually participate in the management or operational affairs of the borrower and not merely have the capacity to influence the borrower, or the unexercised right to control the borrower.

Similarly, the amended law specifically provides protection to the lender who acquires the collateral through foreclosure, deed in lieu of foreclosure, or repossession, and, in turn, attempts to dispose of the property at the earliest practicable, commercially reasonable time and on commercially reasonable terms, taking into consideration market conditions and legal and regulatory requirements. Of course, if as owner of the collateral, the lender goes beyond the safe harbor of the protection of the amendment, for example, by making decisions relating to the handling of hazardous substances, the lender will be exposed to CERCLA liability.

It should be noted that all state environmental laws do not mirror the federal law. Thus, the lender must review applicable state laws to ensure that while it may be in compliance with federal law it is not exposed to liability under state law.

28.05   Environmental Liens and Superliens

Both CERCLA and state laws provide for a lien in favor of the state or federal government to secure the repayment of the costs incurred in the clean-up and containment of the release of the hazardous substance. Under CERCLA, for example, the costs and damages constitute a lien upon the property that has been cleaned up. 42 U.S.C. § 9607(1). As to third parties, this lien is subject to the rights of any purchaser or lender whose interest in the property is perfected before a notice of the environmental lien has been filed in the local records. 42 U.S.C. § 9607(1)(3).

Some states have enacted superlien laws which give the state a priority lien to secure the recovery of its clean-up costs. *See* Conn. Gen. Stat. Ann. § 22a-452a; N.J. Stat. Ann. § 58:10-23.11. Under these laws, the lien given to the state will automatically become prior to the preexisting and future interests of other parties in the property.

28.06   Bankruptcy Implications of Environmental Liability

Once the state has cleaned up the site, the owner's liability to the state is a debt, a liability on the owner's balance sheet. If the owner thereafter goes into bankruptcy, that debt is treated as any other debt and is dischargeable in a bankruptcy proceeding. *Ohio v. Kovacs,* 469 U.S. 274, 105 S. Ct. 705 (1985). If, however, the bankruptcy estate owns a contaminated site, that site cannot be abandoned unless the bankruptcy trustee formulates a plan to protect the public health and safety. Also, the bankruptcy trustee must comply with state statutes or regulations designed to protect the public health and safety, *In re Quanta Resources Corp.,* 739 F.2d 912 (3d Cir., 1995), *aff'd sub nom., Midlantic Nat'l Bank v. New Jersey Dept. of Envtl. Protection,* 474 U.S. 494, 106 S. Ct. 755 (1986), even where such compliance requires the expenditure of funds to comply. *In re Chateaugay Corp.,* 112 B.R. 513 (S.D. N.Y. 1990). Epling, *Environmental Liens in Bankruptcy,* 44 Bus. Law. 85 (1988).

28.07   Dealing with Production of Hazardous Wastes

Certain businesses necessarily involve the production, use, and transport of hazardous materials and wastes. In such cases, the Resource, Conservation, and Recovery Act, 42 U.S.C. § 6901, *et seq.,* and other state and federal laws come into play. Under these statutory schemes, the landowner or generator must obtain a permit for its activity and be subject to inspection by governmental authorities. The government is allowed to act if the process presents a danger to the environment and may require that the operator of the facility take corrective action. After the facility is closed, a notice must be recorded in the land records unless the hazardous waste has been cleaned up and the government waives the recordation requirement. 40 C.F.R. §§ 264.116, 264.119, 265.116, 265.119.

28.08 Liabilities In addition to the statutorily imposed liabilities, an owner, seller, landlord, tenant, real estate broker, and other party that may be involved with a parcel of real property is faced with the same liabilities with respect to environmental and hazardous waste matters as exist with respect to any other matter relating to the property. As discussed elsewhere, a builder or seller may be found liable for the breach of an expressed or implied warranty of habitability or fitness in the context of environmental liabilities. Similarly, a seller, landlord, or broker may be found liable for misrepresentations made to the other parties to the transaction or for active concealment of the hazardous waste condition.

28.09 Underground Storage Tanks Recognizing the threat posed by leaking underground storage tanks, and the propensity of underground tanks to leak, the federal government and state governments have enacted laws governing such tanks and their abandonment. 42 U.S.C. §§ 6991(a)-(i). Under these laws, the government is empowered to respond to leaks from the tanks and order the landowner to take appropriate corrective action in the case of leaks or threats of leaks. These laws also set design standards for the tanks and lay out a method of abandonment of the tanks when they are taken out of service.

From a transactional standpoint, it is important that any purchaser, lender, tenant, or other occupant identify whether the property has any such tanks before entering into a transaction. Once identified, the tanks must be inspected to determine whether they are in compliance with the law and whether they pose a threat to the environment and thus an exposure to liability. Richey, *Regulation of Underground Storage Tanks,* 25 Real Prop. Prob. & Tr. J. 311 (1990).

The 1996 CERCLA amendments also provide protection to lenders who take collateral interests in land on which an underground storage tank is located, if they do not participate in management of an underground storage tank and are not otherwise engaged in the production, refining, or marketing of petroleum. 42 U.S.C. § 6991b(h).

28.10 Fiduciaries The property that trustees, executors, guardians and receivers, and other parties hold for the benefit of others may be environmentally contaminated. As a result, these parties had a justifiable concern that they would be exposed to personal environmental liabilities. Court decisions confirmed these concerns. *City of Phoenix v. Garbage Services Co.,* 827 F. Supp. 600 (D. Ariz. 1993). The 1996 CERCLA amendment gives comfort to these parties, if their actions are within a statutorily defined safe harbor, and they do not negligently cause or contribute to the release or threatened release of the hazardous substance. 42 U.S.C. § 9607(n). These fiduciaries will not be personally liable for taking or directing another to take an environmental response action, addressing a hazardous substance, including and enforcing environmental covenants in their documents, inspecting trust assets, providing financial or other advice to parties to the fiduciary relationship, administering the property that is the subject of the relationship, and terminating the fiduciary relationship. These protections are not available where the fiduciary relationship was created to avoid environmental liability, or where the trust or other fiduciary estate was created for the primary purpose of, or is actively carrying on, a trade or business for profit, unless the estate was created as part of an estate plan or because of the incapacity of a natural person. In addition, protection of the fiduciary from liability does not protect the trust assets from liability.

28.11 Asbestos   Much has been said of the problems created by the presence of asbestos in buildings. Indeed, there is a sort of countercontroversy over what may have been an overreaction to the asbestos problem. The evidence of the adverse health effects of asbestos is well documented. What is to be done when it is found in a building is something else again. Before its use as a building material was banned, it was installed in countless buildings across the country. Lenders and potential property buyers must proceed with caution to ensure that they do not expose themselves to liability and to the cost of removing or containing this material.

Where asbestos-containing materials (ACMs), or potential asbestos-containing materials (PACMs) are present, Occupational Safety and Health Administration regulations require certain protections for employees. These standards apply to any employee, and thus their employers, and those who own the buildings within which the employees work. Before removing any thermal system insulation or materials containing ACMs or PACMs, doing repair work that is likely to disturb ACMs, or doing maintenance or repair work that involves contact with ACMs or PACMs, the building owner must identify the presence, location, and quantity of the ACMs and PACMs. After identifying the materials, the building owner must notify its own employees and other employers whose employees can reasonably be expected to work in or adjacent to the areas where the materials are contained, and tenants who occupy areas containing such materials. The property owner must maintain records about the ACMs and the PACMs and transfer that information to purchasers.

Some local governments have enacted laws that require the removal or encapsulation of asbestos if it becomes damaged or airborne. Further, any renovation or demolition of a building that contains asbestos must be done in a way that prevents the release of the asbestos fibers into the air, and the removed material must be disposed of properly. 40 C.F.R. §§ 61.140-61.157 .

28.12 Radon   Radon is a tasteless, odorless gas that is emitted from the ground. When diffused into the atmosphere, the gas disperses, apparently without danger to people. When the gas is released from the ground into a building, it can reach concentration levels that make it a danger to the health of the building occupants. Typically, the smaller the building, the greater the danger that radon coming through foundation cracks and from the building materials themselves will build to such levels as to cause cancer in the building occupants. The U.S. Environmental Protection Agency has published pamphlets that explain the problem in greater detail and set forth guidelines for the testing of property and determining whether remedial action is necessary.

As a result of the greater awareness of the dangers of radon, buyers, sellers, and lenders are attempting to determine whether radon is present before they become bound to close their transactions. The Federal Home Loan Bank Board requires an environmental assessment of property proposed as security for a loan to be made by a savings and loan association. The property will be unacceptable if high levels of radon are detected. Federal Home Loan Bank Board, Office of Regulatory Affairs, Thrift Bulletin 16 (Feb. 6, 1989). Some states have enacted laws that require radon notification clauses to be inserted into real estate transactional documents, or require the disclosure of any radon tests that have been conducted and any work that the landowner may have done to mitigate the effect of radon infiltration that is revealed by the tests. Kevin L. Shepherd & Kevin A. Gaynor, *Radon: A Growing Menace in Real Estate Transactions,* 3 Prob. & Prop. 6 (May/June, 1989); Office of Air & Radiation & U.S. Dept. of Health & Human Services, *A Citizens Guide to Radon: What It Is and What to Do About It* (1986); U.S. Environmental Protection Agency, *Radon Reduction Methods: A Homeowner's Guide* (1986).

28.13   Lead   Beginning in 1996, purchasers and renters of residential property became entitled to receive disclosures of known lead-based paint hazards if the property being purchased or rented was built before 1978. 42 U.S.C. §§ 4851–4856; 40 C.F.R. pt. 745 & 24 C.F.R. pt. 35. If the property was built before 1978, the year that lead-based paint was banned by the Consumer Product Safety Council, the buyer or renter is to receive specific information on lead-based paint in the property and a federal pamphlet, *Protect Your Family from Lead in Your Home,* which contains practical, low-cost tips on identifying and controlling lead-based paint hazards. The seller or landlord must give a prescribed lead warning statement and disclose known lead-based paint and lead-based paint hazards, and provide available reports to the prospective buyer or tenant. Of course, this disclosure must be made before the parties enter into a contractual relationship, before the buyer or renter signs the contract or lease. Buyers of residential property must be given a ten-day period to conduct a lead-based paint inspection of the property, a time period that may be shortened or waived with the agreement of the buyer. The sales contract or lease must contain certain notification and disclosure language. The seller or lessor and the real estate broker share responsibility for ensuring compliance with the lead disclosure regulations.

Disclosure is all that is required. The regulation does not require testing or removal, nor does the rule invalidate leases or sales agreements. Also, the rule does not apply to housing built after 1977, zero-bedroom units, such as studio apartments, single-room occupancy units and dormitories, housing for the elderly or handicapped unless children are to also be residents, housing that has been inspected by a certified inspector and found to be free of lead-based paint, and foreclosure sales.

28.14   Transactional Implications   Notwithstanding the exposures that these laws present, they have not caused real estate transactions to come to a standstill. Real estate will continue to be a medium of investment and development. The parties to these transactions have learned to deal with these exposures by quantifying them to the extent possible and obtaining protection in the form of environmental audits, insurance, disclosures, indemnifications, and the like. Tod I. Zuckerman, William E. Motzer, Ph. D., Alfred Leonard, Hayden S. Solomon, *Representing Buyers, Sellers, and Lenders in Transferring Contaminated Property: A Primer for Real Estate Practitioners Part I,* 35 Real Prop., Prob. & Tr. J. 305 (2000).

Many transactions involve extensive representations and warranties given by the seller or borrower to the effect that hazardous wastes have not been deposited on the property, hazardous wastes are not present on the property and have not been generated, used, or stored on the property, and that the seller or borrower has not received any notice that there has been any release of hazardous wastes onto or from the property. While the actual representations, warranties, and covenants in a given transaction will typically be much more extensive, the preceding list is a starting point. The more complex the transaction, the more complex these provisions will be.

These provisions are often followed by an indemnity whereby the seller or borrower agrees to indemnify and hold the buyer or lender harmless from losses that may be caused if the other contractual undertakings are breached. While there is some authority to the contrary, *AM Int'l, Inc. v. Int'l Forging Equip. Corp.,* 743 F. Supp. 525 (N.D. Ohio 1990), the better rule is that these provisions will be upheld as between the parties. *Mardan Corp. v. C.G.C. Music, Ltd.,* 804 F.2d 1454 (9th Cir. 1986); *Jones-Hamilton Co. v. Cop-Coat, Inc.,* 750 F. Supp. 1022 (N.D. Cal. 1990); *Rodenbeck v. Marathon Petroleum Co.,* 32 E.R.C. 1236 (N.D. Ind. 1990).

CHAPTER 29

Land Use Controls—
Building Restrictions

29.01 Private and Public Controls Distinguished

Use of land is controlled in two ways, namely, through private controls and through public controls.

> **EXAMPLE:** *A* buys 100 acres of farmland and divides it into 100 residential lots by means of a recorded plat of subdivision accompanied by a declaration of restrictions that specifies that all lots must be used only for the construction of single-family dwellings. This is private control of use of land by means of building restrictions.

> **EXAMPLE:** The city of *X* adopts a zoning ordinance by which part of the city is zoned for residential use, part for stores, and part for industry. This is public control of land use.

Private land use controls rest on the philosophy that where private ownership of land is recognized, ownership includes the right to sell the real estate on such terms as please the landowner, including the right to restrict the future use of the land in some way that seems desirable to the seller.

There is a parallel, but quite different, philosophy that use of land must be controlled, not in the interest of private individuals as such, but in the public interest for the common good. Both methods coexist under U.S. law, with some overlap and some conflict.

Historically, private controls antedate public controls by many years. Hundreds of years ago in England, a landowner might have given away his land and included some whimsical or capricious requirements in his gift that, while legally enforceable, contributed nothing toward the practical control of land use.

> **EXAMPLE:** Gifts on the following conditions were sustained by the courts: that the donor reside in the house on the land; that the donee would lose the land if he were educated abroad; that the donee must always write his name "T. Jackson Mason"; that the minister of donee's church always wear a black gown in the pulpit. Austin Wakeman Scott, *Control of Property by the Deed*, 65 U. Pa. L. Rev. 527 (1916).

In those early days, there was no way for a purchaser of land to prevent a neighboring landowner from constructing a slaughterhouse, tannery, or other offensive use on adjoining land. This continued until 1848, when the courts first evolved the idea that if a land developer deeds out all the lots in the subdivision with identical restrictions providing, for example, that only single-family dwellings are permitted in the subdivision, any lot owner can obtain a court order preventing any other lot owner from violating this restriction. *Tulk v. Moxhay,* 2 Phil. 774, 41 Eng. Rep. 1143 (Ch. 1848). This was one of the great milestones in the history of real estate law.

This development came in the middle of the Industrial Revolution. Factories were springing up everywhere and threatened to engulf all residential areas. By creating these general plan restrictions, enforceable by any lot owner, the courts preserved residential areas from intrusion by factories.

29.02 Private Restrictions—In General

Private restrictions fall into five main categories:

1. Whimsical or capricious restrictions imposed by the seller on a whim or because of a prejudice, such as a restriction that neither tobacco nor liquor shall be used on the premises or that there shall be no card playing on the premises.

2. Covenants for the benefits of land sold or land retained. These are restrictions imposed by a landowner who owns two adjoining tracts of land and sells one of them.

    EXAMPLE: *A,* owning Lots 1 and 2, with a house on Lot 1, sells vacant Lot 2 with a clause in the deed that no building shall be erected in the front thirty feet of the lot. This protects the view from the front of *A*'s house. Alternatively, *A* could have sold the house lot, with a restriction that no buildings shall be erected on the front thirty feet of the lot retained.

3. Restrictions imposed by a land developer with a view to making the development attractive, such as a restriction that only single-family dwellings shall be erected in the subdivision. This is the most important category. These are the restrictions that create a general plan.

4. Affirmative covenants running with the land, discussed later herein.

5. Conditions. These are restrictions providing for a reverter of title if they are violated. They also are discussed later.

29.03 Creation of General Plan Restrictions

To attract lot purchasers, a land developer often evolves a building scheme or general plan for restricting the lots in the development tract to obtain substantial uniformity in building and land use. For example, the plan often contemplates that only residences shall be erected, excluding stores and industrial uses. The effect is to create a restriction that any lot owner may enforce against any other lot owner. Restrictions upon the use of property, imposed as a part of a general plan for the benefit of all lots, give to the purchaser of any lot a right to enforce such restrictions against the purchaser of any other lot. Such restrictions are enforced on the theory that each purchaser buying with knowledge or notice of the general plan impliedly agrees to abide by the plan.

> **EXAMPLE:** The map or plat of a subdivision provides that all of the lots shall be used for residence purposes only. *A,* one of the lot owners, seeks to open a store on its lot. Any lot owner can obtain an injunction preventing *A* from using its lot for store purposes.

To make sure that the restrictions were enforced, developers began to create homeowners associations (HOAs). The declaration of restrictions conferred upon the HOA the power to enforce the restrictions. Finally, developers began to include in the declaration a provision empowering the HOA to levy an assessment in each homeowner to create a fund for the enforcement of the restrictions and other purposes. The declaration explicitly declared that an unpaid assessment was a lien on the land of the delinquent homeowner. The lien usually took effect as of the date of the recording of the declaration. Bessemer *v.* Gersten, 381 So. 2d 1344 (Fla. 1980); *Lakeland Property Owners Assoc. v. Larson,* 121 Ill. App. 3d 805, 459 N.E.2d 1164 (1984); *Prudential Ins. Co. v. Wetzel,* 212 Wis. 100, 248 N.W. 791 (1933).

29.03(a) Notice of General Plan

There are two important ingredients here: (1) the general plan created by the uniform restrictions and (2) notice of the general plan created by recording, usually of the plat or declaration of restrictions.

General plan restrictions were originally created by incorporating identical restrictions in all deeds by the subdivider. This is not the usual practice today. The character that a particular development is to assume is planned at the same time that the acreage is first subdivided into building lots. The developer incorporates into the recorded plat or map of the subdivision itself uniform restrictions to which all lots are subject. Clearly the plan is general. *Case v. Morrisette,* 475 F.2d 1300 (D.C. Cir. 1973). It is best to have each deed state that it is "subject to" the restrictions contained in the recorded plat. Since every lot purchaser at least constructively takes with notice of the recorded plat, the purchaser has constructive notice of the restriction.

These building schemes have become so elaborate that there is not enough room for them on the plat or map, and the restrictions are commonly found in a separate recorded declaration of restrictions recorded simultaneously with the plat and referred to in the plat. Legally, this is as though the restrictions had been set forth in full on the face of the plat. Subsequently, as sales of the lots are made, the deeds contain clauses stating that the land is subject to the recorded restrictions. Robert Kratovil, *Building Restrictions: Contracts or Servitudes,* 11 J. Marshall L. Rev. 465 (1978).

Of course, the privilege of creating restrictions is by no means confined to developers. Any landowner is at liberty to insert restrictions in the deed when the land is sold.

**29.03(b)
Enforcement of
General Plan
Restrictions**

If a general plan restriction is violated, the court will issue an order forbidding the violation, that is, an injunction. Anyone who disobeys the court order can be jailed for contempt of court. Structures erected in violation thereof can be ordered demolished. *Stewart v. Finkelstone,* 206 Mass. 28, 92 N.E. 37 (1910). The general plan creates rights known as "equitable servitudes." The benefit and burden of those equitable servitudes attaches to each lot in the subdivision. For a general plan restriction to be enforced, the one seeking enforcement need only show that the violator purchased its lot with notice of the restriction, either from a recorded document or from actual knowledge of the restriction. The question as to enforcement of a general plan–type restriction, then, arises when one lot owner attempts to violate a restriction and another lot owner seeks a court order prohibiting such attempted violation. The court will ask two questions: (1) Is there a general plan? (2) If there is, did the violator purchase the land with actual knowledge or with notice from the public records of the existence of the general plan? If the answer to these questions is yes, the restriction will be enforced, except in certain situations that are discussed later.

Any lot owner, or tenant or mortgagee, or contract purchaser may enforce a general plan restriction. Maurice T. Brunner, Annotation, *Who May Enforce Restrictive Covenant to Use of Real Property*, 51 A.L.R.3d 556 (1973). As long as the subdivider owns any lot in the subdivision, it also can enforce the restriction. However, when the developer has sold the last lot, it no longer has any economic interest to protect. Nearly all courts say that the developer thereupon loses the right to enforce. *Kent v. Koch,* 333 P.2d 411 (Cal. 1958); *American Cannel Coal* Co. *v. Indiana Cotton Mills,* 78 Ind. App. 115, 134 N.E. 891 (1922). *But see BCE Development, Inc. v. Smith,* 215 Cal. App. 3d 1142, 264 Cal. Rptr. 55 (Cal. App. 1989), which allowed a developer to enforce restrictions even after it sold all of the benefitted property.

The conscientious developer continues to want orderly development of the subdivision even after the last lot is sold. To accomplish this, the developer will create a homeowners' association in the form of a nonprofit corporation. The plat or declaration of restrictions confers on this association the right to enforce the general plan restrictions. Owners of property within the development automatically become members of the association. They pay dues to the association, and a fund is thus formed to finance, among other things, a lawsuit if a violation of the restrictions is threatened. This device is valid. *Neponsit Property Owners Ass'n v. Emigrant Industrial Sav. Bank,* 278 N.Y. 248, 15 N.E.2d 793 (1938); *Merrionette Manor Homes Improvement Ass'n v. Heda,* 11 Ill. App. 2d 186, 136 N.E.2d 556 (1956).

**29.03(c)
Interpretation of
General Plan
Restrictions**

The problem of framing restrictions that will carry out the intention of the developer for years to come, under changed economic and social conditions, is a difficult one. Much litigation has centered around this point.

**29.03(c)(1)   Location
Restrictions**

When the plat or map of a subdivision shows a line designated as a building line extending across a portion of the lots, this is sufficient to create a building line restriction. No substantial parts of buildings may then be erected beyond the building line. Building line restrictions may also be created by restrictions in the deed. The purpose of a building line is twofold: to ensure a certain degree of uniformity in the location of the buildings and to create a right to unobstructed light, air, and sight. The fact that a small porch, awning, stoop, steps, or an overhanging bay window extends beyond the building line will not constitute a violation of the restriction.

In dealing with the interpretation of building restrictions, keep in mind that the courts are trying to discover and give effect to the intention of the developer. Where the developer leaves its intention in doubt, the court faces a difficult problem. It must be as practical as possible. Common sense must be applied. The literal language of the restriction often must be disregarded. Certainly, common sense dictates that minor violations of restrictions must be disregarded. The problem is where to draw the line. What, for example, is a "small porch"? A so-called bay window that is really the front wall of the house is a violation of the restriction. 55 A.L.R. 332, 172 A.L.R. 1324. A carport is part of the house and is a building line violation. *Garden Oaks Board of Trustees v. Gibbs,* 489 S.W.2d 133 (Tex. Civ. App. 1972).

When a restriction provides that no building shall be erected within a certain number of feet of the street line, it is the line where the lot meets the street that is meant. In other words, a plat of a subdivision shows this particular lot as fronting on a street. Where the lot ends, the street begins. Often enough, the city paves only the middle part of the street strip, and laymen sometimes speak of this as the "street." This is technically incorrect. The street extends to the lot line and includes not only the roadway, but also the parkway or planted area, if any, sidewalks, if any, and so on. Building line restrictions are measured from the legal street line, which is not necessarily the curb line. *Trunck v. Hack's Point Community Ass'n,* 204 Md. 193, 103 A.2d 343 (1954).

**29.03(c)(2)
Incidental Use**

A use purely incidental to a permitted use is permitted.

> **EXAMPLE:** Shop in hotel. *Blakeley v. Gorin,* 365 Mass. 590, 313 N.E.2d 903 (Mass. 1974). But solar panels to heat a swimming pool may be prohibited. *Taylor v. Ridge at the Bluffs Homeowners,* 579 So. 2d 895 (Fla. App. 1991).

**29.03(c)(3)
Residence Purposes**

Many restrictions provide that "the land shall be used for residence purposes" or that "only residences shall be erected on this real estate." Under this type of restriction, any kind of building devoted exclusively to residence purposes, single or multifamily, may be erected. This includes a duplex house and an apartment building. Annotation, *Use of Property for Multiple Dwellings as Violating Restrictive Covenant Permitting Property to Be Used for*

Residential Purposes Only, 99 A.L.R.3rd 985 (1980). If the restriction permits construction of only "private," "single," or "detached" residences, only single-family dwellings are permitted. *Flaks v. Wichman,* 128 Colo. 45, 260 P.2d 737 (1953). But they may be rented. *Yogman v. Parrot,* 142 Or. App. 544, 921 P.2d 1352 (1996); *Gilbert v. Shenandoah Valley Ass'n,* 592 S.W.2d 28 (Tex. Civ. App. 1979).

29.03(c)(4)   History of Apartment Rule

When the general plan restriction was born in 1848, apartments were virtually unknown in most of America. The first apartments in Chicago, for example, appeared in the 1870s. In Detroit, the first apartment was built in 1892. It is not surprising, then, that the early restriction schemes, those antedating 1880, were drawn by subdividers and their lawyers or conveyancers on the blissful assumption that all that was needed was protection of homes against factories. The land was restricted to "residential use." When the construction of apartments began, the early restriction schemes were inadequate to protect against apartments. Apartments are a residential use.

29.03(c)(5)   Condominiums

A multifamily condominium is a violation of a restriction that forbids apartments. It is not a group of single-family dwellings. Annotation, *Erection of Condominium as Violation of Restrictive Covenant Forbidding Erection of Apartment Houses,* 65 A.L.R.3d 1212 (1975 Supp. 1998).

29.03(c)(6)   Drafting

A good residential restriction might read as follows:

> Only one detached, single-family dwelling and private attached garage appertaining thereto shall be erected on each lot. No use shall be made of said premises except such as is incidental to the occupation thereof for residence purposes by one private family residing in a detached, single-family dwelling.

This form has the following advantages: The phrase "single-family dwelling" keeps out apartments and other multiple dwellings. Single dwellings will not do the trick because in some states, a restriction against single dwellings does not prohibit a duplex or apartment.

Vocabulary is important. A two-flat is a building with two apartments, one above the other, designed for occupancy by two families. A two-flat is not a single-family dwelling. Annotation, *Use of Property for Multiple Dwellings as Violating Restrictive Covenant Permitting Property to be Used for Residential Purposes Only,* 99 A.L.R.3d 985 (1980). The stipulation as to occupation by one private family keeps out lodgers and prevents doubling up of families.

If a restriction merely specifies the type of building that can be built, but is silent regarding the use of the building, an argument may be advanced that the building can be used for any purpose. As a rule, courts try to give effect to the obvious intention by holding that the use of a structure must conform to the purposes for which it was erected. *Strauss v. Ginzberg,* 218 Minn. 57, 15 N.W.2d 130 (1944).

> **EXAMPLE:** A restriction provided that "no structure shall be built except for dwelling purposes." A dwelling was erected. Later, the owner of the dwelling attempted to use it as a beauty parlor. The court held that the building could be used only for dwelling purposes. *Holderness v. Central States Fin. Corp.,* 241 Mich. 604, 217 N.W. 764 (1928); *J.T. Hobby & Son, Inc. v. Family Homes of Wake County, Inc.,* 302 N.C. 64, 274 S.E.2d 174 (1981).

The restriction should restrict the use of the land as well as use of the building. Again, courts will usually come to the rescue by holding that the intention was to restrict use of both building and land.

EXAMPLE: A restriction provided that no building erected on the land should be used for any purpose other than as a private dwelling place. The landowner attempted to use the vacant land as a parking lot, contending that the restriction applied only to the use of buildings and therefore did not apply to vacant land. The court held that it was the intention to restrict use of both building and land. *Hoover v. Waggoman*, 52 N.M. 371, 199 P.2d 991 (1948); 155 A.L.R. 528, 1007. A restriction calling for only one detached single-family dwelling per lot impliedly forbids occupancy of that dwelling by two families. *Freeman v. Gee*, 18 Utah 2d 339, 423 P.2d 155 (1967).

Evidence of how older restrictions are interpreted in light of new technology is found in the line of cases dealing with satellite dishes. Where the restrictions required the approval by a homeowners' association before the erection of a "structure," the dish could not be erected until the homeowners' association approved. *Shoreline Estate Homeowners' Ass'n v. Loucks,* 84 Or. App. 302, 733 P.2d 942 (1987). Similarly, a restriction that prohibited "outside radio, television, ham broadcasting or other electronic antenna or aerials" prohibited the erection of a satellite dish. *Breeling v. Churchill,* 228 Neb. 596, 423 N.W.2d 469 (1988).

29.03(c)(7) Duplex

A duplex is really two single-family dwellings connected by a party wall built on the lot line, with one building on each lot. *Stephenson v. Perlitz,* 537 S.W.2d 287 (Tex. Civ. App. 1976); *Easterly v. Hall,* 256 S.C. 336, 182 S.E.2d 671 (1971). A duplex is permitted on land restricted to residence purposes. Annotation, *Use of Property for Multiple Dwellings as Violating Restrictive Covenant Permitting Property to be Used for Residential Purposes Only,* 99 A.L.R.3d 985 (1980 Supp. 1998). To keep out duplexes, it is advisable to have the restriction read that only one detached single-family dwelling may be built on each lot. *Freeman v. Gee,* 423 P.2d at 159.

29.03(c)(8) Business Purposes

When the restriction forbids use of the premises for business purposes, the following are not permitted: gasoline filling stations, billboards, and parking for business purposes. Especially in older deeds, one is likely to find restrictions prohibiting use of the property for a "trade or business." Suppose a doctor uses a room of his or her home as an office for the practice of medicine. This would not violate such a restriction because the practice of medicine is not a trade or business; it is a profession. *Auerbacher v. Smith,* 19 N.J. Super. 191, 88 A.2d 262 (1952); E.T. Tsai, Annotation, *Incidental Use of Dwelling for Business or Professional Purposes as Violation of Covenant Restricting Use to Residential Purposes,* 21 A.L.R.3d 641 (1969 Supp. 1998).

29.04 Senior Citizens

There are, of course, numerous subdivisions restricted to senior citizens. This is accomplished by means of general plan–type restrictions in a declaration of restrictions. They are valid. *Riley v. Stoves,* 22 Ariz. App. 223, 526 P.2d 747 (1974); Allan E. Korpek, Annotation, *Validity and Construction of Covenant Restricting Occupancy of Premises to Person Under Specified Age,* 68 A.L.R.3d 1239 (1976 Supp. 1998).

Since the old law frowns on restrictions on the sale of land, frame restrictions in terms of restrictions on occupancy, since these present no legal problem. Because of the shortage of suitable housing and the tendency of condominium developers to bar occupancy by children, the argument is being made that barring children is illegal. This is an unresolved issue. Kristine Cordier Karnezis, Annotation, *Enforceability of By-Law or Other Rule of Condominium or Co-Operative Association Restricting Occupancy by Children,* 100 A.L.R.3d 241 (1980 Supp. 1998).

29.05 Defective Restrictions

Many restrictions are so poorly drafted that they fail to achieve their main purpose.

> **EXAMPLE:** A restriction provided that "no flat roof dwelling house shall be erected." Since no other type of building was mentioned, a flat roof church could be erected. *Corbridge v. Westminster Presbyterian Church & Society,* 18 Ill. App. 2d 245, 151 N.E.2d 822 (1958).

You can see that many restrictions, particularly the older ones, are negative in form. They contain enumerations of prohibited uses, such as apartments and businesses. Such devices are doomed to failure. In the first place, nobody ever makes the list of excluded uses long enough, and nobody, of course, can cover the uses that do not even exist at the time the restrictions are drafted, but will crop up later. This is why, particularly for residential property, modern restriction plans simply specify the one type of permitted use, that is, "only detached single-family dwellings shall be constructed, and the premises shall be used only as a residence for one private family."

29.06 Plans of Buildings

Often a scheme of restrictions provides that no building shall be erected until the plans and specifications therefor have been approved by the developer or an architecture committee. Such provisions are valid, but any refusal to approve plans will be set aside by the courts if such refusal is capricious, arbitrary, or unreasonable. *Hannula v. Hacienda Homes, Inc.,* 34 Cal. App. 2d 442, 211 P.2d 302 (1949); Wade R. Habeeb, Annotation, *Validity and Construction of Restrictive Covenant Controlling Architectural Style of Buildings to Be Erected on Property*, 47 A.L.R.3d 1232 (1973).

29.07 Ingress and Egress for a Prohibited Use

Occasionally, a lot in a restricted residential subdivision is acquired by one who seeks to use it for the benefit of nonresidential land outside the subdivision. This is not permitted.

> **EXAMPLE:** A plat restriction permitted only residential use of the lots. *X,* who owned a restaurant across the street from the subdivision, bought three lots in the subdivision, meaning to use them for access to the restaurant and parking. The court prohibited this. *Bennett v. Consolidated Realty Co.,* 226 Ky. 747, 11 S.W.2d 910,V. Woerner, Annotation, *Maintenance, Use or Grant of Right of Way over Restricted Property as Violation of Restrictive Covenant*, 25 A.L.R.2d 904 (1952).

29.08 Modification, Extension, and Release of General Plan Restrictions

If the right to modify a general plan is not reserved in the deeds, plat, or declaration, it takes a unanimous vote of all lot owners (and probably also their mortgagees) to modify or release the restrictions. *Steve Vogli & Co. v. Lane,* 405 S.W.2d 885 (Mo. 1966); B.C. Ricketts, Annotation, *Validity, Construction and Effect of Contractual Provision Regarding Future Revocation or Modification of Covenant Restricting Use of Real Property*, 4 A.L.R.3d 570 (1966 Supp. 1998). This is rarely obtainable.

> **EXAMPLE:** All owners but one signed a release of the restrictions. The holdout was entitled to enforce the restrictions. *Evangelical Lutheran Church v. Sahlem,* 254 N.Y. 161, 172 N.E. 455 (1930).

In recent restriction plans, developers have often included a clause giving themselves the right to waive or dispense with the restrictions as to some or all of the lots. This is dangerous. A number of courts have held that such a provision destroys the uniformity necessary to a general plan, and therefore the restrictions cannot be enforced by one lot owner against another.

When the right to modify the restrictions is reserved to the developer by the deeds, plat, or declarations, the developer may validly exercise this right. *McComb v. Hanly,* 132 N.J. Eq. 182, 26 A.2d 891.

When the restriction is imposed to satisfy a condition of subdivision approval made by the municipal planning committee, the general public may have to join in any modification or release of the restriction. *Soussa v. Denville Township Planning Bd.,* 238 N.J. Super. 66, 568 A.2d 1225 (N.J. Super. 1990). This may require litigation so as to allow the court to pass on the modification or release.

In providing for periodical extensions and modifications of the restrictions in the declaration, thought must be given to the voting arrangements.

> **EXAMPLE:** There is a difference between "the owners of a majority of the lots" and "a majority of the lot owners."

Where the right to modify restrictions is reserved in the plat, declaration of restrictions, or deeds, any modifications voted by the required majority must be general in their nature.

> **EXAMPLE:** A majority of the landowners voted to take one lot out of the restrictions so that a filling station could be erected on it. This was invalid. *Riley v. Boyle,* 6 Ariz. App. 523, 434 P.2d 525 (1967).

Any amendment must be reasonable and must leave the plan basically intact. *Flamingo Ranch Estates v. Sunshine Ranches Homeowners, Inc.,* 303 So. 2d 665 (Fla. Dist. Ct. App. 1974).

29.09 Mortgage Foreclosure

Care must be exercised where a mortgage is recorded prior to the declaration of restrictions.

> **EXAMPLE:** Owner records a construction mortgage on some vacant land to Lender. Thereafter, Owner subdivides the land and records a declaration of restrictions. Owner then sells a few lots, and deeds are recorded to the buyers. These lots are released from the mortgage. Then, Owner defaults on the mortgage, which is foreclosed. The restrictions are wiped out by the foreclosure. *Boyd v. Park Realty Corp.,* 137 Md. 36, 111 A. 129 (1920); *Sain v. Silvestre,* 78 Cal. App. 3d 144 Cal. Rptr. 478 (1978). Prior in time is prior in right.

The construction mortgage should have stated that it was subject to a declaration of restrictions to be recorded later, or simultaneously with the recording of the declaration of restrictions. The lender could have recorded a subordination of the mortgage to the restrictions. Most land planning procedures require the mortgagee's joinder in the plat of subdivision and consent to the restrictions.

29.10 Minor Violations

Earlier, it was stated that courts will not force removal of trivial encroachments. A court is a tribunal where revenge or punishment in the way of reprisal has no place. *Kajowski v. Null,* 405 Pa. 589, 177 A.2d 101 (1962). The courts will "balance the equities." *De Marco v. Palazzolo,* 47 Mich. App. 444, 209 N.W.2d 540 (1973). If an unintentional minor violation of a restriction is involved, the courts will not compel its removal. This has been explained in connection with location restrictions. The same rule applies to other violations.

> **EXAMPLE:** A restriction limited the height of buildings to twenty-five feet. By mistake, a landowner erected a building that was twenty-six feet high. The court refused to compel the landowner to remove the offending one foot.

> **EXAMPLE:** At times, a lot owner will build a home so that it extends slightly over the building line established by the building restrictions. In the process of balancing the equities, the court will consider that compelling removal of three or four inches of a home is a disastrous burden, but such removal does little for the neighbor. Removal is rarely ordered. Note that encroachments on a neighbor's land of three or four inches are serious. Encroachments over a building line are less serious.

29.11   Factors that Render General Plan Restrictions Unenforceable

In considering what factors render restrictions unenforceable, it is necessary, first of all, to distinguish between restrictions that do not provide for a reverter of title and those that do. We consider first the general plan–type restrictions, which are traditionally enforced by means of an injunction, or court order, forbidding violation. Such orders are not granted lightly. Various circumstances are considered by the courts in determining whether such an order should be granted.

29.11(a)   General Principles

In determining the legal duration of a restriction, keep in mind that courts are practical. Even if the restriction recites that it will exist "forever," courts are likely to terminate it when it has become useless. *Ferguson v. Zion Evangelical Lutheran Church,* 200 Okla. 41, 190 P.2d 1019 (1948).

29.11(b)   Change in Neighborhood

A court will not, as a rule, enforce a restriction by injunction when the neighborhood has so changed in character and environment as to make it unfit to continue the original use. V. Woerner, Annotation, *Change of Neighborhood in Restricted District as Effecting Restrictive Covenant Decisions Since 1927,* 4 A.L.R.2d 1111 (1949); Joseph T. Bockrath, Annotation, *Change of Neighborhood as Affecting Restrictive Covenants Precluding Use of Land for Multiple Dwelling,* 53 A.L.R.3d 492 (1974 Supp. 1998); 26 C.J.S. *Deeds* § 171. The court will "balance the equities." That is, it will not grant an injunction that will do the plaintiff little good but will do the defendant great harm.

> **EXAMPLE:** A restriction provides that lots in the subdivision shall be used only for residence purposes. Gradually, the neighborhood changes character, and stores and factories creep in. This often happens because no single homeowner wishes to incur the expense of hiring an attorney and litigating the right of neighbors to violate the restrictions. When it becomes impossible to characterize the area as residential, courts will refuse to enforce the restriction on the ground that it is no longer possible to carry the original plan into effect. However, if the change in neighborhood affects only a part of the subdivision while the remainder is unchanged, the restrictions may be enforced in the area that remains unchanged. *O'Neill v. Wolf,* 338 Ill. 508, 170 N.E. 669. Suppose *A* owns a house in a restricted subdivision, but six blocks away, a number of violating structures are erected. *A*'s acquiescence in these violations will not bar him from stopping a violation next door to him or in the same block. In other words, these previous violations are so remote that they do not constitute a change in the immediate neighborhood, nor could *A* be charged with undue neglect in enforcing his rights. *Bischoff v. Morgan,* 236 Mich. 251, 210 N.W. 226.

A question on which the courts are not in agreement relates to changes that occur outside the subdivision.

> **EXAMPLE:** A plat restriction limits the subdivision to residential uses. As the surrounding area changes, many stores are built across the street from the subdivision. Some courts insist that the front tier of lots in the subdivision must hold the line and the restrictions continue in force. *Knolls Ass'n v. Hinton,* 71 Ill. App. 3d 205, 389 N.E.2d 693 (1979); *Oritz v. Jeter,* 479 S.W.2d 752; 2 Am. Law Ppty. § 9.39. Since it is not always easy to get people to buy homes across the street from the stores, other courts will allow changes of this nature to sway them

in refusing enforcement of the restrictions. *Hecht v. Stephens*, 204 Kan. 559, 464 P.2d 258 (1970); *Exchange Nat'l Bank v. City of Des Plaines,* 32 Ill. App. 3d 722, 336 N.E.2d 8 (1975).

29.11(c) Numerous Violations

Even when the restricted neighborhood has not changed its general character, the right to enforce a particular restriction may be lost by abandonment. When the property owners in the subdivision have violated the restrictions and the violations have been so general as to indicate an abandonment of the original general plan, the restrictions will not be enforced. The reason for this is that the purpose of the restriction can no longer be carried out. It would be an injustice to a property owner to compel it to conform to a restriction that most of the other owners have violated when such enforcement would be of no benefit to the party seeking to enforce the restriction.

> **EXAMPLE:** A building line was established across a block consisting of fifteen lots. On nine of the lots, buildings were erected that extended across the building line. The owner of a lot that had remained vacant began construction of a building that would also violate the building line. The owner of another vacant lot sought a court order to prevent this violation. The court order was refused. The value of the building line had been destroyed by the numerous violations. *Ewertsen v. Gerstenberg,* 186 Ill. 344, 57 N.E. 1051 (1900).

29.11(d) Abandonment

Even in the absence of numerous violations, a landowner's acquiescence in violations of restrictions may render restrictions unenforceable. Restatement (First) of Property § 561; 26 C.J.S. *Deeds* § 169.

> **EXAMPLE:** A plat restricts all the lots to single-family dwellings. Without protest by others, *A* builds an apartment building on Lot 5 and *B* builds an apartment building on Lot 7. *X* now seeks to build an apartment building on Lot 6, which is sandwiched between the existing apartments. He may do so.

And there may be a partial abandonment. This leaves the remainder of the restrictions enforceable. *Donahoe v. Marston,* 26 Ariz. App. 187, 547 P.2d 39 (1976).

> **EXAMPLE:** A plat restriction provided that all lots were to be used for residence purposes and only single-family dwellings could be erected. A number of two-flats were erected. Now, one lot owner wishes to put in a store. He cannot do so. *Noyes v. McDonnell*, 398 P.2d 838 (Okla. 1965). Likewise, minor violations of a building line furnish no excuse for major violations. *Carter v. Conroy*, 25 Ariz. App. 434, 544 P.2d 258 (1976).

29.11(e) Violations by Party Who Seeks to Enforce Restriction

One who violates a nonreverter-type restriction in some substantial degree or manner cannot obtain an injunction restraining the violation of the restriction by others. Restatement (First) of Property § 560; 26 C.J.S. *Deeds,* § 169, p. 1163; 4 A.L.R.2d 1111 (1949).

> **EXAMPLE:** A plat restriction permits only single-family dwellings to be erected. *A* constructs a two-flat. *A*'s neighbor, *B,* now seeks to erect a three-flat. *A* cannot prevent this.

29.11(f) Delay in Enforcing Restrictions

Where a nonreverter-type restriction, as distinguished from a condition, is involved, a person wishing to prevent a violation must act promptly.

> **EXAMPLE:** A subdivision plat contains a nonreverter-type building restriction forbidding the construction of anything but single-family dwellings. *X,* who owns a house in this subdivision, observes that *Y,* another lot owner, is erecting a gas station. After construction of the station has been completed, *X* files a suit to have it demolished. The court will refuse to interfere. *X* has been guilty of laches or undue delay. R.D. Hursh, Annotation, *Laches or Delay in Bring-*

ing Suit as Affecting Right to Enforce Restrictive Building Covenants, 12 A.L.R.2d 394 (1950); N.J. Dunn, Annotation, *Building Sideline Restrictive Covenants*, 36 A.L.R.2d 861, 870 (1954).

> **EXAMPLE:** A declaration of covenants, conditions, and restrictions established an architectural review committee. A landowner applied to and obtained approval from the committee of the development of a house and satellite dish on the owner's land and the improvements were constructed. A later slate of officers of the homeowners' association sought to cause the removal of what they thought were improvements that violated the restrictions. The suit was not allowed. *Woodmoor Improvement Ass'n v. Brenner*, 919 P.2d 928 (Colo. App. 1996).

29.11(g) Restrictions About to Expire by Lapse of Time

Many restrictions specifically state a time limit for their expiration. Suppose construction of a building that violates the restriction is begun a year or so before the restriction will expire by lapse of time. In this instance, the courts may refuse to enforce the restriction for the simple, practical reason that to do so would be of little practical benefit.

29.11(h) Statutes of Limitations

In some states, laws have been enacted limiting the period of time for bringing a suit for violation of a building restriction.

> **EXAMPLE:** In Missouri, such a suit must be brought within two years after the date the restriction was violated. Mo. Ann. Stat. § 516.095. New York has a two-year limitation on building line violations; in Massachusetts the period is six years. In Massachusetts, building restrictions unlimited in duration expire after thirty years. Basye, *Clearing Land Titles* § 143 (2d ed. 1970). In Colorado, a suit to enforce a restriction must be brought within one year from the date of violation. *Wolf v. Hallenbeck,* 109 Colo. 70, 123 P.2d 412 (1942).

29.11(i) State Laws Placing Time Limits on Enforcement of Restrictions

A number of states—Arizona, Georgia, Massachusetts, Michigan, Minnesota, Rhode Island, and Wisconsin, for example—have enacted laws providing that, after the lapse of a stated number of years, restrictions become unenforceable. *Payne v. Borkat,* 244 Ga. 615, 261 S.E.2d 393 (1979); *Baker v. Seneca,* 329 Mass. 736, 110 N.E.2d 325 (1953); Basye, *Clearing Land Titles* § 143 (2d ed. 1970). And, in all states, having marketability of title laws, restrictions will expire after the permitted time unless the restriction is kept alive by a new recording as provided in the law. *Semachko v. Hopko,* 35 Ohio App. 2d 205, 301 N.E.2d 560 (1973).

29.11(j) Other Factors

Courts are more merciful when the violation is not willful but is due to accident or mistake, as where a surveyor makes an error and, as a result, a building extends over a building line. They are also more merciful toward minor violations than they are toward major violations. Of course, if the party seeking to enforce the restriction has said or done something that would encourage the violator to go ahead with the violation, it will get no help from the courts.

29.12 Conditions

A condition is a restriction that is coupled with a reverter clause. This clause provides that if the restriction is violated, ownership reverts to the grantor in the deed.

> **EXAMPLE:** Owner deeds a lot to Buyer with a provision forbidding sale or use of intoxicating liquor on the lot and that, in case of violation, ownership reverts to Owner. In time, the premises are sold to Buyer 2, who puts in a drugstore with a liquor department. Owner files a suit. The court will give the property back to Owner.

The outstanding characteristic of a condition is the fact that if it is violated, the grantor may get the land back by filing a suit to obtain possession. It need not pay any compensation for the return of the land. Any mortgages or other interests in the land created after the creation of the condition would be extinguished if the condition is enforced, again without payment of compensation to the mortgagee. This rule operates so harshly that courts are reluctant to construe a provision as a condition. In nearly all states, if the restrictive provision is followed by a clause providing that, in the event of a violation of the restrictions, the title to land will revert to the grantor in the deed, the restrictive provision is a condition. If the deed contains no reverter clause, that is, a clause providing for a reverter or forfeiture of title in the event of violation of the restrictions, the restrictive provision is usually a covenant. The nomenclature employed by the parties is by no means decisive as to the character of the restriction created.

> **EXAMPLE:** A deed contained this clause: "These presents are upon the express condition that the said premises shall not be used or occupied as a tavern or public house." There was no reverter clause. It was held to be a covenant. *Koch v. Streuter,* 232 Ill. 594, 83 N.E. 1072 (1908). Violation would not cause a reverter.

Occasionally, the condition is referred to as a reverter.

29.12(a)
Enforcement of
Conditions

When a condition (i.e., a reverter type of restriction) occurs in a deed but the condition forms no part of any general plan, enforcement is relatively simple. The condition can be enforced by the grantor in the deed, or, if the grantor is dead, by the grantor's heirs. Other lot owners in the same subdivision cannot enforce the condition.

A recorded condition can be enforced against any subsequent purchaser or mortgagee of the land. Enforcement of a condition by the grantor in the deed containing the condition, or by the grantor's heirs, if the grantor is dead, extinguishes all subsequent titles and rights in the land.

> **EXAMPLE:** Seller conveys a lot to Buyer 1 with a condition in the deed that the premises shall not be used for the sale of liquor. The deed provides that in the event of violation of this provision, title to the property shall revert to Seller. Buyer 1 sells and conveys the property to Buyer 2, who places a mortgage thereon to Lender. Thereafter, Buyer 2 leases the building to Tenant and the latter uses the property for the sale of liquor. Seller brings suit to recover the land on the ground that the condition has been violated. Seller will be allowed to recover the land and all buildings erected on it without payment of any compensation and will have good title free and clear of the mortgage and lease.

As a result of the operation of the reverter provision, mortgagees may be reluctant to loan money on land that is subject to a condition. In fact, many insurance companies, which are authorized by law to loan money on first mortgages only, cannot legally make a loan on land that is subject to a condition. The problem may be handled in a number of different ways.

1. The person who has the right to enforce a reverter (the grantor in the deed creating the condition, or his or her heirs) may always release the reverter outright to the landowner. Unfortunately, it is sometimes difficult to identify or find all of these parties.

2. The person who has the right to enforce a reverter may subordinate this right to a mortgage by a document stating that the reverter right is subject to the mortgage. If the subordination is unequivocal, the mortgagee, upon foreclosure, completely extinguishes the condition.

3. Many subdividers who place conditions in their deeds also include provisions in their deeds stating that the reverter right is subordinate to all mortgages. These provisions are broad in their terms and protect any mortgagee who may take a mortgage on the land.

4. In some instances, title companies will insure against loss caused by a reverter of title.

29.12(b)   Factors that Render Conditions Unenforceable

In many states, especially where older court decisions are still followed, the factors discussed previously that would prevent enforcement of a nonreverter-type restriction have little application to conditions, that is, reverter-type restrictions. For example, in nearly all states, the grantor in a deed containing a condition, or the grantor's heirs, if the grantor is dead, has the right to enforce a condition even though the neighborhood has so changed that enforcement is of little practical utility. In one or two states, however, the change of neighborhood rule is now also applied to conditions, and conditions will not be enforced where the neighborhood has changed. *Letteau v. Ellis,* 122 Cal. App. 584, 10 P.2d 496 (1932); *Cole v. Colorado Springs,* 152 Colo. 162, 381 P.2d 13 (Colo. 1963); *Koehler v. Rowland,* 275 Mo. 573, 205 S.W. 217 (1918); *Townsend v. Allen,* 114 Cal. App. 2d 291, 250 P.2d 292 (1952).

Again, laws exist in every state allowing a certain time, often as long as twenty years, for the bringing of a suit to declare a reverter of title and to enforce a condition. This period of time runs not from the date of the deed containing the condition, but from the date the condition is violated. Often situations arise where, after the condition has been violated, no action has been taken to enforce the condition, and the landowner continues in possession, perhaps for several years. Mere delay in enforcing a condition, so long as the period allowed by law has not expired, does not, in most states, bar enforcement of a condition. But, if the one who has a right to declare a reverter stands idly by, apparently acquiescing in the violation of the condition, and sees valuable improvements being made by the landowner and delays proceedings to enforce the condition until after the improvements have been completed, some modern courts feel that this conduct is so unfair to the landowner that they refuse to enforce the condition.

29.12(b)(1)   Reverter Acts

In some states, laws have been passed outlawing conditions after a specified period of time has elapsed from the date of their creation. *Trustees v. Batdorf,* 6 Ill. 2d 486, 130 N.E.2d 111 (1955)*; State Highway Div. v. Tolke,* 36 Or. App. 751, 586 P.2d 791 (1978); *Caldwell v. Brown,* 553 S.W.2d 692 (Ky. 1977); Wayne Foster, Annotation, *Validity of Statute Canceling, Destroying, Nullifying, or Limiting Enforcement of Possibilities of Reverter or Rights of Re-Entry for Conditions Broken,* 87 A.L.R.3d 1011 (1978 Supp. 1999). *But see Bd. of Educ. v. Miles,* 15 N.Y.2d 364, 207 N.E.2d 181(1965) (criticized in 1965 *Law Forum* 941). Marketability of title laws also have this result.

29.12(b)(2)   Nominal Conditions

A number of states have statutes that conditions may be disregarded when they become "merely nominal" or "without substantial benefit to the parties." Basye, *Clearing Land Titles* § 143 (2d ed. 1970 Supp. 1983).

> **EXAMPLE:** A subdivider deeded out all lots with a reverter clause against trade or business. After he had deeded out all lots, he could not enforce the conditions. They had only nominal value to him. He could not be hurt by violations. *Ingersoll Engineering & Constructing Co. v. Crocker,* 228 F. 844 (6th Cir. 1915).

29.12(b)(3)   Acquiescence in Violations

Sometimes, a general plan is revealed by the existence of identical conditions in deeds. In such cases, if the owner of the reverter right follows a course of conduct that results in numerous violations of the conditions, he or she will, in some states, be denied the right to enforce any of the conditions. W.W. Allen, *Waiver of, or Estoppel to Assert Condition Subsequent or Its Breach,* 39 A.L.R.2d 1116 (1955).

> **EXAMPLE:** A subdivider sold all the lots in the subdivision by deeds containing conditions against sale of intoxicating liquor. Later, the grantor voluntarily released this clause as to a

number of lots, and saloons were built on the released lots. The grantor was refused the right to enforce any of the unreleased conditions. *Wedum-Aldahl Co. v. Miller,* 18 Cal. App. 2d 745, 64 P.2d 762 (1937).

It can be seen that while the older and stricter court decisions freely allow the enforcement of conditions, the modern decisions are beginning to apply to conditions the same rules that they apply to nonreverter-type restrictions.

29.13 Covenants Running with the Land

This topic is best explained by an illustration.

> **EXAMPLE:** Seller owns two adjoining lots, Lots 1 and 2. Seller sells Lot 1 to Buyer and, in the deed, inserts a clause stating that Buyer covenants to keep in repair the fence between the two lots. Lot 2 enjoys the benefit of this covenant. Lot 1 bears the burden of the covenant. Any subsequent owner of Lot 1 must comply with this covenant and will be liable to pay damages to the owner of Lot 2 if there is a breach. Any subsequent owner of Lot 2 will be able to enforce this covenant. Such an affirmative covenant runs with the land, much in the same fashion as an appurtenant easement runs with the land, the burden of the covenant running with Lot 1 and the benefit running with Lot 2.

In issuing such orders, courts ignore all the technicalities that surround damage suits. As long as a property owner bought the land with notice, either actual or from the public record, that the land was bound by a covenant, the land buyer is subject to court injunctions compelling obedience. In modern times, in other words, the old-fashioned method of enforcing covenants by damage suits that may not be decided by a jury until years after the suit has been filed, and then may offer only a slim chance of persuading a jury or collecting the damages a jury may award, has given way to the new, effective method of enforcing a restrictive covenant by a judge's injunction order that may issue within a few days after suit is filed. Affirmative covenants, such as those requiring payment of assessments for maintenance of common grounds in a planned unit development, still pose the problems relating to covenants running with the land.

CHAPTER 30

Land Use Controls—
Zoning and Building Ordinances

30.01 State Enabling Legislation

For the most part, cities have only such powers as are given them by the state legislature. In 1919, the federal government drafted a suggested state law called the Standard State Enabling Act, setting forth a proposed law that a state could pass to grant cities and villages the power to pass zoning ordinances. Few zoning ordinances were enacted because, at the time, it was thought by many that zoning was of doubtful validity. However, when, in 1926, the U.S. Supreme Court surprisingly held that zoning did not violate the federal constitution, virtually all states passed laws identical to this Standard State Enabling Act. Ever since, municipalities have proceeded to enact zoning ordinances pursuant to the powers granted to them by the states that have enacted enabling legislation. Thus, in zoning law, we are usually dealing with the validity or interpretation of municipal ordinances enacted under the powers granted by laws like the model act.

As a historical fact, the crash of 1929 and the Great Depression that ensued discouraged building and reduced the level of zoning activity. Then, World War II began, and real estate activity remained at a low level. After World War II ended and the veterans began to return to the United States, a huge housing and development boom began, centered in the suburbs and the inexpensive farmland around them. The old residents fought to keep out the developers. Zoning came into its own.

Each state by now has enacted its own zoning law granting cities, villages, counties, and townships the power to enact zoning ordinances. A zoning ordinance must therefore conform to the statute. *FGL & L Prop. Corp. v. City of Rye*, 66 N.Y.2d 111, 485 N.E.2d 986 (1985). In a number of states, "home rule" cities derive their power from the state constitution rather than state legislation. Such cities may enact zoning ordinances that do not conform to the state statute so long as they are reasonable.

30.02 The Ordinance—History of Zoning Ordinances

A zoning ordinance consists of two separate parts. One part contains the text of the ordinance, which refers to the other part, a map of the municipality outlining the various zones. Typically, the zoning map will designate single-family dwelling zones, multifamily zones, commercial areas, and industrial zones. The text of the ordinance refers to the various zones depicted on the map and describes the uses that may be made of the land in a particular zone.

Modern zoning ordinances usually create a greater number of classifications. Residential districts may be divided into single-family districts and multifamily districts. Multifamily zones may be divided into walk-up and high-rise (elevator building) zones. Commercial zones may be divided into retail and wholesale districts and industrial zones into heavy and light industry zones. Small stores may be permitted as accessory uses in apartment buildings and planned unit developments.

30.02(a) History of Zoning Ordinances

The first zoning ordinance was adopted by New York City. Its purpose was to prevent the garment district from spilling over into the fashionable Fifth Avenue shopping area. But the real history of zoning began in 1926, when the U.S. Supreme Court held zoning to be valid. *Village of Euclid v. Ambler Realty Co.,* 272 U.S. 365, 47 S. Ct. 114 (1926). Historically, the village of Euclid was founded by some land surveyors who liked the location they had surveyed and named the town after their favorite mathematician. Today, "cooky cutter" zoning that divides the municipality into rigid zones with rectangular lots in each zone, as was done in the village of Euclid, is derisively referred to as "Euclidean zoning."

Early zoning ordinances generally divided the city into three zones: residential, commercial, and manufacturing. Only residences were permitted in residential districts. Both stores and residences were allowed in commercial zones. All types of uses were permitted in manufacturing zones. This is called "cumulative" zoning.

Since only residential uses were permitted in residential zones, residential use came to be known as a preferred use. All other zones were cumulative. Modern zoning ordinances are generally not cumulative. Rather, there are generally cumulative zoning-within-zoning categories. For example, a zoning ordinance may provide for several densities of multifamily zoning but allow lesser-density uses in the higher-density areas. Similarly, the zoning ordinance may allow certain multifamily uses in commercial areas. This is not strictly cumulative zoning, but is a studied approach that recognizes that complementary uses should be in proximity to each other.

30.03 Noncumulative Zoning

Many zoning ordinances do more than keep industries and stores out of residential zones. They also exclude residences from commercial and industrial zones and allow a mixing of uses that support each other. Ordinances zoning certain areas exclusively for industrial purposes are fairly widespread and are valid. *Roney v. Bd. of Supervisors,* 138 Cal. App. 2d 740, 292 P.2d 529 (1956); *People ex rel. v. Morton Grove,* 16 Ill. 2d 183, 157 N.E.2d 33 (1959); *Lamb v. City of Monroe,* 358 Mich. 136, 99 N.W.2d 566 (1959). Obviously, it is just as injurious to the welfare of the community to permit residential development of land needed for industrial expansion as it is to permit industrial expansion into residential neighborhoods. We must remember that the supply of usable land is limited, and zoning is a primary tool that communities utilize to ensure wise use of our limited land areas.

Interestingly, however, there is a trend away from noncumulative or exclusive zoning. Many zones are mixed-use zones. Stores are common in planned unit developments. Office buildings and theaters are often included in large planned developments.

30.04 Zoning— Validity—In General

Determining the validity of zoning is basically a state court function with a federal constitutional overlay. The U.S. Supreme Court determined the general validity of zoning in *Village of Euclid v. Ambler Realty Co.,* 272 U.S. at 365. It decided that a state, acting under its police power, could enact a zoning law and compel a landowner to accept a substantial reduction in his or her land value as long as there was a corresponding benefit to the public. Thereafter, in *Nectow v. Cambridge,* 277 U.S. 183, 48 S. Ct. 447 (1928), the Supreme Court decided that while a zoning ordinance could be valid in general, it might work such a hardship as to a particular tract of land that it would be held invalid to that tract of land.

> **EXAMPLE:** A zoning ordinance zoned a triangular tract of land for residential purposes. This tract of land was cut off from other residential lots by railroad tracks and was entirely surrounded by property zoned for industrial use. It was worthless as residence property. The zoning map, in other words, put the land in the wrong zone. The court held that the zoning

ordinance was not valid to this triangle. Insofar as the zoning ordinance limits property to a use that cannot reasonably be made of it, it is invalid. *Tews v. Woolhiser,* 353 Ill. 212, 185 N.E. 827 (1933).

Having laid down some general principles, the Supreme Court thereafter refused for a long time to decide zoning cases, leaving the problem of deciding validity to the state courts. Thus, in discussing the validity of a zoning ordinance, we are discussing the validity of the zoning ordinance as applied to a particular tract of land under state law. Each of the fifty states is pretty much at liberty to decide that issue under its own state constitution. The fact that most state constitutions are modeled after the federal constitution is no guarantee of uniformity. Far from it, for judges are people. The decisions exhibit a wild diversity, because judges entertain diverse views on what is proper zoning.

In the ordinary zoning case, we are dealing with a particular tract of land. In general, the landowner is trying to put in an apartment, a planned unit development, a mobile home park, or an industrial plant, and opposition is encountered. There are some approaches to this problem that reveal a degree of uniformity. Since the validity of zoning in general is beyond question, most of the litigation is over amendments or rezoning of a particular tract of land.

There is an unspoken balancing process at work. The court considers the proposed rezoning. Is the new proposed use a nuisance so that it is sure to be harmful to its neighbors? The odds are against it, if it is. If it is relatively benign, such as a strictly residential planned unit development, its chances are good. Does it fit well into the pattern of existing uses so that its neighbors will not suffer too much?

30.04(a)   Validity— Factors to Be Considered

In dealing with questions of zoning validity, one is faced with a variety of situations, namely, (1) the attack may be leveled against the entire ordinance, which is a rarity; (2) the attack may be leveled against the application of the zoning ordinance to a particular tract of land; (3) the attack may be leveled against the granting or refusal of an amendment to the ordinance or a rezoning, a variance, or a special exception.

Except where the issue relates to the validity of the entire zoning ordinance, the following factors will be considered:

1. The character of the neighborhood.

   EXAMPLE: One who seeks to thrust an apartment, industrial plant, or mortuary in the midst of a neighborhood of single-family dwellings will not succeed. Harmony with surrounding uses is one of the objectives of sound zoning.

2. The extent to which property values are diminished by the particular zoning restriction and the extent to which the public is benefitted.

   EXAMPLE: An area is zoned single-family, but one vacant lot sits between two nonconforming apartments. No one thinking realistically would erect a house on this site. The owner must be permitted to erect an apartment. Under the concept of the police power, a landowner cannot be compelled to accept a harmful and sharp reduction in land value unless there is some corresponding benefit to the public. Here, it is obvious that the vacant lot has a very low value if zoned single-family. No public purpose would be served. The land must be rezoned.

   EXAMPLE: In the leading case of *Village of Euclid v. Ambler Realty Co.,* 272 U.S. at 365, the village enacted a zoning ordinance under which Ambler's tract of sixty-eight acres fell into a single-family zone. This reduced its value from $10,000 per acre to $2,500 per acre. Nevertheless, there were residences to the east and west of the property, so that the zoning did indeed benefit large segments of the public. A landowner can be compelled to accept a reduction in land value if the ordinance is reasonable and there is a benefit to the public.

The philosophy here is that in a democracy the people grant to the legislature the power to enact laws. Inherent in this grant of power is the limitation that the power must be exercised reasonably.

Another way of stating this rule is that the ordinance must not be confiscatory to the land in question. If the land is in a residential zone, proof will be required that residential development is not feasible and that use of the property for any of the permitted purposes in the zone is likewise not feasible. *Wackerman v. Town of Penfield,* 47 A.D.2d 988, 366 N.Y.S.2d 718 (1975).

3. The extent to which removal of the existing limitation would affect the value of other property in the area.

    EXAMPLE: In an area zoned for heavy industry, it was irrational to single out the petroleum industry and exclude it. The area was already permeated with odors from existing, legal plants. *Tidewater Oil Co. v. Mayor & Council of Carteret,* 80 N.J. Super. 283, 193 A.2d 412 (1963).

4. The suitability of the property for the zoned purpose.

    EXAMPLE: The land was zoned single-family but was located in a district of predominantly business and industrial uses and was worth ten times more for those purposes than as residential. The zoning is invalid to this tract of land. Here, the harm to the landowner is great, and there is no benefit to the public. *Galt v. Cook Co.,* 405 Ill. 396, 91 N.E.2d 395 (1950).

5. The existing uses and zoning of nearby property.

6. The length of time that the property has remained unimproved under the existing zoning considered in the context of land development in the area.

    EXAMPLE: A tract of vacant land was an island surrounded by business buildings. It was zoned for parking. As such, it remained in use as a parking lot for twenty-five years, although its value for office building use would be much greater. The ordinance was held invalid to this land. *Vernon Park Realty v. City of Mount Vernon,* 307 N.Y. 493, 121 N.E.2d 517 (1954). As to this land, the ordinance was confiscatory. Such well-located property would normally be developed in much less than twenty-five years. While a zoning ordinance need not zone property for its highest and best use, a phrase used by land appraisers, this is a factor to be considered. Moreover, an unspoken factor here is that cities often provide municipal parking lots and, in effect, the city was forcing the landowner to furnish a public service. The land was reasonably adapted to office-building use. No reason can be given why it was not so zoned. Certainly, its use for this purpose would be compatible with existing uses.

    EXAMPLE: The land in question was zoned for residential use. For twenty years it remained vacant. During that period, development was totally stagnant. The only buildings in the area were a stable, a dairy farm, and a city incinerator. The property was worthless for residential purposes. The court held that the zoning was invalid to the land. *Arverne Bay Constr. Co. v. Thatcher,* 278 N.Y. 222, 15 N.E.2d 587 (1938).

7. The relative gain to the public as compared to the hardship imposed on the landowner.

8. A city cannot validly zone private land for what are essentially public purposes.

    EXAMPLE: City rezoned certain land for school purposes. *City of Plainfield v. Borough of Middlesex,* 69 N.J. Super. 136, 173 A.2d 785 (1961). City rezoned certain land as a wildlife preserve. *In re Morris County Land Improvement Co.,* 40 N.J. 539, 193 A.2d 232 (1963). Both ordinances are invalid.

9. The public must be benefited by the zoning of the property.
10. The zoning must do the least possible harm to the landowner.
11. The extent of planning that went into the enactment of the zoning law. If a city has planned the area carefully, a court will be hesitant to disturb the plan by forcing it to accept a use that disturbs the plan.
12. The vigilance with which the municipality has enforced its zoning laws. If enforcement has been lax, the municipality will likely lose many zoning battles.

30.04(b) Validity—Reasonableness as a Test

In recent times, much of the technical verbiage of the older cases has disappeared as courts have focused upon the reasonableness of the zoning. An ordinance requiring all building lots in Manhattan to be of a minimum size of 100 acres would be totally unrealistic. Our forefathers gave our legislatures the power to pass laws, but not to act indiscriminately. If the regulation is totally unreasonable to particular land, it is invalid. *Fred F. French Inv. Co. v. City of N.Y.,* 39 N.Y.2d 587, 350 N.E.2d 381 (1976). Viewed in this light, the task of the courts becomes a good deal simpler and a good deal more sensible. When a court holds that a particular zoning decision is invalid to a particular tract of land, it is holding that, in the circumstances, the zoning is unreasonable. There must be a reasonable governmental interest advanced by the zoning classification of the property and the ordinance must not be purely an arbitrary, capricious, and unfounded exclusion of legitimate land uses. *Hecht v. Township of Niles,* 173 Mich. App. 453, 434 N.W.2d 156 (1988).

30.04(c) Validity—Federal Courts' Role

In determining whether a zoning law or local activity violates the U.S. Constitution, the U.S. Supreme Court has the final word. However, even if that court should hold that the federal Constitution has not been violated, the constitutional question is not yet fully resolved. Each state has its own constitution. What that constitution permits is determined by the state courts. Thus, an ordinance held "valid" by the Supreme Court is valid only so far as federal law is concerned. The State Supreme Court may hold the very same ordinance invalid as a violation of the state constitution. The federal court decisions get the headlines, but, in fact, they are of relatively minor importance. The U.S. Supreme Court has tended to ignore zoning altogether and, when it chooses to decide a zoning case, it takes such a liberal view that land developers have little to fear from the federal courts. Thus, it has been said that "the exercise of sound discretion does not, of course, always require a slavish adherence to federal constitutional minimums." *State v. Smith,* 347 A.2d 8 16 (N.J. 1975). The U.S. Supreme Court has, in fact, encouraged the state courts to exercise their independence. *Oregon v. Hass,* 420 U.S. 714, 719, 95 S. Ct. 1215, 1219 (1975).

30.04(d) Validity—Judgment Declaring Zoning Invalid

It is commonplace, of course, for a landowner to file a suit to have zoning declared invalid as to its land. Suppose the owner wins. The court must then make a further decision. (1) It can declare the zoning invalid as to the land and go no further. The land is then unzoned. A factory could be built. (2) Or, suppose the landowner wants to erect an apartment. The court can rezone the land for apartment use. Purists dislike this approach. Zoning and rezoning are jobs for the legislature. (3) Or, the court can send the case back to the city with an order that the land be rezoned. *Zaagman v. City of Kentwood,* 406 Mich. 137, 227 N.W.2d 475 (1975); Margaret Marshall Prahl, *The Rezoning Dilemma: What May a Court Do with an Invalid Zoning Classification?,* 25 S.D.L. Rev. 116 (1980).

30.05   Rezoning—Referendum

The Supreme Court has held that the U.S. Constitution is not violated by making rezoning subject to referendum approval by the people of the municipality. *City of Eastlake v. Forest City Enterprises, Inc.,* 426 U.S. 668, 672, 96 S. Ct. 2358, 2361 (1976). This leaves the state courts free to deal with this problem as they choose. Some courts will follow the Supreme Court's view that this is simply returning power to the people. Other courts will hold the referendum device illegal.

> **REFERENCES:** *Zoning—Procedural Due Process,* 91 Harv. L. Rev. 1502 (1978); J.R. Kemper, Annotation, *Adoption of Zoning Ordinance or Amendment Thereto as Subject of Referendum,* 72 A.L.R.3d 1030 (1977 Supp. 1988).

30.06   Zoning Exactions

The subject of forced dedication, whereby the municipality approves a plat only if the developer agrees to exactions of some sort (e.g., donation of land to the public), occurs in connection with plat approval. Some municipalities make the same kind of exactions a condition to granting rezoning, a zoning variance, or special exception.

This, predictably, will receive a mixed response in the courts. Most decisions will be favorable if the exaction is reasonable in the circumstances. *Sommers v. City of Los Angeles,* 254 Cal. App. 2d 605, 62 Cal. Rptr. 523 (1967); *Bd. of Education v. Surety Developers, Inc.,* 63 Ill. 2d 193, 347 N.E.2d 149 (1975). Unreasonable exactions are a sneaky way of blocking development. They are invalid. *Bd. of Supervisors v. Rowe,* 216 Va. 128, 216 S.E.2d 199 (1975). Similarly, a municipality cannot use an exaction as the basis for its ruling or expediting its ruling, if the merits of the application would have justified approval of the project.

> **EXAMPLE:** City demanded substantial payments before ruling that a building was not a single-room occupancy project, thereby clearing the way for the development of the site. The court held that City was selling its discretionary determinations and that was improper. *City of New York v. 17 Vista Assoc.,* 618 N.Y.S.2d 249, 642 N.E.2d 606 (1994).

30.07   Churches

It is well established that a zoning ordinance must not exclude churches or synagogues from residential districts. R.P. Davis, *Zoning Regulations as Affecting Churches,* 74 A.L.R.2d 377 (1960). *But see Lakewood, Ohio, Congregation of Jehovah's Witnesses, Inc. v. City of Lakewood,* 699 F.2d 303 (6th. Cir. 1983), holding that a zoning ordinance that prohibits construction of church buildings in residential districts was not an impermissible infringement on religious freedom.

30.08   Schools

Public schools, of course, are not subject to zoning ordinances. *Hall v. City of Taft,* 47 Cal. 2d 177, 302 P.2d 574 (1956). The only controversy, then, relates to private schools. The courts are not in agreement on this question. The more general view is that private schools, like churches, cannot be excluded from residential areas. *Roman Catholic Welfare Corp. v. City of Piedmont,* 45 Cal. 2d 325, 289 P.2d 438 (1955).

30.09   Prohibitory Zoning

Two techniques are available when a village wishes to exclude unwanted uses, such as oil drilling. For example, the zoning ordinance may explicitly prohibit drilling for oil or extraction of minerals. D.E. Ytreberg, Annotation, *Prohibiting or Regulating Removal or Exploitation of Oil and Gas, Minerals, Soil, or Other Natural Products Within Municipal Limits,* 10 A.L.R.3d 1226, 1241 (1967 Supp. 1998). Whether the exclusion will stand up depends on the circumstances surrounding the particular tract of land.

EXAMPLE: A landowner whose land adjoined the city dump applied for rezoning that would permit oil drilling. Refusal of rezoning was held invalid to this land. How could oil drilling possibly debase an area next to the city dump? No public purpose was, in fact, served by this zoning.

EXAMPLE: A landowner applied for rezoning to permit oil drilling. His land was so close to the city water well that it created danger of contamination. Refusal of rezoning was sustained.

As can be seen in both examples, the court considered the validity of the zoning to the particular tract of land.

Another technique simply fails to provide a home in the ordinance for the unwanted uses. *Hohl v. Township of Leadington,* 37 N.J. 271, 181 A.2d 150 (1962); *Wiley v. County of Hanover,* 209 Va. 153, 163 S.E.2d 160 (Va. 1968). The result is the same regardless of the technique involved.

30.10 Development Control Zoning— Sewer, Water, and School Problems— Downzoning

In many cases, municipalities have refused to rezone single-family zones to apartments or other such uses and have given as a reason the shortage of sewer, water, or school facilities. Or, the village may engage in downzoning.

EXAMPLE: The village rezoned *A*'s land from multifamily dwelling to single-family dwelling because it lacked sewer facilities. This was held invalid. *Westwood Forest Estates v. Village of South Nyack,* 23 N.Y.2d 424, 244 N.E.2d 700 (1969). To like effect are *Appeal of Girsh,* 437 Pa. 237, 263 A.2d 395 (1970) and *McGibbon v. Bd. of Appeals,* 369 Mass. 512, 340 N.E.2d 487 (1976).

EXAMPLE: The town increased minimum lot size from 35,000 square feet to three acres and six acres because of lack of sewer facilities. The court upheld the ordinance but admonished the city that the change must be temporary only. *Steel Hill Dev. Inc. v. Town of Sanbornton,* 469 F.2d 956 (1st Cir. 1972). This is also downzoning.

It can be seen from the examples given that the efforts of some villages are bent toward holding the population stable, or keeping things "as they are now," and barring developers who bring in a new, unwanted population. And yet, at times, a genuine health problem or school problem exists.

EXAMPLE: Downzoning by rezoning commercial to residential has been sustained. *Shellburne, Inc. v. Conner,* 315 A.2d 620 (Del. Ch. 1974). But rezoning of a single block to "zone out" apartments has been rejected as "spot zoning," *G. & D. Holland Constr. Co. v. City of Marysville,* 12 Cal. App. 2d 989, 91 Cal. Rptr. 227 (1970).

EXAMPLE: The desire of the villagers to keep the village rural does not justify increasing the minimum lot area from one to two acres and the minimum lot frontage from 100 to 200 feet. *Kavenewsky v. Zoning Bd. of Appeals,* 160 Conn. 397, 279 A.2d 567 (1971); *Oakwood at Madison, Inc. v. Township of Madison,* 117 N.J. Super. 11, 283 A.2d 353 (1971).

The situation seems to break down into several sharply conflicting points of view, namely, (1) the village cannot use its shortage of facilities as an excuse for refusal to grant proper rezoning, *Appeal of Kit Mar Builders, Inc.,* 439 Pa. 466, 268 A.2d 765 (1970); (2) the shortage in facilities is one factor that may be considered in refusing rezoning to the developer, *Adams v. Reed,* 239 Miss. 437, 123 So. 2d 606 (1960); and (3) the village may impose a zoning freeze of limited duration so long as it has a program for correcting the problem.

As can be seen, blanket, haphazard, unplanned restrictions, especially those of indefinite duration, are likely to be held invalid. However, if the development control zoning is carefully planned and is limited in time, it will be sustained by the courts.

In a noteworthy case that exemplifies the planned approach, a municipality adopted a zoning amendment under which the erection of homes by a merchant builder required a special permit. The standards for the issuance of special permits were framed in terms of the availability to the proposed subdivision of five essential facilities or services, specifically, (1) public sanitary sewers or approved substitutes; (2) drainage facilities; (3) improved public parks or recreation facilities, including public schools; (4) state, county, or town roads (major, secondary, or collector); and (5) firehouses. No special permit would be issued unless the proposed residential development had accumulated fifteen development points, to be computed on a sliding scale of values assigned to the specified improvements under the statute. Subdivision was thus a function of immediate availability to the proposed plat of certain municipal improvements, the avowed purpose of the amendments being to phase residential development to the town's ability to provide the previously described facilities or services. This was held valid. *Golden v. Planning Bd. of Town of Ramapo,* 30 N.Y.2d 359, 285 N.E.2d 291 (1972). This is phased development zoning.

All one can say is that the trend seems to be toward the rule that these real or fancied shortages may enable a municipality to declare a brief moratorium on development, but, sooner or later, land that is suitable only for homes will be developed for homes. The villages cannot block this indefinitely.

30.11 Downzoning

Downzoning takes place when property is rezoned to restrict its use from that allowed under the previous zoning ordinance. For example, a village may downzone land from a commercial or high-density multifamily use to a low-density single-family use. This may be done on an areawide or comprehensive basis, or on a piecemeal property-specific basis.

In some states, downzoning is not allowed except to correct an error in the original zoning law or to respond to a substantial change in conditions. *Davis v. City of Albuquerque,* 98 N.M. 319, 648 P.2d 777 (1982). This rule lacks flexibility and unduly constrains the governmental authorities who have the duty to legislate for the public good instead of being bound by the dictates of their predecessors. *Neuzil v. Iowa City,* 481 N.W.2d 159 (Iowa 1990).

The analysis in this area of the law focuses in part on whether the downzoning improperly deprived the landowner of its property without just compensation. In land-use jargon, the issue is stated whether there has been a regulatory taking without just compensation. Downzoning ordinarily deprives the landowner of some uses of the land. The question is whether the zoning ordinance substantially advances public interests and whether the ordinance deprives the landowner of the economically viable use of its land.

EXAMPLE: Tiburon, California, enacted a zoning ordinance limiting the density of a parcel of land to one to five single-family units. The owner sued, attacking the ordinance on the grounds that it deprived him of the value of the property. The court felt that the open-space protection fostered the legitimate governmental purpose of protecting the town from the ill effects of urbanization without denying the owner of an economically viable use of the land. The land could still be developed, but at a lower density. *Agins v. City of Tiburon,* 447 U.S. 255, 100 S. Ct. 2138 (1980).

30.12 Bulk Zoning

Bulk zoning regulates the size and shape of the buildings to be erected and their location on the land. The purpose of this type of zoning is to control the density of the development, open space, and the availability of light and air. The ordinance requires that any building erected must leave specified areas along the front, side, and rear of the lot, which must not be built upon.

30.13 Single-Family Zones

It is so simple to say that in single-family zones only one house per lot occupied by a single family will be permitted. But, as times change, customs change. Many couples choose to live together without marrying. The zoning definition of a "single family" has tended to change. Thus, this area of the law is the subject of some controversy.

The family is perhaps the most revered institution in American life. Hence, any ordinance that forbids members of the same family to live together is invalid.

> **EXAMPLE:** A grandmother cannot be prohibited from living with her grandson. A brother and sister must be allowed to live together. Zoning cannot slice into the family itself. *Moore v. City of East Cleveland,* 431 U.S. 494, 97 S. Ct. 1932 (1977). Similarly, when a family's breadwinner dies, the broader family comes together for mutual assistance. The law cannot forbid this. The law protects the extended family.

Litigation involving single-family zoning ordinances is common. Although there appear to be almost endless differences in the language used in these ordinances, they contain three principal types of restrictions. First, they define the kind of structure that may be erected. Second, they require that a single-family home be occupied only by a "single housekeeping unit." Third, they require that the housekeeping unit be made up of persons related by blood, adoption, or marriage, with certain limited exceptions. Although the legitimacy of the first two types of restrictions is well settled, attempts to limit occupancy to related persons have not been successful. The state courts have recognized a valid community interest in preserving the stable character of residential neighborhoods. That justifies a prohibition against transient occupancy. Nevertheless, in well-reasoned opinions, the courts of Illinois and many other jurisdictions have permitted unrelated persons to occupy single-family residences notwithstanding the existence of an ordinance prohibiting, either expressly or implicitly, such occupancy. *Charter Township of Delta v. Dinolfo,* 419 Mich. 253, 351 N.W.2d 831 (1984*); Borough of Glasborough v. Vallorosi,* 117 N.J. 421, 568 A.2d 888 (1990).

> **EXAMPLE:** Such ordinances must not forbid unrelated widows—widowers, spinsters, or bachelors—from living together to share expenses. *State v. Baker,* 81 N.J. 99, 405 A.2d 368 (1979).

As will be seen, groups of mentally retarded persons or orphans must be permitted to live in single-family homes.

30.14 Apartments

The leading case on zoning held that apartments may be excluded from single-family dwelling zones. *Village of Euclid v. Ambler Realty Co.,* 272 U.S. at 365. The state courts have followed a similar rule. It should be noted, however, that a tract of land can be so located that, as to that tract, single-family zoning would be invalid, for example, a single lot located in a single-family zone between two large nonconforming-use apartments.

30.15 Accessory Uses

Every zoning ordinance recognizes that certain uses are different from, but incidental to, the main use prescribed in the zone. Such uses are legalized under the name "accessory uses." Many accessory uses are found in residential zones.

> **EXAMPLE:** Coin-operated washing machines and dryers in apartment buildings, pay telephones, beverage vending machines, postage vending machines, swimming pools, and skating rinks for which a charge is made, are accessory uses. *City of Newark v. Daly,* 85 N.J. Super. 555, 205 A.2d 459 (1964). Likewise, a food shop in a large apartment hotel is often

permitted. A private garage on a residential lot is universally permitted. A doctor expects to see patients in his or her home even though it is in a residential area.

30.16 Performance Standards

Industrial zoning poses special problems. Some ordinances contain lengthy laundry lists of permitted uses. These ordinances may also list standards that must be complied with, such as limits on the amount of noise, glare, smoke, toxic matter, flammable matter, explosive materials, or radioactive matter that the property may emit.

30.17 Incentive Zoning

Incentive zoning is a type of zoning calculated to induce the landowner to introduce amenities the city deems desirable. This type of zoning typically employs the floor area ratio (FAR) concept.

> **EXAMPLE:** The floor area ratio of a building is the ratio that the floor area within the building bears to the area of the lot occupied by the building. For example, a building occupying 40,000 square feet of lot area in a zone allowing a FAR of 10:1 could have 400,000 square feet of total floor area in all the stories of the building. But a FAR bonus may be given if the building addresses certain needs that the municipality may have, such as providing direct access to the rapid transit system, a plaza, or an on-site day care facility. In such case, the building may be allowed additional floor area. In short, FAR establishes a relationship between total land area and total floor space. Under a FAR regulation of 1:1, a developer could build a one-story structure covering the whole lot, a two-story structure covering half of the lot, or a four-story structure covering a quarter of the lot. Bartke & Lamb, *Upzoning,* 17 Wm. & Mary L. Rev. 701, 705.

An extremely imaginative type of incentive zoning was developed in connection with the Lincoln Center for Performing Arts in New York City. The district zoning permitted developers 20 percent more floor space on provision of certain amenities, notably, pedestrian malls, galleries, covered plazas, and pedestrian-oriented circulation improvements. Elliott & Marcus, *From Euclid to Ramapo: New Directions in Land Development Controls,* 1 Hofstra L. Rev. 56 (1973); Benson, *Bonus or Incentive Zoning—Legal Implications*, 21 Syracuse L. Rev. 895 (1970); Bartke & Lamb, *Upzoning,* 17 Wm. & Mary L. Rev. 701.

30.18 Change of Neighborhood

A change of neighborhood may invalidate existing zoning. *Manger v. City of Chicago,* 121 Ill. App. 2d 358, 257 N.E.2d 473 (1970).

> **EXAMPLE:** In an area zoned single-family, the authorities made no effort to enforce the zoning law. Stores crept in everywhere so that the few remaining vacant lots were surrounded by stores and were totally unfit for residential use. The area had become a business area. The village must permit stores on the vacant lots. *Scott v. City of Springfield,* 83 Ill. App. 2d 31, 226 N.E.2d 57 (1967); *Vigilant Investors Corp. v. Town of Hempstead,* 34 A.D.2d 990; 312 N.Y.S.2d 1022 (1970).

The same result occurs where the city affirmatively causes the situation.

> **EXAMPLE:** The city fathers handed out variances so liberally that nonconforming stores in the area were allowed to expand all over the area. The few remaining lots cannot be held to single-family dwelling use. *Metro. Bd. of Zoning Appeal v. Sheehan Constr. Co.,* 160 Ind. App. 520, 313 N.E.2d 78 (1974).

30.19 Nonconforming Uses

All zoning ordinances make some provision for continuation of nonconforming uses so that new zoning ordinances will not make illegal the use of land that was permitted at the time of the adoption of the new zoning ordinance. *Goodwin v. Kansas City,* 766 P.2d 177 (Kan. 1988).

EXAMPLE: To invalidate an existing store use in a residential area would be unconstitutional deprivation of property. This is a simple proposition.

There is a second type of problem involved here.

EXAMPLE: An area is zoned for multifamily dwellings. A developer buys it and obtains a permit to construct an apartment. The neighbors become aware of the situation and persuade the village to rezone the area to single-family dwellings. If construction has not yet begun, there is, as yet, most courts say, no nonconforming use. Perhaps the developer can attack the new zoning on other grounds, but not on the ground that it has a nonconforming use.

Virtually all courts agree that if construction has begun under a valid permit, nonconforming-use status has been achieved and construction may be completed, even though the zoning as amended after commencement of construction would forbid the erection of such a structure. *Lutz v. New Albany City Planning Comm'n.*, 230 Ind. 74, 101 N.E.2d 187 (Ind. 1951). *But see In re Coleman Highlands*, 777 S.W.2d 621 (Mo. Ct. App. 1989) (where the construction could be and was easily adapted to the use required by the amended zoning ordinance). The construction must be done in good faith and not hastily, simply to obtain nonconforming-use status. In New York, the construction must be substantial. *Reichenbach v. Windward at Southhampton*, 364 N.Y.S.2d 283 (1975).

A generous court has accorded nonconforming-use status after a permit has been issued, survey made, site cleared, and ground leveled. *Griffin v. County of Martin*, 157 Cal. App. 2d 507, 321 P.2d 148 (1958). Some courts have held that nonconforming-use status was not attained where the permit was issued, building plans made, and construction mortgage signed. *Paramount Rock Co. v. County of San Diego*, 44 Cal. Rptr. 74, 180 Cal. App. 2d 217. *Contra Hull v. Hunt*, 53 Wash. 2d 125, 331 P.2d 856 (1958).

This is one of the battlegrounds of zoning law. All courts agree that the constitution protects only vested rights. They disagree, however, on when rights vest. There are several points in time a court can choose, as follows:

1. Rights vest when a landowner has spent money planning construction in good faith even before a permit has issued.
2. No rights vest until a permit issues.
3. Some construction must take place after the permit issues.

A landowner who has achieved nonconforming-use status need not apply to the city or take other affirmative action. The ordinance says that nonconforming uses are protected. Nothing else need be done. When these rights are vested, they are beyond attack by the city. The landowner need not apply for a variance or seek other confirmation of its rights. In some cases, the owner may intensify the use without terminating the permitted nonconforming-use status.

Zoning ordinances, in permitting nonconforming uses, permit ordinary repairs to be made, but sometimes forbid structural alterations of a nonconforming building. A structural alteration would change the physical structure of the building or would change an old building in such a way as to convert it into a new or substantially different structure.

EXAMPLE: *A* operated a milk plant, which was a nonconforming use in a residential zone. His attempt to replace decayed wooden walls with brick walls was a prohibited structural alteration, *Selligman v. Von Allmen Bros. Inc.*, 297 Ky. 121, 179 S.W.2d 207 (1944). Eunice A. Eichelberger, Annotation, *Alteration, Extension, Reconstruction, or Repair of Nonconforming Structure or Structure Devoted to Nonconforming Use as Violation of Zoning Ordinance*, 63 A.L.R.4th 275 (1988 Supp. 1998).

A mere increase in the volume of a nonconforming use without a change in the type of use to which the property is put is not an improper extension of the nonconforming use. *Town of Gardiner v. Blue Sky Entertainment Corp.*, 213 A.D.2d 790, 622 N.Y.S.2d 29 (1995).

Nonconforming uses should be gradually eliminated. *Cole v. City of Battle Creek,* 298 Mich. 98, 298 N.W. 466 (1941). The theory is that zoning seeks to safeguard the future in the expectation that time will repair the mistakes of the past. However, the treatment a particular nonconforming use will receive if it seeks to increase or change its use appears to vary considerably owing to differences in zoning ordinances. Eunice A. Eichelberger, Annotation, *Alteration, Extension, Reconstruction, or Repair of Nonconforming Structure or Structure Devoted to Nonconforming Use as Violation of Zoning Ordinance*, 63 A.L.R.4th 275 (1988 Supp. 1998).

Once a nonconforming owner abandons the use of its property for a nonconforming purpose, it loses its right to make a nonconforming use of the property and must thereafter use it only in conformity with the uses allowed to other properties in the neighborhood. Were the law otherwise, an owner could keep its property in a nonconforming class forever.

EXAMPLE: The owner of a nonconforming slaughterhouse took down the smokestack and discontinued the slaughterhouse business. He thereby lost his right to make a nonconforming use. *Beyer v. Mayor & City Council of Baltimore,* 182 Md. 444, 34 A.2d 765 (1943). Also, where an old nonconforming house trailer was sought to be replaced by a new one, the change was refused because the old use had been abandoned. *Town of Windham v. Sprague,* 219 A.2d 548 (Me. 1966).

A mere temporary discontinuance of the nonconforming use, as when a landowner is temporarily unable to procure a tenant, will not constitute an abandonment of the right to resume such use. *Derby Refining Co. v. City of Chelsea,* 407 Mass. 703, 555 N.E.2d 534 (Mass. 1990); *Landay v. MacWilliams,* 173 Md. 460, 196 A. 293 (1938); *Right to Resume Nonconforming Use After Period of Nonuse or of a Different Use from That in Effect at or Before the Time of Zoning,* 18 A.L.R.2d 725 (1951). Cessation of the nonconforming use caused by the owner's conduct, even without an intent to abandon the nonconforming use, may result in the loss of the nonconforming use. *City of Glendale v. Aldabbagh,* 189 Ariz. 140, 939 P.2d 418 (1997).

If a nonconforming building is either fully or partially destroyed by fire or other casualty, many ordinances forbid rebuilding.

Some zoning ordinances place a time limit on the right to continue a nonconforming use. To the extent that these ordinances amortize and prohibit the continuance of the nonconforming use after the useful economic life of the building has come to an end, they are generally upheld. L.S. Tellier, Annotation, *Power to Terminate Lawful Nonconforming Use Existing When Zoning Ordinance Was Passed After Use Has Been Permitted to Continue,* 42 A.L.R.2d 1146 (1955). Jay M. Zitter, Annotation, *Validity of Provisions for Amortization of Non-Conforming Use,* 8 A.L.R.5th 391. The court must consider (1) the nature of the surrounding neighborhood to determine whether discontinuance of the use will have any beneficial impact and to determine if the nonconforming use, in fact, conforms to other nearby use; (2) the value and condition of the improvements on the premises to determine the amount of damage if the use is discontinued; (3) the cost of relocating the business; and (4) whether the time allowed permits the landowner to make plans for the future of its business. *Harbison v. City of Buffalo,* 4 N.Y.2d 553, 152 N.E.2d 42, 176 N.Y.S.2d 598 (1958).

30.20 Amendments to Zoning Ordinances—During the Permit Period

Under pressure from unhappy neighbors, a city may seek to amend its ordinance at the time a landowner is applying for a permit to build a building the neighbors find objectionable.

> **EXAMPLE:** After *X* had applied for a permit to erect a building that complied with a zoning setback line of 24 feet, the city passed an amendment changing the setback to 49 feet. The court sustained refusal of the permit. *Builders Constr. Co. v. Daly,* 10 N.J. Misc. 861, 161 A. 189 (1932). Until construction begins, the property has not achieved status as a nonconforming use.

In some states, courts will strike down an eleventh-hour attempt to block construction where a landowner has in good faith made plans and applied for a permit in reliance on an existing ordinance. These same courts may sanction the refusal of a permit where the landowner is attempting to rush through a permit with the knowledge that the city is working on an amendment that would block the intended construction, *Chicago Title and Trust Co. v. Village of Palatine*, 22 Ill. App. 2d 264, 160 N.E.2d 697 (1959). Note, *Ex Post Facto Zoning*, 1971 Urb. L. Ann. 63. Jay M. Zitter, Annotation, *Zoning Authority Estopped from Revoking Legally Issued Building Permit*, 26 A.L.R.5th 736 (1992).

If a landowner receives a building permit and commences substantial construction in reliance thereon, the city cannot amend the ordinance so as to block the construction described in the permit. *Preseault v. Wheel,* 132 Vt. 247, 315 A.2d 244 (1974). Basic fairness is the test.

> **EXAMPLE:** *X* applied for and received a permit to build an apartment. *X* graded, excavated, and put in a foundation. The city then attempted to rezone the area to exclude apartments. *X* can go forward with the building. *Deer Park Civic Ass'n v. City of Chicago,* 347 Ill. App. 346, 106 N.E.2d 823 (1952).

When the courts want to protect the landowner, they say the landowner's rights have vested, or the city is estopped to amend its ordinance. Roland F. Chase, Annotation, *Retroactive Effect of Zoning Regulation, in Absence of Saving Clause, or Pending Application for Building*, 50 A.L.R.3d 596 (1973).

30.20(a) Amendments and Rezoning— Spot Zoning

Amendments to the zoning ordinance are constantly being sought by landowners whose land will thereby become more valuable. For example, land is more valuable for industrial or commercial purposes than it is for residential purposes, so rezoning of residential land for industrial purposes will greatly increase its value. Some of such rezoning is invalid. Particularly objectionable is spot zoning, where the city, by amendment of its ordinances, singles out and reclassifies one piece of property in a particular zone without any apparent basis for such distinction. M.O. Regensteiner, Annotation, *Spot Zoning*, 51 A.L.R.2d 263 (1957).

> **EXAMPLE:** A zoning ordinance was amended to permit construction of a mortuary in a residential district. This was held invalid as spot zoning. *Mueller v. Hoffmeister Undertaking Co.,* 343 Mo. 430,121 S.W.2d 775 (1938).

Courts will typically consider several tests to determine whether the zoning of a single piece of a larger area is valid. If the zoning of the individual parcel in question is consistent with a comprehensive plan for the area, if the zoning of the parcel is compatible with the surrounding area, and if the zoning of the subject parcel serves the public welfare rather than conferring a discriminatory benefit on the owner of the parcel, the zoning of the parcel will stand a better chance of being valid. Mark S. Dennison, *Determination Whether Zoning or Rezoning of Particular Parcel Constitutes Illegal Spot Zoning*, 73 A.L.R.5th 223 (1999).

30.20(a)(1) Spot Zoning Rules

The following are some of the circumstances that will validate rezoning that, on the surface, appears to be spot zoning:

> **EXAMPLE:** A large area was rezoned for shopping center purposes because it was at the hub of a natural traffic concentration pattern. *Temmink v. Baltimore County,* 205 Md. 489, 109 A.2d 85 (1954). Traffic is the key to this problem. The same approach is applicable to supermarkets.

> **EXAMPLE:** Four corner lots in a large residential district were zoned for commercial uses. Here, the need for service businesses in a residential area is the key. *Marshall v. Salt Lake City,* 105 Utah 111, 141 P.2d 704 (1943).

> **EXAMPLE:** An area was rezoned to permit apartments in an area of older homes, thus increasing tax revenues of city. *Rodgers v. Village of Tarrytown,* 302 N.Y. 115, 96 N.E.2d 731 (1951).

Illegal spot zoning is basically a reclassification of a small area in such a manner as to disturb or be out of conformity with the surrounding neighborhood. It is a discordant and unneeded use. *Bossman v. Village of Riverton*, 684 N.E.2d 427 (Ill. App. 1997). None of the preceding examples fall in this category.

Where a real change in circumstances has taken place since the original ordinance was passed, an amendment that conforms the ordinance to the new circumstances will be valid.

> **EXAMPLE:** At the time the original zoning ordinance was adopted, the only structure in an area zoned industrial was a factory. Thereafter, many single-family residences were built in the area, but no new factories. To protect the homeowners, the area was rezoned for residential purposes, the old factory remained as a nonconforming use. This is valid rezoning. *Atlantic Coast Line R.R. Co. v. Jacksonville,* 68 So. 2d 570 (Fla. 1953).

> **EXAMPLE:** Where an urban redevelopment displaced many families, creating a need for many units to house those displaced, a single-family dwelling zone could be revised to permit apartments. *Malafronte v. Planning Board,* 230 A.2d 606 (Conn. 1967).

> **EXAMPLE:** *X* owned an area that was zoned commercial. A large city park was opened across the street. The city rezoned the area for apartments. This change in circumstances makes the rezoning valid. *People ex rel v. City of Chicago, 2* Ill. 2d 350, 118 N.E.2d 20 (1954).

Where the original zoning was a mistake, the city can, in most states, correct the error.

> **EXAMPLE:** Because of topography and soil conditions, a parcel was not suitable for single-family dwellings but was included in a single-family dwelling zone. To correct this error, the parcel was rezoned for apartments. This is valid. *Eggebeen v. Sonnenburg,* 239 Wis. 213, 1 N.W.2d 84 (1941).

30.20(b) Amendments— Reliance Rule

In a number of states, the rule is followed that protection ought to be given by the courts to those who bought land in reliance on existing zoning, and that zoning must not be changed unless some change in the neighborhood has taken place. *Northern Trust Co. v. Chicago,* 4 Ill. 2d 432, 123 N.E.2d 330 (1954).

> **EXAMPLE:** An area is built up with homes. There are a few scattered lots. One lot owner has its lot rezoned for apartments. The courts will invalidate this rezoning.

**30.20(c)
Amendments—
Conditional**

At times, a city has rezoned land with a condition in the ordinance that a certain type of building would be erected or other conditions be fulfilled. Older decisions frowned on this. Cities, they said, should not bargain for legislation. Recent decisions sustain conditional amendments. *Christman v. Guilford County,* 370 S.E.2d 579 (N.C. 1988).

> **EXAMPLE:** A zoning amendment was granted on the condition that the land be used for a synthetic gas production plant. It was held valid. *Goffinet v. Christian County,* 65 Ill. 2d 40, 357 N.E.2d 442 (1976); James D. Lawlor, Annotation, *Validity, Construction, and Effect of Agreement to Rezone or Amendment to Zoning Ordinance Creating Special Restrictions or Conditions Not Applicable to Other Property Similarly Zoned,* 70 A.L.R.3d 125 (1976). This is simply a matter of contract zoning now. As this grows more common, villages will be better able to control the quality of new construction. Of course, there will still be decisions that resist the idea. *Ziemer v. County of Peoria,* 33 Ill. App. 3d 612, 338 N.E.2d 145 (1975).

Where the landowner fails to meet the conditions, the village may return to the original zoning.

> **EXAMPLE:** The village rezoned residential to industrial on condition that the property be improved with an industrial plant. The owner failed to comply. The village zoned the land back to residential. *McGowan v. Cohalan,* 361 N.E.2d 1025 (N.Y. 1977).

**30.20(d)
Amendments—
Rezoning Procedure**

When a municipality passes an ordinance of general application, such as a law fixing a maximum speed limit, ordinarily this does not require notice to anyone unless state law requires it. However, where rezoning of a tract of land is involved, that is, amending the zoning ordinance or the zoning map, court decisions regard this more in the nature of a lawsuit between the owner of the land and its neighbors. Of course, every lawsuit requires notice to the landowners affected and an opportunity to be heard. As a matter of constitutional law, an ordinance rezoning land requires notice to the neighbors and an opportunity to state their objections. *Fasano v. Bd. of Commissioners,* 264 Or. 574, 507 P.2d 23 (1973); *Snyder v. City of Lakewood,* 542 P.2d 371 (Colo. 1975); *Fleming v. City of Tacoma,* 81 Wash. 2d 292, 502 P.2d 327 (1972); *West v. City of Portage,* 221 N.W.2d 303 (Mich. 1974).

The constitutional rules of procedural due process require that the notice be appropriate under the circumstances. While a published notice of the adoption of a general zoning law may be adequate, personal notice to the landowner will be required where the landowner's property is specifically and individually targeted for rezoning. *Harris v. County of Riverside,* 904 F.2d 497 (9th. Cir. 1990). Most zoning ordinances now require such notices to neighboring landowners.

> **EXAMPLE:** A zoning ordinance provided that the zoning ordinance could be amended by publication of notice in a newspaper. This is invalid. Neighboring landowners can easily be found and given notice by mail. *American Oil Corp. v. City of Chicago,* 331 N.E.2d 67 (Ill. App. 1975). The rule is that rational planning prior to zoning change also requires such planning to precede the granting of a special exception or variance. *Kristenson v. City of Eugene Planning Comm'n,* 544 P.2d 591 (Or. App. 1976). Listening to the neighbors helps the authorities to make a rational decision.

> **EXAMPLE:** There was a failure to give proper notice as required by the ordinance. The rezoning was held invalid. *Jarvis Acres, Inc. v. Zoning Comm'n,* 163 Conn. 44, 301 A.2d 244 (1972).

30.21 Variances

Even the best ordinance may cause unintentional hardship to particular tracts of land. Some elasticity is needed if these hardship cases are to be dealt with. Most ordinances create a board, usually called the board of adjustment or board of appeals, which is given the power to authorize individual property owners to deviate from the terms of the ordinances where literal compliance would cause undue hardship or practical difficulties. This authorization is called a variance. The courts have worked out a number of requirements that must be met if a variance is to be granted.

1. The hardship must be special and peculiar to the particular property.

   EXAMPLE: A lot is so irregular in shape that if all the front, rear, and the side line restrictions were observed, no building at all could be built on the lot.

   If the hardship complained of is a condition that affects all property in the district, the hardship is not special and peculiar to any lot in the area and no individual lot owner will be granted a variance.

   EXAMPLE: Foul odors from a nearby industrial area exist in an area zoned as residential. No residential lot owner will be granted a variance to build a factory. A plea must be made to the authorities to amend the ordinance.

2. Hardship means that if the landowner complies with the provisions of the ordinance, it can secure no reasonable return from, or make no reasonable use of, its property. With respect to income property, a party seeking a variance must prove that the land in question, if devoted to its existing or any permitted use, will not yield a reasonable return. This involves a detailed showing of the price paid for the property, the taxes assessed, expenses of operation, annual income, and so on. Then, if the net income earned is not a reasonable return on the amount invested, hardship is shown. *Crossroads Recreation v. Broz,* 4 N.Y.2d 39, 149 N.E.2d 65 (1958). The landowner should also show that reasonable return cannot be anticipated from other permitted uses. *Forrest v. Evershed,* 7 N.Y.2d 256, 164 N.E.2d 841 (1959). The fact that more money could be made by devoting the landowner's property to another purpose is not legal hardship.

3. The hardship must not be self-created.

   EXAMPLE: *A* departs from the plans attached to his application for a building permit and builds a home five feet closer to the side lines of the lot than the ordinance allows. When the building inspector stops construction, *A* applies for a variance and will not get it.

   EXAMPLE: The city in question has an ordinance specifying a minimum lot area. *A* owns a building on a legal size lot. *A* then sells the building and enough of the land so that the building still occupies a legal building site. However, the portion of the lot left to *A* is now less than legal size. *A* will not be given a variance to permit a building on the remainder. *Bd. of Zoning Appeals v. Waskelo,* 240 Ind. 594, 168 N.E.2d 72 (1960).

4. The proposed new use must not change the essential character of the neighborhood. It must be consistent with the general plan of the ordinance.

   EXAMPLE: A variance will not be granted to permit introduction of a cemetery into an area zoned residential.

Some courts are so strict on this point that they will not allow a variance that changes the use permitted by the ordinance. In other words, they will allow deviation only from the area, height, and location regulations of the ordinance.

EXAMPLE: Some courts will not permit a variance for an apartment house in a single-family area because this would be a use variance. *Lee v. Bd. of Adjustment,* 226 N.C. 107, 37 S.E.2d 128 (1946).

Most courts will permit a use variance where the hardship is great.

EXAMPLE: *A* owns a vacant lot in a single-family dwelling zone, and nonconforming apartment buildings are neighbors on both sides. These buildings were built before the ordinance was passed and are allowed to continue in operation. *A* will be given a variance for the erection of an apartment building. The sound reason for this variance is that no one can be induced to build a single-family dwelling on such a building site.

In granting a variance, the zoning board may impose conditions. *Vlahos Realty Co. v. Little Boar's Head District,* 101 N.H. 460, 146 A.2d 257 (1958); *Zweifel Mfg. Co. v. Peoria,* 11 Ill. 2d 489, 144 N.E.2d 593 (1957); John J. Michalik, Annotation, *Authority of Zoning Commissioners to Propose, as Condition of Allowance of Special Exception, Permit, or Variance, Requirements as to Highway and Traffic Changes,* 49 A.L.R.3d 492 (1973).

EXAMPLE: The board may put in a condition that the architecture of the permitted building conform to the architecture of neighboring structures, or that certain areas be left open and landscaped.

A variance may be limited in time.

EXAMPLE: A variance given for five years is valid. *Bringle v. Bd. of Supervisors,* 4 Cal. Rptr. 493, 351 P.2d 765 (1960).

Questions may arise as to who may apply for a variance. Clearly the landowner may do so. A contract purchaser is also qualified. However, one who is merely negotiating for the purchase of the land cannot apply for a variance.

The larger the tract of land involved, the greater the likelihood a variance will be held invalid. *Topanga Ass'n v. County of Los Angeles,* 113 Cal. Rptr. 836, 522 P.2d 12 (1974). Large tracts should be dealt with by an amendment to the zoning ordinance.

30.22 Special Exceptions

A common provision in zoning ordinances authorizes the board of appeals to issue special permits for special purposes, such as public utility structures, churches, hospitals, private schools, clubs, or cemeteries. Obviously, institutions of this character must be located somewhere, but some control must be exercised by the zoning authorities over their location so that adverse effects on the other property owners will be held to a minimum. Typically, the ordinance may list a number of different uses that may be licensed "where public convenience and welfare will be substantially served." *Dunham v. Zoning Bd.,* 68 R.I. 88, 26 A.2d 614 (1942). The distinction between special exceptions and variances is a technical one. In the case of variances, the board is given authority to authorize violations of the zoning ordinance in hardship cases. In the case of special exceptions, the ordinance itself lists certain cases in which certain special uses are to be permitted, and the board only determines whether facts exist to bring the particular case within the terms of the ordinance. *Stone v. Cray,* 89 N.H. 483, 200 A. 5 17 (1938). It is not necessary to show "practical difficulties or unnecessary hardship," as is true in variance cases. *Montgomery County v. Merlands Club,* 202 Md. 279, 96 A.2d 261 (1953).

In some states, the special exception is referred to as a "special use" or "special permit." In others, it is called a "conditional use."

30.23 Procedure on Variances and Special Exceptions

A landowner seeking a variance or special exception files a petition with the zoning board. This is not a court. It is an administrative body. It holds hearings like a court, but very informally. Notice of the hearing is given to neighbors, as required by the ordinance. If the issue is not controversial, as where a landowner wants to locate his or her carport two or three feet beyond the zoning setback lines, the hearing is perfunctory. If the landowner wants a special permit to put a gasoline service station in a residential area, a fight may develop, and competing expert witnesses will be called.

In any case, the landowner applies for the permit before construction is begun. Starting construction before the permit issues may result in an automatic refusal to issue the permit. *Wiltshire v. Superior Court,* 218 Cal. Rptr. 199 (1985); W.C. Craig III, *Zoning: Who May Apply for Variance, Special Exception, or Use Permit, or Appeal from Denial Thereof,* 89 A.L.R.2d 663 (1963).

30.24 The Floating Zone

A floating zone is a special-use district. No specific location is assigned to it in the zoning ordinance. When the need for such a zone arises, the same public body that enacted the zoning ordinance will enact an amendment to the ordinance carving a new zone out of some existing zone. It differs from the special exception in that, at least in the earlier ordinances, a zoning amendment passed by the city council or board of trustees was needed to create a floating zone.

Also in this unique type of zoning amendment, the usual rules applicable to zoning amendments are not applied. For example, in some states, for a valid zoning amendment, one must show that a mistake was made in the original zoning ordinance or that the conditions have changed, requiring rezoning. This rule is inapplicable to floating zones. *Haldemann v. Bd. of Comm'rs,* 253 Md. 298, 252 A.2d 792 (1969).

> **EXAMPLE:** Cluster housing in a planned unit development is often allowed to float to any part of the development, while the ordinance will control the number of units, amenities, and so on.

There are a number of decisions sustaining the validity of the floating zone. *Rodgers v. Village of Tarrytown,* 302 N.Y. 115, 96 N.E.2d 731 (1951); *Huff v. Bd. of Appeals,* 214 Md. 48, 133 A.2d 83 (1957); *Treme v. St. Louis County,* 609 S.W.2d 706 (Mo. Ct. App. 1980); *Cheney v. Village 2 at New Hope,* 429 Pa. 626, 241 A.2d 81 (1968). There are a few cases to the contrary. *Rudderow v. Township Committee,* 114 N.J. Super. 104, 274 A.2d 854 (1971).

If one must guess as to the future of the floating zone, the conjecture must be that it is here to stay and will be part of the planning and zoning process. The initial hostility of planning officials has been converted to approbation. Mosher, *The Floating Zone: Legal Status and Application to Gasoline Stations,* 1 Tulsa L.J. 149, 156, 166, 167 (1964). The criticism that zoning amendments lend themselves to political influence is not well taken. It is a well-known fact that zoning ordinances traditionally zone large areas for single-family dwellings in the full knowledge that developers will come forward requesting apartment or other zoning, thus giving the authorities an opportunity to "take a look" at the developer and development.

This argument would invalidate all rezoning. Moreover, the entire zoning view can easily be circumvented under modern ordinances by allowing desired uses, such as research laboratories, to "float" into any zone on issuance of a special exception permit. *Summ v. Zoning Comm'n of the Town of Ridgefield,* 150 Conn. 79, 186 A.2d 160 (1962). Indeed, it has been acknowledged that the special exception technique lends itself to the introduction of desirable uses into residential and other districts. *Lazarus v. Village of Northbrook,* 31 Ill. 2d 146, 199 N.E.2d 797 (1964). Moreover, conditions may validly be attached to a special exception. *Houdaille Constr. Materials, Inc. v. Bd. of Adjustment,* 92 N.J. Super. 293, 223 A.2d 210 (1966). In this manner, the authorities can impose requirements that might be complied with prior to issuance of a building permit, such as greenbelt buffer areas. The proponents of floating zones, it appears, will surely carry the field. Kristine C. Karnezis, Annotation, *Zoning: Regulations Creating and Placing "Floating Zones"*, 80 A.L.R.3d 95 (1977).

30.25 Planned Unit Developments— Cluster Housing

The planned unit development (hereafter referred to as PUD) is the modern concept of governmental control of development, whether town houses, homes, apartments (both garden and high-rise), or combinations of such buildings, industrial or commercial, all with common open areas and amenities. The advantages of this system of development approval are many.

1. Lower-priced homes are available because of the cost savings through more efficient land use and planning.
2. Small, private yards offer a minimum of maintenance chores, whereas a maximum of time and energy can be spent for recreational activities in the common areas.
3. Common areas of green open space provide an attractive setting.
4. Shared facilities are available for swimming, golf, fishing, and so forth, and there is a recreation center for crafts, meetings, and other group activities.
5. Maintenance is furnished by the owners' association.

The phrase "cluster housing" means that the individual homes, usually party-wall row houses, or apartment buildings, are grouped together on relatively small plots of land with large surrounding areas of land left open for common recreational use. The cluster form of development is economical because the clustering of houses with party walls reduces the cost of supplying utilities and roads. Often, a PUD is placed in a floating zone.

The old-fashioned zoning ordinance with its rigid allocation of specific uses to specific zones, its building lines, and its minimum-area requirements does not lend itself to the PUD type of development. Cluster development calls for smaller home sites, with the land subtracted from home sites being added to common areas. The PUD can be listed as a special exception in the zoning ordinance. Alternatively, the zoning ordinance may include a special section devoted to the PUD, calling it variously a "Community Unit Plan," "Dwelling Groups," "Group Housing," "Planned Residential Development" or "Planned Building Groups." Because approving a development of this sort involves a considerable exercise of discretion, it seems wise to provide that final approval of a special exception for a developer's proposal to create a PUD zone should rest with the city council, just as if an amendment to the zoning ordinance were being considered; some ordinances so provide. *Rodgers v. Village of Tarrytown*, 302 N.Y. 115, 96 N.E.2d 731 (1951); *La Rue v. East Brunswick*, 68 N.J. Super. 435, 172 A.2d 691 (1961); *DeMeo v. Zoning Comm'n*, 148 Conn. 68, 167 A.2d 454 (1961). The applicant for such zoning may, under many ordinances, be a government agency, since urban redevelopment plans sometimes call for a PUD.

Where cluster housing occurs in a residential zone that permits the type of housing planned for the PUD, it is simply a form of density zoning and offers no legal problems.

30.26 Contract Zoning

An application by a landowner for rezoning often results in bargaining with the planning board or the city's governing body. At times, a formal covenant is entered into by the landowner and the city contemporaneously with the rezoning.

EXAMPLE: In granting rezoning of land from residential to shopping center use, the city exacted a recorded covenant from the landowner that it would maintain a buffer area of landscaped land between the center and adjoining residential land. This was held valid. *Bucholz v. City of Omaha*, 174 Neb. 862, 120 N.W.2d 270 (1963).

Some courts disapprove of contract zoning. The arguments against contract zoning are as follows:

1. It is illegal to "bargain" for legislation. *Baylis v. City of Baltimore,* 219 Md. 164, 148 A.2d 429 (1959). This argument is specious. Much of the legislation on our books was initiated and lobbied through the legislature by private interests. Moreover, the rezoning could have been enacted without any conditions. *Church v. Town of Islip,* 8 N.Y.2d 254, 168 N.E.2d 680 (1960). Why, then, would the imposition of beneficial conditions invalidate the zoning? Also, since rezoning deals, as it often must, with particular parcels of land, it is difficult to legislate sensibly without taking cognizance of the special conditions relating to that particular parcel.

2. The rezoning is not in accordance with the state zoning enabling act, which contemplates division of the city into zones plainly appearing on the zoning map. Contract zoning introduces a control of land use that appears in the recorder's office, but does not appear on the city's legislative records. *Treadway v. City of Rockford,* 24 Ill. 2d 488, 182 N.E.2d 219 (1962). *Contra Goffinet v. Christian County,* 65 Ill. 2d 40, 357 N.E.2d 442 (Ill. 1976).

It has been suggested that this sort of bargaining is commonplace and stands a good chance of acceptance if it is accomplished by means of "private restrictions" voluntarily created and recorded by the landowner. Hagman, *Wisconsin Zoning Practice,* 11 (1962). At least one court has accepted this suggestion.

> **EXAMPLE:** The city of *X* suggests to *D,* a developer, that a declaration of restrictions restricting a specified area in his development for golf course purposes over a period of twenty-five years be recorded. This is done. In return, the city rezones a part of the area from detached single-family dwellings to town houses. This arrangement is valid. *State ex rel Zupancic v. Schimenz,* 174 N.W.2d 533 (Wis. 1970).

At times, a contract zoning ordinance provides that if the contract is breached, the zoning reverts back to the preexisting zoning. Such a provision is invalid in some states. *Stiriz v. Stout,* 210 N.Y.S.2d 325 (S. Ct. 1960). In other states, it is valid. *Goffinet v. Christian County,* 65 Ill. 2d 40, 357 N.E.2d 442 (1976). Every legislative change of zoning requires a careful weighing of the need for such action in light of the circumstances then prevailing. The automatic reverter provision is the antithesis of proper legislative consideration.

It remains impossible to make a definitive statement of the law on this subject. Some courts reject contract zoning. Others permit it. Others permit a form of it. The trend is in favor of permitting contract zoning. *Goffinet v. Christian County,* 65 Ill. 2d 40, 357 N.E.2d 442 (1976); James D. Lawlor, Annotation, *Validity, Construction and Effect of Agreement to Rezone, or Amendment to Zoning Ordinance, Creating Special Restrictions or Conditions Not Applicable to Other Property Similarly Zoned,* 70 A.L.R.3d 125 (1976).

30.27 Density—In General

Density zoning deals with a number of related items all designed to reduce density of residential occupancy, for example, (1) minimum lot size or area; (2) minimum frontage; (3) front, back, and side yard requirements; (4) maximum lot coverage (open space zoning); and (5) minimum building size. The general purpose, to prevent overcrowding, is valid. *Town of Durham v. White Enterprises, Inc.,* 348 A.2d 706 (N.H. 1975).

In large-scale residential developments, sophisticated density concepts are applied.

> **EXAMPLE:** The ordinance may divide up the residential area of the city into districts of differing residential density. Thus, if the zoning of a particular area permits single-family residences, duplexes, town houses, and apartments, the applicable zoning may permit a density of five dwelling units per acre. The developer of ten acres, let us say, can build fifty single-

family units, or twenty-five duplexes, or five ten-unit buildings, or one fifty-unit building. The usual lot size and building bulk restrictions apply.

Front, back, and side yards require no discussion since they typically occasion no problems. Bulk variances deal adequately with the situation. For example, when sprawling ranch homes became popular after World War II, zoning boards handed out front and side line variances by the thousands.

30.27(a) Density— Minimum Lot Area

Many decisions sanction minimum area residential lot requirements. The theoretical legal basis for such zoning is that spacing buildings farther apart prevents the spread of fire and provides for ample light, air, and adequate sewage disposal. *Simon v. Town of Needham,* 311 Mass. 560, 42 N.E.2d 516 (1942); *Barnard v. Zoning Bd. of Town of Yarmouth,* 313 A.2d 741 (Me. 1974). In a rural area, a minimum lot area of five acres has been sustained. *Honeck v. County of Cook,* 12 Ill. 2d 257, 146 N.E.2d 35 (1957). In connection with the validity of such zoning, courts consider the character of the area. A rural area not in the path of development is a favorable characteristic. Also favorable is the predominance of large tracts in single ownership, as well as the presence of historic sites. The presence of smaller lots in the neighborhood is unfavorable to the validity of the zoning. *Marquette Nat'l Bank v. County of Cook,* 24 Ill. 2d 497, 182 N.E.2d 147 (1962) (minimum area of 20,000 square feet held invalid where neighboring lots were 10,000 square feet in area); *Christine Bldgs. v. City of Troy,* 367 Mich. 508, 116 N.W.2d 816 (1962) (requirement of 21,780 square feet held invalid where most lots were 15,000 square feet or less). Here, the competitive disadvantage makes the larger lots virtually unsalable. An increase in minimum lot area is sometimes characterized as upgrading. Thus, an increase of minimum lot area from two acres to four acres has been sustained. *Senior v. Zoning Comm'n of Town of New Canaan,* 153 A.2d 415 (Conn. 1959). The courts have said that the maximum enrichment of developers is not a controlling purpose of zoning.

In more recent times, environmental factors (e.g., water pollution) have been cited in favor of such zoning. *Steel Hill Dev., Inc. v. Town of Sanbornton,* 469 F.2d 956 (1st Cir. 1973). This type of zoning faces the problem of substandard lots, that is, smaller lots platted and sold before the upgrading by zoning amendment. In general, the courts have required the city to issue building permits or to have invalidated the zoning as to such substandard lots. *Harrington Glen, Inc. v. Mun. Bd. of Adjustment,* 243 A.2d 233 (N.J. 1968); *Fulling v. Palumbo,* 21 N.Y.2d 30, 286 N.Y.S.2d 249 (1967); *Grace Bldg. Co., Inc. v. Hatfield Township,* 329 A.2d 925 (Pa. 1974) (holding that lot owner cannot be required to buy adjoining lot in order to come into compliance with the amendment). *Contra Grobman v. City of Des Plaines,* 322 N.E.2d 443 (Ill. 1975) (denying relief to owners of substandard lot where they refused adjoining owner's offer to purchase).

An occasional decision refuses to protect the purchaser of a substandard lot on the ground that the purchase of the lot was a gamble. The buyer bought the lot fully aware that it was substandard, probably at a bargain price. *Phoenix v. Beall,* 524 P.2d 1314 (Ariz. 1974). This is akin to self-created hardship, which is a valid basis for refusing a variance.

30.27(b) Density— Minimum Frontage or Lot Size

Minimum frontage requirements have been sustained. *Clemons v. City of Los Angeles,* 36 Cal. 2d 95, 222 P.2d 439 (1950). With respect to such requirements, the problem of substandard lots has arisen quite frequently. Many ordinances exempt previously platted lots from this requirement. *Graves v. Bloomfield Planning Bd.,* 235 A.2d 51 (N.J. 1967). In any case, the courts have gone far in protecting substandard lots. *Milano v. Town of Patterson,*

93 N.Y.S.2d 419 (1947) (requirement of sixty-foot frontage inapplicable to previously plat-ted twenty-three-foot lot). Courts have granted flexible relief. *Ziman v. Village of Glencoe,* 275 N.E.2d 168 (Ill. 1971) (court imposed three-foot side yard requirement). But, a denial of a variance will be overthrown. A permit must be granted. *Jacquelin v. Horsham Township,* 312 A.2d 124, 10 Pa. Commw. 473 (Pa. 1973). As in the case of minimum area cases, occasionally, relief is denied to a purchaser who buys with knowledge of the problem, *Klehr v. Zoning Bd.,* 320 N.E.2d 498 (Ill. App. 1974).

The owner of a substandard lot cannot be compelled to buy additional frontage. Nor can the owner be compelled to sell to a neighbor. *Smith v. Smith,* 216 Md. 141, 140 A.2d 58 (1958).

When an owner owns several contiguous substandard lots it must comply with the new frontage requirements. In effect, it must resubdivide the frontage into lots that comply with the new requirements. *Citizens Bank & Trust Co. v. City of Park Ridge,* 5 Ill. App. 3d 77, 282 N.E.2d 751 (1972).

Checkerboarding is always struck down. This is a situation in which an owner of a number of contiguous platted lots conveys out alternate lots in order to qualify each sub-standard lot for a permit. Note, 16 Syracuse L. Rev. 612 (1965).

30.27(c) Density—Minimum Building Area

Prescribing a minimum building area compatible with health requirements is within the po-lice power of the local municipality. *Lionshead Lake, Inc. v. Township of Wayne,* 10 N.J. 165, 89 A.2d 693, *appeal dismissed,* 344 U.S. 919, 73 S. Ct. 386 (1953) (requirement of 768 square feet for one-story building sustained). The only substantial issue in this area is whether such a requirement can occur on a graduated basis, with differing minimum build-ing areas in differing residential zones. One court has rejected this approach. *Medinger Appeal,* 377 Pa. 217, 104 A.2d 118 (1954). The logic of *Medinger* is superficially attractive. If a building area of 1000 square feet suffices to protect public health, it is difficult to sus-tain a requirement of 1800 square feet in zone B. However, this approach overlooks the compatibility argument. Houses of differing value do indeed exist in the various areas of the city, and to keep new houses compatible with existing houses is a legitimate objective of zoning. In line with the compatibility argument, a requirement of large houses in an area characterized by smaller homes could be invalid.

30.28 Exclusionary Zoning

One of the developments in zoning law is the appearance of exclusionary zoning, which oc-curs when a municipality through its zoning law discourages low- or moderate-income housing. This is accomplished by zoning out the uses affordable by members of these in-come groups, for example, by only allowing large lot and commercial development. The at-titude of the courts embracing this doctrine is, in large part, that the public welfare requirement of the police power does not stop at the city limits. Courts cannot think in terms of the welfare of the municipality and its present inhabitants in testing the zoning. The "tight little island" concept of zoning is outmoded. Sager, *Tight Little Islands: Exclusion-ary Zoning, Equal Protection and the Indigent,* 21 Stan. L. Rev. 767 (1969). The wants and needs of all the people living in the region must be considered. The poor people must not be zoned into the decaying areas of the city and zoned out of suburbs. Some early decisions in this area struck down large lot zoning. *Nat'l Land & Investment Co. v. Kohn,* 215 A.2d 597 (Pa. 1965); *Appeal of Kit-Mar Builders, Inc.,* 439 Pa. 466, 268 A.2d 765 (1970); *Bd. of County Supervisors of Fairfax County v. Carper,* 200 Va. 653, 107 S.E.2d 390 (1959). The inequitable aspect of such zoning, bearing heavily as it does on those who cannot af-ford to buy large lots, has long been the subject of discussion.

However, the battle is out in the open. The authorities, and they are numerous, are collected in *Township of Williston v. Chesterdale Farms, Inc.,* 300 A.2d 107 (Pa. 1973). The *Williston* case also collects the authorities on exclusion of apartments from suburbia as a form of exclusionary zoning. Many poor people simply cannot afford to buy a house. An important state court decision on exclusionary zoning is *Southern Burlington County NAACP v. Township of Mount Laurel,* 67 N.J. 151, 336 A.2d 713 (1975). The influence of this case has been felt nationwide. Mount Laurel was a "developing municipality," that is, one with a good deal of vacant land. Its zoning ordinance was a rather typical suburban ordinance. The residential zones permitted only single-family dwellings. Apartments and mobile homes were not permitted. Over 4100 acres were zoned exclusively for industry, even though only 100 acres were occupied by industry. These aspects tended to keep out the poor and were obviously so intended. The court held that virtually the entire ordinance was void because its entire scheme and plan were designed to keep out low- and moderate-income housing. This alone makes the case important. The case held that the public benefit idea that sustains the validity of zoning ordinances in the first place is the public benefit of the region. The zoning must benefit those who live outside the municipality, not simply the residents of the municipality. Outsiders have a right to travel into the municipality and then remain there. The municipality must accept a "fair share" of the disadvantaged. *Urban League v. Mayor & City Council,* 142 N.J. Super. 11, 359 A.2d 526 (1976) (invalidating eleven ordinances); *Surrick v. Zoning Bd.,* 476 Pa. 182, 382 A.2d 105 (1977). It must adopt a new zoning map with smaller lots that the poor can afford. Space must be allocated, the court said, for apartments and mobile homes.

In legal theory, the local governments of New Jersey should immediately have begun the process of amending their ordinances to conform to the *Mount Laurel* decision. Instead they chose to ignore the decision. This was unwise. More litigation ensued and ultimately reached the New Jersey Supreme Court. This time the court dealt harshly with the local governments. It reiterated the earlier holding, but made it clear that if the local governments failed to conform, the courts would take over the issuance of building permits. Evidently, the local governments failed to act, for the New Jersey courts began issuing building permits to builders who could demonstrate that the earlier *Mount Laurel* decision was not being followed. It offered the incentive of higher density as a reward to the builder willing to include low- and moderate-income units in the development. *Southern Burlington County NAACP v. Township of Mount Laurel,* 92 N.J. 158, 456 A.2d 390 (1983); *J.W. Field Co., Inc. v. Franklin Township,* 204 N.J. Super. 445, 499 A.2d 251 (1985).

The result of all of this is the enactment of ordinances and development schemes that allow the developer to build more units per acre if subsidized units are included. Each suburb has its quota of subsidized units.

30.29 Inclusionary Ordinances

To ensure that housing for lower-income people will be built and widely dispersed, several communities have adopted ordinances requiring developers to include a minimum amount of subsidized or low-cost housing in their projects. Thomas Kleven, *Inclusionary Ordinances—Policy and Legal Issues in Requiring Private Developers to Build Low Cost Housing,* 21 U.C.L.A. Rev. 1432 (1974). One such ordinance was held invalid. *Bd. of Supervisors v. DeGraff Enterprises, Inc.,* 214 Va. 635, 198 S.E.2d 600 (1973). But, in California, such ordinances are valid. James D. Lawlor, Annotation, *Validity and Construction of Zoning Ordinance Requiring Developer to Devote Specified Part of Development to Low and Moderate Income Housing,* 62 A.L.R.3d 880 (1975).

30.30 Effect of Zoning Ordinance on Restrictions

Restrictions contained in a deed, plat, or property owner's agreement are neither nullified nor superseded by the adoption of a zoning ordinance. *Chuba v. Glasgow,* 61 N.M. 302, 299 P.2d 774 (1956); *Schwarzchild v. Wolborne,* 186 Va. 1052, 45 S.E.2d 152 (1947).

> **EXAMPLE:** A deed provided that use of the land thereby conveyed was restricted to residential purposes. Thereafter, an ordinance was passed zoning the area for commercial purposes, and the owner attempted to construct a gasoline station on the land. It was held that the deed restriction would be enforced, and a court order was entered forbidding erection of the gasoline station. *Dolan v. Brown,* 338 Ill. 412, 170 N.E. 425 (1930).

However, a change of use in the zoning ordinance does help to show that a change in the neighborhood has taken place, and the court may well decline thereafter to enforce the building restrictions on the ground of change in neighborhood. *Goodwin Bros. v. Combs Lumber Co.,* 275 Ky. 114, 120 S.W.2d 1024 (1938); *Austin v. Van Horn,* 225 Mich. 117, 237 N.W. 550 (1931); 26 C.J.S. *Deeds* § 171 (2). The older zoning ordinances permitted residences to be erected in any zone. This was cumulative zoning. The newer ordinances, by and large, forbid residential uses in commercial and industrial zones. Where the earlier building restriction calls for residential use and the later zoning ordinance forbids residential use, the zoning ordinance supersedes the restriction. *1.77 Acres of Land v. State,* 241 A.2d 513 (Del. 1968); *Grubel v. MacLaughlin,* 286 F. Supp. 24 (1968); *Key v. McCabe,* 54 Cal. 2d 736, 356 P.2d 169 (1960); *Blakeley v. Gorin,* 313 N.E.2d 903 (Mass. 1974); Donald G. Hagman, *Urban Planning and Land Development Control,* 308 (1971).

30.30(a) Mortgages

Zoning laws are binding on mortgagees. When a mortgagee loans money for construction of a building that violates a zoning ordinance, the court will refuse to protect the lender, even though the lender was ignorant of the fact that the ordinance was being violated, since, in dealing with real estate, all who are interested are required to take notice of zoning laws. *Siegemund v. Building Comm'r,* 263 Mass. 212, 160 N.E. 795 (1928). Accordingly, a mortgagee making a construction loan should satisfy itself that the contemplated improvement complies with existing ordinances. Otherwise, the lender may find construction of the building halted by a court order after part of the mortgage money has been paid out.

30.31 Planning

City and regional planning figures prominently in the life of many communities today. State laws authorize the adoption by planning commissions of master plans. Such a commission plans for the systematic and orderly development of the community, with particular regard for the location of future major street systems, transportation systems, parks, recreation areas, industrial and commercial undertakings, residential areas, the creation and preservation of civic beauty, and other kindred matters, all looking not only to the present, but with a view to the orderly development of the unbuilt, as well as the built-up, areas.

Generally, at present, the formulation of a master plan is not a precondition to the enactment of a zoning ordinance. True, the zoning ordinance must be rational and bear within itself some evidence of logical planning, but, if that is present, it suffices. *Angermeier v. Sea Girt,* 27 N.J. 298, 142 A.2d 624 (1958). Increasingly, the courts look for some comprehensive plan to guide them in their decision as to the validity of zoning. If there is a plan and the zoning or rezoning conforms to that plan, the courts are likely to sustain it. If the existing zoning is inappropriate when compared with an existing plan, the courts may strike it down. *Fasano v. Bd. of County Comm'rs,* 264 Or. 574, 507 P.2d 23 (1973).

> **EXAMPLE:** The plan showed the area was ideal for multifamily housing, but the ordinance zoned it as single-family. It must be rezoned multifamily. *City of Louisville v. Kavanaugh,* 495 S.W.2d 502 (Ky. 1973).

If the municipality has no plan at all, the courts are likely to regard this as a good basis for striking down a zoning change. If the city has no plan, any change is, arguably, a planless change. *Forestview Homeowners Ass'n, Inc. v. County of Cook,* 18 Ill. App. 3d 230, 309 N.E.2d 763 (1974). Planless change creates a hodgepodge of incompatible uses. If the court is to decide the validity of a proposed zoning change, it is entitled to know the city's long-range plans for the general area. *Hall v. City and County of Honolulu,* 530 P.2d 737 (Haw. 1975). This is one of the battlegrounds that will surely be fought on, with hammer and tongs. The city fathers prefer to keep their plans secret, meanwhile zoning much land for single-family dwellings or industrial use, with the intent to rezone the land when the "right" developer comes along and they have had a look at his or her proposals. If the city planners must come out into the open and show on their plans that the area has a long-range future for multifamily dwellings, they will have a hard time rejecting rezoning for this purpose. At the same time, the courts want to see "in public" what the long-range plans are so that they can make a rational decision on this score.

Among the states now requiring a city to have a plan are California, Florida, Hawaii, Kentucky, Michigan, Nebraska, Oregon, and Washington. The states in this category apply the rule to rezoning (amendment of zoning ordinance) and to variances and special exceptions. Erwin S. Barbre, Annotation, *Requirement that Zoning Variances or Exceptions Be Made in Accordance with Comprehensive Plan,* 40 A.L.R.3d 372 (1971).

But, most recent decisions continue to reject the notion that a prior plan must exist as a basis for valid zoning. *Quinn v. Town of Dodgeville,* 354 N.W.2d 747 (Wis. App. 1984) (citing many cases).

30.32 Enforcement of Zoning Ordinance

It is usually provided in the zoning ordinance that any property owner wishing to erect a building must first apply to the commissioner of buildings or other proper official for a building permit. Every such application must be accompanied by plans and specifications of the contemplated structure. The official reviews the plans and declines to issue the permit if a violation of the zoning ordinance is disclosed. If, despite the fact that the contemplated structure would violate the zoning ordinance, the building permit is nevertheless issued, any other property owner whose property would suffer special damage by erection of the proposed structure (e.g., a neighbor) may, if he or she acts promptly, obtain a court order prohibiting the erection of the building. *Garner v. County of DuPage,* 8 Ill. 2d 155, 133 N.E.2d 303 (1956). Although it is advisable to do so, the complaining property owner need not first request the public authorities to take action. *Fitzgerald v. Merard Holding Co.,* 106 Conn. 475, 138 A. 483 (1927). If the complaining owner acts promptly in asserting his or her rights, but construction of the building is nevertheless begun, the offending property owner may be ordered by the court to demolish the illegal portion of the structure.

> **EXAMPLE:** Despite protests of an adjoining owner before the commissioner of buildings and the zoning board of appeals, a permit was issued to a property owner to construct an apartment building that violated the zoning ordinance in that it did not have a one-foot setback for every nine feet of rise above a height of seventy-two feet. While litigation was pending to declare the permit invalid, the apartment building corporation proceeded with construction of the building. Eventually, the courts declared the permit invalid, and the adjoining owner filed suit to compel the corporation to reconstruct the building to conform to the zoning ordinance. It

developed that such reconstruction could be accomplished only at a cost of $343,837.07. Nevertheless, the court ordered the building corporation to reconstruct the building to comply with the ordinance. *Welton v. 40 East Oak St. Bldg. Corp.,* 70 F.2d 377 (7th Cir. 1934).

It is held in some states that if a permit is issued and, in reliance thereon, erection of the building is begun, the city cannot thereafter enforce the zoning ordinance if it is discovered that the permit should not have been issued. *Shellburne, Inc. v. Roberts,* 224 A.2d 250 (Del. 1966). The law on this point is chaotic. 1971 Ur. L. Ann. 63.

> **EXAMPLE:** The city allowed an apartment building to stand for over forty-three years although it violated the zoning ordinance. The city then sought to fine the apartment owner. It can do so. The long delay does not bar city action. The philosophy here is that important public rights ought not be lost by inaction of public servants. *G & S Mtg. & Invest. Corp. v. City of Evanston,* 264 N.E.2d 740 (Ill. App. 1970).

As to the matter of a court finding that the village is barred (estopped) from enforcing its zoning laws against a particular tract of land, this usually arises from some action of the village that encourages the landowner to make substantial expenditures in the belief that he or she is acting legally. The village then seeks to invalidate a previously issued building permit, change the law, or otherwise pull the rug out from under the landowner. Courts at times protect the landowner, perceiving the injustice of allowing him or her to spend money in a mistaken belief encouraged by the city. At times, courts permit the city to block construction, often in the unspoken belief that bribery was present. In any event, the decisions are in chaos. In Illinois alone, the decisions number fifty or more. R.P. Davis, Annotation, *Right of Permittee Under Illegally Issued Building Permit,* 6 A.L.R.2d 960 (1948).

**30.33
Telecommunications
Towers and
Satellite Dishes**

The Telecommunications Act of 1996 preempts or prohibits certain aspects of local zoning control over wireless communications. 47 U.S.C. § 332(c)(7). While the local municipality's zoning authority over the placement, construction, and modification of wireless service facilities is preserved, the regulation of the wireless service cannot unreasonably discriminate among providers, and such regulation may not have the effect of prohibiting the provision of wireless service. *Sprint Spectrum, L.P. v. Ontario Planning Bd.,* 176 F. 3d 630 (2nd Cir. 1999). A municipal body must have substantial evidence that the tower will conflict with specific provisions of the zoning ordinance to deny a special use permit. *C-Call Corp. v. Zoning Bd. of Appeals,* 700 N.E.2d 441 (Ill. App. 1998). Generalized opinions of an adverse effect on views and property values are not enough. *Omnipoint Corp. v Zoning Bd. of Pine Grove,* 1998 U.S. App. Lexis 14610 (3rd Cir. 1999).

The FCC has enacted a regulation to preempt state and local zoning regulations dealing with satellite dishes. Through this regulation, state and local zoning and other regulations that differentiate between satellite "receive-only" antennas and other types of antenna facilities are preempted unless those regulations (1) have a reasonable and clearly defined health, safety, or aesthetic objective and (2) do not operate to impose unreasonable limitations on or prevent the reception of satellite-delivered signals by receive-only antennas, or impose costs on users of such antennas that are excessive in light of the purchase and installation costs of the equipment. 47 C.F.R. § 25.104. Enforcement of ordinances that are inconsistent with these requirements will not be allowed. *Neufeld v. City of Baltimore,* 820 F. Supp. 963 (D. Md. 1993).

A recent rule of the FCC allows tenants to install antennas or dishes, subject to the reasonable regulations of their landlords. Thus, landlords may prohibit the drilling of holes or other means of attaching the appliance to the structure in a way that will damage the structure, or prohibit the placement of the receiver in common areas or other places not leased to the tenant.

Similarly, the FCC has ruled that homeowner and condominium associations cannot impair a homeowner or condominium owner's access to satellite signals by placing receivers on property that is within the exclusive use or control of the viewer. F.C.C. Rule 96-328. Thus, a condominium owner should be able to place the satellite dish on the condominium balcony, or on the town-house patio. The association may, however, establish reasonable rules for decor purposes or for the health and safety of the community. These rules may require screening or painting to reduce the visual effect of the antennas.

Cell tower leases present an unusual array of issues in addition to those found in any other leasing transaction. The context of the lease transaction, however, suggests that the parties view those issues differently than they do with the standard industrial lease. Roseleen P. Rick, *Cellular Tower Leases—A Landlord's Perspective (with Form)*, Prac. Real Est. Law. 40 (May 1997).

CHAPTER 31

Land Use Controls—
Land Development, Regulation,
Subdivisions, and Dedication

31.01 Dedication   One long-used element of land development and development regulation is the dedication of land for public use. This occurs where the landowner sets land apart for some public purpose, followed by an acceptance of such donation by the public. No particular form is required for a common law dedication. It is not necessary that there be any written instrument. There merely must be an intention on the part of the landowner to dedicate the land to the public. The landowner must, either by words or actions, offer the land for public use, and the public must accept the offer. When the offer is accepted, the public body acquires an easement in the land dedicated.

> **EXAMPLE:** *A* owned a tract of land. *A* fenced off the tract, locating the fence approximately thirty-three feet north of the south line of his land. This thirty-three-foot strip was used by the public as a road and was later paved by the city. *A*'s acts showed an intention to offer the strip as a street, and the city's acts showed an acceptance of that offer. The city acquired an easement in the land for street purposes. Ownership of the street subject to the road easement remained in *A*. Joyce E. Bagley, *Informal Dedication of Land*, 24 Baylor L. Rev. 592 (1972).

Once an offer of dedication has been accepted by the city, it is irrevocable. M.B. Emma, Annotation, *Revocation or Withdrawal of Dedication by Grantees or Successors in Interest of Dedicator*, 86 A.L.R.2d 860, 877 (1962). Whether it can be revoked before acceptance depends on local law. *Id*. If the intention to dedicate is lacking, there is no dedication.

> **EXAMPLE:** *A* owns land abutting a public street. A store is built on the land some five feet from the street line. To induce the public to look into the store windows on *A*'s land, *A* paves the strip between the store and the street. This does not operate as a dedication of the strip as part of the street. The intention is simply to make a more profitable utilization of *A*'s private property, not to give it to the public. *Nickel v. University City,* 239 S.W.2d 519 (Mo. App. 1951).

For the same reason, a sign placed on such a strip indicating that the area is private property will prevent the creation of a dedication, even though the public is permitted to use such strip. Some owners of private streets or alleys periodically place chains across the street or alley or embed markers in the pavement to show an absence of intention to dedicate the strip or walkway.

It is often said that land can be dedicated only by the true owner thereof. *O'Rorke v. City of Homewood,* 237 So. 2d 487 (Ala. 1970). This is true. Nevertheless, dedications can be and are made by owners whose land is subject to easements or other rights. W.E. Shipley, Annotation, *Right of Owner of Servient Tenement Subject to Right of Way to Dedicate His Land*, 69 A.L.R.2d 1236 (1960).

> **EXAMPLE:** *R* owned land over which *X*, a neighbor, had a recorded driveway easement. *R* filed a plat in which he included the driveway in a public street dedicated by the plat. This is valid. The city acquired its rights subject to the rights of *X* to continue to exercise rights under the driveway easement. This is simply an application of the rule that one acquiring an easement does not acquire the exclusive right to its use.

31.01(a) Nature of Dedication

One common problem with these dedications is the ambiguities found in some plats. For example, it is not uncommon to find a plat with a tract marked "beach" or "park." Does this evidence the intent that the general public may use the area, or was it intended that only owners of lots in the subdivision would be allowed to use the area? The decisions are conflicting. L.S. Tellier, Annotation, *Validity and Construction of Regulations as to Subdivision Maps or Plats*, 11 A.L.R.2d 562 (1950). The developer should make its intention clear by placing a legend on the plat as follows: "A perpetual easement appurtenant to each lot in this subdivision is hereby created for use of the area marked 'beach' as a private bathing beach only for owners of lots in this subdivision, members of their family, and guests. This must not be construed as a dedication to the general public. Ownership of the area is reserved to the developer and does not pass by any deed or mortgage of a lot."

Consideration must be given to the specific use to which the dedicated area may be put. In drafting these provisions, the use of general, ambiguous phrases such as "public square," should not be used. Is the area something like a park? Could a courthouse be built on it? A school? A church? A swimming pool? An athletic stadium? The provision should spell out the specific use contemplated.

The provision should also identify who is to be the legal owner of the dedicated area. The city? The developer? The adjoining landowners? The homeowners' association? There is some advantage to putting ownership in the municipality. This will typically rid the developer of the burden of paying taxes on the area and of personal liability for accidents that may occur on the area. A plat of dedication may give only an easement instead of fee title to the municipality. *Id.* Again, the documents should be clear. The drafter of the dedication should also address whether a present gift is intended or is the dedication to occur in the future? For example, what is meant by the phrase "reserved for park"? Or "proposed park"? *Anderson v. Tall Timbers Corp.*, 378 S.W.2d 16 (Tex. 1964). Does such a phrase create present rights in the lot owners or the municipality, so that the developer may not change its mind a year later and build a house on the tract? Ambiguity should be avoided and the clear intent of the developer set out.

A plat often shows a strip across the rear of the lots marked as an easement for public utilities. Some courts feel that the use of the word "public" makes this a dedication to the public, *Nichol v. Village of Glen Ellyn,* 89 Ill. App. 2d 251, 231 N.E.2d 462 (1967), but other courts disagree. *Island Homes v. City of Fairbanks,* 421 P.2d 759 (Alaska 1966). This should not be left in doubt, for if the strip is not dedicated to the public, there is some control in the landowner over which utilities may come into that strip with their services. A legend should be placed on the plat stating the following: "A perpetual easement is hereby created in favor of all lot owners in this subdivision, over, under, and across the area marked easement for public utilities as an easement appurtenant to each lot in this subdivision for the installation, use, maintenance, repair, and replacement of public utilities, including sewer, water, gas, electricity, cable television, telephone, and telegraph. Said areas are not dedicated to the public."

Even where the public authorities did not accept a particular street, public park, or other public area so designated on a plat, any lot owner in the subdivision has a private right to have the area used as platted and may obtain a court order forbidding any other use. *New-ton v. Batson,* 223 S.C. 545, 77 S.E.2d 212 (1953); *McCorquodale v. Keyton,* 63 So. 2d 906 (Fla. 1953).

Approval of the subdivision plat by the city or other public body is not an automatic acceptance of the streets, parks, and other public areas depicted on the plat. 26 C.J.S. § 479; L.S. Tellier, Annotation, *Validity and Construction of Regulation as to Subdivision Maps or Plats,* 11 A.L.R.2d 574 (1957). Acceptance is shown by the city's paving of the streets, putting in sewers, and so on. V. Woerner, Annotation, *Construction or Maintenance of Sewers, Water Pipes, or the Like by Public Authorities in Roadway, Street or Alley as Indicating Dedication or Acceptance Thereof,* 52 A.L.R.2d 263 (1957). Therefore, if the municipality is to assume immediate responsibility for these areas, the council must pass an ordinance accepting this dedication. And, if you want the city to have complete ownership of a park, for example, it is best to give the city a deed to the area and have the council pass an ordinance accepting it, although in many states acceptance of a plat operates as a transfer of ownership to the city, especially where the plat is executed by the city or village pursuant to an ordinance enacted at the end of the planning process. Once an area has been dedicated, neither the subdivider nor the city can use the land for a purpose other than the dedicated purpose. *City of St. Louis v. Bedal,* 394 S.W.2d 391 (Mo. 1965).

31.02 Plat Approval During the real estate boom of the 1920s, countless subdivisions were created with no thought for potential need. Plats were recorded showing streets and parks that never materialized. Lots were sold to people who had no notion of their true value. When the crash of 1929 arrived, lot sales stopped. The market for vacant lots disappeared. Real estate taxes were not paid. These premature subdivisions became disasters. As a result, laws were passed requiring a developer to submit a plat for approval before it is recorded and, more importantly, before building permits are issued.

In general, the legal philosophy is that if a landowner chooses to subdivide land for development and record a plat for that purpose, the public bodies can legitimately impose reasonable restrictions on the development. The community has a stake in avoiding the problems of unpaid taxes, unusable streets, and other public problems that premature and improperly conceived subdivision creates and an even greater stake in preserving the health of the community through proper sewer and water installations, and traffic control. *Forest Constr. Co. v. Planning Comm'n,* 236 A.2d 917 (Conn. 1967).

Today, subdivision and development of land is subject to strict controls. The governing body of the city or village may retain the power to approve or disapprove proposed developments, or, where the state law permits, this power may be delegated to a planning commission. Control over land development extends over the entire municipality and often a surrounding area of several miles. *Prudential Co-Op Realty Co. v. City of Youngstown,* 118 Ohio St. 204, 160 N.E. 695 (1928); 11 A.L.R.2d 524, *supra.* However, this power to approve plats of land outside the city limits does not confer power to zone the area outside the city. *City of Carlsbad v. Caviness,* 66 N.M. 230, 346 P.2d 310 (1959). The municipality adopts regulations establishing standards of subdivision design, including regulations concerning utilities, streets, curbs, gutters, sidewalks, storm and sanitary sewers, fire hydrants, street lighting, street signs, and width, depth, and area of lots. No subdivision plat may be recorded unless it has been approved. This approval is withheld until the plat complies with the regulations.

In lieu of requiring installation of streets, utilities, and so on, before approval, the commission may accept the developer's agreement to install these improvements, if that agreement is secured by a letter of credit or a surety bond or other credit enhancement guaranteeing that the installation will be made. It is impractical to install streets and then have them pounded to rubble as construction goes forward. Kelley & Shultz, *"Or Other Adequate Security": Using, Structuring, and Managing the Standby Letter of Credit to Ensure the Completion of Subdivision Improvements,* 19 Urb. L. 39 (1987).

Like zoning, subdivision approval is a land-use control that differs from zoning. These are two separate laws that serve different purposes. There is a trend toward combining the functions of zoning and plat approval. The developer proposes a development that requires zoning and submits a plat that conforms to the zoning. The planning process goes forward and the approvals, both planning and zoning, are given.

If a developer records the plat without the required approvals, it runs the risk that the planning board or the municipality will obtain a court order stopping all sales. *Wrongful Subdivision Approval by the Plan Commission: Remedies of the Buyer and City,* 29 Ind. L.J. 408 (1954). Moreover, in most states, the law forbids the recording of a plat unless city approval is endorsed on the face of the plat itself. In many states, selling land in an unapproved subdivision plat is subject to a fine. In some states (e.g., California, Michigan, and New Jersey), the buyer of a lot in an unapproved subdivision may change its mind, terminate its obligations under the sale contract, and obtain a refund of its deposit. Donald W. Brodie, *Platting, Planning & Protection—A Summary of Subdivision Statutes,* 36 N.Y.U. L. Rev. 1205, 1214 (1961). In other states (e.g., Idaho, Iowa, Massachusetts, Michigan, Nebraska, Rhode Island, and Wyoming), the buyer of a lot in an unapproved subdivision may sue the seller for damages. The contract of sale is not void. If the buyer wishes to enforce the contract, it may do so. *Bamberg v. Griffin,* 76 Ill. App. 138, 394 N.E.2d 910 (1979).

31.03 Forced Dedication

As the need for public control of subdivision and development gained acceptance, the pendulum began to swing steadily toward more rigorous controls. The cities, in addition to controlling the size and direction of streets, grading and paving, gutters and drainage, water and utility installation, and so on, began to insist on dedication of land for schools and parks and other contributions to the public. The requirements as to streets, sidewalks, sewers, and water lines have been upheld as valid. Year-Wood, *Accepted Controls of Land Subdivision,* 45 J. Urb. L. 217 (1967); Robert H. Freilich & Peter S. Levi, *Model Regulations for the Control of Land Subdivision,* 36 Mo. L. Rev. 1 (1971). The other requirements have aroused controversy. When it comes to exactions of great magnitude, such as those requiring the developer to contribute parks, school areas, and sewage treatment plants, the problems become very difficult.

The city has two great powers, the police power and the power of eminent domain. The police power is the power to pass reasonable laws for the good of the public. The power of eminent domain is the power to acquire land for public purposes by paying for it. Where forced dedication is employed and sustained, the municipality is saying that this is an appropriate situation for exercising the police power, without the payment of compensation. If the municipal requirement does not bear a relationship to the impact of the development, the court may hold the municipal action to be an unenforceable taking. *Jones Ins. Trust v. City of Fort Smith,* 731 Fed. Supp. 912 (W.D. Ark., 1990). The decisions are not entirely consistent from state to state.

1. Local development ordinances may require that the developer dedicate ample streets, *Ayres v. City of Los Angeles,* 207 P.2d 1 (Cal. 1949), and pave those streets and install utilities, gutters, and storm sewers. *Petterson v. Naperville,* 137 N.E.2d 371 (Ill. 1956); *In re Spring Valley Dev.,* 300 A.2d 736 (Me 1973); *Deerfield Estates, Inc. v. Township of East Brunswick,* 286 A.2d 498 (N.J. 1971); *Brous v. Smith,* 106 N.E.2d 503 (N.Y. 1954).

2. Courts have upheld a requirement that part of a development be set apart for parks and play-grounds, *Aunt Hack Ridge Estates, Inc. v. Planning Comm'ns,* 230 A.2d 45 (Conn.); *Dept. of Public Works & Bldgs. v. Exchange Nat'l Bank,* 334 N.E.2d 810 (Ill. App. 1975); *Frank Ansuini, Inc., v. City of Cranston,* 264 A.2d 910 (R.I. 1970), or pay a fee in lieu of such dedication for park purposes. *Assoc. of Home Builders v. City of Walnut Creek,* 484 P.2d 606 (Cal. 1971). *But see Berg Dev. Co. v. City of Missouri City,* 603 S.W.2d 273 (Mo. 1980).

3. A developer may be required to donate land for a school site. *Krughoff v. City of Naperville,* 369 N.E.2d 892 (Ill. 1977); *Billings Properties, Inc. v. Yellowstone County,* 394 P.2d 182 (Mont. 1964); *Jenad, Inc. v. Scarsdale,* 218 N.E.2d 673 (N.Y. 1966). *But see Ridgemont Dev. Co. v. East Detroit,* 100 N.W.2d 301 (Mich. 1960).

There is a strong current trend toward sustaining this form of land use and subdivision control. Since it is the development that creates the need and demand for greater govern-mental services, it is fair that the developer bear part of the cost of at least creating the fa-cility that will serve the residents or users of the development. This trend was given a great deal of support by the recent U.S. Supreme Court decision in *Nollan v. California Coastal Comm'n,* 483 U.S. 825 (1987). Although that decision struck down a development re-quirement imposed upon the owner of a beachfront home, the Court's reasoning indicates that if there is a sufficient connection between the development requirement and the ob-jective fostered by the development approval body, the development requirement will be sustained. In *Nollan,* the coastal commission required that the landowners dedicate a ten-foot wide easement to the beach in front of their property to offset the reduction in visual access to the beach caused by the construction and to reduce congestion on the beaches. The Court would have allowed height restrictions and the like to provide more views of the beach, but did not find the required connection between the easement and the problems sup-posedly created by the new construction.

> **EXAMPLE:** A city required that a developer dedicate a substantial part of its land to correct existing street alignment problems, even though the planning staff reported that the pro-posed use of the land would not generate greater traffic than the use permitted under the ex-isting zoning. The court held this requirement invalid because it did not have the necessary connection to the rezoning proposed by the developer. *Rohn v. City of Visalia,* 214 Cal. App. 3d 1463, 263 Cal. Rptr. 319 (1989).

The Supreme Court has determined that there must be a rough proportionality between the nature and extent of the required dedication and the impact of the proposed develop-ment. *Dolan v. City of Tigard,* 572 U.S. 374 (1994). *See* Carol M. Rose, *A Dozen Proposi-tions on Private Property, Public Rights, and the New Takings Legislation,* 52 Wash. & Lee L. Rev. (1995).

31.04 Impact Fees   As can be seen from the preceding discussion of forced dedication, it is generally permissible for a municipality to require that the land developer pay an impact fee or exaction to com-pensate the government for the increase in facilities that will be required to service the de-velopment and the people who live there or who use the developed facilities. *Assoc. of Home Builders v. City of Walnut Creek,* 484 P.2d 606 (Cal. 1971); *Downey v. Wells Sanitary Dist,* 561 A.2d 174 (Me. 1989). *But see Eastern Diversified Properties v. Montgomery County,* 570 A.2d 850 (Md. 1990) (which held that a road impact fee was an *ultra vires* tax by the county).

> **EXAMPLE:** The court sustained a San Francisco ordinance requiring that buildings that contain new office space must pay an impact fee before a certificate of occupancy would be issued. *Ross Bldg. Partnership v. City & County of San Francisco,* 750 P.2d 324 (Cal. 1988).

31.05 Development Rights

Under the zoning laws, a tract of land may be developed to a defined level of intensity. For example, a tract of land 500 feet by 200 feet contains 100,000 square feet or about 2.3 acres. If this land is in a downtown section of a city where the property is zoned for office and commercial use and the zone allows development of up to a 7:1 floor area ratio, a 700,000-square-foot office tower could be built. Development and zoning codes often provide incentives to encourage developers to incorporate features into their development that advance public goals. For example, if the developer constructs a public plaza, connects the project to rapid transit lines, and devotes part of the property to day care facilities, a bonus may be allowed. The result could be the development of a larger project that incorporates these features.

If the land has a historic structure, a church, or some other use that does not permit the use of a part of those development rights, these have independent value and may be transferred to nearby property. Development rights are especially valuable in cities where there are several older buildings of historical significance that can be rehabilitated to serve the needs of today's users and preserved to provide a living record of the past. In another use of this practice, a public facility, such as a museum, can be built and the unused development rights transferred to a neighboring property in exchange for funds to pay for the construction and operation of the public facility.

The transfer of these rights can create the potential for increased real estate taxes for the recipient property, even if the transferred development rights are not used. *Mitsui Fudosan v. County of Los Angeles,* 268 Cal. Rptr. 356 (Cal. App. 1990). James M. Pedowitz, *Transferable Development Rights,* 19 Real Prop. Prob. & Tr. L.J. 604 (1984); David Allan Richards, *Transferable Development Rights: Corrective, Catastrophe or Curiosity,* 12 Real Est. L.J. 26 (1983); Neimann, *Historic Preservation and Transferable Development Rights,* Law Forum 927 (1978); Hershel J. Richman & Lane H. Knedig, *Transfer Development Rights—A Pragmatic View,* 9 Urb. L. 571 (1977); Costonis, *Development Rights Transfer and Landmark Preservation,* 9 Urb. L. Ann. 131 (1975).

31.05(a) Development Rights— Farmland—Transfer

A special problem exists with respect to farmlands.

EXAMPLE: *X* owns a farm that has been in the family for many years. As the nearby suburbs expand, the land becomes valuable for a development, and real estate taxes soar. For example, the land might be worth $1,500 per acre for farming, but $10,000 to $25,000 per acre for development. Under state law, all land must be taxed uniformly at its full market value. *X*'s taxes will go up.

One solution to this problem is for the county to buy the farmer's development rights. The farmer is paid the excess in value above the $1,500 per acre. The farmer gives the county a release of the development rights. He and his successors may continue to farm the land, but no one can use the land for development or purposes other than farming. This reduces the land value back to $1,500 per acre. This technique of purchasing development rights was first used to preserve scenic areas, and is currently being used to preserve landmarks and farmlands. John M. Fowler, *Historic Preservation and the Law Today*, 12 Urb. Law 3 (1980).

31.06 Phased Development— Moratoria— "No Growth"

Some municipalities have provided for phased development.

EXAMPLE: In 1966, the town of Ramapo, New York, adopted a master plan for the future development of the town. As part of the plan, the town adopted a comprehensive zoning ordinance. Nine-tenths of the area was zoned residential. To implement the plan, the town enacted a capital budget for the construction of streets, parks, sewers, and so forth. This plan called for installation over an eighteen-year period, with specific phases to be completed at the end of the sixth and twelfth years. In 1969, an amendment to the ordinance was adopted to require that a special permit would be necessary to construct a residence. When a permit was applied for, the zoning board would consider the area to be built upon, including availability of sewers, parks, schools, roads, and firehouses. Each item was assigned a point value. A minimum of fifteen points was required to qualify for a permit. If public facilities were lacking, the developer was at liberty to construct the needed facilities at its own expense. In this fashion, it could proceed with its development as soon as it acquired the required points. The town considered only its own needs. The area outside the town was ignored. A residential developer applied for plat approval. The plan did not conform to the permit requirements. The developer was turned down. The ordinance was held valid. *Golden v. Town of Ramapo,* 30 N.Y.2d 359, 285 N.E.2d 291, 334 N.Y.S.2d 185, *appeal dismissed,* 409 U.S. 1003 (1977). The scheme is called phased development. *See also Estate of Scott v. Victoria County,* 778 S.W.2d 585 (Tex. App. 1989).

A municipality that imposes a moratorium on development because of the unavailability of local services must make a good faith effort to provide those services in order to permit the landowner, particularly the land developer, to proceed. It is only after such efforts have proved fruitless that the moratorium may be continued, and, of course, development must stop because the municipal services are unable to support added population. Richard M. Golden, *The Thirst for Population Control: The Water Hookup Moratoria and the Duty to Augment Supply,* 27 Hastings L.J. 753 (1976). In short, a municipality can reasonably be expected to exert reasonable efforts. It cannot be expected to perform miracles.

EXAMPLE: The town of Petaluma adopted a housing and zoning plan that specified that only 500 new home permits could be issued per year for five years. The federal courts sustained this. *Constr. Indep. Ass'n of Sonoma County v. City of Petaluma,* 522 F.2d 897 (1975); Section of Local Government Law Committee on Land Use Planning and Zoning, *Land Use Planning and Zoning,* 8 Urb. Law 747, 776 (1976); Daniel R. Soegel, *Zoning—Municipal No Growth Limitations Held Violative of the Right to Travel,* 6 Seton Hall L. Rev. 207 (1974); Case Notes, *Boraas v. Village of Belle Terre: The New, New Equal Protection,* 20 S.W. L.J. 794 (1966). The court held that the concept of public welfare is sufficiently broad to uphold Petaluma's desire to preserve its small town character, its open spaces, and low density of population, and to grow at an orderly and deliberate pace. Obviously, some state courts disagree with this point of view, *Stoney-Brook Dev. Corp. v. Town of Penbroke,* 394 A.2d 835 (N.H. 1978); *Harbor Farms, Inc. v. Nassau Planning Comm'n,* 40 App. Div. 2d 517, 334 N.Y.S.2d 412 (1972); C. Davis Hendricks, *Controlled Growth Zoning, Confronting the Inevitable,* 66 Ky. L.J. 99 (1977); Steven G. Melikan, *Municipal Growth Limitations and the Right to Migration,* 52 So. Cal. L. Rev. 1239 (1979), and are not bound by it.

EXAMPLE: In 1974, the U.S. Supreme Court decided the question of the validity of an ordinance of the Village of Belle Terre on Long Island. The ordinance restricted land use to one-family dwellings, thus ensuring that the village would probably grow no larger than its population of 700, living in 220 residences. *Village of Belle Terre v. Boraas,* 416 U.S. 1536 (1974). This decision totally ignored the enormous growth of population taking place in this country. It dealt only with a claimed violation of the U.S. Constitution. Any state court is free to ignore it when determining whether a violation of its state constitution is involved. *State v. Baker,* 81 N.J. 99, 405 A.2d 368 (1978).

The decisions relating to moratoria are quite inconsistent. Where there is a genuine present danger to the public health, a temporary moratorium is valid.

EXAMPLE: The existing sewage system could not handle any additional buildings. Development may be halted temporarily by the city while the system is expanded. *Lom-Ran Corp. v. Dept. of Envtl. Protection,* 394 A.2d 1233 (N.J. 1978).

The key words here are (1) present danger, (2) temporary moratorium, and (3) expansion of existing facilities. The reasoning is elementary. A landowner has the constitutional right to put the land to use. A municipality cannot force a landowner to leave land vacant indefinitely. The U.S. Constitution protects a landowner's ownership of property, and ownership connotes a right to put the land to use. In the exercise of its police power, a local government can act to protect health. But, somewhere along the line, the landowner must be given the right to use the land for some purpose. Land developers frequently encounter questionable conduct on the part of public officials, including delays in acting on applications for building permits and development approvals. The moratorium must be temporary and reasonably limited as to time. *Wheeler v. City of Pleasant Grove,* 746 F.2d 1437 (11th Cir. 1984); *Schavone Constr. Co. v. Hackensack,* 486 A.2d 330 (N.J. 1985); *Smoke Rise, Inc. v. Washington Comm'n,* 400 F. Supp. 1369 (1975); *Collura v. Town of Arlington,* 329 N.E.2d 733 (Mass. 1975); Orlando E. Delogu, *The Misuse of Land Use Control Powers Must End: Suggestions for Legislative and Judicial Responses*, 32 Maine L. Rev. 29 (1980). The municipality must have a plan to solve the problem. *Smoke Rise, Inc. v. Washington Suburban Sanitary Comm'n,* 400 F. Supp. 1369 (1975).

The opposition of existing communities to any growth is reflected in various other measures. Counties around San Francisco have minimum requirements of twenty, forty, and even sixty acres per home in agricultural areas. Local governments draw up boundaries beyond which they will not extend utility lines. Other communities impose a substantial hookup charge of up to $5,000 per home for furnishing of public services. All these steps, together with those discussed in the zoning chapter, are but aspects of the great battle between existing communities and developers who would like to open them up to development.

31.06(a) Phased Development— Concurrency

A relatively new scheme of development regulation that has attracted much attention is Florida's concurrency requirement. This law is a reaction to the population growth in the state and the demands that the increasing population makes on public facilities, such as roads, sanitary sewer systems, solid waste disposal facilities, drainage systems, potable water systems, recreation facilities, and mass transit. Building permits will not be issued unless, concurrently with the impact of the development, sufficient public facilities will be in place. Kobrin & Rubin, *Concurrency,* Fla. B.J. 55 (Jan. 1990).

31.07 Regulations Preserving Light, Air, and View

There is a growing body of opinion that blocks of boxy high-rise office buildings are destroying the attractiveness of downtown areas. Some cities have taken action. In Austin, Texas, building height is restricted where view of the state capitol dome would be obstructed. In Denver, height restrictions were imposed to preserve views of the Rocky Mountains. San Francisco has elaborate regulations designed to reduce shadows on sidewalks. Christopher J. Duerksen & Mary C. Bean, *Land Use and the Law 1985: A Run on the Bank*, 17 Urb. Law 851 (1985). Slender, tapered buildings are encouraged. Steven L. Vettel, *San Francisco's Downtown Plan: Environmental and Urban Design Values in Central Business District Regulations*, 12 Ecology L.Q. 511 (1985).

31.08 Constitutional Issues

As can be seen, development regulation is at odds with the developer's right to use land any way it sees fit for a profitable venture. The municipality's obligation is to protect the public good by seeing to it that responsible development, and not just any development, occurs. As a result, the municipality's obligation is to balance the need for municipal services and the landowner's right to use its land. As with any governmental decision, political considerations, right or wrong, are present. The types of development and land-use regulation vary from area to area depending upon the particular needs of the community and the way the community has chosen to respond to concerns that are common to many areas. Some planning issues are of state- or regionwide concern and are not left for determination by the local municipality.

> **EXAMPLE:** A state may determine that the protection of its shoreline should not be left to local authorities who may have different motivations and expertise. A state coastal commission will be created, and development within the area defined to constitute the "coast" will have to be approved by that commission.

The overriding consideration today is whether the regulation has gone too far and in effect taken the property without the payment of proper compensation to the landowner. *Pennsylvania Coal Co. v. Mahon,* 260 U.S. 393, 43 S. Ct. 258 (1922). It is one thing to regulate, it is quite another where the regulation in effect confiscates the value of the property in the name of regulation.

> **EXAMPLE:** A developer purchased some wilderness property. The county would not issue a development permit because it wanted to keep the land in its natural state. The court held this action by the county to be invalid. If the county wants the wilderness area preserved, it must resort to condemnation. *Harbor Farms, Inc. v. Nassau County Planning Comm'n,* 334 N.Y.S.2d 412 (1972).

The question is when does the regulation go too far and become a "taking" of the property without the payment of just compensation. All regulation will impact upon the value of the land. The standard cannot be that the government can regulate land use only if the regulation does not diminish the value of the property. As long as the landowner is left with an economically viable use of the land, a taking will not be found. *Agins v. Tiburon,* 447 U.S. 255 (1980).

> **EXAMPLE:** In the *Agins* case, the landowner held a five-acre tract that overlooked San Francisco Bay. The municipality enacted an open-space zoning ordinance, which would have allowed the property to be developed with as few as one and as many as five single-family residences. The court felt the zoning ordinance advanced legitimate state interests by protecting the residents of Tiburon from the ill effects of urbanization while not taking the economically viable use of the land from the owner. The property could still be developed, but not to the degree that the landowner wanted.

The process is exemplified in *First English Evangelical Lutheran Church v. County of Los Angeles,* 482 U.S. 304, 107 S. Ct. 2378 (1987), in which a church owned a retreat center and recreational area for handicapped children that were located in a flood plain. Several natural events coincided and a flood destroyed the camp. The county enacted an ordinance that prohibited construction in the flood plain until a flood control plan was developed. The church sued, saying that the county had in effect taken the property as effectively as if it were condemned. This is called inverse condemnation. The U.S. Supreme Court held that even a temporary prohibition on the enjoyment of the use of the land may be prohibited unless the state compensates the landowner. *See also Tahoe-Sierra Preservation Council, Inc. v. Tahoe Regional Planning Agency,* 911 F.2d 1331 (9th. Cir. 1990).

The Court then sent the case back to the state court to determine whether the church was actually deprived of all use of the property and whether the county could avoid the obligation to compensate the landowner on the grounds that the denial of all use of the property was insulated as a part of the state's authority to enact safety regulations. The state court determined that the ordinance did not deprive the landowner of all use of the land (such as hiking and camping in tents) and was a justified enactment for the protection of public safety. *First English Evangelical Lutheran Church v. County of Los Angeles,* 258 Cal. Rptr. 893 (1989).

If the landowner is to be denied the right to develop its land, the denial must be reasonably related to a legitimate public purpose. *Monterey v. Del Monte Dunes at Monterey, Ltd.,* 526 U.S. 687 (1999). The municipality's action must be related to both the nature and extent of the impact of the proposed development.

A recent case demonstrates the kind of problems that can befall the developer.

> **EXAMPLE:** A developer acquired property and entered into a redevelopment agreement approved by the city council. The agreement provided significant tax benefits to the redeveloper of an old building that was not a designated landmark or historic site. The redevelopment agreement provided that it could not be amended without city council approval. During the early stages of the rehabilitation of the property, it was discovered that the building was not structurally adequate to allow the redevelopment to occur without significant additional cost. The developer attempted to abandon the redevelopment plan and demolish the structure. The local government would not grant the demolition permit. The developer brought an inverse condemnation action asserting that, by not granting the demolition permit, the municipality deprived it of the economic value of its asset. The court disagreed and required the enforcement of the contract that required city council approval of a modification. Without that approval, the developer would have to continue with its redevelopment, even if the cost increased considerably. *The Conlon Group, Inc. v The City of St. Louis,* 780 S.W.2d 37 (Mo. App. 1998), *cert. denied* 119 S. Ct. 1786 (1999).

31.09 Estoppel— Vested Rights— Development Agreements

There has always been a reluctance to apply estoppel where a government body is involved. However, in land development matters, courts are increasingly resorting to this doctrine.

> **EXAMPLE:** In zoning cases where a city has issued a permit to a developer and, in reliance on a building permit, the developer has in good faith expended substantial sums (hiring an architect, obtaining a loan commitment, entering into a construction contract), but has not as yet achieved nonconforming-use status, the courts will, at times, hold the city estopped to cancel the permit.

This is simply a legal way of stating that, in the circumstances, it would be unjust to permit a cancellation of the permit. Here, the courts are balancing the obvious injustice to the developer against the public policy favoring an orderly development of land use that permits a city to alter its plans as circumstances indicate the desirability of doing so. Obviously, courts will differ in their approach to the problem. Richard B. Cunningham & David H. Kremer, *Vested Rights Estoppel and the Land Development Process,* 29 Hastings L.J., 623, 651 (1978). The problem is enormously complicated where several different public bodies issue permits for different aspects of the development.

While the courts often approach this problem in terms of whether the developer's rights had "vested," it is hard to distinguish this view from the rule that protects nonconforming-use status. If a final permit has issued, and substantial commitments were made in reliance on a final permit, the courts have to protect the developer.

> **EXAMPLE:** A developer expended $2,800,000 after the county had approved the plat, but had not obtained a final permit for the work. The court refused to protect the developer, since he had not obtained a final permit. *Avco Community Developers, Inc. v. South Coast Regional Comm'r,* 17 Cal. 3d 785, 553 P.2d 546 (1976), *cert. denied* 429 U.S. 1083 (1977). *But see Bd. of Supervisors v. Med. Structures, Inc.,* 192 S.E.2d 799 (Va. 1972).

The *Avco* decision led to dissatisfaction. Ultimately, California passed a law under which a developer can enter into an agreement with the local government. If the developer proceeds in good faith to comply with the agreement, its rights cannot be revoked. Robert M. Kessler, *The Development Agreement and Its Use in Resolving Large Scale, Multiparty Development Problems: A Look at the Tools and Suggestions for Its Application*, L.J. Land Use & Envtl. Control 451 (1986). William G. Holliman, *Development Agreements and Vested Rights in California*, 13 Urb. Law 44 (1981). This is a just result. Especially where the developer has expended substantial sums with the encouragement of local government, the idea is gaining ground that "every citizen has the right to expect that it will be dealt with fairly by the government." *Hollywood Beach Hotel Co. v. City of Hollywood*, 329 So. 2d 10 (Fla. 1976). Robert Kratovil, *Eminent Domain Revisited and Land Use Problems,* 34 De-Paul L. Rev. 587 (1985).

31.10 Interstate Land Sales Act

The Interstate Land Sales Act, 15 U.S.C. § 1701, *et seq.,* and the regulations issued by the Office of Interstate Land Sales Registration (OILSR), 24 C.F.R. § 1700, *et seq.,* are consumer protection devices that regulate land sales by requiring that lots not be sold or leased until a statement of record is filed with OILSR and a property report is given to the buyer. The statement of record is a comprehensive document that contains information relating to the property and its developer. The property report is a condensed version of the statement of record and is written in a question-and-answer format.

The Act requires that the property report be given to the buyer before the contract is signed. If not, the contract may be revoked at any time during the two years after the contract is signed. A violation of the Act may lead to criminal penalties, and a buyer may sue the seller for damages.

The following transactions are exempt from the Act:

1. The sale or lease of lots in a subdivision containing fewer than twenty-five lots.

2. The sale or lease of lots on which there is a residential or commercial condominium, or industrial building, or the sale or lease of land under a contract obligating the seller to build within two years. This is an important exemption because it benefits homebuilders and developers who contract in good faith to build a structure within two years. If, however, the contract provides that the buyer's sole remedy for the builder/seller's breach of the obligation to build the unit within two years is the termination of the contract and return of the earnest money, this exemption will not apply. *Markowitz v. Northeast Land Co.,* 906 F.2d 100 (3rd Cir. 1990). *See also Samari Dev. Corp. v. Marlow,* 556 So. 2d 1097 (Fla. 1990) (where specific performance but not damages was available as a remedy to the buyer). Contracts permitting the seller to breach effectively at will, have no real obligation binding upon the seller. The developer may provide in the contract that the buyer will be entitled to general damages while the contract may exclude special or consequential damages. *Hardwick Properties, Inc. v. Newbern*, 711 So. 2d 35 (Fla. App. 1998). *See* Susan Lee Voss, *The Improved Lot Exemption and the Interstate Land Sales Full Disclosure Act*, Prob. & Prop. 44 (Sept./Oct. 1992).

3. The sale of evidences of indebtedness secured by a mortgage or deed of trust on real estate.

4. The sale of securities issued by a real estate investment trust.

5. The sale or lease of real estate by any government or government agency.

6. The sale or lease of cemetery lots.

7. The sale or lease of lots to any person who acquires such lots for the purpose of engaging in the business of constructing residential, commercial, or industrial buildings, or for the purpose of resale or lease of such lots to persons engaged in such business.

8. The sale or lease of real estate that is zoned or restricted to commercial or industrial development. 15 U.S.C. § 1702(a).

The following transactions are exempt from the disclosure and registration sections of the Act but are subject to the Act's antifraud provisions:

- The sale or lease of lots in a subdivision containing fewer than 100 lots.

- The sale or lease of less than twelve lots in a twelve-month period.

- The sale or lease of lots in separate, unconnected parts of a subdivision, if the part of the subdivision contains less than twenty-one lots.

- The sale or lease of lots that are twenty acres or larger.

- The sale or lease of lots in a municipality or county that has set minimum development standards, if (1) the subdivision meets local codes; (2) each lot is limited by zoning or otherwise to single-family ownership; (3) roads, water, sewer, and other utilities are available to the lot; (4) the seller must give a deed within 180 days after the contract is signed; (5) title evidence is available; (6) the buyer has made an on-the-lot inspection of the property, and (7) there are no high-pressure sales techniques used to sell the lot.

- The sale or lease of a mobile home site, if the lot is sold or leased by one party and the mobile home is sold or leased by another.

- The sale or lease by a developer who is operating on an intrastate as opposed to an interstate basis, if (1) the lot is free and clear of liens; (2) the purchaser has made an on-the-lot inspection; (3) the contract contains an estimate of when roads, utilities, and amenities will be completed, and (4) the buyer has a seven-day "cooling off" period to revoke the contract.

- The sale or lease of lots to buyers within the same "standard metropolitan statistical area," if the same sort of technical requirements set out in the above exemption are met. 15 U.S.C. § 1702(b).

The Act also regulates installment contracts that are not subject to one of the exemptions by forbidding a damage clause that results in the forfeiture of amounts paid by the buyer in excess of 15 percent of the purchase price or the seller's actual damages. 15 U.S.C. § 1703(b)(3). Robert M. Chasnow & Blaise B. Lirot, *The Federal Interstate Land Sales Act: An Overview,* 2 No. 4 Prob. & Prop. 59 (July/August 1988).

31.11 Local Regulations

With regard to sales not covered by the Interstate Land Sales Act, most states have their local laws regulating lot sales. *The Interstate Land Sales Full Disclosure Act*, 21 Rutgers L. Rev. 714, 720 (1967); J. Jackson Walter, *The Law of the Land: Development Legislation in Maine and Vermont,* 23 Maine L. Rev. 315 (1971).

31.12 Endangered Species Act

As can be seen from the discussion of wetlands regulation, there is a host of miscellaneous legislation that can have a serious impact on land development. One such statutory scheme is the Endangered Species Act. 16 U.S.C. § 1531, *et seq. See* Frona M. Powell, *Property Rights, Federalism and the Endangered Species Act*, 29 Real Est. L.J. 13 (2000). This act prevents the modification or destruction of the habitat of endangered species where the development kills or injures protected wildlife by significantly impairing its essential behavioral patterns such as breeding, feeding, or sheltering. The developer may obtain a permit from the U.S. Fish and Wildlife Service, where the developer's action is incidental to an otherwise lawful activity and the developer demonstrates that it has minimized the impact on the habitat. The developer must present a conservation plan to mitigate the destruction and give assurances that the plan is adequately funded.

31.13 Group Homes—In General

Not too many years ago, orphans found refuge in orphanages and mentally disabled persons were confined in asylums. The concept later developed that these persons would fare better if they were placed in residential-type situations. As a result, small groups of orphans were dispersed into neighborhoods to live with foster parents. Similarly, small groups of mentally disabled persons came to live in family-type settings with supervisory couples. The trend was started, and public authorities and private groups began to acquire or lease large homes to house these groups.

When homes are purchased or leased, they are subject to recorded building restrictions. If the recorded restriction limits the use of the home to single-family occupancy, the question arises whether a group of eight or ten mentally disabled children supervised by foster parents constitutes a "single family." Controversies began all over the country, and the decisions are conflicting. Nora A. Uehlein, Annotation, *Community Residence for Mentally Disabled Persons as Violation of Restrictive Covenant*, 41 A.L.R.4th 1216 (1985).

The same question arises under zoning ordinances where the home is in a single-family zone. Note, *Zoning for the Mentally Ill: A Legislative Mandate*, 16 Harv. J. on Legis. 853 (1979); Penelope A. Boyd, *Strategies in Zoning and Community Living Arrangements for Retarded Citizens: Parens Patriae Meets Police Power*, 25 Vill. L. Rev. 273 (1979-1980).

As is evident, a large home must be acquired or leased to house these groups. Neighbors will often be unhappy with their new neighbors and band together to litigate the legal right of the group home to be maintained. The court decisions are not harmonious.

31.13(a)   Group Homes—Zoning

When a group home is established in a single-family zone, the neighbors may argue that only a single family can occupy homes in this zone and that the group is not a single family.

> **EXAMPLE:** A group of six mentally retarded persons living with two foster parents was held to be a "single family" within the meaning of the zoning ordinance. *Costley v. Caromin House, Inc.,* 313 N.W.2d 21 (Minn. 1981).

There are some decisions to the contrary, holding that such a group is not a family. As a reaction, some states have enacted statutes providing that group homes, within limits, are family units under local zoning ordinances. *But see Clem v. Christole, Inc.,* 548 N.E.2d 1180 (Ind. App. 1990) (invalidating such a law).

Exactly the same problem arises with children who, for one reason or another, must live in a foster home.

> **EXAMPLE:** A foster home for disabled children was held to be a family home. *Linn County v. Hiawatha,* 311 N.W.2d 95 (Iowa 1981). Again, there are some decisions holding that unrelated children are not a family.

Many states have enacted laws that prohibit cities from barring these groups from residential neighborhoods. *Mongony v. Bevilacqua,* 432 A.2d 661 (R.I. 1981). These statutes may be inapplicable to group homes that are run by a business rather than by a not-for-profit or philanthropic organization. *Westwood Homeowner's Ass'n v. Tenhoff,* 745 P.2d 976 (Ariz. App. 1988); *Adult Group Properties, Ltd. v. Imler,* 505 N.E.2d 459 (Ind. App. 1987).

31.13(b)   Group Homes—Building Restrictions

There are, of course, many thousands of building restrictions that limit occupancy to a "single family." The same problem of interpretation arises. *Jackson v. Williams,* 714 P.2d 1017 (Okla. 1985). Again, the courts have difficulty with the question of whether a group of children living with foster parents is a family or a group of mentally disabled persons living in a residential setting violates a single-family restriction. *See* Robert Kratovil, *Group Homes,*

15 Real Est. L.J. 223 (1987); Robert Kratovil, *Group Homes: Building Restrictions and the Police Power,* 7 St. Louis U. L. Rev. 465 (1988). Some states have invalidated private building restrictions that preclude group care homes. *Minder v. Martin Luther Home Found.,* 558 N.E.2d 833 (Ind. App. 1990).

31.13(c) Group Homes— Constitutional Issues

The U.S. Supreme Court has held that the exclusion of a group home violates the constitution where the decision is made simply to please the neighbors and is purely arbitrary. *City of Cleburne v. Cleburne Living Center,* 473 U.S. 432 (1985).

31.13(d) Group Homes— Emerging Issues

As is the case with all areas of the law, the law must react to developments in our society. The statutory and case law will develop to respond to societal developments.

> **EXAMPLE:** A city's refusal to grant a special-use permit for a group home for AIDS patients violated the Fair Housing Act. *Assoc. of Relatives and Friends of AIDS Patients v. Regulations and Permits Admin.,* 740 F. Supp. 95 (D.P.R. 1990*); Baxter v. City of Belleville,* 720 F. Supp. 720 (S.D. Ill. 1989). On the other hand, minimum spacing requirements for group homes do not violate the Fair Housing Act. *Family Style of St. Paul, Inc. v. City of St. Paul,* 923 F.2d 91 (8th Cir. 1991).

> **EXAMPLE:** A church operated a shelter for the homeless. A nearby condominium development sought to enjoin the shelter's operation. The court denied the injunction, stating that fears of crime, drugs, prostitution, and the decline of property values did not outweigh the need to address the problem of homelessness in the area. *Greentree at Murray Hill Condominium v. Good Shepherd Episcopal Church,* 550 N.Y.S.2d 981 (1989).

> **EXAMPLE:** A zoning ordinance that requires a special-use permit for a commercial home day care service in a residential area is valid. *Howard v. City of Garland,* 917 F.2d 898 (5th Cir. 1990).

31.14 Historic Buildings and Areas— In General

Federal law provides for the registration in a list, maintained by the Department of the Interior, of buildings worthy of preservation for historic or architectural value. 16 U.S.C.A. § 461; 16 U.S.C.A. § 470. Each state has a procedure for submitting a building worthy of listing. The Secretary of the Interior may also designate a building if it has national historical significance. Rehabilitation of these buildings must follow federal standards. State laws and city ordinances also provide for preservation of historic buildings.

Where local law allows the designation of a building as a historic property without the owner's consent, litigation may result, since often this building would be more valuable if it could be demolished and a new, larger, and more modern building built in its place.

Historic areas, as distinguished from historic buildings, are often designated under state law, often by the use of zoning power. This was done in the case of the area surrounding the Abraham Lincoln home in Springfield, Illinois.

Where the economy of the area depends on tourism engendered by the historic setting, the zoning is likely to be sustained. Historic zoning prevents changes in the historic nature of the area.

Landmarks consisting of isolated buildings present a different problem.

> **EXAMPLE:** In *Lutheran Church in America v. City of New York,* 345 N.Y.2d 121, 304 N.E.2d 371 (1973), an attempt to freeze an individual landmark that was located in a high economic development area failed.

This area of the law has the same constitutional takings issue found in other areas of land-use regulation and zoning. The constitutional issue can be avoided, of course, by payment of compensation. It has been argued that the city could condemn a development easement by paying an award equal to the difference between the fair market value of the land before taking (when the landowner would have the right to demolish and develop to the highest and best use) and the fair market value immediately after taking the development easement. Note, *Landmark Preservation Law: Compensation for Temporary Taking,* 35 U. Chi. L. Rev. 362 (1965). Such a device is virtually certain to stand up if attacked in the courts.

Predictably, area zoning will fare better in the courts than the freezing of individual landmarks. *Fred F. French Inv. Co. v. City of New York,* 39 N.Y.S.2d 587, 350 N.E.2d 381 (1976); *People v. Ramsey,* 28 Ill. App. 2d 252, 171 N.E.2d 246 (1960).

New York introduced a new idea on the subject of landmark preservation. In 1967, the Landmark Preservation Commission declared Penn Central Terminal in New York City a landmark. Penn Central proposed a plan to erect an office tower above the terminal. Permission was refused. The city proposed to transfer development rights to other Penn Central properties. Both the New York court and the U.S. Supreme Court ruled in favor of the city. What is important here is what the courts did not dispose of. In the first place, Penn Central owns other properties in the vicinity of the terminal that derive their value from proximity to the terminal. In other words, the situation as it existed before the development scheme was initiated was a situation that was not harming Penn Central seriously. Penn Central was making money, and constitutional law does not guarantee any landowner more than a reasonable return. People enthusiastic about landmark preservation have hailed the decision. It is an important decision. But much more litigation will be needed before the law can be regarded as settled. *Rebman v. City of Springfield,* 111 Ill. App. 2d 430, 250 N.E.2d 282 (1969) (sustaining establishment of historical zone around the Abraham Lincoln home in Springfield and citing many cases holding that the preservation of historical areas is well within the concept of public welfare). To like effect are *M. & N. Enterprises, Inc. v. City of Springfield,* 111 Ill. App. 2d 444, 250 N.E.2d 389 (1969), and *Fitzpatrick v. City of Springfield,* 10 Ill. App. 3d 317, 293 N.E.2d 712 (1973).

A recent case has upheld New York City's landmark preservation law, which prevented a church from replacing a sixty-seven-year-old church building with an office tower. The court held this law did not violate the free exercise clause of the Bill of Rights since the church can continue its religious practices in the existing facilities. *Rector, Wardens, and Members of the Vestry of St. Bartholomew's Church v. City of New York,* 914 F.2d 348 (2d Cir. 1990). *See also Tourkow v. City of Ft. Wayne,* 563 N.E.2d 151 (Ind. App. 1990) (which upheld a historic commissions ban of vinyl siding).

31.15 Rights of Artists

Many older properties contain works of art, either on the walls in the form of paintings or mosaics, or in the common areas in the form of sculptures in the lobby or garden. Developers seeking to rehabilitate or redevelop properties with these artworks present need to be aware of the federal Visual Rights of Artists Act, 17 U.S.C. §§ 106A, 113. This law gives the artist the right to prevent any intentional distortion, mutilation or modification of the work that would be prejudicial to the artist's honor or reputation, and to prevent the destruction of a work of recognized stature.

Since the purpose of the law is to preserve artwork, *Carter v. Helmsley-Spear, Inc.,* 861 F. Supp. 303 (S.D.N.Y., 1994), *aff'd in part, rev'd in part, vacated,* 71 F.3d 77 (2d Cir. 1995), *cert. denied* 116 S.C. 1824 (1996), developers should take special care to anticipate the impact of their plans on art in projects they intend to develop. If removal of the artwork will not modify or destroy the work of art, the building owner may notify the artist of the intended removal, give the artist ninety days to remove the work, and not be liable under the Act. Similarly, purchasers of property that contains artwork should take care to determine whether any of the artwork is protected by the Act, thereby limiting the flexibility available if the developer intends to rehab or raze the acquired property. Steven W. Snively, *Artists' Rights Meet Property Rights: An Invisible Restraint*, Prob. & Prop. (Nov/Dec 1995).

CHAPTER 32

Land Use Controls—
Wetlands, the Public Trust,
Beaches, and Navigable Waters

32.01 Definition of the Problem

There are two types of wetlands. Inland wetlands are marshes such as those found in every state of the union. Coastal wetlands are estuarian lands or salt marshes. An estuary occurs where an arm of the sea extends inland to meet the mouth of the river. The tides alternately flood and expose tidal marshes. Both types of wetlands are shallow. Land development is possible through "dredge and fill" operations. It is only recently that we have come to realize that our ecological health depends upon these wetlands and that wetlands are disappearing as development progresses.

Wetlands are an important natural resource because of the following:

1. They are nature's way of controlling floods. Wetlands act as giant sponges, absorbing vast amounts of water and then releasing the water gradually. Paving the wetland area creates a flood problem. Estuarian lands, with their mixture of peat, bog, moss, and so forth, absorb the moisture from incoming storms.

2. Inland wetlands maintain groundwater at proper levels. If groundwater is drained, a desert may result.

3. Estuarian lands are an important source of food supply. Carbohydrates and vitamins wash out to sea from the estuaries and greatly increase the number of fish and oysters that the ocean can produce. A large quantity of sea life depends on the estuaries for survival. A great many ocean fish can reproduce only in the estuaries. A classic illustration is that of the salmon that come back to the stream of their birth and go upstream to spawn. Fishermen, fishing villages, and tourist trade depend upon the estuaries. Wild fowl, such as ducks and geese, cannot exist without wetlands. They are necessary for reproduction, migration, and as winter feeding grounds.

4. They absorb polluted air and water and make them clean and wholesome. The following court decision points up the legal problems that arise in the wetlands area.

   EXAMPLE: Ronald and Kathryn Just, land developers, bought a large tract of land in Wisconsin. When their plans became public knowledge, Marinette County passed an ordinance making any reasonable use of wetlands land impossible. Cranberry picking and other low- or no-income activities were permitted. When the Justs went ahead in defiance of the law, they were stopped by the courts. The Wisconsin Supreme Court sustained the law. *Just v. Marinette County,* 56 Wis. 2d 7, 201 N.W.2d 761 (1972). The dilemma is plain. If all developers are allowed to develop wetlands, the landowners are protected from loss of land value, but the surrounding country may be damaged.

The decisions directly relating to wetlands regulation are somewhat in conflict. In *Morris County Land & Improvement Co. v. Township of Parsippany-Troy Hills,* 40 N.J. 539, 193 A.2d 232 (1963), the township had amended its zoning ordinance to create a meadowlands zone designed to preserve the swampland for flood control purposes. Only minor uses were permitted, such as commercial greenhouses. The landowner wished to develop the land for intensive commercial development. The court held for the developer. In *State v. Johnson,* 265 A.2d 711 (Me. 1970), the court held that the preservation of wetlands was a laudable purpose, but that the cost must be publicly borne. The landowner must be paid by the state if development rights are taken. *See also MacGibbon v. Bd. of Appeals,* 350 Mass. 635, 255 N.E.2d 347 (1970); *Presbytery of Seattle v. King County*, 787 P.2d 907 (Wash. 1990). Some cases have been decided against the landowner. *Brecciaroli v. Connecticut Comm'r of Envtl. Protection,* 36 Conn. L.J. 42, p. 4 (S. Ct. Jan. Term 1975); *Potomac Sand & Gravel Co. v. Governor,* 293 A.2d 241 (Md. 1972); *S. Volpe & Co., Inc. v. Bd. of Appeals,* 348 N.E.2d 807 (Mass. App. 1976); *State v. Reed,* 78 Misc. 2d 1004 (N.Y.)

32.02   Wetlands Regulation

The federal Clean Water Act requires that a permit be issued before a nontidal wetland can be filled or dredged materials placed into the wetlands. 33 U.S.C. § 1344. The identification of wetlands is often a problem. While the definition is easy to recite, it is difficult to locate the wetland and define its boundaries on the ground. By definition, a wetland is an area that is inundated or saturated by surface water or groundwater at a frequency and duration sufficient to support a prevalence of vegetation typically adapted to saturated soil conditions. 33 C.F.R. § 328.3. The Supreme Court has recently ruled, however, that a wetland is not found merely because migratory birds may use it as a habitat. *Solid Waste Agency of Northern Illinois v. United States Army Corps of Engineers,* 531 U.S., 148 L.Ed.2d 576 (2001).

The mere designation of an area as a wetland does not constitute a taking, even if that designation results in the requirement that a permit be obtained before development may begin. *Bond v. Dept. of Natural Resources,* 454 N.W.2d 395 (Mich. App. 1989).

Permits for wetland development are issued by the Army Corps of Engineers. The Clean Water Act allows the Corps to issue general permits on a state, regional, or national basis for categories of activities if the Corps has determined that such activities, taken individually or together, are similar in nature and cause only minimal adverse environmental effects. 33 U.S.C. § 1344(e). Of course, these nationwide permits are issued with a related set of guidelines and standards. If more than one-tenth of an acre of wetlands are to be filled, the Corps of Engineers must receive thirty days prior notice before the commencement of the fill. If the fill is to affect more than one-half of an acre or more than 200 lineal feet of stream, an individual permit must be obtained from the Corps. Buffers must be installed around all wetlands, rivers, streams, creeks, and other water bodies. Development activities in flood plains are also severely limited. If any of the permitted criteria are not satisfied, then an individual permit must be obtained from the Corps prior to such development.

32.03   The Public Trust Doctrine

There is another theory that impacts upon the state's ability to regulate and control development in these areas.

> **EXAMPLE:** In *Int'l Paper Co. v. Mississippi State Highway Dept.,* 271 So. 2d 395 (Miss. 1973), a landowner claimed ownership of an island in the Pascagoula River because a prior owner, from whom it had purchased the island, had received a grant from the state. The state of Mississippi argued, and its supreme court held, that ownership of all tidelands, the spaces between ordinary high- and low-water marks, the bed of a bay, and all bodies of land arising from the bay floor are forever held in a public trust by the state. Such land cannot be sold to private persons. The concept is that this area never passed into private ownership and is still owned by the state. Of course, since the state owns the land, it can control whatever is built on it. A number of states follow this public trust rule.

EXAMPLE: The owner of land abutting on the ocean sought to fill and develop the tidelands abutting the property. The court held the power of the state to control its navigable waters; the land beneath them was held in a public trust and was within the absolute control of the state. *Marks v. Whitney,* 6 Cal. 3d 251, 491 P.2d 374, 98 Cal. Rptr. 790 (1971). This was true even though a prior owner had purchased the submerged land from the state.

The test of whether property is subject to the public trust doctrine is whether the property is tidal, not whether the property is in the navigable waters. Even long-standing record title and the payment of real estate taxes is not sufficient to upset the state's constitutionally based claim to land under the tidal waters, even if those waters are not navigable. *Phillips Petroleum Co. v. Mississippi,* 484 U.S.469, 108 S. Ct. 791 (1988). This title or ownership passed to the states at the time of their admission to the Union. After being admitted, each state was free to deal with this land as it saw fit. Many coastal states have granted some or all of these tidelands to adjacent upland owners. Of course, the tidelands have remained subject to the federal navigational servitude, *Appleby v. New York,* 271 U.S. 364, 46 S. Ct. 569 (1925), and the public's right to use for fishing, bathing, and the like. *Bradford v. The Nature Conservancy,* 294 S.E.2d 866 (Va. 1982).

32.04 Navigable Waters

Another approach to the problem rests upon the claims of the federal and state governments to control navigable waters. It is, of course, elementary that both government bodies have and exercise control over both salt and fresh navigable waters. *Phillips Petroleum Co. v. Mississippi,* 484 U.S. 469, 477, 108 S. Ct. 791, 796 (1988). What is surprising is the position they maintain, sustained by the courts, that waters once navigable are always navigable. *United States v. Stoeco Homes,* 359 F. Supp. 672 (D.N.J. 1973). The underlying concept here is that title to the bed of a navigable lake is in the state in trust for the people. *Wilton v. VanHessen,* 249 Ill. 182 (1911). Thus, even though land under navigable water was filled and built on as long as 100 years ago, it is still navigable, and either public body can compel removal of the improvements. Navigable water is subject to federal and state servitudes. Either government can halt construction if it can show that the construction is on "navigable waters." In this context, water is navigable if it is or once was navigable, or if it is or once was part of the tidelands and marshlands of the aquatic ecosystem surrounding the navigable water. *Potomac Sand & Gravel Co. v. Governor,* 266 Md. 358, 293 A.2d 241 (1972).

EXAMPLE: Landowner wanted to dredge in the navigable waters of Boca Ciega Bay in order to create a trailer park. The permit was denied by the United States because construction would have a destructive effect on wildlife. *Zabel v. Tabb,* 430 F.2d 199 (5th Cir. 1970).

EXAMPLE: Where the builder erected mobile homes on coastal marshland without a permit, it was compelled to remove them. *United States v. Moretti,* 478 F.2d 418 (5th Cir. 1973).

32.05 Beaches

Since the history of this country began, it has been assumed that one who buys lands abutting on waters, navigable or nonnavigable, has the right to enjoy the beach as his or her private domain. In lands abutting on tidal waters, this right generally stops at the high-water mark. Landward of that line, the public has no right to picnic or stroll. *In re Opinion of Justices,* 313 N.E.2d 561 (Mass. 1974). The courts have, however, discovered that the public should be allowed to use and enjoy these beaches and have evolved a variety of theories that would enable the public to enjoy such rights, much to the dismay of riparian landowners who paid dearly for their riparian rights and the right to enjoy these beaches in privacy.

Some remarkable decisions have been handed down in order to enable the public to enjoy the beaches.

> **EXAMPLE:** In California, it has been held that where a riparian landowner over a five-year period made no objection to the use of his beach by the public, there exists an implied dedication to the public, and the landowner must allow public use. The reference here is to the beach area above high-water mark, where ordinarily the public has no rights. *County of Orange v. Chandler-Sherman Corp.,* 126 Cal. Rptr. 765 (1973); Charles R. Manzoni, Jr., Comment, *A Threat to Owners of California Shoreline,* 11 Santa Clara L. Rev. 327; Vitauts M. Gullois, Annotation, *Implied Acceptance by Public Use of Dedication of Beach or Shoreline Adjoining Public Waters,* 24 A.L.R.4th 294 (1983).

> **EXAMPLE:** In Oregon, the courts have held that the public has a customary right to the use of the dry sand area. *State ex rel Thornton v. Hay,* 462 P.2d 671 (Or. 1969).

> **EXAMPLE:** In New Jersey, it has been held that land contiguous to a beach is unique and therefore subject to strict zoning. *Frankel v. Atlantic City,* 63 N.J. 333, 307 A.2d 562 (1973). This makes sense. Any person buying beach property ought to recognize that the public will want it kept free from undesirable uses.

> **EXAMPLE:** Under the "public trust" rule, Massachusetts holds that land below the high-water mark, even though sold by the state to a private landowner, remains subject to the public rights of fishing and navigation. *In re Opinion of the Justices,* 313 N.E.2d 561 (1974).

This open-beach easement moves as the lines of mean low tide and of vegetation shift as the beach moves, even as a result of a hurricane. *Matcha v. Mattox,* 711 S.W.2d 95 (Tex. App. 1986). As a result, the beachfront landowner does not know where the seaward line of private property may be from time to time.

No doubt other states will reach out into the beaches to give the public rights in them. As can be seen, the California rule punishes the "nice guy." The Oregon rule, discovering a customary right after millions have been spent by purchasers of riparian land, seems unfair. The fact is that private landowners are now being punished for years of public neglect.

CHAPTER 33

Homeowners' Association

33.01 In General The homeowners' association (HOA) is an interesting legal creature. It derived its early utility in connection with enforcement of general plan building restrictions in the old-fashioned subdivision of single-family dwellings.

> **EXAMPLE:** Developer plats a subdivision of 100 lots and, by using a recorded declaration of restrictions, provides that only single-family dwellings shall be erected and a fifteen-foot front building line shall be observed. The declaration also provides that HOA Corp., a nonprofit corporation whose members are the lot owners in the development, may enforce the restrictions and shall collect an annual assessment from each lot owner to pay the costs of maintaining the common landscaped and paved areas and the amenities, such as the swimming pool and tennis courts. Ultimately, Developer sells all of the lots. Developer then has no interest in protecting the lot owners from violations of the restrictions. Lot Owner begins construction of a store that will come all the way to the street or lot line. Any one homeowner might be disinclined to hire a lawyer and engage in costly litigation to enforce the restrictions. HOA Corp. has the power to cause Lot Owner to discontinue construction and to remove the foundations it has constructed. If Lot Owner does not comply with HOA Corp.'s demands, HOA Corp. may sue to enjoin or stop the violations. The declaration will also typically allow the association to recover the legal fees and costs incurred in enforcing the declaration against Lot Owner; if Lot Owner does not pay these fees and costs, they will become a lien against Lot Owner's property in the development.

Some states have enacted laws governing these associations other than those associated with condominiums and cooperatives. Indeed, a uniform law, the Uniform Common Interest Ownership Act, or UCIOA, has been promulgated to apply to all of such communities where a unit or homeowner pays a share of the real estate taxes, insurance premiums, maintenance, or improvement expenses related to the development.

33.02 Legal Form of Association The HOA is a form of private government. There is something of a misnomer here. Although real estate personnel talk of a "homeowners' association" or "condominium association" they are most often actually referring to a not-for-profit corporation organized pursuant to the declaration of covenants, conditions, restrictions, easements, and liens.

Unincorporated associations must be avoided, for, traditionally, these have very little in the way of legal existence or status. An unincorporated association cannot bring or defend lawsuits in its own name. Instead, it must act through all of its members, an inconvenience at least, and a danger to the members at worst. Of critical importance to the homeowners themselves is the fact that the members of an unincorporated association bear the risk of unlimited liabilities, for example, for personal injuries incurred in areas under the control of the association. In the current setting, those that participate in the governance of a common interest community, and even association members themselves, are exposed to litigation by aggressive owners who challenge the association's actions against them. These fights have become bitter, long lasting, and expensive. The individual owners should not be exposed to liability as a result of the form of the organization being an unincorporated association.

In addition, an unincorporated association cannot hold ownership of land. *Delaware Land and Dev. Co. v. First & Central Presbyterian Church,* 147 A.165 (Del. 1929); Ford, *Dispositions of Property to Unincorporated Non-Profit Associations,* 55 Mich. L. Rev. 67, 235 (1956).

As with any corporation, there are bylaws and a corporate charter. In the beginning, the developer is typically the only member of the corporation. A nonprofit corporation, be it noted, has no shareholders; it has members. As homes are sold, each homeowner automatically becomes a member of the corporation. Typically, when a certain percentage of lots are sold, the developer must relinquish control over the association to the owners. U.C.I.O.A. § 3-103. Of course, even when this point is reached, the developer retains the votes associated with the unsold lots.

33.03 Membership

Membership in the HOA is automatic. Each unit purchaser automatically becomes a member upon acquisition of the property. Membership passes automatically upon the first and any subsequent purchase.

33.04 Meetings

Every corporation holds meetings. All corporate business of importance is conducted at these meetings. The association's board of directors usually meets monthly. The entire membership meets at least once a year, when the annual budget is discussed.

As is true of all corporations, proper notice must be given to all directors of a directors' meeting. Failure to do so invalidates the action taken at the meeting. Likewise, proper notice must be given of any unit owners' meeting.

33.05 The HOA as a Vehicle for Enforcing Restrictions, Liens, and Covenants

In any land development where both an HOA and a declaration exist, the right of enforcement of restrictions, liens, and covenants is transferred by the declaration to the association. *Merrionette Manor Homes Improvement Ass'n v. Heda,* 136 N.E.2d 556 (Ill. App. 1956*); Garden Dist. Property Owners' Ass'n v. New Orleans,* 98 So. 2d 922 (La. App. 1957); *Neponsit Property Owners' Ass'n v. Emigrant Indus. Sav. Bank,* 15 N.E.2d 793 (N.Y. 1938); *Rodruck v. Sand Point Maintenance Comm'n,* 295 P.2d 714 (Wash. 1956). Subsequent owners of the land become burdened with the restrictions of these declarations and covenants and obtain the benefits of the association. *Lincolnshire Civic Ass'n, Inc. v. Beach,* 364 N.Y.S.2d 248 (1975).

At times, it is suggested that the association is acting as an agent of the property owners. *Neponsit Property Owners' Ass'n v. Emigrant Indus. Sav. Bank,* 15 N.E.2d 793 (N.Y. 1938). At other times, it is suggested that it is acting as a third-party beneficiary of the covenants in the declaration. *Anthony v. Brea Glenbrook Club,* 130 Cal. Rptr. 32 (1976). Or, it is acting as the assignee of the developer. Occasionally, it is simply said that the association is a "convenient instrument by which the property owners may advance their common interests." *Neponsit Property Owners' Ass'n, v. Emigrant Indus. Sav. Bank,* 15 N.E.2d 293 (N.Y. 1938); *In re Public Beach, Borough of Queens,* 199 N.E. 5 (N.Y. 1935). It does no harm to combine all these thoughts into the declaration.

33.06 Other Uses of the HOA

Once the HOA had been invented by lawyers and approved by the courts, other uses were found for this device. In a condominium, the HOA operates the property and performs all of the customary business functions traditionally performed by a landlord. Each condominium unit owner, as a member of the HOA, votes to elect a board of directors. In a planned unit development (PUD), the HOA owns and manages the common areas and often provides exterior maintenance of the individually owned home units. In modern condominiums, if the building contains stores as well as residential units, ownership of the stores may be vested in the HOA and leased to retailers, or the stores may be a part of a separate condominium with its own separate owners' association. Often, large- or mixed-use development may be governed by several associations. For example, sequentially developed phases of the development may each have their own association, with a separate association being created for the commercial condominiums; then, a master association may be created to govern the entire complex.

33.07   The Documents

The declaration, the corporate charter and bylaws of the HOA, and the state's not-for-profit corporation law determine the powers, functions, title, rights, and duties of the HOA, its board of directors, and its officers.

> **EXAMPLE:** The bylaws of a condominium forbid any unit owner to rent a unit to a tenant. The HOA may obtain an injunction against any unit owner who rents out the unit. *Le Febvre v. Osterndorf*, 275 N.W.2d 154 (Wis. App. 1978).

The bylaws represent a form of private lawmaking, and unit owners agree to be bound by the bylaws when they acquire a unit in a common-interest community. The unit owners also derive their rights from these documents, and these documents set forth their duties. The members are also obliged to obey the rules adopted by the board of directors.

> **EXAMPLE:** The rules of a condominium forbid leaving baby buggies in the lobby. The HOA may enforce this rule.

33.08   Power of the HOA—Statutes and Regulations

In addition to the powers granted to the board by the declaration and bylaws, the board has all of the powers granted to such boards by state law. Charles C. Marvel, Annotation, *Construction of Contractual or State Regulatory Provisions Respecting Formation, Composition, and Powers of Governing Body of Condominium Association,* 13 A.L.R.4th 598 (1982). These grants typically contain broad language, giving the board the powers necessary or convenient for the operation of the development. There are various forms of disclosures required of developers of common-interest projects. These regulations may be on the federal level, on the state level as required by state land sales acts or subdivision laws, or on the local level as required by county or municipal ordinance. In some instances, there may even be regulation directed specifically at offerings of memberships in HOAs. The task for the developer and its attorney is to determine which regulations apply, and to comply with their requirements.

33.09   Liability of the HOA and Its Officers and Directors

The HOA has control over certain areas in a common-interest community, and makes what are, in effect, business decisions for administering the property. With this control comes liability. This liability may fall upon the association itself, as where someone may be injured because of the defective condition of the property. Liability may also fall upon the officers and directors. Even though these people often serve for the good of the project and for no compensation, their acts may bring personal liability to them. HOA directors' and officers' liability insurance and indemnifications are required if the association is to attract qualified personnel to serve in these important roles. Following are examples of instances where officers or directors of a condominium or PUD were held liable:

- Criminal assault on a unit owner. *Frances T. v. Village Green Owners Ass'n*, 723 P.2d 573 (Cal. 1986); Olar v. Schroit, 202 Cal. Rptr. 457 (1984); Allan E. Korpela, *Annotation, Liability of Condominium Association* or *Corporation for Injury Allegedly Caused by Condition of Premises*, 45 A.L.R.3d 1171 (1972).
- Racial discrimination. *Tillman v. Wheaton-Haven Ass'n*, 517 F.2d 1141 (4th Cir. 1975).
- Failure to establish reserve fund. *Raven's Cove Townhomes, Inc. v. Knuppe Dev. Co.*, 171 Cal. Rptr. 334 (1981).
- Conflict of interest. *Avila South Condominium Ass'n v. Kappa Corp.*, 347 So. 2d 599 (Fla. 1977).

33.10 Master HOA   Many developments take place in stages. Often, the reason for this is a practical business judgment. If phase one sells out nicely, the developer moves on to phase two, and so on. It is a matter of convenience for each phase to have its own HOA and to place a master or umbrella HOA over the entire project. The master HOA employs a general manager and provides services needed for the entire project, such as the maintenance of the facilities that are common to the entire project.

33.11 Stages in Transfer of Control of Common Areas   One can think of the transfer of control over a common-interest development as taking place in phases. First comes the phase of land acquisition and assembly. Then comes the rezoning and plat approval stage. Next comes the preparation, execution, and recording of the declaration. Up to this moment, the declaration lacks legal efficacy, because the developer owns all the land. Easements, covenants, and restrictions require divided ownership, with one property owner enforcing his or her rights against others. Finally comes the phase when the developer makes deeds to unit purchasers, subjecting the units sold and the units retained to the scheme of restrictions, covenants, and easements, and then beginning the transfer of control to the homeowners.

At this stage, the HOA is still under the control of the developer. As the lot or home site sales proceed, under the declaration and corporation documents, the developer's representation decreases, until, ultimately, the developer's rights are phased out. By establishing the HOA, the developer has absolute power in the beginning stages of growth of the development. By appointing the first board of directors, the developer maintains effective control for the first period of the development. As sales continue, the control of the board shifts to the owners through their ever-increasing vote.

When the homeowners have gained control, they may adopt their own bylaws to reflect their experiences and accomplish their purposes.

33.12 Standing to Sue   There is a principle of law that requires a plaintiff who files a suit to have a sufficient interest in the property involved to qualify the plaintiff to bring the suit. Current statutes take this into account, and, although there are earlier decisions to the contrary, current decisions allow the HOA to bring various kinds of suits.

> **EXAMPLE:** An HOA had standing to sue the developer/builder for defects in the building. *Briarcliffe West Townhouse Owners Ass'n v. Wiseman Constr. Co.,* 118 Ill. App. 3d 163, 454 N.E.2d 363 (statute was later amended to make clear that this was the law); *Quail Hollow East v. Donald J. Scholz Co.,* 268 S.E.2d 12 (N.C. App. 1980).

Of course, there are quite a number of cases holding that the HOA lacks standing to sue. *Friendly Village Community Ass'n v. Silva & Hill Constr. Co.*, 107 Cal. Rptr. 123 (1973). Much depends on the type of suit involved.

CHAPTER 34

The Declaration of Restrictions, Easements, Liens, and Covenants: The Master Deed

34.01 In General

In today's developments, property rights of considerable complexity are created. This is true particularly of the condominium, the planned unit development (PUD) or other common-interest community, and multiuse projects that are so common in today's developments. Supplementing and implementing the local zoning ordinance in such developments will be a scheme of annexation agreements, development agreements, and planning conditions, together with private building covenants, easements, liens, and restrictions. Through these documents, the unit owner, by acquisition of its unit, covenants to do a number of things. For example, the unit owner agrees to only use the unit for certain permitted purposes and to pay maintenance assessments, which are foreclosable liens on the individual parcels. These use restrictions are much broader than merely limiting the owner's right to use the property, say, for residential purposes; matters such as fence height, landscaping, exterior maintenance, and the like are also covered.

Through these covenants and restrictions, each landowner will enjoy a number of valuable easements over the other property in the development and have the benefit of a set of development and use controls that burden and benefit all units or parcels of the development. These detailed rights and obligations should be set forth in a declaration of restrictions, easements, liens, and covenants, and only relatively brief reference should be made to them in the deeds of conveyance. In the case of condominiums, this document is, in some states, referred to as the "master deed."

The legality of the establishment of this plan of development and use rests upon the rule that if a recorded document, such as a deed, makes reference to another recorded document, the two are read together. Thus, the provisions of the declaration are treated legally as if they were set out in full in the deed. Wayne F. Foster, Annotation, *Recorded Real Property Instruments as Charging Third Party with Constructive Notice of Provisions of Extrinsic Instrument Referred to Therein*, 89 A.L.R.3d 901 (1979); *Strickland v. Overman*, 181 S.E.2d 136 (N.C. App. 1971).

34.02 History of the Declaration

Originally, the developer used deeds containing identical restrictions in creating general plan restrictions. This proved impractical.

> **EXAMPLE:** Developer recorded a plat dividing land into 200 lots. Developer then conveyed 150 scattered lots by deeds containing identical restrictions. Developer dies. Developer's heirs proceed to sell the remaining 50 lots to anyone who is willing to buy. No restrictions appear in the deeds. Obviously, there is no general plan. The required uniformity is lacking.

Developers began to place the restriction in the recorded plat of subdivision. This served two purposes. Because the plat covers all lots in the subdivision, a general plan of restrictions was disclosed. Since a plat is a recordable document, its recording imparts constructive notice of the restrictions. Also, from a practical perspective, the reference to the terms of the declaration in the deed greatly reduces the size of the deed, an important factor when considered in light of the fact that large developments will involve the recording of hundreds of deeds with the same language repeated over and over in each deed.

As time wore on, restriction plans became complex and lengthy. Physically, there was no room on the face of the plat for these complex restrictions. Hence, the developer simply placed on the plat a legend stating that "All land in this subdivision is subject to the restrictions appearing in a Declaration of Restrictions recorded contemporaneously herewith." When the plat was handed to the recorder, it was accompanied by a separate document, the declaration of restrictions, which sets forth the restrictions and a statement that they were to be treated as part of the plat. This declaration was signed by the developer and duly notarized. This procedure is called "incorporation by reference" and is quite valid.

When PUDs and condominiums came along, a need was perceived for legal machinery to enforce the assessments needed to provide the funds to operate the common areas. The declaration was again utilized, this time to create the lien for the enforcement of the assessments and the covenant by the unit owner to pay the assessment. The declaration thus came to serve an additional purpose.

Finally, some legal body was needed to enforce restrictions, collect assessments, and operate the condominium and the PUD. The homeowners' association was created and brought into the declaration.

As is evident, over a long period of time, the declaration evolved into a very useful and ever longer and more complicated document.

34.03   Declaration and Other Document Provisions

The homeowners' association declaration in a PUD is modeled, in part, after the condominium declaration, which in turn is modeled after the declaration used to create building restrictions. In both the condominium and the PUD, buyers like to see some limit on the increase in annual assessments, but there should be a provision that a stated percentage of unit owners can, at a regularly called meeting, authorize an expenditure that exceeds the maximum. If the roof leaks, for example, it must be fixed regardless of cost.

Every set of bylaws should state a percentage of the membership that will constitute a quorum. It is best to keep this percentage low, since members tend to shun these meetings.

The association should hold meetings in strict accordance with its bylaws and elect officers at the proper time. The elected secretary should keep careful minutes of meetings, custody of the association's books and papers, insurance policies, and so forth. In a PUD, the common area will be covered by title insurance in the name of the association. Of course, the association will take out liability insurance and hazard insurance on buildings owned by the association—for example, on recreation buildings.

If the local law requires the lien of an unpaid assessment to be recorded, the secretary attends to this and keeps the recorded notice of lien in the records. The bylaws will provide for interest on delinquent assessments. Assessments cannot be levied if the purpose is one not authorized by the documents. *Spitser v. Kentwood Home Guardians,* 24 Cal. App. 3d 215 (1972). While the declaration and bylaws may impose many of these obligations on the officers, day-to-day administration is typically handled by a management company that is skilled in the management of condominiums or other common-interest communities. Occasionally, smaller communities are self-managed. If so, the board does not have the support of a trained professional manager and it must be very careful to adhere to the procedural rules and administrative details of running the association.

The declaration is now a standard real estate document, used to create easements, building restrictions, PUDs, and condominiums. Robert Kratovil, *Building Restrictions—Contracts or Servitudes,* 11 J. Marshall J. Prac. & Proc. 465 (1978). When recorded, it imparts constructive notice. *Bessemer v. Gersten,* 381 So. 2d 1944 (Fla. 1980); *Lake Sherwood Estates v. Continental Bank,* 677 S.W.2d 372 (Mo. App. 1984); *Seaton v. Clifford,* 100 Cal. Rptr. 779 (1972); *Strickland v. Overman,* 181 S.E.2d 136 (N.C. App. 1970); *Preston Tower Condominium Ass'n v. S.B. Realty,* 685 S.W.2d 98 (Tex. App. 1985).

34.04 Amendments

All well-drafted declarations contain clauses permitting amendment. This clause should set forth a procedure to be followed. If the procedure is not followed, the amendment will be void. *Wolinsky v. Kadison,* 114 Ill. App. 3d 507, 449 N.E.2d 151 (1983).

> **EXAMPLE:** The declaration calls for a two-thirds vote of all members to modify the declaration. A bare majority voted for the amendment. It did not pass.

An amendment must also be reasonable or it will be declared to be void. *Crest Builders, Inc. v. Willow Falls Improvement Ass'n,* 74 Ill App. 3d 420, 393 N.E.2d 107.

In general, a purchaser of a lot, unit, or condominium apartment is treated as relying on the declaration, as amended, that is on file in the public records when the property is purchased.

Once a declaration has been recorded and some deeds issued, the developer is powerless to change the easements or other provisions of the declaration unless the declaration so provides. *Howorka v. Harbor Island Owners' Ass'n,* 365 S.E.2d 433 (S.C. App. 1987). Many declarations do reserve this power to amend the declaration, add additional property, and so on. This is necessary to allow the developer to conduct its business. Of course, the developer must act reasonably and not to oppress the owners.

34.05 Restrictions

Since all that is needed to create enforceable building restrictions or easements is a recorded document that gives public or constructive notice of the restrictions or easements, a recorded declaration will suffice for this purpose, when followed by deeds referring to the declaration. *Spencer v. Poole,* 207 Ga. 155, 60 S.E.2d 371 (1950); *Davis v. Huguenor,* 408 Ill. 468, 97 N.E.2d 295 (1951); *Kosel v. Stone,* 146 Mont. 218, 404 P.2d 894 (1965); *Lawrence v. Brockelman,* 155 N.Y.S.2d 604 (1956); J.E. Keefe, Jr., Annotation, *Omission from Deed of Restrictive Covenant Imposed by General Plan of Submission,* 4 A.L.R.2d 1364 (1949).

There will be restrictions as to the home sites or apartments and restrictions as to the common areas. For obvious reasons, the developer must not retain the right to modify the restrictions. This may destroy the general plan and render the restrictions unenforceable. 40 A.L.R.3d 864. Also, the declaration must be recorded before any deed or mortgage is recorded, for any deed recorded before the declaration will not be subject to the restrictions, easements, or other rights created by the declaration. All of the deeds from the developer should be expressly subject to the declaration.

The fact that complex building restrictions can be created by a declaration of restrictions does not prevent the creation of restrictions by inserting them in the plat of subdivision. Indeed, that is the logical place for insertion of simple building restrictions, such as setback lines. The declaration is the place for lengthy and more complex matters. Robert Kratovil, *Building Restrictions—Contracts or Servitudes,* 11 J. Marshall J. Prac. & Proc. 465 (1978).

34.06   Easements   Since the law does not specify any particular form an easement must take, the creation of easements by means of a recorded declaration is universally recognized as a proper means of creating easements. The right to use the common areas must be given by the easements and covenants found in the declaration. It should not be done by dedication. A dedication is a giving of rights to the public. Hence, use of the word "dedication" is to be avoided, for this word has no place in the creation of private, as distinguished from public, rights. *Drye v. Eagle Rock Ranch, Inc.,* 364 S.W.2d 196 (Tex. Civ. App. 1962).

When a tall building is divided into multiple uses, such as retail space at the ground floor, office space on the lower floors, and residential apartments on the upper floors, the declaration of easements is quite complicated. It is also accompanied by or incorporated into an operating agreement, which sets out the duties of the party who is to operate the elevators, repair water pipes and electrical systems, and otherwise operate and maintain areas and systems that are common to all uses and ownerships.

34.07   Phased Development   It is quite possible to develop a property in several stages. This is a convenience to the developer. It can limit its investment to sequential or geographic stages. If a stage is not a success, the developer need not develop additional stages. The additional, undeveloped stages can be sold as raw land. It then becomes important to ensure that the building restrictions on developed stages do not "pour over" into the undeveloped stages.

However, as to the common elements (e.g., the swimming pool in stage one), the declaration should make it clear whether the developer has the power to bring in several successive stages, all of which will share the use of the pool.

This may present a problem in the future. What if the project is not as successful as originally planned? What will become of the common elements? If they were built to accommodate the entire complex, they may be too great of a burden on the first phases alone. The upkeep cost to the individual owners may be extreme. Yet, if the project does not succeed, the developer will want the flexibility to deal with the add-on parcels, free from the burdens of the original development scheme. A lot of thought must be given to this issue on both the developer's side and the buyer's side.

34.08   Party Walls   Where party walls are involved, such as in a town house or row house development, the declaration will contain detailed party wall provisions, including a provision that the cost of reasonable repair and maintenance shall be shared by the owners who make use of the wall in proportion to such use.

34.09   Lien of Assessments   Both in the condominium and the PUD, the homeowners' association will want a provision in the declaration giving it the right to levy assessments on the homeowner for maintenance of the common areas.

34.10   Lien and Assessment— Priority with Respect to Mortgages   In both the condominium and the PUD, there will usually be two liens, the lien of the mortgage on the individually owned parcel and the lien of the assessments. Obviously, a question will arise as to whether foreclosure of a mortgage will wipe out delinquent assessment liens or vice versa.

All states have condominium laws. These laws deal with assessments, so that the condominium assessment is largely a statutory lien. Probably, the statute sets forth the requirements for the creation of the lien and assigns it a priority with respect to other liens. The condominium declaration adds other provisions regarding assessments. In making assessments, the board must comply with the statute and the declaration. The priority of a first mortgage over an assessment lien depends on the state law and the language of the declaration.

As regards the PUD, there are very few state laws governing the priority of the assessment liens. And, as to simple subdivisions, the assessments levied to enforce building restrictions are not governed by any laws or ordinances.

In any case, the declaration is likely to contain a clause giving the first mortgagee or institutional lender a lien prior to that of the assessments, and this clause is likely to prevail.

34.11   Covenants

When the declaration is recorded and deeds are given to purchasers, the declaration becomes a covenant running with the land. The benefits and burdens accrue automatically to subsequent purchasers. *Pepe v. Whispering Sands Condominium,* 351 So. 2d 755 (Fla. App. 1977).

34.12   Association as a Vehicle for Enforcing Restrictions, Liens, and Covenants

The enforcement of restrictions, liens, and covenants can legally be transferred through the declaration to an association or not-for-profit corporation formed by the home or apartment owners. *Merrionette Manor Homes v. Heda,* 11 Ill. App. 2d 186, 136 N.E.2d 556 (1956); *Neponsit Property Owners' Ass'n. v. Emigrant Indus. Sav. Bank,* 278 N.Y.249, 15 N.E.2d 793 (1938); *Rodruck v. Sand Point Maintenance Comm'n,* 40 Wash. 2d 565, 295 P.2d 714 (1956).

34.13   Deed Clauses to Implement the Declaration

To fully implement the declaration, it is necessary to insert a clause in the deed from the developer similar to the following:

> Subject to Declaration of Covenants, Conditions, Restrictions, Easements, and Liens dated _____ and recorded in the Office of the Recorder of Deeds of _____ County, _____ as Document No. _____ (the "Declaration") which is incorporated herein by reference thereto. Grantor grants to the Grantee, its heirs and assigns, as easements appurtenant to the premises hereby conveyed, the easements created by the Declaration for the benefit of the owners of the parcel of realty herein described. Grantor reserves to himself, his heirs and assigns, as easements appurtenant to the remaining parcels described in the Declaration, the easements thereby created for the benefit of said remaining parcels described in the Declaration, and this conveyance is subject to said easements and the right of the Grantor to grant said easements in the conveyances of said remaining parcels or any of them, and the parties hereto, for themselves, their heirs, personal representatives, and assigns, covenant to be bound by the covenants, restrictions, and agreements set forth in the Declaration. Said covenants and restrictions are covenants running with the land both as to burden and benefits, and this conveyance is subject to all said covenants and restrictions as though set forth in full herein. The land hereby conveyed is also subject to the liens created by the Declaration, and same are binding on the grantees, their heirs, personal representatives, and assigns. All of the provisions of said Declaration are hereby incorporated herein as though set forth in full herein.

In some decisions, it has been held that the filing of the declaration would suffice to create restrictions, even though they were not mentioned in the developer's deeds. *Kosel v. Stone,* 146 Mont. 218, 404 P.2d 894 (1965); *Steuart Transp. Co. v. Ashe,* 304 A.2d 788 (Md. 1973). But, in California, precisely the opposite has been held. There, the declaration is totally ineffective unless the deeds refer to it. *Smith v. Rasqui,* 1 Cal. Rptr. 478 (Cal. App. 1959). It suffices to state in the deeds that the land is "subject to covenants, conditions, restrictions, and easements of record." *Seaton v. Clifford,* 100 Cal. Rptr. 779 (Cal. App.

1972); *Davis v. Huguenor, 408* Ill. 468, 97 N.E.2d 295 (1951). Alternately, it may be stated in the deed that it is subject to restrictions contained in the Declaration recorded in Book _____, Page _____. *Lake St. Louis Community Ass'n v. Ringwald*, 652 S.W.2d 158 (Mo. App. 1985). It is preferable that the full suggested form be used.

A different rule is applied if all of the restrictions, liens, and covenants are included in a recorded plat of the subdivision. The usual rule is that a deed describing the land conveyed as a lot in a recorded subdivision automatically is treated as if the plat were attached to and formed part of the deed. After all, how can you possibly locate a lot without looking at the plat? And, if you look at the plat, you are bound to see the restrictions. The same rule applies if the plat states on its face that all lots are subject to restrictions set forth in a declaration "recorded contemporaneously herewith." *Spencer v. Poole*, 207 Ga. 155, 60 S.E.2d 371 (1950).

Where the owner of a condominium apartment, PUD unit, or town house is placing a mortgage on the property, a clause is inserted in the mortgage along the following lines:

> Subject to Declaration of Easements, Restrictions, Liens, and Covenants dated _____ and recorded in the Office of the Recorder of Deeds of _____ County in Book _____, Page _____, as Document No. _____, which is incorporated herein by reference thereto. Mortgagor grants to the mortgagee, its successors, and assigns all rights of every description created by said Declaration for the benefit of the mortgaged premises, same to run with the mortgaged land. The provisions of said Declaration regarding liens of assessments are also incorporated herein by reference thereto.

34.14 Subsequent Sales

The declaration should provide that upon sale of the individual parcels, the seller shall not be liable for assessments levied or covenants or restrictions breached thereafter. Unless this clause is included, there is a legal possibility of continuing liability.

34.15 Membership— Homeowners' Association

The declaration will set out the qualifications for membership in the homeowners' association. Usually, membership is automatic and follows the property from one owner to the next. Modern declarations provide for filing with the secretary of the association a notice of which of the multiple owners of a unit will have the right to cast the vote for the unit at any meeting. In this way, only one whole vote per unit will be counted and the association will not be burdened by disputes among co-owners as to which position is to be taken.

34.16 Membership— Clubs Related to the Development

A related question is who is entitled to be a member of any club that might be related to the development. In many cases, property ownership is a prerequisite to club membership. This is especially the case where the development is a golf course residential complex. Other issues remain. May the developer or subsequent owner of the golf course sell memberships to outsiders? Does a member lose membership merely because of a sale of the property? Does the buyer automatically become a club member? If so, does the buyer have to pay an initiation fee? May tournaments and public outings be held at the course and club? What happens if membership is restricted and the development is not as successful as expected? This will place a greater financial burden on those who are members. Will that burden be tolerable?

Sometimes, lot owners agree to become members of the club as long as they continue to own property in the development. What rights and obligations will the members have if the developer sells the club? They may well be bound by their contract to continue as members. *Chesapeake Ranch Club, Inc. v. C.R.C. United Members, Inc.*, 483 A.2d 1334 (Md.

App. 1984). It may be, however, that the obligation to be a club member does not "touch and concern the land" and thus is not binding on future owners merely because they purchase property on resales. *Id.*

34.17 Marketable   Under the Marketable Title Acts, rights in land—including covenants, restrictions, private
Title Acts   assessment liens, and, in some instances, easements—terminate after a stated period of time
unless fresh recordings are made to keep these interests alive.

CHAPTER 35

Planned Unit Developments

35.01 The Planned Unit Idea

The planned unit development (PUD) may consist of attached homes, detached homes, condominiums, garden and high-rise apartments, office and business parks, and mixed use projects, all with common open areas and sometimes with private recreation facilities. The developer is permitted to construct more units per acre than would be allowed under a standard lot and block subdivision. This more efficient land use results in lower prices for buyers.

In residential developments, the purchaser is often free of the work and worry of outside maintenance, which may be transferred to the homeowners' association (HOA). Small private yards and shared recreation facilities reduce the chores associated with any particular unit and give the owners a place for relaxation and enjoyment. The municipality benefits in that cohesive and intelligent planning of the development, and its impact on the community systems, results in a better development.

The PUD is created after the approval by the local municipality. Municipal approval is required because the PUD does not conform with the usual lot and block zoning, and special consideration must be given to the developer in the design of the project. In exchange for these approvals, the developer makes certain agreements regarding the development. In sum, both the municipality and the developer compromise, which results in a project specifically designed to fit the needs of the area. Once approved, a plat of subdivision is recorded to delineate the building lots and common areas. A declaration of covenants, conditions, and restrictions is also recorded to (1) set forth the rules governing the property, (2) create an association that may hold title to the common areas, (3) provide that membership in the association is automatic upon the purchase of a unit, (4) establish voting rights and the rights of the owners to use the common areas, and (5) set out the obligation of unit owners to pay assessments to defray expenses for the maintenance of the common areas and state that such assessments are a lien on the unit until paid.

35.02 Cluster Housing

The phrase "cluster housing" means that the individual homes, row houses, or apartment buildings are grouped together on relatively small plots of land with a larger surrounding area of land left open for common recreational use and open space. The cluster form of development creates economies for the developer because the clustering of houses reduces the cost of supplying utilities and roads.

35.03 Creating a PUD

Before the first lot is sold, the developer obtains zoning and planning approval, incorporates the nonprofit HOA, and records the subdivision plat and declaration of covenants, conditions, restrictions, and easements for all of the land in the planned unit. The plat identifies (1) property to be transferred to public agencies, such as any proposed public streets; (2) the individual home sites; (3) the common areas to be transferred by the developer to the HOA;

and (4) any other parcels, such as a church site or shopping center, to be kept by the developer or transferred to others.

35.04   Zoning   Most states accept the notion of PUD zoning, with its mixed-use and floating zone concepts. The legislation was designed to encourage local governments to tailor their regulations to local needs. Necessarily, bargaining takes place between local government and developers to reach agreement as to unit size, use mix, and so on, so that contract zoning is also involved. *Rutland Envtl. Protection Ass'n v. Kane County,* 31 Ill. App. 3d 82, 334 N.E.2d 215 (1975). In short, all the zoning novelties are present and are acceptable. Often the PUD ordinance is part of the zoning ordinance.

On the whole, the modern decisions sustain the validity of PUD zoning, even though it is a far cry from "cookie-cutter" single-family dwelling zoning, Ferdinand S. Tino, Annotation, *Zoning: Planned Unit Cluster or Greenbelt Zoning,* 43 A.L.R.3d 888 (1972), and even though the density requirements are different from those applicable to conventional subdivisions. *Peabody v. Phoenix,* 485 P.2d 565 (Ariz. App. 1971)

35.05   Plat Approval and Zoning Combined   It is evident that where a local government is called upon to assign a floating zone area to a PUD, it is almost impossible to separate the plat approval or planning process from the rezoning process. Hence, many local governments have adopted a unitary approval process that combines the two operations.

The PUD is often authorized by means of the grant of a special exception permit under the local zoning ordinance. Usually the zoning ordinance contains an elaborate section listing the requirements for the granting of the special permit. Developers usually submit a rough draft of the development scheme and thus obtain the city's views as to what would be acceptable. Commonly, the ordinance provisions also list the requirements for plat approval, and the same department considers the special permit application together with the request for plat approval. At times, annexation or a rezoning may be needed, and a petition for annexation or rezoning must be filed and appropriate notices given to adjoining owners.

At some point there will be a hearing before the planning or zoning board and, ultimately, the city council, where opponents of the development will be given an opportunity to present their case.

35.06   The Common Area   The documents should convey ownership of the common area to the HOA. Indeed, the applicable PUD ordinance may require that ownership be vested in the HOA. The plat of a PUD and the declaration creating it will contain provisions granting the unit owners various easements in the common areas. The village may condition its approval of the plat on the assumption by the HOA of the obligation to maintain the common areas.

Since it is imperative that the common areas be kept in the ownership of the HOA and not dedicated to the public, the recorded plat must bear on its face a legend relative to all the common areas indicating that the area is not dedicated to the public and that its ownership is reserved to the developer (who later will deed it to the HOA). If such a legend is lacking, courts may hold that any area having the appearance of common grounds is, by implication, dedicated to the public. However, since the home buyers will want the developer to deed the land to the HOA, an agreement to do so should be contained in the plat, or in the accompanying declaration, or in a separate contract. Also, appropriate language must be incorporated in the text of the plat to indicate that the individual homeowners take easements in the common properties but no ownership therein. This means that the legend on the plat should be quite comprehensive as follows:

Full ownership of the tracts marked park, playground, private lake, and golf course (describe all other such areas) is retained in ABC (the developer) for ultimate conveyance to XYZ, a nonprofit corporation whose membership will comprise homeowners in this development, all according to the provisions of the declaration of restrictions, easements, liens, and covenants filed contemporaneously herewith, and made a part of this plat. Conveyances of lots in this subdivision shall not be deemed to convey title to any part of the retained areas. Said areas are not dedicated to the public. With respect to the total area embraced in this plat, and all parts thereof, easements, covenants, liens, and restrictions are created in and by such declaration.

35.06(a)   Common Areas—Easements—Paramount Rights of HOA

The declaration should create easements in favor of all of the homeowners in the development for access over the private walks and streets; for utilities, water, sewers, and other services; and for use of the common areas, and so on, but it should make such easement grant expressly subject and inferior to certain rights of the HOA. These rights should include the right of the association to exercise the following rights, free and clear of all private rights created in the homeowners: (1) the right of the association to suspend the enjoyment of the common areas by, and the furnishing of services provided by the association (garbage removal, furnishing water, and so forth) to, any delinquent homeowner while his or her maintenance assessments remain unpaid; (2) the right to manage, maintain, and control the common areas for the benefit of the homeowners and to promulgate reasonable rules toward this end; (3) the right to dedicate part or all of the common properties to the public for public use; (4) the right of the HOA to charge reasonable admission and other fees for the use of the common areas.

35.06(b)   Common Areas—Artificial Lakes

In some planned developments, an artificially created lake is one of the attractive common facilities. It is quite clear that neither the public nor any public body has any rights whatever in lakes so created. The developer has the legal right to reserve to itself the right to dictate who may use the lake, or it may grant this right to the homeowners. *Mayer v. Grueber*, 138 N.W.2d 197 (Wis. 1965); *Thompson v. Enz*, 154 N.W.2d 473 (Mich. 1967).

35.07   The Declaration—Building Restrictions

The declaration will establish a comprehensive general plan of restrictions governing minutely the structures and uses permitted in the development, both on the home sites and on the common areas. The plat of declaration should also vest in the HOA the right to pass upon the plans of any structure to be erected by any home buyer or any alterations to the exterior of any building. John D. Perovich, Annotation, *Validity and Construction of Restrictive Covenant Requiring Consent to Construction on Lot*, 40 A.L.R.3d 864 (1971).

35.07(a)   The Declaration—Covenants

The declaration will contain covenants binding on each homeowner to pay the assessments levied on his or her lot for maintenance charges; these covenants create a personal liability on which a personal judgment can be obtained by the association against a defaulting homeowner. The declaration will also contain covenants by the HOA to (1) maintain and operate the common property; (2) administer architectural controls; (3) enforce other covenants; and, in some cases, (4) maintain all or part of the exterior of individual homes. The covenants provide for amendments, but any amendment requires a vote of the homeowners.

35.07(b)   The Declaration—Lien for Maintenance

The declaration provides for the imposition of a maintenance assessment on each lot in the development. HOA's tend to operate somewhat informally. The danger here is that if procedures grow too lax (meetings held on days other than those set in bylaws, meetings being held without proper notices being given, and so on), the assessments made by the association may be declared invalid. *Noremac, Inc. v. Centre Hill Court, Inc.*, 178 S.E. 877 (Va. 1935).

35.07(c) The Declaration—Restraints on Sales

Any provision in the declaration or deeds that a homeowner cannot sell his or her lot except by consent of a majority vote of the association is invalid. Such a clause is an illegal restraint on alienation (sale). *Mountain Springs Ass'n v. Wilson,* 196 A.2d 270 (N.J. 1963). Also invalid is any clause where only a member of the HOA can purchase a homesite. *Id.* Nor can the declaration or bylaws of the association provide that sales by a homeowner to a future purchaser can only be made to a purchaser approved by the association. *Tuckerton Beach Club v. Bender,* 219 A.2d 529 (N.J. 1966). No refusal to sell can be racially motivated. *Sullivan v. Little Hunting Park, Inc.,* 396 U.S. 229 (1969). It is safe to provide that any home-site purchaser automatically acquires membership in the HOA as a normal incident of home ownership.

35.07(d) The Declaration—Other Provisions

The declaration should also contain, among other things, the following:

1. The name of the PUD and the HOA. A detailed paragraph on the creation of the HOA is needed, listing the obligations of the HOA to operate the PUD, and the rights and duties of the unit members. The HOA should be a state-chartered, nonprofit corporation. Each unit owner is automatically a member of the HOA.
2. A legal description of the land included in the PUD.
3. A description of each unit.
4. A description of the common elements or areas, and a contract by the developer to convey them to the HOA at a specified time.
5. Restrictions on use of the units and the common areas.
6. As in the condominium statute, a provision setting out the procedure for the amendment of the declaration.
7. A provision to set forth the powers of the HOA. These should also be included in the HOA corporate charter.
8. Provision for the levying of assessments by the HOA. The lien and priority of such assessments must be set forth in detail.
9. The developer's warranties of the building, as well as the limitations the developer chooses to place on the warranties. The declaration may provide that a deed of the unit carries the benefit of the warranties.

In some states, the statutes specifically regulate the documents creating the PUD. *See* Uniform Planned Community Act § 2-101. Where this is the case, all of the requirements of the statute must be complied with. However, in most states, the PUD is regulated by local ordinance. Many developers find that the condominium statute has grown so complex with its regulations and disclosure requirements that it is easier to work with the local governments under a PUD ordinance.

35.08 Mortgage Problems

A mortgage on a PUD home site should contain a covenant of the mortgagor to pay all assessments and a covenant not to vote to amend the declaration without the mortgagee's written consent. If there is a prior blanket mortgage, the mortgagee should consent to the creation of the PUD and amend the prior mortgage to allow partial releases from the lien of that mortgage as units are sold. A standard Federal National Mortgage Association (FNMA) mortgage may be used to finance the purchase of a PUD unit, but it must have a PUD rider.

35.09   Taxes on Common Areas

The common areas have no sales value to a third party. They are encumbered with easements that render them valueless to any purchaser. The value of the common areas is reflected in the increased value they contribute to the residential areas. Hence, the tax assessor should not assess the common areas at the value they would have if unencumbered by easements. *People v. O'Donnel,* 139 App. Div. 83, 124 N.Y.S. 36 (1910*); Crane-Berkely Corp. v. Lavis,* 238 App. Div. 124, 263 N.Y.S. 556 (1933).

There is no guarantee of this result until the matter has been worked out with the local assessor. Assessors tend to be rather independent. Basically, the problem is one of persuasion.

35.10   Town Houses and Cluster Homes

Land is the single largest cost component in any housing development. As a result, there is an inverse correlation between the density of a development and the cost of the housing units. A developer can hold down the selling price of the housing units by increasing the density of the development. If land costs $50,000 per acre, the land cost per housing unit in a project with one house per acre is $50,000 per house. If the density is increased to two houses per acre, the land cost per housing unit goes down to $25,000 per unit.

The greatest density comes, of course, in the high-rise development. Town houses or cluster housing present an alternative that is denser than the single-family detached housing development, but not as dense as the high-rise or multilevel project. In the past, this higher-density project would have been accomplished by building rows of attached houses facing a street. The development concept matured, and town house projects were next built with the rows of units being built at right angles to the street. As development patterns evolved, we have come to see more changes, with single-family housing units that are constructed in clusters, on top of one another, on top of or as a part of multiuse projects, or as multiple-unit buildings that have the appearance of a single large house.

Whatever the development scheme, there are some common features to this form of development. There is extensive use of shared walls. This form of development makes extensive use of easements and restrictions, frequently found in a declaration of covenants, conditions, restrictions, and easements. Since the walls are party walls, easements must exist for their construction and use. Also, all of the housing units, except those closest to the street, will need easements of ingress and egress. Additional easements are needed for common gutters and down spouts, common sewers, water pipes, electric lines, telephone wires, cable television lines, and so forth.

In the past, it was not unusual for builders to develop projects of this type with complete indifference to their unique legal requirements. Units would be sold without any mention of the needed easements. Probably, implied easements exist for all of the necessary common uses. *Gilbert v. Chicago Title & Trust Co.,* 131 N.E.2d 1 (Ill. 1955). Obviously, the declaration of easements is the better and more certain way of handling this issue.

There are two legal structures that are used in developing town houses. The condominium form of ownership may be used, in which case the town-house owner will acquire the same ownership as if the condo were in a high-rise, with the exterior of the building, yards, parking areas, and the like being common areas. The other form of ownership will involve the conveyance of the fee to the parcel of land on which the town house sits, with the owner acquiring title to the exterior within the property lines from the center of the earth to the sky. The owner may also acquire some land in addition to that on which the town house sits, such as a yard, patio or garage, and parking area. In either instance, the development will be governed by a declaration of easements, covenants, conditions, and restrictions, as in the case of the fee town house, or, the declaration of condominium, as in the case of the condominium form of town-house ownership. The condominium form of ownership has the advantage of offering a defined body of law and documentation governing the use and occupancy of the development as time goes by.

Developers may opt for the condominium form of town-house development rather than the conventional fee type of conveyance to avoid some of the local governmental administrative rigors that may be applicable to the development of a subdivision but are not applicable to the development of a condominium. This will depend upon state law and practice.

In some states, the town-house development, with its dwelling units and common areas, is depicted on a recorded plat. In other instances, the boundaries of the units and common areas are depicted on a map attached to the declaration.

The typical old town-house development had only a few units and operated without the benefit of an HOA. This form of organization, or lack of organization, has its drawbacks. For example, each unit would carry its own fire insurance. If a unit was severely damaged by fire, the mortgagee on that unit might choose to apply the insurance money to the reduction of the mortgage debt and not to the rebuilding of the town house. This event has obvious detrimental effects on neighboring units. Their salability is severely impaired, and the complex is left with a very visible scar. There is also no organization to enact rules and regulations for the common good of all of the development or to take action against the unit owner or occupant who acts in a manner unacceptable to the rest, as would be the case where a unit owner kept junk cars on the front lawn.

35.11 Business Parks

The history of business parks is comparatively modern when compared with the history of real estate law. To be sure, there are older industrial parks, such as the Central Manufacturing District and the Clearing Industrial District in Chicago. But, as the surge to the suburbs took place after World War II, the industrial developer appeared as a much larger force on the development scene. As communities attempted to attract high-technology industry to keep the work force employed and to build a tax base—or rebuild the older industrial and commercial areas of a city that were abandoned and neglected when smokestack industries closed their doors—the office and industrial park staged a strong comeback.

EXAMPLE: Municipality, recognizing the blighted condition of an old industrial area that has been largely abandoned, passes an ordinance granting development incentives to stimulate the redevelopment of the area. These incentives may include tax increment financing that utilizes the increased real estate taxes generated by the redeveloped property to pay some of the land acquisition costs and job training credits that will help the municipality make some of its citizens employable in a high-tech world. Developer assembles tracts of the land that fall within the incentive district. The developer records a declaration of restrictions that calls for a property owners' association. As the developer sells or leases tracts for office and industrial use, the developer can assure each business owner that the legal problems and development headaches have been solved. The business owner is left to the task of building or leasing the office or plant and commencing operations. The disadvantages are really disguised advantages. The facility is required to observe setback lines, to landscape, and to screen off its trash heaps and truck docks. This can be costly, but these requirements enhance the value of the property. Moreover, the owner knows that neighboring business will be subjected to the same scrutiny.

35.11(a) Advantages of Office and Industrial Parks

Parks of this kind offer many advantages to business. Precious time is not taken up by site preparation or land assembly. The site, with all utilities, is presented to the business for use in the business. Zoning problems are minimized. While the zoning and building codes must be checked to determine whether they will be violated by the particular use contemplated by the individual business, the property will have been rezoned to allow the general run of contemplated businesses. There are no title problems. The developer has usually obtained a clear title policy showing that there are no objectionable building restrictions or easements to impair expected business users' ability to conduct the business.

There are operating economies. For example, the cost of a common sewage plant will be shared by all users. There may also be a shared security force and other shared services. The park is usually protected by building restrictions established by the developer. For example, the developer would have established building lines so that there is ample open space surrounding each business. The developer or an architectural control committee may have the right to pass upon all building plans to assure each owner of an aesthetically pleasing environment developed along a consistent architectural theme. This allows the business owner to omit the precaution of buying excess land to insulate the business from undesirable neighbors. The business user may have an opportunity of preserving working capital by accepting a build-to-suit lease arrangement with the developer or one that the developer has arranged.

35.11(b)   Industrial Parks—Continuing Management Responsibility

Owners of sites in industrial and office parks insist upon a continuing responsibility for the enforcement of site restrictions. This is usually accomplished by the formation of a property owners' association, which is given the legal right to enforce the restrictions in the declaration of covenants, conditions, and restrictions.

35.11(c)   Types of Parks—Legal Aspects

The developer of property of this kind works in one of several ways. Under one format, the developer assembles the land, obtains the proper zoning, brings in the needed utilities, and constructs the roadways and other common facilities. Lots are then sold to the business owners who, in turn, construct the buildings needed to suit their operations. In another development format, the developer does all of the above and also enters into contracts with the business owners to construct buildings to the owner's specifications and lease the facility to the business. In yet another format, the developer will construct building shells without yet having buyers. When buyers are found, the needed interior work will be done to outfit each property to the buyer's specifications.

There are many legal aspects to all of these formats. For example,

1. The zoning must be checked to be sure that it will accommodate a wide variety of office and industrial uses, together with the necessary ancillary uses for a property of this kind. Does the zoning permit the fast-food restaurant that will be needed to support an active park? Depending upon the park's size, a hotel may be needed. Will the zoning permit such a use?

2. A declaration of covenants, conditions, and restrictions will be filed with the plat. This will define the uses that are permitted within the park.

3. A property owners' association will be formed to enforce the restrictions.

4. The subdivision plat will be submitted to the public officials involved in the planning process, and the necessary approvals will be obtained. The plat will be recorded before any lots are sold.

5. Arrangements will be made to bring utilities to the site.

6. Often these properties, especially office parks, are developed with common walls between the businesses. This brings many of the theories of town-house development into play.

When a lot is sold, the developer may wish to reserve an option to repurchase the land within a given number of years at the purchase price if the land remains vacant. This is often done to discourage the purchase of such lots by speculators who are not going to build and use the premises.

**35.11(d) Public
Assistance**

The need for commerce to provide employment, establish a tax base, and generally contribute to the economic life of a community has led to the enactment of various state laws and local ordinances. These enactments are intended to give businesses the economic incentive to locate their enterprise within a particular area. The form of incentives can be, among other things, the governmental purchase of the land for lease to the business; the provision of free offsite and utility service to the property; the reduction of real estate taxes for a stated period; low-interest loans; and more creative devices, such as the training of the community's work force for the future employer's needs. Whatever the incentives may be, the competition among communities, and even states, for the attraction of business is keen, and no developer should overlook the economic advantages that may be available from these sources.

CHAPTER 36
Condominiums

36.01 In General The condominium has come from near obscurity to being a common form of property ownership. Town houses, cluster homes, and apartments become obvious alternatives to detached housing to accommodate today's lifestyles. If those living units are to be individually owned, the condominium form of ownership is an apt vehicle.

The condominium form of ownership may be best explained by physically comparing it with rental apartments. A typical apartment building consists of apartments, lobby, halls, stairways, roof, building walls, garage, grounds, walks, and drives surrounding the building. The apartment unit itself is the private domain of the occupant. Its use is not shared with other occupants. But, the other areas (lobby, halls, stairways, roof, walls, grounds, walks, drives), the common elements, are owned by the landlord and shared by the tenants. In the condominium, the ownership follows this simple pattern. The apartment is purchased and becomes the exclusive domain of the owner, but ownership and use of the common elements are shared with all other apartment owners.

> **EXAMPLE:** Developer acquires a tract of land and obtains a loan to finance the construction of a fifty-unit condominium project. The units are identical. The building is constructed and Purchaser contracts to buy Unit 1. Purchaser really is buying Unit 1 plus the percentage of interest in the common elements assigned to that unit. Technically, the unit is bounded by the inner surface of the apartment walls, and the common elements include everything in the project that is not part of a unit. That is to say that the ground the project is built on, the air space above it, the outside walls of the project, walls between the units, the project's foundation and roof, the basement, stairs, elevators, foyers, swimming pool, janitor's apartment, water tanks, fire escapes, heating plant, air conditioning system, and so on make up the common elements. Purchaser receives a deed becoming the owner of Unit 1 and of an undivided percentage of interest in the common elements.

The purchaser will thus own the unit just as if it were a separate house and will become an owner in common of the common elements with the other unit owners. If the purchaser finances the purchase of Unit 1, the purchaser's lender will have a mortgage lien against Unit 1 and its share of the common elements.

Condominiums are not limited to apartments. Cluster homes, town houses, commercial structures of offices and other uses, campsites, parking spaces, hotels, and other projects have been developed or converted into the condominium form of ownership.

36.02 Public Offering Statement Most modern condominium laws require the developer to file with the state's real estate commission and deliver to each purchaser of a unit a public offering statement. This is a complex document that summarizes the law, the operational system of the condominium, and the facts concerning the physical condition of the building as revealed by an engineer's inspection. The description of the assessment procedure is also included.

36.03 Basic Documents

Several basic documents are typically required or otherwise a part of the creation of a condominium project.

36.03(a) Basic Documents— Declaration

The condominium declaration is the basic organic document or constitution for the condominium. It spells out the extent of the interest that each purchaser acquires and the rights and liabilities of the unit owners. *Pepe v. Whispering Sands Condominium Ass'n, Inc.* 351 So. 2d 755 (Fla. App. 1977). Once the declaration is recorded, the last act in the creation of the condominium is accomplished and the condominium comes into existence. *State Sav. & Loan Ass'n v. Kauaian Dev. Co.*, 445 P.2d 109 (Haw. 1968).

State laws require the declaration to contain the following:

1. The name of the condominium.
2. A description of the property being submitted to the condominium form of ownership. A traditional legal description of the development parcel is used here.
3. A description of each unit. The condominium survey is a three-dimensional marvel of far greater sophistication than the two-dimensional version. It has to be. Condominium units are often cubes of air space, but it is necessary to describe these pieces of real estate with the same precision with which parcels of land are described.

The difficulty with these requirements is that the typical condominium unit is an apartment in a multilevel building. How are the perimeters of an apartment located on the twentieth floor of an apartment building described? Remember that a condominium unit is basically a cube of space. Space is considered to be land that can be deeded and mortgaged, but it is harder to describe than a simple two-dimensional tract of land, such as a lot on which a house has been erected. As regards the house lot, the surveyor can go on the tract of land and place monuments or markers at the lot corners, but markers cannot be placed in the sky.

There are three methods by which a unit of air space can be described:

1. The subdivision plat method. A plat of subdivision of air space and the air lots representing the individual units is recorded by means of a drawing. This will permit conveyance of a particular unit by its number, as shown on the plat.
2. The land and apartment survey. A survey is first made of the land, showing the location of the building. Space surveys of each unit on each floor are then made showing the elevation of the floor and ceiling surfaces, the dimensions of the inside surfaces of the walls of each unit, and their location with reference to the boundaries of the land projected vertically upward. Conceptualize a survey containing three parts. Part one shows the footprint of the building on the land. Part two is a cross-section of the building showing the elevation of the floors and delineating the internal dimensions of the floor and ceilings. Part three is a footprint or floor plan of each floor showing the dimensions of each unit and each of the rooms in the unit.
3. Floor plan method. In lieu of individual apartment surveys, a survey can be made of the land showing the location of the building. This is attached to floor plans showing each unit's location, dimensions, and elevation from the ground floor surface, with a certification by the architect that the building was built substantially in accordance with the plans.

The other, lot, problem is more difficult. Legally, one cannot measure the height of the floor and ceiling from "the ground." The ground is not a stable and definite legal marker. Indeed, in the process of erecting a building, the construction crew invariably levels and changes the grade of the ground. Many condominium apartments are contracted for sale before construction begins.

Engineers have solved this problem.

> **EXAMPLE:** In Chicago, the city, by ordinance, has established an artificial horizontal plane beneath the surface of the entire city. This plane is uniform throughout the city. At many places throughout the city, concrete markers are placed extending about six feet downward from the sidewalk. The sidewalk is used because its grade is rarely altered. Each such monument contains a legend, stating, for example, "twenty feet above Chicago City Datum." The datum is the artificial legal subsurface that extends at the same level throughout the entire city. The markers are called "bench marks." There are hundreds scattered throughout the city, each identified by location and number. Now, a surveyor, plotting a condominium unit on the twentieth floor, can show on his survey that the floor of the apartment is located _____ feet above Chicago City Datum as established by Bench Mark _____. The same is done with the ceiling. With this system, establishing vertical boundaries is a simple task for the surveyor.

The U.S. Geodetic Survey has established its own datum and bench marks. Some surveyors prefer to use these because they are considered more accurate than city datum and city bench marks.

4. A description of the common elements.

5. A description of the limited common elements.

6. A statement of the share of each unit owner in the common elements. This share should be expressed as a percentage rather than a fraction. These shares are allocated upon several bases. In California, each unit, irrespective of its size and value as compared with the other units, has one equal share with the other units. Cal. Civ. Code § 1353(b). In Illinois, the shares are computed on the basis of the value of the unit as compared with the value of the project as a whole. 765 ILCS 605/4. Other states have more complex formulas for allocation. Va. Code Ann. §§ 55-79.55.

7. If the condominium is to be a phased or add-on condominium, the declaration should give the option to add additional property to the condominium, state any limitations on the developer's ability to bring other land under the declaration, and set forth the manner of allocation of common elements, voting rights, and charges for common expenses, upon the joinder of the additional property.

8. If the condominium is a leasehold condominium, the declaration should identify the lease and state the unit owner's rights upon the termination of the lease.

There are other provisions that state law does not require the declaration to contain, but they properly belong in the declaration because they affect the basic rights of the unit owners. They include the following:

1. A provision that ownership of a unit and of the owner's share of the common elements shall not be severed or separated and that any conveyance or mortgage of the one without the other is prohibited. Also, that any partition suit with respect to the common elements is forbidden.

2. A provision that includes giving the condominium association the right to levy assessments on the unit owners for maintenance and so forth; creating personal liability on the unit owner plus a foreclosable lien on each unit for any delinquency in paying the assessments applicable to any unit; and stating the maximum assessment permitted.

3. A provision that in the event of total or substantial destruction of the building by fire or other hazard, or where the property reaches obsolescence, a stated percentage of co-owners' votes shall determine whether to rebuild or sell the property. A number of states have laws on this point.

4. A grant of easements to each unit owner giving the rights of ingress and egress and other easement rights. As time goes by, buildings often settle. Thus, the condominium unit sinks slightly into the common elements (the interior of walls, floors, and ceilings), and common elements

encroach into the units. To deal with this problem, the condominium declaration provides that, as the building settles, the unit owner enjoys an easement to occupy the area not assigned to him or her by the surveys. Comment, 50 Cal. L. Rev. 299, 303 (1962). In tall buildings, the upper floors sway a good deal in a high wind. This is readily perceived when the water in a glass or vase sloshes around and chandeliers hung on chains sway perceptibly. Obviously, a unit in this area trespasses into the air space (a common element) surrounding the building and into the air space of other units. A "sway easement" or encroachment easement should be included in the declaration. Encroachment easements exist by virtue of statute in some states, thereby allowing an easement for encroachment where the encroachment is the result of a deviation from the plat and plans of construction, repair, renovation, restoration, or settling or shifting. This statutory easement will not protect unit owners in the event of their willful or intentional misconduct, or exculpate the contractor from liability for reason of failure to comply with the plans. Va. Code Ann. §§ 55-79.60.

5. Some statement is also needed that the benefit and burden of these covenants run with each unit. A provision should also be included that when any apartment owner sells his or her unit, personal liability of the seller for future breaches of these covenants ends.

6. The condominium owners want to have the ability to control occupancy to avoid the presence of incompatible neighbors. Such control seems to be permitted in some states. Vitauts M. Gulbis, Annotation, *Validity, Construction and Application of Statutes or of Condominium Association's By-Laws or Regulations Restricting Sale, Transfer or Lease of Condominium Units*, 17 A.L.R.4th 1247 (1982). Vincent DiLorenzo, *Restraints on Alienation in a Condominium Context: An Evaluation and Theory for Decision Making,* 24 Real Prop. Prob. & Tr. J. 403 (1989). Rights of first refusal are valid. These give the association the right to buy the unit at the same price a buyer from the unit owner is willing to pay. Practically speaking, these rights are rarely used because the association does not have the funds to make the purchase. Logistically, the unit owner's contract with a buyer must provide for this contingency, and the title company and buyer may require proof that the association was given notice of the sale and did not choose to exercise its right. The right of first refusal is vanishing. The FNMA opposes its use. It lends itself to discriminatory and other arbitrary practices. Another declaration provision prohibits occupancy of the unit (not transfer of the unit) until the occupant is approved by the board. Edward M. Ross, *Condominiums and Preemptive Options: The Right of First Refusal,* 18 Hastings L.J. 585 (1967). Of course, these provisions cannot be used as a means of discrimination. *Phillips v. Hunter Trails Community Ass'n,* 685 F.2d 184 (7th Cir. 1982); Herbert J. Friedman & James K. Herbert, *Community Apartments, Condominiums or Stock Cooperative,* 50 Cal. L. Rev. 299, 317 (1962). The right of first refusal should not apply to a sale made by a mortgagee who has acquired title through foreclosure. *See generally Backus v. Smith,* 364 So. 2d 786 (Fla. App. 1978); *Hoover & Morris Dev. Co. v. Mayfield,* 212 S.E.2d 778 (Ga. 1975); *Gale v. York Center Community Coop., Inc.,* 171 N.E.2d 30 (Ill. 1961); *Lake Shore Club v. Lakefront Realty Corp.,* 398 N.E.2d 893 (Ill. App. 1979).

  Reasonable restrictions against the occupancy of units by children under a specific age are probably valid. Kristine Cordier Karnezis, Annotation, *Enforceability of By-Law or Other Rule of Condominium or Cooperative Association Restricting Occupancy by Children*, 100 A.L.R.3d 241 (1980); *White Egret Condominium, Inc. v. Franklin,* 379 So. 2d 346 (Fla. 1980). This matter is one of state law. It does not follow that this rule will win acceptance in all states. States in the Sun Belt retirement areas are much more likely to sanction barring children than urban, non-recreation–oriented states. State laws forbidding all types of discrimination, including age discrimination, are being widely enacted. These laws may well prohibit restraints against occupancy by children. Some states have enacted legislation that provides that a declaration may legally limit ownership, rental, or occupancy of a unit to persons fifty-five years old and older. 765 ILCS 605/4.1. A social problem of major proportions is developing.

7. The unit owner's right to lease is a hotly debated issue. While estimates vary, somewhere between 25 and 33 percent of condominium apartment units are owned by investors who rent their units to tenants. Increasing opposition to this practice focuses on the alleged inattention of the investor to condominium affairs. The investor owner typically does not attend meetings or serve on committees. This type of owner is indifferent, it is alleged, to tenant conduct that an-

noys owner-occupants and makes the building less desirable. A restriction on the renting of units is valid, if done properly. *Seagate Condominium Ass'n, Inc., v. Duffy,* 330 So. 2d 484 (Fla. App. 1976); *Kroop v. Caravelle Condominium, Inc.,* 323 So. 2d 307 (Fla. App. 1975). Probably a significant restraint of this character ought to be included in the declaration. Courts may refuse to apply the restriction in hardship cases, as where an owner dies and it is convenient to rent the unit while the estate is in probate. Indeed, it would be wise to except this and other hardship cases explicitly from the leasing prohibition so as to discourage courts from holding the entire restriction void for lack of reasonableness.

Unit owners who rent should not use printed tenant-type leases without amendatory language. Ordinary apartment leases contain provisions not suitable for condominiums, such as the landlord will furnish heat, hot water, and so on. The tenant's obligation to care for ordinary repairs should be spelled out. Often, the association requires that all leases be on a prescribed form that causes the tenant to be aware of and agree to conform to the building rules.

Resort-type condominiums present special problems. Suppose the declaration contains a clause that rentals shall be for a minimum of two weeks. This type of restriction eliminates the danger of a motel-type operation. But if the restrictions on renting get too strict, there is the danger that more and more units will be sold to permanent residents, who may amend the declaration to eliminate renting altogether. This, of course, is bad for those who bought the units primarily for investment purposes, hoping to profit through renting the unit most of the year.

8. Most declarations have a clause obligating each unit owner to abide by all the rules or bylaws promulgated by the homeowners' association. Needed flexibility is obtained in this way since new and necessary rules can be enacted through the simple majority vote of a quorum, instead of a majority vote of the apartment owners. It is important that a method of enforcement exists for these rules. The declaration should allow the association to obtain injunctive relief. In this way, the association may, in a serious case, have the court order the violation to cease.

9. The declaration should give the unit owners the right to amend the declaration and provide that the amendment will be binding upon all present and future owners. The declaration should state the procedure for amendment and the number of unit owners who must vote on the amendment for it to become effective.

36.03(b) Basic Documents— Amendments to Declaration

Some courts have taken the position that the declaration is like the constitution of the condominium. Those who buy units in reliance on a recorded declaration cannot be deprived of the rights afforded to them under that declaration by a subsequent amendment. *Pepe v. Whispering Sands Condo Ass'n,* 351 So. 2d 755 (Fla. App. 1977). But, if the declaration specifically permits amendments to be retroactive, other courts will allow retroactive amendments. *Crest Builders, Inc. v. Willow Falls Improvement Ass'n,* 74 Ill. App. 3d 420, 393 N.E.2d 107 (1979).

To illustrate the point, let us assume that a buyer of a condominium unit has a pet dog, and the documents are silent on the subject of pets or retroactive amendments. The courts will not let a subsequent amendment deprive the buyer of the pet. But, if the declaration permits retroactive amendments and an amendment bars pets, the buyer may have to give up the pet.

36.03(c) Basic Documents—Deeds

The individual deed of a unit need not necessarily be a complex document insofar as its legal description is concerned. The basis for such description will already have been provided by (1) the recording of the subdivision or condominium plat and (2) the recording of the declaration with its attached land and unit surveys containing legal descriptions of the various apartments or the land survey and building floor plans.

Thus, in the deed, the legal description of the individual apartment could be as follows:

PARCEL I: The absolute and indefeasible fee simple title to the parcel of land, property, and space designated as Apartment Parcel 100 in the plat of subdivision of the Sandcastle Condominium recorded in the Recorder's Office of _____ County _____ on November 1, 19__, as Document No. 123456 (or, "in the Declaration recorded, etc.," as the case may be).

The description of the common elements could be as follows:

> **PARCEL II:** The absolute and indefeasible fee simple title to an undivided _____ percent interest in the land, property, and space known as Lot 1 in Block 1 in Jones Subdivision, in Section _____, Township _____ North, Range _____ East of the _____ Principal Meridian, excepting from said Lot all the land, property, and space designated as Apartment Parcels 1 to 100, both inclusive, in the plat of subdivision of the Sandcastle Condominium recorded in the Recorder's Office of _____ County, _____ on November 1, 19__, as Document No. 123456 (or, "in the Declaration recorded, etc.," as the case may be).

The apartments excepted in Parcel II should, of course, consist of all the units in the building. Should there be any noncondominium areas of the building that are intended to be rented for commercial facilities, they should not be included among the apartments excepted, since they would be classed as part of the common elements.

An additional paragraph could be included in the developer's deed to the first purchaser of an apartment, conveying all the rights, benefits, easements, privileges, options, and covenants created by the declaration. It will do no harm to repeat in this clause the statement that these run with the land, for it is this document that gives life to the covenants. In addition, if the purchase of the unit carries with it, or the purchaser separately acquires, a parking space, then the deed should specifically describe that space.

Because of a dearth of modern cases touching on the specific question of whether ownership of the space occupied by an apartment or upper floor in a building would survive destruction of the building, it would be advisable to include in the deed a provision that it is the intention of the parties thereto that the ownership rights thereby conveyed shall so survive.

36.03(d) Basic Documents—Bylaws

The bylaws generally control the internal government of the associations, a subject matter that is becoming increasingly important. Bylaws will provide for the following:

1. The election of a board of managers; their term of office, powers and duties; and the election of officers of the board (i.e., president, secretary, treasurer).
2. Notice to the unit owners of the proposed adoption of the annual budget.
3. A yearly accounting to unit owners.
4. Notice to unit owners of board meetings.
5. Quorum requirements for both board and unit owners' meetings.
6. Number and method for calling unit owners' meetings.
7. The maintenance, repair, and replacement of the common elements.
8. The furnishing of a statement of account of any unit owner stating the amount of any unpaid assessments or other charges.
9. The adoption of rules and regulations for the use of units and common areas.

As long as bylaws are reasonable, they are binding. *Ryan v. Baptiste,* 565 S.W.2d 196 (Mo. App. 1978). Most bylaws have been based upon the federal models. The federal model, like everything federal, is complex and often hard to understand. It is best to put important provisions (such as those forbidding occupancy by children) in the declaration. The bylaws are easy to amend. But, when you make it easy to strip a unit owner of his or her rights, you invite litigation. Am. Jur. 2d Rev. Legal Forms, *Condominiums,* § 64.54.

36.03(e) Basic Documents—Rules and Regulations

Rules and regulations on the use of the units and the common areas promote the communal nature of the condominium. 15A Am. Jur. 2d *Condominiums and Cooperative Apartments* § 16. If they are reasonable, consistent with the law, and enacted in accordance with the bylaws, they will be enforced. These are usually contained in a separate document, the "rules and regulations."

Examples of common subjects of valid rules include the following:

1. A rule prohibiting alcoholic beverages in the clubhouse area. *Hidden Harbor Estates, Inc. v. Norman,* 309 So. 2d 180 (Fla. App. 1975).

2. A rule prohibiting the use of washing machines in individual apartments. This prevents water damage to other apartments. *Forest Park Coop., Inc. v. Hellman,* 152 N.Y.S.2d 685 (1956).

3. Reasonable security rules.

4. Restrictions against pets. *Dulaney Towers Maintenance Corp. v. O'Brey,* 418 A.2d 1233 (Md. App. 1980). If the prohibition is adopted after pet owners have taken up occupancy, a lawsuit may develop. To avoid this problem, amendments often permit existing pets to remain. The rule may also take into consideration the nature of the condominium and its surrounding area, such as prohibiting dogs in a high-rise condominium in which the animals must travel a minimum of forty-five floors in an elevator to reach the outdoors, an environment without parks or open space nearby. *Bd. of Directors of 175 East Delaware Homeowners Ass'n v. Hinojosa,* 287 Ill. App. 3d 886, 1079 N.E.2d 407(1997).

5. The requirement that each condominium owner keep the apartment in repair and not to interfere with the exterior of the building or any of the common elements.

6. A rule forbidding overnight parking in driveways. *Holleman v. Mission Trace Homeowners' Ass'n,* 556 S.W.2d 632 (Tex. Civ. App. 1977).

7. A rule giving resident owners priority parking rights over nonresident owners if the allocation scheme provides fair economic benefits to all owners. *Lyman v. Boonin,* 580 A.2d 765 (Pa. Super. 1990).

36.03(f) Basic Documents— Corporate Charter or Articles of Incorporation

Every condominium declaration refers to a homeowners' association (HOA), which is simultaneously created. This is a corporation with its charter issued by the state. This document, together with the bylaws, not-for-profit corporation law, and state condominium law, gives the HOA the power to do all the things necessary or convenient for the operation of the condominium. Every state law gives the HOA the power to adopt bylaws and lists in detail the matters that can be covered by the bylaws. Thus included in the "contract" that defines the unit owners' rights and duties are the declaration, the bylaws, the local condominium law, the HOA charter, the local corporation law, the rules adopted by the board, and the decisions made at meetings of the board and unit holders.

36.04 Procedure

Condominium procedure is governed by the condominium declaration, the corporate charter of the HOA, the local statute relating to such corporations, the corporate bylaws, and the rules adopted by the board. In addition, the local condominium statutes may set forth procedural requirements for the annual meeting, enforcement of assessments, and the giving of timely formal notices to board or association members of meetings where certain actions are taken, such as the election of officers, adoption of a budget, and setting of assessments. If these procedures are not followed, the action taken (e.g., the setting of the assessment), will be void. *Wolinsky v. Kadison,* 449 N.E.2d 151 (Ill. App. 1983). In this way, the "private government" of the condominium is subjected to procedural due process requirements in somewhat the same fashion as local government action.

36.05 Assessments

Every condominium and HOA needs funds to maintain the common areas, staff the project, create reserves for the periodic replacement of major components, and so on. Assessments against the unit owner provide these funds. The owners make monthly payments to fund the association budget, providing an orderly flow of funds to pay bills as they come due.

The declaration should establish the assessment process and a collection mechanism for past-due payments. The declaration should allow the association to sue the delinquent unit owner and foreclose against the unit. In some jurisdictions, the delinquent assessment lien can be foreclosed by the power-of-sale foreclosure process, a quick remedy that does not require court proceedings. To make the association whole, the declaration should provide that delinquent installments bear interest at the highest allowable legal rate, and attorneys' fees and other costs incurred by the association in the collection process are added to the amount of the delinquent installment.

The possibility of foreclosure gives rise to a priority conflict between the association and unit mortgagees. In the typical situation, a condominium declaration is recorded to create the units and establish the lien against the units for assessments. Units are sold, and buyers finance their purchase with mortgages. If state law or the documents do not provide otherwise, the foreclosure of delinquent assessments will extinguish the mortgage, even if the delinquency occurs after the date of the mortgage, *Prudential Ins. Co. v. Wetzel,* 248 N.W. 791 (Wis. 1933); *Washington Fed. Sav. & Loan Ass'n v. Schneider,* 408 N.Y.S.2d 588 (1978); *Bessemer v. Gersten,* 381 So. 2d 1344 (Fla. 1980), though a contrary result has been reached under particular statutory language. *Brask v. Bd. of St. Louis,* 533 S.W.2d 223 (Mo. 1976). This is obviously a situation that chills unit sale financing and works against the long-term best interests of the condominium. A simple provision in the declaration subordinates the assessment lien to first mortgage financing while requiring the foreclosing lender to pay assessments incurred after completion of foreclosure. Robert Kratovil & Raymond J. Werner, *Modern Mortgage Law and Practice* § 26.02 (2d ed. 1981). The secondary mortgage market requires such a provision.

> **EXAMPLE:** Lender financed Buyer's purchase of a condominium unit. If the suggested clause is in the declaration, Lender's lien will be prior to assessment liens against Buyer's unit. If Buyer does not pay the mortgage as installments come due, the assessments will probably also go into default. Lender can foreclose and the purchaser at the foreclosure sale will take the title free of assessments due before the sale date. The buyer at the foreclosure sale, even if the lender is the buyer, will take the title subject only to the lien for those assessments that come due after the foreclosure sale date.

State laws invariably contain provisions regarding the priority of assessment liens. Where the HOA pays for utilities and includes the cost in the assessment, it can cut off a delinquent owner's service, *San Antonio Villa del Sol Homeowners' Ass'n v. Miller,* 761 S.W.2d 460 (Tex. App. 1988).

In some states, (e.g., Illinois), a delinquent unit owner can be evicted just like a delinquent tenant.

The assessment lien process is binding on the original and all subsequent buyers of the units, *Kell v. Bella Vista Village Property Owners Ass'n,* 528 S.W.2d 651 (Ark. 1975); Francis M. Dougherty, Annotation, *Liability of Owner of Unit in Condominium Recreational Development, Time-Share Property, or the Like for Assessment in Support of Common Facilities Levied Against and Unpaid by Prior Owner,* 39 A.L.R.4th 114 (1985), and the assessment percentages allocated to the various units cannot be changed without a unanimous vote unless the declaration clearly provides otherwise. *Thiese v. Leland House Ass'n,* 311 So. 2d 142 (Fla. App. 1975). It is not a defense to the collection of assessments that the association is not properly maintaining the common areas, or that the unit owner is not getting its money's worth. *Agassiz West Condominium Ass'n v. Solum,* 527 N.W.2d 244 (N.D. 1995).

The question of what may be a proper subject of an assessment expense is sure to generate interest and litigation. To date, the courts have given wide latitude to the association as long as it exercises its judgment in good faith for the benefit of the project. Timothy E. Travers, Annotation, *Expenses for Which Condominium Association May Assess Unit Owners*, 77 A.L.R.3d 1290 (1977).

> **EXAMPLE:** The association may purchase a unit for the resident manager of a large complex so he will be available at all hours. An assessment may be levied for this purpose.

As in all cases involving the validity of corporate action, every condominium assessment levied by the board of directors is subject to scrutiny to determine if the power to levy the assessment for the particular purpose was one within the powers conferred on the HOA. In this instance, it is necessary to examine the corporate charter of the HOA, the corporation statute under which it operates, and the condominium declaration. The declaration, as the bill of rights of the unit owners, may limit the powers the corporation might otherwise enjoy. 77 A.L.R.3d 1290, *supra*.

36.06 Termination Due to Destruction of Building
The situation where the building is destroyed by fire or other casualty varies from state to state. Where rebuilding takes place with adequate insurance funds, the problems are not excessively complex. Where, however, a percentage of the owners have the right to vote to sell the property and divide the proceeds, problems exist unless the state law spells out a program. This has been done in some states (e.g., New York, Hawaii, Mississippi, Nevada, Illinois, and Missouri).

36.07 Operational Aspects—New Condominiums
A number of steps must be taken to put a new condominium in operation. Among them are as follows: (1) the election, in accordance with the bylaws, of a governing board by the unit owners (this usually takes place when about 75 percent of the units have been sold and occupied); (2) election of officers; (3) appointment of committees; (4) transfer of control from the developer to the newly elected board; (5) hiring of a new building manager, if it is desired to replace the developer's manager who has functioned from the date of first occupancy to the date the first board was organized; (6) review of insurance placed by developer; (7) review by the board of the completion of the project in accordance with plans and specifications; and (8) adoption of rules governing swimming pools, pets, parking, and so forth.

Upon the transfer of control from the developer to the unit owners, many documents must be turned over to the new board, such as corporate record books, financial records, insurance policies, and management contracts. This is a time for the unit buyer members to settle accounts with the developer. An audit, both financial and operational, should be conducted. In this way, the unit members will have a good base line established to distinguish their acts from the developer's.

After the completion of the building, normal operations include preparation of budgets by the budget committee, setting of assessments by the board, annual audits, approval of sales by unit owners, repair of building, etc. The common elements are operated and controlled by the board and the manager hired by the unit owners in accordance with the rules adopted by the unit owners.

36.08 Board of Directors
As in the case of any corporation, the board of directors controls the destiny of the association. It meets at least monthly. It appoints committees and hears committee reports. Often,

its meetings are open to unit owners. Their complaints and suggestions are heard. The annual budget is a major concern. Fixing assessment rates and enforcing assessments against delinquent owners is another major concern. Dealing with repairs and replacement contracts in larger amounts than those entrusted to the manager is another concern. Hiring a manager, auditor, and attorney will be a board matter, while hiring less important personnel (e.g., security guards), may be left to the manager. Procuring insurance is a board responsibility. Adopting rules (swimming pool hours, etc.) is a board matter. These rules will generally be valid and not bring liability upon the members of the board if they are reasonable. Vincent DiLorenzo, *Judicial Deference to Management Decisions in Planned Unit Developments,* Prob. & Prop. 20 (January/February 2001). Bonding employees who handle money is also a board concern.

36.08(a)   Committees   A variety of committees will serve under the board of directors. There may be an acceptance committee. Its task is to review the building, possibly with the help of an architect, to establish what defects, if any, exist and require correction. The maintenance committee deals with maintenance problems after the building has been accepted. The finance committee reviews budget proposals with the help of the manager and auditor and proposes annual budgets.

36.09   Common Elements   The common elements include every part of the condominium project that is not a unit.

> **EXAMPLE:** A one-acre parcel of ground is developed as a condominium parcel. The building that houses the units covers one-half of the acre. The remainder of the land surface is devoted to the pool, driveway, green areas, and a clubhouse, all of which are common elements. So also are the lobby, elevators, stairways, and roof of the building, the air space above the condominium, and the ground below it.

These common areas are for the common use of all unit owners and are often subject to rules and regulations regulating their use for the mutual enjoyment of all owners.

36.09(a)   Limited Common Elements   Limited common elements are common elements used by less than all unit owners, such as parking or patio area assigned to a unit. These are used exclusively by the unit owners whose units they serve. Even though these areas are not for the use of all unit owners, they are subject to controls by the condo association.

> **EXAMPLE:** Certain limited common elements were originally built as screened enclosures. The unit owner remodeled the area by installing jalousie windows in lieu of the screens. The jalousies had to be removed. *Sterling Village Condominium, Inc. v. Breitenbach,* 251 So. 2d 685 (Fla. App. 1971).

36.09(b)   Common Elements—Invasion by Unit Owners   Many town houses with their location at ground level are being developed as condominiums. These present a temptation for a unit owner to invade the common elements.

> **EXAMPLE:** The building in question was a one-story town house project with units separated by party walls. One unit owner decided to expand its unit, adding a story and excavating beneath the ground floor to add a workshop. The HOA stopped this. It was an invasion of the air space, a common element, and the subsurface, also a common element. *Makeever v. Lyle,* 609 P.2d 1084 (Ariz. 1980). But, a small storage cabinet may not be deemed a violation. *Mission Hills Condominium Ass'n. v. Penashio,* 97 Ill. App. 3d 305, 422 N.E.2d 1125 (1981).

36.10 Real Estate Taxes The real estate taxation issues relating to condominiums are simple but very important. Before a particular condominium is created, the real estate is taxed as a whole.

> **EXAMPLE:** A vacant piece of land has one tax bill; an apartment house has one tax bill.

When these properties are developed into condominiums, either through new construction or conversion, the tax bills must be split. Technically, the tax assessor assesses each condominium unit and its share of the common elements separately from every other unit and its share of the common elements. The laws of most states specifically require this separation of units for real estate taxation purposes.

The condominium owner must determine that this form of separate taxation is in place or, in the case of a new development, being processed. Otherwise, a delinquency in the payment of part of the taxes could result in delinquencies on the entire project. If the tax division is properly done, a unit owner need not be concerned with tax delinquencies affecting any other unit, because a tax sale affecting other parts of the development does not affect its ownership interest. *400 Condominium Ass'n v. Tully,* 79 Ill. App. 3d 686, 398 N.E.2d 945 (1979). *See generally* W.E. Shipley, Annotation, *Real Estate Taxation of Condominiums,* 71 A.L.R.3d 952 (1976).

The problem of assessing for tax purposes a newly converted apartment building is complex.

> **EXAMPLE:** A rental apartment having 100 apartments, if sold as a rental apartment, has a market value of $1,000,000. The converter, in turn, sells the 100 units at $30,000 each. As is evident, this gives the building a value of 100 times $30,000, or $3,000,000. Obviously, each unit owner is entitled to his or her own individual tax bill. But, the aggregate of the tax bills will be higher than the old tax bill on the building when it was a rental property. Meanwhile, the developer makes an estimate of what the tax bill will be. Any contract of sale made before the actual tax is fixed should provide for an escrow of a sum of money to cover a reprorating of taxes when the actual tax bill issues. But, the buyer should be warned that as other conversions in the vicinity push the values up further, the tax bill is likely to increase. It is also possible that the tax division cannot be processed to divide the presently payable tax. Therefore, the converter or developer cannot pay the tax on any particular unit. The buyer must take care that a proper escrow or other device is set up to cause the taxes to be paid.

36.11 Mortgages Since a condominium is a parcel of real estate, the lender must be concerned with the questions that relate to any real property loan. There are additional concerns generated by the unique nature of a condominium.

1. The mortgage should provide (1) that the unit owner's breach of a covenant of the declaration or the failure to pay assessments as they come due are defaults under the mortgage giving rise to the mortgagee's right to accelerate and foreclose; (2) that the mortgagee may pay delinquent assessments and add those sums to the mortgage debt; and (3) that the mortgagor will not vote to amend the declaration without the mortgagee's consent.

2. Any limitation on sale or rental of a condominium unit or any right of first refusal should be expressly inapplicable to a lender who buys the unit at its foreclosure sale or who takes a deed to a unit in lieu of foreclosure.

3. On a newly constructed or converted condominium, unit lenders will likely insist on a presale requirement as a condition to funding any unit loans. The percentage of required sales ranges from 25 to 50 percent. The presale requirement causes the sale contracts to be contingent upon the firming of financing for the outsales.

4. Because financing a condominium unit is really financing part of the building as a whole, the legal framework of the condominium must be examined. An endorsement to the lender's title

insurance policy can be obtained to ensure that the condominium has been legally created in conformity with state law.

5. The developer is dependent upon sales, and sales can only go forward if the outsale lenders find the loans acceptable. The lenders, in turn, look to see if the loans are acceptable on the secondary market and to the FHA.

36.12 Phased Construction

Construction lenders and common sense require that large projects be constructed in stages rather than all at once. The later stages are built if and when sales volume justifies their construction. Phasing also eliminates some problems with the legal logistics of setting up the condominium. Norman Geis, *Representing the Condominium Developer: Tending the Paper Jungle,* 10 Real Prop. Prob. & Tr. J. 471 (1975). Many construction loan documents have presale requirements to be met before partial releases will be available to allow unit sales to close. For example, the lender may require 40 percent of the units to be sold before partial releases for the units will be given. If the total project is 200 units, 80 will have to be sold before closings can occur to give the developer the needed funds to pay down the construction loan and keep total interest costs at a minimum. If the project is built in four phases, only 20 units need be sold before sales can close.

While phasing eliminates some practical problems, it creates documentation problems, which can be solved. Robert Kratovil, *Modern Real Estate Documentation,* § 809, *et. seq.* (1975). Each phase may have its own condominium association. There will also be an umbrella association to manage the recreational and other facilities that serve the entire project. It is also important that the documentation set forth the complete plan for the phasing in of new units and the exact reallocation of each unit's common element percentage as new units are added. *See generally* Gurdon H. Buck, *The Zero Unit Condominium (with Form),* 7 No. 1 Prac. Real Est. Law. 31 (Jan. 1991).

36.13 Leasehold Condominiums

Under the original condominium laws of most states, a condominium could not have been created on a leasehold estate. Statutory revisions have closed this gap in many, but not all, states. *See, e.g.,* Fla. Stat. Ann. § 718.401; Va. Code Ann. §§ 55-79.54(e).

Buyers purchasing units built upon a leasehold estate should take extra precautions. Proper care should be taken to ensure that individual unit owners can protect their interests by making their separate payments of the lease rentals. This may be accomplished by a lease clause allowing a forfeiture to be lodged only against those unit owners in arrears in lease payments. State law may offer some protection in this regard. Va. Code Ann. §§ 55-79.54. The duration of the underlying ground lease must also be checked.

36.14 Developer Control

When the condominium is first created by the recording of the declaration or master deed, the developer owns all of the units and all of the common areas and is the board of directors. Even as units are sold, the developer continues to own the unsold units and have the power within the association that is attributable to ownership of the unsold units.

> **EXAMPLE:** The developer has sold 25 units of a 100-unit condominium project. The developer retains 75 percent of the vote, an enormous power.

Some developers have used this period to their benefit at the expense of unit buyers. Expenses may be loaded toward unit buyers without the developer contributing its fair share. As the holder of the power to contract for the condominium project, some developers would, on behalf of the condominium, make a "sweetheart" contract with a corporation controlled by the developer.

EXAMPLE: The developer, as president of the condominium board, would make long-term contracts with the developer's management company to manage the complex; the developer's janitorial company to clean and maintain the common areas; and the developer's landscaping company to manicure the lawns in the summer and plow snow in the winter.

Perhaps the most notorious of these practices was the recreational lease.

EXAMPLE: The condominium documents would be drafted to exclude the recreational area, that is, clubhouse, swimming pool, pool deck, stairway to beach, and so on. These areas would not be common elements, but would be owned by the developer who, in turn, would enter into a long-term lease with the condominium board, with the developer signing as president of the board.

These arrangements generated a lot of litigation as the unit buyers tried, often without success, to break these agreements. W.E. Shipley, Annotation, *Self-Dealing by Developers of Condominium Project as Affecting Contracts or Leases with Condominium Association*, 73 A.L.R.3d 613 (1976). At times, these cases have been decided on narrow technical grounds that reveal an absence of imagination on the part of the courts.

EXAMPLE: Before any units were sold, Developer entered into a management agreement with a wholly owned subsidiary. The agreement was highly unfavorable to the unit owners. The court sustained the agreement on the ground that no unit owner was injured when the agreement was signed. The court completely disregarded the modern development of the law of fraud, which allows recovery where injury to subsequently interested parties can reasonably be anticipated. *Lyons v. Christ Episcopal Church*, 71 Ill. App. 3d 257, 389 N.E.2d 623 (1979). *But see Mission Hills Condominium Ass'n M-1 v. Corley*, 570 F. Supp. 453 (N.D. Ill. 1983).

The better rule forbids self-dealing by the developer and invalidates such contracts. *Avila South Condominium Ass'n v. Kappa Corp.*, 347 So. 2d 599 (Fla. 1977). The unit owners have, with mixed results, even attempted to use the antitrust laws to avoid these arrangements. *Spitz v. Buckwald*, 551 F.2d 1051 (5th Cir. 1977); *Miller v. Grandos*, 529 F.2d 393 (5th Cir. 1976). *See generally* John R. Lewis & Kenneth A. Jessell, *The Condominium Recreational Lease Controversy*, 9 Real Est. L.J. 7 (1980).

The unit owners have found the real answer in both the market and the legislature. In several areas, units in condominium projects with recreation leases simply will not sell. Many states have amended their condominium laws in two ways. A specific time has been established for the developer to turn control of the property over to the buyers. *See* 765 ILCS 605/18.2; Va. Code Ann. §§ 55-79.74. Contracts and leases made by the developer are cancelable by the owners when they take control. *See* 765 ILCS 604/18.2; Va. Code Ann. §§ 55-79.74; 15 U.S.C. § 3607.

The courts have also begun to treat the developer as having special fiduciary duties toward the unit buyers. *Governors Grove Condo Ass'n v. Hill Dev. Corp.*, 414 A.2d 1177 (Conn. 1980); W.E. Shipley, Annotation, *Self-Dealing by Developers of Condominium as Affecting Contracts or Leases with Condominium Association*, 73 A.L.R.3d 613 (1976). Note, Salvatore LaMonica, *Developer Leases Under the Condominium and Cooperative Abuse Relief Act of* 1980, 15 Hofstra L. Rev. 631 (1987).

36.15 Liability of Developer for Defects

As is the case with respect to any newly constructed residence, the developer/builder implicitly warrants to the purchaser of a condominium unit that the building and the unit are fit for occupancy and free from obvious defects. *Tassan v. United Dev. Co.*, 410 N.E.2d 902

(Ill. 1980); Robert A. Brazener, Annotation, *Liability of Vendor of Condominiums for Damage Occasioned by Defective Condition Thereof*, 50 A.L.R.3d 1071 (1973).

36.15(a) Fraud and Nondisclosure

The law of fraud, including nondisclosure, is much the same with respect to sales of condominium units as it is with respect to any land sale.

> **EXAMPLE:** Condominium Developer was held liable for failure to disclose known structural defects. *Cooper v. June*, 128 Cal. Rptr. 724 (1976); *Governors Grove Condominium Ass'n v. Hill Dev. Corp.*, 414 A.2d 1177 (Conn. 1980).

The association itself has no duty to disclose information to a potential purchaser of defective construction, even if it is in litigation with the developer over those defects. *Kovich v. Paseo del Mar Homeowners' Ass'n*, 48 Cal. Rptr. 2d 758 (Cal. App. 1996). The association may, however, have the duty to disclose certain other information that may lead to the discovery of the defective condition by the purchaser. For example, if the association has the duty to give a copy of the most recent budget to a potential purchaser, the budget may reveal projected costs of litigation with the developer over the defects, or the projected cost of correcting the defect.

36.16 Association— Suits

It frequently develops that the condominium unit owners, individually or collectively, participate in a lawsuit. These suits often involve the buyers' complaints against the developer for faulty construction or to avoid a "sweetheart" contract made by the developer with the association while it was in control of the project. Suits may also be generated by the business transactions of the association (i.e., service contracts such as trash removal, extermination, and the like), or the real property rights relating to the project as a whole (i.e., the encroachment of a neighboring project onto the common elements).

These suits are easier if the association can be the plaintiff rather than all members of the association. Generally, this is not allowed, unless the association is a not-for-profit corporation, but there are some exceptions to this rule. W.E. Shipley, Annotation, *Standing to Bring Action Relating to Real Property of Condominium*, 72 A.L.R.3d 314 (1976). The association can bring suits if

1. The association owns the property that is the subject of the suit. *Raven's Cove Townhomes, Inc. v. Knuppe Dev. Co., Inc.*, 171 Cal. Rptr. 334 (1981).
2. A statute confers *standing to sue* upon the association, 765 ILCS 605/18.3, as construed in *Tassan v. United Dev. Co.*, 88 Ill. App. 3d 581, 410 N.E.2d 902 (1980), regarding condominium unit owners' association. *See also* Cal. Code Civ. Pro. § 74.
3. The suit is to rescind, reform, or seek recovery arising out of unconscionable provisions in recreation leases made while the developer was in control of the association. 15 U.S.C. § 3608.

This is a developing area of the law and local law must be thoroughly reviewed before any action is taken.

36.17 Liability for Injuries—Liability Insurance

The condominium owners are owners and occupants of the common elements. As such owners and occupants, they become liable for injuries sustained by third parties to the same extent as any other owner. This liability corresponds to the liability of a landlord for proper maintenance of facilities enjoyed in common by the tenants, such as common stairways. It is this rule that makes it important for the condominium to have adequate and comprehensive liability insurance. Workers' compensation, elevator liability insurance, and the like are also needed. A closer question relates to the possible liability of the association to a condominium owner.

> **EXAMPLE:** *A,* a condominium owner, sustains injuries because of a negligently maintained common stairway. He sues the association. By the modern rule, he will be allowed to recover his damages. *White v. Cox,* 95 Cal. Rptr. 259 (1971); Note, Recent Cases, *Torts—Condominiums—Condominium Unit Owner Has Standing to Sue Unincorporated Unit Owners' Association for Injuries Inflicted Because of the Association's Negligence,* 25 Vand. L. Rev. 271 (1972). The theoretical legal problems are (1) as an owner, *A* is, in effect, suing himself and (2) there are technical problems in suing an unincorporated association. In some states, one or the other of these obstacles may prevent lawsuits of this nature. *See also* Eric Hollowell, Annotation, *Condominium Association's Liability to Unit Owner for Injuries Caused by Third Person's Criminal Conduct,* 59 A.L.R.4th 489 (1988) (re liability of association to unit owner for injuries caused by criminal acts of third party).

The unit owners will be liable to the injured party in proportion to the share of common elements each owns. Andrea G. Nadel, Annotation, *Personal Liability of Owner of Condominium Unit to One Sustaining Personal Injuries or Property Damage by Condition of Common Areas,* 39 A.L.R.4th 98 (1985).

36.18 Insurance   Insurance of the condominium is a problem that can be solved through coordination of efforts. Each unit owner can obtain fire and other hazard insurance on the apartment and its share of the common elements. Note the problem in insuring a condominium unit, which is a cube of air space. Should a loss occur, the damage to the common elements must be repaired as a single enterprise for the benefit of all owners. The master policy covers the common elements. The laws of some states require that the condominium board obtain insurance on both the common elements and the units. *See* 765 ILCS 605/12. It is extremely important that the coverage between the unit and master policies fits perfectly so that as far as any of the unit owners are concerned, the entire structure and range of risks are covered. This proper match of policies avoids a conflict or gap in coverage for such items as partitions, floor coverings, wall coverings, furniture, and fixtures. This problem can be avoided if the new standard form policies are used and the association and unit owners purchase a package of coverage from the same broker who then tailors the unit owners' policies to meet individual needs.

The standardized master policies provide coverage for the common elements, which, when properly used with the unit owners' policy, constitute the basis for a well-rounded insurance program. The unit owner policy should cover the amount of the interior of the unit not covered by the master policy and personal liability coverage. These master policies waive the subrogation rights of the insurer as against any unit owner.

> **EXAMPLE:** *A,* the owner of Unit 12, falls asleep while smoking. The resultant fire causes smoke and water damage to the hallways. The master policy insurer could pay the loss to the association and by virtue of subrogation rights proceed to recover for the loss as against *A.* The waiver of the subrogation right prevents this from happening. The loss is paid by the insurance company and the matter is over.

Many lawyers feel that losses to the common elements should be paid to the insurance trustee named in the condominium declaration. The trustee is then authorized by the declaration to adjust the loss, that is, to agree with the insurance company as to the amount of loss and be exclusively entitled to hire contractors to rebuild the common elements.

For the unit owner, the policy provides coverage for an amount of unscheduled personal property, and additions and alterations (fixtures, installations, or additions comprising the part of the building within the unfinished interior surfaces of the perimeter walls, floors, and ceilings of the units). The coverages may be increased by a special endorsement that can be tailored to meet the individual needs of the unit owners.

Some points to remember are as follows:

1. The unit owner may want an endorsement (Loss Assessment Coverage) to protect against personal liability if the building's liability insurance is inadequate.

   EXAMPLE: A brain surgeon visiting the building trips on loose flooring in the lobby and is permanently injured. He recovers a judgment of $1,500,000 against the HOA. The HOA carries only $1,000,000 liability insurance. It must levy an assessment of $500,000. Remember that each of the unit owners owns a percentage of the defective floor and is personally liable for such injuries. The endorsement in question covers this assessment.

2. The HOA's liability insurance provides no coverage for injuries sustained in the unit itself.

3. The HOA's insurance does not cover a cabana, storage shed, and so on, owned solely by the unit owner.

4. The HOA's insurance is probably an all-risk policy. Among the common exclusions in such policies are earthquakes, floods, water damage that occurs over a period of weeks (as from small roof leaks), termite damage, wear and tear, and explosion of boilers.

5. The unit owner needs additional living expense coverage for the cost of hotel and meals while his or her unit is inhabitable as a result of fire or other damage.

6. The unit owner needs separate coverage for theft or damage to his or her personal effects, furniture, furs, stereo, cameras, and so on. This should be the replacement value type. The other type is less expensive, but covers the depreciated value.

7. The HOA should buy plate glass coverage if there are many large windows.

8. The HOA needs fidelity coverage on its treasurer and manager, and all persons who handle money.

9. The HOA needs workers' compensation and employer's liability coverage on its guards, maintenance men, and manager.

10. The unit owner's policy should be in the same company used by the HOA. There have been cases where two companies were involved and each pointed the finger at the other.

11. The unit owner may want a medical payments endorsement to cover injuries in his or her unit for which he or she is technically not liable, as where a baby sitter suffers burn injuries while fixing a snack.

12. Since many condominiums provide parking in garages controlled by the HOA, special garagekeeper's liability coverage is needed, to protect the HOA from loss of cars by theft, fire, and so forth.

13. If the HOA operates a snack bar or vending machine, it needs products liability coverage to cover claims for illness due to contaminated food, etc.

14. If the HOA provides a car, uses a pickup truck, or the like, the usual motor vehicle insurance is needed.

15. Officers and directors want officers and directors' liability insurance protecting them against various liabilities, such as failure to take out insurance and a loss occurs, or where a unit owner sues for libel, slander, or invasion of privacy because that owner's name has been posted in the lobby as delinquent in his or her assessments. Some directors feel that liability coverage is not needed where the HOA indemnifies them against liability, as is customary. This is a mistake. The insurance money will be needed by the HOA to pay the claim if the directors are found to be liable.

16. As with other insurance, the HOA can save money by purchasing an insurance policy with a deductible. Liability coverage may carry a deductible as high as $2,500. The wisdom of such a purchase is debatable. One important benefit of liability coverage is the fact that the company is obligated to defend lawsuits at its expense. The expense and nuisance of defending a lawsuit for an amount less than the deductible is considerable. As to deductibles in the hazard insurance part of the policy, a different problem surfaces. If the damage is only to the unit, the deductible is borne by the unit owner. If the damage is to the building, the loss is borne by the HOA.

Of course, some cases present difficult problems.

EXAMPLE: A roof is damaged by storm and rain damage to several units results. Here, the deductible must be spread among the HOA and unit owners involved.

36.19 Title Insurance Requirements

A prudent purchaser of a condominium apartment will demand a title insurance policy. Preferably, the policy will contain specific coverage against mechanic's liens. It should also contain assurance that there are no delinquent condominium assessments, for such condominium assessments are, by law, a foreclosable lien on the unit. To obtain this coverage, the condominium manager furnishes an assessment letter to the title company stating the status of the unit's account. The title company takes the risk of any inaccuracy in this certificate. The title company, in addition to making its usual search of the public records, also searches for assessment liens filed by the management group, for, in some states, these must be recorded. The title company also satisfies itself that the right of first refusal has been properly eliminated, and its policy will insure the purchaser on this score.

To supplement the title coverage, the purchaser may want to request a letter from the secretary of the condominium's board of directors or manager that no special assessments are contemplated. A unit may go on the market because its owner wishes to avoid payment of a large assessment. This is especially the case as buildings age and expensive maintenance must be done. For example, new roofs or windows may be required. Large undertakings such as those will require significant assessments against unit owners if the association has not accumulated reserves for the replacement of these capital items.

In some areas, it is commonly required by purchasers and mortgagees of condominium units that the title company insure that the condominium complies with the local statute. By special request, this insurance can be obtained.

36.20 Regulation

There are various ways that condominiums are regulated. Building codes, zoning laws, and private building restrictions apply to condominiums just as they do to other properties. Some laws are addressed solely to condominiums, regulating their creation and sale. In some states, this is the same format used to regulate any other subdivision, which requires approval of public authorities. For example, in California, a "final public report" issued by the real estate commissioner must be given to a purchaser of a condominium or other subdivided land before a purchase contract is made. Cal. Bus. & Prof. Code § 11018.1. This report discloses all sorts of information about the project, including the condition of title, soil condition, flood problem, nearby schools, and the like. Through these laws, state and local governments exercise their police powers to protect the health, safety, and well-being of local residents under the theory that disclosure of vital information to prospective purchasers allows them to make an informed decision.

36.21 Zoning

Some municipalities have tried to "zone out" condominiums. In this way, a municipality might attempt to enforce a zoning ordinance to block a conversion of an apartment structure to condominiums. Any zoning ordinance that seeks to exclude condominiums while permitting similar tenant-occupied buildings is invalid. Zoning must deal with land use, not land ownership. *Claridge House One, Inc. v. Borough of Verona,* 490 F. Supp. 706 (D.C. N.J. 1980); W.E. Shipley, Annotation, *Zoning or Building Regulations as Applied to Condominiums,* 71 A.L.R.3d 866 (1976).

36.22 Conversion

Hundreds of thousands of rental units have been converted into condominiums and cooperatives. Several factors caused this wave of conversion activity. Increased costs tended to make apartment building construction and ownership an uneconomical business. It became especially unattractive when the value of a structure as an apartment building was compared to the total of the sales prices of the apartment units in the structure. Indeed, the profits of successful conversion caused developers to convert structure after structure in prime areas, such as Chicago's Lake Shore Drive area and the Gold Coast of Florida. The conversion process has begun anew, especially in connection with the reuse of older loft buildings near the center of major cities.

From the tenant/potential unit owner's point of view, the economic advantages and disadvantages are complex and difficult to analyze. It had been the case that the gross costs of condominium unit ownership were more than the costs of renting the same unit. This is less so the case with today's low interest rates, which help make condominium ownership less expensive and more competitive with the cost of renting similar units. These costs may be offset by the equity created by principal payments against the mortgage debt and appreciation in the value of the unit—a very substantial factor, in many cases. It is also probable that the cost to the purchaser of a unit in a converted building will be less than the cost to purchase a comparable unit if it had to be built today. The income tax advantages to the unit buyer must also be factored into the equation.

One other point of view must be considered. The municipality where the condominium is located has a stake. Economically, real estate taxes will probably increase upon conversion. Politically, the city must determine whether the interests of renters and low-income tenants should be fostered or should ownership of a stake in the community be fostered

36.22(a) Conversion Legislation

The first wave of conversion activity brought about a hue and cry of opposition. Tenants, especially senior citizens and handicapped persons, excited the sympathies of the legislatures to enact statutes and local ordinances that in one way or another protect the preconversion occupants of the structure. Unit purchasers benefitted front the flow of recent legislation.

Although the federal government has not specifically legislated in this area, Congress has suggested that states and local governments require that tenants be given adequate notice of the conversion and the first opportunity to purchase converted units. 15 U.S.C. § 3605.

In considering the resultant regulation, it must be remembered that the legislative bodies were reacting to and trying to serve several goals, including the preservation of the community's housing goals (i.e., fostering ownership or tenant rights; the protection of tenants from displacement without the adequate opportunity to find replacement housing; and the protection of unit purchasers).

While the outright prohibition of conversion is invalid, *Zussman v. Rent Control Bd.,* 326 N.E.2d 876 (Mass. 1975), regulation of the conversion process is allowed. *Grace v. Town of Brookline,* 399 N.E.2d 1038 (Mass. 1979). While the form of regulation varies from community to community and reference is directed to local laws and ordinances, the regulations often include the following: moratoria barring conversion for a period; tying government approval of the conversion to apartment vacancy rates; requiring the rent control board's approval of the conversion; requiring a notice to the tenants prior to the conversion of their units; requiring that tenants receive preemptive options to purchase their units, any unit in the building, or even the entire structure; requiring approval of the conversion by a percentage of the tenants; giving senior citizens and handicapped tenants the right to remain as tenants for extended periods of time after the conversion, *Troy Ltd. v. Renna,* 727 F.2d 287 (3d Cir. 1989); *Mountain Management Corp. v. Hinnant,* 492 A.2d 693 (N.J. 1985); requiring the converter to replace the rental units taken from the community by the conversion; giving displaced tenants relocation assistance; and disclosing the physical condition of major structural components of the structure and proposed budgets, past operating statements, and amounts recently spent for repairs to prospective purchasers. Janet Boeth Jones, Annotation, *Validity and Construction of Law Regulating Conversion of Rental Housing to Condominiums,* 21 A.L.R.4th 1083 (1983).

236.22(b)   Areas of Concern for Unit Purchasers

The unit purchaser of a converted unit has some concerns in addition to those of the purchaser of a new unit. The physical condition of the units and the structure as a whole is a prime concern. The report of a reputable engineer is essential as are pest control reports. Warranties will not generally be available for the structure and its components except for work recently done in connection with the conversion. Unless the appliances were replaced in the upgrading of the building for the conversion, they will not have warranties.

When a loft conversion is considered, the ability of the older structure and infrastructure to accommodate today's demands must be considered. Is there adequate electrical power and telephone capacity to service the needs of today's buyer who will install entertainment centers, computer lines, and the like? Will the heating, ventilating, and air conditioning systems provide the level of comfort required by the buyer? In many cases, the building will be gutted and new systems installed. Careful checking of the building's capacities is beyond the means of the single unit owner. The converter's reputation is the key guide to a successful purchase.

36.22(c)   Preconversion Considerations

In addition to the ever-present market analysis, the converter must analyze several other factors in deciding to purchase a project for conversion.

The impact of conversion and tenant's rights laws and ordinances must not be taken lightly. The tenants have awesome power under these laws. The marketing effort can be stopped dead by the legal and political acts of opponents to the conversion. If sales stop while expenses continue, the result is disaster for the converter.

Can the underlying mortgage against the property be paid and how can those payments be made?

> **EXAMPLE:** An owner of an apartment building wants to convert it to condominiums. The building is encumbered with an existing mortgage that permits no prepayment. Conversion is effectively blocked until the lender can be persuaded to accept a prepayment, for which it may well extract a substantial prepayment charge.

The existing mortgage may not be prepayable until a later date or the prepayment penalty may be reduced as the loan ages. Nonetheless, the converter wants to sell the units at an earlier date. Title insurance companies solve this problem by issuing policies that "insure over" the existing mortgage. To do this, the companies require a deposit of cash or triple-A securities that can be used to retire the old mortgage at its earliest due date. Of course, this underlying loan must not have a due-on-sale clause.

Any new financing must provide for partial payment as units are sold. Often, lenders require that a minimum of 25 to 30 percent of the units be sold before the first of the partial releases are available.

> **EXAMPLE:** In a 100-unit conversion, the lender may require that 30 units be sold and closed, with a stated portion of the closing proceeds applied to the loan before the partial release clause becomes effective.

This necessitates a volume closing at a title company when the documents and funds for the thirty units are deposited, and, when all thirty units are ready to close, the appropriate partial releases of the underlying loan are recorded and the loan payment is made by the escrowee. Thereafter, partial releases are available as individual units close.

The assumption of existing encumbrances may greatly assist the converter's payment of the building's purchase price, but additional financing is needed to pay the balance of the acquisition costs and the costs of conversion, such as attorneys' fees, title costs, engineering work, refurbishment, and marketing expenses.

During the time between the signing of the contract and the closing, the converter wants to be able to begin the preliminary work in anticipation of the conversion. For the developer, this is an important period of time; the interest meter is not yet running. The more preliminary items that can be cleared during this preclosing time, the less the cost of the conversion. To this end, the building's purchase contract should give the converter (1) access to the property for the converter's own staff; (2) the ability to communicate with the tenants; (3) access to tenants' lease files; (4) control over leasing activity; and (5) access to operating information (e.g., service contracts, utility charges).

The physical condition of the property and its components (e.g., elevators, climate control system, roof, etc.) must be carefully analyzed.

The tenant roster and rent roll should be examined. Here, the goal is to determine the rights of the existing tenants. Any purchaser of the property will take subject to these rights. Second, an analysis of the tenant roster and rent levels may give some insight into the willingness of existing tenants to purchase units.

Operating statements for recent years will aid in determining the level of assessments to unit buyers, give evidence of repairs and maintenance, and perhaps reveal any special problems that the building may have (e.g., an unusual insect problem).

The condominium documents should comply with the requirements of the GNMA, FNMA, FHLMC, and so on. If not, the units will not be acceptable to permanent lenders because they will not be marketable in the secondary mortgage market.

An interim loan will be necessary to finance conversion costs. The interim lender may require an end-loan commitment to finance outsales to retail buyers. Outsales also necessitate a partial release clause in the interim loan.

The converter should require that the loan documents allow the rental of unsold units during the conversion process to generate funds to help the converter meet expenses.

36.23 Securities Law Problems   Many condominium developments are leisure-oriented projects in vacation areas. The unit purchaser intends to live in the unit for part of the year and hold the unit available for rent for the rest of the year. A managing agent is hired to rent out the various units. This form of operation, however, raises the specter that the development may be subject to both federal and state securities laws.

The Securities Exchange Commission has taken the position that the offering of a condominium must be in compliance with the registration and prospectus delivery requirements of the securities laws if any one of the following are found:

1. The condominiums, with any rental arrangements or other similar service, are offered and sold with emphasis on the economic benefits to the purchaser to be derived from the managerial efforts of the promoter, or of a third party designated or arranged for by the promoter.

2. Participation in a rental-pool arrangement is offered. In a rental pool, all rents are collected by the manager and divided equally among unit owners. *But see Wals v. Fox Hills Dev. Corp.*, 24 F.3d 1016 (7th Cir. 1994) (which requires more than the offer of a rental-pool arrangement, in that there must be a horizontal commonality, or pooling of interests, among the condominium investors and the developer).

3. The offering of a rental or similar arrangement whereby the purchaser must hold the unit available for rental for any part of the year, must use an exclusive rental agent, or is otherwise materially restricted in the occupancy or rental of the unit. Securities Act Release No. 5347, Fed. Sec. L. Rep., (CCH) ¶ 79, 163 (1973).

Registration requirements may also be mandated by state securities or Blue Sky laws.

EXAMPLE: An agreement for the sale of one of six units in a condominium project requires that the buyer enter into an exclusive management and rental agreement. Personal use of the unit was limited, in that the time for use had to be reserved far in advance; the owner had to maintain the unit in a rentable condition and had to pay a flat monthly fee for promotional activities to stimulate rentals. Promotional materials emphasized the investment rather than the residential aspects of ownership. The court found that state securities laws had been violated. *Lowery v. Ford Hill Inv. Co.,* 556 P.2d 1201 (Colo. 1976).

Not all rental arrangements fall under the securities laws, such as when the units are not sold with an emphasis on the economic benefits befalling the purchaser from the managerial efforts of others. A unit buyer may enter into a nonpool rental arrangement with an agent who is not designated or required to be used as a condition of purchase whether or not the rental agent is affiliated with the developer.

EXAMPLE: A developer offers condominium units in an ocean-front high-rise building. The sales emphasis is on the resort aspects of the development, and not on appreciation and return on investment caused by the developer's affiliate real estate management company's activity. In fact, no rental pool agreement is part of the package. The developer does, however, have a local real estate corporation that will, if asked, attempt to rent individual units for periods specified by the owners. No rental pool arrangement is available. No securities law registration is required. *See generally Joyce v. Richie Tower Properties,* 417 F. Supp. 53 (N.D. Ill. 1976).

Condominium resales may be securities sales if the unit is sold with an emphasis on its economic benefits and the unit is offered with a rental arrangement in a single package. *Hockins v. Dubois,* 885 F.2d 1449 (9th Cir. 1989).

36.24 Time-sharing Condominiums

In the mid-1970s, a new form of condominium ownership, the time-sharing condominium, was developed. Found in vacation areas where ownership of the unit for the entire year is unnecessary, expensive, and burdensome for many people, the time-sharing concept allows the buyer to purchase a time slot of ownership. The original time-share developments were in waterfront and recreational vacation areas. The concept spread into urban vacation areas, such as New York, San Francisco, and New Orleans. Indeed, major developers have thriving time-share developments that grow over time into more mature projects.

For the developer, the profit potential is large.

> **EXAMPLE:** A unit in a resort condominium may sell for $100,000. A two-week period of ownership of that same unit may sell for $10,000. Obviously, if all two-week periods can be sold for $10,000, the developer will sell the unit for $260,000. This is not always the case. Recreational and vacation areas are usually seasonal. Only the prime weeks can be sold for the top dollar. The remainder of the year usually sells for rather steep discounts. Marketing costs of time-share condominiums are usually greater than for non-time-sharing units. So are the risks.

For the unit buyer, the property, which would normally be used only occasionally, can be purchased at a much lower price; the lodging costs of vacations are somewhat stabilized; income tax deductions for real estate taxes and interest payments may be available; and ownership burdens are generally reduced. If the owner cannot use the occupancy period, it may be rented, often through the building manager, or, if the owner grows tired of vacationing in the same place every year, the use period can be swapped through nationwide exchange programs for periods in other time-share condominiums all over the world.

Through the time-sharing device, the buyer uses the unit for an agreed segment of the year, with other buyers having the use of the unit for other segments. There are three basic formats used to allocate these ownership rights. First, in the time-span or tenancy-in-common format, the buyers are deeded an undivided interest in a particular unit as tenants in common with other buyers of the unit. At the same time, the buyers agree to limit their use of the unit to a designated time period.

Second, in the interval ownership format, purchasers are granted an estate for years for the agreed time period each year. This revolving estate for years lasts for the expected useful life of the project. At that point, all owners become tenants in common of the whole property.

Third, under a vacation license, the developer retains ownership and agrees to allow the buyers to use the premises for a stated period for a given number of years.

Some states have enacted legislation to specifically authorize and regulate time-sharing condominiums. *See, e.g.*, Fla. Stat. Ann. § 718.103, *et seq.*, W.E. Shipley, Annotation, *Regulation of Time-Share or Interval Ownership Interests in Real Estate*, 6 A.L.R.4th 1288 (1981).

The management of a property of this kind is very important. The unit owners are truly absentee owners. They come to the property for two weeks every year only to return a year later. If a top-flight management company is not in control of the project, it may deteriorate rapidly, taking away many of the joys that the owner anticipated during his or her use period.

36.24(a) Time-sharing Condominiums— Declaration

The declaration for the time-sharing condominiums must address itself to the following special matters:

1. Use and service periods with relevant undivided interests in the common elements.
2. Exclusive right to use, and occupancy of each, of the time-sharing owners for their relevant periods.
3. Collection and payment of costs such as telephone charges, firewood, repairs attributable to any owner's use, and common costs.
4. Waiver of right to partition. This waiver goes beyond the waiver contained in the declaration of a non-time-share condominium by waiving the right to partition between the various time-segment owners of a particular unit.

36.25 Suggestions for the Purchaser of a New Condominium

1. Do the condominium documents conform to state law? If not, dangerous consequences may result. For example, the tax assessor may refuse to separately assess the unit. This problem can be solved by obtaining an endorsement to the unit buyer's title insurance policy insuring that a condominium has been created in accordance with state law.

2. Determine whether the purchase contract gives the developer the right to cancel if a stated percentage of the units are not sold. Check to see how many units are sold to determine whether such clause is likely to be invoked. The buyer may change position by selling existing property, subletting an apartment, and so on, or incur expense by paying loan application fees only to be frustrated if the developer invokes this clause.

3. Check whether the burden of assessments for maintenance, and so forth, falls entirely on the sold units or is shared by the developer in proportion to the units remaining unsold. In general, of course, the entire subject of assessments and the factors that make up the assessment level—maintenance costs, payroll expenses, cost of keeping up the recreational facilities, reserves, and so forth, should be studied. Obtain a copy of the proposed budget. Is it realistic? How many months of advance assessments must be paid by the buyer at the closing? In trying to "sweeten" a deal for a prospective buyer, a developer may price the unit to include a prepayment of assessments for a period, say, six months.

4. Check whether the voting rights of the sold apartments give the unit purchasers at least a minority representation in the homeowners' association. For example, if a majority vote of the units in the building can elect a home association board of directors, the developer will have absolute control until a majority of the apartments are sold.

5. Check whether the documents require all purchasers to get their financing from a specified mortgage lender and, if so, what the lender's terms are likely to be.

6. Consider whether the prospective occupancy is such that the membership is likely to vote future assessments for maintenance and renovation in excess of your financial abilities as a purchaser.

7. The early contracts of sale for a condominium unit will permit the developer to amend or modify the declaration but should not permit the developer to increase the buyer's assessments, or to increase the unit cost, or to reduce the seller's obligation to pay the expenses on unsold units.

8. The contract of sale may state that the purchaser's rights are subordinate to the construction mortgage. This is necessary for the mortgagee's protection. *State Sav. & Loan Ass'n v. Kauaian Dev. Co.,* 445 P.2d 108 (Haw. 1968).

9. Determine what is done with the deposit or earnest money. The most conservative approach is to require that it be held in escrow and not used by the developer to pay construction costs or otherwise. Many buyers who did not protect themselves had their deposits lost when the developer got into financial difficulty. Legislation in some states requires the deposit of these funds into a separate escrow account. *See* Fla. Stat. Ann. § 718.202; Va. Code Ann. §§ 55-79.95.

10. What is the reputation of the management firm? Determine the duration of the management contract, keeping in mind that long-term contracts may lock you into inefficient management. How much authority is delegated to the manager by the association? Too much delegation strips the unit owner of a voice in the running of the project. Who does the hiring and firing of employees? If the board interferes, favoritism can creep in and efficient management becomes difficult. Pay scales of employees should track with pay scales generally.

11. Has the board met regularly and have there been genuinely democratic elections so that no clique runs the operation? In this connection, check the bylaws for duration of the term of board members. Check the present composition of the board. Lawyers and accountants, for example, are likely to do a better job in running the building than nonprofessionals.

12. Look into the physical attributes of the unit. When the purchase is made in reliance upon a model unit, drawing, or promotional material, there is an obvious need to compare the delivered product with the model. Do carpeting, draperies, furniture, and other furnishings in the model go with the unit? Where the unit is not completed, room dimensions, carpet grade, landscaping, finish hardware, appliance quality, and so on must be established. Before the

contract is signed, the particulars of the finished product must be agreed upon and reduced to writing. What of the physical nature of the building and the unit? Is it well constructed, soundproof, and so on? Does the structure conform to local zoning ordinances and private restrictions? Is the unit located near the noisy parts of the building, such as lobby, elevators, trash chute, and so forth? What parking and storage space is allocated to the particular unit? Determine whether the common elements include the recreation areas (swimming pool, tennis courts, and so forth) or whether they are excluded from the condominium, retained by the developer, and then leased to the association on a long-term basis.

13. What is the developer's reputation? Go to other projects the developer has completed. Talk to the residents.

14. What type of insurance does the association buy for the building? What type of insurance does the unit owner have to buy?

15. Are children and pets allowed?

16. What are the rules about window coverings, balcony furnishings, physical changes of the units?

17. If the property is being bought as an investment, other factors must be considered. Are there restrictions on leases? Must a uniform lease form be used? Do you have the ability to check the credit of potential renters? Are you going to turn the property over to a management agent? Will rentals cover ownership costs (i.e., mortgage payments, taxes, insurance, assessments)?

18. Review the basic condominium documentation, such as declaration, bylaws, and lease rules. Will you enjoy living under those rules? Will you enjoy group living generally?

36.26 Resales of Condominium Units

While many states require the developer to disclose certain information to prospective buyers, some states now require disclosures on resales of a unit by an ordinary unit owner. *See* 765 ILCS 605/22.1; Va. Code Ann. §§ 55-79.97. The required disclosures include the basic condominium documents; a statement of anticipated capital expenditures; a statement of the status of the reserve fund; a statement of the fiscal condition of the association; a statement of the status of pending suits involving the association; a statement of insurance coverage; and a statement of the amount of unpaid assessments against the unit.

CHAPTER 37

Cooperatives

37.01 In General

In a condominium, the buyer receives a deed to the apartment. In a cooperative, the buyer receives shares of stock in the corporation that owns the building and a lease or an assignment of the seller's lease of the apartment being sold.

To explain, let us look at an example:

> **EXAMPLE:** Sponsor buys a tract of land that is zoned for apartment purposes, taking title in a corporation. The sponsor owns all the stock and obtains an ordinary mortgage covering the apartment building. Suppose the apartment building contains 100 identical apartments. Sponsor can now sell one share to First Buyer and have that sale and assignment recorded on the books of the corporation. A one-share stock certificate is issued to First Buyer. Sponsor has his corporation give a ninety-nine-year lease, a proprietary lease, to First Buyer for an apartment. A memorandum reciting the making of this lease is recorded in the Recorder's office. First Buyer pays in cash the purchase price for the stock and lease and moves in. The deal is complete.

As can be seen, First Buyer acquires an interest in the corporation that owns the building subject to the large mortgage. First Buyer's lawyer may obtain a photocopy of Sponsor's title policy. First Buyer may or may not receive a title policy covering the lease.

37.02 The Formative Documents

The corporation that owns the building has a corporate charter. In addition to the usual terms of a corporate charter, this document contains special provisions needed for cooperatives.

A form of corporate charter for a cooperative corporation is set forth in 5 Am. Jur. Legal Forms 2d, *Co-ops,* p. 390, § 70.23. Special laws exist in some states for the incorporation of cooperative corporations. A check list for the contents of the corporate bylaws will be found in 5 Am. Jur. Legal Forms 2d, *Co-ops,* § 70.31. The bylaws often provide that the board of directors shall adopt a form of lease so that all leases are uniform in content. 5 Am. Jur. Legal Forms 2d, *Co-ops,* § 70.33. The bylaws provide that a cooperative lease can be assigned only in compliance with the terms of the lease. As can be seen, it is the practice to require the consent of the landlord to any assignment. The landlord is the building corporation, and its directors are elected by the tenant stockholders, so that the tenants can, to a considerable degree, control the occupancy of the building.

37.03 The Blanket Mortgage

The building and land are subject to a large mortgage. All present and future leases contain clauses specifically making the lease subject to this mortgage and all future mortgages. This means that every tenant takes subject to the possibility of loss of their investment by foreclosure. This frequently occurred during the Great Depression. If, for example, 10 percent of the tenants are unable to pay their rent, there is not enough cash flow for the corporation to make the mortgage payments. The mortgage may be foreclosed and all leases extinguished. The apartment becomes a rental apartment.

37.04 The Lease

The lease is called a proprietary lease because it runs for a long term. A form will be found in 5 Am. Jur. Legal Forms 2d, § 70.59.

The lease does not state a fixed rental to be paid each month. Instead the board each year fixes an amount that will be needed to pay the expenses of the building, mortgage debt service, insurance, operating expenses, and so on. A limit may be placed on the amount of rent that can be charged. In some leases, the tenant is given the right to pay a fee and surrender the lease to the corporation, thus terminating his or her liability for rent.

These leases typically require the board's consent to the assignment of a lease to a new owner. This consent cannot be withheld arbitrarily. *Sanders v. Tropicana,* 229 S.E.2d 304 (N.C. App. 1976); *Mowatt v. 1540 Lake Shore Drive Corp.,* 385 F.2d 135 (7th Cir. 1967); *Logan v. 3750 North Lake Shore Drive,* 17 Ill. App. 3d 584, 308 N.E.2d 278 (1974). For example, a refusal of consent based solely on racial grounds would not be allowed by a court. Arbitrary refusals seem to be allowed in New York. *Weisner v. 791 Park Ave. Corp.,* 6 N.Y.S.2d 426, 160 N.E.2d 720 (1950). In California, the landlord's consent is not required.

The lease provides that it is subject to any current or future mortgage placed on the building by the landlord corporation. A mortgage usually requires a two-thirds vote of the tenants. This clause facilitates refinancing of the existing mortgage.

It is significant that both a tenant's interest under a lease and shares of stock are legally considered to be personal property. Thus, a sale of a cooperative apartment is a sale of personalty.

> **EXAMPLE:** *R* entered into a contract to sell a cooperative apartment to *E. E* made an earnest money deposit as is common in sales of land. *E* failed to go through with the deal. *R* declared the earnest money forfeited. *E* sued *R,* and the court held that since a sale of personalty was involved, damages must be determined under the Uniform Commercial Code, which confines the seller's damages to loss on resale to another party and incidental expenses. *Silverman v. Alcoa Plaza Assocs.,* 323 N.Y.S.2d 39 (1971); 21 Buff. L. Rev. 555 (1972); 29 Wash. & Lee L. Rev. 189 (1972).

There are, of course, many other legal consequences of this rule. For example, on the death of an apartment owner, his or her leasehold and shares pass to his or her administrator or executor rather than to his or her heirs. As a result, a simple, informal sale by the executor or administrator is possible without the difficulties attendant upon sale of land owned by a deceased person. *See State Tax Comm'n v. Shor,* 371 N.E.2d 523 (N.Y. 1977).

37.04(a) Stock and Lease Inseparable

The lease provides that ownership of the lease and of the stock must always be in the same person.

37.04(b) Lien on Stock

The corporation retains a lien on any stock where the apartment owner is delinquent in payments.

37.05 The Trust Form

In Illinois, title to a cooperative is often placed in a land trust. The tenants receive certificates of beneficial interest under the land trust. A managing committee takes the place of a corporate board. This can be done in any state that recognizes land trusts.

37.06 Securities Problem

In the cooperative apartment complex that is purchased for residential purposes, there appears to be no problem with entanglements caused by the Federal Securities Law.

> **EXAMPLE:** In a large New York cooperative, prospective purchasers made a recoverable deposit on their apartments by buying shares of stock in the nonprofit housing corporation that held title to the property. The shares of stock were allocated to purchasers on the basis of the number of rooms in their apartments. When the tenant wanted to move out, he had to offer his stock back to the corporation at the initial selling price. The court found that the mere description of the certificates as "stock" did not render them a security subject to the Federal Securities Law. Noting that the purchasers intended merely to acquire a residential apartment for personal use rather than as an investment for profit to be derived from the managerial efforts of others, the court found no security present. *United Housing Foundation, Inc. v. Forman,* 421 U.S. 837 (1975). For similar reasons, a state's Blue Sky laws are inapplicable.

37.07 Conversion

In some areas, particularly New York, apartment buildings are being converted into cooperatives as well as condominiums. Because New York probably has more cooperative units than the remainder of the country, it has a very sophisticated cooperative conversion law. Because the cooperative development is a mix of both real estate and corporation concepts, the law has aspects of both bodies of law. *Richards v. Kaskel,* 32 N.Y.S.2d 524, 300 N.E.2d 388 (1973).

> **EXAMPLE:** Purchasers must be given a cooperative prospectus or offering plan approved by the attorney general in much the same way that a stock offering is approved. N.Y. Gen. Bus. Law Act 23A.

37.08 Warranties of the Building

The cooperative unit owner sufficiently resembles an ordinary tenant so that it is entitled to the benefit of the warranties of the building that characterize an ordinary residential landlord and tenant relationship. *Suarez v. Rivercross Tenants' Corp.,* 438 N.Y.S.2d 164 (1981).

37.09 Sale of Cooperative Apartment

The following suggestions may be appropriate for sellers and purchasers of existing cooperative apartments:

1. Obtain title evidence on the building. Supplement this by getting an affidavit from the secretary of the corporation to the effect that the condition of title remains today as it was on the date of the title evidence, which your lawyer examined, and that no lawsuits are presently pending or threatened against the corporation.

2. Since you are buying the lease and stock of the present tenant, get the secretary of the corporation to sign an affidavit stating the following: (a) that the stock is in fact owned by your seller and is fully paid for; (b) that the lease is owned by your seller, free of any subleases; (c) that the stock and lease are free from any assessments other than the current ones shown on the financial statement submitted to you by the corporation; (d) that the stock is free of restrictions on its transfer or those restrictions have been satisfied, B.C. Ricketts, Annotation, *Transfer of and Voting Rights in Stock Cooperative Apartment Association,* 99 A.L.R.2d 236 (1965); (e) that no defaults have occurred in the lease being sold or in the building's mortgage payments; (f) that none of the other tenants is currently behind in his or her payments; (g) that no proposal to remodel the building or increase assessments has come before the directors within the past year, for this may be why your seller is moving out; (h) determine how much space is rented to persons other than tenant stockholders, for, if this figure gets too high, you may lose your income tax benefits; and (i) determine what insurance is carried presently. Get a certified copy of the cooperative charter and bylaws and the directors' resolution authorizing your seller to sell you the lease and stock, for all cooperatives restrict the right of the tenants to transfer their rights. Check the lease for restrictions (e.g., on remodeling of apartments, or the right to sell, sublease, or operate a business in the apartment) and liabilities (e.g., special assessments) that it creates. Determine what maintenance costs must be paid.

3. It is quite important that an apartment seller who lists an apartment for sale with a real estate broker insert the no-deal, no-commission clause in the listing. This is important because if the cooperative board turns down the purchaser, the seller does not want to be liable for a commission.

4. It is important that the contract of sale specify what appliances and other articles go with the sale of the apartment. The sale does not include these articles unless so specified, and normally, they do not belong to the corporation. The contract should also contain various warranties by the seller, such as a warranty that it owns the shares and lease and will so continue at closing, free of any liens or adverse interests, including mechanic's liens; that the shares are fully paid for; that no lease defaults will exist at closing; and that the seller has no knowledge of building code violations or proposals to increase apartment assessments. For the seller's protection, the contract states that it is subject to approval by the co-op board, and that if the approval is refused, the buyer obtains the return of his or her deposit. The contract clause as to closing costs requires some special attention. The seller normally agrees to pay the corporation's charges for transfer of the shares and lease.

If the buyers are husband and wife who wish to own the apartment in joint tenancy, the contract of sale should so state, and special language may be needed because of the personal property nature of the lease and shares.

> **EXAMPLE:** In Illinois a deed of land to *A* and *B* "in joint tenancy" creates a joint tenancy. But to create a joint tenancy in shares and a leasehold probably requires the phrase "as joint tenants with the right of survivorship and not as tenants in common."

5. In states where a judgment against the owner of a leasehold creates a lien thereon, it probably will be necessary to have a title company make a search for such judgments.

A buyer planning to buy a cooperative unit needs to check quite a number of other things, for example: (1) Is the building mortgage a low-interest loan that will soon mature? If it is, the new loan will call for higher interest, and the monthly rent will increase. (2) Are there adequate reserves that could be used to meet emergency repairs and periodic capital improvements? (3) Does the building have a tax exemption that will soon expire, thereby pushing up the rent? Remember, all building cash flow needs are passed on to the owners. (4) Will the cooperative's documents and the board both allow apartment purchase to be financed by a pledge of the stock the purchaser acquires? Some older cooperatives do not permit share financing. (5) Will renovation contemplated by the purchaser be permitted? This is a thorny problem because the board cannot approve the alterations unless it sees the detailed plans. In other words, the purchaser must hire an architect and may then find it will not be permitted to do the work he or she considers indispensable to the purchaser's happiness. (6) Will the building forbid use of appliances, such as microwave ovens or computers? Many older buildings have inadequate electrical wiring.

Title insurance is available in some areas on sales of a cooperative. The insurer examines the chain of title, the formative documents, the lease, the assignment, and the mortgage documents on the apartment purchase. The title insurer will also require a certificate that the blanket mortgage is not in default and that the lease is in good standing. If title insurance is not available on the purchase of the apartment, the seller may be able to furnish a photocopy of the existing title policy covering the entire building. This will probably be several years old. Title and abstract companies sell searches showing briefly what has happened since the policy was issued as reflected on the public records. For example, if the mortgage debt was increased, such a recorded modification will be shown on the searches. Unpaid taxes will be shown also, and so on.

Both the real estate records and the Uniform Commercial Code (UCC) records should be searched. In either place, a filing may be made that affects the apartments.

The buyer should receive a copy of the bylaws and the rules the board has adopted.

Some corporations impose a transfer fee, which may be substantial, on any assignment.

After closing, the secretary of the board should certify that the assignment of lease and stock have been duly recorded on the corporate records. The buyer receives a stock certificate, an assignment of lease, a copy of the lease, a bill of sale for the appliances, and other customary documents.

The sale contract should require the seller to deliver the keys and the vacant apartment at closing.

Insurance is carried by the corporation and by the individual tenant much as in the case of condominiums.

37.09(a) Mortgage Loans on Sales of Cooperative Apartments

The problem of obtaining a mortgage loan when buying an apartment is great. 46 St. Johns L. Rev. 632. It is a second mortgage, of course, and the blanket first mortgage is apt to be a big one. Many sales are for cash. This is possible because the blanket mortgage is often so big that the seller has only a small equity that the buyer can handle for cash. The buyer who must borrow must seek out a lender who is making cooperative loans. These lenders have standard printed forms. The FNMA requires assurance that the cooperative corporation has marketable title. This process is much like that involved in a sale of the apartment. The stock and the lease are assigned to the lender. The buyer signs a collateral note (with the lease and stock as collateral), which qualifies as a security agreement under the UCC, and a financing statement is filed under UCC requirements.

The lender also requires of the corporation an agreement that the corporation will not, while the mortgage is in force, permit any further assignment, sublease, agreed termination, agreed modification, or junior mortgaging of the lease. The corporation agrees to notify the lender of any default in the payment of rent and to give the lender an opportunity to cure that default. A sore point is the continuing need of the lender to obtain the landlord's consent to the sale of an apartment acquired by foreclosure.

If the lease is of recent vintage, the lender will want a certified copy of the board resolution authorizing the lease. The lender will probably want a memorandum of the lease to be recorded. The assignment of the lease to the lender and the landlord's consent to the assignment are also recorded.

Truth in Lending and the Real Estate Settlement Procedures Act (RESPA) apply to these cooperative loans.

37.09(a)(1) The Secondary Market

Cooperative loans are being sold in the secondary market. Its requirements are not burdensome. Emphasis is on showing that the corporation has good, marketable title to the project, and that the lender has checked all changes since the title policy was issued. The lender's documents must require notice by the corporation of any actual or threatened condemnation, receipt by the corporation of nonrent income exceeding IRS rules, and any defaults in rent. These are requirements that any lender can live with.

37.10 Condominium and Cooperative Ownership Compared

There are significant legal and practical differences between the two types of apartment ownership.

1. The condominium owner holds title to the unit. In the cooperative, the owner buys shares in the corporation that owns the building and enters into an occupancy agreement or proprietary lease for a particular apartment.

2. The mortgage on a condominium unit covers only the unit and its share of the common elements. In a cooperative, the mortgage covers the entire property. If any substantial number of tenants default, the foreclosure would wipe out all tenants. To avoid this result, the nondefaulting unit owners would have to carry the defaulting owners.

The advantage the condominium enjoys with respect to mortgage financing should make it easier to sell or resell than a cooperative, since it enlarges the number of potential buyers.

EXAMPLE: *A* owns a condominium apartment which he can sell to *B* for $130,000. *B* can obtain a mortgage loan of approximately $100,000, so that he needs only $30,000. *A*'s existing mortgage, whatever its amount, would be paid off in the process, just as if *A* were selling a house. If *A* were selling a cooperative in a comparable building on which the building mortgage had been paid down to 50 percent of the property value, *A* would be selling the apartment equity for cash subject to the building mortgage, and he would have to find a buyer who has cash, for many lenders do not lend on cooperatives.

If a person desires a debt-free shelter, as many senior citizens do, a condominium purchaser can pay cash for the apartment. A cooperative purchaser has no choice but to accept the apartment subject to the mortgage on the building.

The condominium, since it is owned by many people, not by a single corporation as in the case of the cooperative, has no feasible way of putting a mortgage on the building in its later years when remodeling or repairs are needed.

3. Cooperative leases provide that the lease may be terminated for failure to meet a monthly assessment or because the apartment owner has become bankrupt or been guilty of objectionable conduct. *Green v. Greenbelt Homes, Inc.,* 232 Md.496, 194 A.2d 273 (1963). The condominium owner is more secure in this regard.

In a cooperative, the apartment owner has the right to leave. If the owner has bad luck and cannot keep up the monthly payments, it can sublease the apartment, sell it, or at the worst, give it back to the landlord corporation. The modern cooperative lease gives the lessee the right to cancel the lease after a specified number of years by surrendering the stock and the lease to the landlord corporation. In the condominium, the owner, having signed a note and mortgage, has no right simply to "walk away." In case of default and foreclosure, there is always the possibility of a deficiency judgment.

Another advantage that the cooperative possesses is the ease with which one can control the type of neighbors one will have in the building. In the cooperative, the lease provides that it cannot be assigned or subleased except with the written consent of the landlord corporation. The stock certificate provides that it can be transferred only in connection with an authorized transfer of the lease. This method has the advantage of simplicity and unquestioned legality. *68 Beacon St. v. Sohier,* 194 N.E. 303 (Mass. 1935); *Weisner v. 791 Park Ave. Corp.,* 160 N.E.2d 720 (N.Y. 1959).

Every cooperative board has an admissions committee. This committee reviews the application of a prospective tenant for permission to buy into the building. It reports to the board, which gives final approval or refusal. The board policy, reflected in a board resolution concerning stated financial requirements, for example, will be helpful in cases where a refused applicant charges discrimination. The board can simply point to its official policy and the failure of the applicant to meet the stated requirements. Many cooperatives look at the applicant's entire package, contract of sale, mortgage application, references, and so on, before scheduling a personal interview. If the applicant cannot meet financial requirements, he or she need not be humiliated by appearing before the board.

Each owner of a condominium apartment holds the apartment subject to a right of first refusal should he or she desire to sell. Such a right of first refusal is probably valid. *Gale v. York Ctr. Community Co-op., Inc.,* 171 N.E.2d 30 (Ill. 1960). However, the method is clumsy. Also, since it calls for the apartment owners to buy the apartment at the price the selling apartment owner can obtain from an outsider, it requires a special assessment on the apartment owners.

Getting rid of an owner who defaults in the payment of monthly payments or fails to abide by the bylaws is easier in the cooperative than in the condominium. Just as an ordinary lease can be terminated for default in rent or breach of covenant, so also a cooperative lease can be terminated for like grounds and the cooperative lessee evicted by quick and inexpensive forcible detainer proceedings. *Green v. Greenbelt Homes, Inc.,* 194 A.2d 273 (Md. 1963). In a condominium, if a particular apartment owner fails to pay the monthly assessments, a lien on the apartment can be foreclosed, just as a mortgage is foreclosed, but the proceeding is costly and time consuming. Making the condominium owner behave, when conduct becomes objectionable, is difficult.

4. In the condominium, the tax assessment is an individual assessment on the unit and its share of the common elements. As long as the tax on a particular unit is paid, failure of other unit owners to pay their taxes does not affect the nondelinquent unit. In the cooperative, there is one tax bill on the entire building. If some owners do not pay their share, the others must carry the entire load or face tax foreclosure proceedings.

5. In a cooperative, work and materials ordered by one tenant can result in a mechanic's lien against the entire building. In a condominium, the lien is confined to the apartment where the work was done.

6. Where for one reason or another it becomes advisable to sell the building and the tenants wish to do so, this can be accomplished in cooperatives by a vote of a percentage of the shareholders (who, of course, are the tenants). A two-thirds vote usually suffices. In the case of a condominium, sale of the building is apt to require a unanimous vote, except in certain special situations, as where the building is destroyed by fire.

7. Both the condominium owner and the cooperative owner have the right to deduct from income for income tax purposes all payments made on mortgage interest and real estate taxes.

37.10(a)   Additional Benefits of Cooperatives

There are additional benefits of the cooperative form of ownership. When a condominium is created, the tax assessor assesses each unit separately. As a result, the total of the tax assessments is far greater than the assessed value of the building viewed as a rental building. A co-op, being a rental building, enjoys the lower overall tax assessment.

Except in New York, cooperatives are not heavily regulated. Condominium regulations, on the other hand, grow more complex each year.

CHAPTER 38

Building Construction and Building Warranties; Mechanic's Liens

38.01 In General

1. An owner of a vacant lot, or a lot improved with an older home, may hire a contractor to build a house on the lot according to certain plans and specifications prepared by the lot owner's architect, or an architect obtained through the builder. This is a construction contract only.

2. A home buyer may pick a lot in a tract being developed by a builder and contract to have the developer build a home in the style of one of the developer's models. This is a contract for the sale of land and for the construction of a house.

3. Similar to the previous two contracts, a home buyer may contract to buy the lot and house that a developer has already constructed on the lot.

The second and third situations involve the sell-and-build type of contract. This type of contract is one for the sale of land and for the construction of a home. *Dieckman v. Walser*, 144 N.J. Eq. 382, 168 A. 582 (1933). It must comply with the requirements of law as to both a contract for the sale of land and a contract for the construction of a home.

EXAMPLE: Developer contracted to sell home buyer a lot and build a home thereon. The contract-of-sale portion was complete, but there were no plans or specifications giving the details of the building. The contract was invalid. *Griesenauer v. Belleau Lake Dev. Co.,* 421 S.W.2d 785 (1967).

A contract to build a home "like" the model the buyer has inspected is a contract to build a home like the model, with all of the inadequacies of the model.

38.02 Sell-and-Build Contracts

The are several types of sell-and-build contracts.

EXAMPLE: Seller contracts to sell a lot to Buyer. The contract requires that Buyer apply for a mortgage loan of $75,000 and is contingent on Buyer's procuring of this loan. When the loan is obtained, the deal is to be closed; thereafter, Seller is to construct the building, using the mortgage proceeds for this purpose. After the closing, the contract between the parties is simply a construction contract.

EXAMPLE: Seller contracts to sell a lot to Buyer, to erect a house thereon, and when the house has been completed, to deed the completed house and lot to Buyer. Here, Seller will obtain a construction loan, build the building with the construction loan proceeds, and deliver the completed package to Buyer. The Buyer's purchase money is then used to pay off the construction loan with the surplus going to Seller. This form of deal has some advantages to Seller. The handling of the construction disbursements does not involve Buyer, whereas in the previous example Seller must go to Buyer for documentation every time a construction disbursement is to be made. After all, in the previous example, it is Buyer's money, which is the proceeds of Buyer's loan, that is being used to pay the cost of the construction.

When a home buyer deals with a developer and builder, the home buyer may be dealing with a person who does not yet own the land that is being sold. Buyer may have only an option or contract to buy the land. If the developer runs into financial difficulties, it may never be able to pay the option price and transfer ownership to the buyer. Moreover, if financial troubles develop, and mechanic's liens are filed and mortgage foreclosures are instituted, the buyer will find that the possibility of acquiring the property at the expected price, or getting any down payment of earnest money back is nil. Therefore, it is best for the buyer to get a deed and title policy, with mechanic's lien coverage for the property as early as possible, before the buyer has put too much money into the house.

Most sell-and-build contracts are on forms prepared by the developer. As such, they are drafted in favor of the developer. When there is a high demand for homes, many developers will not vary the terms of these contracts. When demand is low, the willingness of the developer to make contract modifications increases.

At a minimum, the buyer should have the builder's promise to build the house pursuant to the plans and specifications, or substantially the same as the selected model, and to provide the buyer with an owner's policy of title insurance protecting the buyer against mechanic's liens, matters of survey, and other risks typically included within extended coverage title insurance. The buyer should also be entitled to a preclosing walk-through inspection and to have an architect inspect the home, both during and at the completion of construction. If the walk-through or the architect's inspection results in the discovery of construction defects, so-called "punch-list" matters, some mechanism for resolving those defects must be established. The builder will want the closing to occur and to have the buyer rely on the builder's promise to repair. Many buyers want to hold back some of the purchase price to ensure that the builder carries through with its promise. If these matters are not handled in the contract, disputes may well arise at the closing.

38.02(a) Sell-and-Build Contracts—Execution

Some sell-and-build contracts contain a clause that the seller is not bound unless an officer of the seller corporation signs for the corporation. Obviously, the buyer should not accept a contract signed only by a salesperson. Indeed, it is always advisable to insist on an officer's signature.

38.02(b) Sell-and-Build Contracts—Mortgage Clauses

Most residential sell-and-build contracts have a clause requiring the buyer to apply for and obtain a permanent mortgage loan. If the buyer and the property do not qualify, the deal will be off. The problem with this situation is that most lenders will not lock in an interest rate for the period it will take to construct the home. While the buyer may qualify for the loan at the rates that are prevailing at the time the contract is made, the qualification may be conditional upon a reevaluation when the rate is locked closer to the time of the expected closing.

38.02(b)(1) Sell-and-Build Contracts—Mortgage Clauses—Lender Liability

In the type of sell-and-build contract where the buyer obtains a mortgage that is disbursed as construction progresses, the lender will typically disburse the mortgage proceeds to pay for the construction, rather than merely giving the loan proceeds to the borrower. The reason is obvious. If the lender is counting on the security of the constructed building, the lender wants to be sure that the building is indeed constructed and that mechanics and materialmen are paid as construction progresses.

In this way, the lender gets its security lien free. There is a danger here. Many borrowers feel that the lender is looking out for their interests and expect that the lender will see to the proper disbursement of the loan funds. Some courts will hold in favor of the borrower requiring that the lender has a duty to the owner to exercise reasonable care to see to it that the payments are properly made. *Kalbes v. California Fed. Sav. & Loan Ass'n,* 497 So. 2d 1256 (Fla. App. 1986).

38.02(c) Sell-and-Build Contracts—Delay in Completion

A prospective buyer should read the contract before signing it. The time set for completion is an important matter to a buyer who is planning to sell a current home. Carefully read the *force majeure* clause that gives the builder additional time to complete in the event of unforeseen difficulties, such as acts of God, strikes, and so on. It may be so broad that the completion date is virtually meaningless. Developers will typically give themselves a long period of time to complete the project. It will be hard to negotiate a shorter time until the later stages of the project make the timing of completion more certain.

38.02(d) Sell-and-Build Contracts—Subordination of Contract to Construction Loan

Many sell-and-build contracts contain a clause subordinating the contract to any construction mortgage put on the property by the builder.

> **EXAMPLE:** Builder sells a lot to Buyer under a contract by which Builder will build a home for Buyer like the model home displayed to Buyer. Builder will now put a construction loan mortgage on the lot to Lender. Probably, Lender will want to see the contract to make certain that the land is under contract and to see the sale price. Having actual notice of the contract, Lender's rights would be subordinate to Buyer's rights, and a deed from Builder to Buyer could wipe out Lender's mortgage. To avoid this result, Lender will require that the contract provide that Buyer's rights are subordinate to Lender's lien.

38.02(e) Sell-and-Build Contracts—Builder Liability

Obviously, the seller/builder in a sell-and-build contract has all the liabilities of a building contractor. *Jones v. Gatewood,* 381 P.2d 158 (Okla. 1963).

38.03 Mechanic's Liens

Mechanics and materialmen furnish labor and materials used in the construction of improvements on land. A mechanic or materialman who has furnished such labor or materials on the landowner's order can, by complying with certain formalities, obtain a lien on the land and improvements in question, which can be foreclosed if the landowner does not pay. The lien is called a mechanic's lien, and the person furnishing the work or material is the mechanic's lien claimant.

Generally, lienable work and materials must become a permanent part of the building structure. Thus, for example, medical care furnished to an employee of the contractor, even if the injury was suffered on the building site, is not lienable. Similarly, printing, stationery, and telephone service furnished to the contractor are not lienable.

38.03(a) Performance by Contractor

In general, where the general contractor seeks to assert a lien, it must show that the contract was substantially performed. Likewise, any subcontractor seeking to assert a lien must show that the subcontract was substantially performed. Where the contract specifies that no payment will be made without production of an architect's certificate, a general contractor claiming a lien must produce the certificate and satisfy any other conditions to payment set forth in the contract.

38.03(b) Inception and Priority of Lien

The law as to the particular time when a mechanic's lien attaches to the land varies from state to state. In some states, the lien relates in time to the visible commencement of construction. In other states, the lien relates in time to the execution of the construction contract.

38.03(c) Notice of Lien

In many states, laws require a mechanic's lien claimant to file a notice of the lien in some public office within a specified time, usually within some period after completion of the work. Usually, it is required that the notice state the amount claimed to be due, the name and address of the claimant, the type of improvement, a description of the land, and the name of the landowner or landowners. C.C. Marvel, Annotation, *Sufficiency of Notice, Claim or Statement of Mechanic's Lien with Respect to Description or Location of Real Property,* 52 A.L.R.2d 12 (1957); W.J. Dunn, Annotation, *Sufficiency of Notice, Claim or Statement of Mechanic's Lien with Respect to Nature of Work,* 27 A.L.R.2d 1169 (1953).

38.03(d) Waiver and Release of Lien

As construction or repair work goes forward, liens attach to the land. Both the landowner and any mortgagee involved naturally want to get rid of these liens, which can be accomplished by procuring waivers of their liens from the parties furnishing labor or material. There are partial waivers and final waivers. Suppose that a subcontractor, such as a plumbing, electrical, or plastering subcontractor, has finished half of the job and wants to be paid for that half. When the landowner/developer makes this partial payment, it will demand a waiver of lien from the contractor for the work and materials furnished. This waiver recites that it waives all liens for work and materials furnished. This means, of course, that the lien for work and materials furnished up to the date of the waiver has been waived. The waiver does not affect the lien for the work still to be done.

When final payment is made to the contractor, the landowner/developer will demand a final waiver, which waives all liens for work and materials furnished or to be furnished. This means that the contractor has no lien at all on the land or buildings. Even if the contractor must come back to repair or replace defective work or material, it can claim no lien on the property. This is important, because the objective is always to get the building built at the price and at the bids submitted by the various mechanics. There is trouble ahead if any of the contractors are legally able to assert a lien for a sum greater than the amount agreed to.

When a mechanic has filed a lien claim in some public office as required by law, it becomes necessary to release its lien from the public records, when the claim has been paid or settled. As a rule, a waiver is not appropriate for this purpose. Instead, a release of mechanic's lien is used. It is very similar to a release of mortgage, and is filed in the same office where the lien claim was filed.

38.03(e) Time Limit on Enforcement of Lien

It is usually provided that a mechanic's lien ceases to exist unless steps are taken to enforce or foreclose it within a specified time, usually one or two years, after the filing of the lien claim.

38.04 Extras

Extras are probably the largest cause of disputes between owners and contractors. There is a propensity on the part of some contractors to bid low in order to get the job and then try to bail their way out of a losing job by claiming extras. Also, an owner frequently thinks of items to be added during the course of construction and orders changes or extra work and materials indiscriminately without a definite understanding as to the cost. A contractor who is providing extras does not have to make a competitive bid in order to obtain the work. There is, therefore, a tendency on the part of some contractors to charge more money for extras than the mark-up used in bidding for work.

The contract should, therefore, specifically require that all extra charges be reduced to a written instrument, signed by the owner, describing the work to be performed and the amount to be paid. Such a provision is valid. C.P. Jhong, Annotation, *Effect of Stipulation in Private Building or Construction Contract, That Alterations or Extras Must Be Ordered in Writing*, 2 A.L.R.3d 620, 631 (1965). In the interest of both the contractor and the owner, this procedure should be religiously followed. The owner's architect has no power to waive this provision of the contract. The architect cannot order extras verbally. 2 A.L.R.3d 620, 686, *supra*. However, if the owner verbally orders the extra work, the owner will have to pay. 2 A.L.R.3d 620, 658, *supra*. By ordering the extras verbally, the owner has waived the provision requiring a change order to be in writing. The dispute arises, however, because the contractor says that the owner ordered an extra while the owner states otherwise. Often, there have been conversations, but the owner and the contractor have a different view of the result of those conversations over the change or extra.

Also, the contract should require the owner to deposit additional funds with the mortgage lender in order to assure the contractor and the lender that there will be adequate funds to complete the building including the extra work or materials.

In addition to disputes with respect to the cost of extras, disputes often arise as to whether a given item is an extra or is included under the original contract. If the plans and specifications made a part of the contract are sufficiently detailed, the possibility of a dispute over whether a particular item is an extra can be minimized.

38.05 Progress Payments

If I hire you to erect a building on my land, the contract will almost certainly fix a total price for the entire job. However, your subcontractors will not wait for their money until the building is finished. Therefore, the contract will call for progress payments to the general contractor and the subcontractors as the project is completed. A widely used formula provides for a payment of 35 percent of the contract amount when the house is under roof, 30 percent of the contract price when the house is plastered, and the balance of 35 percent when the building is completed and accepted by the owner. On commercial construction projects, disbursements are typically made on a monthly basis.

The contract often provides that only 90 percent of the full amount of a progress payment due the general contractor is payable when the progress payment falls due. The owner may hold back 10 percent of each payment due to the general contractor (often called a retention) until the project has been completed and accepted by the owner with all lien waivers produced.

As a progress payment is demanded, the contract often calls for an inspection to be made by the owner's architect, who certifies that the work and material for which payment is claimed are in place and that the work has been completed in accordance with the contract. If the owner has no architect, this inspection should be made by the lender. If the lender makes these inspections, it should make it clear to the borrower that the inspections are for the lender's protection only, and the owner/borrower cannot rely on the lender's architect or inspector.

Failure of the landowner to make a progress payment is a material breach of the contract. It entitles the contractor to suspend work until payment has been made. *Watson v. Auburn Iron Works, Inc.*, 318 N.E.2d 508 (Ill. 1974).

38.06 Mortgage Money

Any builder who builds on contract for a landowner should insist that the landowner have a definite commitment for a satisfactory construction loan before construction begins, and the construction contract should be made subject to this condition.

38.07 Cash Down Payments from Home Buyers

Builders usually insist that the home buyer make a cash down payment. What to do with it is the question. Home buyers are often reluctant to pay a builder a large sum of money before construction has begun. Builders are often reluctant to start construction when they have no assurance that the home buyer will be able to come up with the money. One solution is to have the home buyer deposit the down payment with the lender that is financing construction or fund the down payment to the title company that will disburse the construction funds. This is likely to be acceptable to the lender, for, under the typical construction loan agreement, this deposit is used for the initial stages of construction, and the loan proceeds are not used until later stages of construction have been reached.

In some states (e.g., New York), laws require the builder to keep the buyer's deposit in an escrow. In other states, a builder who diverts the deposit to another job is guilty of a crime. *State of Washington v. McDonald,* 463 P.2d 174 (Wash. App. 1969).

38.08   Substantial If a contractor finishes the building in strict accordance with the plans and specifications
Performance and in a good and workmanlike manner, it is, of course, entitled to collect the full contract price. However, it is virtually impossible to complete a building contract in strict compliance with every requirement of the plans and specifications. If the contractor performs substantially according to the contract, it is entitled to collect the contract price, less a deduction that will compensate the owner for the builder's deviations from the contract.

Substantial performance is hard to define. If the owner gets substantially the building that it contracted for, and the deviations are trifling and unintentional, there is substantial performance. For example, a contractor is hired to build a house according to certain plans at a price of $120,000. The contractor fulfills the contract, except that two rooms have the wrong wallpaper, which it would cost $1,000 to remedy. Clearly, there is substantial performance, and the contractor is entitled to collect $119,000.

EXAMPLES: The following are illustrations of cases where substantial performance was found lacking: (1) The footings were inadequate for wet ground, so that the foundations sank and the floors sagged. *White v. Mitchell,* 123 Wash. 630, 213 P. 10 (1923); (2) the contract called for a six-room house, and the builder erected a five-room house; (3) the foundations and walls of the house cracked immediately after completion of construction due to a soil condition that the builder did not properly correct, *Newcomb v. Schaeffler,* 131 Colo. 56, 279 P.2d 409 (1955); and (4) in New York, it is generally held that if the deviations amount to more than 10 percent of the contract price, substantial performance is lacking. *Rochkind v. Jacobson,* 110 N.Y.S. 583 (1908).

If substantial completion is not achieved, one of the following consequences is possible:

1. The owner may accept the building as a complete and satisfactory substitute for the building contracted for. Here, the owner must pay the full contract price. No deductions are allowed because of the defects. *Zambakian v. Lesson,* 77 Colo. 183, 234 P. 1065 (1925).

   EXAMPLE: As the building went up, the owner inspected it and noticed the deviations from the contract. Nonetheless, the owner took occupancy, telling the builder that the building was satisfactory and that the contract price would be paid. This is full acceptance. All deviations were waived. *Hooper v. Cuneo,* 227 Mass. 37, 116 N.E. 237 (1917).

   Often, in these cases, the owner has with full knowledge of the defects paid the entire contract price. Since this is full acceptance, the owner cannot thereafter sue the builder for damages because of defects it knew about when it paid the contract amount. *Houlette & Miller v. Arntz,* 148 La. 407, 126 N.W. 796 (1910). And, there are always words, acts, or both on the landowner's part indicating full acceptance of the building. *Aarnes v. Windham,* 137 Ala. 513, 34 So. 816 (1903). Often, the builder has a printed form that is signed by the owner. This form recites that the building has been constructed in complete conformity with the contract.

2.   The owner may accept the building as substantial performance but reserve the right to deductions because of the deviations.

> **EXAMPLE:** The owner discovers defects as the building goes up, protests the defects, but continues to proceed with the builder on the basis and assumption that their contract is still in force. *Otto Misch Co. v. E.E. Davis Co.,* 241 Mich. 285, 217 N.W. 38 (1928). The builder gets the contract price, less a deduction to compensate for the deviations. *Gray v. Wood,* 220 Ala. 587, 127 So. 148 (1930).

3.   The owner may simply take occupancy of the building because it is on owner's land. The owner's attitude at all times after discovering the defects is that the builder has breached the contract and ought not to be paid anything. Most courts will nevertheless award the builder the value of the building, on the theory that it must be worth something to the landowner and that to give the builder nothing would be unduly harsh. Other courts, however, are less merciful with the builder. They say that the owner has a right to use its land and the buildings on it, and since the builder's performance fell short of substantial performance, the builder is entitled to nothing. 5 Arthur Linton Corbin, *Corbin on Contracts* § 551; G.V.I., Annotation, *What Amounts to Acceptance by Owner of Work Done Under Contract for Construction or Repair of Building Which Will Support a Recovery on Quantum Meruit*, 107 A.L.R. 1411.

4.   If the owner demolishes the structure or refuses to make any use of it, in most states, the builder will be unable to collect a penny. 3 Arthur Linton Corbin, *Corbin on Contracts* § 790.

38.09 Liability of Seller/Builder for Defects in Land or Building

The subject of liability of the seller/builder for defects in the land or building has grown tremendously. The obligations of the seller of a new house under the old law differed from those of the seller of an old house. The obligations of the seller of a completed house differed from those of the seller of a house yet to be constructed. One who sells a house to be constructed has builder liability. One who sells a completed house does not, at least under some older cases. Suppose a builder has a house in the process of construction. *X* sees it and signs a contract to buy it. The builder has builder liability to *X*. As long as the seller has workmen on the job, the house is not fully completed, and, therefore, when the house is sold, the contract is treated as though it were a contract (1) to sell the land and (2) to finish the house. In short, it is a sell-and-build contract.

Builder liability means that the courts hold the builder on two implied warranties. (1) it must build in a good and workmanlike manner and (2) the structure when completed must be reasonably fit for its intended purpose. *Markman v. Hoefer,* 252 Iowa 118, 106 N.W.2d 59 (1960).

> **EXAMPLE:** Exterior stucco peeled off soon after a building was completed. The builder is liable. It has failed to build in a good and workmanlike manner. The same would be true if the concrete footings were faulty and the building settled, causing cracked plaster and ill-fitting doors.

In addition to liability on the two implied warranties, a builder is liable for failure to use ordinary care and skill. This is called negligence liability. For example, a builder must use ordinary care in the selecting of building materials, and if it should carelessly select beams of inadequate strength, it would be liable for injuries resulting from the collapse of the house.

Under the old law, the seller of a completed house had no builder liability for defects in the building, an obvious defect in the law.

Often, but not always, builder liability on implied warranties is employed to hold a builder liable for defects in the building. Negligence liability is employed to recover for personal injuries resulting from defective construction.

38.09(a)   Liability of Builder/Seller for Defects in Building and Injuries Suffered as a Result of Defects in New Building

After World War II ended and veterans began to return home to marry and look for homes, a tremendous building boom ensued. Unscrupulous builders built shoddy homes. In the decade from 1954 to 1964, when the building boom was at its height, hundreds of magazine and newspaper articles appeared about the miserable homes foisted on veterans. The old law was basically "let the buyer beware." Look before you buy. Of course, the unscrupulous builders were clever at hiding the defects. What home buyer looks behind the drywall or beneath the foundation? The courts changed the law.

Beginning in 1964, the courts began to throw the old rules overboard. They began to hold that in every sale of a newly completed residence by a builder/seller there is an implied warranty that the home was built in a workmanlike manner and is fit for habitation. *Carpenter v. Donohoe,* 154 Colo. 78, 388 P.2d 399, 402 (1964); *Bethlahmy v. Bechtel,* 415 P.2d 698 (Idaho 1966); *Waggoner v. Midwestern Dev., Inc.,* 154 N.W.2d 803 (S.D. 1967); *Moore v. Werner,* 418 S.W.2d 918 (Tex. Civ. App. 1967); *Humber v. Morton,* 426 S.W.2d 554 (Tex. 1968); *Theis v. Heuer,* 280 N.E.2d 300 (Ind. 1972); *Tavares v. Horstman,* 542 P.2d 1275 (1976). The philosophy here is that the average buyer of a new home is ill-equipped to detect the defects and shortcomings of jerry-built construction. Annotation, *Liability of Builder-Vendor or Other Vendor of New Dwelling for Loss, Injury, or Damage Occasioned by Defective Condition Thereof,* 25 A.L.R.3d 383 (1969).

It is now the rule that a builder/seller of a home implicitly warrants to the purchaser that the house was, in its major structural features, constructed in a good and workmanlike manner. That is, the structure is of reasonable quality, is reasonably fit for its intended purpose, and is free of building code violations. This rule is based upon the fact that the buyer of a new house relies on the skill of a seller/builder, that the buyer is incapable of detecting defects in construction, and that most defects in construction are hidden from view.

At first, the courts applied this rule only to the benefit of the original purchaser who bought the home from the builder/seller. Recent cases hold that a subsequent purchaser can also sue a builder/seller for defective construction. *Richards v. Powercraft Homes, Inc.,* 678 P.2d 427 (Ariz. 1984); *Redarowicz v. Ohlendorf,* 92 Ill. 2d 171, 441 N.E.2d 324 (1982); *Simmons v. Owens,* 363 So. 2d 142 (Fla. 1978); *Oaks v. Jag, Inc.,* 314 N.C. 276; 333 S.E.2d 222 (N.C. 1985); *Cosmo Homes, Inc. v. Weller,* 663 P.2d 1041 (Colo. 1983); Michael A. Di-Sabatino, Annotation, *Liability of Builder of Residence for Latent Defects Therein as Running to Subsequent Purchasers from Original Vendee,* 10 A.L.R.4th 385 (1981).

EXAMPLE: Builder, operating in termite territory, builds a frame house that rests on the ground instead of being elevated above the surface of the ground. He sells the house to Purchaser who sells it to Second Purchaser. Termite damage is found. Second Purchaser can sue Builder. The implied warranty given to the original purchaser carries over automatically to the subsequent purchaser.

Likewise, the later purchaser can hold the builder liable because the defects were due to the builder's carelessness. The builder must have foreseen that subsequent purchasers would suffer from defective construction. *Cosmopolitan Homes, Inc. v. Weller,* 663 P.2d 1041 (Colo. 1983). Shedd, *The Implied Warranty of Habitability: New Implications, New Applications,* 8 Real Est. L.J. 291 (1980). *See also* Diamond & Raines, *Consumer Warranty Issues in the Sale of Residential Condominiums,* 20 Real Prop. Prob. & Tr. J. 933 (1985). *See, however, Meyer v. Bryson,* 891 S.W.2d 223 (Tenn. App. 1994) (in which the court held the implied warranty extended only to the first purchaser). The implied warranty rule does not apply to commercial buildings. *See Dawson Indus. v. Godley Constr. Co.,* 29 N.C. App. 270, 224 S.E.2d 266 (1976). The rule also applies to sale of condominium units, *see*

Tassan v. United Dev. Co., 88 Ill. App. 3d 581, 410 N.E.2d 902 (1980); to the sale of co-ops, *Suarez v. Rivercross Tenants Corp.,* 438 N.Y.S.2d 164 (1981); and to sale of leasehold, *Lemle v. Breeden,* 462 P.2d 470 (Haw. 1969). The homeowner may bring an action against the subcontractor who actually did the work. *Minton v. Richards Group of Chicago,* 452 N.E.2d 835 (Ill. 1983).

The rule holding the builder/seller liable means the home must be fit for habitation, water will not seep in, the indoor plumbing will work, the foundation and walls will not crack, the well will deliver ample supplies of potable water, and so on.

Many courts today are likely to permit a second purchaser of the home to recover for the defects in the home.

When a client comes to a lawyer with a case involving a defect in a new home, the lawyer must select carefully the theory of liability he or she will urge upon the court. What works in one state may not work in another.

> **EXAMPLE:** Seller knows that there is a dangerous break in the flooring of a dark closet. Seller also knows that it is unlikely that Buyer will discover the danger. Seller fails to warn Buyer. Buyer's wife is injured while hanging clothes in the closet. Seller is liable. *O'Connor v. Altus,* 123 N.J. Super. 379, 303 A.2d 329 (1973), *citing* Restatement (Second) Torts § 353 (1965).

> **EXAMPLE:** There is an unused well on the property, which Seller has covered with sod. Wife of Buyer steps on the sod and the rotten boards break, plunging her into the well. Seller is liable for failure to warn Buyer. *Cooper v. Cordova Sand & Gravel Co., Inc.,* 485 S.W.2d 261 (Tenn. App. 1971).

The builder is going to be liable if it constructs a dangerous structure. *Inman Binghamton Housing Authority,* 3 N.Y.S.2d 137, 143 N.E.2d 895 (1957).

> **EXAMPLE:** The child of a tenant in an apartment building was injured in a fall from a defectively constructed porch. The builder was held liable. *See* Robert Kratovil, *Cardozo Revisited: Liability to Third Parties: A Real Property Perspective,* 7 U. Puget Sound L. Rev. 259, 286 (1984).

The theory of products liability arose in the sale of chattels.

> **EXAMPLE:** Buick Motor Company manufactured a defective automobile. This was sold to its dealer, who sold it to *X. X* suffered injuries owing to the defects and recovered damages from Buick. *MacPherson v. Buick Motor Co.,* 217 N.Y. 382, 111 N.E. 1050 (1916).

Prior to 1916, a person could sue only the person who sold him or her a defective product, for example, the car dealer. Now, it is possible to sue the manufacturer. In its modern version, as expressed in some decisions, products liability does not require the injured party to prove carelessness in manufacture. All that is needed is to show that the product was defective and that bodily injury resulted. The philosophy is that the manufacturer is better able to stand the loss than the injured party. The manufacturer can raise its prices or take out insurance against such risks. *Greenman v. Yuba Power Products, Inc.,* 59 Cal. 2d 57, 377 P.2d 897 (1963); *Products Liability,* 76 Yale L.J. 887 (1987). This view is also applicable in the real estate context.

> **EXAMPLE:** Builder erected a home that had a defective hot water system. The home was sold to Buyer, who rented it to Tenant. Tenant's son was scalded. Builder was held liable. *Schipper v. Levitt & Sons, Inc.,* 44 N.J. 70, 207 A.2d 314 (1965).

This liability extends only to those "in the business" of building. It would not apply to a homeowner selling his or her own home.

38.09(a)(1) Commercial Properties

The implied warranty that a building will be constructed in a workmanlike manner applies to the construction of a commercial building. *Hodgson v. Chin*, 403 A.2d 942 (N.J. 1979).

38.09(b) Liability of Builder/Seller— Personal Injuries

With respect to personal injuries resulting from faulty construction, a new set of rules comes into play. Now we are concerned with the seller's liability, whether or not the seller is the builder. The seller may be liable because it knew of a hidden defect that created a danger to occupants.

38.10 Express Warranties

So far, we have been talking about implied warranties. These involve situations where the documents are totally silent concerning the liability of the builder or seller for defects in the building. Yet, the courts read "warranties" against defects into the contract.

In addition, there are express warranties. These are guarantees that state in so many words that the warrantor will correct any defects at its expense. There are a variety of such warranties.

38.10(a) Express Warranties— New Homes

The National Association of Home Builders is an association of builders engaged in constructing quality homes. Even quality homes develop defects and home buyers need protection against them. To serve these buyers, the Home Owners Warranty Corporation, or a similar entity, issues a warranty on new homes. This warranty offers rather broad protection for two years and protection against major structural defects, guaranteed by an insurance company, for a period of ten years. Subsequent purchasers are also protected. The major coverage is for the first year and is described in detail in the warranty. Also, the builder will typically give a one-year warranty. This warranty ties into the one-year warranty that the seller will obtain from the contractor that built the home.

38.11 Federal Housing Administration and Veterans' Administration Warranties

There are laws allowing the Federal Housing Administration (FHA) and Veterans' Administration (VA) to compensate buyers if their new homes develop certain structural defects. These agencies may correct the defect, pay the homeowner to have it corrected, or acquire the building by buying it from the owner. Where new residential construction is approved for Housing and Urban Development, or HUD, mortgage insurance prior to the beginning of construction, the builder is required to deliver to the purchaser a warranty that construction was carried out in accordance with the plans and specifications. 12 U.S.C. 170 l j-1. While, technically, this is not the same as the responsibility the courts have placed upon builder/sellers, many defects occur because of the builder's noncompliance with the plans and specifications.

> **EXAMPLE:** A foundation may crack because it was installed over ground that did not meet the compaction requirements of the specifications or because concrete of a lesser grade than required in the specifications was used. Furthermore, specifications usually require that work be done in workmanlike manner.

The VA has an almost identical warranty. Both warranties are good for one year from date of completion. The VA has requirements for warranties of good construction if it is to insure the mortgage loan. These requirements are as follows:

1. An insurance-backed warranty for one year against defects caused by poor materials or work-manship.

2. A similar warranty for the first two years against faulty electrical, plumbing, and heating and cooling systems.

3. Direct insurance coverage for years three through ten against structural defects.

4. A system for handling disputes with builders and, if necessary, arbitration arranged by the American Arbitration Association or a similar group. 38 U.S.C. § 1805.

38.12 Seller's Warranties

Of course, one frequently encounters warranties by the seller of a used home. Often, they relate to the heating, air conditioning, electrical, water, and drainage systems. Often, they are placed in the contract of sale. If so, they survive the closing of the deal. They are not merged into the deed. *Rouse v. Brooks,* 66 Ill. App. 3d 107, 383 N.E.2d 666 (1978). The better practice is to provide in the contract that these warranties shall survive the closing.

38.13 Consumer Product Warranties

Typically, a builder incorporates into its structure various items that fall under the term "consumer products" as defined by the Magnuson-Moss Warranty Act. 15 U.S.C. § 2301, *et seq.* Because of this law, the builder must, prior to the sale of any consumer product that is covered by a warranty, fully, conspicuously, and understandably disclose the terms of the warranty and whether it is "full" or "limited" in duration. 15 U.S.C. §§ 2302, 2303. The Federal Trade Commission (FTC) has taken the position that the Act applies to separate items of equipment attached to real property whether or not they are fixtures under state law. The key to understanding the "separateness" test lies in the distinction between the physical separateness of an item and the separate function of that item.

> **EXAMPLE:** A furnace has a mechanical, thermal, or electrical function apart from the realty, whereas roofing shingles have no function apart from the realty. When sold by a builder to a home buyer as part of the home, the furnace is covered by the Act and the shingles are not.

Using this test, the FTC has decided that the following consumer products are covered by the Act when they are sold as part of a home: boiler, heat pump, electronic air cleaner, exhaust fan, thermostat, space heater, furnace, air conditioning system, humidifier, central vacuum system, smoke detector, fire alarm, fire extinguisher, garage door opener, chimes, water pump, intercom, burglar alarm, electric meter, water meter, gas meter, gas or electric barbecue grill, whirlpool bath, garbage disposal, water heater, water softener, sump pump, refrigerator, freezer, trash compactor, range, oven, dishwasher, oven hood, clothes washer, clothes dryer, and ice maker.

Using the same test, the FTC has found that the following are not consumer products when sold as part of a home: radiator, convector, register, duct, cabinet, door, shelving, window, floor covering, wall or wall covering, ceiling, vanity, gutter, shingles, chimney and fireplace, fencing, garage door, electrical switch and outlet, light fixture, electric panel box, fuse, circuit breaker, wiring, sprinkler head, water closet, bidet, lavatory, bathtub, laundry tray, sink, shower stall, plumbing fittings, and medicine cabinet.

A last category or group contains separate items or equipment that are consumer products under the act when sold as part of a condominium, cooperative, or multiple-family dwelling because they are not normally used for personal family or household purposes within the meaning of the Act: fusible fire-door closer, TV security monitor, emergency back-up generator, master TV antenna, elevator, institutional trash compactor. F.T.C. Advisory Opinion, *Trade Regulation Reports,* (CCH) ¶ 2, 1245 (Dec. 17, 1976).

Even though the builder does not make these pieces of equipment itself, the builder is nonetheless bound by the disclosure sections of the act because the builder is a "supplier" under the terms of the Act. 15 U.S.C. § 2301(4).

The builder can comply with the terms of the law by clearly and conspicuously displaying the text or a quote of the text of the written warranty covering the consumer product in close conjunction to each warranted product; or, by maintaining in each of the seller's locations an indexed binder containing copies of all warranties on consumer products; or, if the warranty text is printed on the product box, by displaying the package.

> **EXAMPLE:** When the builder incorporates into its structure dishwashers, disposals, ranges, refrigerators, and range hoods, it should either display next to, or tape onto, the appliances, copies of the warranties given by the manufacturer of those appliances, or keep in the model office a binder that contains those warranties. This binder should be displayed in a conspicuous place and potential buyers should be afforded the opportunity to review its contents prior to the sale. The builder should make similar disclosure of its own warranty if that warranty covers the consumer products. Peters, *How the Magnuson-Moss Warranty Act Affects the Builder/Seller of New Housing,* 5 Real Est. L.J. 338 (1977).

38.14 Warranties of Used Homes

The National Association of Realtors and other service providers have warranty programs that are used in connection with the sale of used homes. Most plans call for an inspection by the warrantor. Items covered usually include central heating and cooling systems; interior plumbing; electrical systems; roof, walls, ceilings, water heaters and softeners; and built-in appliances. Obviously, a buyer who wants such a warranty should require the contract of sale to so specify.

38.15 Disclaimer of Warranties

It is difficult for a seller to disclaim warranties. *Century Display Mfg. Co. v. D.R. Wagner Constr. Co.,* 376 N.E.2d 993 (Ill. 1978*); Peterson v. Hubschman Constr. Co.,* 76 Ill. 2d 31, 389 N.E.2d 364 (1979); *Herlihy v. Dunbar Builders Corp.,* 415 N.E.2d 1224 (Ill. App. 1980*); Schoeneweis v. Herrin,* 110 Ill. App. 3d 800, 443 N.E.2d 31(1982).

What this means, in brief, is that if the builder states in the fine print of the contract that it makes no guarantees whatever as to the presence or absence of construction defects, the courts will ignore this. It really takes a separate agreement, with the statement clearly made therein, that the builder accepts no responsibility for defects in construction. On the other hand, if the seller conspicuously sets out a disclaimer clause in simple and direct language, the courts will enforce it. *Country Squire Homeowner Ass'n v. Crest Hill Dev. Corp.,* 501 N.E.2d 794 (Ill. App. 1986).

CHAPTER 39
Rehab

39.01 In General There is a nationwide enthusiasm for redeveloping old buildings and restoring them to their former glory or turning them into loft residences, with modern plumbing, heating, electricity, and high-tech facilities. This rehabilitation is occurring in both the residential and commercial sectors. These buildings are typically closer to the core of the city where cultural and business activity is centered. The convenience of these projects, when taken together with the aesthetic and economic advantages of this form of residence in a time of low interest rates, is a powerful draw for this form of real estate.

If the structure has a strong shell, as is typical with older brick or stone structures, such as Georgetown row houses, the costs of acquisition and rehabilitation may be considerably less than the cost of new construction. When the income tax treatment of rehab expenses and favorable loan terms are considered, the economics of rehabilitation are even more attractive.

39.02 Appraisals Professional appraisals are required by lending institutions. Appraisers have a number of professional organizations, one of which is the American Institute of Real Estate Appraisers. This organization confers the prestigious title Member Appraisal Institute, or MAI designation, on more experienced and credentialed members. There is also the American Society of Appraisers and the Society of Real Estate Appraisers.

The role of the appraiser in large construction is well understood. But, a great expansion in the use of appraising is taking place as the rehabilitation process continues to assume increasing importance in home renovation. Among other things, the appraiser will consider an economic analysis of the neighborhood; street patterns and the width of streets; convenience to public transportation; the availability of stores and service establishments; community or neighborhood organizations; density of population; degree of home ownership; rent and income levels; and zoning, building codes, and other regulations restricting design or use.

39.03 Architect's Role The architect has an indispensable role in the rehab process. His or her first step is to conduct a feasibility study and provide a realistic estimate of the cost of the rehab, including the cost of bringing the structure into compliance with current building codes. These estimates are based upon actual costs of the same or similar work performed on similar structures and can be made only after a complete detail of exactly what construction work is to be done has been made.

The architect will also help you find a reliable rehab contractor. The loan funds will be disbursed by the lender to the contractor on its production of the architect's approval of the work done and waivers of mechanic's liens by trades involved in the work.

39.04 Building Codes Although building codes are intended primarily for new construction, they are also applied to rehabilitation projects through two widely used regulatory "trigger mechanisms," the "25/50 percent rule" and change-of-occupancy requirements. These are called trigger mechanisms because they "trigger" the application of new construction code requirements onto a rehabilitation project.

The 25/50 percent rule, usually one of the administrative requirements of a typical building code, requires that when the cost of the rehabilitation work to be done exceeds a stated percentage (usually 50 percent) of the value of the building (which, for many urban buildings, may be very low), the entire building must then be brought up to new construction code requirements.

Because building codes have changed over time, most buildings in the United States no longer meet new codes; the imposition of the 25/50 percent rule can and does add costs to the rehabilitation project.

The change-of-occupancy requirement, also usually one of the administrative requirements contained in a typical building code, states that when the occupancy of a building is changed, the entire building must be brought up to the new construction requirements of the building code. An occupancy change, for example, could involve the conversion of an old, large single-family residence into a multifamily residence, care facility, or retail store.

Several cities have enacted revised building ordinances that have taken some of the rigidity out of the old codes, which were primarily enacted to control new construction. These new rehab codes are often written in simplified language understandable to the layman and provide for the creation of a board to grant exceptions from code requirements, if the rehabber's proposal will be equal to or better than the code requires.

39.05 Building Restrictions Sometimes, the building restrictions applicable to a particular piece of property prohibit certain changes or additions. The title commitment must be reviewed to see if such restrictions exist. If so, a full copy of the restrictions and other documents referenced in the title commitment must be obtained from the recorder's office and reviewed by an attorney to see if the contemplated improvements can be made without violating restrictions and other title matters.

39.06 Zoning Ordinances Zoning laws determine how land and buildings can be used. They regulate such things as the amount of land coverage buildings may occupy; front, side, and back setbacks; and the heights of fences and hedges. The local building department should be contacted to determine whether the contemplated use will be in compliance with the zoning laws and, if not, how the use may be changed to accomplish the goals of the rehab developer, yet satisfy the requirements of the zoning laws.

39.07 The Contractor Getting a reliable contractor is a must on any substantial rehab job. Checking with customers who have had recent work done is a must. Bank or thrift institutions that will finance the work are a good source of names. A lawyer can check to see that the contractor is licensed, if local law so requires. Some states have good regulations. If an architect is hired, he or she is sure to know reliable contractors.

39.08 Contractor's Bonds Bonding companies write bonds insuring that the contractor will complete the job. However, most small contractors are not bondable. If the contractor is bondable, it is best for the rehab developer to get the bond, even if the rehabber must pay for it.

39.09 The Contract When the developer gets to the stage where the planning is over and the job is ready to be done, a construction contract is needed. The problem with these types of projects is that until much of the old structure is stripped away, it is impossible to tell exactly what is needed to build it back out. Experienced rehabbers have developed a sophisticated level of expectations, but even they get surprised. Perhaps the best plan is to expect the worst so that only happy surprises result. This way cost estimates can only be bettered and unexpected matters will not take a close job and turn it into an economic nightmare.

It is important that the contract contain enough detail so that there are no later disagreements as to the scope of the contractor's work. If an architect has been retained and the American Institute of Architect's forms of contracts are used, disputes can be minimized. It is best not to take shortcuts. Although these contracts, if properly utilized with detailed plans and specifications, will require a great deal of time to properly prepare, if the thought is not put into the planning of the demolition and build out, the contract will of necessity be on a cost-plus basis, which is bound to be more expensive.

The plans and specifications must be detailed. They must describe the quantity and quality of all of the items of work: how many electric outlets, how many feet of electric wire, will the wood trim be oak or some lesser grade of wood, what size nails will be used for each of the applications, what kind and how many lighting fixtures will be used, and so on. If these points are not agreed upon in advance, the contractor will be left to put in the most minimal items possible that pass code inspections. If these items are not agreed upon in advance, the job is not adequately defined for any contractor to make an effective bid.

Obviously, the contract must establish the contract amount and the start and completion dates. Other items, such as insurance, transfer of manufacturers' warranties, and the like, will also be covered.

39.10 Payment Many contractors ask for a down payment. If the contractor's references have been satisfactorily checked, the rehabber may agree to pay the contractor a small amount down, say, 15 percent. The contractor gets credit from suppliers, but will need to pay wages to workers. On bigger jobs, a final payment on the order of 15 percent will be made after completion of the job. The difference is often paid as the job goes forward.

39.11 Lien Waivers As work is done, the trades expect to be paid. An architect or other job supervisor checks the job first. He or she determines that the work has been done properly and in accordance with the contract plans and specifications. This supervisor also indicates how much money each trade is entitled to receive. Normally, the contract calls for hold backs or retentions. *Holiday Dev. Co. v. J.A. Tobin Constr. Co.,* 549 P.2d 1376 (Kan. 1976); Annotation, *Construction and Application of Provision of Construction Contract as Regarding Retention of Percentage of Current Earnings Until Completion,* 107 A.L.R. 960 (1937); Daniel E. Feld, Annotation, *Building and Construction Contracts: Contractor's Equitable Lien upon Percentage of Funds Withheld by Contractor or Lender,* 54 A.L.R.3d 848 (1973). A common retention is 10 percent of the amount due. As each trade is paid, a partial mechanic's lien waiver is demanded for the work done. When a trade completes its work, a final mechanic's lien waiver is demanded.

39.12 Plan and Specification Analysis Who will review the bids if you have no architect? A subcontractor is not required to do anything other than what the bid or contract, including the plans and specifications, requires to be done. Analyzing the plans and specifications for completeness is important.

39.13 Permits Some fly-by-night contractors never obtain building permits. This may lead to heavy fines if this is discovered by the local building authorities. An architect will not permit work to begin until he or she has verified that proper permits were obtained.

39.14 Rehab Supervision If the rehab work is not supervised by an architect, a building inspector may be hired to do the job. Some inspectors will even give estimates of job cost, which can be used to check the general contractor's bid. Of course, a general contractor undertakes in the general contract to supervise the work of the subcontractors.

If the rehab work is being conducted in a home that is occupied, the owner should make it clear that the contractor is to respect the fact that the work is being done in the owner's home. While it is often foolish to expect too much in this regard, the owner should make it clear that it is expected that the contractor will do the following: arrange a schedule so that the owner will know when the work crew will and will not be on the premises; clean up every night; lay drop cloths and install other protective padding to protect floors and walls; block off work areas with plastic sheeting taped over doors; and take other protective measures to reduce the inconvenience and dirt resulting from the work of improvement. However, the owner should realize that there will be a good deal of dirt and inconvenience resulting from the work no matter how attentive the contractor may be.

39.15 Insurance On a substantial job, talk to an insurance agent. He or she may recommend that the job be covered by special insurance ("builder's risk"). At completion, insurance on the building should be increased to cover the value added by the job.

39.16 Loans Many lenders advance the funds only after the rehab job has been completed. FHA insurance may be obtained for rehab loans before the job begins. Long-term, low-interest loans may also be available under various government programs.

Bear in mind that the rehab construction lender who finances the rehab job has several risks to weigh, namely, (1) the value of the building as is, (2) the value to be added by the rehab job, (3) the ability of the contractor to do the job properly, and (4) the ability of the developer to complete and lease up the project.

It may be possible to get a loan commitment that will become effective when and if the rehab job has been completed. A short-term loan is then obtained from a rehab lender, who will rely on the other loan commitment for ultimate payment. The rehab lender will make periodic inspections so that it is satisfied with the progress and get proper mechanic's lien waivers at each stage of the job.

The secondary market purchasers of mortgages, FNMA and FHLMC, have a program for rehab loans. Patrick A. Randolph, Jr., *The FNMA/FHLMC Uniform Home Improvement Loan Instruments: A Commentary and Critique,* 16 Real Prop. Prob. & Tr. J. 546 (1981).

CHAPTER 40
Mobile Homes

40.01 The Mobile Home Contrasted with the Stick-Built Home

The mobile home industry provides low-cost shelter that is subject to strict federal standards. Most mobile homes are sold fully equipped with major appliances, furniture, draperies, lamps, and carpeting included in the purchase price. Optional features include air conditioning, dishwasher, disposal, and other amenities typically found in a modern home. Warranties on components are available. Under federal law, the "mobile home" is now referred to as a "manufactured home."

40.02 Chattel Aspects

A manufactured home resting on land owned by one other than the homeowner has often been, for that very reason, deemed to remain a chattel. *Farmers Union Mut. Ins. Co. v. Denniston,* 376 S.W.2d 252 (Ark. 1964); *In re Estate of Horton,* 606 S.W.2d 792 (Mo. App. 1980). This is in keeping with a general law of fixtures that a chattel placed on land owned by a third person remains a chattel, since it would be unrealistic to attribute to the homeowner an intention to make the item the property of the landowner. Thus, the mobile home or manufactured home is personal property, governed by personal property law, unless and until it is attached to a parcel of land.

40.03 Fixture Aspects

On the other hand, a manufactured home owned and placed by a landowner on land owned by the landowner is a fixture and is part of the land. Normally, the intention to make the manufactured home a fixture is revealed by the removal of wheels, its attachment to a permanent foundation, and the use of permanent utility connections. *George v. Commercial Credit Corp.,* 440 F.2d 551 (7th Cir. 1971); *Bell v. City of Corbin City,* 395 A.2d 546 (N.J. 1978); *State v. Work,* 449 P.2d 806 (Wash. 1969). Such homes are purchased in home-and-land deals in much the same way as stick-built homes.

40.04 Federal Controls

The construction of manufactured homes is now controlled by the federal government under the National Mobile Home Construction and Safety Standards Act, 42 U.S.C. §§ 5401, *et seq.* 24 C.F.R. pt. 280, *et seq.* This code is promulgated by HUD and has requirements that vary throughout the country to meet geographic conditions. Elaborate federal safety factors are set forth in this regulation. Inconsistent state laws and ordinances are preempted. Each manufactured home is inspected at the factory, where a plate is installed evidencing that the home complies with federal law.

40.05 Mortgage Sources

On the home-and-land type of deal, traditional mortgage financing is available—for example, from a savings and loan association—which will loan up to 90 percent of the total cost of land, home, set-up charges, sales tax, and so forth. FHA and VA loans are available. The mortgages are sold in the secondary market to GNMA and FNMA. These loans, in turn, are pooled; securities are issued against the pool and sold to investors.

Because some states continue to view a manufactured home as having personal property characteristics, it may be necessary in such states to have the mortgage noted as a lien on the certificate of title. 7A Am. Jur. 2d *Automobiles and Highway Traffic* § 31. It may also be necessary for the lender to hold the certificate of title. *Id.* § 39. The law in this area is garbled and complicated. Welsh, *Security Interests in Motor Vehicles Under Section 9-302 of the Uniform Commercial Code,* 37 U. Cin. L. Rev. 265, 286 (1986). *See In re Circus Time, Inc.,* 641 F.2d 39 (1st Cir. 1981) and U.C.C. § 9-302(3).

A buyer of a new manufactured home from a dealer is buying personal property. A search should be made for UCC security filings. Title insurance companies check into this before issuing their policies. It is wise to consult with the title company as to its requirements before drawing up the sale and mortgage documents. In general, on homes that are located on land owned by the owner of the manufactured home, the title company requires proof that the home is permanently connected to the land—that it is connected to sewer, water, electricity, and gas—and that the owner has signed and recorded an affidavit that it is his or her intention that the home be a fixture and part of the real estate.

The FNMA requires that the purchase of the land and the home be a single real estate transaction; that the financing be evidenced by a mortgage recorded in the land records insured by title insurance containing the American Land Title Association (ALTA) Endorsement Form-7 Manufactured Housing Unit; that no chattels, furniture, appliances and so on be included in the mortgage financing; and that the land and home be taxed as land.

40.06 Usury—Federal Preemption Act

The federal usury preemption law applies to manufactured housing. However, to become entitled to the protection of this law, the security instrument must contain provisions requiring a thirty-day notice before foreclosure is instituted. Lacking this provision, the security is subject to state usury laws. *Grant v. Gen. Electric Credit Corp.,* 764 F.2d 1404 (11th Cir. 1985).

40.07 Furniture

Traditionally, mobile homes were sold complete with furniture, carpeting, draperies, and so on. Furniture, of course, is personal property. Where this practice is followed and the home and lot are sold and financed as real estate, a chattel filing under the UCC will accompany the mortgage. This practice is less prevalent today than in the past.

40.08 Building Restrictions

The areas of manufactured housing law that have given rise to much litigation involve building restrictions and zoning. Initially, it should be noted that many of these cases involve an isolated home placed on a lot in a community of stick-built homes. This is a situation that provokes litigation. It is improbable that the new manufactured housing developments will trigger any great volume of litigation.

Many older restrictions prohibit "trailers." Some older decisions hold that a manufactured home of one kind or another cannot be erected where the restrictions prohibit trailers. The more modern better-reasoned decisions hold that a typical manufactured home constructed on the owner's land does not violate a restriction forbidding trailers. *Hussey v. Ray,* 462 S.W.2d 45 (Tex. App. 1970); *In re Willey,* 120 Vt. 359, 140 A.2d 11 (1958); *Manley v. Draper,* 44 Misc. 2d 613, 254 N.Y.S.2d 739 (1963); *North Cherokee Village v. Murphy,* 248 N.W.2d 629 (Mich. App. 1976); *Morin v. Zoning Bd. of Review,* 102 R.I. 457, 232 A.2d 393 (1967); *Douglass Township v. Badman,* 206 Pa. Super. 390, 213 A.2d 88 (1965). This last case is significant. The home involved a structure containing three bedrooms, two full baths, 1440 square feet of floor space, a patio, a 200-square-foot porch, and a 672-square-foot two-car garage. The court commented on the fact that this structure was more handsome and more livable than many stick-built homes. This is obviously the way court decisions will tend. The restrictions using the word "trailer" were framed in an older time, when the double-wide manufactured home was unknown.

40.09 Zoning   The zoning decisions are numerous and conflicting. First of all, there are decisions holding that it is a violation of constitutional law to attempt, directly or indirectly, to bar a poor person's access to the suburbs by excluding manufactured housing. The leading case on this point is *Robinson Township v. Knoll,* 410 Mich. 293, 302 N.W.2d 146 (1981). In that case, a township zoning ordinance attempted to exclude mobile homes except in mobile home parks. The court held this aspect of the ordinance was invalid. The court pointed out that manufactured housing has undergone drastic change and improvement since the days of "trailers"; that many mobile homes compare favorably in appearance, plumbing and health factors with stick-built homes; and that Michigan, by statute, forbids discrimination against mobile homes.

This will become the prevailing view. *See Cannon v. Coweta County,* 389 S.E.2d 329 (Ga. 1990). At least one authority feels that states will step in with state laws, as has taken place in California, to invalidate city ordinances that exclude manufactured housing. Richard W. Bartke & Hilda R. Gage, *Mobile Homes: Zoning and Taxation*, 55 Cornell L. Rev. 491, 514 (1970).

Second, the particular tract of land may be such that a zoning ordinance barring manufactured housing would be invalid as applied. Such homes might provide the only reasonable use for the land. *Czech v. City of Blaine,* 253 N.W.2d 272 (Minn. 1977). 54 Am. Jur. 2d. *Mobile Homes* § 13.

40.10 Exclusionary Laws and Ordinances   The suburbs are generally quite hostile to the introduction of manufactured housing. Most exclusionary ordinances are illegal.

> **EXAMPLE:** An ordinance limiting manufactured housing developments to four new units per year was discriminatory and void where stick-built homes were not so limited. *Begin v. Inhabitants of Sabattus,* 409 A.2d 1269 (Me. 1980).

40.11 Antitrust   Park owners have, at times, enacted rules barring homeowners where the home was not purchased from the park owner. This is called a "closed park." Probably, this is a tie-in sale, illegal under the antitrust law.

40.12 Taxes   In past times, manufactured homes were taxed as motor vehicles or personal property. 71 Yale L.J. 71, 705. Some states levy a license fee. *Id.* Where the landowner owns the home, it is often taxed as real estate. Any discussion of this problem seems pointless. If manufactured housing goes into land developments where the land and home are sold as a unit, these must be taxed as real estate. *See* Larry D. Scheafer, Annotation, *Classification as Real Estate of Personal Property, of Mobile Homes or Trailers for Purposes of State or Local Taxation*, 7 A.L.R.4th 1016 (1981).

40.13 Warranties   Warranties vary among different manufacturers. All retailers are required to have copies of the manufacturers' warranties that are offered on the homes they sell, and they will make them available to buyers upon request. By reading the warranty before purchase, the buyer can make sure the home is covered by adequate warranty protection. The manufacturer's written warranty usually covers substantial defects in workmanship in the structure; factory-installed plumbing, heating, and electrical systems; and factory-installed appliances.

A retailer may offer a written warranty on a home. While all written warranties are not alike, the typical retailer's warranty will state the terms of the warranty; what must be done to keep the warranty in effect; what can reasonably be expected from the retailer; and that the home has been installed according to the manufacturer's specifications and local regulations.

The warranty will also guarantee that the home has a HUD inspection seal and that the optional appliances have been properly installed. The appliances also will be covered by warranties. In many cases, these warranties, along with use-and-care manuals, are provided by the individual appliance manufacturers. In addition, some states require that the home manufacturer's warranty cover the appliances that come with the home.

CHAPTER 41

Basic Landlord and Tenant Law

41.01 In General In the centuries following the Battle of Hastings (1066), when William the Conqueror crushed the English armies and became King of England, the feudal system of real estate law that prevailed in a large part of continental Europe became part of the English way of life. Its intricacies are a twice-told tale and need not be repeated here.

We must, however, look at the bottom rung of the social and economic ladder. Here, we find the landlord renting a small farm to a tenant. Rent was often paid in the form of a share of the crops. Indeed, sharecropping still exists, though on a small scale. The house in which the tenant lived was a primitive structure. The tenant worked with primitive tools. He was a jack-of-all-trades and could repair almost any part of his house and the tools that were used to make a living from the farm. In 1588, England defeated the Spanish Armada. England's ships began their long rule of the oceans of the world, and England became a trading nation. The formation of modern trading law (what formed the basis of our contract law) began. In the meantime, the law of landlord and tenant had been formed. Basically, it was pro-landlord law. The tenant took the premises as they were found. The landlord had no repair obligation.

Then, with the coming of the steam engine in about 1800, the Industrial Revolution changed the face of England. Many men worked in factories. Such a worker was not a jack-of-all-trades. Tenement buildings, the predecessors of modern apartments, began to appear as cities grew up around the factories. Still, the courts applied the old agricultural landlord and tenant law to the new way of life. Beginning about 1970, the courts began to reexamine their thinking. *Javins v. First Nat'l Realty Corp.,* 428 F.2d 1071 (D.C. Cir. 1970), *cert. denied* 400 U.S. 925 (1970). Several things became evident. The tenant, no longer a jack-of-all-trades, lacked the skills to make repairs. Moreover, repairs of any magnitude were beyond the means of the low-income tenant. The repair might have to be made to an area of the apartment to which the tenant did not have access.

Modern courts made a 180-degree turn in their thinking on the law applicable to residential renting. They began to regard the renting of an apartment basically as a contract for the furnishing of services, including the service of maintaining the structure in a habitable condition, free from building code violations. This development made all of the flexibility that is characteristic of modern contract law available to the courts in landlord and tenant matters.

41.02 Leases and Periodic Tenancies The relationship of landlord and tenant may exist by virtue of a formal, written lease or of a periodic tenancy, such as a tenancy from month to month.

> **EXAMPLE:** Tenant sees an "apartment for rent" sign on a building, goes in, makes a verbal arrangement with the owner for the rental of an apartment, pays the first month's rent, and later moves in. This is a tenant from month to month.

> **EXAMPLE:** The facts are the same as in the previous example, but the landlord and tenant, instead of agreeing verbally, sign a lease for one year. Tenant is a tenant under a lease.

One important difference between leases and periodic tenancies relates to the rights and liabilities of the parties during the existence of the landlord-tenant relation. When the relation of landlord and tenant exists without a written lease, the law implies certain rights and liabilities on the part of both. In a month-to-month tenancy, for example, the tenant is entitled to the exclusive possession of the rented premises, and the landlord has no right to enter the premises for the purpose of making repairs. But, in many leases, the parties expressly agree that the landlord shall have this right. In other words, a lease is a contract, and most of the rights and duties of the parties are governed by the provisions of the contract, whereas in a month-to-month tenancy, the rights of the parties are governed by rules of law.

Another difference between a lease and a periodic tenancy relates to the termination of the tenant's right of occupancy. In the case of a lease, at the expiration date fixed in the lease, the tenant need not give notice to the landlord before moving out, nor is any notice needed by the landlord to the tenant. In the case of periodic tenancies, certain notices must be given in order to terminate the tenancy.

41.03   Tenancy from Month to Month

The tenancy from month to month is generally created when no definite term of letting is specified by the parties and the rent is payable monthly. This kind of tenancy is very common. A tenant who pays rent monthly and has no lease is a tenant from month to month.

A tenancy from month to month cannot be terminated except by giving notice. That is, the landlord cannot evict the tenant unless it first gives the tenant the notice required by law. Similarly, the tenant continues to be liable for rent unless the tenant gives the landlord the required notice. In many states, a month's or thirty days' notice is required, but the period varies from state to state.

The notice to terminate a month-to-month tenancy must state a proper termination date and must give the tenant the full number of days' notice to which it is entitled.

> **EXAMPLE:** Landlord rents an apartment to Tenant on a month-to-month tenancy beginning as of the first of the next month. In the state in question a landlord must serve a thirty days' notice to terminate such a tenancy. After some months, Landlord serves a notice on November 1, terminating Tenant's tenancy as of November 30. The notice is void. It gives Tenant a twenty-nine-day notice. Landlord will lose the eviction suit and must serve a new and proper notice.

41.04   Tenancy from Year to Year

A tenancy from year to year is one that continues for a year and then is automatically renewed for another year and from year to year thereafter, unless due notice of termination of the tenancy is given at the time and in the manner required by law for the termination of the tenancy.

While a year-to-year tenancy can be created in other ways, it most commonly is created when a lease for a year or more has expired and the tenant continues in possession paying rent, which the landlord accepts, and the parties have made no other agreement as to the character of the tenant's occupancy.

When a tenant has a lease for a year or longer, and after the lease has expired the tenant remains in possession of the premises, it is said that the tenant holds over. The landlord may, if it wishes, hold the tenant as a tenant from year to year. Observe that it is the landlord who may hold the tenant. The tenant cannot, by holding over, compel the landlord to extend the tenancy. The landlord may evict the tenant if it wishes to do so. If the tenant holds over, even for one day, it becomes liable for another year's rent should the landlord so elect. Once the landlord accepts the rent, it also is bound to the tenancy. And, once the tenancy is established, neither party can terminate it in the middle of the year. If either party wishes to end the tenancy at the end of a yearly period, proper notice must be served for this purpose.

This form of tenancy is virtually obsolete. All printed leases contain a provision under which the parties agree upon what status the tenant will have if it remains in possession after the lease has expired. Often, the lease states that the tenant shall become a month-to-month tenant.

41.05 Tenancy at Will

A tenancy at will may be terminated by either party whenever it wishes to do so.

> **EXAMPLE:** A tenancy at will arises under an agreement that the tenant may occupy until the premises are sold or rented to a third person, until the landlord is ready to construct new buildings, until the land is required by the landlord for its own use, or whenever the letting is for an indefinite term.

41.06 Lease Defined

A lease is both a contract and a conveyance. It is a conveyance by the landlord to the tenant of the right to occupy the land for the term specified in the lease. It contains a contract by the tenant to pay rent to the landlord and usually contains numerous other promises and undertakings by both landlord and tenant. The legal interest of the tenant in the land is called a *leasehold estate* or a *term for years*. It is legally considered to be personal property. 51C C.J.S. *Landlord & Tenant* § 26.

41.07 Requirements of Lease

For a lease to be valid it must identify the parties and the leased premises, and specify the term and rent. As can be seen, the formal requirements are few. In all but a few states, a lease for less than one year may be verbal, but a lease for a period longer than one year must be in writing.

In a number of states, written leases must be executed with the same formality as deeds. In these states, a lease should be under seal. A few states require a lease that exceeds a certain specified duration to be witnessed, and some states require leases that exceed a specified term to be acknowledged. In any case, if the lease is to be recorded, it should be acknowledged. Even though a lease is not recorded, the tenant's possession will normally give the whole world constructive notice of the tenant's rights. However, this rule has been abolished in a number of states with regard to leases exceeding a specified duration.

In most states, the law permits the recording of a brief memorandum of the lease instead of the original lease. This enables the parties to keep the rent and other business terms specified in the lease confidential.

41.07(a) Parties

The landowner and spouse, if the landlord is a married person, should be designated as lessors. The same reasons that make it necessary for the spouse of a landowner to join in a deed require the spouse to join in a lease. *Fargo v. Bennett,* 35 Idaho 359, 206 P.692; *Benson v. Dritch,* 244 S.W.2d 339 (Tex. 1951). As a matter of business practice, short leases, such as one-year apartment leases, are often made by one of the co-owners of the property without the spouse's signature. A lessor should be of age and of sound mind. When the lease is executed by an executor or trustee, the will or other trust instrument must be examined to determine if the party executing the lease has power to make the lease in question. If the lessor is a corporation, the lease must be authorized by the directors or stockholders, as required by the local law.

The signature or execution by the lessor is necessary to give effect to a lease. It is the universal practice to obtain the lessee's signature also, though it is not essential that the lease be signed by the lessee if the lessee accepts the lease and takes possession of the leased premises. *Bakker v. Fellows,* 117 N.W. 52 (Mich. 1908). It is customary to execute leases in duplicate. If the lessor signs one duplicate and hands this to the lessee, and the lessee signs the other duplicate and hands this to the lessor, the effect is the same as if both signatures had been placed on each duplicate. *Fields v. Brown,* 58 N.E. 977 (Ill. 1900).

41.07(b)   Rent   Unless there is an agreement providing otherwise, rent is not due until the end of the rental period.

> **EXAMPLE:** *A* agreed to rent certain premises to *B* as a tenant from month to month. Rent was fixed at $380 per month, but nothing was said about time for payment of rent. The rent is not due until the end of each month.

Most leases, however, provide that rental is payable in advance on the first of each month.

Because of the embarrassment caused a landlord by its inability to put a new tenant in possession, and because of the difficulty attendant upon renting premises out of the normal season, a number of states and lease forms require a tenant who remains in possession after the termination of its lease to pay double rent for the period intervening between the expiration of the lease and eviction. The lease may provide for additional amounts other than double rent.

Under various circumstances, state laws allow an abatement, or reduction of rent. A typical illustration would be found where an apartment landlord fails to furnish hot water, gas, or electricity, or fails to make necessary repairs. Uniform Residential Landlord & Tenant Act § 4.104; Ch. 5 Restatement (Second) Property.

41.07(c)   Description of the Premises   The lease must describe the leased premises with certainty. There is a tendency in short-term leases to designate the leased premises inadequately. Of course, if it is an entire building that is being rented, it is sufficient to describe it by street number, city, and state. Care should be taken to spell out any ancillary property rights, such as easements over adjoining property or parking spaces and storage lockers that the tenant is to have the right to use in addition to the demised premises.

41.07(d)   Duration or Term Lease   Leases are sometimes classified as short-term or long-term leases. This has no great legal significance. With the exception of the rule that leases for more than one year must be in writing, the rules governing short-term and long-term leases are generally the same. Long-term leases often run for ninety-nine years. In some states, laws have been passed limiting the duration of leases. The lease should fix the date on which the term of the lease begins and the duration of the lease. This may be done by a supplemental agreement if the commencement of the term is dependent on the happening of certain events, such as the construction of tenant improvements by the landlord. In fixing the term of the lease, it is better to avoid a description of the term as running from a particular day to another day, since a question may arise as to whether a lease from or to a particular day includes or excludes such day. It is better to describe the term as commencing on a certain day and ending on a certain other day.

**41.07(d)(1)
Condominium Statutes
and Ordinances**

Various laws and ordinances extend the duration of a residential lease when the building is converted to a condominium.

**41.08 Possession—
Landlord's Duty to
Put Tenant in
Possession**

Often, a landlord leases an apartment or store to a new tenant while the old tenant still occupies the premises under a prior but yet unexpired lease, the idea being that when the old lease expires the old tenant will move out. At times, the old tenant fails to vacate the premises. The question then arises as to whose duty it is to put the old tenant out. The court decisions are conflicting. The Uniform Residential Landlord and Tenant Act requires the landlord to put the new tenant in possession (§ 2.102). Many printed residential leases contain a clause to this effect.

If the landlord fails to deliver possession on time, rent abates (is reduced) for the period the new tenant is kept out of possession. Uniform Residential Landlord & Tenant Act § 4.102.

**41.09 Incidental
Rights of Lessee or
Tenant—Services and
Easements**

Among the incidental rights a tenant enjoys, though not mentioned in the lease, are as follows:

1. The right of the tenant, its guests, business visitors, delivery persons, and so on to use the means of access the building provides, namely, front and rear entrances, arcade entrances, lobbies, corridors, stairs, escalators and elevators, suite entrances from reception rooms or private offices (though the landlord, through reasonable regulations, may require delivery to be made at a service entrance, or require freight to use freight elevators, etc.); the right to use common toilets, common laundry facilities, and so on; and the right to have electric wires and conduits, water, steam, and gas pipes cross the landlord's part of the property to service the tenant's quarters. This is an aspect of the law of implied easements, W.R. Habeeb, Annotation, *Easements or Privileges of Tenant of Part of Building as to Other Parts Not Included in Lease,* 24 A.L.R.2d 123 (1952).

   The landlord should try to get a provision giving it the right to make reasonable changes in these facilities. To accommodate a new tenant, for example, the landlord may wish to move the washroom to another floor.

2. The right to have heat, hot water, and so forth furnished where the only means of obtaining them consists of facilities controlled by the landlord for the benefit of all tenants.

**41.10 Liability of
Landlord**

Until recent times, the rule of caveat emptor (let the buyer beware) applied to the landlord and tenant relationship. Unless the lease provided otherwise, the landlord had no duty to the tenant to put the rented premises in a habitable condition or to make any repairs whatever. Even if the building at the time it was rented was in a dangerous or ruinous condition, or wholly unfit for occupancy or use, or if it became so after it had been rented, the tenant had to pay the stipulated rent for the entire term of the lease. This, of course, placed the burden on a prospective tenant of making a careful inspection of the premises before signing a lease and of insisting that the lease contain covenants to keep the premises in repair, if that was the tenant's wish and the landlord was willing to agree.

Since the landlord had no duty as to the condition of the premises, it was not liable to the tenant or the tenant's family for injuries or property damage suffered because of defects in the premises at the time of renting or those occurring thereafter.

> **EXAMPLE:** Landlord rented an apartment to Tenant. The flooring was obviously decayed and dangerous. It collapsed and Tenant was injured. Landlord was not liable to Tenant.

There are some exceptions to these rules:

1. When the landlord lets for a short term of a few days, weeks, or months a fully furnished house supposedly equipped for immediate occupancy as a dwelling, in many states, the landlord implicitly represents that the premises are safe and habitable. If the premises are not habitable, as when they are infested with vermin, the tenant has the right to move out, and its liability for rent ceases. *Young v. Povich,* 116 A. 26 (Me. 1922). Also, the landlord is liable to the tenant and his or her family for injuries sustained from defects in the rented premises or its furnishings. *Hacker v. Nitschke,* 39 N.E.2d 644 (Mass. 1942); *Mease v. Fox,* 200 N.W.2d 791 (Iowa 1972).

2. Where there are concealed defects that would make the premises dangerous to a tenant and the tenant could not discover the defects on an inspection of the premises, but the defects are known to the landlord, the landlord must inform the tenant of the existence of such defects. If the landlord fails to do so and, as a consequence, an injury is suffered by the tenant, the tenant's family, or the tenant's customers or guests, the landlord is liable for those injuries. *Mease v. Fox,* 200 N.W.2d 791 (Iowa 1972). Lawyers call this *fraud liability.*

   EXAMPLE: Premises were leased as a barber shop and residence. Sewer gas often escaped into the premises, which was known to the landlord. The landlord did not disclose this fact to the tenant, and the tenant and the tenant's family became seriously ill from sewer gas. The landlord was liable for the injuries.

3. The landlord normally retains control over parts of the building used in common by the tenants, such as halls, stairs, elevators, and sidewalks leading from the building to the public street or sidewalk. With respect to such common facilities, the landlord must exercise due care to correct any dangerous conditions that develop. It the landlord fails to take such care, it is liable for injuries suffered by the tenant, the tenant's family, customers, or other persons lawfully on the premises, such as delivery men. Allan E. Korpelas, Annotation, *Landlord's Liability for Injury or Death Caused by Defective Condition of Interior Steps or Stairways Used in Common by Tenants,* 67 A.L.R.3d 587, 490 (1975); Allan E. Karpela, Annotation, *Liability of Landlord for Personal Injury or Death Due to Inadequacy or Lack of Lighting on Portion of Premises Used in Common by Tenants,* 66 A.L.R.3d 202 (1975).

   EXAMPLE: Landlord leased a flat in an apartment building to Tenant. The stairways were used in common by the tenants. A stair became defective, and this condition was brought to the attention of Landlord, but Landlord failed to correct it. Tenant slipped on the stair and was injured. Landlord was liable.

   The duty of the landlord to use care to keep facilities used in common by the tenants in repair extends to appliances furnished by the landlord for the tenants' common use, such as laundry appliances, common toilets, playground equipment, and dumbwaiters. It also extends to the roof, chimneys, eaves, flues, outside walls, and swimming pools. George L. Bounds, Jr., Annotation, *Liability of Landlord for Injury or Death Occasioned by Swimming Pool Maintained for Tenants,* 39 A.L.R.3d 824 (1971). This duty extends also to the malls, walks, parking areas, etc., of a shopping center. W.E. Merritt, III, Annotation, *Liability of Owner or Operator of Shopping Center to Patrons for Injuries from Defects or Conditions in Sidewalks, Walks or Pedestrian Passageways,* 95 A.L.R.2d 1341, 1344 (1964).

   This liability of the landlord rests upon the fact that it is in exclusive control of these common areas. With control goes liability. This is a form of occupier liability.

4. Where the landlord, even though not legally obligated to do so, makes repairs, but is negligent in so doing, the landlord is liable for any resulting injuries.

   EXAMPLE: Landlord, though not obligated to do so, repaired a floor in an apartment that was rented to Tenant. The work was carelessly done, and Tenant was injured. Landlord is liable. L.S. Tellier, Annotation, *Breach of Lessor's Agreement as Ground of Liability for Personal Injury to Tenant or One in Privity with Latter,* 78 A.L.R.2d 1238, 1258 (1961).

In California, the courts have decided to hold the landlord liable for injuries to a residential tenant without regard to the presence or absence of negligence on the landlord's part.

EXAMPLE: Tenant in an apartment building owned by Landlord was injured when he slipped and fell through an untempered glass shower door. Landlord was liable. *Becker v. IRM Corp.,* 38 Cal. 3d 424, 213 Cal. Rptr. 213, 698 P.2d 116, *cited in Muro v. Superior Court,* 229 Cal. Rptr. 383 (Cal. App. 1986). This accords with recent decisions extending strict liability to builders of mass-produced homes, which discussions are cited in the *Muro* case.

41.10(a) Liability of Landlord for Injuries to Third Person

As a rule, whenever a landlord would be liable to a tenant, as, for example, when the landlord is careless with respect to care of common stairways, the landlord will be liable to others who stand in the tenant's shoes, such as members of the tenant's family, guests, employees, business visitors, and delivery personnel.

There are other situations where a landlord is liable to a third person.

1. When the landlord rents the premises for a purpose that involves the admission of the public as patrons of the tenant (amusement park, theater, etc.) and if, at the time the lease, or any renewal lease, is signed, the premises are in a dangerous condition (dangerous doorways, steps, floors), the landlord is liable to the tenant's patrons for any injuries they may suffer. *Webel v. Yale University,* 7 A.2d 215 (Conn. 1939); C.P. Jhong, Annotation, *Landlord's Liability to Tenant's Business Patron Injured as a Result of Defective Condition of Premises*, 17 A.L.R.3d 422, 873 (1968).

2. With respect to pedestrians on public walks or streets adjoining the rented premises, there is an additional rule imposing liability on the landlord, namely, when the premises at the time of the renting are in a dangerous and defective condition, the landlord is liable to strangers for injuries resulting therefrom. 52 C.J.S. *Landlord & Tenant* § 417 (20); R.P. Davis, Annotation, *Liability of Owner or Occupant for Condition of Covering over Opening in Vault or Sidewalk*, 31 A.L.R.2d 1334 (1953).

    EXAMPLE: At the time the premises were leased to the tenant, a hole in the sidewalk leading to a coal bin was in a defective condition, and a pedestrian was injured as a result. The landlord was held liable. *Great Atlantic & Pacific Tea Co. v. Traylor,* 195 So. 724 (Ala. 1940). The reason for this rule is that a dangerous condition of premises constitutes a nuisance, and the liability of the landlord results from its leasing premises on which a nuisance exists. *Morgan v. Sheppard,* 156 Ala. 403, 47 So. 147 (1908). The liability exists even though the defect is not concealed. If the premises were safe when originally leased but are defective when the lease is renewed, the landlord is liable for injuries sustained by strangers after the date of the renewal. Of course, the tenant would also be liable for such injuries.

3. Where the lease involves a use of the premises that is inherently dangerous, the landlord will be liable to third persons injured by the tenant's negligence if the landlord failed to exercise due care in selecting a responsible tenant.

    EXAMPLE: The landlord leased a filling station to a tenant who had no experience in this line of work. An explosion occurred and the plaintiff was injured. The landlord was held liable. *Benlehr v. Shell Oil Co.,* 402 N.E.2d 1203 (Ohio 1978).

    If you are curious as to why early landlord-and-tenant law so heavily favored the landlord, remember the American courts tended to follow the rules laid down in England. The English judges were wealthy landlords. It was not until the era of consumerism that the common people received real protections.

4. A landlord will not be liable to third parties for the criminal acts of its tenant, unless the landlord has the legal ability to control the tenant, knows that there is a need to control the tenant, and in fact can control the tenant. *Molosz v. Hohertzl,* 957 P.2d 1049 (Colo. App. 1998). There are

cases to the contrary. Where a landlord knows or has reason to know that the tenant will act tortiously, the landlord may be liable. For example, where a flea-market owner knows or has reason to know that its tenants are selling illegal knock-offs, or is willfully blind to the acts of those parties, it may be liable. *Hard Rock Café Licensing Corp. v. Concession Services, Inc.*, 955 F.2d 1143 (7th Cir. 1992); *Fonovisa, Inc. v. Cherry Oak Street, Inc.*, 76 F.3d 259 (9th Cir. 1996). It is generally held that the landlord is not required to investigate its tenant or prevent infringement.

41.11 Lease Obligating Landlord to Repair

If the lease requires the landlord to make repairs, and the landlord violates this obligation, the tenant may pursue one of the following courses:

1. The tenant may abandon the premises if they become untenantable.

2. The tenant may make the repairs and deduct the reasonable expense or cost thereof from the rent. Jonathan M. Purver, Annotation, *Tenant's Rights Where Landlord Fails to Make Repairs to Have Them Made and Set Off Cost Against Rent*, 40 A.L.R.3d 1369 (1971).

3. The tenant may occupy the premises without repair and deduct from the rent the decrease in rental value occasioned by the landlord's failure to repair. Here, however, the tenant runs the risk of having the lease forfeited for nonpayment of rent if the tenant appraises the situation incorrectly.

4. The tenant may pay full rent and sue the landlord for the decrease in rental value occasioned by the landlord's failure to repair J.A. Bock, Annotation, *Measure and Items of Damages for Lessee's Breach of Covenant as to Repairs*, 80 A.L.R.2d 983 (1961), or for other damages such as emotional distress. *Cherberg v. Peoples Nat'l Bank,* 564 P.2d 1137 (Wash. 1977) (Landlord used situation to pressure tenant to move).

5. The tenant may specifically enforce the landlord's obligation to repair. *Evco Corp. v. Ross,* 528 S.W.2d 20 (Tenn. 1975). *See generally* F.G. Madara, Annotation, *Rights and Remedies of Tenant upon Landlord's Breach of Covenant to Repair*, 28 A.L.R.2d 446 (1953).

When the lease obligates the landlord to repair, and the landlord fails to do so, and the tenant suffers an injury as a result, some courts hold the landlord liable; others do not. The view that the landlord should be held liable is growing in favor. 78 A.L.R.2d 1238, *supra.* Accompanying every contract is an unspoken duty to perform with skill and care and to be liable for negligent performance. 17B C.J.S. *Contracts* § 494(1). In any event, the landlord has no duty to inspect the rented premises it has agreed to keep in repair, for, normally, the landlord has no right to enter on the rented premises without the tenant's consent. It is the tenant's duty to notify the landlord of any condition requiring repair, and no liability on the landlord's part arises until this has been done and the landlord has failed to make repairs as agreed.

41.12 Liability of Tenant for Injuries to Third Person

When a stranger is injured by reason of a defective condition of the premises, it is often difficult to determine whether the landlord or the tenant is liable. If the landlord has made no agreement to repair and the premises were in a safe condition when rented, and if the defective portion is in the exclusive possession of the tenant, the tenant will be liable. The landlord is not liable because the landlord has no control over such premises and is in no position to prevent the dangerous condition.

EXAMPLE: A stranger slipped and fell into a coal hole that was defectively covered but was in a safe condition when the premises were rented. The basement into which the hole opened was used by the first-floor tenant. The tenant alone had a key to this basement, and the landlord had no access. The tenant alone was liable. *West Chicago Masonic Ass'n v. Cohn,* 61 N.E. 439 (Ill. 1901).

Or, suppose the tenant of an upper floor goes out leaving the water running, and the water runs over, drips through the ceiling, and ruins plaster and rugs in the unit beneath. The landlord is not liable since the tenant is in exclusive possession of the unit in which the water was left to run, but the tenant is liable both to the landlord and to the tenant below, because the damage resulted from the tenant's carelessness.

41.13 Insurance

The prudent property owner should protect itself against liability claims by taking out owners', landlords', and tenants' public liability insurance, commonly referred to as OL&T insurance, which provides coverage against legal liability for accidents resulting in bodily injuries or death arising out of ownership, occupation, or use of the premises. Liability for injuries sustained by employees is not covered by this policy, but they should be covered by workers' compensation or employer's liability insurance. Insurance should be obtained protecting the landlord against loss resulting from fire and other casualties. If there is an elevator on the premises, insurance will be needed to protect against injuries arising through operation of the elevator. Special "dram shop" insurance should be purchased if alcoholic beverages are sold on the premises.

41.14 Repairs and Alterations by Tenants—Liability of Tenant to Landlord

When the lease does not provide otherwise, the tenant has no duty to the landlord to make any substantial, extraordinary, or general repairs, such as the replacing of a worn-out furnace. But, it is the tenant's duty to repair broken windows or leaking roofs and to take such other steps as needed to prevent damage from the elements. If the tenant fails to do so, it is liable to the landlord for any resulting damage. *Suydam v. Jackson,* 54 N.Y. 450 (1873).

The tenant must not make any material changes in the nature and character of the leased premises, as by removing walls, cutting new doorways, and the like, even though such alterations increase the value of the property. The theory is that when the tenant vacates the building, the landlord should find it in much the same condition as it was when the tenant took possession. *F.W. Woolworth Co. v. Nelson,* 85 So. 449 (Ala. 1920).

A lease provision for repairs may require the tenant to replace rotten floors, a worn-out furnace, and the like, but not to clean up environmental contamination if the tenant did not cause the contamination. *Griffith v New England Tel. & Tel. Co.,* 649 N.E.2d 766 (Mass. 1995). Also, a provision in a triple net lease requiring the tenant to keep the premises in good order and make necessary repairs "ordinary and extraordinary" will not require the tenant to make or pay for seismic upgrades to a building that otherwise complies with applicable building and safety codes. *Prudential Ins. Co. v. L.A. Mart,* 68 F.3d 370 (9th Cir. 1995). *But see Brown v. Green,* 884 P.2d 55 (Cal. 1994) (requiring the tenant to remove asbestos). A general covenant by the tenant to repair may obligate the tenant to rebuild if the leased premises are destroyed. The tenant will be liable to the landlord for damage occasioned by carelessness, as where damage results from the tenant's negligence in permitting a bathtub to overflow. C.R. McCorkle, Annotation, *Liability of Tenant for Damage to the Leased Property Due to His Acts or Neglect,* 10 A.L.R.2d 1012 (1950). *See* Eugene L. Grant, *First Class Condition: Responsibilities, Rights and Remedies Respecting the Condition of Commercial Leasehold Premises,* 29 Real Prop. Prob. & Tr. J. 737 (1995).

> **EXAMPLE:** A lease required the tenant to maintain the fire protection system of the premises. The premises were damaged by fire and the tenant sued the landlord for negligence. The tenant based his claim on a municipal ordinance requiring the owner of the prop-

erty, the landlord, to maintain a fire protection system. The court held that as between the landlord and the tenant, the parties could allocate their responsibilities, even if the ordinance placed the obligation on the tenant. *Fresh Cut, Inc. v. Fazil*, 650 N.E.2d 1126 (Ind. 1995).

41.15   Damage to or Destruction of the Leased Premises

Unless the lease provides otherwise, the rule is that when both the land and building are rented, the tenant is not excused from paying rent if the building is destroyed by fire, flood, or some other casualty.

> **EXAMPLE:** A lease was made of the premises at 143 and 145 Lake Street, Chicago, Illinois. The buildings were destroyed by fire, but the liability for rent continued. A lease containing a description by street number leases the land as well as the building.

Quite a number of states have abolished this harsh rule. In these states, it is the rule that if a building is destroyed or rendered untenantable, the tenant is relieved of further liability for rent. Many lease forms provide that if the building is destroyed by fire, the lease ends automatically or rent abates in whole or in part until the premises are rebuilt. Predictably, many modern courts will take this approach even where the lease is silent.

The rule that liability for rent continues when the building is destroyed does not apply to a lease of an apartment, flat, office, or floor of a building. Such a lease is not a lease of land. Kristine Cordier Karnezis, Annotation, *Modern Status of Rule as to Tenant's Rent Liability After Injury to or Destruction of Demised Premises*, 99 A.L.R.3d 738 (1980).

When the building is not destroyed, but the apartment is rendered untenantable by fire, leases usually provide that the landlord has a certain time in which to make the necessary repairs, and, in the meantime, the tenant is not liable for rent. Under this clause, if the landlord fails to make repairs during the specified period, the lease ends automatically.

If the lease requires the landlord to repair the building, this may be interpreted as requiring it to rebuild the building if it is destroyed by fire or other casualty. H.D. Warren, Annotation, *Landlord's Duty Under Express Covenant to Repair, Rebuild or Restore, Where Property Is Damaged or Destroyed by Fire*, 38 A.L.R.2d 682, 685 (1954).

The Restatement (Second) of Property § 5.4 takes the position that when the building is destroyed (by fire, windstorm, etc.) without fault on the tenant's part, the tenant may terminate the lease and end his or her liability for rent. This is a sound rule. No doubt most courts will follow this view. Of course, if the tenant is responsible for the damage to the leased premises, the tenant is liable to the landlord for the repair costs. *Regent Ins. Co. v. Economy Preferred Ins. Co.,* 749 F. Supp. 191 (C.D. Ill. 1990); *Teodori v. Werner,* 415 A.2d 31 (Pa. 1980) (tenant's liability for rent ends when building destroyed); 99 A.L.R.3d 738, *supra*; Robert Hickel, *Landlord & Tenant—Liability for Rent After Destruction of Building—Lease of Part of Building*, 34 Mo. L. Rev. 132 (1969); Benjamin N. Henszey & Frederick Pugh, *Tenant's Liability for Rent on Destruction of Leasehold Premises*, 7 Real Est. L. Rev. 187 (1978).

41.15(a)   Damage or Destruction of the Leased Premises Before Tenant Takes Possession

If the rented premises are damaged by fire or other cause, or otherwise rendered unsuitable for the use contemplated by the parties and this occurs before the tenant takes possession, the tenant may terminate the lease without liability to the landlord.

> **EXAMPLE:** The building was destroyed by fire before Tenant took possession. Tenant could cancel the lease. Restatement (Second) of Property § 5.2. The theory is that Tenant has no way of protecting the property before the possession date.

41.16   Taxes   In the absence of a provision in the lease to that effect, the tenant is not obliged to pay real estate taxes on the leased premises.

41.17   Fixtures   The respective rights of landlord and tenant in and to fixtures installed by the tenant are discussed in Chapter 3.

Trade fixtures not removed by the tenant before it moves out become the property of the landlord. The fact that such items are attached to the landlord's building seems to make this result natural and acceptable to the courts. The tenant's ordinary personal property that is not in any way attached to the building—for example, furniture or stock in trade—does not become the landlord's property simply because the tenant has moved out or been evicted. The landlord must keep or store these articles for the tenant. Some state laws cover this point. Many leases provide that personal property left behind by the tenant after it vacates the leased premises shall be deemed to be abandoned and the landlord may dispose of it.

41.18   Cancellation Clause   A lease may contain a clause conferring on the landlord the privilege of canceling the lease in the event of a sale of the property and upon giving a certain specified notice to the tenant. This clause is of value when the landlord sells the premises to a buyer who desires more or less immediate occupancy or to change the use of the property, for example, to change an old factory building to loft condominiums. Great care must be exercised in serving the notice of cancellation. For example, if the lease says that the landlord may cancel the lease in case of a sale, a notice served by its purchaser may be void. T.C. Williams, Annotation, *Construction of Provision for Termination of Lease in Event of Sale of Property*, 163 A.L.R. 1019 (1946). Notice of cancellation should be served personally unless the lease specifically allows notice by mail. Each tenant is entitled to his or her own copy of the notice.

41.19   Assignments and Subleases   Unless the lease provides otherwise, a lessee may assign the lease or sublet the premises. Whether a particular instrument is an assignment or sublease does not depend upon the name given the instrument by the parties. An assignment simply transfers the leasehold estate to a new owner, the assignee. A sublease creates a new and distinct leasehold estate in the sublessee. If the lessee transfers the entire leased premises for the unexpired remainder of the term created by the lease, the instrument is an assignment. If the lessee retains part of the premises or part of the term, however small the part may be, the instrument is a sublease.

> **EXAMPLE:** Landlord leases certain premises to Tenant for a term beginning on May 1, 1996, and expiring on April 30, 1998, at a rent of $1,000 per month. On July 1, 1996, Tenant executes to *X* a "sublease" for a term beginning on July 1, 1996, and expiring April 30, 1998, at a rent of $1,500 per month. The instrument is an assignment.

> **EXAMPLE:** Landlord leases to Tenant certain premises for a term beginning on May 1, 1996, and expiring on April 30, 1998. On July 1, 1996, Tenant executes to *X* an "assignment" of said lease except the last day of the term. The instrument is a sublease. *See* Sidney G. Saltz & Martin P. Miner, *Subleases: A New Approach: A Proposal*, 34 Real Prop. Prob. & Tr. L.J. 1 (1999).

The difference between assignment and sublease is important, since an assignee becomes liable to the original lessor for rent, whereas a sublessee is liable only to the sublessor, who is the lessee under the original lease. Of course, the lessee in the original lease continues to be liable for rent to the original lessor, notwithstanding the assignment or sublease.

If the lease forbids an assignment without the lessor's consent, it does not necessarily prevent a sublease. If the lease forbids a sublease, it does not necessarily prohibit an assignment. As a rule, commercial leases prohibit both assignments and subleases without the lessor's consent. These clauses can be heavily negotiated.

41.20 Deed of Rented Premises

A landlord may, of course, sell the property, and the buyer will take it subject to existing leases and periodic tenancies. The deed alone confers on the buyer the right to collect rent falling due after the sale and the right to declare leases forfeited for nonpayment of rent, if that right is reserved in the lease. *Lipschultz v. Robertson,* 95 N.E.2d 357 (Ill. 1950). So far as the collection of future rent is concerned, it is unnecessary that the lessor execute a formal assignment of its rights under existing leases.

A tenant has the right to continue making rent payments to the original landlord until the tenant is notified of a sale of the property. Therefore, one who buys rented property should promptly notify all tenants that all future rent must be paid to the buyer.

A serious question arises when the tenant prepays the rent called for by the lease and the property is thereafter sold. The buyer of the property no doubt assumes that it will be entitled to collect the future rents called for by the lease. The buyer is then confronted by a tenant armed with the argument that the rent has been paid. In some states, the tenant must pay such rent over again to the new landlord, whereas in other states, the rent payments are good as against the new landlord. 49 Am. Jur. 2d *Landlord & Tenant* § 54. This is typically dealt with in the estoppel agreement that is obtained by the buyer from the tenants before the sale transaction closes. In this way, the purchaser knows what rent has been paid and obtains a closing credit for the advance rent.

41.21 Abandonment of the Premises

Leases usually provide that if the lessee abandons the premises before the expiration of the lease, the tenant shall nevertheless continue to be liable for rent until the expiration of the lease, and any reletting by the landlord shall not relieve the tenant of further liability.

However, upon abandonment of the premises by the lessee, it is the duty of the landlord in most states to mitigate damages, that is, to take charge of the property, and, if possible, relet or rerent it and thus reduce the amount for which the lessee remains liable. E.L. Kellett, Annotation, *Landlord's Duty on Tenant's Failure to Occupy, or Abandonment of Premises to Mitigate Damages by Accepting or Procuring Another Tenant,* 21 A.L.R.3d 534 (1968); Stephanie G. Flynn, *Duty to Mitigate Damages Upon a Tenant's Abandonment,* 34 Real Prop. Prob. & Tr. L.J. (2000). The lessor may deduct the expenses of such reletting, including commissions and decorating, from the rent collected on such reletting, and may apply the balance on the original tenant's liability.

> **EXAMPLE:** Landlord leased premises to Tenant 1 for one year at $500 per month. After six months, Tenant 1 abandoned the premises. The premises were vacant one month and were then relet to Tenant 2 for $400 per month; the expenses of reletting, including commissions and decorating were $500. The landlord thus realized $2,000 on the reletting (five months times $400 per month) minus $500, or $1,500. Tenant 1's liability is $3,000 (six months times $500 per month) minus $1,500, or $1,500.

The courts are not in agreement as to the extent of the landlord's duty where the tenant abandons the premises. Some courts put the landlord under an obligation to seek another tenant so that the damages caused by the tenant's abandonment can be reduced. *Scheinfeld v. Muntz TV, Inc.,* 214 N.E.2d 506 (Ill. App. 1966). Other courts require no affirmative action by the landlord. But, they do compel the landlord to accept a suitable subtenant found by the abandoning tenant. *Reget v. Dempsey-Tegeler & Co.,* 238 N.E.2d 418 (Ill. App. 1968); Howard L. Kastel, *Landlord and Tenant—Duty of Lessor to Accept Tendered Sublease in Mitigation of Abandoning Lessee's Damages,* 48 Ill. B.J. 546 (1959). *But see Vasquez v. Carmel Shopping Ctr. Co.,* 777 S.W.2d 532 (Tex. App. 1989). Often, the lease spells out the landlord's duties.

It is usual to insert a provision in the lease to the effect that the lessor shall not be under any obligation to relet and may permit the premises to remain vacant and sue the lessee for the full amount of the rent. This was the law in most states even in the absence of such a provision in the lease. T.A.M., Annotation, *Duty of Landlord, on Abandonment of Premises by Tenant Before Expiration of Term, to Use Diligence to Procure Another Tenant,* 40 A.L.R. 190 (1926); J.B.G., Annotation, *Duty of Landlord on Abandonment of Premises by Tenant Before Expiration of Term to Use Due Diligence to Procure Another Tenant,* 126 A.L.R. 1219 (1940). Under today's law in most states, the courts will compel the landlord to relet, no matter what the lease says. Ordinarily, the landlord will relet the premises rather than permit them to remain vacant, for rent collections from an existing tenant are money in the landlord's hands, whereas the liability of the previous tenant is, at best, a lawsuit.

If the landlord relets after abandonment of the premises by the tenant, there is danger that this may amount to a surrender or termination of the lease, thus releasing the tenant from further liability for rent. In some states, a reletting automatically releases the liability of the tenant who has abandoned the premises, whereas in other states, the tenant is released unless the landlord gives notice of its intention to hold the tenant liable despite the reletting. R.P.D., Annotation, *When Landlord's Reletting, or Efforts to Relet, After Tenant's Abandonment or Refusal to Enter, Deemed to Be Acceptance of Surrender,* 110 A.L.R. 368 (1937). In the great majority of states, the question is regarded as one of intention. If the landlord's acts indicate an acceptance of the tenant's abandonment and an intention to regard the lease as terminated, the tenant's liability for future rent is terminated. 110 A.L.R. 368, *supra.* In effect, there is a surrender. As previously suggested, the notice given by the landlord is employed to show that the landlord does not intend to treat the lease as terminated by the abandonment.

Suppose, however, that the landlord relets to a new tenant for a new term longer than the remaining term of the original lease. In some states, this is viewed as being inconsistent with the continued existence of the earlier lease, and the earlier lease is thereby terminated. *Ralph v. Deiley,* 141 A. 640 (Pa. 1928); E.W.H., Annotation, *When Landlord's Reletting or Efforts to Relet After Tenant's Abandonment or Refusal to Enter, Deemed to Be Acceptance of Surrender,* 61 A.L.R. 773 (1929). Therefore, the lease provisions covering this point (the abandonment clause) should include a provision giving the landlord the right to relet for a term longer than the original lease without in any way releasing the tenant's liability.

41.22 Surrender A surrender is an agreement by the landlord and tenant to terminate the lease or tenancy, followed by a delivery of possession of the premises to the landlord. A surrender releases the tenant from liability for rent thereafter accruing.

> **EXAMPLE:** Premises were leased by Landlord to Tenant for the term from April 1, 1993, to April 1, 1996. On March 31, 1994, Tenant 1 told Landlord that he wished to give up the lease, and Landlord accepted this offer, telling Tenant 1 to allow a new tenant, Tenant 2, to move in and to turn the keys over to Tenant 2. This procedure was a surrender, and Tenant 1 was not liable for rent accruing thereafter.

Observe that it is the agreement between landlord and tenant that distinguishes a surrender from an abandonment by the tenant.

If the landlord, with the tenant's consent, gives a new lease to a stranger during the existence of the tenant's lease, this also is a surrender.

> **EXAMPLE:** Landlord leased a store to Tenant, who sold the business to Buyer. Landlord then gave Buyer a new lease. This is a surrender of the old lease.

The making of a new lease between landlord and tenant operates as a surrender of a prior inconsistent lease. If the tenant merely abandons the premises, the fact that the landlord accepts the keys does not constitute a surrender.

41.23 Frustration of Purpose

Tenants lease premises for a purpose. They either want to live in the premises or conduct a business from the premises. What happens if the tenant can no longer use the premises for the intended purposes? Can the tenant avoid the lease obligations? If so, the tenant has thereby shifted the risk of this event to the landlord. What if the tenant can use the premises, but not for the primary purposes for which the premises were leased?

Frequently, this issue is raised in the context of a new or changed governmental regulation. A court has recently considered this situation and held that the tenant could not terminate its lease obligations. The court reasoned that while the tenant was prohibited from using the premises for the purpose originally intended, the distribution of chemicals, a serviceable use was still available to the tenant that was consistent with the use clause of the lease. While the lease may have been less valuable to the tenant or even unprofitable, the tenant's use had not been substantially frustrated. *Mel Frank Tool & Supply, Inc. v. Di-Chem Co.,* 580 N.W.2d 802 (Iowa 1998).

41.24 Default— Termination of Tenancy for Nonpayment of Rent

Virtually all leases provide that the lease may be forfeited and the tenant evicted for nonpayment of rent or for violation of the terms of the lease. Many leases distinguish between the termination of the tenant's right of possession and the termination of the lease. If the landlord terminates the lease for the tenant's default, the landlord loses its right to pursue the tenant for future rent. Terminating the tenant's right of possession preserves the landlord's right to sue the tenant and yet allows the landlord to evict the tenant so the premises can be relet.

Although the lease contains a clause permitting the landlord to declare the lease forfeited for nonpayment of rent, the landlord must not suddenly declare a forfeiture if the landlord has been in the habit of accepting tardy rent payments. The landlord must first notify the tenant to pay the rent by a specified reasonable time, and, if the tenant fails to pay within the time specified, then and only then may the landlord declare a forfeiture. *Cottrell v. Gerson,* 371 Ill. 174, 20 N.E.2d 74 (1939).

If the landlord contends that the tenant has defaulted under the lease, the tenant may wish to contest the notice of default. If it is to do so successfully, it must make the argument in good faith, and should begin a declaratory judgment and injunctive proceeding before the cure period expires. *First Nat'l Stores v. Yellowstone Shopping Ctr.,* 237 N.E.2d 868 (N.Y. 1968). To succeed, however, the tenant is advised to begin the cure of any defaults that may exist. *Waldbaum, Inc. v. Fifth Ave. of Long Island Realty Assocs.,* 650 N.E.2d 1299 (N.Y. 1995).

Year-to-year and month-to-month tenancies likewise may be terminated on the giving of a short notice specified by law if the tenant defaults in its rent payments.

When the landlord evicts the tenant because of the tenant's defaults, the tenant's liability for future rent is ended unless the lease contains a clause, called the "survival clause," to the effect that the tenant's liability shall survive such eviction. Such lease clauses are now commonplace.

The issue has become, however, what the landlord's damages may be upon the tenant's default and the termination of the tenancy, or the tenant's right of possession. May the landlord collect all of the rent due for the remainder of the term? In most but not all states, the landlord has the duty to mitigate damages. *Consol. AG of Curry, Inc. v. Rangen, Inc.,* 912 P.2d 115 (Idaho 1996); *Snyder v. Ambrose,* 639 N.E.2d 639 (Ill. App. 1994); *Austin Hill Country Realty, Inc. v. Palisades Plaza, Inc.*, 948 S.W.2d 243 (Tex. 1997). *But see Stonehedge Square Ltd. Partnership v. Movie Merchants, Inc.,* 715 A.2d 1082 (Pa. 1998). *See generally* Marianne M. Jennings, *Those Mitigating Circumstances: Landlords Are Now in Them*, 26 Real Est. L.J. 294 (1998). Christopher Vaeth, *Landlord's Duty, on Tenant's Failure to Occupy, or Abandonment of Premises, to Mitigate Damages by Accepting or Procuring Another Tenant*, 75 A.L.R.5th 1 (2000). Indeed, some cases require the landlord to obtain the market rentals from a replacement tenant, rather than accepting any rent and pursuing the defaulting tenant for the difference. *Temple Bldg. Assocs. v. Somerwille*, 642 N.Y.S.2d 140 (App. Div. 1996).

41.25 Default by Landlord

To the extent that the lease terms do not validly limit a tenant's rights in the event of the landlord's default, the tenant may have the right to collect damages, exercise the right of self-help, seek injunctive relief, or assert that a constructive eviction has occurred. Since the landlord's default may impair a commercial tenant's profitability, the natural reaction of the tenant is to seek recovery of lost profits. Because of the speculative nature of profits, this relief is not readily available. Annotation, *Recovery of Expected Profits Lost by Lessor's Breach of Lease Preventing or Delaying Operation of New Business*, 92 A.L.R.3d 1286 (1979).

Self-help may be available to the tenant, but the tenant must have the financial resources to undertake the cure, and the ability to recover its costs. Leases frequently expressly negate the ability of the tenant to offset its cure costs against rent. If this is the case, the tenant must separately pursue the landlord for recovery of the cure costs. Suits for declaratory judgment and injunction are typically quicker than damage actions, but involve technical requirements and are not available for all of the landlord's defaults. If money damages will suffice, as where an act of the landlord has caused damage to the tenant's property, an injunction will not be available. If, however, the landlord is not providing services to a large building that the tenant cannot provide, such as adequately maintaining the building's air conditioning system thus making the leased premises uncomfortable for the conduct of the tenant's business, the landlord may be subject to injunctive relief at the hands of the tenant.

Before launching into court, the tenant should carefully analyze the lease. It may prevent the tenant from effectively enforcing what would otherwise be its rights. For example, the lease may contain an exculpation clause protecting the landlord from even its own negligence. These clauses may be enforceable. John D. Perovich, Annotation, *Validity of Exculpatory Clause in Lease Exempting Lessor from Liability*, 49 A.L.R.3d 321 (1973). In some states, clauses such as this, or indemnification agreements under which the tenant agrees to indemnify the landlord from loss occurring, even where the landlord is negligent, are unenforceable. 765 I.L.C.S. 705/1. It is also common for the landlord to insert a lease clause that limits the landlord's liability to its interest in the property in which the leased premises is located. These nonrecourse clauses protect the landlord from liability beyond the equity in the property in the case of major liability matters.

41.26   Eminent Domain   When leased property is taken by eminent domain, the lessee is entitled to share in the award paid by the condemning body for the property, to the extent of the value of the leasehold estate. Most leases, being landlord oriented, contain provisions that automatically terminate the lease in the event of condemnation and also specifically provide that the tenant is not allowed to share in the award.. With the lease terminated, the tenant holds no leasehold estate for which compensation would be payable. The automatic cancellation clause contracts away the tenant's right to share in the award. *Rochester v. Northwestern Telephone,* 431 N.W.2d 874 (Minn. App. 1988). Nonetheless, it is good practice for the lease to provide for both the automatic termination and the tenant's disclaimer of any share in the condemnation award, or the agreement of the parties on the tenant's right in any award.

It is not uncommon for the lease to expressly provide that the tenant has the right to a separate award for its relocation costs, to the extent that such costs are reimbursable under applicable law.

CHAPTER 42

Residential Landlord and Tenant Law

42.01 In General The consumerism movement brought with it a body of consumer law applicable to the landlord and tenant setting. While a great deal of this law is unique to the residential tenancy, we should not be mislead to believe that it is entirely inapplicable to the commercial setting. Some of the consumer trends are being applied in the commercial lease context. In this chapter, you will find a discussion of the legal developments in the residential landlord and tenant context. The next chapter will deal with commercial lease issues.

42.02 Repairs— Ordinances and Statutes Imposing Duty to Repair The old rules relieving the landlord of the duty to keep rented premises in repair evolved before the emergence of large cities, with the attendant issues resulting from urban life. Obviously, workers of low income living in tenements in large urban centers cannot afford to keep their premises in repair. If the landlord fails to make needed repairs, they simply are not made. In many states, laws and ordinances have been passed imposing on landlords the duty to keep rented housing accommodations in repair. Restatement (Second) of Property § Ch. 5, note 3(a); E.W.H., Annotation, *Statute Requiring Property to Be Kept in Good Repair as Affecting Landlord's Liability for Personal Injury to Tenant or His Privies*, 93 A.L.R. 778 (1934); W.E. Shipley, Annotation, *Statute Requiring Property to Be Kept in Good Repair as Affecting Landlord's Liability for Personal Injury to Tenant or His Privies*, 17 A.L.R.2d 704 (1951). In California, Montana, North Dakota, and Oklahoma, for example, the tenant is given the right to move out if needed repairs are not made, but if the tenant is injured because of the landlord's failure to make repairs, the landlord is not liable. In some states (e.g., Michigan, New Jersey, and New York), the landlord will be liable if the tenant suffers injuries as a result of the landlord's negligent failure to make repairs. *Altz v. Lieberson,* 233 N.Y. 16, 134 N.E. 703 (1922); 17 A.L.R.2d 708, *supra.*

> **EXAMPLES:** In states following the New York rule, landlords were held liable for the following injuries: tenant injured by falling ceiling; tenant injured as result of landlord's failure to repair hole in bathroom floor; and tenant's child injured when defective radiator valves blew off.

Many of the statutes and ordinances do not even mention the tenant. The ordinance may simply impose a fine on the landlord if, for example, it fails to keep a light burning in a stairway for twenty-four hours a day. Tenants have persuaded courts that such ordinances create an implied right in a tenant to sue the landlord for personal injuries sustained from an accident or other damages that would not have incurred but for the landlord's failure to comply with the ordinance. Prosser, *Selected Topic on the Law of Torts,* 191 (1954).

In many cities, especially home-rule cities, ordinances make the landlord liable for failure to repair or for violation of building codes. *Bell v. Willoughby Tower Bldg. Corp.,* 46

Ill. App. 2d 45, 196 N.E.2d 487 (1964). Other statutes allow the tenant to withhold rent if the landlord fails to repair or provide essential services.

**42.02(a) Repairs—
State Laws Permitting
Tenant to Make
Repairs**

A few states have laws permitting the tenant to make minor repairs where the landlord refuses to do so, typically limited to an amount not exceeding one month's rent, and to deduct this amount from the rent. Restatement (Second) of Property § 112.

**42.03 Warranty of
Habitability**

Perhaps the most meaningful rule of relatively recent times is the rule that rented residential multifamily premises must be habitable and kept this way during the rental period. *Old Town Dev. Co. v. Langford,* 349 N.E.2d 744 (Ind. App. 1976). This is an implied warranty.

What, precisely, is included in this warranty is something that the courts are still in the process of defining. At a minimum, the landlord warrants that the premises are free from substantial building code violations and will remain so during the rental period. Other courts go further, and it seems probable that most courts will expand the warranty beyond freedom from building code violations. Most courts, it is plain, will hold the landlord liable if the premises become unsafe or unsanitary, and thus unfit to live in. *Glasoe v. Trinkle,* 107 Ill. 2d 1, 479 N.E.2d 915 (1985); *Kline v. Burns,* 276 A.2d 248 (N.H. 1971); *Boston Housing Auth. v. Hemingway,* 293 N.E.2d 831 (Mass. 1973).

Many reasons have been marshaled for finding that the landlord warrants the habitability of rented apartments. Tenants do not have the skills to keep apartments in repair and do not have access to many plumbing, heating, and electrical facilities that fall into disrepair. *Javins v. First Nat'l Realty Corp.,* 428 F.2d 1071; *DePaul v. Kauffman,* 272 A.2d 500 (Pa. 1971*); Mease v. Fox,* 200 N.W.2d 791 (Iowa 1972); Jonathan M. Purver, Annotation, *Modern Status of Rules as to Evidence of Implied Warranty of Habitability or Fitness for Use of Leased Premises,* 40 A.L.R.3d 646 (1971).

While this rule has gained wide acceptance in residential leases, it is not the law in all states. *P.H., Inc. v. Oliver,* 778 P.2d 11 (Utah App. 1989).

**42.03(a) Warranty of
Habitability—
Two Flats**

The warranties rule applies to two flats as well as larger multifamily projects. *South Austin Realty Ass'n v. Sombright,* 361 N.E.2d 795 (Ill. App. 1977).

**42.03(b) Warranty of
Habitability—Homes**

The warranty applies to rental of a home just as it does to the rental of an apartment. *Pole Realty Co. v. Sorrells,* 84 Ill. 2d 178, 417 N.E.2d 1297 (1981*); Fair v. Negley,* 390 A.2d 240 (Pa. 1978); *Lemle v. Breeden,* 462 P.2d 470 (Haw. 1969).

**42.03(c) Warranty of
Habitability—
Disclaimer of Warranty**

A clause in the lease under which the tenant waives or disclaims the benefit of any warranty of habitability is against public policy and void. *Teller v. McCoy,* 253 S.E.2d 114 (W. Va. 1979); *Boston Housing Auth. v. Hemingway,* 293 N.E.2d 831 (Mass. 1973).

**42.03(d) Warranty of
Habitability—
Reduction of Rent**

Some courts and state laws allow the tenant a reduction in rent proportionate to the loss of habitability. *McKenna v. Begin,* 325 N.E.2d 587 (Mass. App. 1975); *Javins v. First Nat'l Realty Corp.,* 428 F.2d 1071 (1970); *Hinson v. Deli,* 26 Cal. App. 3d 62; 102 Cal. Rptr. 661 (1972); *Academy Spires, Inc. v. Brown,* 111 N.J.S. 477, 268 A.2d 556 (1970). They have even extended this remedy to public housing. *Housing Auth. of City of Newark v. Scott,* 348 A.2d 195 (N.J. 1975).

Where the building is in violation of the implied warranty of habitability, but the tenant pays full rent, the newer decisions hold that the landlord is liable to repay the excess rent to the tenant. It has been decided that the tenant can even sue the landlord to get back part of the rent paid. *Berzito v. Gambino,* 114 N.J.S. 124, 274 A.2d 865 (1971). The tenant can also sue the landlord for damages. *Marini v. Ireland,* 56 N.J. 130, 265 A.2d 526 (1970); *Winn v. Sampson Constr. Co.,* 398 P.2d 272 (Kan. 1965).

42.03(e) Warranty of Habitability—Lead-Based Paint

As discussed previously, contracts to sell or lease so called "target" residential housing must contain a lead warning statement in a prescribed form, the lessor must disclose known lead-based paint or paint hazards or state that no such hazards exist, provide a list of records pertaining to the paint or hazard, state that the tenant has received the disclosure and list of records and, if a leasing agent is involved, contain the statement of the agent that it has informed the landlord of the lead-based paint obligations.

42.04 Building Code Violations

If the building contains substantial building code violations, a number of consequences may follow: (1) the violations may constitute a breach of the implied warranty of habitability and, in turn, may entitle the tenant to a reduction in rent; (2) the violations may give the tenant the right to withhold payment of rent or to pay the rent into a court or into an escrow provided by law; (3) the situation may give the tenant the right to pay full rent but to sue the landlord for damages; (4) the landlord may be liable for personal injury sustained as a result of the code violations.

The presence of building code violations when the lease is signed may also render the lease void. *Glyco v. Schultz,* 289 N.E.2d 919 (Ohio 1972); *King v. Moorehead,* 495 S.W.2d 65 (Mo. 1973). This rule deprives the landlord of the benefit of all "fine print" in the lease. *Saunders v. First Nat'l Realty Corp.,* 245 A.2d 836 (1968); *Longenecker v. Hardin,* 130 Ill. App. 2d 468, 264 N.E.2d 878 (1970); Recent Case, *Landlord-Tenant—Violation of Housing Regulations Renders Lease Agreement Unenforceable in Action for Possession and Nonpayment of Rent,* 21 Vand. L. Rev. 1117 (1968); *Robinson v. Diamond Housing Corp.,* 463 F.2d 853 (D.C. Cir. 1972). The tenant may choose to declare the lease void. *Mease v. Fox,* 200 N.W.2d 791 (Iowa 1972). If the code violations were not in existence when the lease was made, the lease is not void. *Hinson v. Deli,* 102 Cal. Rptr. 661.

42.05 Landlord's Liability

42.05(a) Landlord's Liability—Criminal Acts of Third Persons

Traditionally, the landlord has been regarded as having no duty to protect its tenants against criminal acts of third parties. However, under the current notion that the lease is a contract for services, courts are beginning to place upon the landlord the duty to protect the tenant against criminal acts of third persons that it should have foreseen. *Kline v. 1500 Mass. Ave. Apt. Corp.,* 439 F.2d 477 (D.C. Cir. 1970). This would be especially true if the landlord's advertisements mention security protection, where the building is in a high-crime area or where the building has a record of criminal activity. There may be a tendency toward the application of a "higher-the-amount-of-rent, the-greater-the-duty-of-care" principle applied in the case of hotel guests. 59 Geo. L.J. 1189; Gary D. Spivey, Annotation, *Landlord's Obligation to Protect Tenant Against Criminal Activities of Third Persons,* 43 A.L.R.3d 331 (1972). Indeed, if the landlord hires security guards, it has a duty to exercise due care in selecting competent guards that will provide the intended protection. *Trujillo v. G.A. Enterprises, Inc.,* 43 Cal. Rptr.2d 36 (Cal. App. 1995).

EXAMPLE: *T,* an elderly tenant, was assaulted and robbed as he entered his apartment. The apartment was in a high-crime area. *T* sued his landlord, *L,* contending *L* was negligent in failing to provide adequate lighting and door locks. *L* was liable. *Johnston v. Harris,* 198 N.W.2d 409 (Mich. 1972); 43 A.L.R.3d 331, *supra.*

EXAMPLE: *L* held liable to *T* where *L* failed to furnish adequate locks. *Dwyer v. Erie Inv. Co.,* 350 A.2d 268 (N.J. 1975). *But see N.W. v. Amalgamated Trust & Sav. Bank,* 554 N.E.2d 629 (Ill. App. 1990). Where the locks are installed and the criminal follows the tenant through the security system, the landlord is not liable. *Robinson v. New York City Housing Auth.,* 540 N.Y.S.2d 811 (1989). The landlord is not required to provide the most advanced security system, only reasonable security is required. *Tarter v. Schildkraut,* 542 N.Y.S.2d 626 (1989).

EXAMPLE: *L* held liable where an intruder set fire to the building, causing damage to *T's* property. *Warner v. Arnold,* 210 S.E.2d 350 (Ga. App. 1974).

EXAMPLE: If a second burglary occurs, *L* is clearly liable. The facts show that burglary was foreseeable, as where there were prior burglaries and the landlord took no steps to prevent future crimes. *Stribling v. Chicago Housing Auth.,* 34 Ill. App. 3d 551; 340 N.E.2d 47 (1975). Allan E. Korpela, Annotation, *Liability of Landlord for Personal Injury or Death Due to Inadequacy or Lack of Lighting on Portion of Premises Used in Common by Tenants,* 66 A.L.R.3d 202 (1975).

This theory of liability presents exposure to property management companies, especially if it can be demonstrated that the management company's employees were in any way involved in the criminal act. *Ctr. Management Corp. v. Bowman,* 526 N.E.2d 228 (Ind. App. 1988).

The landlord may also be liable to passersby who are off the premises, when the injury results from criminal acts taking place on the premises, which were known to the landlord.

EXAMPLE: A pedestrian was shot during a robbery that took place in the landlord's premises, which the landlord knew were used for drug sales. *Muniz v. Flohern, Inc.,* 553 N.Y.S.2d 313 (1990). *But see Waters v. New York City Housing Auth.,* 513 N.Y.S.2d 356 (1987) (where the court held that the criminal acts were not foreseeable) and *Medina v. Hillshore Partners,* 46 Cal. Rptr.2d 871 (Cal. App. 1995) (where the court held that a passerby could not recover from a landlord where a gang incident started from the property).

Much of this relates to the issue of what is foreseeable. Was the occurrence usual or unusual, or was there a history of the kind of events that caused the injury? If so, liability may follow for the injuries caused by the acts of the third party. *Vernon v. Kroger Co.,* 712 N.E.2d 976 (Ind. 1999).

42.05(b) Landlord's Liability—Smoke Detectors

Where the landlord is under no duty to install smoke detectors, the landlord who installs detectors will not be liable because they are not installed near a bedroom. *Dowler v. Boczkowski,* 691 A.2d 314 (N.J. 1997).

42.06 Eviction—Partial Eviction—Constructive Eviction—Partial Constructive Eviction

A landlord who evicts its tenant wrongfully obviously can no longer collect rent. Indeed, even if the eviction is only from part of the premises, the same result follows.

EXAMPLE: Landlord leased Lot 1 to Tenant. The lot was improved with a house and garage. Landlord wrongfully took possession of the garage. Tenant is not liable for rent, even though Tenant continued to occupy the house. *Tuchin v. Chambers,* 439 S.W.2d 849 (Tex. 1969).

If the landlord's conduct makes the premises untenantable, or if the stairways, walks, or elevators become unusable, a constructive eviction occurs, and, if the tenant moves out as a result, he or she is no longer liable for rent. *Mease v. Fox,* 200 N.W.2d 791 (Iowa 1972).

EXAMPLE: Landlord fails to supply heat in the wintertime to an apartment rented to Tenant. Tenant moves out. Tenant is no longer liable for rent.

EXAMPLE: Infestation of a house presents a harder problem because the tenant has some measure of control here. Nevertheless, infestation of a house with rats is a constructive eviction, since this may be beyond tenant's control. *Lemle v. Breeden,* 51 Haw. 426, 462 P.2d 470 (1969). Of course, this would be a constructive eviction in an apartment.

EXAMPLE: Water leaking through a roof or into a basement is a constructive eviction. Robert A. Shapiro, Annotation, *Landlord and Tenant: Constructive Eviction Based on Flooding, Dampness, or the Like*, 33 A.L.R.3d 1356 (1970). So also is the landlord's failure to make necessary repairs.

Matters wholly beyond the control of the landlord are not a constructive eviction.

EXAMPLE: An adjoining tenant had noisy machinery that prevented tenant from holding seminars. There is no constructive eviction. *Finkelstein v. Levinson,* 343 N.Y.S.2d 849 (1973).

Changes are taking place in the old law of constructive eviction. The right to move out is worthless when there is an acute shortage of rental apartments. Thus, the line between actual eviction and constructive eviction has become blurred, and the courts are introducing new ideas that are designed to achieve justice and place little emphasis on labels.

EXAMPLE: Landlord leased a restaurant to Tenant who took possession, not knowing that part of the leased premises was not available for occupancy. The court held this was "actual partial eviction" and that Tenant could occupy the occupiable part without paying rent.

EXAMPLE: Landlord leased Tenant an apartment. Tenant was forced to discontinue use of the terrace because of water dripping from the building's air conditioner. The court permitted Tenant to remain in occupancy and to discontinue paying rent. The court held this was "partial constructive eviction." *East Haven Assoc., Inc., v. Gurian,* 313 N.Y.S.2d 927 (1970); Robert M. Schoenhaus, Annotation, *Landlord and Tenant: Constructive Eviction by Another Tenant's Conduct,* 1 A.L.R.4th 849 (1980).

EXAMPLE: Tenant, an orthodontist, resisted eviction because Landlord was not furnishing proper heating and air conditioning. The court held that because of this breach on Landlord's part, Tenant was not required to pay the rent and could not be evicted. *Demirci v. Burns,* 124 N.J.S. 274, 306 A.2d 468 (1973).

EXAMPLE: Landlord leased a store building to Tenant, with a covenant to repair. Part of the building was destroyed by fire. The court allowed Tenant to occupy the remainder of the building with a reduction of rent. *Coppola v. Tidewater Oil Co.,* 244 N.Y.S.2d 898 (1963).

Statutes are being enacted on the subject of rent withholding and the other new rules. *De Paul v. Kauffman,* 441 Pa. 386, 272 A.2d 500 (1971). The New Jersey statute even includes mobile homes in its retaliatory eviction statute. In Maryland, tenants may repudiate the lease within thirty days of occupancy if the warranty of habitability has been breached.

Up to the present time, the law has been that a tenant who claims that the landlord's conduct amounts to a constructive eviction must vacate the premises within a reasonable time after the landlord has failed to correct the condition. R.W. Gascoyne, Annotation, *Time Within Which Tenant Must Yield or Abandon Premises After Claimed Constructive Eviction,* 91 A.L.R.2d 638 (1963). Some courts will continue to adhere to this view. However, the newer view recognizes the dilemma that confronts the tenant and permits the tenant to use this defense while retaining occupancy of the rented premises. 1 A.L.R.4th 849, *supra.*

Restatement (Second) of Property § 6.1, Comment h, adopts the view of these decisions that the tenant need not abandon the premises where the landlord is guilty of conduct amounting to a constructive eviction. Instead, the tenant may sue for damages or claim an abatement of rent.

42.07 Unconscionability

The notion that the court can strike down an unconscionable lease or any unconscionable provision in the lease has become part of the law of landlord and tenant. Restatement (Second) Property § 5; Section 1.303 Uniform Residential Landlord & Tenant Act.

> **EXAMPLE:** An apartment lease obligated Tenant to pay Landlord an additional rent in attorneys' fees upon commencement of any proceeding by Landlord as a result of Tenant's default. The clause was held void. *Weidman v. Tomaselli,* 365 N.Y.S.2d 681 (1975).

> **EXAMPLE:** Landlord, an oil company, leased a filling station to Tenant under a lease with a clause stating that Landlord would not be liable for loss or damage resulting from the negligence of Landlord's employees and that tenant would pay for any such loss. One of Landlord's employees sprayed gasoline over Tenant, and severe burns resulted. The court held the clause void and awarded damages to Tenant. *Weaver v. American Oil Co.,* 276 N.E.2d 144 (Ind. 1971).

42.08 Fair Dealing

Some courts will strike down any provision of a lease if enforcement would not be considered "fair dealing." Curtis J. Berger, *Hard Leases Make Bad Law,* 74 Colum. L. Rev. 791, 805.

> **EXAMPLE:** Landlord leased commercial premises to Tenant with an option to renew. Tenant failed to exercise the option within the time allowed, but Landlord, after such expiration, notified Tenant that his lease would soon end. Tenant then tendered to Landlord the money needed to renew the lease, but Landlord refused. The court held that Landlord was not injured by the technical defect and compelled Landlord to renew the lease. *George W. Miller & Co. v. Wolf Sales & Serv. Corp.,* 318 N.Y.S.2d 24 (1971).

42.09 Rent Withholding

Until recently, if a tenant failed to pay rent, the landlord could have the tenant evicted. The courts that recognize an implied warranty of habitability and freedom from building code violations have begun to devise additional remedies for the tenant if the premises are in disrepair. One of these is rent withholding, under which the tenant pays the rent to the eviction court. Some cities and states have enacted laws along this line. *McNeal v. Habib,* 346 A.2d 508 (D.C. 1975); *Clore v. Fredman,* 59 Ill. 2d 20, 319 N.E.2d 18 (1974*); Mease v. Fox,* 200 N.W.2d 791 (Iowa 1972), Jonathan M. Purver, Annotation, *Validity and Construction of Statutes or Ordinance Authorizing Withholding or Payment into Escrow of Rent for Period During Which Premises Are Not Properly Maintained by Landlord,* 40 A.L.R.3d 821 (1971). As a rule, when the building code violations have been corrected, the rent deposited in the escrow (or a part thereof) is released to the landlord. *Klein v. Allegheny County,* 269 A.2d 647 (Pa. 1972); *Bell v. Tsintolas Realty Co.,* 430 F.2d 474 (1970); James W. McLehanay, *Rent Withholding,* 29 Md. L. Rev. 202 (1969); 40 A.L.R.3d 821, *supra.* Of course, eviction is postponed as long as the rent is being paid into the escrow. *Kipsborough Realty Corp. v. Goldbetter,* 367 N.Y.S.2d 916 (1975); *Sabul v. Lipscomb,* 310 A.2d 890 (Del. 1973).

Courts have begun to evolve additional new remedies for tenants where building code violations exist. First, the court finds that there is an implied covenant or obligation on the landlord's part to keep the premises free from major building code violations. Then, if the landlord fails to perform this duty, the court finds the tenant is entitled to a rent reduction.

Jack Spring, Inc. v. Little, 50 Ill. 2d 351, 266 N.E.2d 338 (1972). Or, the tenant can make the repairs and deduct the cost from future rents. *Marini v. Ireland,* 56 N.J. 130, 265 A.2d 526 (1970); *Mease v. Fox,* 200 N.W.2d 791 (Iowa 1972).

42.10 Tenant Unions   Because one tenant has little bargaining power against a landlord, tenant unions were formed. Michael O'Conner, *Law, Lawyers and Tenant Unions in Chicago,* 59 Ill. B.J. 732 (1971); H. Edward Hales, Jr. & Charles H. Livingston, *Tenant Unions, Their Law and Operation in the State and Nation,* 23 U. Fla. L. Rev. 79 (1970). These unions engage in collective bargaining with landlords. Tenant organizations have recognized the need for more tenant control and have developed a variety of goals. The most frequently sought goals include the following: (1) negotiation of a new form of lease for use between individual tenants and the landlord; (2) development of a grievance procedure or plan to arbitrate landlord and tenant disputes; (3) recognition of the tenant organization as the exclusive representative of the tenants; (4) formulation of a satisfactory way to handle tenant needs and to bring the buildings into compliance with the building code; (5) participation of the tenant organization in decisions about rent increases; and (6) provision of adequate security. Some tenant unions have engaged in rent strikes. *Tenant Rent Strikes,* 3 Colum. J.L. & Soc. Prob. 1 (1967). Through the use of legal maneuvers, some tenant unions have been able to stall evictions for as long as nine months.

A landlord may not refuse to renew a tenant's lease simply because the tenant has been active in a tenants' union. *Engler v. Capital Management Corp.,* 271 A.2d 615 (N.J. 1970).

42.11 Rent Control   A number of local governments have adopted residential rent control ordinances. Such ordinances have been held valid. *Inganamort v. Borough of Fort Lee,* 62 N.J. 521, 303 A.2d 298 (1973); *Birkenfeld v. City of Berkeley,* 550 P.2d 1001 (Cal. 1976); *Marshall House v. Rent Control Bd.,* 266 N.E.2d 876 (Mass. 1971); Kathi J. Moore, *HUD Preemption of Local Rent Control Ordinances—Tenant Entitled to Due Process Rights,* 30 Rutgers L. Rev. 1025 (1977).

42.12 Retaliatory Evictions   As the renters have grown more militant in reporting building code violations to the city authorities, landlords have retaliated by refusing to renew the leases of the militants. Until recently, the landlord would have been within its rights. Today, many courts would not permit the landlord to evict a tenant where the sole reason for doing so is a desire to retaliate for the reporting of building code violations. *Clore v. Fredman,* 59 Ill. 2d 20, 319 N.E.2d 18 (1974); 40 A.L.R.3d 753, *supra.*

> **EXAMPLE:** *T,* a tenant in an apartment, complained repeatedly to the landlord, *L,* about building code violations. Receiving no satisfaction, *T* complained to the building department, which ordered *L* to cure the defects. When *T's* lease expired, *L* filed an eviction suit. The court refused to evict *T* because *L* was retaliating against *T.* The court allowed *T* to remain in possession until the code violations were eliminated and *T* could find another place to live. *Markese v. Cooper,* 333 N.Y.S.2d 63 (1972).

There are a number of cases holding that the entire doctrine of retaliatory eviction is inapplicable where the landlord simply seeks to oust the tenant so that the landlord can remove a crumbling building from the housing market altogether. *Robinson v. Diamond Housing Corp.,* 463 F.2d 853 (D.C. Cir. 1972). This appears to make sense. If the landlord simply cannot keep the building in good shape, it should be permitted to demolish it. O. Max Gardener, III, *Landlord and Tenant—Retaliatory Eviction and the Absolute Right to Chose Not to Have Any Tenants*, 51 N.C. L. Rev. 162 (1972).

But, if the landlord raises the rent outrageously to get rid of a tenant who complains about building code violations, the tenant can move out and sue the landlord for damages, including damages for mental distress and punitive damages, that is, damages in an amount sufficient to constitute a punishment for the landlord's wrongdoing. *Aweeka v. Bonds,* 97 Cal. Rptr. 650 (1971).

The philosophy that sustains and supports the rule of retaliatory eviction was expounded in *Edwards v. Habib,* 397 F.2d 687 (D.C. Cir. 1968). The court reasoned (1) building codes cannot be enforced unless tenants can report violations without fear of their landlord's vengeance and (2) use of the state courts to evict complaining tenants would be action by the state taken to punish tenants for exercising their constitutional right of free speech. Mack A. Player, *Motive and Retaliatory Eviction of Tenants,* U. Ill. L.F. 610 (1974).

Mere complaints about the condition of the building without reporting the code violations to the municipal authorities may not be enough to make a case for retaliatory eviction. *W.W.G. Corp. v. Hughes,* 960 P.2d 720 (Colo. App. 1998).

42.12(a) Retaliatory Eviction—Motive

To retaliate is to "get even" with someone for something he or she has done. This requires an intention to get even. As to the landlord's motives, *see* Player, *supra.*

> **EXAMPLE:** Tenant complains to the city about building code violations. Immediately, Landlord serves notice on Tenant that his month-to-month tenancy is terminated.

> **EXAMPLE:** Facts as in the example given previously, but Landlord does not act until three years after Tenant's complaint.

Establishing intention to get even is simple in the first example. It is next to impossible in the second example.

Many states have passed laws that fix a time that determines motivation.

> **EXAMPLE:** In California, if Landlord acts against Tenant within sixty days after Tenant has complained, it is assumed that the Landlord is trying to "get even." Other states have other limits. Player, *supra,* p. 615.

42.12(b) Retaliatory Eviction—Landlord's Protected Activities

The landlord is not trying to "get even" if the tenant complains, and the landlord raises rents generally and evenly so that it can pay for repairs. The landlord must spread the cost over the anticipated life of the repairs. Player, *supra,* p. 623.

A landlord may take the entire building off the rental market if the landlord feels the cost of needed repairs would be beyond its means, but the landlord must not single out the tenant who complained and evict only that tenant.

42.12(c) Retaliatory Eviction—Tenant's Protected Activities

Tenant activities against which the landlord must not retaliate include the following: (1) tenants' meetings; (2) complaints to the building code department; (3) forming a tenants' union; and (4) lawful rent withholding. Player, *supra,* p. 614.

42.13   Limitations on the Landlord's Right to Select Tenants, Renew Leases and Tenancies, and to Evict Tenants

Under the old law, which still applies in commercial leases, the landlord could rent to whomever it pleased, refuse to rent, refuse to renew leases, and evict any tenant whose lease or tenancy has been terminated. Now, the court decisions and statutes are beginning to impose limits on the landlord's freedom of action. Where a public body is the landlord, the tenant's tenancy cannot be terminated without a hearing and inquiry into the reasonableness of the termination. *Thorpe v. Housing Auth.,* 393 U.S. 268 (1968). Thus, in the case of such a landlord there are strict limits on the landlord's right to evict. *Chicago Housing Auth. v. Harris,* 275 N.E.2d 353 (Ill. 1971).

It certainly seems logical to hold that where a public body, such as a city or a housing authority, is the landlord, the tenant will have constitutional rights that tenants of private landlords do not have. The notion has gained currency that private landlords who receive government assistance in some form are quasi-public landlords, and their tenants have at least some of the rights of tenants in public projects.

> **EXAMPLE:** Landlord whose building was erected with FHA financing, and who received a real estate tax exemption, could not refuse to accept Tenant because Tenant was a welfare recipient. *Colon v. Tompkins Square Neighbors,* 294 F. Supp. 134 (S.D. N.Y. 1968). Landlord cannot accept benefits from the government and turn its back on the wards of the government.

> **EXAMPLE:** Landlord, in the identical situation of the landlord in the preceding example, refused to renew Tenant's lease. Tenant had been an outspoken advocate of tenants' rights and had organized demonstrations against Landlord. The court held that Landlord could not evict Tenant without giving him notice and a hearing to show that Landlord was acting with good cause. *McQueen v. Drucker,* 317 F. Supp. 1122 (D. Mass. 1970). Tenant had the right to free speech.

> **EXAMPLE:** Some courts require such landlords to give the tenants notice and to hold a hearing when the landlord wants to increase rents, or, when the landlord wants to take action against the tenant in a public housing complex. *Hinojosa v. Housing Auth.,* 896 S.W.2d 833 (Tex. App. 1995).

This court-made law has now been formalized in HUD rules. Freilich, *Recent Developments in Local Government Law,* 8 Urb. Law. 605 (1976).

CHAPTER 43

Commercial Leases

43.01 Term— Options to Renew or Cancel

Leases generally have a term or duration. At the end of the term, the tenant is to vacate the premises and the landlord is free to use the premises for its own purposes or to relet the premises to a third party. Frequently, tenants want options to expand the premises, renew the term of the lease, contract the size of the leased premises by giving some portion of it back to the landlord, or cancel the lease entirely. Obviously, each of these has an economic consequence.

Landlords tend to want certainty and the ability to control the space in their buildings. For example, if Tenant A has an expansion right to be exercised at some future date and the landlord believes it is likely that the expansion option will be exercised, it does not want Tenant B to exercise a renewal option on the space that Tenant A would otherwise occupy upon the exercise of the expansion option. Tenants, on the other hand, want flexibility. With the ever-changing business climate, tenants want the ability to react, even at a price, to what that business climate may bring to them. The right to renew, expand, contract, and terminate gives them that flexibility.

Renewal options should be present agreements to allow the tenant the ability to extend or renew, whether for a new term of the same length as the first or for some other period of time. The terms of the lease for the option period must be certain. While the landlord and tenant may agree upon a mechanism for the determination of certain terms, such as the rent for the option period, they must do more than agree to agree. If they do not agree at the outset on the amount of rent for the option period, they may agree that the rent will be set according to a formula, such as one based on the Consumer Price Index. Alternatively, they may agree that appraisers shall set the rent. These are valid and enforceable provisions. If, however, they leave the amount of future rent to later determination without setting up a mechanism to make that determination, the renewal provision of the lease will not be enforceable. *Cann v. Metropolitan Atlanta Rapid Transit Auth.*, 396 S.E.2d 515 (Ga. App. 1990). *But see P.J.'s Pantry v. Puschak*, 458 A.2d 123 (N.J. Super. 1983) (which holds that an option to renew a lease at a rental reasonably agreed upon is enforceable and requires a fair market value rental for the renewal term). Merely providing that the terms will be renegotiated at the time of renewal is not enough. *R.A.S., Inc. v. Crowley*, 351 N.W.2d 414 (Nev. 1984). If, on the other hand, the lease merely gives the tenant a renewal option and is silent as to rent during the renewal term, it will be implied that the rent during the renewal term will be the same as that due during the original term. *Idol v. Little*, 396 S.E.2d 632 (N.C. App. 1990).

Where the lease establishes a manner in which the lease is to be renewed, such as by requiring that the tenant give the landlord a notice of renewal on or before a certain date, the tenant must follow the procedure exactly and not be tardy. Late notice or notice of renewal not given in the proper manner is generally ineffective. William B. Johnson, Annotation, *Circumstances Excusing Lessee's Failure to Give Timely Notice of Exercise of Option to Renew or Extend Lease*, 27 A.L.R.4th 266 (1984). There are some exceptions, however, such as where the tenant can show that the default was excusable and will work a substantial forfeiture on the tenant; in this case, the landlord will not be prejudiced. *Aickin v. Ocean View Inv., Inc.*, 935 P.2d 992 (Haw. 1997); *Mass Properties Co. v. 1820 New York Ave. Corp.*, 544 N.Y.S.2d 180 (App. Div. 1989); *American Power Indus., Ltd. v. Rebel Realty Corp.*, 535 N.Y.S.2d 99 (App. Div. 1988); Shulman & Chudnoff, *Options to Renew, Expand and Contract (with Forms)*, 7 No. 4 Prac. Real Est. Law. 69 (July 1991).

The courts have held that a landlord must renew a lease if refusal to do so would be unconscionable.

> **EXAMPLE:** Landlord, an oil company, had leased the filling station to Tenant for many years. Tenant had spent a great deal of money in improving the station and building up a business. The court compelled Landlord to renew the lease. *Shell Oil Co. v. Marinello*, 294 A.2d 253 (N.J. 1972); Frona M. Powell, *Unconscionability in the Lease of Commercial Real Estate*, 35 Real Prop. Prob. & Tr. J. 197 (2000).

Many leases condition the exercise of the renewal option upon the tenant not being in default, either at the time the renewal notice is given or at the time of the commencement of the renewal term. There is some authority that the tenant must not be in default in order to exercise the renewal right, even if the lease provision does not so state. *Cowan v. Mervin Mewes, Inc.*, 546 N.W.2d 104 (S.D. 1996)

43.02 Use of the Premises

Many times, there is no reason to restrict the business use to which the tenant puts the demised premises, and it is adequate to simply provide that the tenant can use the property for any lawful use provided that such use is not in violation of any of the private restrictions that encumber the property. It should be understood that the lease will, of course, contain other provisions that control the tenant's actions at and about the property. For example, today's leases will almost always prohibit the tenant's use of hazardous materials in the demised premises, or, if the use of such materials is part of the tenant's business, the lease will require that the tenant use, store, and dispose of those materials in compliance with hazardous waste laws.

Unless the terms of the lease prevent it, the tenant may use the premises for lawful purposes. This use by the tenant is often a point of controversy. Many leases state that the premises are leased for a specific purpose, such as the business of selling tobacco products, newspapers, magazines, and candy, or to be used as a real estate office. Oddly enough, courts seem to feel that such language does not limit the tenant to the stated use. Unless the lease states that the property is to be used only for a particular purpose, the tenant may make any use of the property it wants to, so long as such use is not materially different from that to which the rented premises were customarily put. *Lyon v. Bethlehem Engineering Corp.*, 253 N.Y. 111, 170 N.E. 512 (1930); W.R. Habeeb, Annotation, *Easements or Privileges of Tenant of Part of Building as to Other Parts Not Included in Lease*, 24 A.L.R.2d 123 (1952).

The landlord may want to include a clause under which the tenant covenants to use the property only for a specific purpose, and include at the end of the tenant's covenants a clause giving the landlord the right to terminate the lease if the tenant violates any of the covenants. The landlord must be sure to state clearly what the permitted use includes. For example, if the lease specifies that the tenant is to operate a drugstore, will the tenant be allowed to sell automotive and garden items?

When the lease definitely restricts the use that the tenant may make of the premises and the tenant branches out into some unauthorized use, the landlord need not terminate the lease, even if the lease gives it power to do so. The landlord may, instead, procure a court order forbidding the tenant from engaging in the unauthorized use. This is desirable when the tenant is highly solvent and the rent is favorable to the landlord. It also protects the landlord in those cases where it has agreed with other tenants not to allow competing businesses in the same property.

43.02(a)   Use of Premises—Signs

A lease of business property automatically gives the tenant the right to advertise its business on the leased property if the lease does not forbid this use.

> **EXAMPLE:** In the case of a lease of an entire building, it would give the tenant the exclusive right to place advertising signs on the walls and roofs of the building, for example, to maintain window signs and to have its name on a lobby directory board. In the case of a lease of a portion of a building, the lessee, not the landlord, would have the right to place advertising signs on the exterior walls of the portion leased to the tenant. Boyd J. Peterson, Annotation, *Construction and Application of Restrictive Covenants to Use of Signs*, 61 A.L.R.4th 1028 (1988).

Usually, however, where various floors are leased to different tenants, the landlord is considered as retaining exclusive possession of the roof. And, obviously, if the landlord leases the second floor to *A* and the third floor to *B*, *A*'s signs must not extend above the dividing line between the second and third floors.

Landlords are finding that the roofs of their buildings are valuable for rental to tenants and to third parties for the purpose of installing cellular antennas and other communication devices.

43.02(b)   Use of Premises—Continuous Operation

Related to the use clause is the clause often found in leases of retail space requiring the demised premises to be kept open for business during certain hours and on certain days. There are two reasons for such a provision. In the shopping center situation, it is the joint efforts of the owner of the center and the tenants that breed success. From the tenants' perspective, it is the activity of the group of tenants offering a variety of goods and services that creates the atmosphere in which shoppers come to purchase from store to store. Anchor tenants draw shoppers to the center and feed the specialty stores with traffic. If some stores are not open, the magnet of the variety of open stores is not available for tenants, and the whole center suffers.

The continuous operation clause requires the tenant to keep doing business during the entire term of the lease. Without such a clause, a tenant would be in full compliance with its lease if it shut its doors, but continued to honor the terms of the lease by continuing to pay rent, keep the property insured and in repair, and the like. If the tenant breaches this covenant, it will be liable to the landlord for the loss in value of the shopping center caused by the closure of the tenant's store. *Stein v. Sprainhour,* 521 N.E.2d 641 (Ill. App. 1998); *Hornwood v. Smith's Food King No. 1,* 772 P.2d 1284 (Nev. 1989). Alternatively, the court may order the tenant to stay open for business. *Bradlees Tidewater, Inc. v. Walnut Hill Inv., Inc.,* 391 S.E.2d 304 (Va. 1990). *But see Madison Plaza, Inc. v. Shapira Corp.,* 387 N.E.2d 483 (Ind. 1979). These results naturally follow from the concept that the stores in a shopping center are economically interdependent.

Where the lease does not contain an express continuous operation clause, other lease terms may give rise to the implication that the lease requires the tenant to continue to operate its store. In shopping center lease jargon, the tenant may not "go dark." For example, where the lease specifies a particular use and rent is computed on a percentage of revenue or profit, a court may find that there is an implied covenant by the tenant to use and occupy the premises for the stated purpose to generate the amount of rent contemplated by the parties. *Lippman v. Sears, Roebuck & Co.*, 280 P.2d 775 (Cal. App. 1955); *The College Block v. Atlantic Richfield Co.*, 254 Cal. Rptr. 179 (Cal. App. 1988); *Stein v. Spainhour*, 521 N.E.2d 64 1 (Ill. App. 1988).

The mere presence of a percentage rent clause does not mean that the courts will automatically imply a covenant to continuously operate. Where the base rent was fair at the time the lease was executed, an implied clause will probably not be found. *The Kroger Co. v. The Bonny Corp.*, 216 S.E.2d 341 (Ga. App. 1975); *Carl A. Schuberg, Inc. v. The Kroger Co.*, 317 N.W.2d 606 (Mich. App. 1982). *See also Chicago Title & Trust Co. v. Southland Corp.*, 443 N.E.2d 294 (Ill. App. 1982). Where the base rent was below market rent at the time the lease was made and the percentage rent was substantial in relation to the base rent, a continuous operation clause may be implied. *BVT Lebanon Shopping Ctr., Ltd. v. Wal-Mart Stores, Inc.*, LEXIS 267 (Tenn. App. 1999).

Similarly, the use clause of a lease that allows the premises to be used only for the operation of a grocery supermarket will not prevent the tenant from going dark. *Serfecz v. Jewel Food Stores*, 67 F.3d 591 (7th Cir. 1995).

Continuous operation clauses have been implied from lease clauses other than percentage rent clauses. A clause that permitted the tenant to close for up to sixty days implied that a longer closing would not be permitted. *Slater v. Pearle Vision Ctr., Inc.*, 546 A.2d 676 (Pa. Super. 1988). In other cases, courts have found implied continuous operation covenants merely from the economic interdependence of the tenants. *Ingannamorte v. Kings Super Markets, Inc.*, 260 A.2d 841 (N.J. 1970); *Tooley's Truck Stop v. Chrisanthopouls*, 260 A.2d 845 (N.J. 1970). In each of these cases, the businesses that were closed were of substantial importance to the other businesses located in the landlord's project.

The results of some of these cases may be hard to predict and will depend on the facts of the cases. Patrick A. Randolph, Jr., *Going Dark Aggressively*, Prob. & Prop. 9 (Nov./Dec. 1996). It is clearly best for the landlord and tenant to face this issue at the time of the making of the lease by inserting a clause in the lease that expresses their intent.

43.03 Rent   Today's leases may have several forms of rent. Basically, leases almost uniformly call for the payment of base rent. Simply stated, this is what the tenant must pay to occupy the premises. In real estate finance terms, this is the raw occupancy cost or pure rent. Base rent is often expressed as a flat amount, such as $1,000.00 per month. In more sophisticated leasing transactions, it may be expressed in terms of the rate per square foot of rentable space per year, such as "$17.00 per rentable square foot per year." In such case, the rent will, however, be paid in monthly installments.

Landlords have long since come to the understanding that flat base rents do not accommodate increases in the market rental rates as years go by, especially for longer-term leases. Some leases provide for the base rent to step up or increase in future lease years. For example, a lease may provide for a rental of "$17.00 per rentable square foot during the initial and second Lease Year, $18.00 per rentable square foot during the third and fourth Lease Year. . . ." If the lease does not provide for a step up in base rentals during the lease term, the lease will often provide that rentals will increase as some measurement of inflation or purchasing power is adjusted. Often, the parties will utilize the Consumer Price Index (CPI) as the index to which base rent is tied. At agreed intervals, base rent will be adjusted to coincide with upward movements of the CPI.

Increasing the base rent allows the landlord to, at least in theory, keep rentals somewhat in step with market conditions. Of course, experience indicates that such is not always the case. When there is a glut of office space, base rents on some leases made just a few years earlier are higher than prevailing market rates. Leases with CPI escalator clauses may have driven those leases even higher than market rates. The opposite can also be true. When there is more demand for rentable space than supply, market rates for new leases are higher than the rental rates on existing leases.

In the gross lease, the tenant pays a rental only and makes no separate payment of, or contribution to, real estate taxes and operating expenses. Net leases separate the pure rent from the costs of operation, such as real estate taxes and expenses like security, landscaping, insurance, and maintenance costs, and require the tenant to pay its share of these costs as additional rent. Sometimes, these clauses will have a stop feature, which may either put a cap on the amount of additional rent the tenant will pay or require the landlord to pay the first increment of these expenses and pass on any overage to the tenant. Through this device, either the landlord's or the tenant's share of these expenses is stopped.

> **EXAMPLE:** The lease may require the tenant to pay its share of the real estate taxes to the extent that they exceed $0.50 per rentable square foot, or to the extent that real estate taxes exceed the amount of real estate taxes levied against the property in some base year.

An interesting problem develops where the costs that the tenant agreed to pay or share increase as a result of the landlord's acts, such as extensively remodeling the property in which the leased premises are located. In such case, the increase in real estate taxes resulting from the renovation could not be passed through to the tenant under the tax pass-through provision of the lease. *Design Studio Int'l, Inc. v. Chicago Title & Trust Co.,* 541 N.E.2d 1166 (Ill. App. 1989).

43.03(a) Rent—Office Leases Rent for many types of leases, especially office leases, is based upon the number of rentable square feet in the office space. From the tenant's perspective, it must be remembered that rentable area is always larger than the usable area. There can be many ways to measure the rentable area, but most sophisticated parties have required the use of the "Standard Method for Measuring Floor Area in Office Buildings," adopted as an American National Standard in 1980 to permit the computation of rentable area on an understandable and uniform basis.

The two concepts of rentable and usable area are very important in understanding the economics of office leasing for both the landlord and the tenant. The rentable area includes the tenant's pro rata portion of the entire office floor, excluding elements of the building that penetrate through the floor to areas below. This is the area that is used by the landlord to measure the total income-producing area of the building and to compute the tenant's pro rata share of building expenses and taxes.

> **EXAMPLE:** Suppose that a building has a glass and steel curtain wall that is of almost uniform thickness. If the glass is the dominant part of the wall (i.e., it takes up more than 50 percent of the surface), the rentable area will extend up to the glass, but since the steel portion of the wall is just a few inches inside of the glass, the economic impact to the tenant is minimal. What if, however, there is an interior radiator system that extends eighteen inches into the floor area of the building from the window. Since the rentable area would be measured from the windows, the tenant will lose usable area of one-and-one-half feet per lineal foot of

exterior wall. If the office has 1000 lineal feet of exterior walls and rent was $20.00 per rentable square foot per year, with an additional $7.00 per rentable square foot in expenses and taxes, the tenant will pay $40,500.00 per year for space that is basically not usable (1000 lineal feet $\times$ 1.5 feet of dead space $\times$ $27.00 = $40,500.00).

43.03(b)   Rent— Percentage Leases

Leases of retail locations often provide for a percentage rent. Such a lease usually provides a minimum fixed rent with an additional rent calculated at a percentage of the tenant's gross sales. Commonly accepted percentages for each type of retail establishment are published periodically by various sources. If such a lease is prepared for a multiline store, such as a department store in a shopping center, it may be necessary to fix different percentages for different departments within the store.

Tenants are well advised to carefully analyze the definition of what is included and what is excluded from the calculation of gross sales upon which the percentage rent will be based. Obviously, the tenant wants to pay rent only on the revenue that it receives. Revenue in the form of sales taxes that, in turn, is paid over to the state is one of the categories or components of the total revenue of the tenant, but which should not be included in the gross sales upon which the percentage rent is paid. Similarly, different types of sales may be entitled to different treatment. Where, for example, a store sells lottery tickets, only the commissions earned should be included in the gross sales calculation. *In re The Circle K Corp.,* 19 F.3d 1439 (9th Cir. 1994).

Tenants often negotiate to deduct certain expenses from gross sales. For example, tenants will attempt to subtract from such revenue the discount that is paid to credit card companies to net out their actual revenue. Landlords must take care to not exclude so much of the tenant's revenue so as to transform the provision into a net profit calculation that will be much smaller than gross sales. If this were to be done, the landlord would have to increase the percentage to be made whole. In any event, the landlord wants to measure percentage rent by sales volume and not depend upon the successful or unsuccessful operation of the store for its rent.

Deductions from gross sales are usually allowed for sales and luxury taxes and returned merchandise. Care should be exercised to include in gross sales all income from vending machines, pay telephones, pay toilets, lockers, weighing machines, stamp machines, and so on, as well as services rendered on the premises, such as hairdressing and delivery. Services rendered at cost, clothing alterations and employees' cafeteria, for example, are usually excluded. Income from subtenants and concessionaires is included. The lease should state whether gross income includes sales made by mail and sales to employees. The lease should have a continuous operation clause, for, obviously, if the store is closed, the percentage rent stops or drops. A provision should be included forbidding the establishment of a competing store within a specified radius. Since the landlord is depending on the particular tenant's ability to run a profitable business, the lease should forbid any assignment or sublease or even the occupancy of the premises by anyone other than the tenant unless the landlord consents.

43.04   Assignment and Subletting

As a general rule, a tenant may assign a lease or sublet the demised premises unless the lease provides otherwise. Commercial leases provide either that they are freely assignable or that assignment and subletting are prohibited or controlled. The interests of the landlord and the tenant are somewhat divergent in this area. Landlords want to control the mix and quality of tenants in their property. Tenants want to have flexibility to adapt to changes in their business.

Another economic reason for the debate between landlords and tenants in this area has come to the fore. As between the landlord and the tenant, who should realize the benefit of increases in the market rental price of the premises? If the lease is freely assignable, the tenant can assign the lease to a third party and retain the bonus rent, or the excess of the rent paid by the assignee over the rent paid to the original landlord. If the lease is not assignable, the bonus rent will go to the original landlord.

If the parties face this issue in their negotiations, they may agree upon either a recapture or profit-sharing clause. The recapture clause allows the landlord to recapture the premises if the tenant attempts to assign the lease or sublet the property to a third party. Through the use of this clause, the landlord retains control over the property and the tenant retains business flexibility. Through the profit-sharing clause, the landlord and tenant split the bonus rent, typically after the deduction of the costs of assignment or subletting, such as brokers' commissions and refurbishment.

Clauses prohibiting or limiting the assignability of leases or subletting of the property may be placed in three broad categories. The first absolutely prohibits assignment and subletting. These clauses are generally upheld. *Friedman on Leases*, § 7.403(a) (3d ed. 1990). *But see Warner v. Konover*, 553 A.2d 1138 (Conn. 1989). It is the second and third categories of these clauses that bear a great deal of analysis and thought when they are negotiated and when the parties are forced to deal with the application of these clauses in specific transactional circumstances.

Some leases provide that assignment and subleasing are prohibited unless the lessor consents. Some states imply a condition that the landlord act reasonably in granting or withholding its consent to the assignment or sublease. *Kendall v. Earnest Pestana, Inc.*, 409 P.2d 837 (Cal. 1985). *But see Johnson v. Yousoofian*, 930 P.2d 921 (Wash. App. 1996). A variant of this clause provides that such actions are prohibited without the lessor's consent, which the lessor may withhold in its sole discretion. Most jurisdictions uphold these clauses and give the lessor the discretion that it bargained for. James C. McLoughlin, Annotation, *When Lessor May Withhold Consent Under Unqualified Provisions in Lease Prohibiting Assignment and Subletting of Leased Premises Without Lessor's Consent*, 21 A.L.R.4th 188 (1983).

There are, however, some exceptions. In one such case, the lease prohibited subletting and assignment without the landlord's consent, except with respect to assignments by operation of law. The court, after implying the duty of good faith and fair dealing, held that the lessor's refusal to consent to the assignment of the lease in connection with a sale of the tenant's business, where the lessor did not have a good faith and reasonable basis for such refusal, constituted a breach of contract. *Cohen v. Ratinoff,* 195 Cal. Rptr.3d 84 (1983).

The last type of antiassignment and antisubletting clause provides that assignment and subletting are prohibited without the lessor's consent, which shall not be unreasonably withheld. Here, the contest typically revolves around the reasonableness of the grounds for the refusal of the landlord's consent. The creditworthiness and business character of the assignee, the experience in the business that the assignee proposes to conduct on the premises, the legality and nature of the proposed use of the premises by the assignee, the need to make alterations to the premises to adapt them to the assignee's use, and the effect of the assignee's business on the other tenants are all legitimate bases for a landlord's refusal to consent. *Fernandez v. Vazquez,* 397 So.2d 1171 (Fla. App. 1981); *American Book Co. v. Yeshiva Univ. Dev. Found., Inc.,* 297 N.Y.S.2d 156 (Sup. Ct. 1969). The landlord may not withhold consent solely because the sublessee will not use the premises for the limited purpose set forth in the use clause (i.e., for the sale of bedding, home furnishings, and accessories). *Astoria Bedding, Mister Sleeper Bedding Ctr., Inc. v. Northside Partnership,* 657 N.Y.S.2d 796 (1997)

Where the landlord refuses to approve the assignee or subtenant on the basis of subjective concerns, such as the nature of the proposed assignee's or subtenant's business, even though the business is legitimate, the landlord's subjective concerns must be objectively reasonable. *Ernst Home Ctr. v. Sato*, 80 Wash. App. 473, 910 P.2d 486 (1996).

Where the assignment and subletting clause provides that the landlord's consent shall not be unreasonably withheld, or a requirement of reasonableness is imposed on the landlord by the court, the landlord will not be able to condition the giving of the consent upon the readjustment of the rent, *Chanslor-Western Oil & Dev. Co. v. Metro. Sanitary Dist.*, 266 N.E.2d 405 (Ill. App. 1970); the making of a new lease between the landlord and the proposed assignee, *Ringwood Assocs., Ltd. v. Jack's of Route 23*, 379 A.2d 508 (N.J. 1977); or split the bonus rent, *1010 Potomac Assoc. v. Grocery Manufacturers*, 485 A.2d 199 (D.C. App. 1984), unless, of course, the lease so provides. On the other hand, where the lease does not expressly or by implication require the landlord to consent on reasonable grounds, the landlord may withhold its consent unless it receives some economic benefit from the lease assignment. *Illinois Cent. Gulf R.R. Co. v. Int'l Harvester Co.*, 368 So.2d 1009 (La. 1979).

Another issue that arises in the assignment and subletting context is what actions will trigger the application of the assignment and subletting clause of the lease. Where this issue is addressed in the lease negotiations, the clause may well provide that in addition to an actual assignment or sublease, a transfer of the control of the tenant whether by stock transfer, in the case of a corporate tenant, or the transfer of partnership interests, in the case of a partnership tenant, merger, dissolution, pledge or mortgage, eminent domain proceedings, bankruptcy, death, or execution sale of the tenant's interests, triggers the application of the clause.

A lease is both a transfer of an interest in real estate and a contract. As a result, the tenant will be liable to the landlord under the contract aspects of the lease just as with any other type of contract. If the lease is assigned, the tenant's interest is passed on to the assignee, but the tenant's liability to the landlord under the lease will continue. Of course, the parties may agree upon a different result through the express provisions of the lease. If the lease does not expressly address the termination of the liability of the original tenant upon the assignment, that liability cannot be altered by the provisions of the assignment and assumption agreement. While that agreement is between the assigning original tenant and the assignee, the landlord is typically not a party. For the liability of the tenant to be extinguished, a novation or release agreement must be made between the landlord and the tenant.

43.05 Warranty of Habitability

The courts have generally held that the warranty of habitability applicable in most states to residential leasing transactions is not applicable to commercial leases. *Yuan Kane, Inc. v. Levy*, 326 N.E.2d 51 (Ill. 1975*); Chausse v. Coz*, 540 N.E.2d 667 (Mass. 1989); *Firemen's Fund Ins. Co. v. BPS Co.*, 491 N.E.2d 365 (Ohio 1985). As with other areas of the law, evolution in legal thought has brought change. The courts may see fit to break through this barrier in the proper case.

> **EXAMPLE:** Landlord leased premises to a doctor for use as an office. The landlord failed to provide the agreed-upon services, such as air conditioning, hot water, and janitorial service. Also, the roof leaked. The doctor and his patients were inconvenienced and the doctor moved out. When he was sued for unpaid rent, the doctor defended on the basis that the landlord had breached the warranty of habitability. The court felt there was no valid reason to imply a

warranty of habitability only in residential leases and not in commercial leases. The court defined the commercial warranty to be that, at the inception of the lease, there were no latent defects in the facilities that were vital to the use of the premises for their intended commercial purposes. *Davidow v. Inwood North Prof'l Group—Phase 1*, 747 S.W.2d 373 (Tex. 1988).

43.06   Constructive Eviction

In another carryover from residential landlord and tenant law, courts have also applied the theory of constructive eviction to commercial lease transactions.

> **EXAMPLE:** A tenant of a two-story restaurant was notified of a fire code violation because there was no fire sprinkler on the second floor. The landlord refused to install the sprinkler and the tenant closed the second floor of its restaurant and stopped paying rent. The court ordered the tenant to pay rent for the first floor only because the landlord's actions deprived the tenant of the use of the second floor. *Dennison v. Marlowe*, 744 P.2d 906 (N.M. 1987).

> **EXAMPLE:** Landlord leased premises to a gynecologist who performed abortions. Antiabortion protesters, over a period of time, blocked access to the premises, conducted demonstrations in and outside of the building, and entered the leased premises. The landlord did nothing to deter the protesters, even after the tenant requested. The court held that the tenant was constructively evicted. *Fidelity Mut. Life Ins. Co. v. Kaminsky*, 768 S.W.2d 818 (Tex. App. 1989).

The landlord must do something grave and permanent with the intention of depriving the tenant of the enjoyment of the premises for constructive eviction to be found. Merely temporarily closing an entrance to a shopping center as part of a renovation project will not suffice, even if the tenant is adversely affected. *St. Louis North Joint Venture v. P&L Enters., Inc.*, 116 F.3d 262 (7th Cir. 1997).

43.07   Cross-Default

Landlords with multiple leases with the same tenant, such as an owner of several shopping centers having leases with a national or regional retail tenant, may want to insert cross-default clauses in these leases. Through this clause, a default under one lease will result in a default under the other leases. While this may be appropriate when the landlord makes a portfolio of leases to the same tenant, tenants generally resist this clause. Nonetheless, the clause is valid. *Chrysler Fin. Corp. v. Fruit of the Loom, Inc.*, 1993 Del. Super. LEXIS 28 (1993); *In re Wheeling-Pittsburg Steel Corp.*, 54 B.R. 772 (1985). The clause will not, however, be effective to limit or impair a tenant's ability, as a debtor in a bankruptcy proceeding, to assume and assign an unexpired lease pursuant to section 365 of the Bankruptcy Code. *In re Sanshoe Worldwide Corp.*, 139 B.R. 585 (S.D. N.Y. 1992); *In re Braniff, Inc.*, 118 Bankr. 819 (M.D. Fla. 1990).

The presence of the clause presents an interesting issue in the event of an assignment of the lease. Will the assignee take its interest under the lease subject to the possibility that a default by the assignor under one of the other leases will result in a default under the assigned lease under the cross-default clause? From the assignor's perspective, the same possibility is present. Will a default by the assignee under the assigned lease result in a default under the leases that have not been assigned? Without a modification of the clause at the time of the assignment, the parties are exposed to this possibility.

43.08   Mortgages of the Leasehold

If the lease contains no provision that would prohibit a mortgage of the leasehold, the tenant may place a mortgage on the leasehold estate created by the lease. In such a mortgage, the description of the mortgaged premises should read somewhat as follows:

Leasehold estate created by lease dated May 1, 19____, and recorded in the Recorder's Office of ____ County, ____, on May 2, 19____, as Document 1,000,000 from John Smith, as Lessor, to Henry Brown, as Lessee, demising for a term of years commencing on May 1, 19____, and ending on April 30, 19____, the premises described as follows, to wit: (here insert description of leased premises).

One difficulty with such a mortgage is the fact that the tenant may default in rent payments, and the landlord may declare the lease forfeited. Of course, if default and forfeiture occur, the lease terminates and the mortgage is thereby extinguished. A side agreement between the landlord and mortgagee may provide that before forfeiting the lease, the landlord will give notice of the default to the mortgagee and a stated time to make good the defaults. It may also provide that if the lease is terminated, the mortgagee will be entitled to receive a new lease for the balance of the term on the same rent and under the same conditions as the old lease.

Another question that arises is with respect to the liability of the mortgagee for payment of rent. In title and intermediate states, which regard a leasehold mortgage as an assignment of the leasehold, the mortgagee becomes personally liable to the landlord for rent, under the rule that an assignee becomes liable to the original lessor for rent. *Williams v. Safe Deposit Co.,* 167 Md. 499, 175 A. 331 (1934). For this reason, it is a common practice in leasehold mortgages to omit the last day of the term, so that the mortgage mortgages the leasehold except the last day thereof. By excepting the last day of the term, the mortgage becomes a sublease rather than an assignment, and the mortgagee does not become personally liable to the landlord for rent due under the lease. Mortgages are treated as assignments or subleases depending on whether they cover all or less than all the unexpired term of the lease. In states that follow the lien theory of mortgages, a mere mortgage of the leasehold does not make the mortgagee liable for rent. Robert Kratovil & Raymond J. Werner, *Modern Mortgage Law and Practice,* § 22.09 (2d ed. 1981).

43.09 Integration Clause

Leases typically provide that all of the prior negotiations between the parties, and even any prior writings such as letters that the leasing agent may have written to the then prospective tenant, are merged into the lease and no longer enforceable or of any effect. Courts will generally give effect to these clauses in commercial lease transactions.

> **EXAMPLE:** Tenant was given assurances that a property would be a shopping center containing certain named retailers and would be a retail hub. The shopping center fell on hard times with a high vacancy rate. The court would not consider the prior statements of the leasing agents in light of the integration clause. *Michigan Sporting Goods Distribs. v. Lipton Kenrick Assocs., L.P.,* 927 S.W.2d 570 (Mo. App. 1996).

CHAPTER 44

Discrimination in Real Estate

44.01 History The history of slavery and race relations up to the time of World War I is well documented. The modern history of race relations begins with World War I and much of it occurred in Chicago.

Up until World War I, the segregated neighborhoods of Chicago had been relatively stable. However, during the war, Chicago meat packers began recruiting African American workers from southern states in order to meet the rising demand for meat for the United States and its allies. The African American neighborhoods began to expand into the adjoining white neighborhoods. Tension resulted. Rioting broke out and many deaths occurred.

Property owners in white neighborhoods began to use the restrictive covenant. This document was an agreement designed to cover an entire neighborhood. The property owners in white neighborhoods agreed that their properties would never be occupied by African Americans. The theory was that agreements not to sell to African Americans were invalid under the old English rules forbidding restraints on sales of land. But, a restriction dealing only with occupancy was thought to be valid. *Doherty v. Rice,* 240 Wis. 389, 3 N.W.2d 734 (1942).

In time, these covenants were attacked on the ground that they could be enforced only by court proceedings. Court proceedings are state action, and under the Constitution, state action that produces racial discrimination is forbidden. The Supreme Court ultimately so held. *Shelley v. Kraemer,* 334 U.S. 1, 3 A.L.R.2d 441 (1948).

44.02 Federal Laws The Thirteenth Amendment to the U.S. Constitution abolished slavery. It took effect on December 18, 1865. Many southern legislatures adopted the "Black Codes," which, in effect, placed severe restrictions on the newly won rights of African Americans. Congress, in turn, passed a civil rights bill that became effective on April 9, 1866. Thereafter, the Fourteenth Amendment was ratified on July 28, 1868, and the Fifteenth Amendment on March 30, 1870. On May 31, 1870, a new civil rights act was passed, and on April 20, 1871, Congress enacted another statute, and still another statute on March 1, 1875. 42 U.S.C.A. § 1981, *et seq.* These laws are referred to as the "Civil War laws." Paralleling the new laws creating new rights were new laws giving the federal courts power to enforce these rights.

The Civil War laws were neglected for a long period of time. When they were revived in 1961, there was still no inkling that they would be used by African Americans to enforce their rights in real estate.

Then came the decision in *Jones v. Alfred H. Mayer Co.,* 392 U.S. 409, 20 L. Ed.2d 1189 (1968), decided under the Civil War laws. Please note that this case was pending in the lower courts while Congress was deliberating on the Open Occupancy Law of 1968.

In the *Jones* case, an African American sought to purchase a home from a builder. The builder refused to sell on racially motivated grounds. A suit was filed seeking to enjoin the builder from so discriminating. The court ordered the builder to sell the home to the prospective buyer at the price that was prevailing at the time of the wrongful refusal, a price that was substantially less than the then prevailing price. The Civil War laws were still alive.

44.03 Federal Legislation—The 1968 Law

A federal "open occupancy" law was enacted in 1968. 42 U.S.C.A. § 3601. The law covers dwellings, including homes and multifamily residences (two-flats, duplexes, apartments), and also vacant land acquired for construction for such purposes. No doubt acquisition of vacant land zoned for residential purposes will be regarded as subject to the law. Condominiums and cooperatives also come under the law. The law applies to sales, leases, and all types of rental agreements. It does not include properties used exclusively for commercial or industrial purposes. But, if part of the building is used for residential purposes, the building is subject to the law.

The law creates new and important rights. Some are spelled out fairly clearly. Others came into sharper focus only after the Supreme Court interpreted the law. Some observations can be made. Where bias against a person is based on race, color, religion, or national origin, it is unlawful to

1. Refuse to sell or lease, or refuse to negotiate for sale or lease, because of such bias, or to discriminate in the furnishing of services or facilities.

   EXAMPLE: A landlord cannot furnish maid service to white tenants and refuse this service to minorities.

2. Discriminate in the terms of the sale or lease, for example, by asking a higher price because of the race of the buyer.

3. Advertise in the newspapers or post notices on the building that particular races will not be welcomed as buyers or tenants.

4. State that a dwelling is not available, where such statement is made because of the race of the party seeking to buy or lease.

5. Refuse to make a loan or to insist on higher interest rates or harsher loan terms for racial reasons.

6. Refuse membership in brokers' organizations or multiple-listing services because of racial reasons.

7. Induce a person to sell by creating fears of racial change in the neighborhood.

Enforcement of the law is complex. In general, the Secretary of the Department of Housing and Urban Development (HUD) is entrusted with some of the machinery of enforcement. The following procedures are available:

1. If there is a substantially equivalent remedy under a state law or ordinance, HUD notifies the appropriate state officials to enforce the law.

2. The party discriminated against may file a suit for damages. *United Stages v. Peltzer,* 377 F. Supp. 121 (N.D. Ala. 1974).

3. The court may issue an injunction restraining violation of the law, and set aside a deed or lease, except that no deed or lease shall be set aside if entered into before a court order has issued and the grantee or lessee had no actual knowledge of the proceedings. One is left with the inference that a court that sets aside a sale to a white person can order a sale of the property to

an African American who made an earlier comparable offer and was rejected because of racial bias.

4. The U.S. Attorney General may obtain injunctions restraining violations of the law if a "pattern or practice" is evident. *United States v. Mintzes,* 304 F. Supp. 1305 (D. Md. 1969).

5. In certain instances, the law provides for fines against, or imprisonment of, persons using force or threat of force to bring about racial discrimination in housing.

44.04   Federal Legislation—The Civil War Laws

The Civil War laws provided that U.S. citizens of every race and color shall have the same right throughout the country to purchase, lease, sell, hold, and convey real and personal property. Laying stress on the phrase "the same right," the Supreme Court has held that this law prohibits all racial discrimination, private and public, in the sale and rental of property. Thus, every "racially motivated refusal to sell or rent" is prohibited. *Jones v. Alfred H. Mayer Co.,* 392 U.S. 409 (1968).

This law to some extent overlaps the Open Housing Act of 1968, to some extent goes beyond it, and to some extent omits protection afforded by the 1968 law. 42 U.S.C.A. § 1981, *et seq.*

> **EXAMPLE:** *A,* a white person, owns a home occupied with his family. This is the only land he owns. *A* offers it for sale without employing a broker, but declines to sell to *B.* His refusal is motivated by *B*'s race. This refusal is wrongful under the Civil War laws. Such a situation is expressly omitted from the coverage of the 1968 law under which a person owning only one home and selling it without a broker is not forbidden to discriminate.

> **EXAMPLE:** *A* refuses to sell his store to *B; A*'s refusal is racially motivated. This refusal is prohibited by the Civil War law, but does not come under the 1968 law.

> **EXAMPLE:** *A* owns a large apartment building. For racial reasons, he refuses to rent an apartment to *B.* Both laws forbid this type of discrimination.

As the Supreme Court has pointed out, the Civil War law does not

1. Forbid discrimination on grounds of religion or national origin.

   > **EXAMPLE:** *A,* a member of XYZ Church, owns only one home. He offers his home for sale without the aid of a real estate broker. As purchasers appear, he states verbally that he will sell only to members of XYZ Church. The 1866 law does not forbid such action.

2. Deal specifically with discrimination in the provision of services or facilities in connection with the sale or rental of a dwelling, for example, furnishing maid service to apartment tenants.

3. Prohibit advertising or other representations that indicate discriminatory preferences.

4. Refer explicitly to discrimination in financing arrangements or in the provision of real estate brokerage services.

5. Enable a rejected purchaser or tenant to call upon the Attorney General or any other federal officer for aid.

6. Make an express provision for the bringing of damage suits by rejected purchasers or tenants, but the court has indicated it has kept an open mind on the question of whether a right to damages could be implied or inferred from the language and purpose of the law.

44.05   Remedies for Racial Discrimination

In considering the remedies available for racial discrimination, one must remember that today's courts do not hesitate to improvise remedies where the statute is silent. These are called *implied remedies.* Damages have been allowed. Annotation, *Recovery of Damages as Remedy for Wrongful Discrimination Under State or Local Civil Rights Provisions*, 85 A.L.R.3d 351 (1978).

> **EXAMPLE:** Landlord refused to rent to Tenant because she was African American. She recovered damages of $10,000 for emotional distress and $10,000 punitive damages (to punish Landlord). *Parker v. Shonfeld*, 409 F. Supp. 876 (N.D. Cal. 1976).

> **EXAMPLE:** A white plaintiff can sue a landlord who refuses to rent to her because she has an African American husband. *Hodge v. Sieler*, 558 F.2d 284 (5th Cir. 1977).

44.06 Fair Housing Developments— Zoning

In instances of isolated individual discrimination, the court decisions appear to give adequate implementation to state and federal legislation. The damage awards for individual acts of racial discrimination are sizeable. They are calculated to deter individuals and groups, such as real estate boards, that might otherwise be tempted to perpetuate discriminatory practices. With respect to villages that seek to perpetuate geographic racial discrimination, the litigation has been largely ineffective. It has been protracted and indescribably expensive. Case after case has yo-yoed up and down from trial courts to reviewing courts, running up astronomical attorneys' fees and court costs.

The U.S. Department of Justice, in consequence, made a frontal attack on suburban segregation policies, hoping to open up white villages to minorities. The philosophy here, in addition to the strictly legal notion of achieving the racial equality mandated by the Constitution, is that of providing homes for minorities close to the places of employment offered by prospering suburbs.

> **EXAMPLE:** Black Jack was an unincorporated area in St. Louis County. Developers announced a plan for low-income, multiracial housing. The community incorporated as a city and passed a zoning ordinance that excluded multifamily dwellings. A federal court struck down the ordinance as palpably discriminatory. The plaintiff developers then sought a court order compelling the village to admit multiracial housing. The court of appeals ordered the city to come up with a plan that would provide low-income housing. *Park View Heights Corp. v. City of Black Jack,* 605 F.2d 1033 (8th Cir. 1979).

These decisions are indicative of the assumption by the U.S. Department of Justice of an activist role in this area. In general, where the public authorities are taking action that will concentrate the location of low-income housing in racially segregated areas, most courts will endeavor to block this move.

> **EXAMPLE:** A developer wanted to build a multifamily residential housing project and sought rezoning for that purpose. It was refused. However, the courts found that the refusal to rezone was due to the racial opposition of residents. The court ordered rezoning. *Dailey v. City of Lawton,* 425 F.2d 1037 (10th Cir. 1970), 5 J. L. Reform 357 (1972).

44.07 Permitted Discrimination

The federal law does not prohibit an owner from considering any factors other than race which the developer feels are relevant in determining whether to rent to one individual or another. Such factors, which an owner might consider, include the credit applicant's standing; assets and financial stability; reputation in the community; age; family size; children's ages; the applicant's past experience as a lessee or tenant; length of time the applicant plans to occupy the premises; and whether the applicant is a transient.

The owner may also consider more subjective factors in determining whether it will rent to one individual or another. Thus, the owner may consider the applicant's appearance, demeanor, the owner's estimate of the applicant's trustworthiness or truthfulness, or other subjective factors. Indeed, businesspersons utilize such conclusions and opinions in their daily affairs.

Nonetheless, the owner may later be called upon to demonstrate in court that these and not racial motivations were responsible for the owner's decision in refusing to rent or sell to a particular person. Subjective factors are by their nature difficult to prove and often have little more than the credibility of the individual witness behind them.

An owner may even refuse to rent to an individual simply because the owner does not like the applicant. No one is required to rent or sell to an individual he or she doesn't like. As in other cases, however, the owner may later be called upon to demonstrate in court that the personal dislike of an individual, rather than the individual's race, was responsible for the decision to refuse the applicant as a tenant.

Any factor, other than race, that is relevant to a decision whether to rent or sell to an individual may be considered, and the list of factors set forth previously is not intended to be, and could not constitute, an exclusive list.

> **EXAMPLE:** *A* refused to rent to *B,* an African American, because *B* did not meet *A*'s requirement that a tenant have an income equal to 90 percent of the rent. This was not discriminatory. *Boyd v. Lefrak Org.,* 509 F.2d 1110 (2d. Cir. 1975); Recent Developments, *Class Actions,* 89 Harv. L. Rev. 1631 (1975-76); Ann Graf McCormick, *Fair Housing—Private Landlord May Exclude Potential Tenants on the Basis of Economic Criteria Which Have Racially Discriminatory Effect,* 7 Seton Hall L. Rev. 168 (1975).

44.08 State Constitutions, State Laws, Court Decisions, Ordinances, and Commission Rulings and Orders

An increasing number of states and cities have enacted laws and ordinances forbidding racial discrimination in housing. Such laws set up commissions to hear complaints of racial discrimination. The following are illustrations of state commission orders and court decisions enforcing local open housing laws.

> **EXAMPLE:** A white apartment owner discriminated against an African American prospective tenant by refusing to rent him an apartment. The prospective tenant filed a complaint with the state commission. An order was entered requiring the owner to rent an apartment to the prospective tenant at the regular prevailing rental rate and to desist from acts of discrimination in rental practices against the prospective tenant or any other persons because of race, religion, or national origin. *In re Ruth,* 12 Race Rel. Rep. 1703. (Cal).

> **EXAMPLE:** A commission ordered the landlord to rent to a prospective tenant who had been refused occupancy for racial reasons. Tenants who later moved in with knowledge of the problem were required to vacate. *City of N.Y. v. Camp Constr. Co.,* 11 Race Rel. Rep. 1949 (N.Y.).

> **EXAMPLE:** The court sustained a commission order ousting a white tenant because he was not a bona fide tenant ignorant of the landlord's earlier attempt to discriminate against an African American seeking to rent the same apartment. *Feigenblum v. Comm'n on Human Rights,* 278 N.Y.S.2d 652.

> **EXAMPLE:** A white subdivision was subject to a recorded declaration giving the homeowners' association a preemptive option, that is, the right to buy any home site at the same price another party would offer. A homeowner entered into a contract to sell to an African American. The contract was specifically made subject to the recorded declaration. The association then gave notice of exercise of its preemptive privilege. The court held that exercise of such a privilege would be illegal under the state fair housing law if done solely because of racial bias. *Vaught v. Village Creek,* 7 Race Rel. Rep. 849.

44.09 Landlord and Tenant Quite a number of cases arising either under federal or state law have held the landlord guilty of racial discrimination.

> **EXAMPLE:** The landlord accepted an African American tenant and then resorted to incredibly evasive tactics to discourage the tenant. He was held liable for damages. *Jackson v. Concord Co.,* 253 A.2d 793 (N.J. 1969).

> **EXAMPLE:** The landlord refused to rent a house to an African American, and a relative of the landlord agreed to cover up for the landlord by buying the house. Both were held liable. *Rody v. Hollis,* 500 P.2d 97 (Wash. 1972). The damages awarded can be great ($20,000). *Parker v. Shonfeld,* 409 F. Supp. 876 (N.D. Cal. 1976).

> **EXAMPLE:** The owner of an apartment complex restricted African Americans to buildings 65 and 66, and there were only two African American families in the remainder of the complex. Racial discrimination was established. *Midland Heights Homes v. Pennsylvania Human Relations Comm'n,* 333 A.2d 516 (Pa. 1975).

> **EXAMPLE:** The commission found the landlord guilty of discrimination in rejecting an African American tenant, but refused to oust a white tenant to whom the landlord later rented the apartment. The white tenant was an innocent party unaware of the discrimination. The court sustained this ruling. *Comm'r v. City Builders, Inc.,* 277 N.Y.S.2d 434 (1967).

> **EXAMPLE:** Evicting African American tenants to create an "all adult" building is discriminatory and damages must be paid. *Betsey v. Turtle Creek Assocs.,* 736 F.2d 983 (4th Cir. 1984).

> **EXAMPLE:** Exclusive rental agents found to have refused to rent to plaintiffs on the basis of their race are liable under the law for their unlawful conduct, even where the management agreement stated that leases and tenants shall be approved by owner and where their actions are at the behest of their principal. *Jeanty v. McKey & Poague, Inc.,* 496 F.2d 1119 (7th Cir. 1974).

> **EXAMPLE:** A landlord had no right to evict a white tenant because the tenant married an African American. *Prendergast v. Synder,* 50 Cal. Rptr. 903, 413 P.2d 847 (Cal. 1966).

But, at times, the court finds that discrimination is not present.

> **EXAMPLE:** L refused to rent to an African American lawyer, claiming that L disliked all lawyers and regarded them as troublemakers. No discrimination was shown. *Kramarsky v. Stahl Management,* 401 N.Y.S.2d 943 (1977).

44.10 Brokers A broker may lose its license under state law if it is guilty of racial discrimination.

> **EXAMPLE:** B, a broker, told an African American that a home was not available for sale. In fact, it was available. B was suspended. *Strickland v. Dept. of Registration & Education,* 376 N.E.2d 255 (Ill. App. 1978).

> **EXAMPLE:** B, a broker, engaged in "blockbusting," that is, B represented that the area was changing, values were declining, and women were not safe. B was disciplined. *In the Matter of Butterfly & Green, Inc. v. Lomenzo,* 30 N.Y.S.2d 250, 326 N.E.2d 799 (1975).

Of course, if the broker complies with a prospective purchaser's request to be shown homes in an integrated area, as opposed to an all white area, the Fair Housing Act is not violated. *Village of Bellwood v. Dwivedi,* 895 F.2d 1521 (7th Cir. 1990).

Quite a number of city ordinances forbidding discrimination—for example, by real estate brokers—have been upheld as valid. *Chicago Real Estate Bd. v. Chicago,* 36 Ill. 2d 530, 224 N.E.2d 793 (1967).

Federal and state legislation forbidding blockbusting by real estate brokers is also valid. Erwin S. Berbrem, Annotation, *Validity and Construction of Anti-Blockbusting Regulations Designed to Prevent Brokers from Inducing Sales of Realty Because of Actual or Rumored Entry of Racial Group into Neighborhood*, 34 A.L.R.3d 1432 (1970); *United States v. Hunter,* 459 F.2d 205 (4th Cir. 1972).

> **EXAMPLE:** A broker is forbidden to tell property owners that the neighborhood is "going colored." This is true even if the prospective buyer asks this question. *Brown v. State Realty Co.,* 304 F. Supp. 1236 (N.D. Ga. 1969).

> **EXAMPLE:** The rule against blockbusting applies even to statements such as "This is a changing neighborhood." *United States v. Mintzes,* 304 F. Supp. 1305 (D. Md. 1969).

A broker who violates either law is liable for damages.

44.11   Seller and Buyer

Racial discrimination by a seller is illegal.

> **EXAMPLE:** An African American bought a vacant lot adjoining the white seller's home, using a white nominee to accomplish the purchase. When the seller discovered the identity of the real purchaser, he brought suit. The court refused to set aside the transaction. *Hirsch v. Silberstein,* 227 A.2d 638 (Pa. 1967).

44.12   Mortgages— Redlining

It is illegal for mortgage lenders to "redline" minority neighborhoods. The word *redlining* comes from the practice of marking African American neighborhoods in red on a map, thus indicating the areas where loans will not be made. This practice is, of course, the subject of much federal, state, and local regulation.

44.13   Mortgages— Foreclosure

A mortgage lender must not discriminate against minorities in its foreclosure practices.

> **EXAMPLE:** If a mortgagee routinely grants a sixty-day grace period, it must do so for all mortgagers.

44.14   Builder/Seller Discrimination

A builder/seller must not discriminate among its customers.

> **EXAMPLE:** A Corp. had *X, Y,* and *Z* as its shareholders. It engaged in the building and selling of homes in an African American neighborhood of Chicago. *X, Y,* and *Z* also had other corporations engaged in building identical homes in white neighborhoods of the Chicago metropolitan area. In the African American neighborhood, A Corp. sold only on installment contracts, even where the buyers could make large cash payments and obtain mortgages. It sold at prices higher than it charged for identical homes in white neighborhoods. The corporation and *X, Y,* and *Z* were held guilty of racial discrimination. *Clark v. Universal Builders,* 501 F.2d 324 (7th Cir. 1974); Recent Cases, *Black Homebuyers Are Entitled to Damages Equal to the Increments in Price of Homes in Black Neighborhood that Resulted from Dual 1975 Housing Markets Caused by Racial Discrimination,* 88 Harv. L. Rev. 1610; Notes, *Housing and Section 1982: The Endorsability of Extending the Statutory Mandate Beyond Acts of Traditional Discrimination,* 1975 Duke L.J. 781 (1975); Charles D. Pulmen, *USC 1982: An Exploitation Theory,* 12 Houston L. Rev. 476 (1974–78); Case Comments, *Constitutional Law—Civil Rights—Section 1982 Prohibits "Exploitation" of Racially Segregated Housing Market,* 28 Rutgers L. Rev. 1009 (1975).

44.15   Public Housing

Many local housing authorities and HUD have been instructed by the courts to develop housing projects in predominantly white neighborhoods. Low-income developments must not be confined to minority neighborhoods in the inner city. *Hills v. Guautreaux,* 425 U.S. 284, 96 S. Ct. 1538, 47 L. Ed.2d 792 (1976).

44.16   City Services   The city must not discriminate racially in its provision of municipal services.

> **EXAMPLE:** In one town, 97 percent of the homes that fronted on unpaved streets and were not served by sewers were occupied by African Americans; street lights were installed in white neighborhoods, not in African American neighborhoods; surface water drainage, traffic control signs, and so forth were all in white neighborhoods. This was invalid. *Hawkins v. Town of Shaw,* 437 F.2d 1286 (5th Cir. 1971).

44.17   Proof of Discrimination   Basically, what current legislation forbids is discrimination. Discrimination is not merely a state of mind. Prejudice is a state of mind, but discrimination is prejudice coupled with action or inaction motivated by that prejudice.

Discrimination can be shown by express proof of intention. *Hawkins v. Town of Shaw,* 461 F.2d 1171 (5th Cir. 1972).

> **EXAMPLE:** A builder stated that "no one is going to force me to sell a house in this development to a black." This proves discrimination if followed by sales only to white persons. *Jones v. The Haridor Realty Corp.,* 37 N.J. 384, 181 A.2d 481 (1962).

Or, it may be established by circumstantial evidence.

> **EXAMPLE:** *A* offered a house for sale for $75,000 on terms set forth in a broker's listing. Promptly, *B* tendered an offer at the price and terms stated. *A*'s refusal of *B*'s offer would be evidence of discrimination, especially if *A* sold later to a white person at the same price, thereby showing that the refusal of *B* was not motivated by a desire to withdraw the house from sale.

> **EXAMPLE:** The fact that there are no African American tenants in an apartment building will weigh against the owner, and the refusal of even one financially qualified African American applicant for an apartment may be sufficient proof of discrimination. *United States v. Real Estate Dev. Corp.,* 347 F. Supp. 776 (N.D. Miss. 1972).

44.18   Impact or Intent   A deeply troubling question relates to the necessity of establishing the presence of discriminatory intent where racial discrimination is charged. If the lawsuit charges a violation of the federal Constitution, one frequently cited decision holds that it is necessary to prove an intention to discriminate.

> **EXAMPLE:** The village of Arlington Heights (a suburb of Chicago) had a traditional zoning ordinance, establishing some single-family zones. A developer sought a rezoning of land in such a zone so that it could construct low-income housing, which would accommodate minorities. The village population was white. The village refused the rezoning. The Supreme Court held that no violation of the Constitution was shown. There was no intention to discriminate, *Village of Arlington Heights v. Metro. Housing Dev. Corp.,* 429 U.S. 252, 50 L. Ed.2d 450 (1971).

In a later phase of this case, the issue was whether the Open Housing Act of 1968 had been violated.

> **EXAMPLE:** In this lawsuit, the court pointed out that the construction of the apartments would give the village its first subsidized low-cost housing. This would enable minorities to move into a village that theretofore had been exclusively white. Thus, the village's refusal to rezone had a discriminatory impact in that it perpetuated segregation in Arlington Heights. A violation of the statute had been established. *Metro. Housing Dev. Corp. v. Village of Arlington Heights,* 558 F.2d 1283 (7th Cir. 1977).

These cases exemplify what is called the disparate impact theory. Under this theory, discrimination is found in those situations where parties engage in apparently neutral practices, not justified by business necessity, that have a disproportionate effect on a protected group. *Huntington Branch, NAACP v. Town of Huntington,* 844 F.2d 926 (2d Cir. 1988), *aff'd* sub nom *Town of Huntington v. Huntington Branch, NAACP,* 488 U.S. 15 (1988). *Saville v. Quaker Hill Place,* 531 A.2d 201 (Del. 1987); *Middlesboro Housing Auth. v. Kentucky Comm'n on Human Rights,* 553 S.W.2d 57 (Ky. App. 1977); *Guyan Valley Hospital, Inc. v. West Virginia Human Rights Comm'n,* 382 S.E.2d 88 (W.Va. 1989). *But see North Carolina Human Relations Council v. Weaver Realty Co.,* 340 S.E.2d 766 (N.C. App. 1986). A difference between these two theories lies in the fact that a defendant may avoid liability under the disparate impact theory by establishing that the practices at issue were justified as serving a sufficiently important interest.

> **EXAMPLE:** A statute required residential facilities for mentally ill and retarded persons to be a minimum distance apart. This statute was challenged on the grounds that it unlawfully discriminated against handicapped persons in violation of the Fair Housing Act. Although the law had a disparate impact on handicapped persons, the law was upheld on the ground that it was necessary to promote a compelling governmental interest, the deinstitutionalization of mentally ill and retarded persons by dispersing their facilities throughout the community. *Familystyle of St. Paul v. City of St. Paul,* 923 F.2d 91 (8th Cir. 1991).

44.19 Testers and Steering

A group of African Americans visited real estate brokers in the village of Bellwood, Illinois, asking to be shown homes. In point of fact, they were not genuine purchasers. They were "testing" the brokers. The brokers attempted to steer these purported purchasers to African American neighborhoods of the village. The court held that steering was illegal and that testers could sue to have a court prohibit this steering. *Gladstone Realtors v. Village of Bellwood,* 441 U.S. 91, 99 S. Ct. 1601 (1979).

Where, however, affirmative marketing efforts attempt to steer white buyers into purchasing houses in African American neighborhoods, no violation of the Fair Housing Act will be found. *South-Suburban Housing Ctr. v. Greater South Suburban Bd. of Realtors,* 713 F. Supp. 1068 (N.D. Ill. 1988).

44.20 Advertisements

Real estate advertisements that picture only white models in advertisements for housing located in predominately white buildings or neighborhoods may violate the Fair Housing Act. This type of advertisement may violate the prohibition of the act making it unlawful to publish any advertisement, with respect to the sale or rental of a dwelling, that indicates any preference based on race. *Ragin v. New York Times Co.,* 923 F.2d 995 (2d Cir. 1991).

44.21 Discrimination—Age

It has long been a practice that a landowner will attempt to limit the nature of the occupancy of land. These restraints are typically contained in deeds, mortgages, leases, and declarations of covenants, conditions, and restrictions. Such devices have encountered legal obstacles and, in some cases, have been invalidated. *Martin v. Palm Beach Atlantic Ass'n, Inc.,* 696 So.2d 919 (Fla. App. 1997). All states have some form of the so-called rule against unreasonable restraints on alienation or sale.

> **EXAMPLE:** Father makes a deed to Son. The deed provides that the real estate will never be sold. This restriction is invalid.

As pointed out earlier, this rule does not apply to restraints on occupancy. Hence, lawyers tend to prefer to create restrictions on occupancy rather than restrictions on sale. Today, we have statutes and court decisions that limit the extent to which restrictions on occupancy may be imposed.

It is good to reflect on the development of the law in this area and the relationship of that development to social and economic events. Viewing only the relatively recent past, we have seen discrimination reflected in the use of restrictions that prohibited the occupancy of property by African Americans. Those restrictions were used as a result of a social view. In reaction to such restrictions, laws were enacted and court decisions were made that held such provisions to be invalid.

To much the same extent, we see today a social contest of sorts where the interests of the aging population to live in an environment conducive to its needs may come in conflict with the interest of families with children in finding suitable and affordable housing. In this context, we do not have any necessarily morally correct position. Both groups have legitimate concerns, which our government, and thus the law, must accommodate.

The discrimination does not always take the form of a direct prohibition, say, against children under the age of twenty-one. It may be a more subtle style of prohibition or regulation.

EXAMPLE: A landlord imposed rules that children could not play or run around inside an apartment building. The court found this rule violated the Fair Housing Act. *Fair Housing Congress v. Weber*, 993 F. Supp. 1286 (C.D. Cal. 1997).

44.21(a) Retirement Communities

There are many retirement communities in this country. The restrictions and declarations recorded by the developers of these communities usually forbid occupancy by children under twenty-one years or some similar age. Since public schools are not needed, real estate taxes are lower. Playground facilities are not needed. Moreover, public opinion polls show that older people prefer the quiet of an environment without children. It seems likely that the courts will sustain as valid restrictions of this nature. *Riley v. Stoves,* 526 P.2d 474 (Ariz. 1974); *Preston Tower Condo Ass'n v. S.B. Realty,* 685 S.W.2d 98 (Tex. Civ. App. 1985); *Ritchey v. Villa Nueva Condo Ass'n,* 146 Cal. Rptr. 695 (1978).

The Fair Housing Act, 29 U.S.C. § 3601, *et seq.,* exempts housing for older persons from the prohibition against discrimination based on familial status. The regulations require that a development seeking this exemption must be intended and operated for people fifty-five years old and older; at least 80 percent of the occupied units in the development must have at least one occupant that meets this age criteria; and the facility must both publish and follow policies that demonstrate the intent to qualify for this exemption. Thus, the law has again reacted to the socioeconomic needs of the time.

44.21(b) Zoning

The zoning decisions exemplify the conflicting pressures that this area of the law involves. Some courts have ruled that zoning ordinances restricting units that would be suitable for families are invalid. *Duggan v. County of Cook,* 324 N.E.2d 406 (Ill. App. 1975); *Molino v. Mayor of Glassboro,* 281 A.2d 401 (N.J. Super. 1971); Michael A. Haber, Case Notes, *No Dogs, Cats or Voluntary Families Allowed,* 24 DePaul L. Rev. 784 (1975). Other courts have held that it is unlawful to zone out senior citizens. *Shepard v. Woodland Township Planning Bd.,* 320 A.2d 191 (N.J. 1974). Other courts have held that a municipality may limit a particular residential zone to senior citizens. Their needs (e.g., curb ramps for wheelchairs) are largely peculiar to the elderly, and they need a zone that caters to these needs.

Hinman v. Planning & Zoning Comm'n, 214 A.2d 131 (Conn. 1965); *Taxpayers' Ass'n. v. Weymouth Township*, 364 A.2d 1016 (N.J. 1976); *Maldini v. Ambro*, 330 N.E.2d 403 (N.Y. 1975).

As can be seen, the needs of one age group may be adverse to the needs of the other age group. If the zoning ordinance limits occupancy of an area to senior citizens, it zones out children. If the zoning decisions prohibit the barring of children from residential areas, the establishment of retirement communities is made more difficult. Public policy decisions must be made, and those decisions must relate to both public and private land use control devices in a way that accommodates the needs of both age groups. Gary Person, *Weymouth Township: Age Restrictions in Zoning*, 31 Ark. L. Rev. 707 (1978); Ed Stafman, *Housing for the Elderly: Constitutional Limitations and Our Obligations*, 5 Fla. St. U.L. Rev. 423 (1977); Mary Doyle, *Retirement Communities: The Nature and Enforceability of Residential Segregation by Age*, 76 Mich. L. Rev. 64 (1977); Joel E. Shutte, Annotation, *Validity of Zoning for Senior Citizen Communities*, 83 A.L.R.3d 1084, 1103 (1978).

**44.21(c)
Condominiums**

Condominium documents that forbid occupancy by children have been sustained. *Starlake North Commodore Ass'n, Inc. v. Parker*, 423 So.2d 509 (Fla. App. 1982); *Constellation Condominium Ass'n, Inc. v. Harrington*, 467 So.2d 378 (Fla. App. 1985); *Covered Bridge Condominium Ass'n v. Chambliss*, 705 S.W.2d 211 (Tex. App. 1985). Retirement is a major industry in some states such as Florida, and many retirees live in condominiums. These court decisions are sensitive to that fact.

**44.21(d) Mobile
Home Parks**

Limiting occupancy to adults in mobile home parks has been sustained. *Dubrevil v. West Winds Mobile Lodge*, 213 Cal. Rptr. 12 (1985).

**44.21(e) Statutes
and Ordinances**

A number of states (e.g., Arizona, California, Connecticut, Delaware, Illinois, Maine, Massachusetts, New Jersey, New York, and Oregon) have laws or ordinances prohibiting housing discrimination against children. In some states, these laws forbid landlords to bar children. *Marina Point, Ltd. v. Wolfson*, 30 Cal. 2d 721, 180 Cal. Rptr. 496, 640 P.2d 115 (1982). In other states, landlords are not affected. *Dept. of Civil Rights v. Beznos Corp.*, 336 N.W.2d 494 (Mich. App. 1983). In California and Oregon, the law applies to condominiums. *O'Connor v. Village Green Owners Ass'n*, 662 P.2d 427 (Cal. 1983). State laws and local ordinances must be carefully checked.

The federal government has reacted by prohibiting discrimination under the Fair Housing Act on the basis of familial status. 42 U.S.C. § 3600, *et seq.* Familial status is defined to include situations where children under the age of eighteen live with their parents or other person having legal custody of them, or the child lives with a person designated in writing by the parent or legal custodian of the child. 24 C.F.R. § 100.20. The protections against discrimination on the basis of familial status shall apply to any person who is pregnant or in the process of securing custody of a child under eighteen. 24 C.F.R. § 100.20.

Recognizing the need for older people to live in environments especially adapted to their lifestyle and needs, the prohibitions against this form of discrimination do not apply to housing developments intended for and solely occupied by persons over sixty-two years of age. 24 C.F.R. § 100.303. A further exemption is applicable to housing developments intended for occupancy by persons over fifty-five and which have significant facilities and services specifically designed to meet the physical or social needs of older persons. 24 C.F.R. § 100.304.

44.22 Marital Status

Again, driven by social developments, the law is reacting to the situation where unmarried people live together. As may be predicted, the courts are reaching inconsistent decisions. In some instances, it has been held that it is not prohibited to refuse to rent to unmarried persons of the opposite sex, even where a state law, 77ILCS 5/102, 103, prohibits discrimination on the basis of marital status. *Mister v. A.R.K. Partnership,* 553 N.E.2d 1152 (Ill. App. 1990); *Cooper v. French,* 460 N.W.2d 2 (Minn. 1990). The decisions in these cases were influenced by anti-fornication-type laws, a totally unrealistic premise for such decisions. Other courts have reached contrary results. *See Foreman v. Anchorage Equal Rights Comm'n,* 779 P.2d 1199 (Alaska 1989); *McCready v. Hoffius,* 586 N.W.2d 723 (Mich. 1998); *Shadow Lake Village Condominium Ass'n v. Zampella,* 569 A.2d 288 (N.J. Super. 1990).

44.23 Discrimination— Handicapped Persons

Using the same method that it used to outlaw discrimination against people based on race, sex, age, marital status, and the like, the federal government has outlawed discrimination based on handicap or disability. Both the Americans with Disabilities Act, 42 U.S.C. §§ 1201, *et seq.,* and the Fair Housing Act, 42 U.S.C. §§ 3600, *et seq.,* require that certain broad categories of real estate be constructed or remodeled to be accessible by the handicapped and disabled population. The Acts establish a timetable, which began on March 31, 1991, for the construction and reconstruction of affected properties.

The most sweeping of these provisions is found in the Americans with Disabilities Act, which prohibits discrimination against disabled persons in (1) employment; (2) access to the services, programs, and activities of a public entity, such as a state or local government or agency; or (3) the ability to enjoy the goods, services, facilities, privileges, advantages, or accommodations of any place of public accommodation. This latter category has the greatest impact on real estate.

The Act broadly defines a public accommodation to include the following: places of lodging, such as hotels, motels and inns; places where food or drink are served; places of exhibition or entertainment, such as movie theaters and stadiums; places where the public gathers, such as convention centers; sales or retail establishments, such as grocery stores and shopping centers; service establishments from laundromats to law offices; passenger terminals and depots; places of recreation, such as health clubs; and other public places, such as museums, libraries, amusement parks, schools, and social service centers.

The Act makes the failure to remove structural architectural barriers that can be removed without much difficulty or expense a discriminatory practice. A problem arises in that the degree of difficulty or expense involved is not easily determined. It takes a balancing of factors, including the cost of the removal and the financial resources of the owner of the property.

Properties being remodeled or rehabbed must be made readily accessible to and usable by disabled persons. New properties must be readily accessible to and usable by disabled persons, unless it is structurally impractical to meet the requirements of the Act. Developers and landowners should become familiar with the Accessibility Guidelines for Buildings and Facilities. 24 C.F.R. Part 1191, *Appendix.*

The Fair Housing Act amendments of 1988 make it illegal to discriminate against handicapped persons in the sale and rental of dwellings. Like the Americans with Disabilities Act, this law defines discrimination to include certain actions or inactions. For example, it is discriminatory to fail to design and construct multifamily units so that (1) the public and common areas are readily accessible to and usable by handicapped persons; (2) the doors are wide enough to accommodate wheelchairs; (3) light switches, electric outlets, and environmental controls are accessible; (4) bathroom walls are reinforced to allow installation of grab bars; and (5) kitchens and bathrooms allow a person in a wheelchair to maneuver. *See* 24 C.F.R. §§ 100.200, *et seq.*

It is also discriminatory to refuse to allow a handicapped person to make reasonable modifications to a dwelling so that the handicapped person can fully enjoy the living unit, if the modifications are made at the expense of the handicapped person.

The courts have begun to construe and enforce these new laws. One court has found the law to be violated where a housing authority rejected housing applicants because of their inability to live independently, since only handicapped persons were rejected on that basis. *Cason v. Rochester Housing Auth.,* 748 F. Supp. 1002 (W.D. N.Y. 1990). A similar result was reached under a different statute, the Federal Rehabilitation Act. In that case, the court blocked the eviction of a mentally ill tenant who suffered from hallucinations, striking the walls of the apartment. The court held that the eviction would be discriminatory and that any damage to the apartment would be superficial and reimbursed under a federal program. *City Wide Assocs. v. Penfield,* 564 N.E.2d 1003 (Mass. 1991).

Landlords should be careful in the application process. They may not ask whether the prospective tenant or a family member has a disability, or inquire into the nature or severity of the disability, or require the production of medical records. If, however, the proposed tenant seeks a unit designed for a disabled person, the landlord may require documentation of the disability.

A new area of concern is the requirement that under the Fair Housing Amendments Act, the association must set aside a parking space to accommodate a disabled unit owner. *Gittleman v. Woodhaven Condominium Ass'n, Inc.,* 972 F. Supp. 894 (D. N.J. 1997).

The full ramifications of these laws are yet to be played out. How do these rules apply to group homes, for example. A court has held that the enforcement of a single-family covenant against a group home for AIDS sufferers violates the Fair Housing Act because it would have a disparate effect upon handicapped persons and violates the obligation to make reasonable accommodations to handicapped persons. *Hill v. Community of Damien of Molokai,* 911 P.2d 861 (N.M. 1996).

CHAPTER 45

Real Estate Taxes and Special Assessments

45.01 In General

General taxes are levied by various taxing bodies, such as states, cities, villages, counties, or school districts, to raise revenue needed for the performance of various public functions, such as maintaining roads, schools, parks, police departments, fire departments, county hospitals, and mental institutions. One of the most important sources of revenue is the tax on real estate. Although this tax is encountered in most, if not all, states, laws regarding levy, assessment, and collection of the tax vary considerably, so that few general statements can be made that will be universally true.

45.02 Steps in Taxation

The nine principal steps in real estate taxation are as follows: budgeting; appropriation; levy; assessment; review of the assessment; equalization; computation; collection of the tax through voluntary payment by the taxpayer; and collection of the tax through compulsory methods, such as a tax sale.

45.02(a) Budgeting

Budgeting involves an annual determination of how much money is to be spent by each taxing body and for what purposes. Keep in mind that in each state there are numerous bodies—cities, villages, counties, school boards, and sanitary districts—that have the power to levy taxes, and each body must prepare its annual budget and make its annual appropriation and tax levy.

45.02(b) Appropriation

Appropriation is the step where the taxing body formally enacts into law its decision to spend the money, with a specification of the particular purpose for which the money is to be spent, the amount to be spent for each purpose, and the source from which the funds are to come.

45.02(c) Levy

The appropriation usually provides that part of the money to be spent is to be raised by property taxation. It then becomes necessary to levy a tax for this purpose. When the legislative body of some taxing unit, such as a village board or a school board, votes to impose a tax of a specified amount on persons or property, this action is known as the levy of a tax. The levy is an indispensable step in arriving at a valid tax.

Various technical defects will invalidate part or all of the tax levy, and attorneys for big taxpayers are most astute in discovering these technical defects. As a rule, only those taxpayers who file proper objections may take advantage of these technical defects. Taxpayers who pay their money without formal objection cannot get their money back if the tax is later held invalid.

45.02(c)(1)   Tax Rate Limitations

In levying taxes, taxing bodies must see to it that they do not spend more than the law allows. Tax rate limitations, or caps, will be found in both state constitutions and state laws.

45.02(d)   Assessment

Assessment of real estate for taxation involves determining the value of each parcel of land to be taxed. In assessing real estate, a book or list is first prepared by the proper officer containing a description of all of the taxable real estate in the town, county, or district and the names of the owners of that property. This book is turned over to the tax assessor, who proceeds to place a valuation on each parcel of land and enters this valuation in the tax list or assessment roll.

In assessing land, the assessor should consider various factors, such as market price of similar land, income, depreciation, obsolescence, and reproduction cost of buildings. Actual methods vary widely. Farmland is still usually taxed at its market value, but urban land is often assessed differently. In assessing urban land, assessors often place a value on the land as though it were vacant and then value the building at what it would cost to build today, deducting from this figure an allowance for depreciation. The two valuations are then added together to fix the total assessment. Assessors may employ experts and use scientific procedures as a basis for their valuations. But, any wholesale turning over of valuation to experts would be illegal, for it is the assessor's judgment, based perhaps on expert advice, that the law requires.

In some states, it is the practice to assess property at a certain percentage of its true value. This is not objectionable as long as the assessor assesses all property at the same proportion of its true value. Likewise, if all the property is uniformly overvalued, the courts will not intervene. The main thing is uniformity. If a taxpayer can show that its property is assessed at its full value, whereas the rest of the property in the district is uniformly assessed at less than its full value, the court will lower the assessment complained of to the general level.

45.02(d)(1)   Uniformity

Under various constitutional provisions, it is required that the taxation of property be equal and uniform, so that taxpayers owning tracts of substantially equal value will pay substantially the same amount of taxes. *Walsh v. Property Tax Appeal Bd.*, 692 N.E.2d 260 (Ill. 1998). This is an ideal difficult, if not impossible, to attain, and courts are aware of that fact. Hence, if the assessor has made an honest mistake in assessing a particular tract of land, the courts, as a rule, will not intervene. Courts do not sit to correct mere errors in an assessment. The error can be corrected only by an appeal to the board of review or other body designated to review and correct the assessor's valuations.

Where, however, there is systematic discrimination in the assessment of properties of the same class, the courts will order the property to be reassessed.

EXAMPLE: A county assessed real property at 50 percent of its value as determined from the declarations accompanying recorded deeds. As can readily be seen, this system produced quite accurate valuations for recently transferred properties. Unfortunately, property not recently transferred was not reassessed at reasonable levels, with only modest adjustments being made to their assessed valuations for real estate taxation purposes. Over time, this system resulted in great disparities, with some newly transferred properties being assessed and thus taxed at up to 35 times the assessed value and tax amounts of comparable properties. This system of assessment violated the Equal Protection Clause of the Fourteenth Amendment to the U.S. Constitution. *Allegheny Pittsburgh Coal Co. v. County Comm'n of Webster County, West Virginia*, 109 S. Ct. 633 (1989). *But see Nordlinger v. Hahn*, 50 U.S. 1, 120 L. Ed. 2d 1 (1992).

The *Allegheny* case exemplifies the fact that tax assessment procedures must pass both the uniformity test of the state constitution, and the equal protection test of the federal Constitution. The West Virginia Supreme Court of Appeals upheld the system of assessment that the U.S. Supreme Court struck down. *See In re 1975 Tax Assessments Against Oneida Coal Co.,* 360 S.E.2d 560 (W.Va. 1987).

It is interesting to note that this area of the law involves challenges to the practices that have been used for many decades. In some cases, we see examples of the living law adjusting to the economic and social change. In other cases, we see fundamental principles somewhat belatedly catching up with governmental and business practices. In yet other cases, we see the courts balancing the fiscal realities of our time with the constitutional mandates that must be followed.

> **EXAMPLE:** Montana adopted a system under which 20 percent of all tax parcels were to be reassessed each year. The system fell behind in its timetable and an indexing system was adopted with a formula based upon recent sales prices. The problem was that the formula produced results that did not reflect the market value of the property, with some properties being underassessed and some overassessed. The court found the system to be unconstitutional, but to head off an impending financial crisis gave the legislature until the end of the tax year to correct the situation. *Montana Dept. of Revenue v. Barron,* 799 P.2d 533 (Mont. 1990).

45.02(d)(2)
Exemptions

Each state grants various exemptions from taxation. The nature and form of these exemptions vary from state to state. Common exemptions are those extended to public property, charitable organizations, schools, religious institutions, and cemeteries. There are also some states that extend partial exemptions to senior citizens.

45.02(d)(3) Review
of Assessment

All states provide some method by which the taxpayer can have the assessor's valuation reviewed and corrected by some higher authority. The procedures vary widely. In New England, the reviewing board is often a town tribunal, such as the selectmen. In other areas, the reviewing officials may be called a board of equalization or a board of review. In some states, a further appeal is provided to a higher board of review. In other states, the decision of the first board of review can be appealed directly to some court. As a rule, the taxpayer cannot appeal to the courts unless it has first appeared before the board of review or other initial reviewing body. *First Nat'l Bank v. Bd. of Comm'rs of Weld County,* 264 U.S. 450 (1924).

45.02(d)(4)
Equalization

Equalization is the raising or lowering of assessed values in a particular county or taxing district in order to equalize them with the assessments in other counties or taxing districts.

> **EXAMPLE:** The board of equalization deducts a certain percentage from all assessments made in a certain township because the township assessor valued the property on a higher level than did the assessors of other townships.

This function is usually performed by a board known as the board of equalization. The board of equalization does not handle complaints of individual taxpayers, but raises or lowers the assessment of each county or taxing district as a whole in order to bring the assessment into line with assessments in other counties or taxing districts.

45.02(e)
Computation of Tax

The amount of the tax that a particular tract of land must pay is computed by multiplying the equalized assessed value of the tract by the tax rate applicable to the land in that particular taxing district. The tax is then entered on the tax books.

45.02(f)   Lien   Tax laws usually provide that real estate taxes are a lien on the land. Often, it is provided that such a lien is prior and superior to all other liens, both those that antedate and those that come after the date on which the tax lien attaches to the land.

45.02(g)   Payment   Payment to the proper official at the proper time discharges the lien of the tax. When the tax records show a tax is paid, a purchaser or mortgagee who relies on such records is protected against enforcement of the tax should it later develop that the tax actually remains unpaid. *Jackson Park Hosp. v. Courtney,* 4 N.E.2d 864 (Ill. 1936). A number of states make provision for the issuance of a certificate by some tax official showing all unpaid taxes on the property. Purchasers who rely on such certificates are generally protected against errors in the certificate. *Burton v. City & County of Denver,* 61 P.2d 856 (Colo. 1936); *Amerada Petroleum Corp. v.* 1010.61 *Acres of Land,* 146 F.2d 99 (5th Cir. 1944); C.S. Patrinelis, Annotation, *Effect of Certificate, Statement (or Refusal Thereof) or Error by Tax Collector or Other Public Officer Regarding Unpaid Taxes or Assessments Against Specific Property,* 21 A.L.R.2d 1273 (1952). When a landowner redeems from a tax sale and the certificate of redemption shows that all delinquent taxes have been thereby redeemed, a purchaser or mortgagee who relies on such a certificate will be protected if it later develops that some delinquent taxes in fact remain. *Jones v. Sturzenberg,* 210 P. 835 (Cal. App. 1922).

A purchaser or mortgagee is not ordinarily protected in relying on a tax receipt showing full payment of the taxes. Despite issuance of the receipt, the tax collector is allowed to show that a part of the tax remains unpaid.

45.03   Proceedings to Enforce Payment of Taxes   Various special remedies are provided by local law for the collection of unpaid real estate taxes. A tax sale is a common method. It is usually preceded by the giving of notice to the delinquent taxpayer. Unless the taxpayer appears and defends this proceeding, which it may do if the tax is illegal or if the taxpayer has some other defense, a judgment will be rendered for the amount of the tax and penalty due. This judgment orders the land to be sold. Thereafter, notice of the coming sale is published, and, on the date fixed for sale, the land is sold at public sale. Usually, a certificate of sale is issued to the purchaser, stating that it will be entitled to a deed at the expiration of the redemption period if no redemption is made. In some states, the state, county, or city is permitted to bid at the tax sale.

The landowner or other persons interested, such as mortagees, may redeem the land from the tax within the period specified by the local law. If redemption is not made, a tax deed is issued to the purchaser.

Although state laws vary as to the validity of tax titles, a tax title acquired through normal tax sale usually constitutes the flimsiest sort of title, since deviation from the technical requirements of the law will invalidate the title. In some states, however, a tax deed is regarded as a conveyance of good title to the land. *Shapiro v. Hruby,* 172 N.E.2d 775 (Ill. 1961); *Thomas v. Kolker,* 73 A.2d 886 (Md. 1950).

An alternative method of enforcement of the tax lien is by foreclosure, the procedure being similar to that employed in mortgage foreclosure. In some states, a good title can be acquired through tax foreclosure.

45.03(a)   Validity of Tax Sale—Notice Requirements   The U.S. Constitution, as do most state constitutions, requires that actions that deprive a party of its property must comply with procedural due process requirements. This means that the party must be given a notice, which is reasonably calculated under the circumstances, to apprise interested parties of the pendency of the action and afford them the opportunity to present their objections. *Mullane v. Cent. Hanover Bank & Trust Co.,* 339 U.S.

306 (1950). This notice must be given to every party who owns an interest in the property or who has a lien or encumbrance on the property that would be extinguished by the tax sale proceeding. The practice of notice by publication will not suffice if the party to be affected by the proceeding can be identified. *Campbell v. City of New York,* 546 N.Y.S.2d 781 (1989). The Supreme Court has held that a tax sale is ineffective to extinguish a mortgage unless at least a mailed notice has been given by the tax collector to a mortgagee whose interest would be extinguished. *Mennonite Bd. of Missions v. Adams,* 103 S. Ct. 2706, 77 L. Ed.2d 180 (1983). In Illinois, the courts get around this decision by requiring the tax sale purchaser to notify the mortgagee before the tax deed issues. *Rosewell v. Chicago Title & Trust Co.,* 99 Ill. 2d 407, 459 N.E.2d 966 (1984). Of course, each state has its procedure, which should comply with the notice standard set by the *Mennonite* decision.

45.03(b) Effect of Tax Sale on Junior Interests

When real estate taxes obtain priority over junior interests, either because they were a lien prior to the creation of the junior interests or by force of law, the law of many states results in a purchaser at a tax sale taking a title that is free of encumbrances, such as mortgages, liens, and so forth.

45.03(c) Termination of Easements and Restrictions by Tax Sale

An almost insoluble problem exists with respect to the effect of a tax sale of the servient tenement. The owner of the easement, of course, receives the tax bill on the dominant tenement. It does not even receive the tax bill on the servient tenement.

> **EXAMPLE:** *A* owns Lot 1 and *B* owns Lot 2. *A* grants to *B* an easement for ingress and egress for driveway purposes over the southern twenty feet of Lot 1. *A* fails to pay the taxes on Lot 1 and all of Lot 1 is sold to *X* at a tax sale. Under the law in this state, a tax sale wipes out all prior easements. Obviously, *B* must arrange to keep a check on the taxes on *A*'s Lot 1 and pay them, if necessary, to prevent loss of the easement. *B* can include a provision in the easement grant requiring *A* annually to furnish *B* a paid tax bill, and also a provision that any taxes advanced by *B,* or his successors, will be a foreclosable lien on Lot 1.

The law on this subject has been in some confusion. In some states, a tax sale does not destroy easements. *Northwestern Imp. Co. v. Lowry,* 66 P.2d 792 (Mont. 1937); *Arizona R.C.I.A. Lands, Inc. v. Ainsworth,* 515 P.2d 335 (Ariz. 1973); *Clippinger v. Birge,* 547 P.2d 871 (Wash. 1976); Restatement, Property § 509(2)(e). One basis of this rule is the thought that the assessment of the land was based upon its value. That value was determined by taking the easement into consideration.

> **EXAMPLE:** Tract A is valued at $10,000 without being encumbered by an easement. Assessment is based upon this value. If the property were encumbered by an easement, its value would be $9,000. The assessment in the later case would be based upon $9,000.

By this same theory, the holder of the dominant estate is protected in that the easement will continue for the benefit of the land irrespective of the failure of the owner of the servient estate to pay taxes. The result is justified by the theory that the easement enhances the value of the dominant estate, and assessment of the dominant estate is based upon this enhanced value. In almost all states, laws have been passed to conform to the above. The minority view is discussed elsewhere. *See Powell on Real Property,* § 686.

In a similar view, a tax sale will generally not extinguish a restrictive covenant to which the land is subject. G. Van Ingen, Annotation, *Easement or Servitude or Restrictive Covenant as Affected by Sale for Taxes,* 168 A.L.R. 529, 536 (1947). *But see Lake Arrowhead Community Club v. Looney,* 748 P.2d 649 (Wash. App. 1988). Robert Kratovil, *Tax*

Titles: Extinguishment of Easements, Building Restrictions, and Covenants, 19 Hous. L. Rev. 55 (1981).

45.04 Special Assessments

There is a distinction between public improvements, which benefit the entire community, and local improvements, which benefit particular real estate or limited areas of land. The latter improvements are usually financed by means of special, or local, assessments. These assessments are, in a certain sense, taxes. But, an assessment differs from a general tax in that an assessment is levied only on property in the immediate vicinity of some local public improvement and is valid only where the property assessed receives some special benefit differing from the benefit that the general public enjoys. *Prod. Tool Supply Co. v. City of Roseville,* 253 N.W.2d 350 (Mich. App. 1977). In fact, if the primary purpose of an improvement is to benefit the public generally, as with, for example, the erection of a county courthouse, it cannot be financed by special assessments, even though it may incidentally benefit property in the particular locality. Special assessments are often imposed for opening, paving, grading, and guttering streets, construction of sidewalks and sewers, installation of street lighting, and so on.

Index